Introductory Readings on Language

Introductory Readings on Language

FOURTH EDITION

Wallace L. Anderson
Bridgewater State College

Norman C. Stageberg
University of Northern Iowa

Holt, Rinehart and Winston, Inc.
New York   Chicago   San Francisco   Atlanta   Dallas

Library of Congress Cataloging in Publication Data

Anderson, Wallace L., ed.
Introductory readings on language.

Includes bibliographies.
1. English language—Addresses, essays, lectures.
2. Language and languages. I. Stageberg, Norman C.,
joint ed. II. Title.
PE1072.A5 1975   401   74–16229

ISBN: 0–03–089578–2

TO THE INSTRUCTOR

An instructor's manual is available for this fourth edition. It contains information that supplements the text, suggestions for teaching, questions for review, useful references for the instructor, additional assignments and exercises, and, where feasible, answers to questions in the suggested assignments of the text. To receive a copy, please write on departmental stationery to:

> College Department
> Holt, Rinehart and Winston, Inc.
> 383 Madison Avenue
> New York, New York 10017

In this edition, essays that have been found too difficult for freshmen have been removed. We have also excised the section on clear thinking in the belief that students will learn these matters elsewhere. New material has been added on language origins, dictionaries, etymology, names, Black English, body language, psycholinguistics, and animal "language." Thus this edition is notably greater in breadth.

This book is designed primarily as a text for freshmen English, though it should also prove useful in undergraduate English courses devoted to the study of language. It has four major purposes:

1. To present basic information about language as a subject interesting and important in its own right. The intent is to make the students aware of the nature of language and some of its multifarious aspects.
2. To make students more perceptive of the artistic uses of language in literature.

3. To arouse the students' intellectual curiosity about language to the point where they want to know more about it.
4. To influence the students' own use of language and to enable them to cope more successfully with the welter of words, both spoken and written, that surrounds us all.

College freshmen are, for the most part, linguistically unsophisticated. Their attitudes toward language are often naïve; indeed, they have many misconceptions about language—misconceptions that they share with the general populace. One function of the English instructor is to rid college students of these misconceptions, to replace false beliefs with a more enlightened view of language in general, and of their own language in particular. For many college students, the freshman course is the sole course in English that they will take. Freshman English is the only place where these students will have the opportunity to gain real insight into the workings of language. They should not come to us naïve and leave older but still naïve in a matter of such vital import—hence this book of readings on language.

We realize that other kinds of content may be justifiably defended in a freshman English course, but we also believe that the rationale offered here has a cogency that cannot be lightly dismissed.

These essays constitute an introductory course in language. Although they deal with various linguistic topics, they are not a course in linguistics. They are intended to be complementary to a composition text or handbook; hence matters of rhetoric and mechanics have for the most part been excluded. The readings have been selected on the basis of three criteria: (1) that they be soundly informative, (2) that they be in line with current linguistic thought, and (3) that they be within the intellectual reach of the average freshman. We have been particularly mindful that these readings are for beginning college students. The topics chosen are basic to an understanding of the nature of language; yet they do not presuppose previous technical knowledge. In the main the selections themselves are nontechnical. The single exception is the essay on the classification of English vowels and consonants, pages 181–187; here of necessity phonetic terminology and symbols are used. (This essay should precede the others in the section.) The few technical terms that do occur are clearly defined in the text or in footnotes of definition and illustration that we have provided.

In addition to the explanatory footnotes, we have included three kinds of editorial assistance: headnotes, suggested assignments, and lists of further readings. These are an integral part of the book. The headnotes prepare the students for the reading to follow by providing background material and by raising questions. Their purpose is to arouse interest, to stimulate thought, and to direct attention to the particular issues involved. The "assignments" are in a sense extensions of the readings themselves. Their purpose is to make the readings more meaningful by giving the students an opportunity to come to grips with specific issues by means of a variety of oral and written assignments. Many of the assignments are adaptable to either discussion or written work. The readings are included as a source of information for research papers; they may also serve to open more doors for those students desirous of gaining further insight into the nature of language.

The arrangement of topics is one that makes sense to us. However, it is not inflexible. The most appropriate order will depend, as it should, on the ingenuity of the instructor and his or her view of the course.

W.L.A.
N.C.S.

December 1974

TO THE STUDENT

To use language is the mark of a human being; to understand language, in the deepest sense, is the mark of an educated human being. From about the age of six, you have been using language with really a high degree of efficiency. And so have 300 million other speakers of English. But your understanding of your native tongue is probably fragmentary and riddled with misconceptions. In the course of twelve years of schooling, if you are like many college freshmen, you have gathered into your intellectual granary sundry notions about language, varying in worth from known truths to half-truths down to palpable nontruths. An illustration will make this clear. With which of the following propositions would you agree?

1. The languages of primitive peoples are simpler than those of more advanced nations.
2. An excellent way to find the correct pronunciation of a word is to look it up in the dictionary.
3. If you pronounce *pursuing* to rime with *ruin*, you are dropping the *g*.
4. The word *humor* should be pronounced with an *h* because it is spelled with an *h*.
5. Since the real meaning of *awful* is "full of awe," this word should not be used as a general term of condemnation.
6. Individual words have a specific and universal connotation.
7. In the question "Who is it for?" one should say *whom* because it is the object of the preposition *for*.
8. Words labeled "Colloq." in your dictionary should not be used in cultivated conversation.
9. Cultured speakers of New England and the Eastern coast prefer "He doesn't" to "He don't."
10. Dialect words should be avoided in serious and formal writing.

If you agree with any of these, you are in error, for each states or implies a concept that is to some degree untrue. These errors, however, are no cause for alarm, since we all entertain misconceptions in areas of knowledge with which we are unfamiliar. But the situation is one that demands correction because, as you go through college, you will gain much of your education through the medium of language. You will listen to classroom lectures where you will have to catch and interpret words on the fly. You will have heavy reading assignments where you will have to read closely, with sharp attention to nuances of meaning. You will have compositions and papers to write where you must use language with scrupulous precision. All of these activities you should be able to perform more capably when you understand the language matters presented in this book—such matters, for example, as the symbolic nature of language, the uniqueness of meanings, the bases of good usage, the values of metaphor, the information a dictionary affords, the importance of context, the ever-present hazards of ambiguity, the dangers of classification, and the formation of words.

Language study, in addition to being a practical pursuit, is also a cultural subject. It is a social science, concerned with an aspect of our behavior that sets us apart from the lower animals—our use of an intricate system of speech sounds to communicate with our peers and our use of written symbols to transmit the accumulated knowledge of the race to our descendants. You will get an inkling of the scientific side of language study when you read the selections on linguistic geography, psycholinguistics, sociolinguistics, and animal behavior. You will discover fragments of history embedded in words when you dig into etymology. You will touch upon philosophy when you inquire into the symbolic nature of words. And you will deepen your understanding of literature when you examine the means by which the richness and complexity of imaginative writing are achieved.

Of the whole fascinating drama of language behavior, you will receive a series of quick, revealing glances as scholars draw the curtain aside on various scenes. And you will emerge, it is hoped, with a deepened comprehension of the foundation stone of our humanity—language.

6. ONOMATOLOGY

7. THE SOUNDS OF LANGUAGE

11. SEMANTICS

12. KINESICS: NONVERBAL COMMUNICATION

13. PSYCHOLINGUISTICS

14. ETHOLOGY: THE STUDY OF ANIMAL BEHAVIOR

15. STRUCTURAL AND TRANSFORMATIONAL GRAMMAR

16. LANGUAGE AND LITERATURE

1

THE ORIGIN
OF LANGUAGE

In the Beginning

John and Joan Levitt

"In the beginning was the Word," according to St. John. The Greek term was *Logos*, which carried with it the sense of reason, order, and purpose. Ultimately it referred to the creative principle of the universe. It is well at the outset to be reminded of the significance of language in the development of humankind, for it is largely through language that we sort out our universe and give intelligent direction to our lives. Man learned to speak many, many millennia before he devised the earliest writing systems known to us, which go back only about 5000 years. How did he develop this skill? The question is tantalizing, and the answer is hidden in the mists of prehistory. Nevertheless, numerous scholars, including eminent names of the past, have succumbed to the urge to speculate on the matter. This introductory essay surveys the major theories on the origin of language and presents the types of evidence employed. John Levitt is a staff tutor at the University of Keele. His wife, Joan, has been a teacher of English.

The Problem

The problem of how human speech originated is one which will never be solved; and it is one which, at the same time, men will never cease to explore. The chief reason for trying to discover a solution is a very human one—the

From *The Spell of Words*, by John and Joan Levitt. Published by Darwen Finlayson, Ltd., Shopwyke Hall, Chichester, Sussex, England. Copyright © 1959 by John and Joan Levitt and published by their permission.

mere fact that the problem exists; just as, in the words of a famous mountaineer, the chief reason for trying to climb mountains is the fact that mountains exist.

Men have speculated for centuries on the origin of languages; and though from time to time particular people have produced theories which satisfied themselves, they have not often managed to convince other people. Nevertheless, in their enquiries they have been led to study a number of topics connected with human language; and these topics have their own interest, however much or little they bear on the major mystery. This is the chief justification for the present chapter, which will not offer any new theory about speech.

The Great Original

Two things of importance to people's ideas about language happened in the nineteenth century. In the first place, it became apparent that the length of human history was far greater than had previously been imagined; and that men had been talking to each other, not for thousands of years, but for tens of thousands. It is strange to reflect that when John William Burgon called the city of Petra "A rose-red city, half as old as time," he may well have meant it quite literally. Archbishop Ussher in the seventeenth century had worked out that the date of the Creation was 4004 B.C.; many cities are half as old as that.

In the second place, the idea of evolution entered men's minds. It became normal to think of existing creatures as having evolved through time into what they are at present, rather than having been created in their special shape and remaining unchanged through the whole of time. In the study of languages, this is the period when the scholar came to assume that present-day languages had similarly evolved out of earlier ones. It was a profitable assumption to make. . . .

These two things taken together affected the question of the origin of speech. Before the nineteenth century, it had been the usual assumption that the original of all known languages was one of the languages still spoken, or one which had only recently (that is, in the last thousand years or so) fallen into disuse. The German philosopher Leibniz, in the eighteenth century, had suggested that no existing language was the "original"; but his ideas were not taken up until the next century.

Almost every language spoken in the civilised world was at some time suggested as the original. Hebrew was the language of the peoples of the Old Testament, and was thus a favourite choice.[1] ("We are sure, from the

---

[1] Samuel E. Morison reports about Columbus' first voyage: "Luis de Torres, a . . . converted Jew, was taken along as interpreter because he knew Hebrew and a little Arabic. It was then commonly supposed that Arabic was the mother of all languages, so Torres was expected to make shift at conversing with the Grand Khan and other oriental potentates." *Admiral of the Ocean Sea*, pp. 145–146. [eds.]

names of persons and places mentioned in Scripture before the Deluge, not to insist on other arguments, that Hebrew was the primitive language of mankind." This was written by Bentley, a great eighteenth-century English scholar.) In the seventeenth century a Swedish writer had an interesting alternative theory: he believed that in the Garden of Eden, Adam and Eve had spoken Danish; the Serpent, French; and God, Swedish. As late as 1934 a meeting of Turkish scholars had solemnly declared that Turkish was the language from which all others originated. But Greek has also been frequently put forward by classical scholars; a sixteenth-century Dutch scholar suggested Dutch; Celtic has been suggested by Irishmen and Welshmen; and Gothic was suggested by a Renaissance German. Anyone could guess, and these guesses had the virtue of patriotism.

The Royal Experiment

At least three times in history an oddly inhuman experiment seems to have been tried; and since the three experimenters were all kings, it deserves the title of "The Royal Experiment." It was thought that, if a number of small children were isolated at birth from all sound of human speech and brought up together in silence, then, when they did start talking, it would be the original language of mankind that they would use. The first king to try it was the Egyptian Psammitichos (the Greek historian Heredotus tells of it). His victims are supposed to have said first *Békos*; which happened to be the Phrygian word for "bread." This solved the mystery to the king's satisfaction.

Later, the Emperor Frederick II (who died in 1250) tried the same experiment but failed, because the children he used died inconveniently before saying anything at all. Later still, James IV of Scotland (who died in 1513) made an attempt. In the result, he declared that the children came to speak "very good Hebrew."

The Bow-wow Theory

Nineteenth-century theories about the origin of language were more plausible. Many of them fall into convincing categories; there are four types of theory, which have been put forward from time to time. Scholars have given them nicknames. The *bow-wow* theory is the first of them. This is, quite simply, the theory that human speech originated in imitation of the noises of animals. A man, hearing a dog, might have imitated its bark; and, if he did this when with companions, they might have understood that he was drawing their attention to the dog. In this way a barking sound (or something similar) might have become the first word.

To this, at least one objection can be made. Man could always make noises of his own; did these mean nothing until he imitated the animals?

The Ding-dong Theory

This is similar to the last; it suggests that the first sounds that had meaning for men were those they made in imitation of natural sounds, such as the falling of stones or the running of water. There may, indeed, have been a great deal of imitation in early speech. Words (such as *hubbub*, *splash*, and *boom*) quite frequently owe their origin to the sounds they stand for. But this simple explanation does not seem adequate; there are many more sounds in the experience of even the most primitive man than the sounds of nature; why should the theory be so limited?

The Pooh-pooh Theory

This is the theory that language originated in the involuntary expression of emotions. Of course, any sort of creature that we can imagine as a man at all must give expression to his feelings; and in our own speech, emotional noises occur pretty frequently. *Ow! Oooch! Ah!*—these are some of them. But it is an odd fact that these noises do not function as normal words such as nouns, adjectives and verbs. They are classed as interjections; and they never have any place in the grammar of a sentence. It is hard to see how noises of this sort could have given rise to ordinary words; but of course it is even harder to see how language came to exist at all.

The Yo-he-ho Theory

This suggests that language started with the unintentional noises which we make when we are doing some physical work. These noises are often rhythmical, and rhythmical noises are useful when people are working in company with each other, since they help to keep their efforts co-ordinated. (Sea-shanties are rhythmical songs which grew up to help sailors pull together at such jobs as hauling sheets or turning a windlass.) Unintentional exclamations may have evolved into something like songs, and from these songs language may have originated.

Gesture Theories

Several theories popular today suggest that language began as some form of *gesture*. Although we usually think of gestures as movements of the hands and arms, it is possible to make gestures with the head and lips. A man with a burden in his arms might want to indicate something; whilst making a head movement, he could quite naturally make a voice-noise as well, to draw attention to it. Different gestures, involving all the muscles of the head and mouth, would result in different noises; and it would soon become apparent from the noise alone what gesture caused it. These noises would therefore come to stand in the place of the gestures, rather than accompanying them; and words would have been born.

It is a curious fact that many of the personal pronouns in various languages seem to fit in with this theory. A man who tries to indicate himself by a gesture of the mouth and head might naturally draw his lips tighter and backwards; the word *me* is pronounced with much the same lip movements as these. A man gesturing towards someone else might do the opposite: that is, he might push his lips forward in the direction of the person he is indicating. The English *you* and *thou,* the French *vous,* and the German *du* have this sort of lip-action.

Gesture theories are more complicated than this, but these examples give an indication of their nature. The chief British advocate of the gesture theory was Sir Richard Paget, who went to great trouble to work out details for his theory. He made a list of various ideas which a primitive man might need to express; then, whilst his hands were tied he tried to make gestures to express them. The noises he produced were taken down as "words"; and these he sent to a number of scholars who were experts in early languages. He claimed that many of his words were matched by words of similar meanings in these languages, and took this as a confirmation of his theory. Other people, however, have been less impressed.

Lines of Approach to the Problem

Most of the theories so far discussed have been no more than guess-work; and it is useful at this stage to pause and ask what sort of actual evidence might be used if a sounder theory were to be constructed.

There are four sorts of evidence which appear at first sight promising. There is the evidence of early languages. . . . How far could one work back in time, . . . and would the result help with the problem of the origin of speech?

There is also the evidence of "primitive" languages. The speech of peoples who live today at a very humble level of civilisation might be thought to have some bearing on the problem.

The Royal Experiment, inhuman as it was, perhaps suggests another line of approach. Children learning to speak may perhaps reveal something about the way mankind as a whole learnt to speak.

Finally, there are other forms of life. Man is part of the pattern of evolution. Animals and birds do communicate with each other in certain ways, and these ways may indicate something about human communication.

Unfortunately, there are serious drawbacks to each of these types of evidence.

The Early Stages of Language

The drawback here is that the evidence does not go far enough. Man-like creatures appeared on the earth a million years ago; and creatures who, from their brain-capacities, could have learned to speak, emerged about 30,000 years ago. The evidence of existing languages and their reconstructed ancestors goes back hardly more than five thousand years; beyond that, all suggestions are so highly speculative as to be worthless. There is a great gap of unbridged time, during which any sort of speech must have altered very greatly. Attempting to discover what the first language must have been like from the evidence of the historical development of known languages is like trying to discover what happened last century on the evidence of last week.

"Primitive" Languages

Languages change and develop with civilisation; so it is, on the face of it, reasonable to suppose that those societies, which exist today on a lower level of civilisation than we have ourselves, may offer us a better idea of what language must have been like before men were civilised at all.

Unfortunately, it is easy to underestimate the complexity of the civilisation possessed by even the most backward societies. "Primitive" man is in many ways surrounded by a far more complicated system of beliefs, habits, and emotions, than civilised man. His language is also frequently more complicated than more "advanced" languages.

Moreover, we have no grounds for supposing that any one language has an earlier origin than any other. Everything we said in the last section about the dangers of arguing from existing, known languages to assumptions about the first language is again applicable.

We may *think* that the society and civilisation of the Australian aborigines has remained unchanged for many thousands of years, but we have no evidence for it. We may assume that the life of the Bushman represents an earlier, fossilised stage of our own progress towards civilisation; but this is only an assumption, and a risky one at that.

The Speech of Children

The trouble with the evidence from children's speech is this—no child ever learns to talk under the same conditions that early man must have experienced. Children learn to talk in the middle of families that already know how to talk. A child grows up in a world of words; learning to speak is learning to understand the words that are always in his ears, as well as learning to make words for himself.

There is a second point about children. We often assume that a child, growing up, passes through the same stages that mankind as a whole must have passed through in its evolution. We regard children as undeveloped adults; and we assume that our early ancestors were also undeveloped creatures of a similar nature. This assumption is very questionable; there is no real justification for thinking that the modern child can tell us anything about human life many thousands of years ago.

The Communication of Other Living Creatures

There is in this case a different difficulty; human beings can never enter directly into the minds of animals. Animals make cries, which have, apparently, some meaning. We can never *know* this meaning; we can only guess at it. We assume that animals can express emotion, though we cannot know that when an animal makes a cry this represents anything that we ourselves could ever experience, or would be justified in calling an emotion in the normal human sense of the word. Some animal cries express desires; we know this by deduction—because the cry stops when we satisfy what we think the desire was (as when we give milk to a mewing cat).

There is only a very small range in which the cries of any one animal can vary. Animal cries have a monotonous simplicity which is so unlike human language that we can see no likely way by which they could evolve into it. Animal cries do not communicate ideas or facts; they merely express feelings and desires.

There is one class of living creatures, however, who are able to communicate very precise information to each other; and that is the bees. A bee returning to a hive can tell other bees where pollen is to be found, and can give both the distance and direction of it very exactly indeed.[2] Bees also have a way, when swarming, of debating with each other about the site for a new hive. In its results, the language of bees is far more like human language than anything which birds, dogs or other creatures exhibit, but the physical differences between bees and men are so great that these facts can help us very little with the problem of the origin of language; and, moreover, the bees' language is not a matter of spoken words, but of *dances*.

Sound, Meaning and Sociability

To look critically in this way at these four possible sources of evidence is discouraging—but only if we still hope for certainty in our guess-work about the origin of language. Once this hope is abandoned, however, and we seek no more than a speculation which is less improbable than others, there is some comfort to be had; for on a number of points the early stages of existing languages, the languages of primitive peoples, and the child's experiences with language, seem to agree.

[2] For the language of bees, see pages 361–364. [eds.]

It has been said that the speech of primitive peoples is usually far more complicated than that of more advanced peoples. In some primitive languages there may be a separate word for each sort of tree in the community's experience, but no one word meaning "tree." The Cherokee Indians have no word for "wash," but they have these other words instead: *kutuwo*, "I wash myself"; *kulestula*, "I wash my head"; *testula*, "I wash some-one else's head"; *kukuswo*, "I wash my face"; *takutega*, "I wash dishes." A second point about primitive languages is that, on the whole, far more sounds are needed to express a given meaning than in more advanced speech. A third point is that primitive speech, on the whole, is much more frequently a matter of expressing friendliness between speakers than of communicating thoughts and facts.

It does seem that the very early stages of modern languages resemble primitive speech in some of these ways. In them, there are often fairly large numbers of very different words which have only slightly different meanings, as in the Cherokee examples given above. Grammar is invariably more complicated than in the later stages, rather than simpler as might be expected; and it is conceivable that there was, in general, more sound for less meaning.

When children learn to speak the first stage is that of babbling. A child in his cot discovers that he can make noises; and is soon putting out a long stream of sounds, with no deliberate meaning in them, for the fun of it. When his mother makes meaningless sounds back at him, he is pleased. This is, though he would not call it that, his discovery of the use of language for expressing simple sociability.

Later, and accidentally, he makes a stream of sound such as *mamamama-mamama*—and his mother interprets this as his use of her name: *mama*. She is wrong, in the first place; but the child finds that the more often he makes these sounds, the more often his mother will come to smile at him and respond to him. Sooner or later he starts using the word deliberately; not with a "meaning" in the normal sense, but with an intention. The word produces some sort of action; his language becomes a way of getting things to happen. Other words, *dada*, *tata*, etc. are learnt similarly.

If these ideas from primitive languages, the early stages of modern languages, and the speech of children, are put together, a very tentative theory emerges. Man may first have discovered the pleasure of rhythmical sound for its own sake—long strings of sound, like the child's babble. Next, the pleasure of making such sounds in company with others could have been discovered; and the knowledge that, to make such sounds, is to provoke that pleasure. At this point speech becomes something that can have a purpose. Various accidental things might now come together—in the same way that, for a child, the response of his mother to his *mamamama* sound could have been an accident; and the sound which was being made when the accidental event occurred could gain an association with that sort of event in the speaker's mind. The sounds are more likely, it seems, to have become associated with the emotions caused by the events, than with the events themselves.

Over a long stretch of time, amongst a group of early men living near each other and coming together for sociability, such word-sounds may have become fixed, in the sense that they called up the same emotions or situations for all that heard them. The pleasure in sound for its own sake would have remained, however, together with the pleasure in sound for the sake of sociability. As language evolved, and men got more accustomed to facing situations that were not actual, but merely evoked by words, their thoughts (which is to say, their abilities to summon up such mental situations at will, in greater complexity) would come to have more importance than they previously had; and language would become shaped to assist them. The amount of "meaning" in the sounds would become more concentrated and the length of the soundstrings would be cut down.

The story would certainly have been more complicated than this; it is only a very simplified sketch of a theory which its chief proponent—the Danish scholar, Otto Jespersen—has worked out in more detail. Jespersen's theory is the best so far; but, good as it is, it remains no more than a guess.[3]

[3] See Jespersen's *Language, Its Nature, Development and Origin*, Chap. XXI, "The Origin of Speech" (New York, 1922). [eds.]

The Origin of Language

Claire and W. M. S. Russell

In the preceding essay we encountered the major theories of the past on the origin of language. All are highly speculative. In this essay we are presented with scientific evidence from which can be inferred the time that human language came into existence and the stimulus that brought about this development of language. Claire and W. M. S. Russell are a team of eminent ethologists. Among their many publications are *Human Behavior: A New Approach* and *Violence, Monkeys, and Man*. Dr. W. M. S. Russell is a lecturer in Social Biology at the University of Reading, England.

From *Linguistics at Large,* edited by Noel Minnis. Copyright © 1971 by Claire and W. M. S. Russell, published by Victor Gollancz. Reprinted by permission.

So far, we have no evidence of any animals spontaneously evolving true language without anybody to teach them. Man *did*. How, and when, did this happen? What are the origins of human language? Our study of animal signals may help in some ways towards answering these questions.

How old is human language? Obviously it is at least as old as writing. The art of writing evolved rapidly in ancient Iraq between 3500 and 2900 B.C. A series of tablets from Erech, Jamdat Nasr, Ur and Fara tell the story of a transition from pictured objects and numbers to true writing with conventional signs for the syllables of the spoken language. But of course, even the first stage presupposes language itself, which must therefore be older than 3500 B.C. Much earlier than this, some time between 9000 and 6500 B.C., there lived at Ishango, on the shores of Lake Edward in the Congo, a people, apparently Negro, of great technological achievement for their time. The excellent bone harpoons they manufactured were exported as far as the Upper Nile and almost to the coast of West Africa. A bone tool-handle found at Ishango is marked with 3 series of notches grouped together in sets. One series has 11, 13, 17 and 19 notches—the 4 prime numbers between 10 and 20. Another has groups suggesting multiplication—3 and 6, 4 and 8, 10 and 5 and 5. The third series has 11 (10 + 1), 21 (20 + 1), 19 (20 − 1) and 9 (10 − 1), suggesting a decimal system. If these people really had a number system, they certainly must have talked, and we can put the age of language back to at latest 6500 B.C.

Now let us go back to the other end of man's story. Man-like beings who made and kept stone tools seem to have been at Olduvai Gorge in Tanzania 1,750,000 years ago, to judge from potassium dating. Now human language is connected with another peculiarity of man: his brain functions in an asymmetrical way. Language is controlled by the left side of the brain in 97 per cent of human adults. The asymmetry also appears in the fact that most people are right-handed, whereas in monkeys right- and left-handedness appear to be about equally common. E. H. Lenneberg has suggested, for complicated reasons, that there is a *necessary* connection between the two things, language and an asymmetrical brain. Washoe has, perhaps, proved him wrong in one way; but the idea may still be relevant for the *initial spontaneous evolution* of language, as opposed to the capacity to learn it.[1] It is said that the earliest human stone tools show evidence of a predominance of right-handed tool-makers; so if Lenneberg is right, man had the potentiality of developing language from his earliest beginnings.

But did he develop it at once? For nearly all of his 1,750,000 years, man continued to make simple hand-axes and flake tools. All these crude stone implements look virtually alike to those of us who are not experts in prehistoric archaeology; there is scarcely any obvious difference between hand-axes hundreds of thousands of years apart. Then, suddenly, in the last Ice Age, about 100,000 years ago, there was a breakthrough: people began to

[1] See the Russells' "Language and Animal Signals," pp. 371–374. [eds.]

manufacture more and more elaborate stone and bone tools in greater and greater diversity. To us, the conclusion has seemed inescapable that this efflorescence was made possible by the emergence of true language.

We reached this conclusion a few years ago, and have since found we are not the first to reach it. In 1951, in his Inaugural Lecture as Derby Professor of Zoology in the University of Liverpool, R. J. Pumphrey presented just this hypothesis. Throughout those hundreds of thousands of years, he wrote, "the hand-axe and flake cultures show an extraordinary conservatism of type and an improvement in the technique of manufacture so gradual as to make the intervention of what we should call 'reason' unlikely in the extreme. . . . And then in the last Ice Age the picture changes . . . with dramatic suddenness." Pumphrey had already stressed the relationship between true language and planning for the future ("forward planning about lions"). He noted that in the last Ice Age a wide range of stone tools began to be designed and made *to make other tools* by boring, scraping, cutting and polishing bone and antler, "clear evidence of an objective reached through a planned and orderly succession of *different* operations." And so, he suggested, "characteristically human speech" appeared about 100,000 years ago in the last Ice Age.

A similar idea had apparently suggested itself independently to the Australian archaeologist V. Gordon Childe. In an article published in 1953, he too noted the enormous acceleration of technical progress in the last Ice Age, and concluded that this "apparent change in tempo might reasonably be attributed to the increasing use of a more flexible system of symbols with which to 'operate in the head' as a substitute for physical trial-and-error processes."

Suppose that true language did originate in or just before the last Ice Age: we have still to consider what stimulated this momentous development. Now we [know] that monkey bands are regulated by automatic codes of signals, and that these signal codes *vary* between bands of the same species. This creates no new problems of communication, for when monkey bands meet they do not normally mix, interacting only by a set of common threat signals, simpler than those used within the band. When bands of howler monkeys meet, for instance, each band sets up a howl, and the louder band must be the larger; the smaller and less noisy band discreetly withdraws. Human beings originally moved about in similar small groups, and there was probably comparatively little contact between these groups. While still living under these conditions, they developed the manufacture of durable tools. They could very well manage to continue to function thus, tools and all, on the basis of automatic monkey-like codes of signals. Chimpanzees are known to shape sticks and straws to size, for fighting leopards and for luring termites out of their nests, respectively.

But about 300,000–400,000 years ago, man achieved control of fire, gathered on lavafields or from lightning brush fires and carefully kept burning, and some time between then and the last Ice Age he discovered how to *light* fires himself. These tremendous advances gave him a new control over his environment, notably in defence against predators and protection from the cold; the world human population increased considerably, and spread out over the continents, invading temperate and even colder regions for the first time. Now there were many more small groups, and more likelihood of their meeting frequently. Moreover, tools at last began to become gradually more elaborate and diversified from group to group. With this frequent contact between groups, and this incentive to borrow and copy each other's tools, a new development began. The old automatic signal codes would not work *between* groups (compare the Carniolan and Italian honeybees).[2] The automatic noises and gestures that had formerly sufficed would eventually have to be replaced by *words*—overriding and controlling automatic moods—intelligible and intelligent between groups with different cultures. In this way man was stimulated to break the link between signal and automatic mood, and begin the logical combination of signals, or true language. Claire Russell has shown that a connection between the dawn of language and contact between culturally different groups can be detected in myths from several parts of the world. Gordon Childe has summarized the considerable evidence for trade and technical influence, and hence for communication, between culturally different groups great distances apart in the last Ice Age. So we may plausibly suppose that increasing contact between culturally separate groups was the stimulus for the evolution of true language. Even today, intercultural relations can stimulate new combinations of words—as in the case cited earlier of East African recruits and the phrases *colour of blood* and *colour of leaves*.[3]

It remains to ask, why vocal rather than sign language, especially since chimpanzees and other advanced monkeys are, as we have seen, so geared to visual signals? Now we have also seen that where visibility is poor, calls predominate, as in dolphins or monkeys of dense forest. Martin Moynihan studied a Central American monkey active at night—the night monkey. Though this species has only 10 calls, it has even fewer visual signals, and uses the calls far more. Now human eyes are not much use at night, and one of the results of man's control of fire was a new ability to continue his activities after sundown. Kenneth Oakley has suggested that "the lighting aspect of fire was probably almost as important as its heating aspect in extending man's range northwards." But visibility is *far from perfect* on a dark night around a flickering fire, and we may suppose that, as man became active at night, the value of vocal signals would greatly increase. So, we may conjecture, when true language appeared, it was conveyed by voice and not by gesture, until the deaf and their teachers, and certain monks, evolved sign languages to translate existing spoken ones. . . .

[2] See the Russells' "Language and Animal Signals," pp. 361-364. [eds.]
[3] See the Russells' "Language and Animal Signals," p. 359. [eds.]

SUGGESTED ASSIGNMENTS

1. The Ding-Dong theory, you will remember, maintains that language had its origin in words whose sound imitated natural sounds, like *clink, roar, hiss, ripple, grumble, whisper, click, murmur*. Let us speculate a little, however wildly, about this theory.

   a. List all the imitative words (like the above) that you can think of in ten minutes. In class, all such words found by class members can be put on the board for the next step.

   b. Indicate the part of speech of all these imitative words.

   c. How many prepositions are there among these words? How many conjunctions?

   d. Is it possible to have a language that does not express the relationships and meanings carried by prepositions and conjunctions? (Test: Choose any page of English, cross out the prepositions and conjunctions and see what this does to the meaning.)

   e. Open your dictionary to any page. Count the number of words on that page. Then count the number of imitative words on that page. What is the proportion? When all class members pool their figures, you will have a very rough estimate of the proportion of imitative words in English.

Now, sum up what seem to be the weaknesses of the Ding-Dong theory.

2. Report all the things you have learned in the last week without the use of verbal language. When the class has reported its experiences, try to make a general statement about the methods, scope, and effectiveness of such non-verbal learning.

FURTHER READINGS

Gaeng, Paul A. *Introduction to the Principles of Language*. New York: Harper & Row, 1971. See pp. 1–10.

Hockett, Charles F. *A Course in Modern Linguistics*. New York: Macmillan, 1958. See pp. 569–586.

Langer, Suzanne. *Philosophical Sketches*. Baltimore: Johns Hopkins Press, 1962. See "Speculations on the Origins of Speech and Its Communicative Function," pp. 26–53.

Ornstein, Jacob, and William W. Gage. *The ABC's of Languages and Linguistics*. New York: Chilton Books, 1964. See pp. 16–24.

Sturtevant, Edgar H. *An Introduction to Linguistic Science*. New Haven: Yale University Press, 1947. See pp. 40–50.

2
THE NATURE
OF LANGUAGE

The Nature of Language

W. Nelson Francis

At this point you have had a glimpse of the beginning of language, and have witnessed the all-important role that language plays in the development of society, as described in the preceding selection. Now we turn our attention to the nature of this civilizing tool we call language. The way to ascertain the nature of language in general is to abstract those characteristics that individual languages have in common. This is done by W. Nelson Francis in the present selection. Mr. Francis is Professor of Linguistics at Brown University and is the author of *The Structure of American English*.

. . . Language is interesting in itself. After all, it is a universal form of human behavior, and all of us are interested in what people, including ourselves, do.

English is, of course, only one of the many languages, perhaps as many as three thousand, which are spoken today. These languages are very different one from another. Indeed, it is primarily the fact that they are so different as to be mutually unintelligible that allows us to call them separate languages. A speaker of one of them, no matter how skillful and fluent, cannot communicate with a speaker of another unless one of them, as we say, "learns the other's language." Yet these differences, great as they are,

Reprinted from *The English Language, an Introduction, Background for Writing*, by W. Nelson Francis. By permission of W. W. Norton and Company. Inc. Copyright © 1963, 1965, by W. W. Norton and Company, Inc.

are differences of detail—of the kinds of sounds used and the ways of putting them together. In their broad outlines, in their basic principles, and even in the way they approach certain specific problems of communication, languages have a great deal in common. It is thus possible to make some observation about language in general. . . .

In the first place, any language is **arbitrary**. This means that there is nothing—or at most very little—in the nature of the things we talk about that dictates or controls the language we use to talk about them. When we are children we do not know this. We believe that the connection between an act or an object and the word which refers to it is somehow a natural and inevitable one. If you ask a child why he calls a certain object a *clock*, he will probably answer, "Because it *is* a clock." We can see the error of this belief in this childlike form. But it is likely to persist in a somewhat more sophisticated form in the minds of those who have not thought or studied about language. All of us have heard people make statements like "The real name for these things is *crullers*, but I call them *doughnuts* because everybody else around here does." Note the assumption that there is a *real*—natural or inevitable—name for something, even though nobody uses it. Only when we learn a foreign language do we become completely disabused of this notion. When we discover that *horloge* and *Uhr* seem to other people just as natural names for a timepiece as *clock*, we come to realize that none of them is really natural, but all are arbitrary.

Primitive peoples often build much of their religious and cultural behavior on this belief in the natural relationship of word and thing. For example, they believe that to know the name of an object, person, or deity is to gain a certain control over it: in "Ali Baba and the Forty Thieves," the words "Open Sesame!" cause the stone doors of the cave to move aside. Conversely, certain powers in the universe are thought to dislike the use of their names by mortals. Words are therefore tabooed, or euphemisms and descriptive phrases are invented such as *the little people* instead of *fairies*. The Greeks came to call those vengeful mythological creatures whose "real name" was *Erinyes* (or Furies) the *Eumenides* (or "good-tempered ones").

Although we consider ourselves too civilized for such superstitious behavior, vestiges of it remain in our conduct still. Many people will not speak of "death" or "dying" but use expressions like "passing away," "going to rest." A group of words that virtually everybody knows, most of them referring to universal bodily functions, are taboo in polite society, though polysyllabic synonyms for them are quite all right. Many of us knock on wood or cross our fingers when we say certain things, pretending—usually humorously—that this conduct will counteract the risk incurred by using powerful or dangerous words. But on our rational side we know that the only real connection between the word and the thing is in the minds of the people who speak our language.

There is, of course, a small area of language which is less arbitrary than the rest because it makes use of imitation. A child may call a clock a *tick-tock* or a train a *choo-choo*. Even here, however, there is a considerable degree of arbitrariness. The pendulum clock in the room where I am writing is making a rhythmic sound, but it certainly would not be described as "tick-tock" by an impartial—Chinese or Martian—observer. And the disappearance of the steam locomotive has removed from the scene anything making a sound even remotely resembling "choo-choo." Even supposedly imitative words of this sort are usually learned from others rather than made up in spontaneous imitation of other sounds.

Secondly, language is **conventional**. Its effectiveness rests upon a kind of unspoken public agreement that certain things will be done in certain ways. This is one consequence of its arbitrariness. Speakers of English are agreed upon calling a certain animal a *horse*. This is an arbitrary agreement. The principal function of language, communication, would break down if everybody insisted on using his own private arbitrary names for things. It is true that the agreement is often not complete. People may argue over whether or not whales are fish or spiders are insects. Such arguments, however, are wholly within the conventional field of language. They are concerned not with the basic agreements about words but with how much of the world of things a given word can be agreed upon to cover, which, in turn, may vary with the circumstances. It suits biologists to limit the class of things which they agree to call insects to those which have six legs, but most of us in our daily lives are agreed on including the eight-legged spiders as well. It is sometimes necessary, therefore, to specify what convention we are operating under at any given time. That is, when we are using language carefully, we must define our terms.

A third important quality of language is that it is **culturally transmitted**: it is passed on from generation to generation as a form of learned, rather than physically inherited, behavior. Nobody inherits the ability to use a particular language; everybody must learn it from other people who have themselves learned it at an earlier time. This learning begins in infancy and continues in varying intensity throughout life. The biggest part of the job is done between the ages of one and six, but it is not necessary to remind students that a good part of both their formal and their informal education consists of extending and sharpening their use of language.

An important consequence of this quality of language is that since individual people differ greatly in their capacity to learn, they also differ greatly in their command of language. This is true of all culturally transmitted activities—dancing, for example, or drawing. Some people simply have more aptitude for them, or have received more training, or both. At one end of the scale are those whose use of language and interest in it are the minimum needed to get them through routine work and simple play. At the other are writers (especially poets), actors, and others for whom the elaborate and subtle use of language is the central activity of life. Most of us fall somewhere between, depending on the nature of our work and play.

A second consequence is that like other aspects of human culture, language is subject to change. Our clothes, our food, our tools, and our speech vary from generation to generation just as they do from age to age. This change is sometimes fast and sometimes slow, sometimes radical and sometimes superficial, but it goes on all the time. Its causes are many and varied, and some of them are not fully understood. There may be a kind of slow, imperceptible, glacierlike drift, such as that which has brought about the differences in pronunciation between the English of America and the English of England. Or there may be striking innovation, taken up and circulated by fashion, like that which has added such new expressions as *hipster, blast off*, and *cosmonaut* to our vocabulary. The cumulation of such changes, going on in different ways in different places, may eventually cause what were once local versions of the same language to become distinct, mutually unintelligible languages like French and Spanish, or English and German. We don't know in how many different places language began—perhaps several, perhaps only one—but we do know that the great diversity of tongues among the peoples of the world today is almost wholly due to this process of divergent change.

The fourth and last general quality of language that will be mentioned here is that it has a very complicated **multiple structure**. This is necessary if language is to discharge the most important function that is asked of it: the communication of an infinite number of different messages, made up from a small number of vocal signals which can be learned by any human of normal intelligence. Language, in other words, is open-ended; there is no limit to the number of things that can be said. This is made possible by the mathematical possibilities of combination. Out of a relatively small group of sounds—fewer than a hundred—that any normal person can learn to produce can be made hundreds of thousands of words, which in turn can be combined according to the rules of grammar into a virtually endless number of different sentences. All languages have this complex, many-layered structure. That is what makes them adequate to the needs of their users. Contrary to some popular impressions, the word and sentence structure of the langauge of the most primitive people is highly complex. Anyone who undertakes to study an American Indian language, with its long, intricately complicated word structure and its delicate nuances of grammar, many of them very different from those we are used to in English, discovers immediately how preposterous is the widespread notion that the first Americans communicated largely by grunts, by sign-language, and by smoke signals. No matter where language is used—in the jungles of Africa or South America, the mountains of Tibet, or the islands of the Pacific—it has a complex, versatile, and adaptable structure.

Editors' note: Professor Francis' fourth observation on language, that it has a very complicated multiple structure, is deserving of specific illustration. So let us examine a few examples of the multiple structure of English.

1. English speech sounds in the word are constrained to follow certain rules or order. An English word can begin with a cluster of three consonants but no more, as in *spring*. When a word does begin with a three-consonant cluster, the first sound must be /s/. The second sound must be a /p/, /t/, or /k/. And the third must be an /l/, /r/, /y/, or /w/. Some examples are *spring, strength, scratch, spew, squirt*. Here you must be careful not to confuse letters with speech sounds. For example, *scratch* begins with the sounds /s/ + /k/ + /r/; *spew* with /s/ + /p/ + /y/; and squirts with /s/ + /k/ + /w/.

2. Words are formed of meaningful parts called morphemes. The word *strengtheners*, for example, is formed by the morphemes *-en, strength, -s*, and *-er*. The important thing to notice here is that these morphemes must appear in a fixed order, and no order but one can form the word *strengtheners*. Try another word for yourself: Take the morphemes *-ize, -al, structure*, and *-ation* and make a word of them. You will see again that only one order is possible.

3. When a noun is modified by a single word, this modifier precedes the noun. Thus we can say *excellent strengtheners, only strengtheners, those strengtheners*, and *muscle strengtheners*. Now try putting all these single-word modifiers before *strengtheners*. You will find that one and only one order is possible.

All the above examples illustrate one aspect of the multiple structure of English, namely, the order of parts. And it is a structural fact that the order of parts in these and many other sentence situations is not random but firmly fixed. The multiple structure of English in its entirety is so manifold and complex that no grammarian has ever succeeded in describing it completely.

SUGGESTED ASSIGNMENT

Professor Francis points out that language is arbitrary and conventional. The meaning of a word is arbitrary because the word could be made to stand for anything; and its meaning is conventional because speakers, by a general unstated convention or agreement, have accepted a given meaning. We can sum up these two characteristics by calling words "conventionalized symbols."

Almost anything can become a conventionalized symbol if human beings choose to make it so. For example, what do the following symbols convey: a class ring, college letters on a sweater, a particular mode of dress, ownership of a particular make of car? What other conventionalized symbols do you observe around you? Are such symbols useful? Explain.

Language, Logic, and Grammar

L. M. Myers

Language, we have seen, is a system of conventionalized symbols by which we communicate with each other. One would think that, since we use the same symbols, we would always understand one another. Yet we do not always say what we mean, nor do we always understand what other people mean. If we do not know the meaning of a particular word, we are told, we can always consult the dictionary. But what do we find in the dictionary? Other words! In one sense these other words are the meaning of the first word. But aren't we only saying that both mean the same thing? What is this other meaning? Is meaning only verbal? This whole question of the meaning of meaning is of fundamental importance in the study of language. In the following essay, L. M. Myers, Professor of English Emeritus at Arizona State University, identifies three kinds of meaning.

A language may be defined roughly as consisting of a set of words and some habitual ways of putting them together. Dictionaries deal primarily with the individual words; grammars with characteristic forms and with ways of arranging words in coherent communications. There is inevitably some overlapping between the two.

WORD-FORM AND WORD-ORDER

In some languages the connections between words are shown largely by changes in form. Thus in Latin, "Marcus vidit Quintum" and "Marcum vidit Quintus" mean quite different things, although the same three words are used in the same order. The first means that Marcus saw Quintus; the second, that Quintus saw Marcus. The endings in -*us* and -*um* show which is the subject and which is the object of the action, regardless of the order.

From *American English, a Twentieth-Century Grammar* by L. M. Myers. Reprinted by permission of the author, copyright 1952. Published by Prentice-Hall, Inc.

In some other languages, like Chinese, words never change their form. The meaning of a group of words therefore depends on the choice of words and the order in which they are arranged.

Originally, English was very much like Latin in this respect. Most words were *inflected*; that is, they had a number of forms that showed variations in their basic meanings, and indicated their relations to each other. Now most of these inflections have been lost, and the structure of the language has become more like that of Chinese. Even the endings that remain have lost most of their power to show distinctions. Look at the following sentences:

He and I saw it yesterday.
Him and me seen it yesterday.

There are good reasons . . . for avoiding the second. But we understand it as readily as the first, and take it to mean the same thing. Our usual way of showing differences in meaning is by varying the *order* of words, as in the following sentences.

John hit Tom.
Tom hit John.

On the other hand, there are times when changes in the forms of words make a considerable difference in the meaning:

The man helps the boys.
The men helped the boy.

A study of English grammar therefore involves both the forms and the order of words.

THE PROBLEM OF MEANING

If we want to keep our feet on the ground while we are making such a study, we had better begin by trying to understand something about how words came to "mean" anything at all. If we simply take it for granted that they do and go on from there, we will never have any real understanding of the language, no matter how many grammatical rules we memorize.

Let us suppose that on an uninhabited island a freak rock-formation has resulted in the white streaks on a cliff forming the letters P A I N. This would mean absolutely nothing to the animals, the trees, or the rocks themselves. It would still mean nothing if an illiterate savage landed on the island and looked at it. But if an American landed, the letters would look to him like a familiar word, and would call up reactions connected with earlier acquaintance with that word. For the first time the letters would suggest a meaning—"pain." This meaning would occur in the man's mind. The cliffs and the letters would be no more intelligent than before.

If a Frenchman landed on the island and noticed the same letters, an entirely different meaning would be suggested, since it happens that in French the letters P A I N also form a word—but the word means "bread," and not an uncomfortable sensation.

Most of us probably have a feeling that the letters must somehow mean something all by themselves, even if there is nobody there to appreciate them; but it is hard to see how they could mean two such different things as "pain" and "bread." If we think the matter over, we are forced to agree that meaning is the product of human nervous systems, and does not reside in the letters on the cliff.

The next question that comes up is, would the letters on the cliff have a meaning of their own if they had been deliberately written to form a word? Suppose the American had written down the sentence, "I have a *pain* in my back," and had then torn up the paper so that one piece contained just the word "pain." If the Frenchman happened to pick that piece up, it would suggest to him the idea "bread." Would the word "really" mean what the American intended to convey, or what it happened to suggest to the Frenchman?

THREE KINDS OF MEANING

We could argue this point forever without getting anywhere, for the fact is that we use the words *mean* and *meaning* in a number of different ways; and if we don't keep at least three of these carefully separated in our minds, we can become badly confused.

Meaning (1) What the speaker intends to indicate.

Meaning (2) What is suggested to a particular listener.

Meaning (3) A more or less general habit of using a given word to indicate a given thing.

A good many writers on the language neglect the first two of these and treat the third far too rigidly, as if the connection between the word and the thing were absolute, instead of a never-quite-uniform habit. You have probably heard such statements as: "*Buffalo* does not mean the American bison, but an entirely different animal"; or: "*Penny* really means an English coin—the American coin is a *cent*."

This is putting the cart before the horse. We can discover meaning (3)—often referred to as the "real" meaning—only by observing the occurrences of meanings (1) and (2). To deny that these meanings are real is as unreasonable as it would be to deny the reality of a family of two or eleven on the grounds that the "average" family consists of five. It is quite true that the English used the word *penny* for one kind of a coin before we used it for another. But it is equally true that the newer meaning is very common in America; and it is *not* true (in spite of what some dictionaries say) that this meaning is merely "colloquial." Even our most formal writers might say, "He had a dime, two nickels, and three *pennies*," though they probably express the total by saying "twenty-three *cents*."

Of course we could not communicate at all without some sort of agreement that certain words are to be used to stand for certain things. Therefore meaning (3)—"a more or less general habit of using a given word to indicate a given thing"—is also perfectly legitimate. But we should not pretend that this more or less general habit is absolutely uniform, or that any number of books or teachers can ever make it so.

We can only guess how the habit started, and a number of very different guesses have been made. A linguist can trace the connection between English *father* and Latin *pater*, or between English *fish* and Latin *piscis*; but he cannot give a satisfactory reason why one of these pairs of words should be applied to male parents and the other to animals that live in the water. They would work exactly as well if their meanings were reversed. This last point is important. The "agreement" to use certain words for certain things is basically arbitrary. It is also, in the main, informal, habitual, and unenforceable.

WHY COMMUNICATION IS NEVER PERFECT

We cannot understand each other unless we approximate the habits of those with whom we communicate; but we can only approximate. Until we find two people with identical physical equipment, nervous systems, and backgrounds of past experience, we cannot expect to find even two people who use a language in exactly the same way.[1] Schools and other forces tend to keep our language habits somewhat similar, but perfect uniformity is not even theoretically possible. This is true of both individual words and of ways of putting them together. Moreover, it is true of the ways we react to language as well as of the ways we express it.

Let us look at a single short sentence:

[1] For a more detailed treatment of this concept, see R. H. Moore's "Contexts," pp. 298–302. [eds.]

John hurt Mary.

Most of us would say offhand that we understand this perfectly. Yet it conveys, by itself, very little definite information, as we can see by trying to answer the following questions: Are John and Mary people, pigs, or one of each? Are they real or imaginary? Was the hurting mental, physical, or what?

Suppose that as I wrote the sentence I was thinking of one pig biting another; that Jim Smith, as he reads it, gets the impression of one child scratching and kicking another; and that Sally Jones builds up the picture of a love affair marked by deep spiritual suffering. Each of these "meanings" is perfectly legitimate; but unless we can somehow get closer together, our communication will not be very successful. From the *words themselves* we get only the following information.

1. *John* is presumably male and animate, and there is some probability that he is human. He may be either real or imaginary.
2. *Mary* is presumably female. Her other possibilities are parallel to John's.
3. *Hurt* indicates some sort of action with an unpleasant effect that has already occurred.
4. The position of the words indicates that the direction of the action was from John to Mary.

Thus each word, by itself, *limits the possibilities* a good deal; and the relative position of the words limits them still further. The question is, can we limit them enough to communicate our ideas accurately and effectively?

We can make some progress in this direction by using additional words. Suppose I expand the sentence to read: "My little black pig, John, hurt my little white pig, Mary, by biting her in the left ear." This answers two of the questions listed above—John and Mary are pigs rather than people, and the hurting was physical. The reader may even accept the fact that the pigs are real rather than imaginary, although this cannot be proved by words alone. But other questions remain—how big is *little*, how much it hurt, and so forth. No matter how many words we use, or how carefully we arrange them, we can never directly transfer an idea from one mind to another. We can only hope to stimulate in the second mind an idea *similar* to that in the first. The words pass through our minds. The pigs, we hope, stay in their pens. And the exact nature of the connection between the words, the minds, and the pigs is not the easiest thing in the world to explain. At the very least we have to consider:

1. The relation between the words and the minds of the people who use them.

2. The relations between the words and the things and activities they stand for.
3. The relations of the words to each other.

WORDS AND THE HUMAN NERVOUS SYSTEM

The human brain operates something like an electronic computing machine. It contains millions of short nerve-lengths comparable to wires, and millions of nerve-connections comparable to switches. The workings of this complex system are not fully understood, but we do know that electrical impulses pass through it at a very regular speed of about four hundred feet per second. It is the passage of these impulses that constitutes our thinking.

Even the simplest thought requires the passage of a current over a complicated circuit containing innumerable switches. When an impulse starts, it might follow any one of an enormous number of routes, depending on how the switches click. But once a route has been selected, there is some tendency for the switches to set, so that a second impulse starting from the same point as the first can more easily duplicate the route than pick out a new one of its own. It is by this setting of the switches that memory and habits develop. It may take a number of repetitions to have a significant effect.

A switch may be set so firmly that a possible connection is blocked out temporarily, or even permanently. For instance, most of us have had the experience of doing a complicated problem of arithmetic, in the midst of which we have made a very obvious mistake, such as multiplying two by two and getting two as the result. We have then checked it over several times without finding the error—two times two still seems to give us two. One of our switches has temporarily been jammed in the wrong position. Fortunately, not every passage of a nerve impulse jams a switch; it merely makes it easier for it to turn one way than another.

There are always a number of impulses passing through different circuits, and these affect each other. The way we think at a given time is therefore determined largely by our previous experiences—not only the things we have encountered, but the particular paths that our nerve impulses have followed as a result of encountering them. No two of us started out with exactly the same wiring system, and the original differences have been increased by later activity.

The explanation just given is greatly oversimplified, but perhaps it will help us to understand something about the way we use words. Early in life we learn to associate words with people, things, events, and relations. Words as such are not permanently stored in the brain like cards in a filing cabinet. When a man hears or sees a word he receives an impulse which must pass along some circuit, determined by his previous experience with both words and things. When he hears it again, the new impulse tends to follow the same circuit, unless some intervening experience modifies it. On the other hand, when some other stimulus sends an impulse along part of the same circuit, he "remembers" the word. Meanwhile it, as a word, has completely disappeared from his mind. But the effect it has had on his nervous system, by operating some of the switches, persists. Consequently, if he has associated the word with a given situation, the recurrence of some aspect of that situation, either in physical fact or in mental review, is likely to reactivate the circuit, and he is again conscious of the word.

For instance, I look into a pen and see one animal bite another, and hear the second one squeal. I would not say anything, even to myself, unless I was to some extent interested in the activity. But if I was interested enough to notice it, part of the reaction of noticing would probably be the passing of words through my mind. The particular words that passed would be determined by my previous experiences. If I had seen similar animals before, I might say "One pig bit the other," or "One pig hurt the other," depending on whether I was more impressed by the action or its effect. If they were my own animals, I would probably think of them as individuals rather than simply as pigs, and might therefore say, "John hurt Mary."

Simple as this sentence is, I could not possibly have said it without having had a number of past experiences—enough to guess at the probable effect of John's teeth on Mary's ear and nervous system, and the significance of her squeal. Not being, myself, a small female pig, I must base my guess on a whole chain of assumptions; but I can be reasonably confident of its accuracy.

Certain events in the outside world have made impressions on my nervous system. I have associated words with these *impressions*, and not directly with the events themselves. If I attempt to communicate by the use of words, I must try to arouse *similar impressions in the nervous system* of the man I am talking to. Similar, not identical. His own past experiences, which cannot possibly be exactly the same as mine, are bound to affect his reactions. Even if he realizes that I am talking about my two pigs, his internal response may be quite surprising. I am expecting him to feel something like "Isn't that too bad?" but his actual sentiments may be "So what?" or even "Three cheers for John!"

We may be tempted to say: "Oh, he understands, all right. He just reacts differently." But what we call his understanding is merely a part of his total reaction, and cannot be separated, except verbally, from the rest of it. If you don't believe this, try telling a mother some time: "Oh, your boy is all right; he just broke a leg and a couple of ribs." The only thing she will understand from the word *just* is that you are an inhuman brute. As for the rest of the sentence, you have sent out a message saying "The damage to your son is temporary, so there is nothing to worry about." She has received one saying: "My darling is suffering, and there is no justice, and how do I know that one of his ribs hasn't punctured a lung?" And if you try to tell her that that is not a reasonable interpretation of your words, she will simply say (if she is still bothering to speak to you), "You have never been a mother." Her past experiences and her set of values are different from yours, especially where her son is concerned. Even if you had been more tactful in your report, your words could not possibly "mean" to her what they "mean" to you.

WORDS AND THINGS

The second relation—between words and the things they stand for—also needs some attention. We have already seen that the connection between a word and a thing is neither necessary nor direct. It is also important to realize that it is never quite the same twice, because the thing itself is always changing. If you buy a quart of milk, drink half of it, leave the rest in a warm kitchen for a couple of days, and then drink *that*, are you drinking the *same* milk?

The question cannot be answered intelligently without realizing that two quite different ideas are indicated by the word *same*. In the sense of continuity, it *is* the same milk you left there. In the sense of identity of structure, it is *not*. Important changes have taken place, and your tongue recognizes the effect of some of these changes at the first sip. Moreover, these changes have been taking place every instant that the milk has been there, and other changes have been taking place in the bottle. Such changes are not always perceptible, and we can often afford to disregard them, but they are inevitably taking place *all the time*; and the fact that we don't notice them does not prevent them from being real. It does no good to say that for "all practical purposes" a thing remains the same, unless we are quite sure that we can predict in advance what "all practical purposes" will be. If the bottle crystallizes and breaks at a tiny jar, or the milk picks up and multiplies germs that kill us, we cannot dispose of the unfortunate results by insisting that the "same" things were perfectly all right a while ago.

To go one step further into the matter, we may bring up the question of whether anything is the same, even at a given instant, to two different observers. Again the answer seems to be no. Since our senses, nervous systems, and backgrounds of past experience vary, no two people can get identical impressions of the "same" thing. The actual thing (unless it is something like a bullet or an axe) does not get into our heads. What does get in—what we are conscious of and what we talk about—is merely the impression made on our nervous system. Therefore when two people look at a Pekingese dog, and she says, "Oh, the cute little darling!" while he says "What a disgusting little slug," they are not applying different words to the *same* thing. Each of them is describing, not the physical dog, but the impression created in his own mind by a combination of his present sense-perceptions and his past experiences. Even if they agree verbally that it is a Pekingese, the meaning of their minds is not complete; because the word Pekingese still "means" something different to each of them.

It follows that "using the same words for the same things" is not even theoretically possible, because there simply aren't any "same things." The best we can hope for is a reasonable approximation. Our remote ancestors, when they developed the language, did not know this. A few of them had imaginative glimpses of the truth, but on the whole they believed very firmly that many things were identical, permanent, and alike to all observers; and the structure of the language, like the structure of their physical theories, reflected this belief. Until the development of modern physics and neurology there was no definite proof that they were wrong.

A good many men, for a good many centuries, have been trying to devise and encourage the use of a language suitable for perfect communication— a language in which every word has a fixed meaning, which any properly trained person can recognize; and in which the arrangement of words is completely systematic and "logical." [2] We can now see that such a language would be possible only if words operated in a vacuum, or at least in a perfectly uniform medium, of which each human skull somehow contained a part. We must therefore lower our sights.

Of course an approximate agreement as to the significance of words and word-arrangements is possible, or we could not communicate at all; and among people of similar backgrounds and training, communication over a limited range of subjects may reach a high degree of reliability. Dictionaries and grammars, if they are well made and sensibly used, may increase the uniformity of our language habits and thus improve the quality of our communication. But they may do us more harm than good if we let them blind us to the fact that language is not, and never can be, an independent, objective structure governed by its own laws. At its theoretical best, language can only stimulate similar (never identical) reactions in necessarily different nervous systems. Aside from its effect on these nervous systems, it has no importance at all.

The man who goes through life complaining that his friends (a) don't say what they mean, and (b) don't understand him when he speaks plain English, deserves pity rather than blame. He suffers from a delusion that makes it hard for him to look through the words and find out what the man behind them means; and equally hard for him to select and arrange his own words with some attention to the response that they probably will arouse, rather than the one they "should" arouse. If his delusion makes him haughty

---

[2] A large number of artificial languages for international use have been invented, fifty-three between 1880 and 1907. Volapük and Esperanto are the two most notable. Recently the International Auxiliary Association of New York proposed a new one, Interlingua, made up of components common to the languages most widely used today. [eds.]

and ill-tempered, it is probably because of continual frustration rather than natural viciousness.

The Relation of Words to Each Other

We must now turn our attention to the third relation—that of words to each other. In the light of what has already been said, we will remember that it is only the emphasis of our interest that is changed—the three relations continue to function together. We may begin by looking at three sentences:

(1) The boy kicked a dog.
(2) The man saw a stone.
(3) The question demanded an answer.

We have already seen that any sentence can represent an indefinite number of situations. These sentences themselves do not overlap—no reasonable interpretation of any of one of them could be applied to either of the others. Moreover, the general structure of the kind of situation to which each could refer is quite different, as we can see by analyzing the activity represented by each. In the first, the boy definitely did something to the dog. In the second, we *say* that the man did something to the stone; but what really must have happened is that light, reflected from the stone, did something to the nervous system of the man. And in the third, we don't know whether anything was done or not, though we can feel reasonably sure that if it was, the question did not do it.

Yet the formal or grammatical structure of all three sentences is exactly the same. We can call the second word in each of them the "subject," the third word the "verb," and the fifth word the "complement" or "direct object." A single diagram would apply to all the sentences, in spite of the differences between the three situations.

This formal similarity has a dangerous tendency to make different situations seem more alike than they actually are. When the sentence structure is obvious, we may forget to examine the structure of events—or even to make sure that there is one. A good many readers will accept perfectly meaningless statements like "The high temperature caused the heat," or "The increased prices made the goods more expensive," without noticing that the writer is shooting blanks. This explains the popularity of certain books.

Nevertheless, the familiar patterns are indispensable, since they help us to organize our reactions. Without them a writer would simply jumble words into a "sentence" in haphazard order, and it would be a coincidence if any two readers took them as indicating the same relations. . . .

Differences in Language Patterns

As a very simple example of the kinds of difference that occur, speakers of English have somehow managed to agree to put a modifier before a substantive rather than after it, while speakers of French use the opposite order. As a result, we automatically take *blue sky* to refer to a weather condition, and *sky blue* to a color; while the French take *bleu ciel* to be the color, and *ciel bleu* the weather condition. There is no use arguing about which is the better method. Either one seems to work satisfactorily as long as we know what to expect.

Sometimes the order is unimportant. *Beautiful house* causes no confusion if it is switched to *house beautiful*. But there is a distinct difference between our reactions to *government business* and *business government*, *American ideal* and *ideal American*, and thousands of other reversible combinations. It must be emphasized that the difference is simply in our habitual reactions. There is no intrinsic difference in the word-order itself, or the French practice would be impossible.

Such differences as these indicate that we should be wary of grammatical rules laid down in the name of logic, especially when they assert that common constructions "really mean" something quite different from what most speakers intend. Meaning occurs in human nervous systems, not in vacuum; and our ability to communicate depends on the agreements that, consciously or subconsciously, we have actually made—not on the ones that we "should" have made.

The Scope and Purpose of Grammar

Unfortunately, not all our agreements are as strong or as general as the one about modifier-substantive order. There are a good many points, involving both the forms and the order of words, on which practice is far from uniform. Is it better to say "He done it" or "He did it," "It is I" or "It is me"? Are there any dependable rules about the uses of compound verbs? Is it legitimate to split an infinitive, to begin a sentence with *and*, or to end one with a preposition? How many of our words change form, and how, and what is the general effect of each change? When is the order of words automatic, and when does it have to be carefully considered? A grammar is simply an organized study of such questions as these.

Uniform habits make for better communication and a grammarian has a perfect right (if he likes) to do what he can to encourage uniformity, as long as he doesn't try to subordinate the facts to his theory, or twist the evidence as to what the facts are. If he can show that one construction is more likely to be clearly understood than another, or that it actually enjoys a greater prestige, a good many people will modify their habits accordingly.

But a grammarian has no more right to say what our habits ought to be than a chemist has to say how molecules ought to react to changes in temperature.

One more point must be made. The idea that grammar is a logical system has a tendency to make us concentrate on the "concepts" involved, and to turn us away from the study of the actual phenomena of language. A great deal of the material that appears in many texts leads only to the ability to talk *about* the language according to a set of artificial conventions, and has no value whatever in increasing our ability either to use or to understand it.

For instance, it is necessary to distinguish between "direct" and "indirect objects" in Latin for the simple physical reason that they take different forms. In English the distinction, however fascinating, is completely useless. A four-year-old can make and understand sentences like "He gave me a book"; and he won't be able to do either a bit better for learning that *me* may be called an "indirect object" and *book* a "direct object." We do not have separate dative and accusative cases in English; and since the boy is not in the least likely to say "He gave I a book" or "He gave a book me," no question of either form or position is involved. If we force him to "distinguish between these constructions" we are not teaching him anything about the use of the language, but only about an unnecessarily complicated linguistic theory.

It may be that all knowledge is good in itself, and that the question "Good for what?" is impertinent. But only those who choose to do so need learn about butterflies or old postage stamps; and the one justification for the widespread belief that everybody should learn something about grammar is the theory that a knowledge of it is directly useful in communication. Considering the amounts of time, money, and effort invested, we cannot afford to accept this theory in blind faith.

As a matter of fact, a good many of our educators have stopped accepting it, and have announced that there is no discoverable connection between training in "formal grammar" and ability to use English effectively.

But instead of recommending changes in our "formal grammar," they have usually been satisfied that it should be abandoned entirely. This is throwing out the baby with the bath. English is not so different from all other subjects that a systematic study of it is worthless. We need only make sure that the system is soundly organized on the basis of the facts, and that we concentrate our attention on the choices we have to make, not on things to say when there is no question of choice.

SUGGESTED ASSIGNMENTS

1. Most words are imprecise. For example, think of the disappointments in store for you when you order a *cheese sandwich*. (What kind of bread? White? Rye?

Whole wheat? Pumpernickel? Substantial home-made? Frothy commercial? What kind of cheese? Swiss? Cheddar? Brick? Limburger? Natural cheese? "Cheese food"? Strong? Mild? Hard? Soft? What proportion of cheese to bread? And so on.) Because of this imprecision, a given word will have different meanings, ranging from slightly different to vastly different, to different persons. Consider, for example, this sentence:

I'm going to buy a *car*.

What is the word *car* likely to mean if the speaker is seventeen-year-old Sammy? His fifty-year-old father? This leads to an important question that you can probably answer just as well by class discussion as by reading: Why does a given word mean different things to different persons?

2. A Greek philosopher once said, "You cannot cross the same river twice." And Thomas Wolfe entitled a novel *You Can't Go Home Again*. Both of these statements express the same idea. Think them over and be prepared to explain the idea in class.

3. Write a brief theme in which you describe an experience of a misunderstanding caused by the speaker and the listener understanding a word in different senses.

The Uses of Language

Irving M. Copi

Language has many uses, and often several uses are operative in the same set of words. Consider for example the boy who asked to go for a ride one Sunday afternoon in the new family car. His father refused the request with "Sorry, Jim, but it looks like rain today. Let's wait till the sun is out." The following Sunday was a beautiful sunny day, and Jim said to his father expectantly, "Daddy, the sun is shining." Here one set of words not only conveys information but makes a request that may lead to action. And what uses of language are embodied in the words of the jealous wife who greeted her late-arriving husband with "There's lipstick on your collar"?

Three major uses of languages are here sorted out and described by Irving M. Copi. Copi, a logician, is Professor of Philosophy at the University of Michigan.

1. THREE BASIC FUNCTIONS OF LANGUAGE

Language is so subtle and complicated an instrument that the multiplicity of its uses is often lost sight of. Here, as in many other situations, there is danger in our tendency to oversimplify things.

A not uncommon complaint of those who take too narrow a view of the legitimate uses of language concerns the way in which words are "wasted" at social functions. "So much talk, and so little said!" sums up this kind of criticism. And more than one person has been heard to remark, "So and so asked me how I felt. What a hypocrite! He doesn't care in the least how I feel!" Such remarks reveal a failure to understand the complex purposes for which language is used. It is shown also in the deplorable conduct of the bore, who, when asked how he feels, actually proceeds to tell about the state of his health—usually at great length and in much detail. But people do not usually talk at parties to instruct each other. And ordinarily the question "How are you?" is a friendly greeting, not a request for a medical report.

One very important use of language is to communicate information. Ordinarily this is accomplished by formulating and affirming (or denying) propositions. Language used to affirm or deny propositions, or to present arguments, is said to be serving the *informative function*. In this context we use the word "information" to include misinformation: false as well as true propositions, incorrect as well as correct arguments. Informative discourse is used to *describe* the world, and to reason about it. Whether the alleged facts that are being described are important or unimportant, general or particular, does not matter; in any case the language used to describe or report them is being used informatively.

We may distinguish two basic uses or functions of language in addition to the informative, and refer to them as the *expressive* and the *directive*. Just as science provides us with the clearest examples of informative discourse, so poetry furnishes us the best examples of language serving an *expressive* function. The following lines of Burns:

> O my Luve's like a red, red rose
>> That's newly sprung in June:
> O my Luve's like the melodie
>> That's sweetly play'd in tune!

are definitely not intended to inform us of any facts or theories concerning the world. The poet's purpose is to communicate not knowledge but feelings and attitudes. The passage was not written to report any information but to *express* certain emotions that the poet felt very keenly and to evoke feelings of a similar kind in the reader. Language serves the *expressive* function whenever it is used to vent or communicate feelings or emotions.

Not all expressive language is poetry, however. We express sorrow by saying "That's too bad," or "Oh my," and enthusiasm by shouting "Wow!" or "Oh boy!" The lover expresses his delicate passion by murmuring "Darling!" or "Oh baby!" The poet expresses his complex and concentrated emotions in a sonnet or some other verse form. A worshipper may express his feeling of wonder and awe at the vastness and mystery of the universe by reciting the Lord's Prayer or the twenty-third Psalm of David. All these are uses of language not to communicate information but to express emotions, feelings, or attitudes. Expressive discourse *as expressive* is neither true nor false. For a person to apply only the criteria of truth or falsehood, correctness or incorrectness, to expressive discourse like a poem is to miss its point and to lose much of its value. The student whose enjoyment of Keats' sonnet "On first looking into Chapman's Homer" is marred by his historical knowledge that Balboa rather than Cortez discovered the Pacific Ocean is a "poor reader" of poetry. The purpose of the poem is not to teach history, but something else entirely. This is not to say that poetry can have no literal significance. Some poems *do* have an informative content which may be an important ingredient in their total effect. Some poetry may well be "criticism of life," in the words of a great poet. But such poems are more than merely expressive, as we are using the term here. Such poetry may be said to have a "mixed usage," or to serve a multiple function. This notion will be explained further in the following section.

Expression may be analyzed into two components. When a man curses to himself when he is alone, or a poet writes poems which he shows to no one, or a man prays in solitude, his language functions to express or evince his own attitude but does not serve to evoke a similar attitude in anyone else. On the other hand, when an orator seeks to inspire his audience—not to action, but to share enthusiasm; when a lover courts his beloved in poetic language; when the crowd cheers its athletic team; the language used not only evinces the attitudes of the speakers but also is intended to evoke the same attitudes in the hearers. Expressive discourse, then, is used either to *evince* the speaker's feelings or to *evoke* feelings on the part of the auditor. Of course it may do both.

Language serves the *directive* function when it is used for the purpose of causing (or preventing) overt action. The clearest examples of directive discourse are commands and requests. When a mother tells her little boy to wash his hands before supper, she does not intend to communicate any information to him or to evince or evoke any particular emotion. Her language is intended to get results, to cause action of the indicated kind. When the same mother asks the grocer to deliver certain goods to her house, she is again using language directively, to motivate or effect *action*. To ask a question is ordinarily to request an answer, and is also to be classified as directive discourse. The difference between a command and a request is a rather subtle one, for almost any command can be translated into a request by adding the word "please," or by suitable changes in tone of voice or in facial expression.

In its nakedly imperative form, directive discourse is neither true nor false. A command such as "Close the window" cannot be either true or false in any literal sense. Whether the command is obeyed or disobeyed does not affect or determine its truth-value, for it has none. We may disagree about whether a command has been obeyed or not; we may disagree about whether a command should be obeyed or not; but we never disagree about whether a command is true or false, for it cannot be either. However, the reasonableness or propriety, the unreasonableness or impropriety of commands are properties somewhat analogous to the truth or falsehood of informative discourse. And questions of the propriety of given commands can be raised and resolved in ways that are strictly within the scope of logic.

2. DISCOURSE SERVING MULTIPLE FUNCTIONS

In the preceding section the examples presented were chemically pure specimens, so to speak, of the three basic kinds of communication. The threefold division proposed is illuminating and valuable, but it cannot be applied mechanically, because almost any ordinary communication will probably exemplify, to a greater or less extent, all three uses of language. Thus a poem, which is primarily expressive discourse, may have a moral and be in effect a command to the reader (or hearer) to lead a certain kind of life, and may also convey a certain amount of information. On the other hand, although a sermon is predominantly directive, seeking to cause certain appropriate action by members of the congregation (whether to abandon their evil ways, or to contribute money to the church, or what not), it may evince and evoke sentiments, thus serving the expressive function, and may also include some information, communicating some factual material. And a scientific treatise, essentially informative, may evince something of the writer's own enthusiasm, thus serving an expressive function, and may also, at least implicitly, serve some directive function or other, perhaps bidding the reader to verify independently the author's conclusion. Most ordinary uses of language are mixed.

It is not always the result of any confusion on the part of the speaker when his language serves mixed or multiple functions. It is rather the case that *effective* communication demands certain combinations of function. Few of us stand to each other in the relation of parent to child or employer to employee. And outside the context of such formal relationships as these, one cannot simply issue an order with any expectation of having it obeyed. Consequently a certain indirection must be employed: a bald command would arouse antagonism or resentment and be self-defeating. One cannot cause action by merely voicing an imperative; it is necessary to use a more subtle method of stimulating the desired action.

Action may be said to have very complex causes. Motivation is more properly to be discussed by a psychologist than a logician, but it is common knowledge that actions are usually caused by both desires and beliefs. A man who *desires* to eat food will not touch what is on his plate unless he *believes* it to be food; and even though he *believes* it to be food he will not touch it unless he *desires* to eat. This fact is relevant to our present discussion because desires are a special type of what we have been calling "attitudes."

Consequently actions may be caused by evoking appropriate attitudes *and* communicating relevant information. Assuming your listeners to be benevolent, you may cause them to contribute to a given charity by informing them of its effectiveness in accomplishing benevolent results. In such a case your use of language is ultimately directive, since its purpose is to cause action. But a naked command would be far less effective in this situation than the informative discourse used. Suppose, on the other hand, that your listeners are already persuaded that the charity in question does accomplish benevolent results. Here again you cannot simply command with any great hope of being obeyed, but you may succeed in causing them to act in the desired fashion by somehow arousing a sufficiently benevolent feeling or emotion in them. The discourse you use to realize your end is expressive discourse; you must make a "moving appeal." Thus your language will have a mixed use, functioning both expressively and directively. Or finally, let us suppose that you are seeking a donation from people who have *neither* a benevolent attitude *nor* a belief that the charity serves a benevolent purpose. Here you must use *both* informative and expressive language. In such a case the language used serves all three functions, being directive, informative, and expressive all at once, not accidentally as a mere mixture that just happens to occur, but essentially, as necessary to successful communication.

Some writers on language have suggested that discourse serves more than these three distinct functions. It is possible, however, to understand any other function as a mixture or combination of two or possibly all three of the basic uses that have been distinguished here. The most important of these others has frequently been called the "ceremonial" use of language. Included within this category are many different kinds of phrases, ranging from relatively trivial words of greeting to the more portentous discourse of the marriage ceremony, phrasings of state documents, and the verbal rituals performed on holy days in houses of worship. But these can all be regarded as mixtures of expressive and directive discourse, rather than some altogether different and unique kind. For example, the usual ceremonial greetings and chit-chat at social gatherings serve the purpose of evincing and evoking goodwill and sociability. Perhaps for some speakers they are intended also to serve the directive purpose of causing their hearers to act in certain definitive ways, to patronize the speaker's business, to offer him employment, or to invite him to dinner. At the other extreme, the impressive language of the marriage ceremony is intended to emphasize the solemnity of the occasion (its expressive function), and also to cause the bride and groom to perform in their new roles with heightened appreciation of the seriousness of the marriage contract (its directive function).

SUGGESTED ASSIGNMENTS

1. Study the six selections below and be prepared to point out the uses of language in each

A BIRTHDAY

My heart is like a singing bird
   Whose nest is in a watered shoot:
My heart is like an apple-tree
   Whose boughs are bent with thickset fruit;
My heart is like a rainbow shell   5
   That paddles in a halcyon sea;
My heart is gladder than all these
   Because my love is come to me.

Raise me a dais of silk and down;
   Hang it with vair and purple dyes;   10
Carve it in doves and pomegranates,
   And peacocks with a hundred eyes;
Work it in gold and silver grapes,
   In leaves and silver fleurs-de-lys;
Because the birthday of my life   15
   Is come, my love is come to me.

CHRISTINA ROSETTI

b. Sea King Sailing Surf Board. Wonderful for summer sailing—you don't have to be an expert. Easy to handle aluminum boom. Non-sinkable balsa wood flotation. Special non-skid deck for safety; removable centerboard, kick-up rudder for shallow water. 14-ft. Fiberglass covered hull. With 3-ft. beam. Maximum 10 in. deep 14-ft. gunwale length; transom 18 in. wide by 4 in. deep.

A MAIL-ORDER CATALOG

c. Every Price Cut $1. Famous Pinehurst at Low Prices. It's like walking on air. Heel-to-toe foam rubber shock absorbing cushion for greater foot ease. Fashioned of extra fine leathers. Finest Goodyear welt construction. Super-tex lining resists athlete's foot. $11.99.

A MAIL-ORDER CATALOG

d. None of them knew the color of the sky. Their eyes glanced level, and were fastened upon the waves that swept toward them. These waves were of the hue of slate, save for the tops, which were of foaming white, and all of the men knew the colors of the sea. The horizon narrowed and widened, and dipped and rose, and at all times its edge was jagged with waves that seemed thrust up in points like rocks. Many a man ought to have a bath-tub larger than the boat which here rode upon the sea. These waves were most wrongfully and barbarously abrupt and tall, and each froth-top was a problem in small-boat navigation.

STEPHEN CRANE'S "THE OPEN BOAT"

e. One day somebody should remind us that, even though there may be political and ideological differences between us, the Vietnamese are our brothers, the Russians are our brothers, the Chinese are our brothers; and one day we've got to sit down together at the table of brotherhood. But in Christ there is neither Jew nor Gentile. In Christ there is neither male nor female. In Christ there is neither Communist nor capitalist. In Christ, somehow, there is neither bound nor free. We are all one in Christ Jesus. And when we truly believe in the sacredness of human personality, we won't exploit people, we won't trample over people with the iron feet of oppression, we won't kill anybody.

MARTIN KING'S "A CHRISTMAS SERMON ON PEACE"

f. These are the times that try men's souls. The summer soldier and the sunshine patriot will, in this crisis, shrink from the service of their country; but he that stands it *now*, deserves the love and thanks of man and woman. Tyranny, like hell, is not easily conquered; yet we have this consolation with us, that the harder the conflict, the more glorious the triumph. What we obtain too cheap, we esteem too lightly; it is dearness only that gives every thing its value. Heaven knows how to put a proper price upon its goods; and it would be strange indeed if so celestial an article as FREEDOM should not be highly rated.

THOMAS PAINE'S "THE CRISIS"

2. Assume that you are the representative of a business firm that has sent you to investigate Community X as a possibility for future expansion of the business— a branch office, a new factory, or something of the sort. Write a theme in the form of a report to the company, making either a positive or negative recommendation. Your intent is to be informative. As a contrasting exercise, assume that you are the Secretary of the Chamber of Commerce of Community X. Write a theme in the form of a letter to the same company. Your purpose is to induce the company to establish its business in Community X. Make an analysis of how the two themes differ in their use of language.

3. Assume that you are Chairman of the Board of Student Governors at your college. You are disturbed at the apathy of some student organizations for failing to send representatives to the monthly meeting of the Board. Write a letter, directive in intent, to the presidents of the sluggard organizations, announcing the next meeting. You want their representatives to attend the

meeting. Keep in mind as you write that you want to gain their support, not to lose it completely.

4. Professor Copi discusses three basic uses of language—the informative, the expressive, and the directive, and mentions a fourth, the ceremonial use, which some writers consider very important. In addition there are other uses, such as these:

   a. Language can be used to conceal thought.
   b. Language can be used to conceal ignorance.
   c. Language can be used to confuse one's listener.
   d. Language can be used to release tension.
   e. Language can be used to soothe feelings.

   Give one example of each of these five uses. Which of these uses might be included under Copi's three major functions?

The Gift of Tongues

Clyde Kluckhohn

For several decades anthropologists have concerned themselves with a concept that has come to be known as the Whorfian hypothesis, so called because Benjamin L. Whorf presented it cogently in his writings. The gist of this hypothesis is that the language we happen to speak directs our perceptions into predetermined channels, and influences the ways in which we think; in short, it affects the "world of reality" in which we live. The late Clyde Kluckhohn was Professor of Anthropology at Harvard University.

. . . We live in an environment which is largely verbal in the sense that we spend the most of our waking hours uttering words or responding actively or passively to the words of others. We talk to ourselves. We talk to our families and friends—partly to communicate to them and to persuade them, partly just to express ourselves. We read newspapers, magazines, books, and other written matter. We listen to the radio, to sermons, lectures, and movies. As Edward Sapir says:

> Language completely interpenetrates direct experience. For most persons every experience, real or potential, is saturated with verbalism. This perhaps explains why so many nature lovers do not feet that they are truly in touch with nature until they have mastered the names of a great many flowers and trees, as though the primary world of reality were a verbal one, and as though one could not get close to nature unless one first mastered the terminology that somehow magically expresses it. It is this constant interplay between language and experience which removes language from the cold status of such purely and simply symbolic systems as mathematical symbolism or flag signalling.[1]

. . . Because anthropological linguists have usually been trained as ethnologists and have often done general field work, they have tended less than other students of language to isolate speech from the total life of the people. To the anthropologist, language is just one kind of cultural behavior with many interesting connections to other aspects of action and thought. Analysis of a vocabulary shows the principal emphases of a culture and reflects culture history. In Arabic, for example, there are more than six thousand different words for camel, its parts, and equipment. The crudity and the special local words of the vocabulary of Spanish-speaking villages in New Mexico reflect the long isolation of these groups from the main stream of Latin culture. The particular archaisms used show that the break with the main continuity of the Spanish language occurred during the eighteenth century. The fact that the Boorabbee Indians of Panama use words like *gadsoot* (gadzooks), *forsoo'* (forsooth), *chee-ah* (cheer), and *mai-api* (mayhap) suggests a possible connection with Elizabethan buccaneers. . . .

We are always bringing together by words things that are different and separating verbally things that are, in fact, the same.[2] A Christian Scientist refused to take vitamin tablets on the ground that they were "medicine"; he willingly accepted them when it was explained that they were "food." An insurance company discovered that behavior toward "gasoline drums" was ordinarily circumspect, that toward "empty gasoline drums" habitually careless. Actually, the "empty" drums are the more dangerous because they contain explosive vapor.

The semantic problem is almost insoluble because, John Locke said, "So

---

[1] From "Language," by Edward Sapir, *Encyclopedia of the Social Sciences,* vol. ix. Copyright 1933 by The Macmillan Company and used with their permission.
[2] For example, the word *building* brings together such different things as a gymnasium, a library, and an outhouse; and the word *player* brings together such different persons as Wilt Chamberlin, Arthur Rubinstein, and Bobby Fischer. On the other hand, the words *mind* and *body* separate verbally things that are, in fact, the same. And the Eskimo words *qana* (falling snow) and *piqsiroq* (drifting snow) separate verbally what are, for Americans, the same thing. [eds.]

difficult is it to show the various meaning and imperfections of words when we have nothing else but words to do it by." . . . Anyone who has struggled with translation is made to realize that there is more to a language than its dictionary. The Italian proverb *"traduttore, tradittore"* (the translator is a betrayer) is all too correct. I asked a Japanese with a fair knowledge of English to translate back from the Japanese that phrase in the new Japanese constitution that represents our "life, liberty, and the pursuit of happiness." He rendered, "license to commit lustful pleasure." English to Russian and Russian back to English transmuted a cablegram "Genevieve suspended for prank" into "Genevieve hanged for juvenile delinquency." . . .

The British and the Americans are still under the delusion that they speak the same language. With some qualifications this is true as far as denotations are concerned, though there are concepts like "sissy" in American for which there are no precise English equivalents. Connotations, however, are often importantly different, and this makes for the more misunderstanding because both languages are still called "English" (treating alike by words things that are different). An excellent illustration is . . . supplied by Margaret Mead:

> . . . in Britain, the word "compromise" is a good word, and one may speak approvingly of any arrangement which has been a compromise, including, very often, one in which the other side has gained more than fifty per cent of the points at issue. On the other hand, in the United States, the minority position is still the position from which everyone speaks; the President *versus* Congress, Congress *versus* the President, the State government *versus* the metropolis and the metropolis *versus* the State government. This is congruent with the American doctrine of checks and balances, but it does not permit the word "compromise" to gain the same ethical halo which it has in Britain. Where, in Britain, to compromise means to work out a good solution, in America it usually means to work out a bad one, a solution in which all the points of importance (to both sides) are lost. Thus, in negotiations between the United States and Britain, all of which had, in the nature of the case, to be compromises, as two sovereignties were involved, the British could always speak approvingly and proudly of the result, while the Americans had to emphasize their losses.[3]

The words, then, that pass so readily from mouth to mouth are not entirely trustworthy substitutes for the facts of the physical world. The smooth-worn standard coins are slippery steppingstones from mind to mind. Nor is thinking simply a matter of choosing words to express thoughts. The selected words always mirror social situation as well as objective fact. Two men go into a bar in New York and are overcharged for bad liquor: "This is a gyp joint." The same thing happens in Paris: "The French are a bunch of chiselers."

[3] Margaret Mead, "Where Were You Born?" *Child Study* (Spring 1941).

Perhaps the most important contribution of anthropological linguistics has come from the difficulties the anthropologist goes through in trying to express the meanings contained in speech structures completely foreign to the pattern of all European tongues. This study and this experience has forced upon the anthropologist a rather startling discovery which is fraught with meaning for a world where peoples speaking many different idioms are trying to communicate without distortion. Every language is something more than a vehicle for exchanging ideas and information—more even than a tool for self-expression and for letting off emotional steam or for getting other people to do what we want.

Every language is also a special way of looking at the world and interpreting experience. Concealed in the structure of each different language are a whole set of unconscious assumptions about the world and life in it. The anthropological linguist has come to realize that the general ideas one has about what happens in the world outside oneself are not altogether "given" by external events. Rather, up to a point, one sees and hears what the grammatical system of one's language has made one sensitive to, has trained one to look for in experience. This bias is the more insidious because everyone is so unconscious of his native language as a system. To one brought up to speak a certain language it is part of the very nature of things, remaining always in the class of background phenomena. It is as natural that experience should be organized and interpreted in these language-defined classes as it is that the seasons change. In fact the naïve view is that anyone who thinks in any other way is unnatural or stupid, or even vicious—and most certainly illogical.

In point of fact, traditional or Aristotelian logic has been mainly the analysis of consistencies in the structures of languages like Greek and Latin. The subject-predicate form of speech has implied a changeless world of fixed relations between "substances" and their "qualities." This view, as Korzybski[4] has insisted, is quite inadequate to modern physical knowledge which shows that the properties of an atom alter from instant to instant in accord with the shifting relationships of its component elements. The little word "is" has brought us much confusion because sometimes it signifies that the subject exists, sometimes that it is a member of a designated class, sometimes that subject and predicate are identical. Aristotelian logic teaches us that something is or isn't. Such a statement is often false to reality, for both-and is more often true than either-or. "Evil" ranges all the way from black through an infinite number of shades of gray. Actual experience does not present clear-cut entities like "good" and "bad," "mind" and "body"; the sharp split remains verbal. Modern physics has shown that even in the

---

[4] Alfred Korzybski, foremost proponent of General Semantics, wrote *Science and Sanity: An Introduction to Non-Aristotelian Systems and General Semantics,* a difficult but significant book on language and human behavior. Korzybski's views have been popularized by S. I. Hayakawa, Stuart Chase, and others. [eds.]

inanimate world there are many questions that cannot be answered by an unrestricted "yes" or an unqualified "no."

From the anthropological point of view there are as many different worlds upon the earth as there are languages. Each language is an instrument which guides people in observing, in reacting, in expressing themselves in a special way. The pie of experience can be sliced in many different ways, and language is the principal directive force in the background. You can't say in Chinese, "answer me yes or no," for there aren't words for yes and no. Chinese gives priority to "how?" and nonexclusive categories; European languages to "what?" and exclusive categories. In English we have both real plurals and imaginary plurals, "ten men" and "ten days"; in Hopi plurals and cardinal numbers may be used only for things that can be seen together as an objective group. The fundamental categories of the French verb are before and after (tense) and potentiality vs. actuality (mood); the fundamental categories of one American Indian language (Wintu) are subjectivity vs. objectivity, knowledge vs. belief, freedom vs. actual necessity.

In the Haida language of British Columbia there are more than twenty verbal prefixes that indicate whether an action was performed by carrying, shooting, hammering, pushing, pulling, floating, stamping, picking, chopping, or the like. Some languages have different verbs, adjectives, and pronouns for animate and inanimate things. In Melanesia there are as many as four variant forms for each possessive pronoun. One may be used for the speaker's body and mind, another for illegitimate relatives and his loincloth, a third his possessions and gifts. The underlying conceptual images of each language tend to constitute a coherent though unconscious philosophy.

Where in English one word, "rough," may equally well be used to describe a road, a rock, or the business surface of a file, the Navaho language finds a need for three different words which may not be used interchangeably. While the general tendency is for Navaho to make finer and more concrete distinctions, this is not inevitably the case. The same stem is used for rip, light beam, and echo, ideas which seem diverse to speakers of European languages. One word is used to designate a medicine bundle with all its contents, the skin quiver in which the contents are wrapped, the contents as a whole, and some of the distinct items. Sometimes the point is not that the images of Navahos are less fluid and more delimited but rather just that the external world is dissected along different lines. For example, the same Navaho word is used to describe both a pimply face and a nodule-covered rock. In English a complexion might be termed "rough" or "coarse," but a rock would never, except facetiously, be described as pimply. Navaho differentiates two types of rough rock: the kind which is rough in the manner in which a file is rough and the kind which is nodule-encrusted. In these cases the differences between the Navaho and the English ways of seeing the world cannot be disposed of merely by saying that the Navaho language is more precise. The variations rest in the features which the two languages see as essential. Cases can indeed be given where the Navaho is notably less precise. Navaho gets along with a single word for flint, metal, knife, and certain other objects of metal. This, to be sure, is due to the historical accident that, after European contact, metal in general and knives in particular took the place of flint.

Navahos are perfectly satisfied with what seem to Europeans rather imprecise discriminations in the realm of time sequences. On the other hand, they are the fussiest people in the world about always making explicit in the forms of the language many distinctions which English makes only occasionally and vaguely. In English one says, "I eat," meaning. "I eat something." The Navaho point of view is different. If the object thought of is actually indefinite, then "something" must be tacked on to the verb.

The nature of their language forces the Navaho to notice and report many other distinctions in physical events which the nature of the English language allows speakers to neglect in most cases, even though their senses are just as capable as those of the Navaho to register the smaller details of what goes on in the external world. For example, suppose a Navaho range rider and a white supervisor see that a wire fence needs repair. The supervisor will probably write in his notebook, "Fence at such and such a place must be fixed." If the Navaho reports the break, he must choose between forms that indicate whether the damage was caused by some person or by a nonhuman agency, whether the fence was of one or several strands of wire.

In general, the difference between Navaho thought and English thought —both as manifested in the language and as forced by the very nature of the linguistic forms into such patterns—is that Navaho thought is ordinarily much more specific. The ideas expressed by the English verb "to go" provide a nice example. When a Navaho says that he went somewhere he never fails to specify whether it was afoot, astride, by wagon, auto, train, airplane, or boat. If it be a boat, it must be specified whether the boat floats off with the current, is propelled by the speaker, or is made to move by an indefinite or unstated agency. The speed of a horse (walk, trot, gallop, run) is expressed by the verb form chosen. He differentiates between starting to go, going along, arriving at, returning from a point. It is not, of course, that these distinctions *cannot* be made in English, but that they *are not* made consistently. They seem of importance to English speakers only under special circumstances.

A cross-cultural view of the category of time is highly instructive. Beginners in the study of classical Greek are often troubled by the fact that the word *opiso* sometimes means "behind," sometimes "in the future." Speakers of English find this baffling because they are accustomed to think of themselves as moving through time. The Greeks, however, conceived of themselves as stationary, of time as coming up behind them, overtaking them, and then, still moving on, becoming the "past" that lay before their eyes.

Present European languages emphasize time distinctions. The tense systems are usually thought of as the most basic of verbal inflections. However, this was not always so. Streitberg says that in primitive Indo-European a special indicator for the present was usually lacking. In many languages, certainly, time distinctions are only irregularly present or are of distinctly secondary importance. In Hopi the first question answered by the verb form is that of the type of information conveyed by the assertion. Is a situation reported as actuality, as anticipated, or as a general truth? In the anticipatory form there is no necessary distinction between past, present, and future. The English translation must choose from context between "was about to run," "is about to run," and "will run." The Wintu language of California carries this stress upon implications of validity much farther. The sentence "Harry is chopping wood" must be translated in five different ways, depending upon whether the speaker knows this by hearsay, by direct observation, or by inference of three degrees of plausibility.

In no language are the whole of a sense experience and all possible interpretations of it expressed. What people think and feel and how they report what they think and feel are determined, to be sure, by their personal history, and by what actually happens in the outside world. But they are also determined by a factor which is often overlooked; namely, the pattern of linguistic habits which people acquire as members of a particular society. It makes a difference whether or not a language is rich in metaphors and conventional imagery.

Our imaginations are restricted in some directions, free in others. The linguistic particularization of detail along one line will mean the neglect of other aspects of the situation. Our thoughts are directed in one way if we speak a language where all objects are classified according to sex, in another if the classification is by social position or the form of the object. Grammars are devices for expressing relations. It makes a difference what is treated as object, as attribute, as state, as act. In Hopi, ideas referring to the seasons are not grouped with what we call nouns but rather with what we call adverbs. Because of our grammar it is easy to personify summer, to think of it as a thing or a state.

Even as between closely related tongues, the conceptual picture may be different. Let us take one final example from Margaret Mead:

> Americans tend to arrange objects on a single scale of value, from best to worst, biggest to smallest, cheapest to most expensive, etc., and are able to express a preference among very complex objects on such a single scale. The question, "What is your favorite color?" so intelligible to an American, is meaningless in Britain, and such a question is countered by: "Favorite color for what? A flower? A necktie?" Each object is thought of as having a most complex set of qualities, and color is merely a quality of an object, not something from a color chart on which one can make a choice which is transferable to a large number of different sorts of objects. The American reduction of complexities to single scales is entirely comprehensible in terms of the great diversity of value systems which different immigrant groups brought to the American scene. Some com-

mon denominator among the incommensurables was very much needed, and over-simplification was almost inevitable. But, as a result, Americans think in terms of qualities which have uni-dimensional scales, while the British, when they think of a complex object or event, even if they reduce it to parts, think of each part as retaining all of the complexities of the whole. Americans subdivide the scale; the British subdivide the object.[5]

Language and its changes cannot be understood unless linguistic behavior is related to other behavioral facts. Conversely, one can gain many subtle insights into those national habits and thought ways of which one is ordinarily unconscious by looking closely at special idioms and turns of speech in one's own and other languages. What a Russian says to an American doesn't really get across just from shuffling words—much is twisted or blunted or lost unless the American knows something about Russia and Russian life, a good deal more than the sheer linguistic skill needed for a formally correct translation. The American must indeed have gained some entrance to that foreign world of values and significances which are pointed up by the emphases of the Russian vocabulary, crystalized in the forms of Russian grammar, implicit in the little distinctions of meaning in the Russian language.

Any language is more than an instrument for conveying ideas, more even than an instrument for working upon the feelings of others and for self-expression. Every language is also a means of categorizing experience. The events of the "real" world are never felt or reported as a machine would do it. There is a selection process and an interpretation in the very act of response. Some features of the external situation are highlighted; others are ignored or not fully discriminated.

Every people has its own characteristic classes in which individuals pigeonhole their experiences.[6] These classes are established primarily by the language through the types of objects, processes, or qualities which receive special emphasis in the vocabulary and equally, though more subtly, through the types of differentiation or activity which are distinguished in grammatical forms. The language says, as it were, "notice this," "always consider this separate from that," "such and such things belong together." Since persons are trained from infancy to respond in these ways, they take such discriminations for granted as part of the inescapable stuff of life. When

[5] Margaret Mead, "The Application of Anthropological Techniques to Cross-National Communication," *Transactions of the New York Academy of Sciences* (February, 1947).

[6] Classification is mandatory. Franz Boas explains it thus: "An infinite number of words, one for each sense experience, would make language impossible, because the same experience is never repeated in an identical way. It has been pointed out that classification is unavoidable. The same dog in different positions or activities, or every individual dog as it appears at different times, is not designated, each by a specific word; rather, all kinds of dogs in all conditions and activities may be classed under one term." *General Anthropology* (New York, Heath, 1938), p. 126. [eds.]

we see two peoples with different social traditions respond in different ways to what appear to the outsider to be identical stimulus situations, we realize that experience is much less an objective absolute than we thought. Every language has an effect upon what the people who use it see, what they feel, how they think, what they can talk about.

"Common sense" holds that different languages are parallel methods for expressing the same "thoughts." "Common sense," however, itself implies talking so as to be readily understood by one's fellows—in the same culture. Anglo-American "common sense" is actually very sophisticated, deriving from Aristotle and the speculations of scholastic and modern philosophers. The fact that all sorts of basic philosophic questions are begged in the most cavalier fashion is obscured by the conspiracy of silent acceptance which always attends the system of conventional understandings that we call culture.

The lack of true equivalences between any two languages is merely the outward expression of inward differences between two peoples in premises, in basic categories, in the training of fundamental sensitivities, and in general view of the world. The way the Russians put their thoughts together shows the impress of linguistic habits, of characteristics ways of organizing experience, for

> Human beings do not live in the objective world alone nor alone in the world of social activity as ordinarily understood, but are very much at the mercy of the particular language which has become the medium of expression for their society. It is quite an illusion to imagine that one adjusts to reality essentially without the use of language and that language is merely an incidental means of solving specific problems of communication or reflection. The fact of the matter is that the 'real world' is to a large extent unconsciously built upon the language habits of the group. . . . We see and hear and otherwise experience very largely as we do because the language habits of our community predispose certain choices of interpretation.[7]

EDWARD SAPIR

A language is, in a sense, a philosophy.

SUGGESTED ASSIGNMENTS

1. We tend to think in terms of polar opposites because we have pairs of words like the following: *conservative-liberal*; *drunk-sober*; *work-play*; *intelligent-stupid*; *fat-thin*; *good-bad*; *sane-insane*; *guilty-innocent*; *open-shut*; *on-off*. But

---

[7] Edward Sapir, "Language," *Encyclopedia of the Social Sciences,* vol. ix (New York, The Macmillan Company, 1933).

there are few real either-or situations, offering a choice of only two possibilities. Here are five other kinds:

a. Third possibility between. "Did we win or lose?"
b. Neither possibility. "Is Smith a Baptist or a Methodist?"
c. Infinite possibilities between extremes. "Is it cold this morning?"
d. Limited possibilities between extremes. "What was his rank in the army?"
e. Both possibilities. "Is the blueprint of your house accurate?"

Confused thinking and trouble can occur when a person applies a two-possibility choice to one of the other kinds of situations; for example, "The judge said, 'Were you drunk or sober at the time of the accident? Don't beat about the bush, but answer me in one word.' "

Write a theme on the dangers of thinking in terms of polar opposites.

2. Languages vary in the words they have to slice up distance away from the speaker or listener. English has two words, *here* and *there*. Spanish has five: *aquí, acá, ahí, allá, allí*. Ask a native speaker of Spanish to explain the meaning of these words.

3. Our American use of personal names has its own language. If, for instance, you were introduced to an eminent speaker who has come to your university, and soon after you addressed him by his first name, your act would carry the message of effrontery. Our whole system of using first names, surnames, nicknames, and titles is a delicate one. Which one should you use with whom on what occasions? Who initiates the use of first names? How long should you use "Miss" before adopting "Helen"? How can you tell when to change, and in what way do you make the change? Write a theme on the use of names in social, business, and academic intercourse.

FURTHER READINGS

Berlin, Brent, and Paul Kay. *Basic Color Terms*. Berkeley: University of California Press, 1968. See pp. 1–14.

Bloomfield, Leonard. *Language*. New York: Holt, Rinehart and Winston, 1933. For meaning, see chs. 2 and 9.

Brown, Roger. *Psycholinguistics: Selected Papers*. New York: Free Press, 1970. For Whorfian Hypothesis, see pp. 235–256.

————. *Words and Things*. New York: Free Press, 1958. For Whorfian Hypothesis, see pp. 229–263.

Carroll, John B. *The Study of Language*. Cambridge, Mass.: Harvard University Press, 1953. For a definition of langauge and discussion of the work of linguistic scientists, see pp. 7–15. For the Whorfian Hypothesis, see pp. 43–48.

Gleason, H. A., Jr. *An Introduction to Linguistic Science*. New York: Holt, Rinehart and Winston, 1955 and 1961. For language, see ch. 1.

Hayakawa, S. I. *Language in Thought and Action*. New York: Harcourt Brace Jovanovich, 1949. For the uses of language, see ch. 5 and 7.

Herskovits, M. J. *Man and His Works*. New York: Alfred A. Knopf, 1947. For the Whorfian Hypothesis, see pp. 440–457.

Hoijer, Harry. "The Relation of Language to Culture," in A. L. Kroeber, ed., *Anthropology Today*. Chicago: University of Chicago Press, 1953. For the Whorfian Hypothesis, see pp. 554–573.

Lee, Irving J. *Language Habits in Human Affairs*. New York: Harper & Row, 1941. For meaning, see pp. 29–51.

Lévy-Bruhl, Lucien, *How Natives Think*. New York: Alfred A. Knopf, 1925. For the Whorfian Hypothesis, see pp. 139–180.

Lorenz, Konrad. *King Solomon's Ring*. New York: Thomas Y. Crowell, 1952.

Wallis, Willis D. *An Introduction to Anthropology*. New York: Harper & Row, 1926. For the Whorfian Hypothesis, see pp. 416–431.

Whatmough, Joshua. *Language: A Modern Synthesis*. New York: St. Martin's Press, 1956. For the uses of language, see ch. 6.

3
LANGUAGE HISTORY

English: Its Origin and Relation to Other Languages

Henry Alexander

Languages, like people, have relatives, close and distant. Dutch, for example, is a close relative to English, while Danish is more distant, and Greek still more distant. The position of English in its own family of languages, Indo-European, and its development in England are the subjects of the simple sketch that follows. Dr. Henry Alexander is an outstanding Canadian linguist and was, before his retirement, Professor of English at Queen's University, Kingston, Ontario.

In tracing the history of English it is convenient to distinguish three different periods. First, there is the earliest age, from the arrival of the English in Britain down to about 1100. This is usually called the Old English (O.E.) or Anglo-Saxon period. From 1100 to about 1500 we have Middle English (M.E.). Finally there is Modern English (Mod. E.) from 1500 to the present day. Although the migration of the English people from the Continent of Europe took place mainly in the fifth and sixth centuries, we have very few records of anything written in English before about the year 700, after which we find an unbroken sequence of documents from which the nature of the language can be seen. If we take 700 as our starting-

From *The Story of Our Language* by Henry Alexander. Reprinted by permission of the author, publisher, copyright 1940. Published by Thomas Nelson & Sons, Ltd.

point, and 1900, which is close enough to the present day, as our final date, we get a convenient division into three periods of 400 years each.

O.E.   700–1100
M.E.   1100–1500
Mod. E.   1500–1900

The outstanding literary work of the O.E. period is the epic poem *Beowulf*, written about 700; the most important M.E. work is the poetry of Chaucer, who died in 1400; while in Mod. E., starting with Spencer and Shakespeare in the sixteenth century, there is a continuous series of great writers down to our own day.

We must not imagine the change from one of these periods to the next as abrupt and sudden, that on a certain day or week people stopped speaking Old English and started to speak Middle English. The process was rather like passing from one country to another when traveling; there is little at any one moment to show the change, but after a time one finds oneself in a new region. The evolution of the language was always gradual and just as imperceptible as it is at the present day; in any age there must have been considerable overlapping between old and new, the older generation, more conservative, retaining the earlier forms of speech, the younger adopting innovations. Even in the work of an individual writer we can often find a mixture of old and new forms. It must also be borne in mind that these changes were largely unconscious; they were not due to any deliberate effort on the part of the speaker.

English is not the original language of England but, like the English people themselves, came over from the continent of Europe. We cannot say what was the first language in England; that lies far back in the mists of prehistory. But we do know that, before the arrival of the English people and their language, there had existed for several centuries a tongue belonging to quite a different family of languages, the Celtic group. This was spoken by the ancient Britons. During the Roman occupation of Britain (43–410) Latin must also have been widely used. Both these earlier languages have left some traces on Old English. It was not until the middle of the fifth century, when the invading Teutonic tribes from the continent began to conquer the Britons and to impose on the country their own speech and social organization, that the history of the English language in England began. It had of course a long previous history on the continent, but to consider this would take us too far afield.

These continental tribes came from different parts of Northern Europe. Their exact origin is still an unsolved problem. With regard to two branches —the Angles and the Saxons—the historians are fairly well agreed; they came from a region around what is now Northern Germany. But in addition there was a third tribe, whose original home is less certain. These were the Jutes, who, according to the traditional view, migrated from Jutland, the northern part of Denmark; many modern historians, however, do not accept this explanation, which is based largely on the resemblance of the two names, Jutes and Jutland. The Angles settled mainly in the north and central portions of England and gave their name both to the country and its language; the Saxons settled mainly in the south; the Jutes in Kent, the south-eastern corner of England, and in the Isle of Wight. Mingled with these three main races there may well have been representatives of several other tribes, such as the Frisians, who inhabited what is now part of Holland, and even possibly the Franks. Because of this mixed strain in the English people the term Anglo-Saxon is not quite accurate. To use Anglo-Saxon-Jute . . . etc. would be awkward; so the modern practice is to employ Old English to indicate this early stage of our language. This also has the advantage of being parallel to Middle English and Modern English and to the terminology applied to other languages, e.g. Old, Middle and Modern French. It also suggests the continuity of our language from its earliest stages. The Old English writers themselves used the term *englisc* or *engliscgereord*, "the English language." The use of "Anglo-Saxon" to indicate the English people and their language prior to the Norman Conquest arose at a relatively late period, in the sixteenth century.

We will now indicate how English is related to other languages. One of the far-reaching discoveries of the nineteenth century was that many languages show important resemblances in their structure, and that these features are to be explained, not by a process of borrowing but by descent from a common ancestor. Languages are like plants or animals, which may differ considerably today but may still exhibit certain characteristics pointing to a common origin or parent stock. By grouping together those which show these similarities we are able to draw up various genera, families and classes. Languages, too, may be divided into families. To indicate a common descent for a group of languages or a group of words we use the term *cognate*. Some idea of the evidence on which these relationships are based may be obtained from the following facts.

Let us make a list of some common terms in several European languages and compare their appearance. We may take the first four numbers and the

English	German	Dutch	Swedish	Danish
one	ein	een	en	een
two	zwei	twee	två	to
	(German $z = ts$)			
three	drei	drie	tre	tre
four	vier	vier	fyra	fire
	(German $v = f$)			
father	vater ($v = f$)	vader	fader	fader
mother	mutter	moeder	moder	moder
brother	bruder	broeder	broder	broder
sister	schwester	zuster	syster	søster

Notice also the pattern of the verbs:

	English	German	Dutch	Swedish	Danish
Infinitive	sing	singen	zingen	sjunga	synge
Past Tense	sang	sang	zong	sjöng	sang
Part Participle	sung	gesungen	gezongen	sjungit	sungen
	(O.E. gesungen)				
	fish	fischen	visschen	fiska	fiske
	fished (-ed pron. t)	fischte	vischte	fiskade	fiskede
	fished	gefischt	gevischt	fiskat	fisket

closest family relationships; many striking resemblances will emerge, which cannot be accidental.

These and other similarities of an equally fundamental nature point to a common ancestry for this group of languages. They are called the Teutonic or Germanic group and are usually divided into three sub-groups, North Teutonic, East Teutonic and West Teutonic. All these are descended from one parent language, which is called Primitive Teutonic. The relationship can best be shown by the following table, which includes only the more important languages.

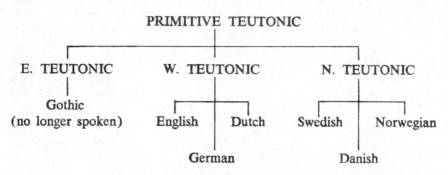

PRIMITIVE TEUTONIC

E. TEUTONIC   W. TEUTONIC   N. TEUTONIC

Gothic
(no longer spoken)   English | Dutch   Swedish | Norwegian

German   Danish

This, however, is not the whole story. If we go a stage further and compare this Teutonic group with non-Teutonic languages, we discover equally remarkable resemblances. Taking some of the words used before, let us

English	Latin	French	Greek
one	unus	un	cf. oinos
			one (on dice)
two	duo	deux	duo
three	tres	trois	treis
father	pater	père	pater
mother	mater	mère	meter
brother	frater	frère	phrater

compare their forms in English, representing a Teutonic language, with those found in Latin or Greek which belong to two different branches, the Italic and the Hellenic respectively. We might also include French, which is a modern development from Latin, just as Modern English is from Old English.

The resemblances are not so close as before, but they are too great to be merely accidental. A similar comparison with other languages, such as the Celtic group, would reveal more features in common. As a result of this evidence we can now draw up a more complete table to show the relationship between these larger linguistic units, the Teutonic, Italic, Hellenic, Celtic and other groups. There are altogether nine of these,[1] and they include most of the European and some of the Indian languages. For this reason they are often called the Indo-European family of languages. Another term is the Aryan family. Aryan is thus not a racial but a linguistic label. The people who speak the Aryan or Indo-European languages are not a racial unit; they include, and no doubt always included, many varied stocks. It is difficult to say when or where the parent language from which these groups are descended—primitive Aryan or Indo-European—was originally spoken, except that it was some time before 2000 B.C., possibly 3000 or 4000 B.C. Scholars formerly thought that the original home of this ancestral tongue was somewhere in Asia, but the modern view is that it was more probably in Northern or Central Europe.

The accompanying diagram shows the relationship of English to the Indo-European family. Again, only the more important languages and groups have been included—the table is considerably reduced and simplified; only six of the nine (or eleven) branches are shown.

A glance at this genealogical table will show that the nearest relatives of English are German and Dutch; the Scandinavian languages are also very close, in some respects actually closer. Rather more distant are Greek and Latin (with its modern descendants French, Spanish and Italian) and the Celtic languages, including the language of the ancient Britons, and modern Celtic forms of speech, such as the Gaelic still spoken in the Highlands of Scotland and in parts of Canada, especially Nova Scotia, the recently revived Irish language of Eire, and the Cymric of Wales.

Outside the Indo-European family and, as far as we know, quite unrelated to it, are many other groups of languages, for instance, the Semitic group to which Hebrew and Arabic belong, another group which includes Chinese, and several besides these. Although they have attained a dominating position because of the political power and prestige of the nations who use them, the Indo-European languages thus constitute only a fraction of the world's total linguistic resources. They may not always maintain that supremacy. . . .

---

[1] Or eleven, if we include the results of recent discoveries.

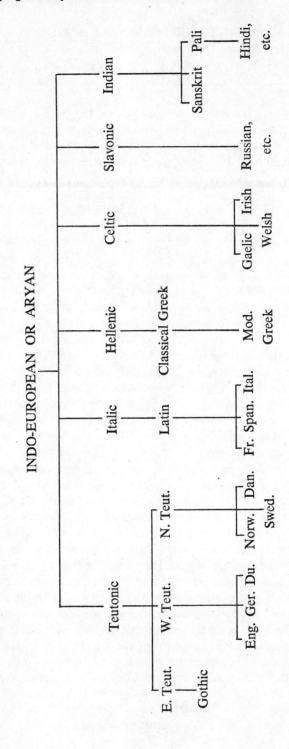

SUGGESTED ASSIGNMENTS

1. The three versions below of the first thirteen verses from the seventh chapter of *The Gospel According to St. Matthew* are examples of our language as it appeared in the Old English, Middle English, and Early Modern English periods. The O.E. text (ca. A.D. 995) shows how our language looked a millenium ago. Although you will recognize a few words, this is essentially a foreign language to the reader of today. The M.E. text (ca. 1389) is from Wycliffe's *New Testament*. Here the language is beginning to look familiar, and you can read it without much trouble. The third example represents Early Mod. English. It is from Tyndale's translation of the *New Testament*, printed in 1525 or 1526, which influenced greatly the King James Version of 1611. This is our own modern English, save for occasional differences in grammar, spelling, sound, and meaning.

    You will find the exercise that follows these selections illuminating with respect to changes in English grammar.

Old English:

CHAP. VII. 1 Nellen ge déman, đæt ge ne sýn fordémede;

   2 Witodlíce đam ylcan dóme đe ge démaþ, eow biþ gedémed, and on đam ylcan gemete đe ge metaþ, eow byþ gemeten.

   3 To hwí gesihst đú đæt mot on đínes bródor égan, and đú ne gesyhst đone beam on đínum ágenum eagan?

   4 Odđe húmeta cwyst đú to đínum bréđer, Bróđur, þafa đæt ic út-ádó đæt mot of đínum eagan, đonne se beam biþ on đínum ágenum eagan?

   5 Lá đú líccetere, ádó ǽrest út đone beam of đínum ágenum eagan, and beháwa đonne đæt đú út-ádó đæt mot of đínes bróđur eagan.

   6 Nellen ge syllan đæt hálige húndum, ne ge ne wurpen eowre mere-grotu tofóran eowrum swýnon, đe-læs hig mid hyra fótum hig fortredon, and hig đonne ongean gewende eow toslýton.

   7 Biddaþ, and eow biþ geseald; séceaþ, and ge hit fíndaþ; enuciaþ, and eow biþ ontýned.

   8 Witodlíce ǽlc đæra đe bit, he onfehþ; and se đe séeþ, he hyt fínt; and dam cnuciendum biþ ontýned.

   9 Hwylc man is of eow, gyf his sunu hyne bit hláfes, sylst đú him stán?

  10 Odđe gyf he bytt fisces, sylst đú him næddran?

  11 Eornustlíce nú ge, đe yfele synt, cunnun góde sylena eowrum bearnum syllan, mycle má eower fæder đe on heofenum ys syleþ gód đam đe hyne biddaþ?

  12 Eornustlíce ealle đa þing, đe ge wyllen đæt men eow dón, dóþ ge him đæt sylfe, đæt ys sóþlíce ǽ and wítegena bebod.

  13 Gangaþ inn þurh đæt nearwe geat; forđon đe đæt geat is swýđe wíd, and se weg is swíđe rúm đe to forspillednesse gelæt, and swýđe manega synt đe þurh đone weg faraþ.

Wycliffe:

CHAP. VII. 1 Nyle ʒe deme, that ʒe be nat demyd;

2 For in what dome ʒe demen, ʒe shulen ben demyd, and in what mesure ʒe meten, it shal be meten to ʒou.

3 But what seest thou a festu in the eiʒe of thi brother, and thou seest nat a beme in thin owne eiʒe?

4 Or what maner saist thou to thi brother, Brother, suffre that I caste out a festu fro thin eiʒe, and loo! a beme is in thin owne eiʒe?

5 Ypocrite, cast out first a beme of thin eiʒe, and than thou shalt see for to cast out a festu of the eiʒe of thi brother.

6 Nyl ʒe ʒeue holy thing to houndis, nether sende ʒe ʒour margaritis before swyne, lest perauenture thei defoulen hem with theire feet, and lest *houndis* turned to gidre al to-breke ʒou.

7 Axe ʒe, and it shal be ʒouen to ʒou; seke ʒe, and ʒe shulen fynde; knocke ʒe, and it shal be opnyd to ʒou.

8 For eche that axith, takith; and he that sechith, fyndith; and it shal be opnyde to a man knokynge.

9 Other who of ʒou is a man, who ʒif his sone axe breed, wher he shal dresse to hym a stoon?

10 Other ʒif he shal axe a fishe, wher he shal dresse to hym a serpent?

11 Therfore ʒif ʒe, when ʒe ben yuel men, han knowen for to ʒeue good thingus ʒouen to ʒoure sonys, hou myche more ʒoure fadir that is in heuenes shal ʒeue good thingis to men axinge hym?

12 Therfore alle thingis, what euer thingis ʒee wolen that men don to ʒou, and ʒe do to hem, forsothe these thingis *ben* the lawe and prophetis.

13 Entre ʒe bi the streyt ʒate; for the gate that ledith to perdicioun is brode, and the weye large, and ther ben many that entren bi it.

Tyndale:

CHAP. VII. 1 Iudge not, lest ye be iudged;

2 For as ye iudge, so shall ye be iudged, and with what mesur ye mete, with the same shall it be mesurd to you agayne.

3 Why seist thou a moote in thy brothers eye, and percevest not the beame that ys in thyne awne eye?

4 Or why sayest thou to thy brother, Suffre me to plucke oute a moote oute off thyne eye, and behold! a beame is in thyne awne eye?

5 Ypocryte, first cast oute the beame oute of thyne awne eye, and then shalte thou se clearly plucke oute the moote off thy brothers eye.

6 Geve not that which is holy to dogges, nether cast ye youre pearles before swyne, lest they treade them vnder their fete, and the other tourne agayne and all to rent you.

7 Axe, and it shalbe geven you; seke, and ye shall fynd; knocke, and it shalbe opened vnto you.

8 For whosever axeth, receaveth; and he that seketh, fyndeth; and to hym that knocketh it shalbe opened.

9 Ys there eny man among you, which wolde proffer his sonne a stone, if he axed him breed?

10 Or if he axed fysshe, wolde he proffer hyme a serpent?

11 Yff ye then, whiche are evyll, cann geve to youre chyldren good gyftes, howe moche moore shall youre father which ys in heven geve good thynges to them that axe off hym?

12 Therfore, whatsoever ye wolde that men shulde do to you, even so do ye to them, this ys the lawe and the prophettes.

13 Enter in at the strayte gate; ffor wyde is the gate; and broade ys the waye thatt leadeth to destruccion, and many there be which goo yn there att.

Now we shall examine these passages to note how a few particulars of grammar and meaning in the language of former days differ from those of today.

a. What was the M.E. plural form of *shall* (Wycliffe, verses 2 and 7)? Did this form survive into Early Modern (Cf. Tyndale)? What was the M.E. plural form of *will* (Wycliffe, verse 12)? The M.E. singular form was both *wil* and *wol*. How do you explain the vowel in "I won't"?

b. In what respect was the use of *thy* and *thine* like that of *a* and *an* today (Wycliffe, verse 3)? Had this usage changed by Tyndale's time?

c. In Wycliffe, verse 6, identify the objective form of *they*. No, this is not a misprint. This form has since been regularized to make it fit into the paradigm of they, their, ———— . All three are not from O.E. but were borrowed from Old Norse, whereas *hem* in this passage is a surviving O.E. form.

d. *Ye* and *you* are plural forms. Each is restricted to its own grammatical situations in the sentence. Using both Wycliffe and Tyndale as your data, formulate a statement of the uses of these two pronouns. If *you* was a plural, objective form in the sixteenth and early seventeenth centuries, how can we justify its use today as a singular, nominative form?

e. Today the plural of *is* is *are*. What was it in Wycliffe and Tyndale (verse 13)?

f. Today we use the inflectional ending *-s* for the third-person present singular of the verb, as in "He asks." What was Tyndale's ending in this situation (verse 8)? By Shakespeare's time, the *-s* ending had come into London English, and we find both in the plays of the Bard, as in

Who want*eth* food and will not say he want*s* it?

PERICLES

What advantage was the presence of these two forms to a poet who wrote in meter?

g. What did *deem* and *doom* mean in Wycliffe, verse 2? Which one has undergone a change of meaning since that time?

h. In Wycliffe, verse 6, the word *houndis* is used to express the general meaning of *dogs*. Today the meaning of *hounds* has been narrowed, or specialized, to denote particular breeds of dogs. For a discussion of this type of meaning change, see Simeon Potter on specialization, pp. 123–124.

The questions in the first six subdivisions above illustrate the concept that grammar is a description of usage and that as usage changes, grammar must change.

Early American Speech: Adoptions from Foreign Tongues

Thomas Pyles

The English language is one of the great word-borrowers in history. About one-half of our word stock has been borrowed into English from Latin and its Romance descendants, and in the Renaissance alone words were adopted into English from more than fifty languages. This process did not stop when the English language was brought to our shores, and in the selection below Thomas Pyles describes how our early settlers took over the words they needed from the tongues with which they came in contact. Mr. Pyles is Professor of English and Linguistics Emeritus at Northwestern University and is the author of *The Origin and Development of the English Language.*

Before there was any permanent settlement of English-speaking folk in this land, a number of Indian words had made their way into the language of England by way of Spanish or Portuguese—words from Nahuatl, the tongue of the Aztecs, who were the most highly advanced of the Indians that the Spanish found in Mexico, as well as from various Indian dialects spoken in Central and South America and the West Indies. Some of these words came in time to be current in all the languages of Europe.

The English language in those exuberant days of Elizabeth, of Raleigh, Drake, Hawkins, Bacon, Marlowe, Jonson, and Shakespeare, had been particularly receptive to augmentations of its already rich word stock from foreign sources—the so-called "inkhorn" terms from the classical languages, along with words from French, Spanish, Italian, and Portuguese.[1] Words from the New World must have had all the charm of lush exoticisms in a period when the language was being enriched from so many nearby Continental sources, though they seem for the most part commonplace enough today—words like *potato, tomato, chocolate, cocoa, canoe, cannibal, barbecue, maize,* and *savannah,* which must have been known to the first Englishmen to come to these shores with any intention of staying. One of them, *maize,* was by a strange perversity of linguistic fate to be replaced by *corn* in the English of America. The British use *corn* in the sense "wheat," while retaining the older meaning of "grain," as in the "Corn Laws." Another of them, *cannibal,* a modification of *Caribal* "Caribbean native," was used in slightly different form by Shakespeare in his play about the "vexed Bermoothes," for *Caliban,* if not simply a metathesized [2] form of *can(n)ibal,* is a variant of *Cariban,* itself a variant of *Caribal. Barbecue,* while appearing first in British English, is nevertheless much more familiar in America, and its use to designate an outdoor social or political meeting at which animals are roasted whole is exclusively American. But these words, while native to the New World, must be distinguished from those which entered the language of Englishmen who chose or were forced to transplant themselves permanently in this strange and savage land.

The colonizers of this country were confronted with a land whose topography, meteorological phenomena, trees, plants, birds, and animals were frequently quite different from what they had known in England. Inasmuch as an understanding of the principles of semantics is not congenital, people generally are wont to ask when they see some new object, "What is it?" and expect in answer to be told its name, supposing then that they have learned something really significant about it. This procedure, or something very similar to it, must have been gone through a great many times in the early days of the colonization of America when Indians were friendly enough to be asked and bright enough to divine what was being asked of them. Sometimes, too, these first white Americans made up their own names for what they saw, if there was no one to tell them the "true" names or if the "true" names were too difficult for them to pronounce. . . . They frequently combined or modified English words, as in *bullfrog* and *jimson weed* (originally *Jamestown weed*); sometimes they made use of sound alone, as in *bobolink.*

The situation with regard to the American Indian languages, with many tribes speaking apparently unrelated languages which are in turn subdivided

---

[1] In sixteenth-century England, many scholars and writers believed that the English vocabulary was poverty-stricken and set about to enrich it by inventing and using new words formed from Latin and other tongues. These words were called "inkhorn terms." Thousands of them appeared in print. Many have vanished, like *adminiculation, annect, deturpated, inquisiturient, matutine,* and *temulent.* But numerous others, serving a useful purpose, have lived on, like *anachronism, decorum, education, extravagant,* and *scientific.* [eds.]

[2] Metathesis is a transposition of sounds (or letters) as in *aksed* for *asked.* [eds.]

into dialects, is extremely complex. Fortunately it need not concern us here, for to American English only one stock, the Algonquian, is important. This huge group of tribes, comprising among others the Arapaho, Blackfoot, Cheyenne, Cree, Delaware, Fox, Micmac, Ojibwa (Chippewa), and Penobscot, formerly occupied a larger area than any other North American Indian stock. It was they whom the first English settlers in Virginia and Massachusetts came in contact with.

As early as 1608 Captain John Smith in his *True Relation of . . . Virginia Since the First Planting of That Collony* recorded *raccoon*, though he did not spell it that way. He wrote it in various ways—for instance, *raugroughcun* and later, in his *General Historie of Virginia, New-England and the Summer Isles* of 1624, *rarowcun*—in his effort to reduce to symbols, which were, incidentally, ill-adapted to that purpose, what he heard or thought he heard from the Indians. It is highly unlikely, as a matter of fact, that a single English word of Indian origin would be immediately intelligible to an Indian today, for words have been clipped, like *squash* (the vegetable), which was originally *askutasquash*, folk-etymologized[3] like *whiskey-John* "blue jay" from *wisketjan*, or in one way or another made to conform to English speechways.

Early Indian loan words naming creatures neglected by Adam are *opossum, moose, skunk, menhaden, terrapin, woodchuck,* and *caribou. Opossum* usually occurs in speech and often in writing in an aphetic form as *possum,* as does *raccoon* as *coon. Woodchuck* is a folk-etymologizing of Cree or Ojibwa *otchek* or *odjik.* Noah Webster was quite proud, by the way, of deriving *woodchuck* from an Avestan word meaning "pig" and made frequent reference to this acute etymological discovery in lectures and prefaces. *Caribou,* as the spelling of its final syllable indicates, comes to us by way of Canadian French; an Englishman would have been more likely to write *cariboo.* These words, all of Algonquian origin, designate creatures indigenous to North America. Ojibwa *chipmunk* would seem to belong to this group, though it was first recorded considerably later, in Cooper's *Deerslayer* (1841); it was certainly in use much earlier.

A good many native plants, vegetables, trees and shrubs bear names of Indian origin; *hickory, pecan, poke(weed), chinquapin, squash, persimmon,* and *catalpa,* all but one of which are Algonquian. That one, *catalpa,* is of Muskhogean origin. A good many Southern place names are of this linguistic stock, which includes Creek, Chickasaw, and Choctaw, but *catalpa* (with its variant *catawba*) and the topographical *bayou* (from Choctaw *bayuk* "stream," coming to us by way of Louisiana French) are the only widely known words other than place names taken from the languages of these Indians, who formerly occupied an area of our country including most of Georgia, Alabama, and Mississippi and parts of Tennessee, Kentucky, Louisiana, and Florida.

---

[3] See p. 72, suggested assignment 5.

Other early borrowings from the Indians include words denoting foods, customs, relationships, or artifacts peculiar to the Indians at the time of borrowing: *hominy, succotash, johnnycake, pone, pemmican, moccasin, tomahawk, totem, wigwam, toboggan, powwow, mackinaw, caucus* (perhaps), *wampum, sachem, papoose,* and *squaw. Toboggan* and *mackinaw* are first recorded later than the others in this group, though their earliest use in English certainly goes back considerably beyond their first recording. Both entered English by way of Canadian French; the latter word has a half-French spelling, *Mackinac,* when used as a name for the strait, the island, and the town in Michigan. The first element of *johnnycake* is probably from *jonakin* or *jonikin,* apparently of Indian origin and meaning a thin griddle cake made of corn meal. *Johnnycake* was folk-etymologized to *journey cake,* which Noah Webster thought the original form; he assumed that it meant cake to eat when one went on a journey. It has also been suggested that the word is a corruption of *Shawnee cake,* a kind of cake supposed to have been eaten by the Shawnee Indians—an explanation which Mr. Mencken in *The American Language, Supplement One* (New York, 1945) considers "much more plausible" than any other. *Jonikin* (usually spelled *johnnikin*) is still used for a corn griddle cake in the eastern part of the Carolinas and on the Eastern Shore of Maryland. . . .

All the other words in this last group save *johnnycake* have made the Atlantic crossing, and most of them are now about as familiar to the English as they are to us. In fact, all of them except *mackinaw* are listed in Wyld's *Universal Dictionary;* only *succotash* and *johnnycake* are labeled "U.S.A." The usual British pronunciation of *wigwam* rimes with *big dam,* a pronunciation never heard in this country. *Pemmican,* the Indian name for dried meat pounded into paste, mixed with fat and dried fruits, and then compressed into cakes, has even acquired the figurative meaning in British English of "condensed statement." On the continent of Europe also, most of these words are quite well known as a result of literary transmission, for generations of European children have thrilled to the novels of James Fenimore Cooper, as well as of his European imitators.

Tammany as a political designation is a well-known Americanism of Indian origin. Tammany was a Delaware chief who flourished in the latter part of the seventeenth century and who was jocularly canonized as an American saint in 1771. His name was later used to designate a political club which ultimately grew into the present powerful Democratic organization in New York City. References to *Tammany* as the name of club, which was founded in 1789, occur from 1790 onwards. The organization uses *the Wigwam* as a designation for Tammany Hall, *sachem* for high official of the society, and *brave* (not of Indian origin, but long used to mean an Indian warrior) for a rank-and-file member.

A good many other words of Indian origin are included in the *Dictionary of American English,* but most of them are not in wide current use: *tuckahoe* "edible part of a fungus found on roots of trees," which is also used to designate a poor white in Virginia and West Virginia, *carcajou* "wolverine," *manito* or *manitou* "a god," *quahog* or *quahaug* "hard clam," *sagamore* "chief," *samp* "corn porridge," *tamarack* "the American larch," *mugwump* "great man," and others considerably less familiar. *Mugwump*, though known much earlier, came into real prominence in the presidential campaign of 1884, when it was applied to those independent Republicans who, affecting an attitude of superiority, refused to support James G. Blaine as their party nominee. Nowadays the word is chiefly notable for the oft-recorded definition by a Congressional wag (would there were more of his kidney!) to the effect that a mugwump was one who always had his *mug* on one side of the fence and his *wump* on the other.

Some early Americanisms were translations or supposed translations of Indian words or phrases, for example, *paleface* (first used by James Fenimore Cooper), *war paint, warpath, firewater, pipe of peace, medicine man, Great Spirit, big chief, to scalp,* and *to bury the hatchet.* Frequently *Indian* was used in conjunction with another word, as in *Indian meal, Indian file, Indian summer,* and *Indian gift,* originally a gift for which one expected something of more value in return, but later a gift which the giver took back. *Indian giver* is first recorded, as far as we know, in Bartlett's *Glossary* of 1848, with the notation that "this term is applied by children to a child who, after having given away a thing, wishes it back again," though *Indian gift* occurs much earlier. The *Dictionary of American English* lists almost a hundred such combinations, though not all are early, for instance, *honest Injun,* which is not recorded until 1875. . . .

Before passing on to other non-English influences it is interesting to note that British English borrowed *Mohawk,* which it usually spelled *mohock,* early in the eighteenth century to designate, according to the *Oxford English Dictionary,* "one of a class of aristocratic ruffians who infested the streets of London at night," but the term has only a historical interest today. It has never had any currency in American English save among professors of eighteenth-century English literature. The *Apache* of *Apache dance,* a rowdy, sexy dance performed by a pair of dancers attired as a Parisian gangster and his "moll," did not come to us directly from the well-known American aborigines of that name. It came instead by way of French, which in the early twentieth century borrowed the name of the Indian tribe, Gallicized its pronunciation, and used it to designate a Parisian street bully.

It is perhaps not surprising, considering the ultimate reduction of the American Indians to the status of a conquered people, that the Indian element in American English is no larger than it is. As a matter of fact, if we leave out of consideration place names, of which there are an overwhelming number—more than half our states bear Indian names, and a large portion of our rivers, lakes, mountains, towns, and cities as well—the Indian influence on our vocabulary must be characterized as slight.

The Indian languages were not, however, the only non-European influence upon the English of America in colonial days. More than a year before the Pilgrims landed on Plymouth Rock in search of religious freedom, a group of people were against their will brought here from the west coast of Africa—principally from Senegal, Gambia, Sierra Leone, Liberia, the Gold Coast, Togo, Dahomey, Nigeria, and Angola—and forthwith sold into slavery. The traffic in Negro slaves continued until shortly before the Civil War, though slackening somewhat after 1808, when the Slave Trade Act went into effect. A great majority of these Negroes were brought direct from Africa; some, however, had previously lived in the British West Indies, where they had picked up a bare working knowledge of English.

Most of the descendants of these transplanted Africans living in the South now speak conventional American English. Because of lack of social contacts with whites and lack of schooling, relics of older standard speech may occasionally be heard from them, such as the pronunciation *deef* for *deaf* and *obleege* for *oblige*. When a colored charwoman with some embarrassment informed me that her small daughter had suffered an injury in her *grine*, she was not using an un-English, "darky" pronunciation, but merely saying *groin* in a manner which went out of fashion in more sophisticated usage years ago. There is, of course, no connection whatever between race and the ability to articulate given speech sounds, though it is popularly believed that the Southern Negro speaks as he does because of a peculiar conformation of speech organs, aided and abetted by indolence and stupidity. I was once gravely informed by a professor of government that the Negro does not have an *r* sound (my informant was of course referring only to *r* before a consonant sound in final position) because the "letter *r*" did not exist in African languages—not one of which he had any acquaintance with, incidentally. When I presumed to disagree with his explanation, a corollary of which was that the speech of white Southerners was *r*-less because of the linguistic influence of Negro "mammies," and to point out that an Ohio-bred Negro has no difficulty whatsoever pronouncing *r* in all positions, he was grievously offended with me. The fact is that uneducated Negroes in the South by and large differ little in their speech from the uneducated whites. As for the presence of archaisms, they may also be heard from whites who have lived for a long time in cultural isolation, for instance, the Southern mountain folk.

There are, however, communities of Negro Americans engaged largely in the cultivation of rice, cotton, and indigo along the coastal region of South Carolina and Georgia, both on the Sea Islands and on the mainland, who have lived in cultural and geographical isolation for many generations. Most of them have had little contact with whites; some, indeed, have seldom seen white people. These Negroes, numbering about a quarter of a million, speak a type of English which has been so heavily influenced by the African languages native to their remote ancestors that it is not readily intelligible to people, white or colored, from other parts of the country. Their language,

Gullah or Geechee, retains a good many African characteristics in its system of sounds, its syntax, its morphology, its vocabulary, its methods of forming words, and, most striking of all to one hearing it for the first time, its intonation. The word *Gullah* is probably either from *Gola*, the name of a Liberian tribe and its language, or from *Angola*. *Geechee*, also used in the up-country of South Carolina as a derisive nickname for a low-country white, particularly one living in the Charleston area, is probably derived from the name of another Liberian tribe and language.

It was very unlikely that Africans from the same tribe or language area would find themselves thrown together on a single plantation in sufficient numbers to enable them to maintain their native languages. The chances were all that they would be considerably dispersed upon their arrival at the various southern ports. Consequently, it became necessary for them to learn English as well as they could. It is not likely that anyone helped them to do so, unless there were prototypes of Mrs. Stowe's Little Eva gliding or floating about the plantations (for Little Eva seldom merely walked) in the seventeenth and eighteenth centuries. The only English many of them ever heard from native speakers was that of the illiterate or semiliterate white indentured servants with whom they worked in the fields or who were set over them as overseers. It was for them not simply a matter of translating word for word their native idioms into English. This cannot be done successfully even with related languages, where it may result in something intelligible if un-English, like *the bread is all*, a Pennsylvania Germanism (though heard in other parts of the country) from German *das Brot ist alle*. It was for these Negroes a matter of acquiring a quite different linguistic psychology, a new attitude towards the phenomena of life as expressed by language. It is not surprising that their accomplishment fell considerably short of perfect. Their English was a sort of jargon or pidgin, which passed into use by their descendants as a native language. This type of so called creolized language has been preserved largely in the speech of the Gullahs, Negroes who "stayed put" in a region in which they have always been far more numerous than whites and in which they have developed the only distinctive Negro speech in this country.

The principal importance of Gullah, aside from its intrinsic interest as a remarkable linguistic development, is that recent studies of it have been the means of identifying beyond a doubt the African source of a number of words in Southern American English, a few of which have passed into other types of American English and one of which, *banjo*, if it is indeed of African origin, is part of the English language wherever it is spoken. Until Lorenzo Dow Turner began his investigations about twenty years ago, Gullah was traditionally regarded as "a quaint linguistic mongrel," to quote from one serious commentator; it was thought to be characterized by "intellectual indolence," "slovenly and careless," a debased form of the "peasant English" of poor whites, a sort of baby talk. One writer even went so far as to attribute its phonological characteristics to the "clumsy tongues," "flat noses," and "thick lips" of the Negroes who speak it.

Professor Turner's studies of Gullah, culminating in his *Africanisms in the Gullah Dialect* (Chicago, 1949), identify thousands of words in Gullah which have or may have African sources. Unlike earlier commentators, who assumed that many words which seemed strange to them were either non-sense words or mispronunciations of English words, Turner, himself of African descent, took the trouble to acquire a good working knowledge of West African languages. His studies and conclusions have made short shrift of some of the theories of previous writers, who assumed, for instance, that a Gullah word for "tooth" which sounded to them something like *bong* was merely a childish, clumsy-tongued, flat-nosed, thick-lipped mispronunciation of English *bone*, and that the Gullah word *det* or the expression *det rain* "a long, hard rain" was really *death rain*, which involved the further assumption that to the Gullahs a long, hard rain is an omen of death to come—as it were, folklore made to order. The fact that in the Wolof language, spoken in Senegal and Gambia, the word for "tooth" is very like *bong* (it is impossible to indicate the exact pronunciation of the un-English final sound of this word, a palatal nasal, without using phonetic symbols) and that in the same language the word for "long, hard rain" is *det* ought to dispose of the "baby talk" explanation for good and all—though of course it will not, for most people prefer "quaint" explanations of linguistic phenomena to the true ones.

From many Gullah informants, some of them bearing names which are a delight to contemplate—among them Saki Sweetwine, Prince Smith, Samuel Polite, Sanko Singleton, Balaam Walker, Scotia Washington, Shad Hall, and Paris Capers—Dr. Turner collected more than five thousand African words in the Gullah region. About four-fifths of these are now used only as personal names, but most of the remainder are everyday words in the speech of the Gullahs. Some of these words, doubtless the common possession of Negroes in all the slaveholding states, passed into the vocabulary of whites at what must have been a very early date.

How did words from the language of humble slaves get into the speech of their white masters? M. M. Mathews, who devotes the final chapter of his *Some Sources of Southernisms* (University, Ala., 1948) to Africanisms in the word stock of Southern American English, speculates with some reason that such words were transmitted by white children, who would not have resisted the influences of what their elders considered an inferior culture. Dr. Mathews cites his aged aunt's aversion to the "Negro word" *cooter* "turtle" and her regret that her brother, Mathews' father, had sullied the "purity" of his speech by ever using the word.

Actually, the African contribution is rather meager. The remarkable thing is, considering the social and economic relationship of black to white, that there should have been any contribution. Many a white Southerner has imbedded in his vocabulary words whose African origin he probably never suspects. *Banjo* and *cooter* have already been cited. The first word has usually been considered as originating in a Negro mispronunciation of *bandore*, an English word of Spanish transmission denoting a musical instrument whose similarity to the banjo consisted mainly in the fact that it had strings to be plucked. According to Turner, the most probable source is Kimbundu, a language spoken in Angola, in which the word *mbanza* refers to an instrument very similar to the banjo. *Cooter* is very likely from *kuta,* a word appearing in two French West African languages, Bambara and Malinke, in which it has the same meaning as in the language of the Gullahs and in the English of many white Southerners.

Goober "peanut" is a modification of Kimbundu *nguba*, with similar forms occurring in Imbundu (also spoken in Angola) and Kongo (Belgian Congo and Angola). *Pinder,* with the same meaning, is from Kongo *mpinda.* Both these words are freely used on a colloquial level in the South; the first has probably gained a limited national currency.

A number of gustatory and culinary terms of African origin testify to the skill of Negro cooks. Many of these, however, are local terms, like *cush* "corn meal stuffing" and *cala* "sweetened rice"—the latter term confined to the New Orleans area. *Gumbo* is confined to no locality or region, nor is *yam,* which is found also in British English and which is of Portuguese transmission; in Scotland it is used for the common white potato. If the word *yam* was brought to these shores by our early settlers, as it may have been, it is of course not to be regarded as belonging with the group of words under discussion; but there is no reason to insist that, because it occurs also in British English, we could not have got it independently. The same people from whom the Portuguese got the word were right here, and the word might well have entered the American vocabulary, as Dr. Mathews points out, from the language of the slaves. At the least, its use in American English would have been reinforced by their use of it. The word survives as an Africanism in the Gullah dialect (in the form *yambi*) to mean a red sweet potato, which is its usual meaning in Southern American English.

Buckra "white man" is also of African origin, appearing as *mbakara* in Efik and Ibibio, spoken in Southern Nigeria. Loss of the initial nasal sound in the word probably occurred in Negro speech before the word was transmitted to whites and is due to the influence of English on the speech of the Negroes. Simplification of the initial consonant combinations *mb-, mp-, nd-, nt-,* and *ng-,* which do not occur in this position in English, is frequent in the Gullah pronunciation of African words.

The great blue heron is frequently called *poor Joe* (or *po' Joe*) in those regions of the South in which the bird is found. There can be no doubt that this is the same word as Vai (Liberia and Sierra Leone) *pojo* "heron." It is likely that *chigger* and its variant *jigger*—the dictionaries give a spelling *chigoe* which suggests a pronunciation seldom if ever heard—are of African transmission as far as their use in American English is concerned, and perhaps of African origin as well. At any rate, *jiga* "flea" is found in a number of African languages spoken in Senegal, Gambia, Togo, Dahomey, and Northern and Southern Nigeria. The word got into British English probably by way of the British West Indies and has been thought to be of Carib origin. It is likely, however, that its use in American English is due independently to Negro transmission, regardless of its ultimate origin.

Pickaninny, which is probably used nowadays by whites more frequently than by Negroes, is of African transmission, but its source is Portuguese *pequenino* "very little." It is not impossible that the last part of the Portuguese word may have been identified by the Negroes with the Mende (Sierra Leone) word *nini* "female breast," *pequenino* being folk-etymologized into *pickaninny* after these Negro acquired their English. The word is not exclusively American (the same is true of *buckra*, *jigger*, and others), though it is probably more commonly used here than elsewhere. It is, nevertheless, recorded in British English almost a century and a half earlier than in American English.

Hoodoo and its New Orleans variant *voodoo* are Africanisms. Both forms are in use by the Gullahs. They have, however, become somewhat differentiated in meaning, the latter usually referring to the cult which flourished in the West Indies and was later introduced into this country. *Hoodoo* is applied to a person or object that is thought to bring bad luck, *to hoodoo* consequently meaning "to bring bad luck to someone." Voodoo worship was introduced into Louisiana very early by slaves from the French colonies of Martinique, Guadeloupe, and Santo Domingo, where the cult—probably of African origin, as its name would indicate—raged furiously. It would seem to have grown rather slowly at first, but was a source of worry among the whites by 1782, when the Spanish governor of Louisiana probibited further importation of Negroes from Martinique because slaves from there were thought to be "too much given to voudouism and make the lives of the citizens unsafe." Later, and partly for the same reason, a similar prohibition was extended to Negroes from Santa Domingo. After the American occupation, however, there were no such restrictions, and with the sudden influx of Negroes into Louisiana by way of New Orleans between 1806 and 1810, voodoo began to exert a strong influence upon the Louisiana Negroes. For a long time thereafter—until well after the Civil War, in fact—voodoo "queens" and "doctors" were persons of tremendous power and prestige among the Negroes, and even to some extent among the lower-class whites.

The most famous of the queens, who were the priestesses of the cult and much more influential than the doctors who shared with them their powers of sorcery, was the remarkable Marie Laveau, a free mulatto of striking beauty in her younger years, who was by profession a hairdresser and by avocation a procuress for white gentlemen. For more than forty years absolute ruler of the cult, she has remained a legend to this day. The visitor to

New Orleans, if he is lucky, may still hear old Oscar "Papa" Celestin, a Robert Frost in ebony, sing *Marie Laveau*, an original composition which recounts some of the miracles performed by this celebratetd "cunjer-lady."

Transmission into general use of African *zombi*, a word intimately associated with voodooism, is probably rather recent, though it must have been known to whites in certain areas of the South at an early date. Its present familiarity may well be credited to the cycle of "horror" films some years ago. The word originally designated the snake god which was the object of adoration in the voodoo cult. It later came to mean a supernatural force thought to restore corpses to life, and ultimately a corpse brought to life by means of this force. Recently it has been used, with an obvious appropriateness, to designate a mixed drink of (usually) rum and brandy.

Juke, which has come into general use among whites comparatively recently, mainly in the compounds *juke box* and *juke joint*, has been a part of the vocabulary of the Gullahs for a long time in the sense "disorderly," particularly in the combination *juke house*. Turner shows that the word is of African origin. In standard colloquial use its meaning has been considerably toned down, as has been that of *jazz* which, though of unknown origin, is said to have been long used by Negroes, particularly in the New Orleans region. *Jazz* is very likely of African origin, though no African etymon has been found. These two words are included here because they have probably appeared in the English or creolized English speech of Negroes since pre-Revolutionary days, even though they may have been late in reaching the standard language. Their very nature would of course sufficiently explain the fact that they were not earlier transmitted to whites. *Jazz* as a verb is, as a matter of fact, sometimes used by whites, though only on a rather low social level, in the sexual sense which it seems originally to have had among the Negroes.

It would be pleasant to be able to record that Professor Turner's researches in Gullah have cleared up the origin of *to tote*, long an etymological puzzle, but there are circumstances in respect to it which indicate that final judgment had better be reserved. It is true that no satisfactory English etymon has been found. *Tote* is one of that sizable number of words of which the dictionaries can say only "orig. uncert.," "unknown origin," or something to that effect. Professor Turner found possible African sources in Kongo and Kikongo *tota* "to pick up," with related words in other West African languages mean "to carry." The fact that *tote* is used in Gullah does not rule out the possibility of an unknown English source, for very many English words are used by the Gullahs. It is likely, however, that if the word is not of African origin, its use has been reinforced, at least in the South and particularly among the Gullahs, by the African words. Though it is usually thought of as a Southernism, *tote* was first recorded in New England in the seventeenth century; it has also been found in upstate New York, northern Michigan, and northern Minnesota, occurring alone and in the combinations *tote road, tote wagon, tote team*, and *tote sled*. The fact that the word crops up in parts of the country where Negro influence is highly unlikely suggests that there may after all be an English source for the word which has been lost to us. If so, the fact that words of similar sound and meaning occur in West African languages would have to be due to sheer coincidence, like the similarity in American Indian *Potomac* and Greek *potamos* "river."

Contacts with other colonizing peoples have also contributed to the American vocabulary. Relations between the English and the New Amsterdam Dutch were, it is true, never very friendly; nevertheless from the language of these Dutch settlers American English gained *coleslaw, cooky, cruller, boss, dope, hay barrack, spook, stoop* "porch," *poppycock* (from *pappekak* "soft dung"), *patroon* (which the Dutch had in turn taken from Latin *patronus*), *sleigh, scow, to snoop, bowery* "a farm" (but now more famous as the street name), *pit* "fruit stone," *boodle, Santa Claus, waffle,* and probably *Yankee*. In addition American English incorporated a number of geographical terms used in the region of the Hudson: *kill* "creek, stream, river," *dorp* "village," and *clove* "valley," which also appear in place names. Many of these Dutch words were not used by writers until well into the nineteenth century, but we may be fairly sure that they occurred in English contexts much earlier; and we may be equally sure that many more Dutch words than are recorded were once in use. *Hay barrack* represents what English-speaking people did to Dutch *hooi-berg*. *Coleslaw* is from Dutch *koolsla* "cabbage salad"; folk etymology frequently converts it to *cold slaw*. *Dope* has acquired a good many slang uses, as in *to dope out, to get the dope on*, and *he's a dope* (i.e., a dolt). It seems to have begun its career in American English meaning a drug, later adding the connotation "narcotic." *Boss*, from *baas* "master," was a very useful word, for it allowed the American working man to enjoy the satisfying if purely verbal illusion that he had no master; only slaves had masters in early American democracy. *Father Christmas*, not *Santa Claus*, visits good English children on Christmas Eve. Our name for the jolly saint is from *Sante Klaas*, a Dutch dialect form of *Sant Nikolaas*, that is, "St. Nicholas"; it seems to have taken a long time catching on, and was probably not very common until the nineteenth century. In my childhood *Santa* was always pronounced *Santy* even by the most highly cultured; people nowadays have become much more conscious of spelling and may use a pronunciation which the spelling *Santa* seems to indicate to them.

The source of *Yankee* is uncertain, but the word is most probably from *Jan Kees* (a variant of *Jan Kaas*, which has been in Germany and Flanders a nickname of long standing for a Hollander), used by the English to designate a Dutch pirate, a sense in which it apparently came also to be used in New York as an expression of the contempt in which the English held the Dutch. Because of the final *-s*, the name seems to have been misunderstood to be a plural; the form *Yankee* is thus what is known to linguists as a back formation, like *shay* from *chaise*.[4] It should also be noted that *j* in Dutch has the sound of English *y*; hence the initial sound of the English form of the word. It is a little difficult to understand why the word was transferred from Dutchmen to people of English descent. Perhaps the shift in application was the result of the same type of humor involved in nicknaming the fattest boy in school "Skinny"—the *lucus a non lucendo* principle. . . .

The meaning of *Yankee* has been anything but static. By the mid-eighteenth century its use in this country to designate a New Englander seems to have been well established. During the Civil War Southerners were employing the term, usually derogatorily, for any Northerner, and it was not long before it acquired what was in the usage of many Southerners the inseparable prefix *dam*, as in *damyankee*.

Since the Revolutionary War the British have used the word to designate any American, with connotations no more derogatory than those of the word *American* itself as it is used by them. It is difficult to imagine any experience more painful to most deep Southerners than to be called *Yankees*; yet there is only sporadic evidence that G.I.'s of southern origin stationed in England during either World War ever objected very vigorously to the appellation. *Yank* is about as common in British colloquial usage as the unabbreviated form; the clipped form has never been very frequent in American use, though it was the title of a magazine distributed to American soldiers and occurs in a line of the World War I song *Over There* ("The Yanks are coming").

Despite the large number of Germans in this country long before the outbreak of the Revolution, few German words entered the American vocabulary until about the middle of the nineteenth century, when many new immigrants from Germany arrived. The first large groups of Germans came from the Palatinate; they arrived on Delaware Bay in the early years of the eighteenth century, and, finding that the good lands around Philadelphia were already taken by descendants of Penn's colonists, proceeded to settle the back country. Those who subsequently moved on to other parts with the Scotch-Irish soon abandoned their native language. Those who stayed on in Pennsylvania kept pretty much to themselves—on farms and in villages where they continued speaking their dialect of German, which was in time considerably influenced by English but which had no appreciable effect upon English outside the areas in which they were settled. *Sauerkraut* appears in British English as early as 1617, though neither the word nor the food it designates ever really caught on in England. It is most likely that it was borrowed independently in this country. Similarly, *noodle* is recorded in England before its first known appearance in America, but was probably reborrowed here.

[4] For back-formation, see p. 108. [eds.]

It is not improbable that other words which entered American English through Pennsylvania German were known outside the immediate German settlement area before the nineteenth century, but most of them are of such a nature that we should not expect to find them recorded as early as the eighteenth century. Some of them, like *ponhaus* "scrapple," are not listed in modern abridged dictionaries, probably because lexicographers do not consider them "standard," despite the fact that they are known and used by many speakers of standard American English at the present day. *Rainworm* "earthworm" is used in settlements of German origin and is probably a translation of *Regenwurm*. It occurs in the Pennsylvania German area and in the German settlements on the Yadkin in North Carolina, as well as in Nobleboro, Maine, which was settled from the Palatinate. Old English *regenwyrm* is doubtless the ancestor of the term as it occurs elsewhere, for instance, on Buzzards Bay in Massachusetts. *Sawbuck* is now widely disseminated but it originated in German and Dutch settlements from, respectively, *Sagebock* and *zaagbock*. The fact that each end of the rack on which wood is sawed is shaped like the letter X—the Roman symbol for ten—has given rise to the slang use of the term for a ten-dollar bill. *Woodbuck* is also heard over the entire German settlement area, obviously a partial translation of German *Holzbock*. *Hex* "a witch or the spell cast by a witch" and *to hex* "to cast a spell on" are fairly well known all over the country nowadays. *Ponhaus* (also occurring as *ponhoss*, *ponhorse*, *ponehoss*, and *pondhorse*) corresponds to standard German *Pfannhase*; it is current from the Pennsylvania German area proper westward to Ohio and is also well known in northwestern Maryland and northeastern West Virginia. Other gastronomical and culinary terms of Pennsylvania German origin are *sots* "yeast"; *snits* (also *schnitz*) "dried apples, pieces of fruit cut for drying" (also used as a verb "to cut into pieces"); *fat-cakes* "doughnuts" (*fettkuche*), *fossnocks* (*fasnachskuche* "Shrovetide cakes"); *thick-milk* "curdled milk" (*dickemilich*); *smearcase* "cottage cheese" (*schmierkäs*); and possibly, but by no no means certainly, *applebutter*. *Clook* "setting hen," with its less frequent variant *cluck*, is from Pennsylvania German *kluck* (standard German *Klucke*). According to Hans Kurath's *Word Geography of the Eastern United States* (Ann Arbor, 1949), "the derogatory phrase *dumb cluck* obviously contains this word." *Belsnickel* (or *Belschnickel*) was, and still is, the southern Pennsylvania equivalent of *Santa Claus*; the last part of the name is an affectionate diminutive form of German *Nikolaus*. Another name of long standing for the unhappily commercialized saint who rewards good children at Christmas is *Kriss Kingle* (or *Kriss Kringle*); it is a modification of *Christkindl* "Christ child." *To dunk* "to dip (doughnuts usually) into coffee or milk" is from Pennsylvania German *dunken* "to dip," corresponding to standard German *tunken*. It has not really been widely current for more than about twenty years, although it spread very rapidly once it caught on. There is no usage label for the word in the *American College Dictionary*, so that it is apparently considered standard American English nowadays. *Dunker* (or *Dunkard*) is the popular name of a member of the German Baptist Brethren, a pietistic sect which practices baptism by immersion, that is, by dunking.

From French explorers and colonizers American English acquired, usually by way of the Canadian border, such words as *prairie, bateau, voyageur, chowder, buccaneer, carryall* (vehicle), *lee, calumet,* and perhaps *gopher. Chowder* is a modification of *chaudière* "caldron." Although it is recorded first in England, *buccaneer* should probably be regarded as an *Americanism* by virtue of its many American historical associations; it is ultimately a Carib word, but comes to English by way of French *boucanier. Carryall* is a folk-etymologizing of *cariole. Gopher* is most likely from *gaufre* "honeycomb," in reference to the animal's burrowing habits. *Prairie* is of frequent occurrence in American English, alone and in a number of compounds such as *prairie dog, prairie wolf* "coyote," and *prairie schooner* "small covered wagon." The word is now perfectly familiar in British English also. *Levee* is a derivative of French *lever* "to raise." Its use to designate an embankment for preventing the overflow of a river is largely confined to the South, as is also its later sense "landing place for vessels." *Calumet,* ultimately a derivate of Latin *calamus* "reed," was the word used by the French explorers for the ceremonial tobacco pipe of the Indians.

A number of Spanish words, such as *mosquito* "little fly," *negro* "black" (an adjective which was soon converted into a noun), *pecadillo* "little sin," *armada* "armed (naval) forces" (originally a past participle), and *alligator* (from *el lagarto* "the lizard"), along with Nahuatl words adopted by the Spanish, such as those cited at the beginning of this chapter, entered the English language as early as the sixteenth century. These words, though some of them are more frequently used in this country than in England, should be distinguished from words taken from Spanish by English-speaking people settled on this continent. Such words are very numerous at a later date but very rare before the nineteenth century. *Calaboose* "jail" is a modification of Spanish *calabozo*, used chiefly in the southern states; it is recorded first in the latter years of the eighteenth century. *Cockroach* (as *cacarootch*) first appears in the *General Historie* of Captain John Smith, who refers to it in a somewhat ambiguous passage as "a certaine India Bug, called by the Spaniards a *Cacarootch*, the which creeping into Chests they [that is, the "cacarootches"] eat and defile with their ill-sented dung." The word used by Smith is a modification of Spanish *cucaracha* "wood louse," or possibly a variant form of it. It was later folk-etymologized to *cockroach* (just as Latin *asparagus* is converted by some speakers into *sparrow grass*) and subsequently clipped to *roach* in this country, American verbal prudery perhaps playing some part in the elimination of the first element of what deceptively appeared to be a compound of *cock* and *roach*. *Key* "reef or low island" from Spanish *cayo* was in English use before it was recorded in America, but its use is now mainly confined to this country, particularly to Florida. *Key West* is a modification of *Cayo Hueso* "bone key." The form *cay*, riming with *day*, is now more usual in British English than *key*. *Stevedore*, from Spanish *estivador*, occurs first in the form *stowadore* by association with English *to stow*.

SUGGESTED ASSIGNMENTS

1. Using a detailed map and, if necessary, the aid of a foreign-language student for data, write a composition on one of these subjects:

   a. Spanish place names in the Southwest
   b. French place names in the Mississippi Valley
   c. French place names in Louisiana
   d. Dutch place names in the Hudson Valley
   e. German place names in Pennsylvania

2. If you live in a town that retains some Old World flavor derived from its early foreign settlers, write a theme about the words of foreign origin that are generally known to the community. You might consider such questions as these: Have their pronunciations changed? Have their referents changed? What areas of life do they represent? Why are they used instead of American words? Have they become naturalized; for example, do they take *-s* plurals or verbs ending in *-ed* and *-ing*?

3. If you have studied Latin, write a composition on Latin words and phrases in English. Consider such matters as these: How have the meanings changed? Is the pronounciation Latin, English, or a combination of the two? Do the words fulfill a useful purpose? Among useful references for this assignment are these: Edwin Lee Johnson, *Latin Words of Common English*; E. E. Burriss and Lionel Casson, *Latin and Greek in Common Use*; and Jerome C. Hixson and I. Colodny, *Word Ways*.

4. Two historical dictionaries devoted to American English are *A Dictionary of American English*, edited by Sir W. A. Craigie and J. R. Hulbert, and *Dictionary of Americanisms*, edited by Mitford Mathews. Use these dictionaries to look up the following words to see when they are first recorded in American English and where they came from: *raccoon, skunk, moccasin, prairie, bureau, gopher, waffle, cockroach, mosquito*.

5. To understand the process of folk etymology, let us begin with examples. (1) The French *carriole* (a light cart) was borrowed into American English in the eighteenth century and soon was transformed to *carry-all*, thus conforming to the English verb-object pattern of compound nouns, as in *cure-all, cutthroat,*

killjoy, and *spitfire.* (2) In the eighteenth century the English word *pentis* meant a sloping-roofed structure attached to a main building. Since it was used for living quarters, it was changed to the more familiar and more English-looking *penthouse.* (3) British folk humor of the 18th century invented the term *Welsh rabbit* for melted cheese over toast, just as in the United States *Cape Cod turkey* was used for the humble codfish and *prairie oysters* for eggs. Later, because *Welsh rabbit* seemed an inexplicable form for its referent, the more reasonable *Welsh rarebit* was substituted. This process of changing words, in part or in whole, to make them more understandable, or more natural, or more reasonable, or more familiar, is called folk etymology. The resulting word is also called a folk etymology.

Although desk dictionaries tend to neglect folk etymologies, you will find enough information in *Webster's New Collegiate Dictionary* (8th edition) to enable you to infer the process by which the following folk etymologies came into being: *crayfish, chaise lounge, cold slaw* (look up *coleslaw*), *shamefaced, belfrey, sand-blind, bridegroom.*

FURTHER READINGS

Barber, Charles L. *The Story of Speech and Language.* New York: Thomas Y. Crowell Co., 1964.

Brook, G. L. *A History of the English Language.* New York: W. W. Norton & Company, Inc., 1958. (Paperbound in the Norton Library, 1964.) On the development of English, see pp. 28–58.

Chadwick, John. *On the Decipherment of Linear B.* New York: Random House, Inc., 1968.

Hughes, John P. *The Science of Language.* New York: Random House, Inc., 1962. On the languages of Europe, see pp. 73–93.

Marckwardt, Albert H. *American English.* New York: Oxford University Press, 1958.

Myers, L. M. *The Roots of Modern English.* Boston: Little, Brown & Company, 1966.

Pyles, Thomas. *The Origin and Development of the English Language.* New York: Harcourt Brace Jovanovich, Inc., 1964. On recent British and American English, see pp. 217–261.

4
DICTIONARIES

How to Find Fault with a Dictionary

Paul Roberts

A good up-to-date dictionary is a valuable tool for a college student, no matter what his specialty is. But, like any tool, it will be of greatest benefit only after one has acquired skill in using it. In the selection below, the author first sketches a history of dictionaries in English and then provides helpful suggestions on the uses of a desk dictionary. Dr. Paul Roberts was a professor at San Jose State College and is the author of five textbooks on English grammar.

DICTIONARY WORSHIP

It is probably fair to say that most present-day Americans show rather more respect for the dictionary than they do for the Bible. It is significant that we speak of "the dictionary" rather than "a dictionary," as if there were only one. When we say, "The dictionary says so," we feel that we have settled the matter once and for all, that we have carried the appeal to the final authority. The popular feeling seems to be that the dictionary editor visits heaven every few years to receive the material for the next edition.

Well, modern dictionaries are good, but they're not that good. It is true that they are generally more sophisticated linguistically than the people that use them; that they are prepared with great care at considerable expense by squads of experts; that keen competition for a large market keeps them up to date, well presented, and generally sharp. But it is also true that they are prepared by men and women liable, like all men and women, to error. It is further true that the nature of their subject—the word units of a vast, boiling, constantly changing language—makes it impossible, or at least economically unfeasible, for them to be prepared by what could be called scientific methods.

It is the intent of this [essay] to look at dictionaries in perspective, to trace their growth briefly, and to see what they offer their modern users.

THE EVOLUTION OF THE MODERN DICTIONARY

It has been said wisely that nobody ever begins anything. Look behind every bright idea and you find some earlier bright idea that contains its kernel. This is so at least with the English dictionary. It is hard to say which the first one was because we find word lists of one kind or another going deep into the Middle Ages. But these early lists were two-language dictionaries—e.g., Latin words with English translations. The first English-English word list was published in 1603, and this is usually called the first English dictionary.

Interestingly enough, it was not called a dictionary. Its title was *A Table Alphabeticall* and its author a man named Robert Cawdrey. Cawdrey's dictionary contained about 2500 words. They were all "hard words," words that readers, or at least inexperienced readers, might be expected to stumble over. The definitions were fairly primitive—synonyms usually, and not always accurate.

Cawdrey did not pick his 2500 words out of the air. For the most part he got them by copying from an earlier Latin word list. Thus at the very beginning was born that splendid tradition of plagiarism in dictionary-making that has lasted nearly to the present day. Plagiarism in dictionary-making is next to inevitable. Suppose you wanted to produce a dictionary. How could you, how could anyone, arrive at all the words except by looking in dictionaries already in existence? Presumably you would have your own contribution to make, but you would be a plain fool if you didn't check your competitors' books to make sure you hadn't overlooked something important. There is, as it happens, one other way of going about it, but it is fearfully toilsome, and it has been undertaken only once, as we shall see.

Anyway, Cawdrey copied from his predecessors, and his successors copied from him. But each lexicographer produced not only his predecessor's word list but also more words that he had dredged up by himself, and as the seventeenth century wore on, dictionaries, as they had come to be called, grew larger and larger. By the end of the century they were crowding 25,000 words.

They were getting better as well as bigger. Generally they copied not only one another's word lists but one another's definitions as well; nevertheless, there was steady improvement in the definitions. Being much worked over, they grew more accurate, more elaborate, and more refined.

In the second half of the seventeenth century an important addition to the dictionary was made: etymologies. The etymology is that part of the dictionary entry which explains the history of the word. It is now an essential part of dictionaries and is most carefully and accurately done. In the beginning the etymologies were slipshod and primitive. Usually they consisted of a single letter—F or L or G—to indicate whether the word was borrowed from French, Latin, or Greek. Many words were not labeled at all. But once somebody thought of putting in etymologies, all his successors had to include them too or risk losing the market; and, like the definitions, the etymologies, worked over decade after decade, became better and better. Thus free enterprise triumphed again.

The dictionaries of the seventeenth century were all hard-word dictionaries. Nobody made any attempt to include all the words of the language, but only those likely to give a reader trouble. However, shortly after 1700 a man named John Kersey took the step of including common words too. His purpose presumably was to provide a complete spelling list, but he didn't shrink from the difficult task of providing definitions for the common words. These are sufficiently crude. The word *an,* for instance, is given thus "An: as, *an* apron." This may make us smile until we try to define it ourselves. Ultimately the only important thing we can do with words like *an, the, of, with, some* is to show how they are used.

Kersey was a new breed—a man whose main business was making dictionaries, a professional lexicographer. Another was Nathaniel Bailey. Bailey produced several dictionaries, one of which appeared through the eighteenth century in thirty different editions. Presumably most literate homes of that century possessed a Bailey dictionary. So many were printed that they are still readily available on the second-hand book market, and can be bought cheap, despite their age, by collectors of old dictionaries.

DR. JOHNSON

But the great figure of lexicography in the eighteenth century was Dr. Samuel Johnson, the king of literary London in the time of George the Third. Johnson made his reputation with his dictionary, published in 1755 after seven years of labor. It was originally intended . . . to regulate the English language. It didn't do that, of course, but it did contribute much to the growth of lexicography and indeed exerted considerable influence on English writing.

Students of literature are likely to pass rapidly over the dictionary and concern themselves with Johnson's literary works and with Boswell's great biography of Johnson. They note the dictionary only as the subject of a famous letter to Lord Chesterfield in which Johnson repudiates help offered too late, or as a book containing occasionally waspish definitions:

> PENSION: An allowance made to anyone without an equivalent. In England it is generally understood to mean pay given to a state hireling for treason to his country.
>
> LEXICOGRAPHER: a writer of dictionaries; a harmless drudge.

But Johnson's dictionary, as his contemporaries well knew, was not a collection of amusing definitions but a serious and important work.

Johnson had, first of all, a rare ability for definition, a greater one, possibly, than anyone before or after him. His definitions, sometimes overcomplicated, are mostly strong and clear. He also made a couple of lexicographical innovations. One was the practice of separating and numbering word meanings, thus:

> MAN: 1. Human being. 2. Not a woman. 3. Not a boy. 4. A servant; an attendant; a dependent. 5. A word of familiarity bordering on contempt. 6. It is used in loose signification like the French *on,* one, any one.

This is now of course standard procedure in dictionaries.

Another, even more important innovation, was the citing of contexts to show word meanings or particular usages. As he worked on the dictionary, Johnson read widely in earlier literature and marked passages for secretaries to copy out, and many of these passages found their way into the dictionary. Definition-by-context is not carried through in anything like a complete or systematic way. But in a great many entries, the reader is given not only Johnson's definition but a sentence to show how the word was used by Shakespeare or Milton or Addison or Swift.[1]

Johnson's dictionary went through four editions in his lifetime and more after his death. In the early nineteenth century it was revised by Todd, and in one form or another it continued to be "The Dictionary" in England much as Noah Webster's became "The Dictionary" in America.

Others, however, were making their contributions to lexicography. In the late eighteenth century synonymies were added to entries in dictionaries. These are lists of close synonyms. Thus after *courage* one might find *bravery, boldness, valor, heroism, fortitude,* etc. In the course of time lexicographers undertook to define the shades of meaning between such synonyms. This is not only an integral part of modern dictionaries but has been expanded outside the dictionary proper. We now have "dictionaries of synonyms," such as *Roget's Thesaurus* or *Webster's Dictionary of Synonyms*, devoted entirely to the listing and explication of synonymous words.

[1] Or others. [*eds.*]

Also in the second half of the eighteenth century, dictionaries began to include guides to pronunciation. A pioneer in this department was Thomas Sheridan, the father of the playwright Richard Brinsley Sheridan. The elder Sheridan was also connected with the theatre, as were other people experimenting with pronunciation guides. They of course set down as "correct pronunciation" the pronunciation current in their own theatrical circles. This had a considerable effect on how people thought they ought to pronounce words, if not on how they actually did pronounce them. Probably its effect is still going on.

THE OXFORD ENGLISH DICTIONARY

The greatest lexicographical effort in England in the nineteenth century —perhaps the greatest of any century anywhere—was the *Oxford English Dictionary*. This has gone under various names in its long career. It is sometimes called the *Oxford Dictionary*, the *Historical English Dictionary*, and the *New English Dictionary*, and it is variously abbreviated the OED, the OD, the HED, and the NED. It is usually bound in ten or twelve or twenty volumes, and it costs in the neighborhood of 250 dollars.

The idea for the *Oxford English Dictionary* was born and nurtured in the Philological Society in England. In the year 1857 one of its members read a paper criticizing existing dictionaries. He pointed out that the best of them were hit-and-miss affairs, unscientifically produced, impressionistic. He suggested that the Society undertake a new dictionary to be planned along quite different lines. The Society agreed enthusiastically, not knowing that none of them would live long enough to see the project completed.

The idea was that the dictionary would draw its data from English writing and would not only give word meanings but would systematically cite contextual evidence to verify the meanings given. The dictionary would include all words in use between the year 1100 and the date of publication. It was intended to cite the first occurrence of each word in English writing and the last occurrence if the word had dropped out of use, together with other citations across the centuries to show developments in meaning. It was decided that all extant English writing dating from before 1500 should be read and as much of the later writing as possible. In the end, practically all of English literature was covered, together with great quantities of cookbooks, religious tracts, trade manuals, newspapers, and the like.

The reading was done by thousands of volunteers. If you volunteered to read for the dictionary, you would be assigned, say, the works of Jane Austen. You would be told to read the novels carefully, looking for any unusual word, any word unusually used, any word that struck you as new or old or in any way remarkable. When you came on such a word, you wrote it on a slip together with the sentence in which it occurred, noting the page or chapter number and the edition. You were also instructed to excerpt as many ordinary words and their contexts as time permitted. In the end some five million quotations were gathered of which about a million and a half appeared in the dictionary.

As the slips came in, they were sorted and filed in storehouses and eventually studied by the editors and their assistants. When an editor came to write the entry for the word *buxom*, for example, he began by assembling all the slips on *buxom*. He then deduced its meaning and its changes of meaning from those slips. It didn't matter what he thought it meant or ought to mean or what other dictionaries said about it. He was bound by the slips. They gave him all the variant spellings and different usages and displayed the whole history of the word. Everything he had to say about *buxom* came out of those slips, and in the finished article, he included quotations to demonstrate the meanings given.

In the first quarter of a century, progress on the dictionary was spasmodic. The Philological Society found the undertaking vaster than it had imagined; financial troubles arose; editors died; interest flagged. But in the 1880's a man named James Murray was hired as editor, and the work picked up again. Murray got out the first volume, A to Ant, in 1884. About this time Henry Bradley, a young philologist, was hired as coeditor, and the pace was doubled. After the turn of the century, two more editors, William Craigie and Charles Talbot Onions, were added to the staff. These last were the only ones who saw the work completed in 1928. Murray and Craigie were knighted for their work on the dictionary.[2]

Anyone with any curiosity at all about words should make the acquaintance of the *Oxford English Dictionary*. It is to be found in the reference room of any college library, along with its abridgement, the two-volume *Shorter Oxford*. You may find it rather a maze at first. The entry on the word *set*, the longest entry in the dictionary, runs to some twenty-three small-type, triple-columned pages; there is a good deal to say about *set* if you say everything. But brief acquaintance will quickly make the plan and possibilities clear. You will find there everything known about most English words and, through the words, the key to much in the development of English culture. The *Oxford* has contributed to thousands of scholarly studies that would have been altogether impossible without it. The *Oxford* is itself one of scholarship's greatest triumphs and a monument to the thousands of men and women who contributed their leisure hours for years and decades, for neither money nor fame but only for the satisfaction of extending human knowledge.

---

[2] The last volume of the *OED*, Vol. X, Part II, V–Z, is dated 1928. A supplement was published in 1933 to treat new words and meanings and also to correct and amplify the entries already in print, by means of readers' contributions that have flowed in continuously during the compilation of the entire dictionary.

In 1972 appeared Vol. I, A–G, of a projected three-volume *Supplement to the Oxford English Dictionary*, designed to replace the 1933 supplement. [eds.]

DICTIONARIES IN AMERICA

In America the great pioneer in lexicography was of course Noah Webster, whose name came to be closely linked with lexicography in this country as Johnson's was in England. Webster was a Connecticut school teacher, a graduate of Yale. He early became a producer of spelling books and an advocate of spelling reform and this interest led him into the making of dictionaries. His *Compendious Dictionary*, published in 1806, included such spellings as *fether* (feather), *hed* (head), *masheen* (machine), *bilt* (built), *leen* (lean), *thum* (thumb), *magic* (for *magick*), *color* (for *colour*), *center* (for centre). Most of these sensible suggestions were rejected by the writing public, and it could not be said that Webster was greatly effective in simplifying English spelling. On the other hand, he was more effective than anyone else had been.

But Webster is famous not as a spelling reformer but as the Webster of Webster's dictionary. Webster brought out his last and greatest effort in lexicography in 1828 under the title *An American Dictionary of the English Language*. This work is in a sense the American counterpart of Johnson's dictionary. Neither is scientifically controlled in the sense that the *Oxford* was to be. But neither is a mere plagiarism either or a hasty commercial effort. Both Webster and Johnson were intelligent men of strong and independent minds. Both were sufficiently crotchety and opinionated and likely to indulge idiosyncracies now and then. But they were mostly sane and wise, and they brought more genius to the field of lexicography than it was used to at the time.

Webster's book was revised once in his lifetime. In 1843 the rights were purchased by Charles and George Merriam, and the Merriam firm continued, and continues, to bring out editions of all sizes, all bearing the Webster name. This name quickly acquired enormous commercial value, and one of the problems of the Merriam Company was how to keep it as their very own. Other publishers would, for example, hire somebody named Joseph Webster and publish a "Webster's Dictionary," neglecting to mention that the Webster involved was Joe and not Noah. The consequence was a series of court battles decided now one way and now another. Today one of Merriam's chief competitors in the college field, the World Publishing Company, publishes a dictionary called the *Webster New World Dictionary*. This is done legally and with acquiescence, but not with as much cheerfulness on either side as one would like to see.

The Merriam Company has always enjoyed enough challenge to keep it up to the mark and to maintain a rather heady excitement in American lexicographical circles. One of Noah Webster's early competitors was a man named Joseph Worcester, who followed the Johnson tradition more closely than Webster deigned to. Worcester's dictionary also had its violent partisans, and for some decades it was possible in American literary circles to work up heated argument about whether Webster's or Worcester's was to be accepted as the authority. Even institutions took sides. Yale embraced the work of Webster, its famous son, whereas it was late in the nineteenth century before Harvard men were permitted to peep into anything but Worcester's.

In the late nineteenth and early twentieth centuries Merriam's chief competition came from Funk and Wagnalls, publishers of the *Standard Dictionary*. This competition produced, from edition to edition, added features in both dictionaries: improved synonymies, illustrations, biographical and geographical lists, improved methods in presentation, more research. It also produced more words.. It was quickly apparent that the customer eyed with favor that dictionary which contained most words, and the result was that editors bringing out a new edition would make sure that it contained everything the other company's had and then dredge up a few thousand more. Under this stimulus the number of entries in the "unabridged" versions rose to around 600,000. They stopped there, not because the editors ran out of words but because the dictionaries are advertised as portable, and 600,000 words seems to be as many as one can carry from one room to another.

The dictionary popularly called "Webster's Unabridged" has more exactly the title *Webster's New International Dictionary*, second edition. It was published in 1934. It seems to be the intention of the Merriam Company to publish revisions of the big book about every twenty-five years. The *New International* is not comparable to the *Oxford*. Its editors did not enjoy the resources available to the editors of the *Oxford*, and they labored under certain commercial limitations, principally that of space. Even so, the *New International* is (not to search too hard for a metaphor) a great storehouse of information. Its principles are, at least in theory, those of the *Oxford*: the word is defined by the contexts in which it occurs, and the editor is bound by those contexts in writing his article. The Merriam Company keeps a staff of editors and assistants and special experts at work to keep its files up to date and to prepare for the next edition.[3]

COLLEGE DICTIONARIES

Almost from the beginning of lexicography there has been a market for dictionaries smaller than possible: college dictionaries, high school dictionaries, pocket dictionaries, office dictionaries. The Merriam Company for a

---

[3] In 1961 appeared *Webster's Third New International Dictionary*. This volume employed the findings of linguistic science in its treatment of pronunciations, definitions, and usage labels. The furor that it raised can be studied in *Dictionaries and THAT Dictionary* by James Sledd and Wilma H. Ebbitt. [eds.]

long time enjoyed an advantage in the college field as well as in the unabridged class. Until the end of the Second World War, the outstanding
dictionary in the college field was the *Webster Collegiate*, fifth edition,
published in 1936. A whole generation of college students carried the *Collegiate* from class to class, blissfully unaware that any other dictionaries
existed. . . . Few good ones did in America at that time.

By 1945, however, the *Collegiate* had come under serious criticism,
particularly from linguists. It was argued that the *Collegiate* was not only
old but stodgy; that it was authoritarian, laying down the law about correctness, instead of objectively reporting the usage of educated people; that its
treatment of pronunciation and other features was unrealistic; that its
definitions needed a breath of clarity. Some of this criticism was no doubt
justified; some of it stemmed possibly from the tendency of the Merriam
Company to give the impression that its dictionaries were produced under
the general supervision of the angel Gabriel.

At any rate, shortly after the end of the Second World War, the Merriam
monopoly was vigorously challenged. In 1947 Random House and Harper
& Brothers jointly brought out *The American College Dictionary* (ACD).
In 1949, Merriam answered with a revision of the *Collegiate* under the title
Webster's New Collegiate Dictionary (WNCD). A few years later the World
Publishing Company put the *Webster New World Dictionary* (WNWD) into
the ring. The editor of the ACD, Clarence Barnhart, produced the *Thorndike-Barnhart Dictionary* for Scott Foresman. This is similar to the ACD
in many features, but of smaller scope.

It should be said first of all that all of these postwar dictionaries are good
books. The college student who owns either the WNCD, the ACD, or the
WNWD owns a dictionary that is adequate for his normal needs, that is
reasonably accurate and up to date, and that is sufficiently easy to use.
Whichever one you buy, you buy a lot of scholarship for five or six dollars.
Salesmen for the other two dictionaries will take a pretty gloomy view of
your chances for success and happiness, but you may not feel especially
handicapped. The writer of this [essay] owns all three of these college dictionaries, and he tends to use the one that happens to be closest to hand
when he wants to look something up. . . .

The student's problem is not really what dictionary to buy. This is likely
to be settled for him by his college bookstore or his instructor. His task is
rather to inform himself on what is in whatever dictionary he owns and to
learn how to use it.[4]

---

[4] Since the publication of this material, three more acceptable desk dictionaries
have appeared: the *Standard College Dictionary* (Funk & Wagnalls Co., 1963); the
American Heritage Dictionary of the English Language (American Heritage
Publishing Company and Houghton Mifflin, 1970); the *Random House Dictionary
of the English Language*, 1966, 1967). [eds.]

INSIDE THE DICTIONARY

The big college dictionaries run to around 130,000 or 140,000 main entries. These are the black-type headings. Obvious derivatives are usually listed within the main entries. Thus, *intelligently* will not a rate a paragraph of its own, but will be listed in small type under *intelligent*. But *intelligence* will have an entry of its own. Some prefixes—like *un, non, and ex*—attach to thousands of words. The dictionary will not list all the possibilities, but will give a number of examples, usually in smaller type at the bottom of the page.

In addition to ordinary words, dictionaries list a great many names of people and places. The WNCD lists these in two separate sections at the back of the book—a biographical index and a pronouncing gazetteer. The other modern dictionaries throw everything into one alphabetical list. Thus in the ACD you find *Disraeli* between *disquisition* and *disrate*. In the WNCD he's in the back of the book between *Disney* and *Ditmars*.

The college dictionaries contain all the words the student is likely to look up in ordinary work. It is only if your interest is quite special—as when you are working in very specialized science or dialects or old literature— that the college dictionary will fail you. Then you will have to turn to the *Oxford* or the *New International* or a special dictionary for your subject.

GRAMMATICAL DESIGNATIONS

Right after the word in the alphabetical list, the dictionary will give an abbreviated designation of its "part of speech"—as *n., v., prep.,* for *noun, verb, preposition,* respectively. The grammatical system used is the traditional one. . . . It should be remembered that in this as in other matters the dictionary can give only ordinary usage, not all possible usage. It may, for example, list *horse* only as a noun, though it obviously occurs also as a verb, as in "Don't horse around."

If the word occurs in two or more grammatical categories, the dictionary will give the definitions for each. For example, the word *face* will be given as *face, n.,* followed by definitions of *face* as a noun. Then, in the main entry, you will find the abbreviation *v.t.,* followed by definitions of *face* as a verb. *T.* here means *transitive,* and that means that the verb occurs in the pattern N-V-N; *v.i.* means *verb intransitive,* which means that the verb occurs in the pattern N-V. *Face* is *v.t.* because we ordinarily say "He faced something" and not just "He faced."[5] You will find these and other abbrevia-

---

[5] N-V-N means noun-verb-noun and refers to the subject-verb-object structure, as in "He read a book." Here *read* is a *v.t.* because it takes an object. N-V means noun-verb and refers to the subject-verb structure, as in "He read." Here *read* is a *v.i.* because it has no object. [eds.]

tions explained in the front or back of your dictionary, usually on the cover. Abbreviations very frequently used are explained at the bottom of each page.

DEFINITIONS

Since Johnson's time dictionaries have recognized that words have multiple meanings and have undertaken to separate and number them. A word in a college dictionary may have fifteen or more numbered meanings. The careless student looking up a word is likely to settle for the definition at the top of the list, which may not be what he's after at all. Often you have to search around a bit.

Note also that dictionaries differ in the way in which they arrange the different meanings. The Merriam-Webster dictionaries, like the *Oxford*, list the meanings in historical order. The oldest meaning that the word has had in English is given first, then the one that developed next, and so on. The ACD and the WNWD try to give the meanings in the order of current frequency. Both methods have advantages and disadvantages. The order in the WNCD gives you something of the history of the word; its semantic development unfolds as you read the definitions. On the other hand, the definition your eye first lights on is likely to be obsolete and useless to your present purposes.

ETYMOLOGIES AND SYNONYMIES

All modern college dictionaries contain two features which can be of much service to you in strengthening and sharpening your vocabulary. These are the etymologies and the synonymies. The etymology is a very brief explanation of the history of the word, the route by which it has come into English, the elements of which it is made, and so on. The etymology is given in square brackets. In the WNCD and the WNWD it appears at the head of the entry, just after the pronunciation. In the ACD it follows the definitions.

Etymologies are very highly abbreviated in order to conserve space. The abbreviation key is given on the cover of the dictionary, common symbols at the bottom of the page. Thus, in the ACD the etymology of *diminutive* is [ME, t. ML; m.s. *diminutivus*, der. L. *di-*, *deminutis*, pp., *lessened*]. Reference to the symbols will allow you to translate this as "This word, which occurs in Middle English, was taken from Medieval Latin; it is a modification of the stem of *diminutivus*, which derives from Latin *diminutis* or *deminutis*, a past participle meaning 'lessened.' " A very little practice will make the symbols readily familiar to you. The etymologies of all the college dictionaries are quite accurate, the history of words having been thoroughly studied for centuries. Naturally there is no space to give more than an outline of the word's history. . . . .

Do get in the habit of glancing at the etymology when you look up a word. You will begin to see patterns in word-building that will help you retain words in your vocabulary. You will also make your way into a field most interesting in itself.[6]

The synonymies are also interesting and sometimes helpful. Lists of synonyms are given mostly for abstract words, like *courage, pride, cleverness*. The synonymy will be given only once for one group of synonyms. For example, if you look up *arrogance*, you may be directed to *pride* for the synonymy. There you will find not only the list of synonyms— *pride, arrogance, haughtiness*, etc.—but also an attempt to explain the shades of difference between each word.

STATUS DESIGNATIONS

Words which are in anything less than general respectable use are marked in the dictionary by such designations as *slang, colloquial, provincial, dialectal, vulgar, archaic, obsolete*. These are generally abbreviated, as *obs.* for *obsolete* or *col.* for *colloquial*. Words or meanings pertaining to special fields are so labeled, as *Law, Med.* (medicine), *Teleg.* (telegraphy). Geographical limitations are also given: *U.S.* (United States), *Brit.* (British). Words for which there are no status designations are presumably in current, general, polite use.

It should be said that in applying status designations dictionaries do not walk on very firm ground. . . . The lines between slang and colloquial and between colloquial and elegant are not sharp lines, and there is really no controllable procedure by which the lexicographer can decide whether to pin on the label *slang* or *colloquial* or to let the word slip by unreproached. Presumably he often studies all the available evidence and then flips a coin. Here as elsewhere the student will do well to use his own ears and eyes. They may prove the dictionary wrong. You use the dictionary to improve your language only when better means are not available.

Remember also that a status designation does not necessarily mean that the word should not be used under any circumstances. *Colloquial*, for example, means simply that the word is more likely to occur in conversation than in writing. *Dialectal* means that there are geographical restrictions on it, as, for instance, that it is current only in southern Utah. If you live in southern Utah, you would not conclude from this that you and your neighbors are subnormal because you use the word; you would simply not expect it to be understandable or to sound natural in Buffalo.

[6] For a more thorough treatment of etymology, see Umbach's "'Etymology," pp. 91–100. [eds.]

PRONUNCIATION

All modern dictionaries indicate a pronunciation of each word, usually in parentheses right after the entry. For all dictionaries this remains one of the weakest features, though the lexicographers are not obviously to blame for the shortcomings. . . . In practice, dictionaries include a lot of nonsense about "short vowels" and "long vowels," and often festoon the vowels with various squiggles called "diacritical marks." From all this one can, with application, get a rough notion of how the editor wants the word to be pronounced, but the procedure could scarcely be called efficient. . . .

There has been much improvement in the last [decade]. The editors of the ACD adopted the symbol called *schwa*: ə. This represents the so-called neutral vowel which is very common in syllables that do not have primary or secondary stress. It is for most speakers the first vowel in *event* and *above*, the last two in *sensible*. By adopting *schwa*, the dictionary was able to get rid of a whole host of diacritical marks. The same practice is followed by the WNWD, by the *Thorndike-Barnhart Dictionary*, and by others. The Merriam dictionaries cling to the old system with its confusion of diacritical marks, but they are not likely to do so forever.[7] . . .

The system of representing pronunciation in your dictionary may be overly complicated, but a little practice and reference to the symbol key at the bottom of the page will quickly initiate you. Even the diacritical marks of the WNCD are fathomable with only a little application. Much more important is the whole question of "correct pronunciation."

There is a widespread notion that every word has one and only one correct pronunciation, and that this is inscribed in phonetic symbols on a scroll in heaven or perhaps carved on the wall of Plato's Cave. One feels that there is some principle somewhere, some rules or set of rules, which the dictionary-maker applies to determine which pronunciation is correct. Actually, the only arbiter of pronunciation is usage. There is no other. None whatsoever. If a pronunciation is correct it is so because people, or more likely those particular people whom one admires and wishes to emulate, pronounce the word that way, and for no other reason.

It seems to be very hard to grasp this. The writer recalls a speech teacher who liked to begin his course with a demonstration of the ignorance of the students. He would write a word on the blackboard—say, *illustrate*—and ask each student to pronounce it in turn. Like as not each one would put the stress on the first syllable: *íllustrate*. "You see," the teacher would say triumphantly, "not one of you knows how to pronounce it. The correct pronunciation is *illústrate*." But observe the flaw. The students were themselves members of the educated class. Many of them were sons and daugh-

---

[7] The last two Merriam college dictionaries—*Webster's Seventh New Collegiate Dictionary* and the eighth edition, called *Webster's New Collegiate Dictionary*, 1973—both employ the *schwa*. [eds.]

ters of educated people and moved in circles where the English spoken was good and decent and admired and admirable. If they had not encountered the pronunciation *illústrate*, this was substantial evidence that the pronunciation was not current in educated circles. All the teacher succeeded in proving was that he didn't know how to pronounce the word.

A popular book on pronunciation published some decades ago began with a list of words and the comment that not three educated people out of five hundred could pronounce them correctly. Again, observe the flaw. If 498 educated people pronounced them one way, the inference is that the other two were eccentric. But this seemed not to have occurred to this expert on pronunciation.

Modern dictionaries do much better than this. To be sure, they do not publicize the methods by which they decide what pronunciations to favor. Perhaps they send around questionnaires, or perhaps the editor just asks his secretary what she thinks he should put down. But in general they try to list pronunciations that are current and common and not just traditional. Often they will give two or more pronunciations for a word, listing them in the order of frequency.

Remember also that many words, and particularly many of the words we are likely to look up in the dictionary, do not really have stable pronunciations. These are what are sometimes called "eye words," words that we write and read but do not often speak and hear. If the word is not spoken, it cannot develop a standard pronunciation. Nobody can be altogether sure how to pronounce *schism*, because he so seldom hears it pronounced.

YOU AND THE DICTIONARY

It has been said that when an educated American has a word problem he tends to consult the dictionary; when an educated Englishman has a word problem he tends to consult his memory, to recall how the word is used or pronounced by his friends and relatives. The latter is certainly the more reasonable approach, though of course it won't always work. The proper procedure is to solve the problem on the basis of your experience if it lies within your experience; if it does not, you consult the dictionary.

Observe, however, that the dictionary is a more reliable guide in some areas than in others. If the question is one of spelling, you can depend on the dictionary absolutely; all you have to be sure of here is that you are using an American dictionary and not a British one. In etymologies also you can take the dictionary's pronouncements as nearly gospel. Errors in etymology do occur, and occasionally the editor is a little more positive about the history of the word than he ought to be, but such matters will not trouble you until you get pretty well along in the study of philology.

Definitions are a somewhat different matter. As we have seen, the ultimate definer is the context. All the editor can do is make a generalization or a series of generalizations from contexts available to him. It may be that these will not apply exactly to the context you are concerned with. Here you use the dictionary to fill out and clarify what you learn from the passage itself.

In word status and pronunciation you are even more on your own. The only real teacher here is observation of what goes on in the circle you belong to or in the one to which you aspire. The dictionary gives you a more or less informed opinion, but it cannot override the facts that confront you. Don't start correcting your betters if they pronounce a word one way and the dictionary suggests another.

Above all, remember that the dictionary does not make laws. It reports usage, usually accurately, sometimes not. It reports mostly the usage of educated people, therefore of the class to which you belong or into which you are moving. It reports, in some degree, your usage. . . . You're a member of the educated class or at least hovering on its outskirts. You're going to college, aren't you?

SUGGESTED ASSIGNMENTS

1. Using your desk dictionary, find out how the following words are pronounced: *advertisement, aunt, chaise longue, chic, cinquecento, derby, despicable, duty, envelope, exquisite, garage, lingerie, root, tomato.*

2. Using your desk dictionary, look up and write down the meaning of the following words: *analphabetic, antediluvian, cinquecento, donnybrook, megabuck, uxorious, mendacity, leman, femme fatale.*

3. Using your desk dictionary, look up and write down the etymology of the following words: *arrive, boor, pajamas, ransack, tantalize, jeans.*

4. Use your desk dictionary to find out the usage status of the italicized words in the following sentences. (That is, are they nonstandard, dialectal, slang, colloquial, obsolete, archaic, vulgar, British, Scottish; or do they have some other usage label? Remember that any item without a usage label is considered acceptable in educated use.)
   a. That was *real* nice of you.
   b. You'd better go *slow*.
   c. He looked *like* he was frightened. (*Like* as a conjunction.)
   d. Jane was *disinterested* in sports cars. (For *uninterested*.)
   e. Have you *drank* your medicine yet? (For *drunk* as a past participle.)

5. In your desk dictionary, study the front matter that explains how to use it. Then, combining this information with what you know from experience, write a short theme explaining to an incoming freshman how to make efficient use of his dictionary.

EXCERPT FROM THE OXFORD ENGLISH DICTIONARY

Fun (*fvn*), *sb.*   [prob. f. FUN *v.*]

†1. A cheat or trick; a hoax, a practical joke.

a **1700** B. E. *Dict. Cant. Crew*, *Fun*, a Cheat or slippery Trick. **1719** D'URFEY *Pills* (1872) V. 259 A Hackney Coach-man he did hug her, And was not this a very good Fun?

2. Diversion, amusement, sport; also, boisterous jocularity or gaiety, drollery.

(Johnson **1755** stigmatizes it as 'a low cant word'; in present use it is merely somewhat familiar.)

1727 SWIFT *Misc. Epit. By-words*, Tho' he talk'd much of virtue, his head always run Upon something or other she found better fun. **1749** FIELDING *Tom Jones* IX. vi, Partridge .. was a great lover of what is called fun. **1751** E. MOORE *Gil Blas* Prol. 25 Don't mind me tho', for all my fun and jokes. **1767** H. BROOKE *Fool of Qual.* I. 99 Vindex .. looked smilingly about him with much fun in his face. **1768–74** TUCKER *Lt. Nat.* (1852) II. 313 It is fun to them to break off an ornament, or disfigure a statue. **1790** BURNS *Tam o'Shanter* 144 The mirth and fun grew fast and furious. **1837** DICKENS *Pickw.* ii, 'What's the fun?' said a rather tall thin young man. **1845** S. C. HALL *Bk. Gems* 90 His wit and humour delightful, when it does not degenerate into 'fun'. **1849** E. E. NAPIER *Excurs. S. Africa* II. 331 Being better mounted than the rest of his troop, [he] pushed on to see more of the fun. **1887** SHEARMAN *Athletics & Football* 325 Most footballers play for the fun and the fun alone. **1889** J. K. JEROME *Idle Thoughts* 42 There is no fun in doing nothing when you have nothing to do. **1891** BARING-GOULD *In Troubadour-Land* iv. 50, I do not see the fun of going to hotels of the first class.

b. Phr. *To make fun of, poke fun at* (a person, etc.): to ridicule. *For or in fun*: as a joke, sportively, not seriously. (*He, it is*) *good, great fun*: a source of much amusement. *Like fun*: energetically, very quickly, vigorously. *What fun!* how very amusing!

1737 H. WALPOLE *Corr.* (1820) I. 17, I can't help making fun of myself. **1840** HOOD *Up Rhine* 157 The American .. in a dry way began to poke his fun at the unfortunate traveller. *a* **1847** MRS. SHERWOOD *Lady of Manor* III. xxi. 250 Then you won't make fun of me, will you? **1848** LOWELL *Biglow P.* Ser. I. IV. 98 Stickin' together like fun. **1849** LYTTON *Caxtons* 19 You would be very sorry if your mamma were to .. break it for fun. **1857** HUGHES *Tom Brown* II. iii, The bolts went to like fun. **1860** GEN. P. THOMPSON *Audi Alt.* III. cxxvi. 82 Who knows but Volunteer Rifles may make a campaign in the Holy Land, and mount guard over the production of the holy fire at Easter? 'What fun!' **1875** JOWETT *Plato* (ed. 2) I. 151 He may pretend in fun that he has a bad memory. **1877** M. M. GRANT *Sun-Maid* iii, The races are great fun. **1891** N. GOULD *Double Event* 1 He's such good fun, and he's so obliging. **1895** H. A. KENNEDY in *19th Cent.* Aug. 331, I suppose the wood-carver was poking fun at him?

3. *Comb.*, as *fun-loving* adj.

1775 PRATT *Liberal Opin.* (1783) II. 119 This fun-loving Alicia. **1892** *Daily News* 14 July 5/1 A fun-loving, jolly, prankish elf of a woman.

Fun (*fvn*), *v.*   [Perh. a dialectal pronunc. of FON *v.*, to befool (not recorded after 15th c.).]

1. *trans.* To cheat, hoax; also, to cajole. Const. *of, out of. Obs. exc. dial.*

1685 *Roxb. Ball.* VII. 473 She had fun'd him of his Coin. *a* **1700** B. E. *Dict. Cant. Crew* s.v., What do you Fun me? Do you think to Sharp or Trick me? **1744** OZELL tr. *Brantome's Sp. Rhodomontades* (ed. 2) 44 He that funs me out of her, may boldly say, he has fun'd the best Sword in France. **1785** GROSE *Dict. Vulg. Tongue* s.v., Do you think to fun me out of it. **1812** *Sporting Mag.* XL. 86 Sure your lordship wouldn't be funning me. **1847–78** HALLI-WELL, *Fun*, to cheat, to deceive, *Somerset*. **1886** ELWORTHY *W. Somerset Word-bk.* s. v., He've a-fun me out o' vower poun.

Reprinted from the *New English Dictionary* by permission of The Clarendon Press, Oxford.

Etymology

William E. Umbach

Etymology is the history of words. You can often enrich your understanding of a word by a knowledge of its etymology. Take, for example, the word *assassin*. If you look this up in the second edition of *Webster's New World Dictionary*, a college desk dictionary, you will find this etymological information: "[Fr. < Ar. *hashshāsīn*, hashish users < *hashish*, hemp]." This means that the English word *assassin* is borrowed from the French word, which in turn is derived from the Arabic plural *hashshāsīn*, meaning hashish users, which comes from the Arabic *hashish*, hemp. And hemp, as you probably know, is the source of several powerful drugs. Meaning number one continues the story, as the meanings in this dictionary are in a logical semantic order, from the original meaning up to the present meanings. Meaning number one informs us: "1. [A–] [Editors' Note: This means assassin is capitalized.] a member of a secret sect of Moslems who killed Christian leaders during the Crusades, supposedly while under the influence of hashish." From this it is a short, comprehensible step to the present more general meaning given next: "2. a murderer who strikes suddenly and by surprise; now generally used of the killer of a politically important person."

The essay below provides background historical information that will help you understand the compressed and abbreviated etymologies given in your desk dictionary. Dr. William E. Umbach has been a professor, dean, and vice-president at Redlands University and is etymological editor of the *Webster's New World Dictionary*.

. . . The ancient notion that there is a single, true meaning for a word has been replaced by the concept that words are essentially nothing more than conventional symbols whose use and pronunciation may vary even from person to person, let alone generation to generation. Over the course of the centuries such variations may so alter the form and meaning that only patient study can trace the course by which the modern world has come to its present sense and form.

In this process of unraveling the fabric of modern languages, the etymologist comes upon evidence of the effect which the associations of ancient and modern people have had upon the range of concepts and objects represented by the vocabulary, as well as upon the form and content of the word symbols for them. Much worn and altered, many prehistoric artifacts of language are still in active use, and may be identified in numerous languages. Thus the names of family members—father, mother, brother—appear in relatively similar form in numerous languages; *mother*, for example, is represented by German *Mutter*, Old Irish *mathir*, Old Slavic *mati* (genitive form *matere*), Latin *mater*, Greek *meter*, and Sanskrit *matar*. The familiar *mouse* is represented by German *Maus*, Old Saxon and Old Norse *mus*, Latin *mus*, and Sanskrit *mus*. Such similarities are certainly not pure coincidence, and the etymologist is concerned with the nature of their relationships.

It is well known that a number of modern languages, among them French, Spanish, Portuguese, and Italian, have come into being as a result of gradual changes of Latin. Examination of older manuscripts clearly reveals the stages in the development of each of the modern languages, and makes it possible to identify certain regular patterns of change by which each of the modern representatives of Latin came to have its unique form and character.

In the same way, historical retracing of other languages reveals a similar gradual development of some modern languages from a common parent tongue which may not, however, be as well documented as is Latin. Thus it is clear that English is closely related to Dutch and German, that this group is in turn related to the Scandinavian languages and to the language of the medieval Goths, and that all of these, known as the Germanic languages, are ultimately derived from an unrecorded ancient language known to scholars as proto-Germanic or Primitive Germanic.

Similar studies of the various Celtic languages, of the Slavic languages, and of some other groups, indicate that each group has had its common parent. But this process of historical reconstruction has gone farther, to reveal that the groups of languages have been derived from a still more ancient, unrecorded language which scholars call Indo-European. . . .

Indo-European, it is important to note, includes only a small fraction of all of the world's languages, although at least one half of all of the world's population has a language of this family as its mother tongue. Similar families have been identified, but there is only fragmentary evidence of a still older relationship between Indo-European and the others. Yet regardless of genetic relationship, there is abundant evidence in the vocabulary of many languages that words have been borrowed by those who encountered names for new ideas or objects in the languages of other peoples with whom they came into contact. Such borrowings might be between languages belonging to one family, or between languages totally unrelated. Thus Greek includes words originally of Sanskrit, or even of Semitic or Egyptian origin, and some of these loanwords have in time come to be part of our modern

English vocabulary (see *costmary, gum, sack, canna, hyssop*). Numerous among the Greek loanwords from Semitic languages are those related to the Judeo-Christian religion, which were introduced through the Septuagint and the New Testament, and which continue in many modern languages, English among them (see *Beelzebub, Sabbath, Messiah*). Latin, like Greek, contains many loanwords which are now a part of our own vocabulary (see *car, biretta, gantry, lantern*).

It was inevitable, in the many encounters of different peoples during the migrations of the Middle Ages, that a residue of borrowed words would remain in various languages even after some of the groups had moved on to new homes, or had lost their separate identity and with it their own language. English has derived from French many words which had been borrowed from Germanic tribes, Franks, Goths, Norsemen, as well as from Celts; from Italian, loanwords from the Goths and Lombards, and from the Arabs; and from Spanish, words borrowed from Gothic as well as from the Arabs and Celts.

The process is still going on in the modern languages, and the vocabulary of English, more than that of any other language, has been enriched by its appropriation of foreign words. In some modern nations, notably France and Germany, there have been repeated efforts to avoid the intrusion of foreign words and to substitute native coinages to take their place. English, throughout its history, has had all of the delicate sensitivity of a powerful vacuum cleaner. Thus the warp of genetic derivation is interwoven with the woof of great numbers of words borrowed from related and unrelated languages; the resulting fabric has a richness and variety unequalled by any other language past or present.

Genetically, English is a descendant of the Germanic dialects spoken by the Angles, Saxons, and Jutes who invaded the British islands, beginning about the middle of the fifth century. They were members of a group of tribes whose homes had been near the North Sea. . . .

The Anglo-Saxon tribes, on invading the British islands, encountered inhabitants speaking various Celtic languages, and found areas in which the earlier Roman occupation had left some Latin influence on vocabulary. To this day, the place name *Chester*, either independently or as a prefixed or suffixed element, is a reminder of the Latin *castra*, "camp," from which Old English borrowed it in the form *ceaster* (thus *Winchester, Chesterfield, Rochester*). A second form of Latin invasion, the coming of Christian missionaries, from 597 on, supplemented the earlier Latin remains, as has the influence of the church until our own day. Other invaders, chiefly Danes and Norsemen, added to the complex. As various groups established settlements, they added to the dialect differences already present between the tribes of the Anglo-Saxon invasion. But in the main the Scandinavian settlers . . . gradually adopted the language (Old English) of the Anglo-Saxon group, while adding to it many of their own words, some of which appear in modern English as *husband, sky, skin, scathe, club, gape,* and the suffix -*by.*

Old English, under these conditions, was composed of numerous dialects, some of whose differences went back to those between the dialects of the Angles, Saxons, and Jutes. But interwoven with these hereditary variations were the many strands, often local or regional, of Celtic, Latin, and Scandinavian influence. To this already complex pattern the Norman invasion and conquest (1066–69) eventually brought lasting new motifs. The Normans, descendants of Scandinavian invaders who had settled on the south coast of the English Channel some centuries earlier, spoke a form of French. This became the official language of the court after the Conquest. It came, in time, also to be the language of the merchants and the learned. The common people continued to speak their various dialects of English, but French influence gradually added significant elements to the vocabulary, especially in the areas of law and government. By 1200 the language had altered to such an extent that it is designated as Middle English. It is significant that about half of the vocabulary of modern English is of Romance origin.

Since the Norman invasion, the influences which have altered the texture of the English vocabulary have not come from actual intrusions of a foreign people, although immigrants from various places have made their contributions (*pal,* a comrade, and *rye,* a gentleman, for example, are from the language of the Gypsies). As the English-speaking peoples have themselves invaded other areas, or have established trade relations, in America, Africa, Asia, and the islands of the South Pacific, there have come the influences of exotic objects and foreign cultures: *tobacco, cannibal, banana, taro, quinine, mango, jujitsu, pajama, jodhpur, manioc, pagoda, tapioca;* the long list grows year by year.

Study of classical and ancient civilizations has added, through direct appropriation, vast numbers of words from Latin and Greek; science and invention have mined the rich metal of the same languages to coin names of new creations or concepts: *halogen, pentstemon, triskaidekaphobia, metronome, acrophobia, helium, aerodynamic, neurotomy, euphenics.* Even the stripteaser calls upon Greek (*ecdysiast*).

World-wide exploration, followed by jet travel and instantaneous communication, has made the remote and isolated familiar and even commonplace, and foreign names have become part of the common tongue. Indeed, to read the menu of even a simple meal is to recapitulate a portion of the experience of English-speaking people with remote places: potatoes or yams, hamburger with ketchup, tomatoes or succotash, a lettuce salad with Roquefort dressing or mayonnaise, and perhaps chocolate cake—none would have appeared in Old English, and only the lettuce salad and cake (but not chocolate) in Middle English.

In America a flood of new words has resulted from confrontation with the native Indian population, with the French in Canada and in the lower

Mississippi basin, with the Spanish in the Southwest, and with African natives who came against their will, as well as with immigrants from all parts of the world who came for freedom, fortune, or the excitement and danger of the frontier. From the Indians, the settlers learned the names of *squash, hominy, pemmican, raccoon, skunk, chipmunk, caribou, tamarack, toboggan, tomahawk, moccasin, persimmon,* and *wampum*; from the French: *lagniappe, prairie, craps, praline, picayune, brioche, butte, crevasse, chowder*; from the Spanish: *corral, chaps, lariat, poncho, bonanza, placer, savvy, canyon, ranch, hackamore, hoosegow, loco.* The Chinese brought us *chop suey, chow mein,* and *tong* wars. From the Japanese, we learned of the *kudzu* vine, *nisei,* and *hara-kiri.* The Swedish immigrants acquainted us with the *smorgasbord,* the Czechs with the *sokol.* Germans added to the vocabulary not only many items of the diet (*pretzel, pumpernickel, zwieback, smearcase, wieners*), but *steins, delicatessen, kindergartens, turners, loafers, hoodlums,* and the adjective *dumb* (in the sense "stupid"), the verb *canoodle,* and—recently, in connection with rocketry and space travel—the term *glitch.* The Yiddish-speaking portion of our population brought, from homes in Germany and in other parts of Europe, *gefilte fish, bagels, blintzes, borscht, kibitzers, shtick, schmalz,* and the expressive *phooey.* From Italian immigrants, we have gained *spaghetti, macaroni, ravioli, pizza, minestrone, arugula,* and the *mafia.* The Dutch have given us *coleslaw, cookies, bedspreads, dope, crullers, boss, snoop,* and *spook.* And from Africa, black people brought *jazz, goobers, juke* boxes, *jumbo, voodoo, gumbo, okra,* the *marimba, yams,* and the verb *tote.* Chiefly through Spanish, we have gained from Nahuatl, the language of the Aztecs, *tomato, avocado, chocolate, chili, tamale, mesquite, peyote,* and *coyote.*

Together with the many words which English has inherited or borrowed (even if somewhat altered in form and meaning), the vocabulary possesses others which have been the product of conscious invention (*rayon, nylon, Emmy, Corfam*), of contracting or clipping longer words (*bus, hi-fi, prof*) or combining initial letters (*radar, laser*), of imitation of sounds (*blimp, whiz*), of scribal or typographical errors (*celt, collimate, cycad*), of use of personal or place names for objects or processes (*frisbee, watt, pasteurize, tuxedo*), and of the intentional merging of words (*brunch, smog*). Some are effusions of an exurberant whimsy (*hornswoggle*) or of a capricious transposition of sounds (*sockdolager*). Occasionally a borrowed word is translated (*masterpiece*), or altered by the process of folk etymology to conform to an assumed proper form (*carryall, shamefaced, country dance, singletree, sparrowgrass*). Some words have been created (by "backformation") on the assumption that they were the root forms from which others had been created (*diagnose* from *diagnosis*; *evaluate* from *evaluation*; *edit* from *editor*; *shay* from *chaise*). And the language of very fastidious people contains, without their being aware of the fact, words from the argot of thieves, convicts, gamblers, and harlots.

Words, like poetry, can be treated as arbitrary mathematical symbols or formulas. Sometimes this is necessary simply as a material for the cutting of refractory substances. Seen as the product of perhaps three thousand years of human experience, a word may not only have many facets, but may somehow reflect with brilliant intensity the concentrated experience or insights of the generations. It is still true that words can have a mysterious power to conjure up images, to evoke visions, or stir up emotions deep-seated in the shared experience of mankind.

Thus the etymologist is engaged in no esoteric pursuit, but one which can help bring the use of the magnificent complex which is the English language an understanding of meanings, distinctions, and implications which are not merely conventional but rooted in the long history through which we have received it.

Editors' note: It will be useful now to review in capsule form those salient facts mentioned by Umbach that are most relevant to the understanding of dictionary etymologies.

Ca. A.D. 450 and on.

Germanic peoples—Angles, Saxons, Jutes, and Frisians—settled in England, bringing with them their Germanic tongues that as a whole we call Old English (OE) or Anglo-Saxon (AS). This OE developed during the course of fifteen centuries into the language we speak today. Examples of OE words: *and, hē, fram* (from), *cann* (know how), *fugol* (bird), *steorfan* (die), *tūn* (enclosure, form), *hund* (dog), *cnafa* (boy), *dēor* (beast).

Ca. 600 and on

The Germanic inhabitants of England became Christianized. This resulted in the building of churches, monasteries, and schools and in the study and use of Latin. So Latin words were borrowed into English at this time, for example, *angel, noon,* and *master* [here in modern English form]. And borrowing from Latin has continued in English up to the present day.

Ca. 800–1066

Norsemen and Danes invaded and settled in northern England. Because the Anglo-Saxons and the settlers from Scandinavia lived together in the same territory and because their languages were similar, numerous Old Norse words were borrowed into OE, common words like *ill* and *skirt*, place names like *Derby*, and even the pronouns *they, their, them*. Often, however, they do not appear in records until several centuries later.

Ca. 1066–1500

The Norman French crossed the English Channel, conquered England, and became the ruling class in all walks of life—in the church, in government, in commerce, and in society. Thus, two languages—the Norman French (called Old French OF) of the upper class and the English (now called Middle English ME) of the lower class existed side by side. During this period thousands of OF words were adopted into English. And borrowing from French, like that from Latin, continued up to the present. Examples of English borrowings from the OF are: *chief, pavilion, charm, dame, tavern, tabernacle, poison.*

You must not forget the relationship of Old French to Latin. After the Roman legions invaded and conquered Gaul (now France) in the first century B.C., Gaul became a Roman province. Soldiers were given land and settled down in their new home. Administrators, traders, merchants, and other settlers followed. All of these spoke Vulgar Latin, which means merely the language of the common people and which differs in some respects from Classical Latin, which was a literary language. It was this Vulgar Latin that, in the course of nine centuries, developed into Old French, which in time became Middle French, then modern French. Thus French, like Italian, Spanish, Portuguese, and Romanian, is simply a later-day form of Latin.[1] Your dictionary will often give you just L (Latin) for a source word because the VL (Vulgar Latin) form is not known for many words.

Ca. 1500 and on

The Renaissance was a period of worldwide exploration, resulting in trade and in cultural contacts with many foreign lands. With trade came new things, and with these things came the names for them. Words from numerous languages, especially from French, Italian, and Spanish, entered English. And throughout the following centuries, as travel and intercommunication increased, new words continued to pour in and enrich our language. Examples of Renaissance borrowing are: *rendezvous, piazza, alligator, mosquito.*

During the Renaissance there was a resurgence of interest in classical languages; consequently many Latin words came into English, among them: *education, fact, circus, arena.*

1609 and on

The settlement of North America brought the English language into contact with Indian languages. Also, it produced a renewed contact with French, Spanish and Dutch, and later, with the languages of immigrant groups—the Norwegians, Danes, Germans, Czechs, Poles, German Jews, black slaves, Italians, and others. All of these added their bit to the vocabulary of the English language.

SUGGESTED ASSIGNMENTS

1. Look up the etymologies of the following words in your desk dictionary; or, for fuller information, use one of these etymological dictionaries in the library: C. T. Onions, *The Oxford Dictionary of English Etymology*; Walter W. Skeat,

---

[1] These are called Romance languages because they came from the language of the Romans (Latin). [eds.]

An Etymological Dictionary of the English Language; Ernest Weekley, *An Etymological Dictionary of Modern English*; Ernest Klein, *A Comprehensive Etymological Dictionary of the English Language*. In your desk dictionary, the etymology is given in brackets, either right after the entry word or at the end of the definitions. You may disregard whatever follows the expression "akin to." This material consists of related words in other languages.

1.	foot	11.	tulip
2.	school	12.	muscle
3.	street	13.	jovial
4.	window	14.	easel
5.	fellow	15.	hazard (noun)
6.	skirt	16.	umbrella
7.	student	17.	thrill (verb)
8.	veto	18.	curfew
9.	salary	19.	punch (beverage)
10.	campus	20.	nice

2. Here is a list of prefixes and "combining forms" from the Greek that are used as word-parts in the formation of English words, mostly of a learned character. A combining form is one that cannot be used alone but only in combination with other forms. Linguists call such forms bound morphemes. Your instructor may give you an assignment involving these combining forms.

Combining Form	Meaning	Example
1. anthrop anthropo	man (in general sense), human	anthropoid
2. aster astro	star	astronomy
3. aut auto	self, same one	autobiography
4. bi bio	life	biography
5. biblio	book	bibliography
6. cephal cephalo	head	microcephalic
7. chron chrono	time	chronology
8. cosmo	universe	cosmology
9. cracy	form of government	democracy
10. dema demo	people	democracy
11. dox	opinion	orthodox
12. ec eco	environment	ecology
13. ge geo	earth	geology
14. gamy	marriage	monogamy
15. graph graphy gram	something written, writing	geography
16. gyn gyno gyne gyneco gynous	woman	gynecology
17. hyper	above, beyond	hypertension
18. logy	oral or written expression; doctrine, science, theory	geology
19. mega	great; million	megacephalic
20. metry	measure	chronometry

21. micr micro	small	microfilm
22. mis miso	hatred	misogynist
23. mon mono	one, single	monogamy
24. morph morpho	form	anthropomorphic
25. nomy	laws governing, knowledge about	astronomy
26. orth ortho	straight, upright	orthodox
27. pathy	feeling, suffering	sympathy
28. path patho	disease	pathology
29. phil philo phile	love, loving	philanthropic
30. phobe	one fearing	xenophobe
31. phon phono	sound, voice, speech	telephone
32. phot photo	light	photograph
33. poly	many, much	polygamy
34. psych psycho	spirit, mind, mental processes	psychology
35. scope	means of viewing	telescope
36. sophy	knowledge, wisdom	philosophy
37. sym syn	with, together	sympathy
38. tele	far	television
39. therm thermo	heat	geothermal
40. xen xeno	strange, foreign	xenophile
41. zo zoo	animal	zoology

3. Here is a list of common Latin prefixes and combining forms used in the formation of English words. You may be given an assignment in the use of these terms.

Latin Form	*Meaning*	*Example*
1. ab	away from, down	abstain
2. ad	to, toward	admit
3. ante	before	antebellum
4. bellum	war	bellicose
5. bi (not to be confused with Greek *bi* or *bio*, life)	two	bilingual
6. cap cept	take	capture, accept
7. cide cis	cut, kill	suicide, incision
8. circum	around	circumlocution
9. cogni	know	recognize
10. com con	with	compose, convene
11. cor	heart	coronary
12. cult	care for	cultivate
13. curr curs	run	current, cursive
14. de	off, down	deemphasize
15. dent	tooth	dentist

16. dict	say	dictate
17. duc duct	lead	induce
18. ex e	beyond, from, out	export, eject
19. extra	outside	extracurricular
20. fac fect	make	factor, effect
21. fin	end	finish
22. in	not	insecure
23. im	on, in, toward	import
24. inter	among, between	international
25. intra	within	intrastate
26. ject	throw	projectile
27. loqui locut	talk	loquacious, locution
28. luc	light	translucent
29. mal	bad	malfunction
30. mit miss	send	remit, mission
31. mare	sea	mariner
32. mor mort	dead	mortal
33. nauta	sailor	nautical
34. navis	ship	naval
35. ped	foot	pedestrian
36. pel puls	drive	compel, impulse
37. pon posit pose	place	position
38. port	carry	portable
39. post	after	postpone
40. pre	before	preschool
41. pro	forward	propeller
42. re	again, back	return
43. rupt	break	eruption
44. scrib script	write	scribble, scripture
45. spect	look	inspect
46. sub	under	submarine
47. super	above	superior
48. tain ten	hold	contain, tenure
49. tang tact	touch	tangible, tactile
50. trans	across, over	transatlantic, transfer
51. uni	one	uniform
52. vene vent	come	convene
53. vers vert	turn	adverse
54. vid vis	see	video, vision
55. voc	call	vocation

N.B. English uses both the Latin infinitive and the past participle form of a root verb. Since these forms have different spellings, the English words formed from them do also. Latin: *vid*ere, to see (infinitive); *vis*us, seen (past participle). English: e*vid*ence, pro*vid*ence, *vis*ion, re*vis*e. Latin: *mitt*ere, to send (infinitive), *miss*us, sent (past participle). English: sub*mit*, ad*mit*, trans*miss*ion, *miss*ile.

FURTHER READINGS

Gove, Philip, ed. *The Role of the Dictionary.* New York: Bobbs-Merrill, 1967. A collection of articles about *Webster's Third New International Dictionary.*

Lodwig, Richard R., and Eugene F. Barrett. *The Dictionary and the Language.* New York: Hayden Book Co., 1967. A simple introduction to dictionaries and their uses.

Mathews, M. M. *A Survey of English Dictionaries.* New York: Russell and Russell, 1966.

Partridge, Eric. *The Gentle Art of Lexicography.* New York: Macmillan, 1963. Pleasant miscellaneous essays on dictionary making.

Sledd, James, and Wilma R. Ebbitt. *Dictionaries and THAT Dictionary.* Chicago: Scott, Foresman, n.d. Largely reviews and articles illustrating the reception, often hostile, of *Webster's Third New International Dictionary.*

Wilson, Kenneth G., R. H. Henrickson, and Peter Alan Taylor, eds. *Harbrace Guide to Dictionaries.* New York: Harcourt Brace Jovanovich, 1963. Articles related more or less directly to dictionary-making and the contents of dictionaries.

5
WORDS:
FORMS AND MEANINGS

Morphemes and Words

Dwight Bolinger

As language continues to grow, its word stock is constantly changing. While some words sink into disuse and disappear, others are being added to meet new needs. Your grandfather, for instance, could have driven a *runabout* or a *touring car*, whereas now, two generations later, you are likely to be behind the wheel of a *hardtop* or a *station wagon*. The additions to our word stock are of two kinds. One consists of borrowings from other languages. In English this borrowing has gone on without stop ever since our language first appeared in England 1500 years ago. It is illustrated in the preceding selection by Thomas Pyles and in Umbach's "Etymology," pages 91–100. The second kind of addition consists of new words formed from existing materials. That is to say, words and word-parts are re-formed into new combinations.

Some of these words and word-parts are called morphemes. Professor Dwight Bolinger of Harvard University here explains what morphemes are and how they are combined into words. We might truthfully say that a morpheme is the smallest meaningful element of language; and we could provide, as examples, words of one morpheme (*hope*), of two morphemes (*hopeful, misguide, unwise*), of three morphemes (*insufferable*), and of four morphemes (*ineffectively*). All this seems simple enough. But you will soon see that not all cases are so clear cut. The morpheme, as Professor Bolinger demonstrates, is a genuine but elusive element of language.

From *Aspects of Language* by Dwight Bolinger. Copyright © 1968 by Harcourt Brace Jovanovich, Inc., and reprinted with their permission.

The organic function of language is to carry meaning. Meaning must therefore have something to do with the workings of the linguistic cell. We often speak of words as if they were the cells of meaning. To be precisely that, the simplest meaning would have to stand in a one-to-one relationship with a word; but this is not always true. We would like to say that *roadblock* is "a word," yet it is made up of elements that are themselves words. And certainly *un-American* is a word, yet it is made up of an independent word, *America*, plus a prefix *un-* and a suffix *-an*, for each of which we seem to discern a kind of meaning—as is quickly confirmed by listing other places where they occur: *unhealthy, unwise, unsteady; Hawaiian, Alaskan, Russian*. It hardly seems that in our dissection of cells we can stop with the word.

The apparently meaningful bits that are smaller than words are termed morphemes. A sentence like *Every/one/admire/s/Bill/'s/man/li/ness* breaks up into nine morphemes bunched into four words: *everyone* is a compound containing the morphemes *every* and *one* (which also happen to be words when used separately), *admires* is a verb containing the stem *admire-* and the suffix *-s* meaning "third person singular," and so on. The word *morpheme* itself contains *morph-* and the suffix *-eme*, which also appears in *phoneme*.

If morphemes are the minimal units of meaning, one begins to wonder what words are good for—or even what words are. Is popular thinking about words an illusion? Do we only imagine that *roadblock* is one word but *road machinery* is two?

If it is only imagination, people are strangely consistent, for nearly everyone would make this distinction between these two examples. There is pretty general agreement on whether to regard a particular segment of speech as one word, two, or more. What is it that makes us feel that certain units are somehow distinct and inseparable?

Linguists sometimes answer this question by defining the word as "the smallest unit of language that can be used by itself," that is, used to form an utterance: *Go!, Henry* (in answer to *Who was it?*), *Tomorrow* (in answer to *When are you going?*), and *Nice* (in answer to *What do you think of it?*) qualify as words under this definition. But a good many forms that we like to regard as words don't qualify: one can't make an utterance with just *the* or *from* or *and*. Either they are not words, or the separateness of words does not always go so far as potentially complete independence.

Nevertheless, there is a mark of a lower degree of independence that does correlate very closely with our notion of what constitutes a word. This is our freedom to insert, between one word and the next, a vocalized hesitation—typically, the sound *uh*: *The—uh—workman—uh—who—uh—put up—uh—that—uh—roadblock—uh—didn't—uh—leave—uh—any—uh—warning-light.* Murder would be too merciful for a speaker who put in all these hesitations, but one or two, at any of the points indicated, would be perfectly normal for someone who must pause to gather his thoughts. The gaps agree remarkably well with our feel for separations between words.[1] No pause can be inserted between the morphemes in *workman*, *roadblock*, *didn't*, or *warning-light*. A pause can be inserted between *the* and *workman*. The one apparent disagreement, the unlikelihood of a pause between *put* and *up*, coincides with our uncertainty about whether to regard such forms as one word or two—grammarians often call *put up, leave out, take off*, and so on "two-word verbs."

The possibility of hesitating most likely reflects the freedom we have to insert other words at the same point. Instead of separating the words of the example which repeated *uh's* we could separate them with other words: *The careless workman there who supposedly put up just that one roadblock surely didn't dutifully leave in view any red warning-light.*

This is the physical evidence, but it is less important in itself than as a symptom of the role that words play in a language. A word is evidently "something that is not to be broken up." Words are prefabricated units. Language in action is a process of fabrication that takes two forms: the fabrication of larger segments using words and the fabrication of the words themselves. The first we call syntax. It goes on whenever a speaker says anything: *I got Mary some buttered popcorn at the movies last night* is a sentence that the speaker may never have said before in his life; he throws it together out of the prefabricated units he has at hand, to fit a situation. Once said, that sentence may never again be repeated and it may well be forgotten, as if the parts were disassembled and returned to the stockroom. But the parts themselves, the prefabricated units, are not forgotten and will be used again.

But what about the fabrication of words? Obviously, this is not something that happens every time we speak. If it were, the Oxford Dictionary could not tell us that the word *frontage* appeared for the first time in English in the seventeenth century while the words *slippage* and *roughage* appeared in the latter part of the nineteenth century. It may be hard to decide sometimes who first used a word, or where and when it was first used, and many words are doubtless created independently by more than one speaker. But that is nothing new in the history of invention. The fact remains that a word is tied to its moment in history. If something is prefabricated there must have been a time when the job was done.

Words are not the only prefabricated units, of course. There are also idioms, platitudes, and proverbs. But words are the prefabricated units of

---

[1] LeRoy Little, *The Syntax of Vocalized Pauses in Spontaneous Cultivated Speech.* Dissertation, George Peabody College for Teachers, 1963. Abstract in Linguistics 11.105–6 (1965). See also the studies that show audible changes in the phonemes (referred to as "junctural" changes) to be lacking between morpheme and morpheme but present between word and word—for example, Ilse Lehiste, "An Acoustic-phonetic Study of Internal Open Juncture," supplement to *Phonetica* 5.1–54 (1960).

syntax. The larger prefabs do not typically become parts of larger structures but are the complete structures themselves. They tend to be sentences, not parts of sentences.

The morpheme is now a bit easier to define. It is the semi-finished material from which words are made. Semi-finished means second-hand. The times when speakers set about constructing words out of the pure raw material of phonemes and syllables are few and far between—an occasional trade name such as *Kodak* or an acronym (word made up of initial letters) like *Unesco*—and these are almost always of one part of speech, nouns. Practically all words that are not imported bodily from some other language (this too is an abundant source) are made up of old words or their parts. Sometimes those parts are pretty well standardized, like the suffix *-ness* or the prefix *un-*. Other times they are only broken pieces that some inventive speaker manages to re-fit, like the *bumber-*, altered from *umbr-* in *umbrella*, and the *-shoot*, based on the *-chute* of *parachute*, that go to make up the word *bumbershoot*. In between are fragments of all degrees of standardized efficiency and junkyard irregularity. *Hamburger* yields *-burger*, which is reattached in *nutburger, Gainesburger,* and *cheeseburger. Cafeteria* yields *-teria*, which is reattached in *valeteria, groceteria,* and *washateria.* Trade names make easy use of almost any fragment, like the *-roni* of *macaroni* that is reattached in *Rice-a-Roni* and *Noodle-Roni.* The fabrication may re-use elements that have been re-used many times, or it may be a one-shot affair such as the punning reference to being a member of the *lowerarchy,* with *-archy* extracted from *hierarchy.* The principle is the same. Scientists and scholars may give themselves airs with high-bred affixes borrowed from classical languages, but they are linguistically no more sophisticated than the common speakers who are satisfied with leftovers from the vernacular. The only thing a morpheme is good for is to be melted down and recast in a word.

Word-making, for all its irregularity, has two fairly well defined processes. One process uses words themselves as raw material for new words. It is called *compounding.* The other attaches a lesser morpheme—an affix—to a major morpheme a—stem, frequently a word. It is called *derivation. Road-block* and *warning-light* are compounds. *Worker* is a derivative (so, prob-ably, is *workman,* since *-man,* pronounced *m'n,* has been reduced to an affix in English). *Troubleshooter* embodies both processes, derivation in *shoot* + *-er* and compounding in *trouble* + *shooter.* An affix that is rather freely used to make new derivatives is termed active. When one man referred to the occupants of flying saucers as *saucerians,* he was using the active suffix *-ian.*[2] An affix that is not freely used is inactive, though one can never pronounce any element completely dead. The suffix *-ate* is a Latinism that can hardly be used to make new words—until some wag comes forward with *discom-*

---

[2] *Look,* March 21, 1967, p. 76.

bobulate and makes it stick. If a word fragment like *-burger* can be used as if it were an affix, nothing prevents any piece of a word, inactive or not, from being reused.

There are other processes. A fairly common one is reduplication, where the same morpheme is repeated in the same or slightly altered form: *hush-hush, mishmash, helter-skelter, fiddle-faddle.*

The meanings of morphemes can vary as widely as their forms. This is to be expected of second-hand materials. When an old dress is cut down to a skirt its former function may be partly remembered, but when a remnant of it becomes a dustcloth the old function is forgotten. Almost no morpheme is perfectly stable in meaning. The morpheme *-er* forms agentive nouns—a *builder* is one who builds, a *talker* one who talks, a *wrecker* one who wrecks; but an *undertaker* is no longer one who undertakes—the morpheme has been swallowed up in the word. The suffix *-able* suggests something on the order of "facilitation," but this would be hard to pin down in words as various as *charitable, likable, tangible, terrible, reputable,* and *sensible.* Language is not like arithmetic; numerical composites are strictly additive: the number 126 is an entity but it is also the exact sum of $100 + 20 + 6$. When morphemes are put together to form new words, the meanings are almost never simply additive. This is because a word is coined after the speaker has the meaning before him. If he can lay hold of parts whose meanings suggest the one he had in mind, so much the better, but that is not essential. The speaker who first put together the word *escapee* was not bothered by the fact that he should have said *escaper,* since *-ee* is etymologically for persons acted upon, not for persons acting. He wanted something to suggest the same "set category of persons" idea that is carried by words like *employee* and *draftee,* and he twisted *-ee* to his purpose.

The high informality of word-making in English, the clutching at almost anything to nail up a new prefab, reflects the vast expansion of our culture. A supermarket that in 1966 stocked eight thousand items and by 1971 is expected to stock twelve thousand[3] is one ripple in a tide of growth that carries our vocabulary along with it. We have to have names for those new items. All cultures exhibit this to some extent: the list of content-carrying words—nouns, verbs, adjectives, and most adverbs—is the one list in the catalog that has no limit. Phonemes, syllable types, rules of syntax, and certain little "function words" are "closed classes"—they are almost never added to; but the major lexicon is open-ended. The relationship of morphemes to words is therefore the hardest thing in language to analyze. Asking what morphemes a word contains and what they mean is asking what the coiner of the word had in mind when he coined it and possibly

---

[3] Estimate by American Paper Institute, *Consumer Reports,* September, 1966, p. 425.

what unforeseen associations it may have built up since.[4] It is less an analytical question than a question about history.

The morpheme at best continues to live a parasitic life within the word. It remains half-alive for one speaker and dies for the next; or it may be revived by education. A child who calls a tricycle a *three-wheeled bike* and later discovers other words with the prefix *bi-* may reanalyze *bicycle* into two morphemes instead of one. Hundreds of morphemes lie half-buried in the junkheaps of the etymological past. A corner of the Latin *pre-* sticks out in words like *predict, prearrange, predetermine,* and maybe *prepare*—we sense that *pre-* here has something to do with "before"; but in the verb *present* it is almost hidden and in *preserve, pregnant,* and *prelate* it is lost from sight. No one but an etymologist remembers what the *luke-* of *lukewarm* means (it originally signified "lukewarm" by itself—*lukewarm* = "lukewarmly warm"). The *re-* of *reduce* and the *di-* of *digest* are only meaningless syllables to speakers of English, even though their sources are the same as the *re-* of *readjust* and the *dis-* of *distrust.*

Still, in spite of the difficulties, looking for morphemes is a necessary part of linguistic analysis. This is true partly because not all languages are quite so unsystematic (or so burdened with conflicting systems, which comes to the same thing) as English; some of them have more regular habits of word formation. It is also true because even in English there is one class of morphemes that are more orderly in their behavior.[5]

SUGGESTED ASSIGNMENT

Point out the morphemes in these words and give the meaning of each.

1. wise, wisely, unwise
2. large, enlarge, enlargement, larger, largest
3. wide, widen, widened
4. sense, sensible, insensible, nonsense
5. oyster, oysters
6. sun, sunny, sunshine
7. hunt, hunter, hunters, hunter's
8. sweet, sweetness
9. even, uneven

[4] How we analyze a word into morphemes can change in the course of the word's history. A *wiseacre* is generally thought to be someone who acts wise but is not entitled to—*wise* is morphemicized by the speaker in spite the fact that *wiseacre* originally meant "soothsayer" and the *wise-* part is related to *witch.* . . .

[5] The orderly class of morphemes consists of the inflectional suffixes, such as the *-s/es* plural, the *-er* comparative, and the verbal *-ing.* English has only about eight of these, the exact number depending on the system of analysis one uses. [eds.].

10. tie, untie
11. true, truth
12. exact, inexact
13. hopeful, hopefully, hopeless, hopefulness
14. equal, equalize
15. play, replay
16. sharp, sharpen, resharpen, resharpened
17. beauty, beautify
18. king, kingdom, bestsellerdom
19. deodorizer, deordorization
20. immeasurable

Word-Making in English

Henry Bradley

In the preceding selection you were presented with three processes of word-making—compounding, derivation, and reduplication. Here you will meet three more such processes that are productive in modern English. "Productive," as used here, is a linguists' term. It means that these processes are in active use to *produce* new forms. Henry Bradley was one of the distinguished editors of the *Oxford English Dictionary*, that monumental lexicon.

BACK-FORMATION

There are many words in English which have a fallacious appearance of containing some well-known derivative suffix. It has not unfrequently happened that a word of this kind has been popularly supposed to imply the existence of a primary word from which it has been derived in the usual way. The result of this supposition is the unconscious creation of a new word, which is made out of the old one by depriving it of what is thought to be its suffix, or sometimes by the substitution of a different suffix. According to some eminent scholars, the verb *to beg* has been in this way formed from *beggar*, which is thought to be adopted from the old French *begar*, a mem-

From *The Making of English* by Henry Bradley. Reprinted by permission of Collier-Macmillan, Ltd., and St. Martin's Press, Inc., copyright 1904.

ber of the religious order called Beghards, who supported themselves, like the friars, by begging. This etymology is disputed; but there are many other instances of the process which are not open to question. The noun *butcher* is really from the French *boucher*, and the ending is not etymologically identical with the common English suffix of agent-nouns,[1] but in many dialects people have come to use the berb *to butch*, and to speak of "the butching business." Other dialectal back-formations are *buttle*, to pour out liquor, from *butler*, and *cuttle*, to make knives, from *cutler*. The noun *pedlar* is older than the verb *to peddle* or the adjective *peddling*, and *broker* than the verb *to broke* (now obsolete) and the verbal noun *broking*. *Grovelling* was originally an adverb, meaning "face downwards"; it was formed out of the old phrase *on grufe* (which had the same meaning) by adding the suffix *-ling*, which occurs in many other adverbs, now mostly obsolete, such as *backling*, backwards, *headling*, head-first. But *grovelling* was misunderstood as a present participle, and the verb *grovel* was formed from it. Similarly the verbs *sidle* and *darkle* have been formed out of the old adverbs *sideling* and *darkling*. Probably the modern verb *nestle* is not, as is commonly said, the same as the Old English *nestlian* to build a nest, but has been evolved from *nestling*, an inhabitant of a nest, used adjectively as in "nestling brood." Many of the words that have been formed by this process are so happily expressive that the misunderstanding that has given rise to them must be accounted a fortunate accident. . . .

An excellent illustration of the working of this process is seen in the origin of the verb *edit*. The Latin *ēditor*, literally "one who gives out," from the verb *ēdere* to give out, was after the invention of printing often employed in a special sense as denoting the person who "gives to the world" a book or other literary work of which he is not the author. In this sense it has passed into English and other modern languages. But under modern conditions there are two different classes of persons concerned in the production of a book, to either of whom the word might be applied in its literal meaning with equal propriety. The "giver-out" of a book—for instance, of a classical text which has never before been printed—may mean what we now call the "publisher," the man who bears the expense of printing it and makes the arrangements for its circulation among the public, or it may mean the scholar who puts the text into order for publication and provides it with such illustrative matter as it is deemed to require. In early times these two functions were often united in the same person, but they are now ordinarily divided. Now while in French *éditeur* ("editor") has come to mean "publisher," in English it has become restricted to the other of its possible applications. When we use it we no longer think of its literal sense: the prominent function of an "editor" is not that of issuing a literary work to the

---

[1] The English agent-noun suffix is *-er*, as in *writer, singer*. It indicates one who performs the action named by the stem of the word. [eds.]

public, but that of bringing it into the form in which it is to appear. Although *editor* is not a word of English formation, it has an ending which coincides in form with that of English agent-nouns, so that it has naturally suggested the coinage of a verb "to edit," meaning "to prepare for publication as an editor does," *i.e.*, to put into such a form as is thought suitable for the public to read. . . .

SHORTENING

The substitution, in hurried, careless, jocular or vulgar speech, of a part of a word for the whole, is common in most languages, and is especially congenial to the English fondness for brevity of utterance. It does not, by itself, constitute a mode of word-formation: the vulgar *taters* and *bacca*, for *potatoes* and *tobacco*, cannot be called new words, any more than any other mispronunciations can be so called. But when, as very often happens, the original word and its shortened form come both to be generally used by the same speakers with different meanings, or even only with a difference in the implied tone of feeling, a real addition has been made to the vocabulary of the language, and the lexicographer is bound to recognize the shortened form as a distinct word. Shortening, in such cases, is in the strictest sense a kind of derivation; and it is a process which has contributed not a little to increase the English store of words.

Even when the abbreviated form expresses precisely the same meaning as the original form, the two must often be reckoned as separate words, because the longer form is reserved for more dignified or more serious use. *Omnibus* and *bus* are synonymous in the sense that they denote the same objects; but they are not absolute synonyms, because the one is more familiar in tone than the other; the two are used on different occasions. . . .

But very frequently a word which has been formed by shortening undergoes a sense-development of its own, in which the original word does not share. Even if anybody is pedantic enough to deny that *bus* is a distinct word from *omnibus*, he cannot refuse to admit that *cab* is a real word, though it was originally a shortened pronunciation of *cabriolet*. A cab and a cabriolet are not the same kind of vehicle at all. So, too, *Miss*, the title given to an unmarried woman, and *Mrs.* (pronounced *Missis*) are now quite different in meaning from each other, and from *mistress*, from which both are derived by shortening. There was a time when *gent* was used by educated people as a familiar abbreviation for *gentleman*, without any depreciatory implication. But in this use it was gradually discarded from the speech of the upper classes, and came to be a contemptuous designation for the vulgar pretenders to gentility in whose vocabulary it still survived. . . .

Some words that originated as playful abbreviations of other words are now used without any consciousness of their origin. *Extra*, in such phrases as "an extra allowance," is not the Latin word, but an abbreviation of *extraordinary*. An *extra*, meaning an edition of a newspaper out of the usual course, was at one time called "an *extraordinary*." . . . And only students of etymology know that *chap* is a shortening of *chapman*, properly meaning "trader."

In the Middle English and early Modern English periods it was very common, in the hurry of pronunciation, to drop an initial vowel which immediately preceded the stressed syllable of a word. In this way many words beginning with a vowel come to have an alternative form from which the first syllable was omitted; and almost in every case in which both forms have survived a difference of meaning has been developed. *Assize* and *size* are so different in sense that no one could think of them as the same word, and yet the one is only a shortened pronunciation of the other. The standard magnitude of an article of commerce was settled by an "assize" or sitting of some constituted authority. Hence the standard or authorised magnitude of anything was called its *assize* or *size*, and afterwards the latter form came to mean magnitude in general. *Tend*, as in the phrase "to tend the sick," was originally the same word as *attend*; but the two verbs are no longer synonymous. *Alone*, which stands for an earlier *all one*, was in the Elizabethan period shortened into *lone* when used as an adjective. The Middle English phrase *on live*, equivalent to "in life," was commonly pronounced *alive*, and this, by shortening, afterwards yielded the adjective *live*. *Mend* was originally the same word as *amend*. The shorter form, as usual, serves for the trivial occasions of ordinary life, while the longer form is of more dignified application. We speak of *mending* a stocking, but of *amending* an Act of Parliament. Sometimes other prefixes than those consisting only of a vowel were dropped in the same way. The verb to *vie* is shortened from *envie*—not the same word as the modern *envy*, but adopted from the French *envier*, which comes from the Latin *invitare* to challenge; so that *vie* and *invite* are in ultimate etymology the same. *Fence* is *defence* without its prefix; and *fend*, from which *fender* is derived, is short for *defend*. Several words that originally began with *dis-* or *des-* now begin with *s*. *Stain* is a shorter form of *distain*, which is the Old French *desteindre*, to take out the dye of anything, from the prefix, *des-*, *dis-*, and *teindre* to dye. *Despite*, from the Old French *despit*, the Latin *despectus*, a looking down, despising, has become *spite*. No word now sounds more thoroughly English than *sport*, which has, indeed, been adopted from English into foreign languages; yet it is a shortening of *disport*, which is a word of French origin. To "disport oneself" is, literally interpreted, "to carry oneself in a different direction" from that of one's ordinary business; and hence *disport* and *sport* came to mean amusement or pastime.

Besides the new words that owe their origin to shortening in pronunciation, there are others which have arisen out of abbreviations used in writing. Sometimes the mere initials of a phrase come to be treated as a word, the written letters being represented in pronunciations by their names. Thus we speak of "a question of £ s.d. (*el ess dee*)"; or, again of "an M.P. (*em pee*)," or "a D. C. L. (*dee cee el*)," meaning a person who is entitled to write those initials after his name. Sometimes, again, a word or phrase as abbreviated in writing happens to yield a pronounceable sequence of letters, and takes its place in the language as a word.[2] This occurs most frequently with Latin phrases. Many of the shortened forms are vulgar[3] or jocular, as *infra dig, incog, nem. con.,* "the *pros* and *cons.*" But *per cent, cent per cent,* from the Latin (*centum*) *per centum,* are part of the ordinary English vocabulary. The most curious instance of the formation of a word by this process is *culprit.* Its origin is to be found in the strange corrupt Norman French once used in our courts of justice. When a prisoner had pleaded "not guilty," the reply made on behalf of the Crown was "culpable; prest." This means "(he is) guilty, (and we are) ready (to prove it)." In the reports of criminal cases the phrase was commonly abbreviated *cul. prest,* and afterwards corruptly *cul prit.* Then in some way, not very clearly understood, it seems to have come about that the clerks of the Crown, modelling their procedure on the pattern set in the written reports, fell into the practice of using the syllables *cul prit* as an oral formula; and as this formula was followed by the question, "How will you be tried?" addressed to the prisoner, it was popularly apprehended to mean "guilty man." The custom survived in the courts down to the eighteenth century but when *culprit* became a current word with a new sense, it was probably felt that there was an injustice in addressing a prisoner by a term which presumed his guilt, and the use of the formula was discontinued.

ROOT-CREATION

Perhaps few, even among professed students of the language, are aware how large a portion of the English vocabulary has, in the ordinary sense of the word, no etymology at all. We do not mean merely that there are many words the origin of which is and will always remain unknown because of the imperfection of our means of discovery. This is no doubt quite true. But there are also many words which were neither inherited from Old English, nor adopted from any foreign language, nor formed out of any older English or foreign words by any process of composition or derivation. It is to instances of this kind that the name of "root-creation" may be fitly applied.

One of the principal forms of root-creation is that which is known by the name of Onomatopoeia. The word is Greek, and literally means "name-

---

[2] Such a word is now called an acronym. Examples: AWOL, NATO, RADAR. Many acronyms appeared during and after World War II. [eds.]

[3] By *vulgar* Bradley does not mean "indecent." He is using the word in the linguists' sense of "belonging to the common people." [eds.]

making." It was used by the Greeks to express the fact (common in their own as in other languages) that a noise, or the object producing it, sometimes *makes its own name*: that is to say, is denoted by a word formed in imitation of the sound.

The number of "echoic" words (as they have been called by Dr. Murray) which have arisen in Middle and Modern English is very considerable. We may mention as examples *bang, boo, toom, cackle, cheep, fizz, gibber, giggle, hiss, hum, mumble, pop, quack, rumble, simmer, sizzle, titter, twitter, whirr, whiz, whip-poor-will,* and the reduplicated words *bow-wow, ding-dong, flip-flop, hee-haw, ping-pong, pom-pom, rub-a-dub, tick-tack.*

It is possible that some of the words in the first part of this list may go back to Old English; words of this kind are much more common in speech than in literature, and we are certainly far from knowing the whole of the Old English vocabulary. However, even if they are much older than they can be proved to be, there is no doubt that they are imitative in origin.

The imitation of inarticulate by articulate sounds can never be accurate. Perhaps one or two birds *do* really "make their names"; though even in the case of the cuckoo it is not quite certain that we actually hear the two consonants. But the cries of birds and animals produced by organs having more or less similarity to our own, may be regarded as in some measure articulate. In general the rendering of noises into the sounds of human speech involves some play of fancy, like that which is exercised when we see faces in the fire, or landscapes in the clouds. The resemblance which an imitative word is felt to bear to the inarticulate noise which it names consists not so much in similarity of impression on the ear as in similarity of mental suggestions. For instance, it is not at all literally true that a gun, or a heavy body impinging on a door, says "*bang.*" But the sequence of three sounds of which the word consists is of such a nature that it can easily be uttered with force, so as to suggest the startling effect of a sudden violent noise, while the final consonant admits of being prolonged to express the notion of a continued resonance. In this instance and in many others, the so-called "imitative" word represents an inarticulate noise not so much by way of an echo as *symbolically.* That is to say, the elements composing the sound of the word combine to produce a mental effect which we recognise as analogous to that produced by the noise.

In much the same way, the sound of a word may suggest "symbolically" a particular kind of movement or a particular shape of an object. We often feel that a word has a peculiar natural fitness for expressing its meaning, though it is not always possible to tell why we have this feeling, and the reasons, when we can trace them, are different in different cases. Sometimes the notion of natural fitness is an illusion, due to the fact that the word obscurely reminds us of the sound of several other words which happen to have meanings somewhat similar to that which it expresses. But quite often the sound of a word has a real intrinsic significance. For instance, a word with long vowels, which we naturally utter slowly, suggests the idea of slow movement.[4] A repetition of the same consonant suggests a repetition of movement, slow if the vowels be long, and rapid if the vowels be short.[5] The vowels that are produced by the passage of the breath through a narrow opening, such as *ee* or *ĭ*, are suited to convey the notion of something slender or slight, while a full vowel such as *oo* suggests a massive object.[6] A syllable ending in a stopped consonant, especially an unvoiced one like *p*, *t*, *k*, preceded by a short vowel, affords a natural expression for the idea of some quick and abrupt action.[7] Sequences of consonants which are harsh to the ear, or involve difficult muscular effort in utterance, are felt to be appropriate in words descriptive of harsh or violent movement.[8] It would be possible to say a great deal more about the inherent symbolism of sounds; but it is not necessary here to pursue the subject in further detail. The point that needs to be remarked is that this phonetic symbolism (which probably had a large share in the primary origin of human language) has led to a very large amount of root-creation in Middle and Modern English. It is worthy of note that many of the words that have in this way been invented as instinctive descriptions of action or form occur in groups of two or three, in which the consonants are alike, while the vowel is varied to express differences of mental effect. Thus we have *bleb, blob, blub-cheeked*, all denoting something inflated. The initial *bl* was perhaps suggested by the verb *blow*; the pronunciation of the syllables involves an inflation of the cheeks which is symbolical of the notion common to the three words, and the different degrees of fulness in the vowels are obviously significant of differences of size in the object denoted. Other instances in which the notion expressed by the consonantal skeleton is modified by difference in the vowel are *jiggle, joggle*; *flip, flap, flop*; *chip, chap, chop*; *fimble, famble, fumble*; *flash, flush*.

Among the many words that owe their origin to a sense of the intrinsic expressiveness of particular combinations of sound are *bob, brob, brunch, dab, dodder, fiddle-faddle, fidge, fidget, flabbergast, fudge, hug, huggermugger, hump, jog, see-saw, squander, squelch, throb, thump, thwack, twiddle, wobble*. Some of these, it is true, may in a certain sense be said to have an etymology; but their actual meaning is not due to the word, native or foreign, that may have suggested their formation in the first instance, but to the impression which is made by their mere sound.[9]

Many excellent examples of intentional root-creation may be found among the invented words (not intended to be permanent additions to the

[4] For example, water *seeps*. [eds.]
[5] For example, *cock-a-doodle-doo, titter*. [eds.]
[6] For example, for smallness: *little, slim, bit, teeny, wee*. [eds.]
[7] For example, *clap, flap, pat, crack, knock, flick*. [eds.]
[8] For example, "When Ajax strives some rock's vast weight to throw." Pope [eds.]
[9] For an application of the ideas above to literature, see "Phonetic Symbolism in Poetry," pp. 436–449. [eds.]

language) in Lewis Carroll's *Alice in Wonderland, Through the Looking-Glass,* and *The Hunting of the Snark.* These clever coinages derive their effect partly from their suggestion of obscure reminiscences of existing words, and partly from real phonetic expressiveness. Two of them, *galumphing* and a verb *to chortle,* have come into pretty general use, and have found their way into our dictionaries.

SUGGESTED ASSIGNMENTS

1. English has two homophonous *-ish* morphemes that are currently in use to form new words. One is *-ish* in the sense of "somewhat," as in *reddish, fortyish, sickish.* The other is *-ish* as a pejorative suffix, that is, one that conveys a depreciatory meaning. For example, *womanish* is pejorative, contrasting with *womanly,* which is laudatory. We add this *-ish* to a noun when we wish to disparage, as in *childish, bookish,* and *tomboyish.* Cite three words containing the approximative *-ish* and three containing the pejorative *-ish.* You may invent them if you wish.

2. The suffix *-ee* is often used to make a passive noun. For example, a *trainer* (active) is one who trains, but a *trainee* (passive) is one who is trained. Occasionally *-ee* is used to form an active noun, as in *escapee,* meaning one who escapes. Thus we have here two morphemes: (1) *-ee* (= doer) in active nouns, and (2) *-ee* (= receiver) in passive nouns. Tell whether each of the following nouns is active or passive: *draftee, nominee, returnee, appointee, inductee, employee, standee.*

3. One important kind of compound word is exemplified by *bláckbird.* The first part is given the stronger stress, and this part modifies the second part. This type of compound is sometimes printed as two words, for example, *hót dog,* but it is nevertheless considered a single compound word if it meets the two qualifications mentioned. Thus both *sídewalk* and *drúg store* are compounds. Some compounds like these have a counterpart in a two-word combination of modifier plus noun. In these the stronger stress is on the second part, as in *black bírd* (any bird that is black in color) and *hot dóg* (a dog that is hot). The left-hand list below is composed of compounds and the right-hand list of their two-word counterparts. Explain the difference in meaning.

bláckberry	black bérry
Whíte House	white hóuse
géntleman	gentle mán
gáme fish	game físh
blúe book	blue boók
hígh chair	high cháir
súrplus store	surplus stóre
dáncing girl	dancing gírl
móving van	moving ván

4. In the light of the exercise above, explain the ambiguity in these sentences:
   a. The lawyer lost a brief case.
   b. I am an outdoor lover.
   c. Our school has two French teachers.
   d. The firemen burst into the smoking room.
   e. In the old creek bed he found a mammoth tooth.

5. What onomatopoetic words do you find in these quotations?
   a. And the silken, sad, uncertain rustling of each purple curtain. (*Poe*)
   b. And murmuring of innumerable bees. (*Tennyson*)
   c. I hear lake water lapping with low sounds by the shore.[10] (*Yeats*)
   d. And the plashing of waterdrops
      In the marble fountain.[11] (*Amy Lowell*)
   e. With lisp of leaves and ripple of rain. (*Swinburne*)

6. Are any of these words not onomatopoetic: *thunder, tinkle, clink, boom, bubble, tick, whisper, wheeze, chug, coo, pop*?

7. A blend is a word consisting of the first part of one word plus the last part of another word. Thus, *chuckle* and *snort* are blended into *chortle*, and *breakfast* plus *lunch* produce *brunch*. What words were used to form the following blends: *motel, smog, telecast, electrocute, splatter, escalator, blurt, happenstance, contrail, motorcade, irregardless*. Hard evidence for the origins of blends is often lacking, and the best one can do in many cases is to give an educated guess.

8. Otto Jespersen, the eminent Danish grammarian, classified reduplicatives into three main groups, according to their form. Using the following examples, ascertain these three groups: *chug-chug, zig-zag, hurly-burly, razzle-dazzle, riff-raff, pom-pom, pitter-patter, hotsy-totsy, pooh-pooh, hanky-panky, ticktock, hush-hush, dilly-dally, hoity-toity, hodge-podge, chit-chat, goody-goody, sing-song, clack-clack, hocus-pocus*.

9. Our English word stock is filled with inconsistencies and gaps. Among the reflexive pronouns we find *himself* not *hisself but *myself* not *meself. Impossible is the negative of *possible*, but *impassive* is the same as *passive*. One who professes *heterodoxy* is a *heretic*, but one steeped in *orthodoxy* is not an *orthetic. We have many negative adjectives, like *inane, incessant, uncouth, insipid*, which do not have their logically positive forms of *ane, *cessant, *couth, and *sipid. This nonrational characteristic of English makes possible the kind of verbal play which we find in the poems that follow.[12] Explain each nonword.

[10] Reprinted with permission of The Macmillan Company from *Collected Poems* by William Butler Yeats. Copyright 1906 by The Macmillan Company. Renewed 1934 by William Butler Yeats.

[11] From Amy Lowell, *Complete Poetical Works*. Boston: Houghton Mifflin Company, copyright 1955.

[12] These poems are from Felicia Lamport's *Scrap Irony*. Copyright © 1961 by Felicia Lamport Kaplan. Reprinted by permission of the publisher, Houghton Mifflin Company. Permission also granted by Victor Gollancz, Ltd.

SENSICAL SITUATION

Men often pursue in suitable style
The imical girl with the scrutable smile.

HMM...

Nothing gives rise to such wild surmise
As the peachable widow with consolate eyes.

FINE OLD PROFESSOR

The students who had gnored him
Universally adored him
And he died beknownst and famous
A gnonimious gnoramus.

UTTERABLE WISDOM

The wife of a brilliant, becilic professor
Should never show anity too.
Unless she admits that her brain is the lesser
Their marriage will never stay skew.

Analogical Creation

Charles F. Hockett

New word-forms and patterns in language are created by a simple but important process called analogy or analogical creation. You will understand analogy when you know why a child says *goed* for *went* or *deers* for *deer*, or why you sometimes make a slip of the tongue with a form like *teached*. You will hear examples of analogy nearly every day if you listen attentively to the language around you. Charles F. Hockett is Professor of Linguistics at Cornell University.

It has been said that whenever a person speaks, he is either mimicking or analogizing. Often we cannot know which is the case. A few years ago we might have heard someone say *shmoos*, under circumstances which led us to believe that he had never said it before. We would still not know, however, whether he had previously heard the plural form *shmoos*, or had heard only the singular *shmoo* and was coining the plural on his own.

When we hear a fairly long and involved utterance which is evidently not a direct quotation, we can be reasonably certain that analogy is at work. There is even more certainty when a speaker produces some form which deviates from what he could have heard from others. Examples are especially common in the speech of children. Regularized plurals, like *mans* and *sheeps*, probably are produced by every English-speaking child. *Clothes* (usually pronounced /klówz/) is today an isolated plural; one child supplied the singular /klów/. Interpretation of singulars ending in /z/ or /s/ as though they were plurals is likewise common. *What's a poy?* is one instance. Another is the following. At breakfast, a woman said *Daddy, please pass the cheese.* Her small daughter then said *Mummy, I want a chee too.*

Having frequently heard his father say *Don't interrup(t)*, one boy returned the admonition in the form *Daddy! You're interring úp!* On the basis of *look at* /lúkət/ *this*, some children have said *I'm looketing.* As a five-year-old girl was improperly sliding from her chair to go under the lunch table, her parents said *Don't disappear*; she continued the motion, saying *I'm dissing a peer.* When told *You must behave*, a child may reply *I'm being haive.* One child used *bate* as the past tense of *beat* (= "finish first"); compare our approved *eat* : *ate*. Four planes overhead are in a *formation*; two planes are therefore in a *twomation*. When it was more excessively hot than would warrant the comment *It's too hot*, one child said *It's three hot.* (All of these instances are attested.)

Adults produce forms like these too, but they are more apt to be received either as slips of the tongue, perhaps through weariness, or as feeble attempts at humor. Examples of the former are the writer's *I could eat a whole nother apple*, or what he has twice caught himself saying after answering the phone: *It's for she.* An example of the latter is *You're looking very couth and kempt today.*

In all the cases so far cited, a clear analogical basis for the coinage can be discerned. *A whole nother apple*, thus, solves a phonemic proportion like

a big apple	:	*a whole second apple*	::	
a second apple	:	*a whole big apple*	::	
another apple	:	*X.*		

It's for she is based on sets like

John is wanted on the phone	:	*It's for John*	::
You are wanted on the phone	:	*It's for you*	::
She is wanted on the phone	:	*X*.	

SUGGESTED ASSIGNMENTS

1. If you wished to use the past tense of *ding,* a verb employed by Robert Burns, what two forms would come first to your mind? What is the analogical basis of each one?

2. What analogical patterns might bring about the use of the following non-standard forms: *knowed* for *knew*; *brang* for *brought*?

3. Here is a stanza of Burns showing his use of the past tense of *ding,* which was mentioned in item one above:

O ay my wife she dang me,
   An' aft my wife she bang'd me,
If ye gie a woman a' her will,
   Gude faith she'll soon o'ergang ye.

4. On the analogy of

my	mine
thy	thine

what nonstandard analogical forms have been created?

your	_____
his	_____
her	_____

5. On the analogy of

my	myself

what nonstandard analogical form has been created?

his	_____

6. On the analogy of

our	ourselves

what nonstandard analogical form has been created?

their	_____

7. The colloquial present forms of *do*, in the negative, are these:

I don't	we don't
you don't	you don't
he doesn't	they don't

What change might you expect to occur here through the pressure of analogy? For facts on this usage, see "*Linguistic Atlas* Findings," page 234.

Etymology and Meaning

Simeon Potter

In the first two essays of this section we saw how changes in words and word forms are brought about. In the next two essays we shall see how word meanings are also altered. Meanings, as subjective phenomena, are especially unstable and elusive, and have not yet been subjected to the scientific analysis that other aspects of language have undergone. However, as we look back into linguistic history and observe successive changes in word meanings, we can discern specific directions in which words change. These directions, or "semantic categories," as Professor Potter calls them, are the subject of the essay that follows. Professor Simeon Potter, who was educated at the University of London and Oxford University, has taught in European universities and is now Professor of English at the University of Liverpool.

Few words have fixed significations like the pure numbers of mathematics or the technical formulas of chemistry. The mathematical sign π denotes a constant, namely, the ratio of the circumference of a circle to its diameter, or 3.14159 . . . The chemical formula NaCl denotes a substance, sodium chloride, or salt, and it always means that substance and nothing else. These symbols π and NaCl cannot vary with time or circumstance, nor do they ever change with their contexts. Few expressions in daily use have such simple and direct denotations as these. Even words like *mother* and *father*, *sun* and *horse*, denoting primary human relationships or natural objects and

From *Our Language* by Simeon Potter. Reprinted by permission of the publisher, Penguin Books Ltd., copyright 1950.

creatures, are not quite so definite. All four words occur in Old English and their meanings have not changed in twelve centuries. But in such sayings as "Westminster is the mother of Parliaments," "The child is father of the man," "He seeks a place in the sun," and "He rides the high horse," the primary meanings of these words are manifestly transcended.

What is the *sun*? According to *The Oxford English Dictionary* it is "the brightest (as seen from the earth) of the heavenly bodies, the luminary or orb of day; the central body of the solar system, around which the earth and other planets revolve, being kept in their orbits by its attraction and supplied with light and heat by its radiation." And what is the *horse*? It is "a solid-hoofed perissodactyl quadruped (*Equus caballus*), having a flowing mane and tail, whose voice is a neigh." Now are these so-called "dictionary definitions" really definitions, or are they not descriptions? As long ago as 1891, when he was writing his magistral *Essai de Sémantique*, Michel Bréal demonstrated that the cause of shifting meaning in so many words lay in the impossibility of complete definition and in the varying complexity of the word-thing relationship. "Language," he wrote, "designates things in an incomplete and inaccurate manner: *incomplete*, since we have not exhausted all that can be said of the sun when we have declared it to be shining, or of the horse when we say that it trots; *inaccurate*, since we cannot say of the sun that it shines when it has set, or of the horse that it trots when it is at rest, or when it is wounded or dead."

Could the word or symbol *sun* ever alter its reference and come to mean "moon," or "star," or something else? That, surely, is inconceivable. *Sun* is an ancient word, indicating the same "heavenly body" as its ancestral equivalent in Indo-European five thousand and more years ago. Day by day during those five thousand years, man has observed it "coming forth as a bridegroom out of his chamber, and rejoicing as a giant to run his course." Nevertheless, it has happened that üλ, the etymological equivalent of *sun* in Albanian, has come to mean "star"; and *haul* and *súil*, its equivalents in Welsh and Erse respectively, have come to mean "eye." At some period in the history of each of these three languages that apparently simple and rigid relationship between word and thing, between *symbol* and *referent*, has been distorted. The meaning, we say, has been changed. The seemingly impossible has occurred and any notions that we may have entertained concerning the indissolubility of the links connecting *etymology* and *meaning* have been rudely dispelled. The shock is, to say the least, disconcerting. We should so much prefer to regard a "speech-form as a relatively permanent object to which the meaning is attached as a kind of changeable satellite" (Leonard Bloomfield, *Language*, p. 426). The study of language would be so much easier for us if we could be assured that the etymology of a word is not only something *real* and *true* (as, indeed, the Greek *etymon* implies) but also that it is something permanent; and that the basic form or *root* of a word has some inherent connexion with the thing, quality or action denoted.

Primitive peoples still believe that word has power over thing, that somehow the word participates of the nature of the thing. The word, in fact, is the symbol and it has no direct or immediate relation with the referent except through the image in the mind of the speaker. As Henri Delacroix once said (in *Le Langage et la Pensée*), "All thought is symbolic. Thought first constructs symbols which it substitutes for things." The symbol *sun* has no connexion with the celestial luminary other than through the thoughts or images in the mind of the speaker and the hearer. Unless these two images are identical, there can be no complete understanding.

Latin grammarians sometimes taught wrong etymologies long ago and more recent writers, who should have known better, have occasionally had recourse to fictitious etymologies in order to buttress a theory or to point a moral. Carlyle liked to define *king* as "he who can," associating the word with German *können* "to be capable, to know how to"; and Ruskin found pleasure in reminding the married women in his audience that since *wife* meant "she who weaves" their place was in the home. On the other hand, a speaker may knowingly or unwittingly ignore an etymology. He may refer to a "dilapidated wooden shed," although *dilapidated* is strictly applicable only to a building of stone (Latin *lapis, lapidis*). He may say that "the battalion was well equipped," although *to equip* (French *équiper*, from Old Norse *skipa*) means historically "to fit out a ship." He may say that "the lifeboat was manned by Wrens,"[1] "the ocean liner sailed," and "the cattle were shepherded into their stables." A rediscovered etymology may be highly informative and may give pleasure. Those two attractive birds, the nuthatch and the redstart, have most interesting names. The nuthatch is that little creeping bird that breaks or *hacks* the nuts in order to feed on the kernel. For the alternation between final plosive and affricative in *hack* and *hatch*,[2] you may like to compare *bake* and *batch*, *dike* and *ditch*, *lyke-wake* and *lich*gate, *mickle* and *much*, *wake* and *watch*. The redstart is still called the firetail in some dialects and *start* "tail" survives in *Start* Point "tail-shaped promontory" and *stark*-naked, older *start*-naked. It is interesting to recall that a *governor* is etymologically a "steersman," a *marshal* a "horse-servant," and a *constable* a "companion of the stable." A *companion* is "one who eats bread" with another, a *fellow* is "one who lays down money," a *comrade* a "chamber-fellow," and a *friend* "one who loves."

If the meanings of words are not fixed, if they are liable to flux and change, is there any way of predicting in which direction they are most likely to change? Do changes in meaning admit of empirical generalizations? It is the aim of students of *semantics or semasiology* to find the answers to these questions. So far there has been little coordination of semantic research and

---

[1] Wren is a member of a British World War II organization, the Women's Royal Naval Service. [eds.]

[2] Here the plosive, also called a stop, is the *k* sound; the affricative, or affricate, is the *ch* sound, as in *church* [eds.]

semantics – branch of linguistics concerned w/ nature, structure, develop. & development & changes of meanings v. speech form investigators have fallen into two groups according to their preoccupation with mental processes (Bronislaw Malinowski, C. K. Ogden, and I. A. Richards) or with mathematical symbols (Ludwig Wittgenstein, A. N. Whitehead, Bertrand Russell, and Rudolf Carnap). At present these two groups—the linguistic psychologists and the mathematical logicians—seem to be moving on different planes. The student of language sees many parallels, and he is able to distinguish certain semantic categories, but he inclines to the view that generalizations are dangerous and unprofitable.

The most obvious semantic category is that involving specialization or narrowing. When a speech-form is applied to a group of objects or ideas which resemble one another in some respect, it may naturally become restricted to just one object or idea, and if this particular restriction gains currency in a speech community, a specialized meaning prevails. *Meat*, as in *sweetmeat* and as in the archaic phrase "meat and drink," meant any kind of food. It now means "edible flesh," a sense formerly expressed by *flesh* and *flesh meat*. *Deer*, like Dutch *dier* and German *Tier*, used to mean "animal" in general, as in Shakespeare's "mice and rats and such small deer." Latin *animal* and French *beast* have taken its place as the general words and *deer* now means "wild ruminant of a particular (antlered) species." *Fowl*, like Dutch and German *Vogel*, denoted "bird" in general as in Chaucer's "Parlement of Foules" and Biblical "fowls of the air" and as in modern names of larger kinds of birds used with a qualifying adjective, such as *sea fowl*, *water fowl*, and *wild fowl*. Otherwise, of course, *fowl* normally means a domestic cock or hen, especially when full grown. *Hound* formerly meant a dog of any breed and not, as now, a hunting-dog in particular. *Disease* was still conceived in Chaucer's day as being dis-ease "absence of ease." It might point to any kind of temporary discomfort and not, as now, to "a morbid physical condition." To *starve*, like Dutch *sterven* and German *sterben*, meant "to die," not necessarily from lack of food. In modern Yorkshire dialect a body can still "starve of cold." A *wed* was a pledge of any kind. In conjunction with the suffix *-lock* forming nouns of action, it has come to be restricted to "the marriage vow or obligation." To the Elizabethans an *affection* was a feeling of any kind and both *lectures* and *lessons* were "readings" of any kind. *Doctrine* was still teaching in general and *science* was still knowledge in general.

Sometimes a word has become restricted in use because a qualifier has been omitted. *Undertaker*, like French *entrepreneur* and German *Unternehmer*, used to mean "contractor, one who *undertakes* to do a particular piece of work." It is now used exclusively in the sense of *funeral undertaker*, although *mortician* has already superseded it in the cities and towns of America. In daily conversation *doctor* "teacher" means "medical doctor" and normally refers to a "general practitioner." Many words have both wider and narrower senses in the living language and many others have varying senses according to the persons addressed. *Pipe*, for example, evokes different images in the mind of the smoker, the plumber, the civil engineer, the geologist, the organist, and the boatswain. The *line* means a clothesline to the laundrywoman, a fishing line to the fisherman, the equator to the seaman (as in Joseph Conrad's *Crossing the Line*), a communication wire to the telephonist, a succession of descent to the genealogist, and a particular kind of article to the man of business. To the geographer *cataract* means a cascade or waterfall, to the engineer a hydraulic controller, but a disease of the crystalline lens to the oculist.

The processes of specialization and extension of meaning may take place in a language side by side. For instance, as we have just seen, *hound* has been restricted in the course of a thousand years from a dog in general to a hunting-dog in particular; contrariwise, *dog* . . . has been extended from "a dog of ancient breed" to include any sort of dog, ranging from a formidable Alsatian to a puny and insignificant lap-dog. *Bird* meant "young birdling," just as *pigeon* meant "young dove" and *pig* "young swine." *Place* has had a remarkable history in English, where it has largely superseded the older words *stead* and *stow*. It derives from the feminine form of the Greek adjective meaning "broad," as in *plateîa hodós* "broad way." In one of its senses it still means "a group of houses in a town or city, now or formerly possessing some of the characters (positive or negative) of a square," like its well-known cognate in French, as in *Place de la Concorde*, or like Italian *piazza*, Spanish *plaza*, and German *Platz*. Now, however, it is also used in a hundred ways. . . .

If we assume that the central meaning of *place* is still "square" and that these other diverse uses *radiate* from the centre, we might equally well put it into our third semantic category: radiation, polysemia, or multiplication. Another excellent example is the word *paper*. It is the same as *papyrus*, the paper-reed of the Nile from the thin strips of which writing-sheets were first made as a substitute for parchment. The name was naturally transferred to paper made of cotton and thence to paper of linen and other fibres. To-day a paper may mean a document of any kind, for instance, a Government White Paper; an essay, dissertation or article on some particular topic, especially a communication read or sent to a learned society; a set of questions in an examination; a journal or a daily newspaper. *Power* "ability to do, state of being able" may hold radiating meanings as diverse as "capacity for mental or bodily action" (power of intellect, power of movement); "mechanical or natural energy" (horse-power, candle-power, electric power-station); "political or national strength" (the balance of power); "possession of control or command over others, dominion, sway" (the power of the Cabinet); "a political state" (the four great powers); and "a mathematical conception" (5^4 or five to the fourth power). Because the *head* is that part of the human body containing the brain, it may be the top of anything, literally or metaphorically, whether it resembles the head in shape (the head of a nail, screw, pin, hammer, walking-stick, flower, or cabbage) or in position (the head of the page, the list, the bed, the table or the stairs); or it may signify the person who is the chief or leader (the head of the school, the business, the family, the house, the State, the Church). It may denote the head of a coin (that side of a coin bearing the sovereign's head); a headland or promontory (St. Bees Head, Great Ormes Head, or Beachy Head, from tautologous Beau Chef Head); a single person or beast (lunch at five shillings a head, fifty head of cattle); or one of the main points or logical divisions of a subject or discourse (dealing with a theme under several heads). These and other senses do not derive from one another. They radiate from a common centre and are therefore mutually independent. Some of these senses will be translated by German *Kopf*, by French *tête*, by Spanish *cabeza* or by the ordinary word for *head* in other languages, but many senses will not permit of such direct translation. Each sense must be considered separately and in the process of translating our linguistic knowledge may be severely put to the test. It is surprising that in ordinary conversation in English there is so little ambiguity.

It is surprising, too, that every day we use words in both literal and metaphorical senses and that there is little danger of being misapprehended. We may speak as we will of "bright sunshine" or "a bright boy"; "a sharp knife," "a sharp frost" or "a sharp rebuke"; "a cold morning" or "the cold war"; "the Black Country" or "the black market." A person who is slow-witted may be described metaphorically as "dull," "obtuse," or "dim," the latter term being associated with the German *dumm* meaning "stupid," although cognate with our *dumb*. "Dumb" in German is now *stumm*, which is related etymologically to our *stammer*. Many words are themselves old metaphors: *dependent* "hanging from" (Latin *dē-pendens*); *egregious* "selected from the herd" (Latin *ē* for *ex + grex, gregis* "herd"); *precocious* "too early ripe" (Latin *praecox* from *prae* "before" + *coquere* "to cook, ripen").

Our next category of semantic changes may be labelled concretization. The naming of abstract qualities, such as *whiteness, beauty,* and *justice,* comes late in the evolution of a language because it results from conscious or unconscious comparison in the mind of man. Does *beauty* really exist apart from beautiful things? On this question the medieval schoolmen argued for centuries. No sooner are abstract nouns formed than men tend to think of each appearance of a quality or action in the abstract as a separate entity and so, by concretization, they make abstractions tangible and visible once more. *Youth,* "youngness" in the abstract, becomes a "young man." In the form *geogop* this word occurs eleven times in *Beowulf,* five times with the abstract meaning "youth," but six times with the concrete and collective meaning "young men." In much the same way Latin *multitūdo* "maniness, the quality of being many" came to signify "a crowd" and *congregātio* "flocking together" came to mean "a body of people assembled." Barristers appointed counsel to the Crown are named *King's Counsel.* A judge is addressed as *Your Honour* and an archbishop as *Your Grace*. *Health* is the quality of being *hale* or *whole*, soundness of body and mind. Modern man seeks diligently to maintain physical, mental, and social health. It is Greek *hugíeia* (from the adjectival form of which comes our *hygiene*), Latin *salūs*, French *la santé*, and German *die Gesundheit*. Clearly these are all highly abstract forms. Nevertheless, even *health* becomes concrete in the sense of a toast drunk—"Here's a health unto His Majesty!" *Wealth* was primarily "weal," "welfare," or "well-being," the state of being "well." In the old assonantal formula "health and wealth" the two abstract substantives were practically synonymous. But side by side with this meaning of *wealth* the concretized sense of "worldly goods, riches, affluence" also developed. The expression *wealth of nations*, denoting "the collective riches of a people or country," was certainly current before it was adopted by Adam Smith in 1776 as the title of his epoch-making book. "Money," wrote John Stuart Mill in 1848, "being the instrument of an important public and private purpose, is rightly regarded as wealth." "Let us substitute welfare for wealth as our governing purpose," said Edward Hallett Carr in 1948, exhorting us, in fact, to restore to the word *wealth* its older meaning. *Kindness, mercy, opportunity*, and *propriety* are historically abstractions, but today we speak of *kindnesses* in the plural in the sense of "deeds of kindness," *mercies* as "instances or manifestations of mercy," *opportunities* as "favourable chances or occasions," and *proprieties* as "proper forms of conduct." Similarly *provision* "foreseeing, foresight" has come to be applied in the plural to "stores of food."

Sometimes words, like men, "fall away from their better selves" and show deterioration or catachresis. *Silly* once meant "happy, blissful, holy," as in the "sely child" of Chaucer's Prioress's Tale. Later it signified "helpless, defenceless," becoming a conventional epithet in the "silly sheep" of Milton, Cowper, and Matthew Arnold. Then it descended yet lower and came to imply "foolish, feeble-minded, imbecile." *Crafty* "strong" and *cunning* "knowing" were once attributes of unmingled praise. A crafty workman was one skilled in a handicraft; a cunning workman was one who knew his trade. *To counterfeit* meant simply "to copy, reproduce," conveying no suggestion of fraud. "What finde I here?" asked Bassanio, as he opened the leaden casket, "Faire Portias counterfeit." (*The Merchant of Venice*, III, ii. 115.) It was, in fact, no counterfeit in the modern sense, but a true and lifelike delineation that came "so near creation." A *villain* once meant "a slave serving in a country-house or *villa*," a man occupying a lowly station in life. Caucer's *vileynye* already showed depreciation, for it connoted the opposite of *courteisye*, that comprehensive term for a noble and chivalrous way of life, implying high courtly elegance and politeness of manners. A *knave*, like German *ein Knabe*, was just "a boy"; later, as in "the kokes knave, thet wassheth the disshes" of the *Ancrene Riwle*, "a boy or lad employed as a servant"; later still, "a base and crafty rogue." Like *rogue* and *rascal*, *knave* may still be used jocularly without seriously implying bad qualities. *Varlet,* a variant of *valet,* has shown an almost identical catachresis. *Nice* has become just a pleasant verbal counter: anything or everything may be nice. But *nescius,* its Latin antecedent, had the precise meaning "ignorant, unaware," a meaning maintained in Chaucer side by side with that of "foolish." From "foolish" it developed the sense "foolishly particular about small things," and so "fastidious, precise," as in "nice in one's dress." Later it was made to refer to actions or qualities, as in "a nice discrimination" and "a nice sense of honour." Since then, as H. W. Fowler has sagaciously observed in *A Dictionary of Modern English Usage,* "it has been too great a favourite with the ladies, who have charmed out of it all its individuality and converted it into a mere diffuser of vague and mild agreeableness." It is a pleasant, lazy word which careful speakers are bound to avoid using in serious contexts. *Propaganda,* which now implies an organized and vicious distortion of facts for a particular purpose, has suffered sad depreciation in recent years. In 1622 Pope Gregory XV founded a special Committee or Congregation of Cardinals for the Propagation of the Faith, in Latin *Congregātion dē propāgandā fide.* That marked the beginning of the history of this word, which, you see, is the ablative singular feminine form of the gerundive of *propāgāre* "to fasten or peg down slips of plants for growth, to multiply plants by layering." Most appropriately the Latin metaphor is agricultural and botanical. *Propaganda* should mean, in its extended sense, the dissemination of news of any kind. Unfortunately, since the year 1880 the meaning of the word has been poisoned.[3] Propaganda and trustworthy news are dissociated in our minds. We even hear of propaganda and counter-propaganda! . . .

SUGGESTED ASSIGNMENTS

1. Look up the derivation of the following words and indicate which process each exemplifies, specialization or extension: *dunce, minister, butcher, pocket, box, campus, colossal, poison, liquor, bootleg.*

2. Spend an hour poking around in your desk dictionary and collecting interesting etymologies. In some cases you may wish to refer to an unabridged dictionary for further information. Then write a theme on what you found, using some such title as "An Etymological Excursion through a Dictionary," or "Glimpses of the Past in a Dictionary."

---

[3] Professor Potter explains as follows: "When I wrote that this semantic 'poisoning' has gone on 'since the year 1880' I was thinking more especially of British political life and of that bitterly contested General Election in that year which brought Benjamin Disraeli's glorious Ministry to an end. Since then the word has been in frequent political circulation as a smear-word, far removed from its first modern use by the Roman Catholic Church in 1622." [Letter to Joseph C. Bohme, Jr.] [eds.]

Changes in Meaning

Charles Barber

This essay continues the story of semantic changes. It suggests causes, shows collateral effects, and presents more word histories in some detail. Charles L. Barber is a senior lecturer at the University of Leeds, England.

When we use the word *meaning* here, we are talking about the relationship between language and the real world, between the signalling system and the things that the signals refer to or stand for. We can call this *referential meaning*. We can only detect referential meaning by observing how language is used in actual situations, and this is how a child discovers the meaning of words and sentences when it learns its mother tongue. Often, of course, the verbal context by itself can show us what a word means, and if we are trying to discover the meaning of a word in, say, sixteenth-century English, we simply examine a large number of passages of sixteenth-century English in which the word occurs. But we can only discover meaning in this way because (1) we have already learnt the meanings of the other words in the passages by meeting them in actual situations, and (2) the passages are therefore able to present us, by what they say, with fairly clear situations.

Change of Meaning and Polysemy

This essay is about changes in referential meaning which henceforth I shall simply refer to as meaning. . . . Changes in meaning do not lend themselves to systematic treatment, because there are no regular laws or large-scale trends such as we find in phonology or in grammar. However, we can still see some kind of order in these changes of meaning: changes of various kinds can be distinguished, and similar causes can often be seen at work to bring them about. In this essay I shall look at a few examples of change of meaning in English, and illustrate some of the common types of change. . . .

When a word develops a new meaning, it sometimes loses the old one. Thus the word *wan* (Old English *wann*) at first meant 'dark', or even 'black', being applied for example to a raven and to night. In late Middle English it developed its modern sense of 'pale'. This remarkable change of meaning seems to have taken place partly through the application of the word to human faces discoloured by disease, and partly through its use to describe the color of lead. From meaning 'darkened by disease' it came to mean 'livid', 'the colour a person's face is when they are ill', and hence 'pale'. When one word has two such contradictory meanings as 'dark' and 'pale' there are grave dangers of confusion, and it is not surprising that one of them died out; the meaning 'dark' is last recorded in the sixteenth century.

Often, however, there is no such sharp contradiction between the old and the new meaning; or each meaning is found in one characteristic kind of context so that there is no danger of confusion; and in such cases the two meanings may continue to exist side by side, and even branch out again and give more meanings. Thus the original meaning of *horn* was 'one of a pair of pointed projections on the heads of oxen, sheep, goats, etc.'; but already in the Old English period it was extended to mean 'one of these used as a musical instrument'. Later, similar musical instruments were made of other materials, such as brass, but they were still called horns; and later the word became used for other kinds of noise-producing instruments, like those used on motor-cars. There is really no danger of confusion from the coexistence of these different meanings, because they all occur in characteristic contexts: 'He plays the horn in the Hallé'; 'Jack jammed on his brakes and sounded his horn'; 'Let's take the bull by the horns.' And the word has more meanings yet. Besides meaning 'a wind instrument', it can mean 'a person who plays such an instrument' ('for five years he was first horn in the Hallé'). Besides referring to the projections on the heads of animals like cows, it can be used for projections on the heads of insects and snails, and for tufts of feathers on the heads of birds; it is the snail usage that has given us the phrase 'to draw in your horns'. It can also be used as the name of the material that animals' horns are made of ('a handle made of horn'). And we still have meanings like 'drinking vessel', and the horns of a bow, or of the moon, or of a dilemma. And all in all you will agree that the word *horn* now has a positive welter of meanings, which have all developed out of the original one referring to the things on an animal's head.

The coexistence of several meanings in one word, which is extremely common, is called *polysemy*. Some words develop a whole family of meanings, each new meaning often forming yet another starting point for more; if in a good dictionary you look up such words as *natural, good, loose, free,* and *real*, you will be surprised at the number of meanings listed. If you look them up in the big *Oxford English Dictionary*, available in any big public library, you will find brief dated quotations illustrating each meaning, including the first recorded example of each in English; from these you can get some idea of the way in which the various meanings have evolved.

It sometimes happens that a word develops meanings very remote from one another, and the reader of a dictionary will be puzzled or intrigued to find a word operating in such different fields. Such is the word *collation,* which in present-day English has two main meanings: 'the act of bringing together and comparing (different manuscripts or editions)' and 'a light meal'. How does it come to have such oddly assorted meanings? The first of the two meanings is very close to the meaning of the Latin word *collatio* to which the English word ultimately goes back, and which meant 'a bringing together'. In Late Latin, *collatio* also had the meaning 'a conference, discourse', and this too was one of the early meanings of English *collation,* though it has not survived into our time. In Benedictine monasteries, it was the custom before Compline for the monks to hear a reading from a Latin work on the lives of the fathers, the *Collationes* ('Conferences, Discourses') of Cassian; and the name *collation* was then applied to these readings. Next, it seems, it became applied to the light meal which the monks took after the readings. This can easily have happened simply from the constant closeness of the two events in time: a reference to something happening before or after the collation, for example, might often equally well refer to the readings or to the meal. Having become the name of this particular meal, the word was later extended to refer to any light meal.

When a word develops very different meanings like this, and has no intermediate ones to link them together, the native speaker may feel that there are two different words, not one word with two meanings. Thus historically the word *mess* meaning 'group of people who take their meals together' is identical with *mess* meaning 'state of disorder'; but most people probably feel these as two separate words, because they occur in such different contexts. In such cases, it sometimes happens that two different spellings develop for the word, one for each meaning. This is so with *mettle,* which historically is the same word as *metal.* The specialized meaning 'temperament, spirited temperament, ardour' arose from the figurative application of *metal* (referring to the temper of a sword blade) to the qualities of human beings or animals. But this meaning is so remote from the other meanings of metal that the word has split in two, and this is reflected in the spelling. The same is true of *flower* and *flour,* which are simply spelling variants of what was originally the same word. One meaning that developed for *flower* was 'the best part' (as in 'the flower of chivalry'), and *flour* is simply 'the best (or finest) part of the wheat'. . . .

Changes in the Referent

One reason why a word changes its meaning is that the thing it refers to changes. The word *ship* has been used in English for over a thousand years to denote a vessel for travelling on the sea, but the kind of machine actually used for this purpose has changed enormously: the word used of the long boats of the Vikings is now also used of a modern liner or aircraft carrier, and it seems reasonable to say that its meaning has changed. The same applies to other products of our material culture, like *house, lamp, weapon, hat*. It also applies to the names of institutions, like *parliament, king*, and *law*, for they too have changed. And it applies to words that involve moral or aesthetic judgments: the words *good, virtuous, modest*, and *beautiful* do not mean the same today as they did in 1600, because our moral and aesthetic standards have changed: our idea of what constitutes virtuous conduct, or a modest woman, or a beautiful painting does not tally with the ideas of Shakespeare and his contemporaries.

Shift in the Focus of Interest

At first sight it might seem that the change in meaning of the word *horn* (from 'animal weapon' to 'musical instrument') was also of this kind: just as ships changed from sail to steam, but kept the same name, so musical instruments were made of a new material, but were still called horns. But the change in *horn* is not as simple as this: even before horns came to be made of brass, it is clear that a new meaning had appeared, namely 'musical instrument'. This meaning had arisen by a shift in the speaker's and hearer's centre of interest when the word was used—from animals and their weapons to the fact that a noise could be produced from the thing; and the shift arose because the implement came to be used regularly in a different kind of situation. Consequently, when the word *horn* was used in certain types of context, it had a musical meaning.

Many changes of meaning are of the kind where a shift takes place in the focus of interest, in the aspect which is given prominence, though the mechanism of change is not always identical with that for *horn*. The adjective *fair* (Old English *fæger*) originally meant 'fit, suitable' . . . but in Old English it had come to mean 'pleasant, joyous, agreeable, beautiful'. When used of conduct, it must have been used frequently in situations in which 'pleasant conduct' meant 'conduct free from bias, fraud, or injustice', so that *fair* came to mean 'equitable, just'; this meaning is recorded from the fourteenth century, and remains one of its chief ones. In the sense of 'beautiful', *fair* is often used of human beings, and especially women, from Old English times onwards; but for various historical reasons, . . . the ideal of beauty in medieval and early modern English was a blonde one: hair and complexion had to be light in color. Consequently, a beautiful woman was also a blonde one, and *fair* came to mean 'light in colour', a meaning first recorded in the mid-sixteenth century. The existence side by side of the meanings 'beautiful' and 'blonde' is demonstrated by a famous Shakespeare sonnet, in which he asserts that his love is fair although she is dark. But the existence of these two different meanings, which would obviously occur in similar contexts, offers too many possibilities of ambiguity, and the meaning 'beautiful' has dropped out of use, except in a few consciously archaic (and often jocular) phrases like 'a fair lady' and 'the fair sex'. On the other hand, there is little danger of conflict between the meanings 'equitable' and 'blonde', because the context usually shows clearly whether we are talking about conduct or appearance.

Somewhat similar is the way in which words denoting occupation or social rank often develop meanings referring to the moral or intellectual qualities (real or supposed) of people in that station. When the word *gentle* was borrowed from French in the Middle English period, it was used mainly to refer to social rank, and meant 'well-bred, of good family'. The meanings 'docile, courteous, merciful', and so on, arose because these were the qualities conventionally attributed to people of that class. Of course, we know that not all gentlemen were gentle, but the idealized picture that a ruling class has of itself may be more influential than the actual facts. The influence of the dominant social class in these matters is shown by the rather different history of the word *villain*: this originally meant 'peasant,' but then came to mean 'scoundrel, criminal'. In this case, plainly, it is the gentleman's view of the peasant that has determined the change of meaning, not the peasant's view of himself. The word *lady,* similarly, from meaning 'woman of the upper classes', has come to mean also 'woman of delicacy and refinement'. And *noble*, from meaning 'pertaining to the aristocracy', has come to mean 'lofty, magnanimous, imposing, holding high ideals', because these qualities, as we know, are especially characteristic of members of the House of Peers. Other examples are *churl* (originally 'man of low rank'), *boor* (originally 'peasant, countryman'), and *bourgeois*.

A particularly striking example of a change of meaning arising from a movement of the focus of interest within a situation is given by the word *bead*, discussed in detail by Gustaf Stern in his book on change of meaning in English.[1] The word originally meant 'prayer'. The meaning 'small pierced ball for threading on a string' arose from the medieval habit of counting one's prayers on a rosary: *to tell your beads* meant 'to count your prayers', but what anyone would actually *see* when a man was 'telling his beads' was the movement of the small balls on the rosary; hence the word *beads* came to be apprehended as referring to these balls, and the modern meaning arose.

THE INFLUENCE OF FORM

Sometimes a change of meaning is caused by the *form* of a word: one word is confused with another that resembles it in some way, or its meaning is affected by the meaning (or supposed meanings) of its constituent parts. For

[1] Gustav Stern, *Meaning and Change of Meaning.* Göteborg, 1931. This is a seminal book on meaning-changes. [eds.]

example, in early Modern English, *obnoxious* often had the meaning of its Latin original, "liable to harm or punishment, exposed to injury'; its modern meaning, 'offensive, objectionable', is due to the influence of the word *noxious*.

This kind of change is encouraged in English by the large number of words of Greek or Latin origin, which are often 'opaque', that is, their meanings cannot be deduced from their constituent parts by an unlearned speaker. Our literature is full of comic characters who use long words incorrectly, like Sheridan's Mrs. Malaprop, who says 'illegible' when she means 'eligible', and remarks that she has very little affluence over her niece. Indeed, Mrs. Malaprop has given a new word to the language, *malapropism,* and it is perhaps significant that English speakers feel a need for such a word. Of course, one malapropism doesn't make a change of meaning; but if there is some factor that causes a large number of people to make the same mistake, then a new meaning will indeed arise. Malapropism, for example, may have played a part in the development of a new meaning for . . . *disinterested* ('not taking an interest' instead of 'impartial') and *protagonist* ('supporter' instead of 'main character') . . . . The new meaning of *disinterested* [is probably due] to confusion with *uninterested.* The change in *protagonist* is probably due to the influence of *antagonist*: speakers feel half-consciously that these two words contain the prefixes *pro-* ('for') and *anti-* ('against'), and are therefore the opposites of one another. It is quite true that the first syllable of *antagonist* represents *anti-*, but the first syllable of *protagonist* is from the Greek *protos* ('first'), and the word originally meant 'first competitor' or 'first actor'. These particular changes of meaning are still not accepted by all speakers, but the new usages are extremely common, and look like obtaining ultimate acceptance.

A rather different kind of influence of one word on another is illustrated by the adjective *fast* (Old English *fæst*). Today this has two main meanings: (1) 'firmly fixed' (*make a boat fast with a painter*); and (2) 'swift, rapid' (*a fast train*). The first meaning was the original one. . . . Then, in the second half of the fourteenth century, we suddenly find alongside this meaning the new one of 'swift, rapid' (in phrases like a *fast fleeing*), with no intermediate ones to form a bridge. The explanation is that the adjective *fast* was influenced by the related adverb *fast* (Middle English *faste*, Old English *fæste*), in which we can trace a continuous chain of meanings from 'firmly' to 'rapidly'. Like the adjective, the adverb at first had a passive kind of meaning, 'firmly, securely', and is found in Old English in phrases like *fæste tosomne gelīmed* ('firmly cemented together'); this meaning, of course, it still possesses. However, when it was used with verbs like *to hold*, it could easily acquire a more active sense, 'strongly, energetically, vigorously', because in order to hold a thing securely you often have to exert effort. Next it was used with verbs like 'strike, beat, fight', in which it could only have an active meaning, 'strongly, vigorously, violently'. Among other verbs of vigorous action, it was used with verbs of motion, like 'run' and 'ride'. But to run vigorously or strongly usually means to run *quickly*, and in the second half of the thirteenth century the word acquired this meaning; this becomes clear round about 1300, when *faste* begins to be used in the sense 'rapidly' with verbs not denoting motion, like *sell, eat,* and *fail*. Once the adverb *faste* had acquired the meaning 'rapidly', it was not long before the adjective *fast* acquired the parallel meaning 'rapid'; this is an example of analogy, for related pairs of adjectives and adverbs usually have related meanings.

NARROWING AND WIDENING OF MEANING

One common change is a narrowing or widening of reference. An example of narrowing is the verb *to starve* (Old English *steorfan*), which originally meant simply 'to die'. In Middle English it was sometimes specialized to mean 'die of cold' (and in some northern English dialects it still means 'to be cold'), but a sixteenth-century specialization, 'die of hunger', is the meaning that has survived in the modern standard language. This is a grim reflexion on the hardships of our ancestors, since it implies that a verb meaning 'to die' was very often used in contexts where the death had in fact occurred from lack of food. Similarly, *accident* once meant 'happening, chance event'; *science* meant 'knowledge' (while what we call science was called *natural philosophy*); a *desert* was 'any uninhabited place'; and an *undertaker* was 'anybody who undertakes something'. Other examples are *deer,* which originally meant 'animal' (like German *Tier* and Swedish *djur*), and *meat,* which originally meant 'food', a meaning which survives vestigially in stereo-typed phrases ('meat and drink', 'one man's meat is another man's poison'). More recent examples are *photogenic*, which used to mean 'suitable for being photographed' but which has now been narrowed to 'good-looking, glamor-ous', and the verb *to discipline*, which used to mean 'to provide discipline, to train', but which is now commonly used in the sense 'to punish'.

An example of widening is the word *rubbish,* which in early Modern English meant 'rubble', but which soon developed the wider meaning of 'waste matter, anything worthless'. Words often take on a wider meaning when they move out of the language of some special group and get adopted by the speech community as a whole. For example (since we are talking of rubbish) the word *junk* was originally sailors' slang, and meant 'old rope', but now that it has moved out of that restricted sphere it has the wider meaning of 'useless stuff, rubbish'. Similarly, *gambit* is a technical term in chess, meaning 'an opening in which White offers a pawn sacrifice', but when it is used outside chess it means simply 'opening move'. Similar widenings of meaning can be seen in the popular use of words from other fields: *allergic* from medicine, *complex* from psychology, *alibi* from the law courts, and so on.

AMELIORATION AND DETERIORATION

A special kind of narrowing of meaning is the acquisition by a word of favourable implications (called 'amelioration') or of unfavorable ones (called 'deterioration'). Amelioration is seen, for example, when *success* changes its meaning from 'result' to 'favorable result', and when *knight* changes from 'servant' to (among other things) 'loyal and chivalrous servant'. Amelioration is often the result of a general change in social or cultural attitudes. Thus in the late seventeenth century the words *enthusiasm* and *zeal* were pejorative, implying violence and fanaticism, at any rate in the mouths of polite society, because of their association with revolutionary puritanism, but as English society changed and the civil wars were forgotten these associations were lost. . . . Among political words, we may note *politician*, which in Shakespeare's day was a sinister word (implying scheming and machiavellian trickery), and *democratic*, which is now usually a term of praise, but which not so very long ago was more often a term of reproach (like *red* today).[2]

Human nature being what it is, deterioration is commoner than amelioration: we are only too prone to believe the worst of anybody, and this is reflected in the way our words change. An example is *lust*, which in Old English meant 'desire, pleasure', but which today means 'illicit or intemperate sexual desire'. We have already noticed the deterioration of *villain*, which from 'peasant' came to mean 'scoundrel'; a similar example is *knave*,

---

[2] In British English, "politician" has a favorable meaning, like "statesman," but in American English it has retained the old unfavorable meaning. To illustrate, here is an entry from H. W. Horwill's *Dictionary of Modern American Usage*, reprinted by permission of The Clarendon Press, Oxford:

> politician, politics. The following passage is taken from a leading article in the *N.Y. Evening Post* of March 2, 1923: 'The Chancellor of the British Exchequer remarked at the Pilgrims' dinner Wednesday that our common language carries an impediment to full Anglo-American amity because it makes people of the two lands feel that they have nothing more to learn about each other. Mr. Baldwin of all men should know that it has still another grave disadvantage. The slight differences in our speech open up many pitfalls of misunderstanding. He recently referred to the fact that the debt agreement would have to be submitted to "politicians" from "pastoral districts" of the West. In Britain the word "politician" is applied without a thought of reproach, while Mr. Baldwin meant the word "pastoral" in simple literalness. In Am. "politician" carries a tinge of opprobrium, while we think raillery implied in any reference to the "pastoral" regions. Hence indignation in Congress, consternation in Mr. Baldwin's breast. Editors of the *Britannica* hardly understood the anger of some Americans at finding Newton D. Baker described as a "politician" therein.' A striking confirmation of the 'tinge of opprobrium' attaching to the word in Am. was given by Miss Ellen Wilkinson, M.P., in the *Star* of March 25, 1931. 'Once,' she says, 'when lecturing in Am., I made the obvious statement that I was a politician. I felt my audience stiffen. My anxious chairwoman-cum-hostess said to me in tones of agony afterwards, "My dear, *don't* say that again. It sounds so *dreadful*".' A former Cabinet minister records a similar experience. 'Speaking to an Am. audience a few months ago I referred to myself as a politician. I saw that they were shocked' (II. B. Lees-Smith, in Daily Herald. Nov. 9, 1934). [eds.]

which at one time meant 'boy, servant', but which now means 'rogue'. Another such case is *lewd*, which in Old English meant 'lay' (as opposed to 'clerical'), and so also 'ignorant'; hence it came to mean 'common, vulgar', and in early Modern English this progressed to the present meaning of 'unchaste, lascivious'. Other adjectives which are now pejorative, but which formerly were not, include *coy* ('quiet, modest'), *cunning* ('skilful'), *gaudy* ('brilliant, gay'), *notorious* ('well known'), . . . and *uncouth* ('unknown'); the meanings given in brackets are ones found in Middle English or early Modern English. . . .

LOSS OF INTENSITY

Another type of change going on all the time is loss of intensity. When you want to emphasize the strength of your feelings about something, or to impress your hearer suitably, you tend to exaggerate. But of course the meaning of a word is determined by the situations that it is normally used in. So if, for example, the word *hellish* becomes commonly used to describe, not the agonies of the damned or sufferings resembling them, but the kind of discomfort experienced in the rush hour in the London tube, then it comes to *mean* a discomfort of this degree of intensity. The word fades, or loses its intensity. The word *awful,* which once meant 'causing reverence and fear', has been weakened to a kind of omnibus term of deprecation ('The weather was awful') or omnibus intensifier ('It's an awful nuisance'). Similar weakening has occurred in the words *dismal, dreadful, fearful, frightful, horrible, horrid, monstrous,* and so on. The very fact of loss of intensity leads to rather a rapid turnover in words of this kind, since they wear out so quickly, and new words have to be found in their place. But it is not only words of this type that suffer loss of intensity. In Shakespeare's English, the word *naughty* meant 'wicked, evil', and *to annoy* meant 'to harm, to injure'. In the nineteenth century the adjective *fair,* some of whose meanings we have already examined, lost its intensity in some types of context and came to mean 'moderately good' (as in 'He has a fair chance of success'). The adverb *quite* still retains in some contexts the meaning 'entirely' (I think she is quite superb'), but in others has been weakened to mean 'fairly, in a moderate degree' ('I think she is quite good'). Fading often occurs in words to do with punctuality, since we have an incurable tendency to exaggerate our own promptitude: thus Old English *sōna* meant 'immediately', but has become Modern English *soon*; and in early Modern English, *presently* meant 'immediately, at once', but has now been weakened to 'soon, after a short time'.[3]

---

[3] In current English "presently" is often used in the sense of "now," as in "He is presently working at a service station." [eds.]

FIGURATIVE LANGUAGE

Many of the changes of meaning that we have examined have been slow and insensible affairs; even when not slow, they have mostly been unintentional, as with malapropisms. However, some changes of meaning are conscious affairs. This is the case, for example, when we use a word in a figurative sense, which in due course becomes one of its meanings. The first man to speak of the *foot* of a hill or of the *mouth* of a river was consciously coining a metaphor; but, by constant use, these innovations have ceased to be figurative: they are simply two common meanings of the words *foot* and *mouth*. Language is full of dead metaphors of this kind. They are especially common in words for mental phenomena, and indeed for abstract things in general, since originally these often took their names from some physical or concrete analogy. Thus we talk about *grasping* an idea, on the analogy of the action of the hand; the verb *to comprehend*, similarly, comes from a Latin word which originally meant 'to grasp, to seize', and then came to be used of mental acts as well; we say that we *see* when we mean that we understand; and *lucid* comes from a Latin word that means 'bright, shining'. Metaphors of this kind are old and deeply embedded in the language, but new figurative uses constantly arise: consider in our own times such words as *target* (of production), *ceiling* (of prices, wages, aircraft, mental attainments), *freeze* (of wages, prices), *bottleneck* (in a transport system, on a production line), *blanket* (meaning 'comprehensive, all-embracing'), *package* ('group of proposals which must be accepted or rejected as a whole'), and *headache* ('problem'). These usages are still felt as figurative, but they are well on the way to becoming simply new meanings, dead metaphors.

THE ARGUMENT FROM ETYMOLOGY

It is perhaps change of meaning that produces the most violent reactions among those who are conservative about language, and there are frequent letters to the papers condemning the misuse of this or that word. Every speaker has the right to refuse to adopt an innovation in the language, and we all draw the line somewhere. But, if we refuse to adopt a new meaning, we should often be prepared to recognize that we are fighting a lost cause, and that, after a certain stage has been reached, it is mere pedantry to insist that the earlier meaning is the 'right' one. Above all, we should be wary of resorting to the argument that the 'real meaning' of a word is so and so. There is no intrinsic meaning to any word. A word means what the speech community makes it mean, and if people use the word *aggravate* in the sense 'annoy', then it *means* 'annoy'.[4]

[4] *Aggravate* has an earlier sense of "make worse" from Latin *aggravare*, "to make heavier, to make worse, to annoy." Note that, in English as in Latin, the sense has moved from "make worse" to "annoy." [eds.]

Sometimes the opponent of the new meaning triumphantly produces the etymology of the word, to prove that his meaning is the right one: the word *climax* is from the Greek *klimax*, he says, and so the English word does not mean 'culmination' but 'rising series of events leading to a culmination'. But the meaning of a word in English is the meaning that speakers of English give to it, not the meaning of some earlier word from which it is descended. Besides, if we are to play this game of etymological meanings, where are we to stop? After all, the *original* Greek meaning of *klimax* is not 'rising series of events', but 'ladder, staircase'; so why should we not argue that this is the 'real' meaning of English *climax* ('He climbed up the climax to clean the window')? And if we are going to claim that meanings must be etymological, we shall have to say that *wan* means 'dark', *idea* means 'look, form', *idle* means 'empty', *idiot* means 'a private person', *deer* means 'animal', *try* means 'rub down, pulverize', *beam* means 'tree', and so on.

I am not arguing that we should accept all innovations automatically and uncritically: but that we should accept the fact that change exists, and come to terms with it.

SUGGESTED ASSIGNMENTS

For each word on the following list, you are shown an earlier and a later meaning. Label the semantic change of each with one of these symbols:

G Generalization, or widening, or extension
S Specialization, or narrowing
D Deterioration, or degeneration
A Amelioration, or elevation.

Symbol	Word	An Earlier Meaning	A Later Meaning
d	hussy	housewife	brazen woman
a	fame	common talk	renown
e	box	receptacle made of boxwood	receptacle
d	saloon	elegant dining room	inelegant drinking joint
___	naive	unlearned, artless	credulous, simpleminded
___	marshall	groom, stableman	high official
___	citizen	city dweller	a member of a country
___	stink	smell	bad smell
___	queen	woman	female ruler
___	wench	girl	wanton woman
___	pastor	shepherd	religious leader
___	dose	something given	unpleasant substance to be swallowed.
___	clerk	learned man	worker at a sales counter

_____ campus	field, plain	college grounds
_____ reek	to smoke	to smell bad
_____ governor	pilot	chief executive of a political unit
_____ harlot	fellow (male or female)	prostitute
_____ mansion	residence	sumptuous residence
_____ naughty	good-for-naught	mischievous
_____ gossip	baptismal sponsor	talebearer
_____ front	forehead	forward part of anything
_____ cupboard	shelf for cups	cabinet for kitchen utensils
_____ wife	woman	married woman
_____ spill	to destroy	to allow to flow accidentally
_____ operate	to function	to function as a surgeon
_____ butcher	one who kills he-goats for meat	one who kills animals for meat

The Euphemism: Telling It Like It Isn't

Time Magazine

This essay deals with euphemisms. A euphemism is a softened, agreeable, or indirect expression used instead of the one that seems too harsh, indelicate or direct. For example, _he passed away_ and _he is gone_ are euphemisms for _he died_ and _he is dead_. Circumlocutions like these may arise from the desire to avoid giving pain and in such cases must be accounted useful terms. At times, however, euphemisms are employed merely through hypersensitivity or excess of delicacy. The Victorian use of _white meat_ to avoid saying _breast_, and the Ozark woman's use of _lay down_ to avoid the indelicate suggestiveness of _go to bed_ seem to us cases of overconcern hinting of prudery. There is still a third reason for the use of euphemistic terms: to enhance prestige. The job of a hairdresser, for example, seems more prestigious if he or she is called a cosmetologist, and a secondhand car seems more desirable if it is labeled a preowned car.

Modern American speech, while not always clear or correct or turned with much style, is supposed to be uncommonly frank. Witness the current explosion of four-letter words and the explicit discussion of sexual topics. In fact, gobbledygook and nice-Nellyism still extend as far as the ear can hear. Housewives on television may chat about their sex lives in terms that a decade ago would have made gynecologists blush; more often than not, these emancipated women still speak about their children's "going to the potty." Government spokesmen talk about "redeployment" of American troops; they mean withdrawal. When sociologists refer to blacks living in slums, they are likely to mumble about "nonwhites" in a "culturally deprived environment." The CIA may never have used the expression "to terminate with extreme prejudice" when it wanted a spy rubbed out. But in the context of a war in which "pacification of the enemy infrastructure" is the military mode of reference to blasting the Viet Cong out of a village, the phrase sounded so plausible that millions readily accepted it as accurate.

The image of a generation blessed with a swinging, liberated language is largely an illusion. Despite its swaggering sexual candor, much contemporary speech still hides behind that traditional enemy of plain talk, the euphemism.

NECESSARY EVIL

From a Greek word meaning "to use words of good omen," euphemism is the substitution of a pleasant term for a blunt one—telling it like it isn't. Euphemism has probably existed since the beginning of language. As long as there have been things of which men thought the less said the better, there have been better ways of saying less. In everyday conversation the euphemism is, at worst, a necessary evil; at its best, it is a handy verbal tool to avoid making enemies needlessly, or shocking friends. Language purists and the blunt-spoken may wince when a young woman at a party coyly asks for directions to "the powder room," but to most people this kind of familiar euphemism is probably no more harmful or annoying than, say, a split infinitive.

On a larger scale, though, the persistent growth of euphemism in a language represents a danger to thought and action, since its fundamental intent is to deceive. As Linguist Benjamin Lee Whorf has pointed out, the structure of a given language determines, in part, how the society that speaks it views reality. If "substandard housing" makes rotting slums appear more livable or inevitable to some people, then their view of American cities has been distorted and their ability to assess the significance of poverty has been reduced. Perhaps the most chilling example of euphemism's destructive power took place in Hitler's Germany. The wholesale corruption of the language under Nazism, notes Critic George Steiner, is symbolized by the phrase *endgültige Lösung* (final solution), which "came to signify the death of 6,000,000 human beings in gas ovens."

ROSES BY OTHER NAMES

No one could argue that American English is under siege from linguistic falsehood, but euphemisms today have the nagging persistence of a headache. Despite the increasing use of nudity and sexual innuendo in advertising, Madison Avenue is still the great exponent of talking to "the average person of good upbringing"—as one TV executive has euphemistically described the ordinary American—in ways that won't offend him. Although this is like fooling half the people none of the time, it has produced a handsome bouquet of roses by other names. Thus there is "facial-quality tissue" that is not intended for use on faces, and "rinses" or "tints" for women who might be unsettled to think they dye their hair. In the world of deodorants, people never sweat or smell; they simply "offend." False teeth sound truer when known as "dentures."

Admen and packagers, of course, are not the only euphemizers. Almost any way of earning a salary above the level of ditchdigging is known as a profession rather than a job. Janitors for several years have been elevated by image-conscious unions to the status of "custodians"; nowadays, a teenage rock guitarist with three chords to his credit can class himself with Horowitz as a "recording artist." Cadillac dealers refer to autos as "preowned" rather than "secondhand." Government researchers concerned with old people call them "senior citizens." Ads for bank credit cards and department stores refer to "convenient terms"—meaning 18% annual interest rates payable at the convenience of the creditor.

Jargon, the sublanguage peculiar to any trade, contributes to euphemism when its terms seep into general use. The stock market, for example, rarely "falls" in the words of Wall Street analysts. Instead it is discovered to be "easing" or found to have made a "technical correction" or "adjustment." As one financial writer notes: "It never seems to 'technically adjust' upward." The student New Left, which shares a taste for six-syllable words with Government bureaucracy, has concocted a collection of substitute terms for use in politics. To "liberate," in the context of campus uproars, means to capture and occupy. Four people in agreement form a "coalition." In addition to "participatory democracy," which in practice is often a description of anarchy, the university radicals have half seriously given the world "anticipatory Communism," which means to steal. The New Left, though, still has a long way to go before it can equal the euphemism-creating ability of Government officials. Who else but a Washington economist would invent the phrase "negative saver" to describe someone who spends more money than he makes?

A persistent source of modern euphemisms is the feeling, inspired by the prestige of science, that certain words contain implicit subjective judgments, and thus ought to be replaced with more "objective" terms. To speak of "morals" sounds both superior and arbitrary, as though the speaker were indirectly questioning those of the listener. By substituting "values," the concept is miraculously turned into a condition, like humidity or mass, that can be safely measured from a distance. To call someone "poor," in the modern way of thinking, is to speak pejoratively of his condition, while the substitution of "disadvantaged" or "underprivileged," indicates that poverty wasn't his fault. Indeed, writes Linguist Mario Pei in a new book called *Words in Sheep's Clothing* . . . , by using "underprivileged," we are "made to feel that it is all our fault." The modern reluctance to judge makes it more offensive than ever before to call a man a liar; thus there is a "credibility gap" instead. No up-to-date teacher would dare refer to a child as "stupid" or a "bad student"; the D+ student is invariably an "under-achiever" or a "slow learner."

FORBIDDEN WORDS

The liberalization of language in regard to sex involves the use of perhaps a dozen words. The fact of their currency in what was once known as polite conversation raises some unanswered linguistic questions. Which, really, is the rose, and which the other name? Is "lovemaking" a euphemism for the four-letter word that describes copulation? Or is this blunt Anglo-Saxonism a dysphemism[1] for making love? Are the old forbidden obscenities really the crude bedrock on which softer and shyer expressions have been built? Or are they simply coarser ways of expressing physical actions and parts of the human anatomy that are more accurately described in less explicit terms? It remains to be seen whether the so-called forbidden words will contribute anything to the honesty and openness of sexual discussion. Perhaps their real value lies in the acidic, expletive power to shock, which is inevitably diminished by overexposure. Perhaps the Victorians, who preferred these words unspoken and unprinted, will prove to have had a point after all.

For all their prudery, the Victorians were considerably more willing than modern men to discuss ideas—such as social distinctions, morality and death —that have become almost unmentionable. Nineteenth century gentlewomen whose daughters had "limbs" instead of suggestive "legs" did not

---

[1] Dysphemism is the substitution of a disagreeable word for an agreeable one, like *brat* for *child*. [eds.]

find it necessary to call their maids "housekeepers," nor did they bridle at referring to "upper" or "lower" classes within society. Rightly or wrongly, the Victorian could talk without embarrassment about "sin," a word that today few but clerics use with frequency or ease. It is even becoming difficult to find a doctor, clergyman or undertaker (known as a "mortician") who will admit that a man has died rather than "expired" or "passed away." Death has not lost its sting; the words for it have.

PSYCHOLOGICAL NECESSITY

There is little if any hope that euphemisms will ever be excised from mankind's endless struggle with words that, as T. S. Eliot lamented, bend, break and crack under pressure. For one thing, certain kinds of everyday euphemisms have proved their psychological necessity. The uncertain morale of an awkward teen-ager may be momentarily buoyed if he thinks of himself as being afflicted by facial "blemishes" rather than "pimples." The label "For motion discomfort" that airlines place on paper containers undoubtedly helps the squeamish passenger keep control of his stomach in bumpy weather better than if they were called "vomit bags." Other forms of self-deception may not be beneficial, but may still be emotionally necessary. A girl may tolerate herself more readily if she thinks of herself as a "swinger" rather than as promiscuous. Voyeurs can salve their guilt feelings when they buy tickets for certain "adult entertainments" on the ground that they are implicitly supporting "freedom of artistic expression."

Lexicographer Bergen Evans of Northwestern University believes that euphemisms persist because "lying is an indispensable part of making life tolerable." It is virtuous, but a bit beside the point, to contend that lies are deplorable. So they are; but they cannot be moralized or legislated away, any more than euphemisms can be. Verbal miasma, when it deliberately obscures truth, is an offense to reason. But the inclination to speak of certain things in uncertain terms is a reminder that there will always be areas of life that humanity considers too private, or too close to feelings of guilt, to speak about directly. Like stammers or tears, euphemisms will be created whenever men doubt, or fear, or do not know. The instinct is not wholly unhealthy; there is a measure of wisdom in the familiar saying that a man who calls a spade a spade is fit only to use one.

SUGGESTED ASSIGNMENTS

1. Give a euphemistic substitute for each of the following expressions:
   sweat
   insane asylum

to steal
painful (as used by a.dentist)
prostitute
mentally retarded child
the excreted waste of dogs and birds
the rear part of the human body between the waist and the thighs
toilet

2. Delineate a human situation in which you would find it advisable to use euphemisms and show how you would handle the situation.

3. Report on euphemisms used in the undertaker's trade. Here are two good sources:

   a. Evelyn Waugh's *The Loved One*, a delightful satirical novel that you can finish in a few hours.

   b. H. L. Mencken's *The American Language*, abridged by Raven I. McDavid, Jr., pp. 341–343. This is a one-volume condensation of three volumes by Mencken, each of which contains material on this subject. They are titled *The American Language*, *The American Language, Supplement* I, and *The American Language, Supplement* II.

4. Restate the following in a way that will soften the blow.

   a. You are discharged.
   b. You are wrong.
   c. The price of Gooey Bread will be increased two cents a loaf beginning March 17.
   d. You have been cut from the basketball squad
   e. Your application for a scholarship has been rejected
   f. We cannot give you a job.
   g. Your salary will be cut beginning next week.
   h. You are getting fat.

5. Read or listen to a political speech, or an interview, or a panel discussion dealing with a serious issue, like war, crime in the streets, poverty, dishonesty in politics, or relations between the sexes. Note the euphemisms used and try to ascertain the reasons for their use. Then write a theme with some such title as "Euphemisms on TV" or "Euphemisms in Politics." There is an element of luck in this assignment. You may come across a mealy-mouthed politician whose speech is loaded with euphemisms, or you may listen to a straightforward speaker who calls a spade a spade.

FURTHER READINGS

Brook, G. L. *A History of the English Language*. New York: Oxford University Press, Inc., 1958. On meaning and meaning changes, see Chapter 8.

Bryant, Margaret M. *Modern English and Its Heritage*, 2d ed. New York: Crowell-Collier and Macmillan, Inc., 1962. On meaning changes, see Chapters 28, 29, 30.

Burriss, Eli E., and Lionel Casson. *Latin and Greek in Current Use*. Englewood Cliffs, N.J.: Prentice-Hall, Inc., 1939.

Estrich, Robert M., and Hans Sperber. *Three Keys to Language.* New York: Holt, Rinehart and Winston, Inc., 1952. On meaning and meaning changes, see Chapters 9, 10, 11, 12.

Friend, Joseph. *An Introduction to the English Language.* New York: World Publishing Co., 1967. On morphemes, see pages 35–48.

Greenough, James B., and George L. Kittredge. *Words and Their Ways in English Speech.* New York: Crowell-Collier and Macmillan, Inc., 1900, 1901. (Paperbound by Beacon Press) Although 74 years old, this book, which is both scholarly and popular, is still a valuable source of information about English words. For meaning changes, see Chapters 17, 18, 19, 20.

Grose, Francis. *A Classical Dictionary of the Vulgar Tongue,* edited by Eric Partridge. London: Routledge and Kegan Paul, Ltd., 1963. Accounts of the lower levels of eighteenth-century vocabulary. Very entertaining.

Hixson, Jerome C., and I. Colodny. *Word Ways.* New York: American Book Company, 1946. On meaning changes, see Chapters 12, 13. On slang, see Chapter 16.

Johnson, Edwin L. *Latin Words in Common Use.* Boston: D. C. Heath, 1931. Excellent and abundant material on the Latin element in English.

Marchand, Hans. *Categories and Types of Present-Day English Word-Formation,* 2d edition. München: C. H. Beck'sche Verlagsbuchhandlung, 1969. On backformation, see Chapter 6. On clipping, see Chapter 9. On blends, see Chapter 10.

Mathews. M. M. *Words: How to Know Them.* New York: Holt, Rinehart and Winston, 1956. See Chapter 6 on meanings and etymologies.

Mencken, H. L. *The American Language.* Fourth edition and two supplements abridged with annotation and new material by Raven I. McDavid, Jr. New York: Alfred A. Knopf, 1963. On euphemism, see pages 339–367.

Potter, Simeon. *Language in the Modern World.* Baltimore: Penguin Books, Inc., 1960. On the making of words, see Chapter 5.

————. *Modern Linguistics.* London: André Deutsch, 1957. This discussion is more detailed and technical than that in the preceding book.

Quirk, Randolph. *The Use of English.* New York: St. Martin's Press, 1962. On words, see pages 115–132.

Serjeantson, Mary S. *History of Foreign Words in English.* New York: E. P. Dutton, 1936.

Sheard, J. A. *The Words of English.* New York: W. W. Norton, 1966. A survey of the history of the English lexicon from the beginning to the present. A treasury of information.

Steiner, Franz. *Taboo.* Baltimore: Penguin Books, Inc., 1956. A detailed account of the practice and theory of taboo.

Ullmann, Stephen. *Semantics: an Introduction to the Science of Meaning.* Oxford: Basil Blackwell, 1962. On taboo, see pages 204–209.

Vallins, G. H. *The Making and Meaning of Words.* London: Adam and Charles Black, 1949.

Wentworth, Harold, and Stuart B. Flexner. *Dictionary of American Slang.* New York: Thomas Y. Crowell Co., 1960, 1967. On slang, see the preface.

6
ONOMATOLOGY

People Have Names

John and Joan Levitt

The study of names is a fascinating area of investigation. The origin of some of the names we bear, like *John* and *Mary*, goes far back into pre-Christian times, and each succeeding era has contributed its share to our vast onomasticon. Names, like other words, undergo transformations of form and meaning. Who would suspect, from the forms today, that *John* originally meant in Hebrew "Jahveh [= God] is gracious," that *Jones* is merely the possessive of *John*, and that *Johnson* is the same word as *Ivanovitch* in Russian and *Ionescu* in Rumanian? The authors, John and Joan Levitt are identified on page 1.

> With Bill Brewer, Jan Stewer, Peter Gurney, Peter Davey, Dan'l Whiddon, Harry Hawk, Old Uncle Tom Cobbleigh and all.
>
> TRADITIONAL

THE NEED FOR SURNAMES

The date when surnames first came to be used in England can be determined fairly simply. Records of one sort or another—wills, grants of land,

From *The Spell of Words,* by John and Joan Levitt. Published by Darwen Finlayson, Ltd., Shopwyke Hall, Chichester, Sussex, England. Copyright © 1959 by John and Joan Levitt and published by their permission.

royal writs and charters—have been kept in this country from long before the Norman Conquest. After 1066, there were many more records. Domesday Book, completed in 1087, was the Conqueror's first inventory of his new dominions, and the first great expression of the Norman genius for administration. After that, until the present, the volume of paper-work produced by government (and by other activities of society) has been ever-increasing.

It is possible to see, from these records, that surnames came gradually into use in this country between 1066 and about 1400. Before 1066, a person usually had one name only—a Christian name, belonging to himself and not necessarily to his father or grandfather. After 1400, people almost always had a family surname as well as a Christian name, as we have today. (This happened in England before it happened in Wales or Scotland.) Almost all the names now in use have a history going back to this period, after which very few new names appeared.

The growth of surnames is a consequence of two things: the growth of population, and the expansion of government. A small population living an almost unchanging life in small villages could manage quite well with no more than one name for each person. Such communities would probably have a big enough store of names from which to choose, when naming their children; so that the confusion caused by two people having the same name and living in the same village need not arise too frequently. Occasions when their names would need recording would be rare. If, however, the population of the country and of the local communities in it grows, it is clear that this system might prove inadequate.

It is thought that the population of England rose from about two millions in 1066 to about four millions in 1400. Towns were larger and more numerous; people travelled from place to place more often; trade brought more strangers into contact with each other.

At the same time, the Conquest gave England a line of kings with a genius for government. There was both a need for more systematic administration, and an ability in the Normans to fill that need. Under William and his successors, as has been said, records become more elaborate and voluminous. The old system of "one man, one name" was no longer workable, and had to be replaced. This replacement was gradual; it took about three centuries to complete; and by 1400 the present system had come into being.

The present system is of course one whereby surnames belong to families, and are handed down unchanged in the male line from one generation to the next. There was a time when an earlier system was in use, though only for occasional men. The last English king before the Conquest was Harold, the son of Godwin. Harold was known as *Harold Godwinsson*—Harold, son of Godwin. This is a surname of sorts; Harold bore it all through his life. But it was not a *family* name, it was a *personal* one. Harold's father, Godwin was not called *Godwinsson*—he really *was* Godwin. And Harold's son would not have been called that either; he would have been *Haroldsson*. Harold's second name was thus not passed down from one generation to another, but it was used as a surname in all other ways. It is easy to see the difference between this and the modern system; and it is also easy to see how this system could change into the modern one fairly naturally. It did in fact do so.

THE TYPES OF SURNAMES

In the foregoing section we approached the questions "When," "Where?," and "Why?" surnames came about. The question "How?" still requires an answer.

Surnames, it has been seen, arose to avoid confusion between people. If we can imagine a situation in which surnames have ceased to exist, we may think of ways in which they could have come to exist. Suppose it were necessary to distinguish two people who had the same single Christian name, and no other name. It would be necessary, in talking about them, to distinguish them from each other by alluding to the things which they did not have in common. If, for instance, the names of their fathers were known and were not identical, this would be helpful. "Jack, Harry's son" could be distinguished from "Jack, Will's son". Alternatively, these two people might follow different trades; in which case "Jack, the Miller" could be distinguished from "Jack, the Weaver". If they lived in different places, or came originally from different towns or villages, there would be a third way. Thus "Jack from the Wood" or "Jack from Lincoln" would be all that was needed. Finally, these men may have personal characteristics which could be referred to; in other words, they could be given nicknames. These, then, are four possible ways of solving the problem, and it is curiously difficult to see any other ways. In fact, all surnames started in one or other of these four ways.

Names which distinguish a person by reference to his father are known as *patronymics*. Those which refer to a person's trade or calling are *occupational names*. Names which refer to a person's home, or place of origin, are *local names*; and the fourth class is that of *nicknames*.

PATRONYMICS

Names in this class are on the whole easy to pick out; and the easiest of all are those which end in *-son*: *Harrison*—"the son of Harry"; *Johnson*—"the son of John"; and similarly, *Edwardson, Thomson, Robertson, Williamson*, etc.

Not all patronymics end in -*son*, however; the ending -*s* is also common. (This is simply the possessive ending of a word, written today as the "apostrophe *s*." *William Johns* is "John's William", or "William, Son of John". Similar surnames are *Jacks, Edwards, Thoms, Roberts, Jones, Williams*, and *Evans*. (Many of these are Welsh; Welsh surnames include more patronymics than English.) There was a famous Yorkshire public house, the scene of an ancient murder and now demolished, called "The Bills o' Jacks". This shows the beginnings of patronymics of this sort.

Surnames of this sort become more complicated when "pet" forms of the Christian names involved in them are considered. Today, the name *Robert* is often shortened to *Rob*; and this may be given an affectionate ending, as in *Robbie*; or it may become *Bob*, or *Bobbie*. Many other Christian names have similar shortened or affectionate forms. This is no new thing, although in the past the pet forms for common names were not always those we use today. *Robert*, in the three centuries of which we are writing, could be *Rob, Robin*, or *Hob*. Moreover, in the way that we today often add -*ie* or -*y* to a name—*Billy*, for instance—our ancestors would often add -*kin* or -*lin*. (*Tamlin*, the hero of an old ballad, is "Little Tom".) Any of these pet forms could be used to form surnames; and surnames could be formed from them by either the -*son* or the -*s* endings. So, from the name *Robert*, with its pet forms *Rob, Robin, Hob, Hobkin*, etc., there could arise the following, all meaning "son of Robert": *Robertson, Roberts, Hobson, Hobbes, Robson, Robinson, Robbins, Robens*, (the last two being merely alternative spellings), *Hopkinson*, and *Hopkins*. In the same way, from *Richard* could arise *Richards, Richardson, Dickson, Dixon, Dicks, Dickinson, Dickens, Hickson, Higson, Hicks, Hickes, Higginson*, and possibly others. From *Thomas*: *Thomas, Thomasson, Thomson, Thompson, Tomson, Thoms, Tomlinson, Tomkinson, Tomlins*, etc.

Occasionally the -*son* or -*s* endings are added, not to the Christian name, but to the occupational name of a person's father to give a patronymic. These names are of a mixed form, therefore. The nursery rhyme tells of Tom the piper's son; in the same way, *Smithson* is the smith's son, *Taylorson* the tailor's, and so forth.

In Scotland and Wales other ways were used to make patronymics. Instead of the -*son* ending, as in England, the word *Mac* was used at the beginning of the name. *MacPherson* is "son of the parson"; *MacNab*, "the son of the abbot", etc.

The Welsh equivalent of -*son* is the small word *ap*, placed before the name and having the same meaning. But the rather complicated sound-changes that occur in the Welsh language have often confused the picture. *Ap* often fuses with the word which follows it, and becomes altered in form. The vowel may drop out; and the *p* may survive as either a *p*, a *b*, or an *f*. The name *Lloyd* in this way would give, first, *ap Lloyd*; and this may survive today as *Flood, Blood*, or *Floyd*. *Preece* is *ap Rhys*; *Probert* is from *Robert*;

and so too is *Probyn* (*ap Robin*). *Prothero* comes from *Roderick,* and *Apjohn, Upjohn* and *Applejohn* from *John.*

OCCUPATIONAL NAMES

Many of these—and there are many of them—are easy to understand. Where they become difficult is in those occupations which are no longer followed today. *Clark, Miller, Baker, Smith, Carpenter, Tailor,* and others —these mean what they say. If the reader bears a name such as this, it is probable that at least one of his ancestors followed the calling it indicates.

Of obsolete words which survive in surnames and indicate occupations which have either died out or are now called something different, the name *Theaker* is interesting. It occurs in this form in the north, and shows marks of the dialects which were spoken in areas of Danish occupation. The equivalent southern form of it is *Thatcher.* The name is not a very unusual one, and its extent shows the importance of the thatcher before the days of tiled roofs.

A *Chandler* was a candle-maker; a *Fletcher* was the same as an *Arrowsmith*—the first of these is a word of French origin, and the second is native English. A *Barker* was a *Tanner*—bark is used in tanning. A *Chapman* was a merchant, usually travelling about the countryside; connected with this name are the words *chaffer* ("to haggle"), *chapbook* (a small book of ballads or popular tales, sold in markets and on thresholds); and the place-name *Cheapside,* the site of a market. A *Webster* was a *Weaver.*

It is amusing to notice that some aristocratic names are occupational in origin; though the occupations they are taken from may be themselves quite humble in their beginnings. A *Marshall* is a dignified figure in State processions, and so forth; the name itself comes from a word which meant "horsegroom". The royal name *Stuart* is from the word "steward"; and *steward* itself is *stye-ward*—the man who looked after the styes.

LOCAL NAMES

Local names are of two sorts. First, there are the actual names of places —villages, towns or hamlets. These would probably be applied to a person moving into a new locality. A man from Lincoln might be called "Jack from Lincoln", or perhaps "Jack o'Lincoln", if he went to live elsewhere; but he would be unlikely to gain this name if he remained in the town of his birth, since it would serve no distinguishing purpose.

Examples of particular place-names which have given rise to surnames are: *Preston, Lancaster, Carlisle* (or *Carlyle*), *Manchester, Doncaster,* and

Churchill.[1] The last of these shows that a place need be neither large nor well-known to give rise to a surname; it is a fairly common place name—there are at least eight places bearing it—but all of them are small and none particularly famous.

Of course, when a surname has been traced to a place-name, its final origin has not been discovered; for it is then natural to ask about the origin of the place-name itself. . . .

The second group of local surnames are formed from words which do not refer to places which necessarily have proper names of their own, but to features of the countryside which may be found close to any settlement in which people live. *Hill, Brook, Beck, Wood, Mill,* and *Bridge*; names like this are sufficient to identify a man in his own village. Take a village on the slopes of a hill, with a large wood nearby, and a stream or beck below it. Each of these features may have its own particular name. The hill may be *Castle Hill*; the wood, *Mollicar Wood*, and the stream, *Fenay Beck*. Yet, to distinguish a man who lived on Castle Hill, "John from the Hill" would be enough of a name to give him.

It is worth noticing that these "topographical" names, as they are called, need not always refer to natural features of the landscape; man-made features will be equally useful. The examples of *Mill* and *Bridge* are found frequently enough, and others can easily be added.

NICKNAMES

Nicknames form a much less definite class, and are on the whole harder to understand. There are still many names whose origins are not clear, and these tend to be treated as nicknames if they are fairly clearly neither patronymics, occupational names nor local names.

It is impossible, also, to arrange nicknames into groups as neatly as other classes. Men can gain nicknames for all sorts of reasons: their personal appearance, their habits, their favourite oaths, the fact that they once played a part in amateur dramatics, and almost anything else.

Some of the more obvious nicknames are those referring to personal appearance. *Redhead* is one; *Blacklock* almost certainly belonged to a dark-haired man; *Beard* and *Tooth* explain themselves; and *Prettybody* needs little thinking about. Some personal appearance names are not, by modern standards, very nice; the Norfolk name of *Whalebelly* is an instance.

Some names come about, apparently, because of the sort of clothes people wore. *Bracegirdle* is one example, and *Shorthouse* (which is "short hose") is another.

---

[1] The syllable *-ton* meant enclosure, farm, town; *-caster* and *-chester* meant a fortified Roman city; *Carlisle* originally meant city of Lugus, a Celtic god. [eds.]

A strange little group of names actually refer to what were presumably the favourite oaths of their first possessors. *Pardy* or *Purdy* is from the French words "par Dieu." *Godbehere* is from an English oath which needs no translation.

Habits and characteristic gestures may give rise to other nicknames. There has been, from time to time, a certain amount of fanciful speculation about the name *Shakespeare*; and all of it has been unnecessary, for the name means exactly what one would expect it to mean. If a parallel name is required, one can point to *Wagstaffe*, which suggests a similar sort of gesture. *Drinkwater* is an English name of the same meaning as the French name *Boileau*; clearly, a nickname given to an early abstainer. *Doolittle* again means what it says; and *Lovelace* is probably from "love-lass"—a name given to a young man, perhaps, whose fancy too lightly turned to thoughts of love.

THE SPELLINGS OF SURNAMES

The search for the origins of surnames is often complicated by the fact that different spellings for the same name are often adopted by different families—who may also dictate their own preferences as to the pronunciation of the names. Some of these family varieties are only slightly different from each other; *Smythe* is recognisable as *Smith*, and *ffellowes* uses no more than an old typographical convention of doubling a letter instead of making a capital. But others are more difficult.

These facts mean that, though anyone can guess at a name, and though the outlines of the study of surnames are fairly simple, the detailed investigation of them is unfortunately a matter for experts. The ordinary reader would be well advised to refer to them. The recently published *Dictionary of British Surnames*, by P. H. Reaney, is an excellent reference book.

Editors' note: Most of the names discussed above are of British origin. In the United States the name situation is complicated by the fact that many immigrant groups brought names from their native countries. These fall into the same general categories given above, but are disguised by the foreign language. Thus, German *Schneider* is a tailor, an occupational name. Greek *Giannopoulos* is the son of John, a patronymic. Swedish *Sjöstrand* is seashore, a place name. French *Bon Coeur* is good heart, a nickname. Names in a foreign language often undergo a change in our country, to make them appear English, or to shorten them, or to make them more pronounceable for Americans. Much information is given on such changes in H. L. Mencken's *The American Language*, in the one-volume edition abridged by Raven I. McDavid, Jr., published in 1963, on pages 572–610.

SURNAMES OF SOME ENGLISH POETS

BLAKE	= "Black". Dark-complexioned.	*Nickname*
BUTLER	From French, *Bouteillier*. The servant in charge of the wine (Bottles).	*Occupational*
BYRON	*Either* from Byron: Place name (Lancs and W. Yorks).	*Place-name*
	Or from "At the byres" = "he who lives at the cowsheds".	*Topographical*
COLERIDGE	Perhaps from Coldridge in Devon; "ridge where charcoal was burned".	*Place-name*
COWPER	="Cooper". Cask-maker.	*Occupational*
DONNE	="Dunn". Dark or swarthy.	*Nickname*
DRINKWATER	—means what it says.	*Nickname*
DOWSON	Son of Dow = David (pet form).	*Patronymic*
GRAY	*Either* "Grey-haired"	*Nickname*
	Or from Graye in Normandy.	*Place-name*
HOGG	"Pig".	*Nickname*
HUNT	From Old English *hunta* "hunter".	*Occupational*
KEATS	*Either* from *kite*—a rapacious person	*Nickname*
	Or from Old English *cyte* = "a hut", possibly for sheep; so "herdsman".	*Occupational*
LOVELACE	"Love-lass"; nickname for a libertine.	*Nickname*
MILTON	Many places are called this; "the Middle place" or "the place with the mill".	*Place-name*
POPE	"Pope". Nickname for either a solemn man, or one who played the Pope in a pageant play.	*Nickname*
SHELLEY	Six or seven places are called this.	*Place-name*
SUCKLING	from "to suck".	*Nickname*
TENNYSON	= Dennison, etc. Son of Dennis.	*Patronymic*
WALLER	*Either* "a builder of walls";	*Occupational*
	"a dweller by a stream",	*Topographical*
	or "a coxcomb."	*Nickname*
YEATS	From Old English *geat* "gate" = "a barrier or opening". One who dwells there.	*Topographical*

SUGGESTED ASSIGNMENTS

1. The following are the eighteen most frequently occurring surnames in the United States, listed according to order of frequency: Smith, Johnson, Brown,

Williams, Miller, Jones, Davis, Anderson, Wilson, Taylor, Thomas, Moore, White, Martin, Thompson, Jackson, Harris, and Lewis. Classify as many as you can into these categories:

Category	Examples
1. Patronymic	MacDonald, Olson
2. Occupational names	Baker, Carpenter
3. Local names (of places)	Brook, Newton
4. Nicknames	Drinkwater, Moody, Stout

2. Another frequency list, this one containing the top twenty-one names in New York City, gives us the following new names: Cohen, Green, Lee, Schwartz, White, Levy, Levine, Rodriguez, Friedman, Taylor, Clark. Classify as many as you can into the categories above.

3. Write a short theme on "Choosing a Name for a Baby Girl." Use your student directory for a list of possible names. As you look over the names, you will probably notice various categories, such as floral (Rose), Biblical (Sarah), mythological (Diana), descriptive (Constance), feminine form of masculine name (Josephine). These classes may suggest ideas for your theme.

Place Names

George R. Stewart

To investigate the origins of place names is an alluring pursuit. Some names, like *Blooming Prairie*, are transparent; others, like *What Cheer*, kindle the imagination. In the United States, with its written records and recent history, such investigation is less onerous than in Great Britain. There we find place names that go back to prehistoric times, and only painstaking linguistic and historical research can recover their sources. Dr. George R. Stewart, professor emeritus at the University of California (Berkeley), has published widely in biography, American folkways, and place names. His latest book is a highly lauded dictionary entitled *American Place Names*.

From "Names [in Linguistics]" in the *Encyclopaedia Britannica*. 14th ed. Reprinted by permission of the publishers.

The giving of local names depends, much like that of personal names, upon (1) a sense that a place is an entity which possesses an individuality differentiating it from other places, and (2) a sense that a place is useful and therefore worth naming. The recognition of these requirements necessitates no high degree of intelligence and onomastic reaction is easy. Hence place names arose at a very early period, and occur in all recorded languages.

Originally place names need not have been fully differentiated from common nouns. Just as people now living near a large river say ordinarily "the river," so a primitive tribe thus located, and perhaps knowing no other river, must have spoken. Place naming in a fuller sense would have begun when the people recognized two examples of the same class, and distinguished "the red river" from "the black river," whence eventually Red river and Black river. The original quasi-place name thus became what is now called, by biological analogy, the *generic* (river), and the element used to distinguish between examples of the same class became the *specific* (red, black). This principle, in fact, it not limited to toponomy, or to nomenclature in general—*father* may be any father or *Father* (Jones). In many instances, however, the development proceeded conversely, so that the original common noun became a specific, *e.g.*, from Anglo-Saxon words meaning "the river" several English streams now bear the name Ray or Rea.

The specific-generic principle of place naming, which is highly efficient and so widespread as to be considered universal, rests upon the basic linguistic principle of classification. Ordinary practice in most languages permits the combination of generic and specific into one "word," *e.g.*, Charlestown, and also the omission of either half under the proper circumstances, so that people may say or write either "the Ohio," or "the river," at the same time knowing the full name to be "the Ohio river." In English the specific generally precedes, but it may follow (Lake Mead) or be appended in a phrase (the Bay of Islands).

In spite of the widespread use of the specific-generic principle, different languages naturally differ in their methods of forming place names. . . . French and Greek employ the article more freely than English does, but Latin lacks an article and so cannot omit it as a mark of a name. The fully developed place name in English generally omits the article; *e.g.*, France, Long Island. The article, however, is used with plurals (the British Isles), and commonly with certain generics, *e.g.*, desert, sea.

This complicated subject of the omission of the article is involved in English with the distinction between evolved and bestowed names. The former begin as mere makeshift identifications; *e.g.*, "the river where the pine trees grow." This can become "the river of the pines," and then "the pine river," and finally "Pine river," or the evolution may be somewhere arrested. At a point sometimes difficult to sense the identification assumes the quality of a name. Bestowed names, on the contrary, arise when a place is consciously labeled by some definite act of naming. Since such a name is likely to be a fully developed one, evolution does not commonly occur, although it may take over to simplify an overcomplicated name, as when El Pueblo de la Reina de los Angeles de la Porciúncula is shortened to Los Angeles.[1]

The giving of place names, as already stated, depends upon entity and use. Primitive peoples, lacking large geographical conceptions, have names for small and obviously useful natural features such as springs, but are not likely to have a sense of the entity of a long river or to have any sense of its usefulness as a whole. Therefore they may not have a single name for it, but may have names of particular pools, reaches and rapids. A mountain is likely to be even harder to conceive as an entity; a range of mountains, still more so. As knowledge increases, larger features are named, often by the process of extending a name in its application; for instance, Italy, Africa and Siberia were originally but small parts of the areas later so denominated. With the development of civilization and geographical knowledge names must be applied to larger and more abstract entities, such as oceans, continents and archipelagos, and eventually to features such as submarine basins, of which earlier peoples were necessarily ignorant.

At the same time a developing civilization gives rise to numerous man-created entities, such as villages, towns, fortresses, provinces and streets, and these also are named. A significant distinction, however, exists between such names and those of natural features. The man-created entities are somewhat less definitely "places" than are natural features, being less surely connected with an actual spot. Towns have changed location, moving the name with them. Primitive villages may bear merely the tribal name, and shift location with the tribal migrations. Even a modern city is often conceived as consisting not of the place, but of the people; its name, then, approaches the status of a collective personal name. In addition, any sovereign or corporate entity such as a city or state possesses a name much as a corporation does. Nevertheless these "habitation-names" are usually considered to be place names, partly because they have a geographically definable location and partly because many of them, such as Liverpool, go back to evolved names of natural features. More doubtful, but sometimes considered to be place names, are the names of such things as bridges, tunnels and individual buildings.

TYPES OF SPECIFICS

The number of specifics is very large, but their usage may be considered under nine heads, and a useful classification of place names thus results, even though the existence of many borderline examples must be recognized.

---

[1] The Spanish name means "The City of the Queen of the Angels of the Little Portion." Porciúncula is a Franciscan shrine near Assisi, Italy. [eds.]

It must also be emphasized that this classification is of kinds of usage, not of the specifics themselves. Thus a specific such as Lincoln might give rise, according to circumstances, to an incident name, a possessive name, a commemorative name or even to something else.

Descriptive names employ a specific indicating a long-enduring quality of the generic (Clear brook, Roaring river, Stinking spring, Pliocene ridge). Less purely descriptive, but generally so classified, are names that identify by means of a possibly impermanent association (Boundary mountain, Mill river, Lone Pine creek). Similar to these latter are the relative descriptive names which identify by indicating a relation to something else (North sea, Ten Mile creek, Fourth crossing). Many counterpart names thus arise, *e.g.*, Big river may not actually be very large, but may be named because it is larger than a neighbouring Little river.

Incident names arise from an incident occurring at the place and making it memorable (Massacre lake, Hungry Moose creek). Names of persons are often applied to natural features for this reason, as are also the names of animals. Thus, Crocodile river need not indicate that those beasts were especially numerous there, but merely that a single crocodile happened to impress himself upon early explorers. Nearly all names used by primitive peoples are either descriptive or incident names.

Possessive names spring from the idea of ownership, whether legal or informal (Culp's hill, Bakersfield), though the possessive form of the noun need not be maintained. Under this heading may be included most ethnic names (Zululand, Cheyenne river) and many mythological names derived from the names of gods and spirits. These two subclasses, however, are also closely connected with associative-descriptives and with commemorative names. Possessive names appear at an early stage of culture, but probably arise subsequently to the first two classes.

Commemorative names are those given consciously "in honour of" someone or something (many religious and patriotic namings); here are to be included most transfer names (Megara from Greece to Sicily; Boston from England to the United States).

Euphemistic names are those bestowed with the idea of making a good impression or establishing favourable auspices (Euxine sea, Beneventum, Greenland, Cape of Good Hope). Commemorative and euphemistic names may be considered to arise somewhat later in cultural development than the above-mentioned classes.

Manufactured names are those constructed from recombined sounds or letters, out of fragments of old words, from initials, by backward spellings etc. (Tesnus, from Sunset; Tonolo, from an arrangement of selected letters). Such names are probably of comparatively late origin; no certain example seems to be known before 1600.

Shift names result from the mere shift of the specific from one generic to another in the vicinity (White lake, though it may not be white, takes that name because it is near White mountain). The resulting group is called a *name-cluster*.

Folk-etymologies, though they may be said merely to transform old names, really produce what are essentially new names, through the mishearing and misinterpretation of an obsolete or foreign word (Picketwire from Purgatoire)....[2]

Mistake names arise from failure in transmission, either oral or written (Oregon, from an error on a map). These last three classes differ from the others in that they arise secondarily from other names, and seldom by a conscious process of naming.

The number of names in a given area will be greater because of any factor that increases the number of places easily to be conceived as having entity (*e.g.*, more variegated topography), and also because of any factor leading to more intensive use of land (*e.g., denser population*). Longer continuous linguistic and cultural tradition is also an important factor, since names established for any reason tend to persist. From such factors, and doubtless from others less easily appraised, spring varying local habits of name giving: thus in some countries every farm and even every field bears a name, but elsewhere such units do not. The density of names thus differs greatly in different areas (according to estimates. South Dakota, .2 to the sq. mi.; U.S., 1; Keos, Greek island, 17; Norway, 40; Bohuslän, Swedish province, 150). Such differences, however, result partly from differences in judgment as to what is to be considered a place name.

Notable periods of naming occur when an uninhabited country is being explored or developed, or when the speakers of a new language are imposing themselves upon a country. In such periods not only are names established for the most important natural features but also for many of the habitation sites that will later become the cities. Because of the general turmoil associated with such a situation, the names are lakely to be impermanent. Thus, during the period of the settling of the United States, thousands of names appeared, only to disappear; five once-current European names are recorded for Hudson river, in addition to North river, still in limited use.

Once established firmly, however, place names cling with great pertinacity, and frequently survive, though suffering great change of form, even through periods of shift in population and language.[3] This tenacity renders place

---

[2] Folk etymology is the process of changing the form of a word to make it more understandable and more like familiar English words. Examples: (1) In Arkansas a town that had been named *De Geoijen* after a Dutch capitalist was folk-etymologized to *De Queen*. (2) In England the Cornish place name *Pen Lestyn* (= chief lodging place) was changed by folk etymology to *Palestine*. [eds.]

[3] A good example is *York*. In early Celtic this name was *Eboracon*. In the ninth century the Anglo-Saxons changed it to *Eferwic*, abandoning the meaningless *-acon* and substituting -wic, their word for village. Later they changed the first part of the name to *eofor*, boar. So, by now, the name had become completely understandable—*Eoforwic*, boar village. Then came the Scandinavians, who wrote the name as *Iórvik*; and finally, by the thirteenth century, it had evolved to *York*. [eds.]

names valuable to the study of history and prehistory, and necessitates careful study of the alterations to which they are subject. In general, being a part of language, place names change pronunciation along with the rest of the language. Thus, when the pronunciation of English vowels shifted in the later middle ages, this change occurred in place names as in other words. Certain special factors, however, must be noted. (1) Place names, consisting of specific-generic, are on the average at least twice as long as ordinary words, and so are especially subject to the linguistic forces applicable to long words. (2) Many place names, whether because originally from foreign words or because long-enduring and therefore affected by the obsolescence of native words, are or become meaningless to the ordinary speaker, and thus are peculiarly subject to the processes of folk-etymology. (3) The usage of most place names is highly local, and they are thus susceptible to dialectal variation and even to personal whim. Place names thus tend to depart from the rest of the language and to become unintelligible to the ordinary person, except insofar as they are "re-interpreted" by folk-etymology. By means of earlier recorded forms and by the methods of comparative philology, however, the trained linguist is able to penetrate most of the disguises, and even the most cryptic are not beyond his attempts. As a result the study of place names has proved highly rewarding, and has been assiduously pursued during the 20th century, particularly in western Europe. . . .

PLACE NAMES OF THE UNITED STATES

The place-name pattern of the United States is typical for countries whose development lies mainly in the historical period. The discoverers found a situation such as is to be expected in a region thinly inhabited by primitive tribes. Names were rather sparse; they were descriptive or incident names; according to the principles of entity and use only such features were named as were of interest to a primitive people and were recognizable by them. Europeans adopted some of these names, but since these were generally unintelligible, they were used as mere counters and often misapplied. Thus Connecticut, "at the long estuary," applying only to the river near its mouth, was extended to the whole stream, and then to the colony. At a later period Indian names that had acquired sentimental value were transferred to new sites; a striking example is Wyoming, originally applied to a small valley in Pennsylvania.

Much more commonly the Europeans, of whatever nationality, gave names in their own languages. These were often descriptive (Colorado river, Marblehead, Detroit), or sprang from incidents (Cape Fear, Ranchería de la Espada). Many were commemoratives (Virginia, numerous saints' names in French and Spanish territory), and many of these were transferred from "the old country" (Thames river, Harlem). During more than three centuries, while the country was being explored and settled, thousands of names, and eventually millions, arose by bestowal and evolution. All possible methods of naming were represented; all phases of the history and social development of the American people were enshrined in the names. Enlarged geographical conceptions and an increased density of population resulted in more and more naming. The necessity of establishing so many names in such a short time, because of the rapidity of settlement, resulted in much repetition and in a great use of transfer names taken in seemingly haphazard fashion from various parts of the world; *e.g.*, Toledo, Athens, Odessa. Nevertheless not a little ingenuity was also displayed, and occasionally some sense of poetry, as in John Frémont's naming of the Golden Gate.

The typically American use of the manufactured name seems to have arisen in an attempt to gain more variety. Although beginning as early as Saybrook (1635), it was a special development of the last half of the nineteenth century and subsequently. Many manufactured names are *boundary names*, such as Calexico and Mexicali (both from California and Mexico), and Texarkana (from Texas, Arkansas and Louisiana).

Toward the end of the nineteenth century the "big names" had all been fixed, and the process became one of filling in. Significant dates are the fixing of the last state-name (Wyoming. 1868) and the establishment of the Board on Geographical Names (1890), a federal agency to regulate governmental naming. Place-naming in the United States, however, is still in a comparatively active period because of the constant naming of towns, districts and streets, and the filling-in by the naming of lesser natural features.

PLACE-NAME SCHOLARSHIP

As a result of the differences in the nature of the problems in Europe and in the United States, the method and interest of onomatologists have differed greatly. European scholars, lacking historical information, have generally worked by linguistic methods, drawing what help they could from geography, history and anthropology. They have been essentially etymologists. The usual European scholar has little interest in names that have arisen since the middle ages, and are therefore of no etymological interest. Many European scholars have been intensely concerned with the ancillary use of place-name study as a tool for the investigation of prehistory.

American scholars rely mainly on the methodology of history. Not primarily etymologists, they are likely to consider the establishment of the etymology as a mere primary step, of not much significance unless the reason for the application can be established. They are more likely than European scholars to be informed as to the processes of place-naming and more likely to be interested in recent and current naming.

Since the study of place names deals with an important human activity, it is justified in its own right, but it is also of ancillary value to many other studies, such as linguistics, history, geography, archaeology, anthropology and folklore. A zoologist may study place names to establish the former habitat of an animal. Probably the greatest "external" triumphs of the study have been in connection with the establishment of the locations, and something of the social organizations, of various peoples when historical records are lacking. Thus place names make certain a Saxon occupation of the Calais region in France at some time during the period of Germanic migrations. Similarly such study, almost without historical aid, has established that many Norwegians settled in northwestern England (about 900), and is even able to support the assertion that these came in small groups, not in an invading army, had an Irish element mingled with them, and lived on comparatively peaceable terms with the English.

Nevertheless, evidence derived from the study of place names must be used with caution, and is seldom conclusive except when a whole "pattern" can be demonstrated. Individual names may show close resemblance or even be identical as the result of coincidence, as with Georgia in the Caucasus and Georgia, U.S., or Miami (Ohio) and Miami (Fla.), and many others. In the newer countries, such as those of both the Americas, there has been constant transfer of names at a sophisticated level and for what may be called somewhat extraneous reasons. Thus California has been shown to be derived from a Spanish romance. Corinto in Nicaragua resembles the Greek Corinth only by being a port. Odessa in the U.S. may indicate not a settlement of Ukrainians but a wheat-growing district.

Without historical evidence coincidences are often baffling, as with the three widely separated tribes known to the ancient Greeks as Enetoi. Such cruxes can only be approached by a meticulous combination of linguistic, historical, archaeological, geographical and anthropological techniques.

SUGGESTED ASSIGNMENTS

1. Of the hundreds of morphemes (= meaningful parts) that enter into English place names, here are a few of the more common ones, together with their meanings. You will use these in the exercise which follows. Self-evident ones have been omitted, those like *hill, ridge, pool, stone, mouth, wood, ford*

1. ac	oak	30. hurst	wooded hill
2. ash	ash tree	31. ing	son of; descendent of; follower of, dweller at
3. bar	barley	32. kirk	kirk, church
4. bent	bent grass	33. Lan	river Lune
5. berk	birch	34. lang	long

6. borough   fortified town
7. brad   broad
8. buck   Bucca (proper name)
9. bur   (same as *borough*)
10. burn   stream
11. bury   (same as borough)
12. by   town
13. caster   Roman fort or city
14. chester   (same as *caster*)
15. chis   cheese
16. clif   cliff
17. combe   valley
18. comp   (same as *combe*)
19. dal, dale   valley
20. der   animal
21. dor   Dorset
22. dun   hill

23. farn   fern
24. gate   road, street, way
25. ham   home
26. hamp   (same as *ham*)
27. hart   hart
28. Hast   (Haesta, proper name)
29. hat   heather

35. ley   meadow, lea, grassland
36. mar   pool, lake
37. mere   (same as *mar*)
38. mor   moor
39. nor   north
40. over   river bank
41. rug   rook (bird)
42. sea   lake, sea
43. shaw   grove, wood
44. ship   sheep
45. stan   stone
46. sted, stead   place
47. sut   south
48. thorn   thorn tree
49. thorpe   farmstead, village
50. thwaite   clearing, meadow
51. ton, tun, tin, ten   enclosure, hamlet, town
52. Wassa   (a proper name)
53. whit   white
54. wich   village, farm
55. wick   (same as *wich*)
56. wor-   tribe of Wigoran
57. worth   farm, village

Using the list above, give the original root meanings of the following place names; for example, *Norton* means north town; *Bradwell* means broad well; *Butterwick* means a farm where butter is made.

1. Bradford
2. Norby
3. Sutton
4. Eastthorpe
5. Westbury
6. Highgate
7. Newstead
8. Sandwich
9. Shipley
10. Derby
11. Hartford
12. Berkeley
13. Ashton
14. Buckhurst
15. Blackburn
16. Acton
17. Mapleborough
18. Applethwaite
19. Greensted
20. Seaton
21. Grasmere
22. Butterworth
23. Hasting
24. Buckingham
25. Washington
26. Combe
27. Chester
28. Whitby
29. Dunham
30. Woodcote
31. Barton
32. Bentley
33. Worchester
34. Clifton
35. Compton
36. Cowley
37. Dalton
38. Dorchester
39. Farnsworth
40. Greenwich
41. Hampton
42. Thornbury
43. Oxford
44. Hatfield
45. Oxwick
46. Petersgate
47. Kirby
48. Lancaster
49. Langdon
50. Martin
51. Morton
52. Morby
53. Norwich
54. Norfolk
55. Overton
56. Shaw
57. Shipley
58. Stanford
59. Burnham
60. Fishwick

2. Open a road map of your state and spend half an hour classifying as many names as you can according to the first five classes of Stewart's nine-point classification. You will have to guess at times, but some of your guesses can be checked in class by the use of Stewart's *American Place Names*.

3. Many common nouns have come from place names. Look up the source of the following words: *jeans, denim, sandwich, wiener, hamburger, frankfurter, bologna, jovial, cashmere, pheasant, sherry, port, bourbon, gin, limousine, cantaloupe.*

FURTHER READINGS

Ekwall, Eilert. *A Concise Oxford Dictionary of English Place-Names*, 4th ed. Oxford: Oxford University Press, 1960.

Hughes, James P. *How You Got Your Name*. London: Phoenix House, 1959.

Matthews, C. M. *English Surnames*. New York: Scribner's Sons, 1966–67.

McKnight, George H. *English Words and Their Backgrounds*. New York: D. Appleton, 1923. See Chapters XXIV and XXV.

Mencken, H. L. *The American Language*, 4th ed., and the two Supplements abridged, with annotations and new material, by Raven I. McDavid, Jr. New York: Alfred A. Knopf, 1963. See Chapter X.

Reaney, P. H. *The Origin of English Place-Names*. London: Routledge and Kegan Paul, 1960.

————. *The Origin of English Surnames*. New York: Barnes and Noble, 1967.

Smith, Elsdon C. *The Story of Our Names*. New York: Harper & Row, 1950.

Stewart, George R. *American Place-Names*. New York: Oxford University Press, 1970.

Weekley, Ernest. *Surnames*. New York: E. P. Dutton, 1927.

Withycombe, E. G. *Oxford Dictionary of English Christian Names*. New York: Oxford University Press, 1944.

7
THE SOUNDS
OF LANGUAGE

The Sound System of English

Norman C. Stageberg

Language is based on speech sounds, not written letters. Writing is a derived form composed of symbols once removed from the original speech sounds. Important as the written symbols are in fastening down and making more or less permanent what otherwise would be gone with the wind, they nonetheless limit our perception of the nature of language. Such basic matters as vowels and consonants, for example, are misunderstood by those who think of them in terms of the letters of the alphabet rather than in terms of the sounds themselves.

This essay deals with matters of fundamental importance in understanding language as a system of sounds, especially with the production and classification of speech sounds. The material is technical but not difficult, and it is fundamental to the three succeeding essays. In fact, you really cannot discuss pronunciation intelligently unless you know how speech sounds are made and what their system is. Since not all linguists use exactly the same set of symbols to represent the sounds of language, the essay is followed by a table of all the symbols that you will meet in the essays of this section.

Adapted from *An Introductory English Grammar*. Reprinted by permission of the publisher, Holt, Rinehart and Winston, Inc., copyright © 1965.

THE SPEECH-PRODUCING MECHANISM

Speech sounds are sound waves created in a moving stream of air. They are disturbances of the medium such as you would observe if you were to drop a stone on the quiet surface of a pool. The air is expelled from the lungs, passes between the two vocal cords in the larynx (Adam's apple), and proceeds upward. As you will note on diagram 1, this moving stream of air has two possible outlets. It can pass through the nasal cavity and emerge through the nose, or it can pass through the oral cavity and come out through the mouth. But why doesn't it go through both passages, which are shown to be open on the diagram? Because in speech one of them is ordinarily closed. And how does this happen? Let us consider the oral sounds first. On diagram 1 you will notice the velum, marked V. This is a movable curtain of flesh. If you will run your finger back along the roof of your mouth, you will feel at first the bony structure of the hard palate, marked *P*. Just behind this hard palate you will feel the soft flesh of the velum. It ends in a pear-shaped pendant, called the uvula, which you can see hanging in your throat if you look in the mirror. Now, when you produce any oral sound, one that goes out through the mouth, for example a-a-a-a-a-a, you at the same time raise the velum until it touches the back of the throat, cutting off the nasal cavity. You can actually see this raising of the velum if you will open your mouth wide, look in the mirror, and say a-a-a-a-a-a several times in succession. The process is illustrated in diagram 2.

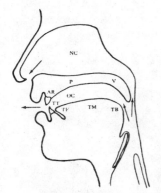

Meaning of abbreviations:
AR = alveolar ridge
NC = nasal cavity
OC = oral cavity
P = soft palate
TT = tongue tip
TF = tongue front
TM = tongue middle
TB = tongue back
V = velum

DIAGRAM 1. Speech-producing mechanism.

Now let us turn from the oral sounds to the nasals, those that pass through the nasal cavity. To make the three nasal sounds of English, you leave the velum in the position shown on diagram 1 and block off the oral cavity in one of three ways: with the lips (diagram 3), with the tongue tip (diagram 4), or with the tongue back (diagram 5).

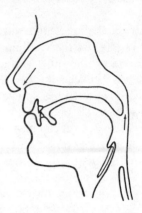

DIAGRAM 2.
  Air passing through oral cavity.
  Tongue position for /a/

DIAGRAM 3.
  Air passing through nasal cavity.
  Lip position for /m/

Thus, with the oral cavity blocked off, the sound can emerge only through the nasal cavity. It is evident now that every speech sound we utter is either an oral or a nasal sound. For illustration of oral and nasal sounds, try pronouncing the list of words below and hold the final sound for some time. As you hold each final sound, stop your nose with your fingers. If this action stops the sound, the sound is obviously a nasal. But if the sound continues, then close your lips. The sound will thereupon be cut off, demonstrating that it is an oral sound. The words are: *rim, saw, bin, see, sing, tall, trim, pain, wrong.* You may wonder about the "nasal twang" that you occasionally hear.

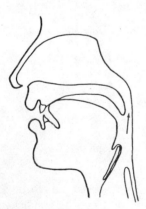

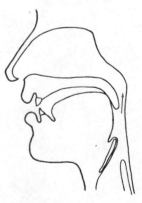

DIAGRAM 4.
  Air passing through nasal cavity.
  Tongue position for /n/

DIAGRAM 5.
  Air passing through nasal cavity.
  Tongue position for /ŋ/

This is caused by the habit of slightly lowering the velum for sounds that are normally oral, thus permitting some of the air to go out through the nasal cavity. You have now learned the three nasals of English, which we symbolize in a special notation as /m/, /n/, and /ŋ/. The /m/ is a bilabial nasal, made by closing the two lips. The /n/ is an alveolar nasal, made by stopping the flow of air with the tongue tip against the alveolar ridge. The /ŋ/ is a velar nasal, made by stopping the flow of air with the back of the tongue against the velum. In all three the air moves through the nasal cavity. They are illustrated on diagrams 3, 4, and 5. But one element is missing from our description of the three nasals. Where does the sound come from? To answer this question we must examine the vocal cords. Inside the larynx (Adam's apple) are two short bands of flesh and muscle stretching from front to rear. In breathing and during the production of some speech sounds, like *f* and *s*, these are held open, allowing free ingress and egress of air, as shown in diagram 6. But with many sounds they are pressed tightly together, and the air passing between them causes them to vibrate, as shown in diagram 7.

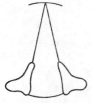

DIAGRAM 6.
Position of vocal cords
during exhalation

DIAGRAM 7.
Position of vocal cords
when vibrating

[Reprinted by permission of the copyright owners, the Regents of the University of Wisconsin, from R.-M.S. Heffner. *General Phonetics,* 1950, the University of Wisconsin Press.]

These vibrations are given resonance by the cavities of the mouth and nose and the result is the phenomenon called voicing. In the making of every speech sound, then, these vocal cords are either vibrating or not vibrating. If they are vibrating, the sound is called voiced. If they are not vibrating, the sound is called voiceless. In order to hear for yourself the voicing and voicelessness of speech sounds, hold your hands tightly over your ears and pronounce the last sound in each of the following words. You will hear clearly the hum of the vibration of your vocal cords for the voiced sounds, and this hum will be absent for the voiceless sounds. The words are: *less, hum, if, pin, sheath, among, mush, fin, song.* Now try the same thing with the first sound of these words: *fine, vine, thin, then, seal, zeal, shock, late, rate.*

THE PHONEME

Before continuing with an inventory of English speech sounds and the ways of producing them, we must clearly understand one basic concept—the phoneme.

The phoneme is easily understood: it is a speech sound that makes a difference in meaning. Consider, for example, the words *dime* and *dine*. They sound exactly alike except for the /m/ and the /n/, yet their meanings are different. Therefore it must be the /m/ and the /n/ which make the difference in meaning, and these two nasals are thereby established as English phonemes. Likewise, if we compare the sounds of *sin* and *sing*, we find only one difference between them: *sin* ends in the alveolar nasal /n/ and *sing* in the velar nasal /ŋ/. (Don't be deceived by the spelling of *sing*; the letters *ng* represent a single sound /ŋ/, one which you can prolong as long as your breath holds out.) This contrast is evidence that /n/ and /ŋ/ are both phonemes. Pairs of words like those above which demonstrate a phonemic contrast are called minimal pairs. A phoneme may be pronounced in different ways, depending on its position in the utterance, and still remain the same phoneme. As an example, let us take /l/. If you pronounce *lit* and *well* slowly and distinctly, you will hear two different [l]s. The second one seems to be preceded by an "uh" sound. With a little practice you can place your tongue tip on the alveolar ridge and change from the first to the second [l] without moving the tongue tip. Now, if you pronounce *well* with the [l] of *lit*, the word will sound different, a little un-English, but the meaning will not be changed. The use of one or the other of these two [l]s never makes a difference in meaning; hence they are not two phonemes but merely variants of the /l/ phoneme. You will sometimes hear still another [l] in words like *play* and *sled*. Here there may be a voiceless [l], whereas the [l]s of both *well* and *lit* were voiced. But whether you pronounce *play* and certain other words with a voiced or a voiceless [l], the meaning remains unchanged; so this third [l] is another variant of the /l/ phoneme. Such variants of a phoneme are called allophones. Allophones are enclosed in brackets with the occasional addition of diacritical marks to indicate the exact pronunciation. Phonemes are enclosed in slants. Thus we may say that the /l/ phoneme has three allophones: [l] as in *lit*, [l] as in *well*, and [l] as in *play*. A phoneme then is not an individual sound but a small family of similar sounds.

With this introduction to the concept of the phoneme, we are now ready to continue the inventory of English phonemes.

THE ENGLISH PHONEMIC SYSTEM: VOWELS

The classification of English vowels is a complex and controversial matter; it is even difficult to define a vowel with precision. But we can make four statements about vowels that will help to show their nature.

1. All vowels are oral sounds. In some dialects and in certain contexts, vowels may become partially nasal, but normally they are orals, not nasals.
2. All vowels are voiced.
3. Vowels are characterized by a free flow of air through the oral cavity.
4. The distinguishing features of the different vowels are determined largely by tongue position.

English may be said to have 12 vowels—five front, four back, and three central vowels—which we shall now take up systematically.

FRONT VOWELS.   If you pronounce the final sound of *be*, symbolized by /i/, and hold the /i/, you will find that the tongue front and middle is humped high in the mouth, leaving a narrow passage for the flow of air between the hard palate and the surface of the tongue. The tongue position of /i/ is the top one on diagram 8. Next, say the same vowel /i/, holding your jaw in your hand, and then say the first sound of *add*, symbolized by /æ/. You will observe a considerable drop of the jaw and some flattening of the tongue. The tongue position of the vowel /æ/ is the bottom one on diagram 8. To fix these differences of position in your mind, hold your jaw and say /i/, /æ/ rapidly a number of times in succession.

Between these two extremes, /i/ and /æ/, are three other vowels. To hear them in order from the top tongue position to the bottom one, pronounce the following words, noting the middle sound: *beat, bit, bait, bet, bat*. Now say just the vowels in the same order, holding your jaw, and observe how the jaw drops a little as each one is uttered. These five vowels are called the FRONT VOWELS, because they are formed in the front of the mouth by the position of the tongue front. For each front vowel the lips are spread, or unrounded. The tongue positions are shown on diagram 8. English spelling cannot be used to represent accurately the speech sounds of English because of its inconsistencies. How, for example, would you symbolize the vowel of *bait* in English spelling? By *ai* as in *wait, eig* as in *reign, ey* as in *they, ay* as in *say, a* as in *late, ei* as in *vein, au* as in *gauge, ea* as in *steak*? So to represent the sounds of words, we shall use a special alphabet in which one symbol always represents one and the same speech sound, and each sound is always represented by only one symbol. In this alphabet the five illustrative words in the preceding paragraph are written as follows:

beat = /bit/   bit = /bɪt/   bait = /bet/   bet = /bɛt/   bat = /bæt/

The phonemic symbols and words written in these symbols are enclosed in slants, like /bɛt/.

BACK VOWELS.   Pronounce the final sound of *too*, symbolized by /u/. For this vowel /u/ the lips are rounded and the back of the tongue is raised to a position near the velum, leaving a little space for the air to flow. The

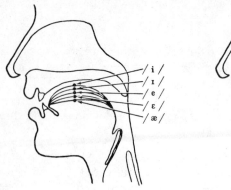
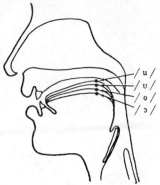

DIAGRAM 8. Front vowels   DIAGRAM 9. Back vowels

tongue position is the top one on diagram 9. Now pronounce the sound you make when you say "aw," as in "Aw, come on." For most Americans this is the vowel of *saw, raw,* and *jaw.* It is symbolized by /ɔ/. The tongue position is the bottom one on diagram 9. Next, utter the vowels /u/ and /ɔ/ in rapid succession, with your hand on your jaw. This will show you the upper and lower extremes of the range of the four vowels that are called back vowels. If you will also look in the mirror while uttering the successive /u/s and /ɔ/s, you will see the close rounding of the lips for /u/ and the open rounding for /ɔ/.

As the back of the tongue is lowered from the /u/ position, it reaches in turn the positions for the three other back vowels: /ʊ/ as in *pull,* /o/ as in *note,* and /ɔ/ as in *ought, law,* and *ball.* And at each of these three positions the rounding of the lips is successively opened, as you can observe in the mirror. The four back vowels, from top to bottom, are illustrated by this series:

fool = /ful/   full = /fʊl/   foal = /fol/   fall = /fɔl/

CENTRAL VOWELS. English has three central vowels. The first central vowel requires special consideration. If you pronounce *fur, sir, her,* you are uttering, as the final sound, a central r-colored vowel, that is, if you belong to the majority of Americans who do not "drop their r's." But there are other Americans who pronounce words like these with a /ə/ plus an r sound, as in hurry /həri/, instead of with the single r-colored vowel. Thus we shall use the pair of symbols /ər/ to represent both pronunciations—the single, central, r-colored vowel and also the schwa[1] plus an r sound.

----

[1] See paragraph below. [eds.]

The second central vowel may be illustrated by the first sound of *up* and *upon*. It is written /ə/, like an upside-down e, and its position is shown in diagram 10. It is heard as the pronunciation of the italic vowels in the following words:

Stressed: s*u*n, d*o*ne, fl*oo*d
Unstressed: sof*a*, *a*lone,
            princ*i*pal, spec*i*men, sci*e*nce,
            kingd*o*m, c*o*nnect,
            diffic*u*lt, s*u*ppose

The /ə/ is a vowel of high frequency in English, especially in unstressed syllables, and is technically called "schwa." . . .

The third central vowel is the sound you make when the doctor says, "Open your mouth wide and say a-a-a-a." For most Americans this is the vowel of *not* and the first vowel of *father*. It is symbolized by /a/. In sounding this vowel you will note that the mouth is widely opened and that the tongue is nearly flat. The tongue position is the bottom one illustrated in diagram 10. The central vowels from, top to bottom, are illustrated in this series:

purr = /pɚr/   pup = /pəp/   pot = /pat/

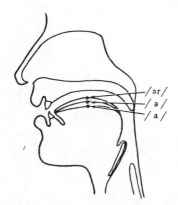

DIAGRAM 10.   Central vowels

The twelve vowel phonemes of English can be seen in relation to one another on the vowel chart below.

This is a two-dimensional grid of tongue positions, the mouth being at the left and the throat at the right. Using this chart we can easily give to the twelve vowels descriptive names which will be useful in discussing them. The names are these:

/i/ High front   /u/ High back rounded
/ɪ/ Lower high front   /ʊ/ Lower high back
                                                        rounded

/e/ Higher mid front   /ər/ Higher mid-
                                  central   /o/ Mid back rounded

·/ɛ/ Lower mid front   /ə/ Lower mid-
                                  central   /ɔ/ Low back rounded

/æ/ Low front   /a/ Low central

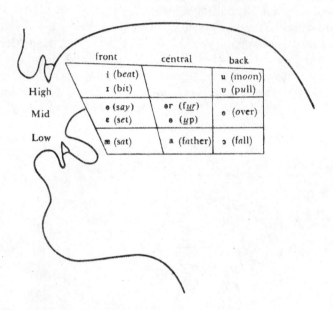

Chart of English vowel phonemes

[Adapted from *Discovering American Dialects* by Roger Shuy. Reprinted by permission of the author and the publisher, The National Council of Teachers of English, copyright, 1967.]

It must be realized that the classification of vowels by tongue position is imprecise and generalized. Also, there are further classifications—tense, lax; close, open; narrow, wide; long, short—that we are bypassing in the interest of a stringent simplicity. But by and large the above description and classification of vowel phonemes will serve for the fleeting glance to which we are limited.

THE SYLLABLE.   Before moving ahead to the next group of phonemes, the diphthongs, it is necessary for us to examine the nature of the syllable.

When we speak we can observe that certain sounds have a greater sonority or carrying power than others. For example, in *soap* /sop/, the /o/ has greater sonority than the /s/ or the /p/, even though all are spoken with equal force. If /sop/ is spoken at some distance from the listener, he may hear distinctly only the /o/. In *potato* /pəteto/, the /ə/, /e/, and /o/ are more sonorous, more audible, that the /p/ and the /t/s. The sounds which have this greater inherent sonority or carrying power are mostly the vowels. Thus, as we utter connected discourse, we become aware of a peak-and-valley effect of sonority or audibility. The peaks of sonority are the vowels; and the valleys of less distinctness are the consonants, as in *echo*/ɛko/, or the slight diminution of loudness, as in *create*/kri-et/. This brings us to the syllable. A syllable is a sound or a short sequence of sounds which contains one peak of sonority. This peak is usually a vowel, and the vowel is said to be the center of the syllable. A segment of speech, then, contains as many syllables as there are peaks. Here are some examples of words with the peaks, or syllabic centers, underlined.

One syllable	be	/bi̱/
	string	/strɪ̱ŋ/
Two syllables	believe	/bə̱liv/
	being	/bi̱ɪŋ/
	stirring	/stə̱rɪŋ/
Three syllables	believing	/bə̱livɪŋ/
Four syllables	unbelieving	/ənbə̱livɪŋ/
Five syllables	unbelievingly	/ənbə̱livɪŋli/

We have seen that the vowels are peaks of sonority and are therefore syllabic centers: But there are four consonants—/m/, /n/, /ŋ/, and /l/—which also have considerable sonority and which can constitute syllables.

As our first example, let us take the two-syllable expression *stop 'em*. This can be uttered in two ways. The first is /stapəm/. After the lips are closed to make the /p/, they are opened for the /ə/, and closed again for the /m/. The second way is /stapm/. Here the lips are closed for the /p/ and remain closed for the /m/. Try it and see for yourself. While you are making the /p/, no air can escape from the mouth. The closed lips shut off the mouth exit and the raised velum shuts off the nasal exit. Now, holding the lips closed, you open the velum by lowering it, and what happens? The air escapes with a slight explosion through the nasal cavity. This is what happens in /stapm/. Here the /m/ is a peak of sonority and by itself constitutes a syllable. This /m/ is called a syllabic /m/. For illustration, pronounce the following, leaving your lips closed at the /p/: *leap 'em, rob 'em, open.* The last will sound like /opm/.

The syllabic /n/ is formed similarly. Consider for example *button.* You may pronounce it /bətən/ by dropping the tongue from the /t/ position on the alveolar ridge, uttering the /ə/, and then replacing the tongue for the /n/. But you can also pronounce *button* without removing the tongue, as in /bətn/. At the /t/ position the air is prevented from escaping by the tongue against the alveolar ridge and by the closed velum, which shuts off the nasal cavity. If you hold the tongue in the /t/ position and open the velum, you will get an /n/ as the air escapes through the nasal cavity. For illustration, pronounce the following words without removing the tongue after it is touching the /t/ position: *beaten, cotton, sudden.* The syllabic /ŋ/, which is less frequent, is heard in expressions like *Jack and Jill,* /jækŋjɪl/. At the /k/ position the air is held in by the back of the tongue against the velum and by the velum, which has been raised to cut off the nasal cavity. With a lowering of the velum, the nasal cavity is opened and the syllabic /ŋ/ is heard. For illustration, pronounce the following expressions without removing the tongue after it has reached the /ŋ/ position: *back and forth, bag and baggage, rack and ruin.* The syllabic /l/ is somewhat differently articulated. To make the common /l/, you place the tongue on the alveolar ridge, vibrate the vocal cords, and let the air flow over and off the tongue on one or both sides and escape through the mouth. Now, to make the syllabic /l/, as in *rattle,* you first have the air completely closed off by the tongue in the /t/ position on the alveolar ridge and by a raised velum cutting off the nasal cavity. Then you open one or both sides of the tongue, without removing the tip from the alveolar ridge, letting the air go around the tongue and out the mouth. As illustration, pronounce the following words by keeping your tongue at the /t/ or /d/ position while pronouncing the syllabic /l/: *cattle, saddle, beetle.*

Although it is easy to locate the peaks of sonority that indicate syllable centers, the vowels and syllabic consonants, it is sometimes impossible to find the boundary between syllables, that is, the point of minimum sonority. In the two-syllable *hushing* /həšɪŋ/, for example, where is the syllable boundary? After the /ə/? Before the /ɪ/? Or in the middle of /š/? It is like trying to establish in a valley the exact line separating the two hills on either side. For our purpose here we need not be much concerned with syllable division, and where the boundary is not audible, we can resort to an arbitrarily selected break.

DIPHTHONGS. A diphthong consists of two vowels which occur in the same syllable, the tongue moving smoothly from one position to the other without hiatus, as in *sigh,* /sai/, *sow* (female pig), /sau/, and *soy,* /sɔi/. The two vowels together represent the peak of sonority, though one always has greater prominence than the other. Many of our vowels are diphthong-

ized in various subareas of English, and four of them are normally diphthongized in Standard English: /i/, /e/, /u/, and /o/. For these, however,
we shall use the symbols just given, since there is no phonemic difference
between the pure vowels and the diphthongized vowels.[2] According to the
system we are using, the diphthong PHONEMES are only three: /ai/ as in *by*,
/au/ as in *bough*, and /ɔi/ as in *boy*. Under the heading of "diphthongs"
we shall consider the "r" sounds. You have already met the /r/ consonant
as in *race* /res/ and the central r-colored vowel as in *cur* /kər/. This leaves
us to consider the "r" sound that occurs after vowels in the same syllable.
Our practice here will be to consider these "r"s as consonantal and to transcribe them with the /r/ symbol, thus: *farm* /farm/; *pore* /por/; *poor*
/pur/; *fair* /fɛr/; *fear* /fɪr/. The symbols /ər/ will be reserved for occasions
when this sound is the center of a syllable, as in the two-syllable *stirring*
/stərɪŋ/ contrasted with the one-syllable *string* /strɪŋ/.

		Labio-dental	Inter-dental	Alveolar	Alveo-palatal	Velar	Glottal
	Bilabial						
Stops							
vl	p			t		k	
vd	b			d		g	
Fricatives							
vl		f	θ	s	š		h
vd		v	ð	z	ž		
Affricates							
vl					č		
vd					ǰ		
Nasals							
	m			n		ŋ	
Lateral							
				l			
Glides							
				r	y	w	

Chart of English consonant phonemes.

Vowels, you have learned, are characterized by a free flow of air.
Consonants, on the other hand, are produced by stopping or obstructing
this flow of air, except for the three nasals. The first six consonants presented
here are those produced by a stoppage of air: /p b t d k g/.

---

[2] You may think that you are uttering single vowels in words like *cease*/sis/,
maim/mem/, *noon*/nun/, and *moan*/mon/. But the vowel sounds you are actually
making are diphthongized vowels something like these: 1. [ɪi], 2. [ei], 3. [ʊu], and
4. [ou]. If you can find a tape recorder which plays backward, you can easily hear
them for yourself: simply record these four words and then play them backward.

STOPS.   /p/, /b/. If you hold your velum and lips closed and exert outward air pressure, nothing will happen except that your cheeks may puff out. Now if you suddenly open your lips the air explodes outward and you have made a /p/. This consonant is called a voiceless bilabial stop because (1) the vocal cords do not vibrate, (2) two lips are used, and (3) a complete stop of the air flow is made. If during the same process you vibrate your vocal cords, you will produce a /b/, a voiced bilabial stop.

/t/, /d/ Instead of using the lips, you can stop the air flow by holding the tongue against the alveolar ridge, with the velum closed. A sudden removal of the tongue will then produce a /t/, a voiceless alveolar stop. But if the vocal cords vibrate during the process, you will produce a /d/, a voiced alveolar stop.

/k/, /g/. The third pair of stops is produced by raising the tongue back against the velum, which is also raised to cut off the nasal cavity. When the tongue back is released, the outrushing air results in a /k/, a voiceless velar stop, or a /g/, a voiced velar stop, depending on whether or not the vocal cords are vibrating.

To increase your awareness of the three stop positions, pronounce slowly and in succession /p/, /t/, and /k/, and try to feel, tactually and kinesthetically, what is going on inside your mouth. Do this six times and then repeat the sounds in reverse.

FRICATIVES.   English contains nine consonants which are produced by an obstruction of the air stream causing audible friction. These nine fricatives are:

$$/f\ v\ \theta\ \eth\ s\ z\ \check{s}\ \check{z}\ h/$$

We shall discuss the first eight in pairs, beginning with those in the front of the mouth and moving to the back.

The first pair, /f/ and /v/, are heard in *fail* and *vale*. They are produced when the outgoing air is obstructed by the lower lip touching the upper teeth. The /f/ is called a voiceless labiodental fricative, and /v/ a voiced labiodental fricative. They differ only in the fact that /v/ is voiced. You can feel the vibration of the vocal cords for /v/ if you press your fingers around the top of the larynx, sound a continuous /f/, and then change without stopping to a /v/. The next three pairs of fricatives can be tested in the same way for voicelessness and voicing.

The second pair, /θ/ and /ð/, are heard in *ether* and *either*. They are made with the tongue obstructing the air stream between the upper and lower teeth, or at the bottom of the upper teeth. The /θ/ is a voiceless interdental fricative, and /ð/ a voiced interdental fricative.

The third pair is /s/ and /z/, as in *face* and *faze*. These are pronounced by the tongue permitting a small stream of air to hiss over its surface at the alveolar ridge. The /s/ is a voiceless alveolar fricative, and /z/ a voiced alveolar fricative.

The fourth pair of fricatives are /š/, the third consonant in *dilution*, and /ž/, the third consonant in *delusion*. These are made by the friction of moving air between the tongue front and the palatal region just behind the alveolar ridge. The /š/ is a voiceless alveopalatal fricative, and /ž/ a voiced alveopalatal fricative. To get the feel of the voiceless alveolar and alveopalatal fricatives, take a deep breath and on a continuous stream of air repeat /s/ and /š/ in alternation, noting the movements of the tongue and the lips.

The last fricative is /h/, as in *hat* contrasted with *at*. This is produced by the breath rushing through the open vocal cords. The fricative's tongue and lip position is that of the following vowel. You can see this easily by preparing your mouth to say *ha, he, who*. It is called the voiceless glottal fricative, the glottis being the space between the vocal cords.

AFFRICATES.   English has two affricates—the voiceless /č/ as in *chill*, and the voiced /ǰ/ as in *Jill*. The /č/ begins with the voiceless stop /t/, which is exploded as a voiceless fricative /š/. Thus it is sometimes written /tš/. It is known as the voiceless alveopalatal affricate. The /ǰ/ consists of a voiced stop /d/, which is exploded as a voiced fricative /ž/, and is sometimes written /dž/. It is called the voiced alveopalatal affricate.

NASALS.   The three nasals—/m/, /n/, and /ŋ/—have already been described above.

LATERAL.   The lateral, /l/ as in *louse*, is made by placing the tongue tip on the alveolar ridge and vibrating the vocal cords as the air passes out on one or both sides of the tongue. To feel the tongue position, hold the tongue firmly at the alveolar ridge and make a series of /l/s and /n/s, noting how the sides of the tongue open and close as you alternate sounds.

GLIDES.   The three glides—/y/, /r/, and /w/—are signalized by a moving, not stationary, tongue position. They are all voiced.

With /y/, as in *yoke* contrasted with *oak*, the tongue begins in the /i/ region and moves toward the position for the following vowel. It is called the high front glide. In the case of /r/, as in *rate* contrasted with *ate*, the tongue begins in the position of the r-colored vowel of *purr*, /ər/, and moves toward the following vowel. It is known as the retroflex alveolar glide, though this name is not descriptive of some /r/s. The third glide is /w/, as in *will* versus *ill*. Here the tongue takes a /u/ position and then moves into the following vowel. It is called the high back glide.

We have now covered briefly the 12 vowels, 3 diphthongs, and 24 consonants of English. The vowels and consonants are charted on the diagrams on pages 172 and 175.

SUGGESTED ASSIGNMENTS

(The first three exercises will give you practice in reading phonemic script, which will help you with the next three selections in the book. At the same time they will reveal the systematic aspect of four English inflectional endings.)

1. If asked to tell how the past tense of our regular verbs is formed, most people would say by the addition of *d* or *ed* to the stem form; e.g., *love* plus *d* is *loved*, *walk* plus *ed* is *walked*. Such a description is based on spelling and does not accurately describe the different sounds involved. Actually, this past-tense ending takes three phonetic forms. To find out what these three forms are, first read the following transcriptions and write after each its spelled form.

pæst _____	rabd _____	ratəd _____
læft _____	simd _____	lodɔd _____
mapt _____	lond _____	sitəd _____
bækt _____	rɔŋd _____	sadɔd _____
rəšt _____	hɔgd _____	nidəd _____
rɛnčt _____	rcvd _____	ripitəd _____
	mɔld _____	
	stərd _____	

Now, in the spoken language, what are the three endings that signal the past tense? These endings are not distributed randomly but according to a system. You can easily discover this system if you will compare the voicing or voicelessness of the last sound of each verb stem with that of the ending.

2. In English spelling we have two "s" plurals, *-s* and *-es*. But in spoken language there are three "s" plurals with a systematic distribution. To discover these three plurals and the system of their distribution, first read the following transcriptions and write after each its spelled form.

staps _____	mabz _____	glæsəz _____
raits _____	raidz _____	rozəz _____
keks _____	frɔgz _____	dišəz _____
məfs _____	wevz _____	gərajəz _____
brɛθs _____	səmz _____	dičəz _____
	sənz _____	ɛjəz _____
	sɔŋz _____	
	dalz _____	
	fɪrz _____	

3. Is the same system as in exercise 2 operative for the noun possessive? Compare, for example, /jæks/ (= Jack's), /janz/ (= John's), and /jɔrjəz/ (= George's). And is this also true of the third person present singular of the verb, as in /lɪfts/ (He *lifts*), /ridz/ (He *reads*), and /mɪsəz/ (He *misses*)?

(The next three exercises will give you transcription practice and at the same time illustrate some of the irregularities of English spelling.)

4. Transcribe the following words with phonemic symbols and notice all the ways in which the phoneme /i/ is spelled.

feet _____	beat _____	ravine _____
me _____	deceive _____	key _____
Caesar _____	amoeba _____	quay _____
people _____	relieve _____	

5. Transcribe the following words with phonemic symbols and notice the various phonemes which the letter *a* represents.

dame _____	father _____	lunar _____
fare _____	ball _____	opera _____
pan _____	pillage _____	

6. Transcribe the following words with phonemic symbols and notice the silent letters.

corps _____	debt _____	pneumatic _____
island _____	reign _____	colonel _____

7. By transcribing the following words, you will meet all the vowels, diphthongs, and consonants of the preceding essay.

palm _____	ether _____	rang _____
taste _____	sister _____	root _____
keen _____	song _____	wade _____
coon _____	wash _____	your _____
bought _____	voted _____	have _____
dull _____	breathe _____	boy _____
gadding _____	lazy _____	house _____
chicken _____	measure _____	few _____
dredge _____	lamb _____	mine _____
fig _____	gnawed _____	physics _____

8. Some words have two pronunciations, one that we learn by ear, called the traditional pronunciation, and a second that we derive from the spelling of a word, called the spelling pronunciation. An example is *breeches*, a word that seldom occurs in current speech. Its traditional pronunciation, the one that your grandfather learned by ear, is /brícɔz/; but as most of us learn it from print, it has acquired the spelling pronunciation of /bricɔz/. It is not unusual for a spelling pronunciation to gain general acceptance and replace the traditional pronunciation. Your own pronunciation of *fault, author, host,* and *theater* illustrates spelling pronunciations that have ousted the traditional ones.

Look up these words in your desk dictionary, and where you find two pronunciations, try to decide which one is the spelling pronunciation:

1. almond	6. forehead
2. arctic	7. clothes
3. often (cf. soften)	8. vehicle
4. falcon	9. pall-mall
5. nephew	10. coxswain

TABLE OF SOUND SYMBOLS USED IN THIS BOOK

	Symbol	*Example*
Consonants		
Stops	p	*p*are, s*p*are, sto*p*
	b	*b*are
	t	*t*are
	d	*d*are
	k	*c*are
	g	*g*et
Fricatives	f	*f*ish
	v	*v*ase
	θ	*th*ink
	ð	*th*en
	s	*s*ink
	z	*z*inc
	š, ʃ	*s*ure
	ž, ʒ	plea*s*ure
	h	*h*ow
	ç	*h*uge (with friction between tongue front and palate)
Affricates	č, tʃ, tš	*ch*urch
	ǰ, dʒ, dž	*j*ud*g*e
Nasals	m	*m*y
	n	*n*ose
	ŋ	si*ng*
Lateral	l	*l*ike
Glides	r	*r*ye
	y, j	*y*es
	w	*w*ait
	ʍ, hw	s*w*eet (voiceless *w*), *wh*y
Vowels		
Front	i	m*ee*t
	ɪ	s*i*t
	e	r*a*te
	ɛ	p*e*t
	æ	p*a*t
Central	ər, r, ɝ, ɚ	f*ur*
	ə, ʌ	sof*a*, *u*p
	a, ɑ	f*a*ther
Back	u	f*oo*l
	ʊ	f*u*ll
	o	n*o*te
	ɔ	s*aw*
	ɒ	n*o*t British (slightly rounded)
Diphthongs	aɪ, ai, ɑɪ, ɑi	m*i*ne
	ɔɪ, ɔi, oɪ, oi	b*oy*
	aʊ, au, ɑʊ, ɑu	h*ow*
	iu	f*ew*
	ju	*u*se

Primary and secondary stresses are shown by vertical lines. A high vertical line indicates that the following syllable has primary stress. A low vertical line indicates that the following syllable has secondary stress. Example: ǀsɛkrəǀteri. Primary stress is also shown by a ′ after the syllable. Examples: bihev′, ımpor′tənt.

Phonetic Change: Assimilation

Charles Kenneth Thomas

You probably have wondered why it is that the word *cupboard*, which is obviously a compound of *cup* plus *board*, is not pronounced in accordance with its spelling. If you were to write *cubberd* for *cupboard*, you would be branded as an illiterate, even though *cubberd* represents the pronunciation, certainly as old as "Old Mother Hubbard," more accurately than the standard spelling. As a matter of fact, *cubberd*, along with *cubbourd, cubboorde, cubbord* and others, was a common spelling during the sixteenth and seventeenth centuries. It was not until the eighteenth century that the spelling became standardized as *cupboard*, but people went right on saying *cubberd*. Clearly something interesting is at work in the spoken language that is not adequately reflected in writing.

When we speak we do not utter a series of individuated units of sound. Rather we speak in a continuous flow of sounds; vowels and consonants are constantly jostling each other, often blurring or wearing away the edges of adjoining sounds especially. In other words, under certain conditions phonetic changes take place. One·type of phonetic change is assimilation, which Charles Thomas, Professor of Speech at the University of Florida, discusses in the following essay. An understanding of assimilation will let you in on the secret of some of the mysteries of English pronunciation.

Variations in pronunciation . . . should convince us that language is not static and uniform, but that it develops and changes. We notice this development even more if we read the literature of earlier periods. Shakespeare's English is noticeably different from our own, even though our present-day archaic spelling masks some of the differences. To understand Chaucer we must frequently refer to a glossary; to appreciate his rhythms and rhymes we must also know something about the language spoken in fourteenth-century London. To read Old English, of the time of King Alfred for instance, we must study it as we would a foreign language.

Changes in the language are usually imperceptible till afterward, and often seemingly capricious. Analysis of the historical changes shows, however, that the patterns of development are usually clear in retrospect, and that definite causes can be assigned to some of them. . . . We are going to examine one type of historical change, in order to throw light on the changeable nature of present-day speech.

ASSIMILATION

The usual pronunciation of *income* is ['ɪn͵kʌm],[1] with primary stress on the first syllable, secondary stress on the second syllable, and a distinct syllabic division between [n] and [k]. When we use the word as an adjective, however, in the phrase *income tax,* the pronunciation may be ['ɪn͵kʌm 'tæks], but often it changes to ['ɪŋkəm ͵tæks]. The reduced vowel represents reduced stress. The change from [n] to [ŋ] illustrates what is known as *assimilation,* a type of phonetic change which occurs frequently enough to warrant detailed examination.

When *income* becomes part of the larger unit, *income tax*, we scan the details more rapidly. The succession of three stressed syllables conflicts with our normal rhythmic patterns, and we weaken the second syllable from [ʌ] to [ə]. The phrase as a whole telescopes within itself, and the amount of time available for the shift from one syllable to the next is shortened. The tongue, however, requires an appreciable amount of time to shift from the alveolar contact of [n] to the velar contact of [k]. If the time is too short, the tongue anticipates the velar contact by shifting from [n] to [ŋ], since the sequence [ŋk] can be made with a single contact of the tongue, instead of the sequence of contacts required for [nk]. Furthermore, as Kent has pointed out,[2] thought constantly outstrips utterance, and this mental anticipation is closely associated with the mechanical adjustment just described.

Assimilation may therefore be defined as the process whereby one sound is changed to a second under the influence of a third;[3] in *income tax* the alveolar [n] changes to the velar [ŋ] under the influence of the velar [k]. Another useful definition is that of Bloomfield,[4] who points out that the position of the speech agents for the production of one sound is altered to a position more like that of a neighboring sound.

All assimilations start in a manner similar to that of *income tax*. The change may take place as soon as the two original sounds come close together: we have every reason to suppose that the sequence [ŋk] formed as

---

[1] For a table of phonetic symbols, see p. 180. [eds.]

[2] Roland G. Kent, "Assimilation and Dissimilation," *Language,* XII (1936), pp. 245–258.

[3] Compare Daniel Jones, *An Outline of English Phonetics,* 8th ed. (New York, E. P. Dutton & Co., Inc., 1956), pp. 217–218.

[4] Leonard Bloomfield, *Language* (New York, Holt, Rinehart and Winston, Inc., 1933), p. 372.

soon as the word *sank* was formed. On the other hand, the change may take place more slowly if, as in *income tax,* the sequence is brought gradually together in the act of compounding. That is, many assimilations start as accidental mispronunciations of an accepted sequence of sounds. Some never progress beyond this stage, for they may be noticeable enough to cause adverse criticism, and to induce speakers to avoid the assimilation.

A substandard pronunciation of *length* illustrates this accidental type of assimilation. The shift from the velar [ŋ] to the linguadental [θ] is apparently too great for some speakers' muscular control. Consequently the tongue anticipates the dental position, [ŋ] changes to [n] in anticipation of the following [θ], and we hear the new pronunciation [lɛnθ], rhyming with *tenth* [tɛnθ]. The pronunciation [lɛnθ] has never, however, risen to the standard level, because it has always been noticeable enough to provoke adverse criticism. Most people pronounce *length* as [lɛŋθ] or [lɛŋkθ], the added [k] serving as a kind of insulation against assimilation.

On the other hand, some assimilations are adopted so promptly and generally that adverse criticism is futile. For example, derivatives of the Latin preposition *cum* occur in English with all three nasal consonants. The original [m] of *cum* survives in such words as *combine* [kəm'baɪn], *compare* [kəm'pɛr], and *comfort* ['kʌmfət]; but it has become [n] in such words as *contact* ['kan₁tækt], *condemn* [kən'dɛm], and *constant* ['kanstənt]; and has become [ŋ] in such words as *congress* ['kaŋgrəs] and *conquer* ['kaŋkə]. A glance at the consonant which follows the nasal shows that in every word the nasal has approximated the position of the following consonant; [m] has assimilated to [n] before alveolar consonants, and to [ŋ] before velars. Many of these assimilations took place in the Latin period.

The assimilative process is essentially the same, whether in *length, income tax, condemn,* or *congress,* but the effect of adverse criticism has been selective. There was probably no appreciable criticism of the assimilations based on Latin *cum;* most of them were completely established and accepted before English adopted the words from Latin or French.

Between the extremes of accidental, substandard assimilations of the type of [lɛnθ] and established, standard assimilations of the type of ['kaŋgrəs] lie a few instances on which a final verdict has not yet been made. Some people object to ['ɪŋkəm ₁tæks]; others accept it, not only without objection, but often without even being aware that any change in pronunciation has taken place. Some people object to the assimilated ['hɔrʃ'ʃu] for *horseshoe;* others accept it without noticing that they have lost the [s] of *horse* [hɔrs]. The fate of these and similar assimilations will be decided only in the future. In and of themselves, assimilations are neither good nor bad. General acceptance or rejection of a particular assimilation is completely irrelevant to the assimilative process.

When we consider the inherent nature of the assimilative process, we notice that in all the illustrations used thus far the preceding sound has been influenced in anticipation of the sound that follows. Though this is the most common type,[5] the direction of influence may be otherwise.

Americans who pronounce *tune* [tun] and *duty* ['duti] often wonder why British and Canadian speakers sometimes insert a seemingly gratuitous [ʃ] in *tune* [tʃun] and *duty* ['dʒutɪ]. Far from being gratuitous these sounds represent the assimilations that sometimes develop from [tjun] and ['djutɪ]. The sequences [tj] and [dj] are unstable, not because of the distance through which the tongue must move, but because of the delicacy of adjustment required. In [tʃun], the tongue has moved forward from the position of [j] to that of [ʃ], which blends more readily with [t]. In ['dʒutɪ], the tongue has moved forward from the position of [j] to that of [ʒ]. Thus [t] has assimilated [j] to [ʃ]; [d] has assimilated [j] to [ʒ]. The articulation of [t] and [d] is vigorous enough to move the place or articulation forward for the following sound, and the voiceless quality of [t] also carries over to the following sound. . . . In all these instances in which the preceding sound influences the sound that follows, classify the assimilation as *progressive*. When the second sound influences the first, as in *length* and *congress*, we call it *regressive*.

Finally, there is a third assimilative classification known as *reciprocal*, in which the two sounds influence each other and combine to produce a single sound which is a compromise between the two. The word *sure*, for instance, was formerly pronounced [sjʊr]; but the sequence [sj] required a more delicate adjustment than most speakers gave it. Consequently, the tongue slipped further back for [s] and further forward for [j], perhaps through some intermediate stage like [ʃj] or [sç], until the two sounds came together at the position for [ʃ] and gave us our present pronunciation [ʃʊr].

A similar reciprocal assimilation has taken place in *vision* ['vɪʒən], from earlier ['vɪzjən]. In *issue* and a few similar words, Americans habitually use the assimilated ['ɪʃu]; the most frequent British pronunciation seems to be the unassimilated ['ɪsju].[6] . . .

ASSIMILATION AND VOICING

From the direction of influence in the assimilative process we now turn to the nature and varieties of the physical changes. First, assimilation may produce a change in the voicing of consonants. In *north* [nɔrθ] and *worth* [wɝθ], the final consonant is voiceless, but in *northern* ['nɔrðæn] and *worthy* ['wɝði], the voiceless [θ] has been assimilated to the voiced [ð] by the voiced quality of the following vowels. In *thieves* [θivz] in comparison with *thief*

---

[5] See Roland G. Kent, "Assimilation and Dissimilation," *Language*, XII (1936), 246; Leonard Bloomfield, *Language* (New York, Holt, Rinehart and Winston, Inc., 1933), p. 372; E. H. Sturtevant, *Linguistic Change* (Chicago, University of Chicago Press, 1917), p. 49.

[6] See the 1956 edition of Daniel Jones, *An English Pronouncing Dictionary*.

[θif], [v] results from an earlier assimilation to a vowel which is now no longer pronounced.

Instances of the change from a voiced to a voiceless consonant are more numerous. The inflectional ending -ed . . . ends in [d] so long as the ending remains a separate syllable and [d] follows either of the voiced sounds [ɪ] or [ə], as in *heated* [ˈhitɪd] or *heeded* [ˈhidɪd].[7] But when inflectional -ed becomes nonsyllabic, it remains [d] after voiced sounds, as in *begged* [bɛgd], but assimilates to the voiceless [t] after voiceless consonants, as in *baked* [bekt].

Similarly, inflectional -es continues to end in [z] when the ending is syllabic, as in *guesses* [gɛsɪz]. When reduced to nonsyllabic status, inflectional -es and -s remain [z] after voiced sounds, as in *begs* [bɛgz], but assimilate to the voiceless [s] after voiceless consonants, as in *bakes* [beks].

A double assimilation takes place in the phrase *used to*. The verb *used* [juzd] has been assimilated to [just] by the following [t], and has acquired the meaning "formerly accustomed." The unassimilated pronunciation, with looser juncture, has been kept for the meaning "utilized." Thus, *the pen he used to* [ˈjustə] *write with* means the pen he was accustomed to write with; *the pen he used to* [juzd tə] *write with* means the pen he utilized for writing.

Something similar occurs in the phrases *have to* and *has to* when they denote compulsion. *That is all I have to* [ˈhæftə] *do* means that that is all I am compelled to do. *That is all I have to* [hævˈtə] *do* means that that is all I have on hand at the moment to do. In the sentence, *That is all he has to do*, [ˈhæstə] and [ˈhæz tə] indicate the same distinction in meaning. The form [ˈjustə] is fully established in standard speech; the assimilated [ˈhæftə] and [ˈhæstə], despite their usefulness, still impress some conservatives as substandard.

A few minor instances, such as the occasional assimilation of *width* [wɪdθ] to [wɪtθ] and *breadth* [brɛdθ] to [brɛtθ], complete the list of changes from voiced to voiceless consonants. There is an element of unvoicing in the assimilation of [sj] to [ʃ] in *sure* and of [tj] to [tʃ] in *tune*, but these assimilations are primarily positional. . . .

ASSIMILATION OF NASAL CONSONANTS

Another class consists of those assimilations which involve a change in the place of articulation of nasal consonants. We have already seen this class illustrated in such derivatives of Latin *cum* as *compound* [ˈkɑmpɑʊnd], *combine* [kəmˈbaɪn], and *comfort* [ˈkʌmfɚt], which retain the unassimilated [m] before labials and labiodentals; and *content* [kənˈtɛnt], *condemn* [kənˈdɛm], *constant* [ˈkɑnstənt], *conquer* [ˈkɑŋkɚ], and *congress* [ˈkɑŋgrəs], which illustrate assimilation of the nasal to the place of articulation of the following consonant.

[7] The inflectional ending -ed is syllabic when it follows a base which ends in *t* or *d. Heated* and *heeded* are also pronounced [hitəd] and [hidəd]. [eds.]

Other illustrations in this class usually depend on the loss of an "insulating" sound. After the loss, an instable sequence results, and assimilation is likely to take place. Thus if *open* ['opən] loses [ə] and becomes ['opn], it is likely to assimilate to ['opm], the alveolar [n] giving way to the labial [m] under the influence of the labial [p]. Similar assimilations may take place in *ribbon,* which may change from ['rɪbən] to ['rɪbn], and then assimilate to ['rɪbm]; in *bacon,* which may change from ['bekən] to ['bekn], and then assimilate to ['bekŋ], in *wagon,* which may change from [wægən] to ['wægn], and then assimilate to ['wægŋ]; *grandpa,* which may change from ['grænd-pɑ], to ['grænpɑ], and then assimilate to ['græmpɑ]; and in *pumpkin,* which may change from ['pʌmpkɪn] to ['pʌmkɪn], and then assimilate to ['pʌŋkɪn].

PARTIAL ASSIMILATIONS

Most of the assimilations discussed thus far are readily audible, even to speakers with little or no phonetic training. Most of them involve shifts from one phoneme to another. There remain some minor assimilations in which the change is slight enough not always to be audible to the untrained listener. Most of these changes involve only a shift from one allophone to another.[8] Thus the [g] of *goose* has the normal contact of the back of the tongue with the soft palate. The [g] of *geese,* however, is a different allophone, partially assimilated to the front vowel [i] which follows it, and articulated farther forward in the mouth, sometimes as far forward as the back part of the hard palate. . . . The [t] of *eighth* [etθ], the [d] of *width* [wɪdθ], the [n] of *tenth* [tenθ], and the [l] of *health* [helθ] are not ordinarily the usual alveolar allophones, but are usually assimilated to the dental position in anticipation of the dental [θ].

In initial sequences of voiceless consonants followed by voiced semivowels [= glides], the voicing of the semivowel may be slightly delayed by assimilation to the preceding voiceless consonant. This assimilation is most noticeable after voiceless fricatives. *Sweet* [swit] may become [sʍit] or [sʌit]; *thwart* [θwɔt] may become [θʍwɔrt] or [θʌɔrt].[9] *Sled, frame, flame, throw,* and *shred* may have voiceless or partly voiceless [l] and [r] instead of the usual voiced allophones.

---

[8] The term *allophone* can be easily explained. The first consonant sound in *goose* is not exactly the same as the first consonant sound in *geese.* You can test this easily by whispering these sounds. Yet, though both are a *g* sound, the difference between the two never makes a difference in meaning in English. We call each of these *g* sounds an allophone of the *g,* which is called a phoneme. A phoneme is a speech sound, which may have allophonic variations, that makes a difference in meaning. Our *g* is a phoneme because it distinguishes the meaning of *goose* from *loose, moose, noose,* and so on. A phoneme is usually written between slants, e.g., /g/, and an allophone is written between brackets, e.g., [g]. [eds.]

[9] The /ʍ/ is a voiceless /w/, which often occurs after a voiceless consonant. You can make this sound by pursing your lips for a /u/ and then blowing through them. [eds.]

After voiceless stops, the assimilative unvoicing is a little less noticeable, but *twice* [twaɪs] may become [tʌwaɪs] or [tʌaɪs]; *quart* [kwɔrt] may become [kʌwɔrt] or [kʌɔrt]; and *play, pray, tray, clay,* and *crane* may have partly or completely unvoiced allophones of [l] or [r]. *Smell* and *snail* may have partly unvoiced [m] or [n].

Except for the idiomatic phrases *used to, have to,* and *has to,* single words have been used to illustrate the assimilative process. But assimilation may also take place at the junction of words, whenever the words are spoken without a pause. Thus we may hear such assimilations as *Miss Shaw* [mɪʃ ˈʃɔ], *Miss Young* [mɪʃ ˈjʌŋ] or [mɪʃ ˈʃʌŋ], *did you?* [ˈdɪdʒə], *was sure* [wəʒ ˈʃʊr] or [wəʃ ˈʃʊr], and *in court* [ɪŋ ˈkɔrt]. Though the social status of some of these illustrations is not secure, it must be realized that they look stranger than they sound.

The question of standard speech is, as we have seen, quite distinct from that of assimilation. The latter is a phonetic process, continually taking place, and restricted at times by conservative opinions. Many of the results of the assimilative process have been accepted on the standard level, immediately or eventually. Some of the assimilated forms characterized in this chapter as substandard may come to be accepted as standard in the future. Others may continue indefinitely to carry the stigma of substandard usage. The classification of particular assimilations as standard or substandard is therefore but one aspect of the question of standard or substandard speech in general. Questions of standards involve the judgments of speakers and critics of the language; they must not be confused with the "natural history" of the language itself.

SUGGESTED ASSIGNMENTS

1. A device that writers use to characterize illiterate persons is to represent the way they talk, for example, "I da wanna go!" or "I betcha can't." Often the result in print produces a humorous effect, as writers of humorous stories and comic strips well know. Examine a comic book that contains dialogue of this sort and see to what extent the distorted spelling represents assimilations that are normal in colloquial language. Write a theme on your findings, identifying and explaining the assimilations you come across.

2. The Latin prefix *in-* (= not) has come into English and is widely used as an English negative prefix, as in *inactive, incomplete, inability.* In four situations it changes form. It assimilates to an initial /m/, /l/, and /r/, becoming identical with them, as in *immovable, immoderate, illegal, illegible, irregular, irrelevant.* But in the fourth situation, before an initial /p/, it becomes /m/, as in *impossible, impure, imprudent.* Explain this assimilation in terms of the way /m/ and /p/ are articulated.

3. In American English a /t/ between two vowels tends to be pronounced as a short /d/, as in these examples: *city* /sɪdi/; *letter* /lɛdər/; *it is* /ɪdɪz/. Explain

this assimilation in terms of voice. The next instance is similar but not identical. (1) Latin *pater* /patər/ developed into Spanish *padre* /padre/. Explain the assimilation.

4. The word *is* is pronounced /ɪz/. But in *it's* the /z/ changes to /s/. Explain.
5. What happens to the final /s/ of *this* in the phrase *this sugar*? Explain.
6. Compare the pronunciation of *south* and *southern*. Explain the assimilation.

The Music of English

Ray Past

Many subtleties and shades of meaning in English are expressed by features of the living voice—its stresses, pitches, and pauses. As a simple example, let us consider this statement: "The boss is going to get a new secretary," and the ensuing question "Who?" If this *who* is spoken with rising pitch, it will elicit the answer "the boss." But if uttered with falling pitch, the answer will be the name of the new secretary. With other question words, like *when* and *where*, the same principle is operative: Rising pitch signals a request for repetition, and falling pitch indicates a desire for more information. Professor Ray Past is head of the Department of Linguistics at the University of Texas at El Paso. He is the author of an English grammar entitled *Language as a Lively Art.*

Once we have understood the concept of the phoneme and become familiar with the English vowels and consonants we are in position to go on and examine another set of phonemes, those known as the "suprasegmentals." In a sense you might say that so far we have dealt only with the skeleton; we need to flesh it out to have anything approaching the living language. Man does not speak by vowels and consonants alone but orchestrates them into what we could call the "music" of the language—the voice rises and falls, hesitates and accelerates, softens and becomes louder, all giving to the language its peculiar "flavor." In the bilingual community where I live, for instance, you can frequently tell what language a nearby person is speaking even when you can't quite hear what he's saying. The tip-off is this "music." English and Spanish don't sound alike even when you can't make

Written especially for this book and used by permission of the author.

out the vowels and consonants. As Thoreau might have said, they march to the music of different drums.

Probably the first thing we should consider about the suprasegmentals is why they are called that. The "supra-" would suggest that these are phonemes somehow laid on "over" phonemes that are "segmental," and this is exactly the case. The now-familiar vowels and consonants are called "segmental phonemes" because with them we *segment* the living, fluid stream of speech. But speech is not a neat parade of separate phonemes following one another like boxcars in a string; rather it is a fusing and blending of speech sounds into one another. For example, if you were to say "pooch" and "peach" you would find that the instances of /p/ are different, for even as you release the /p/'s your lips are already in position for the following vowels. Try saying "I'm gonna do it" rapidly as it would occur in normal speech—something like /aimganaduit/—and ask yourself where the separation between the phonemes *really* occurs. Of course we see that there is no separation and that writing phonemes as we do is actually a bit of make believe. It has its uses, though, and it deceives no one so long as we are aware that what we are doing is simply a convenient fiction. In any event, this is why the vowel and consonant phonemes are called segmentals: With them we segment, compartmentalize, the continuous stream of sounds that comprise language. However, as we are now observing, other phenomena occur simultaneously with them—the *supra*segmentals.

Let us consider briefly an often-reprinted ambiguous sentence:

He fed her dog biscuits.

The two meanings are quickly apparent: Either he fed dog-biscuits to an animal belonging to "her," or we have the slapstick situation in which he fed "her" (his date?) a hard and not-very-tasty snack. Perhaps you also noticed—and if you didn't, please do—that this sentence is ambiguous only on paper. When you bring it to life by *saying* it you will automatically give it one meaning or the other. See what happens when you put just a little extra emphasis on "her," pause slightly, raise the pitch of your voice sharply on "dog" and let it fall through the rest of the phrase. Or, on the other hand, suppose you rip right along at a good clip through "dog," letting your voice rise both in pitch and volume on that word. Then pause slightly and add "biscuits." These descriptions are pretty primitive, but I think they can be followed well enough for you to see that in the first reading "she" gets the biscuits, and in the second the dog gets them. Finally, be sure to observe that either way you read it, the *segmental* phonemes are exactly the same.

We note that the two readings do indeed have different meanings. And we remember the principle of the minimal pair: i.e., when two utterances with different meanings are alike in all respects but one, then that single difference is a phonemic difference. In this pair of readings, then, since the vowels and consonants are identical we must be dealing with phonemes that are not segmental. And we are. We are dealing with the suprasegmental phonemes of pitch and stress.

Let us consider another example, this one taken from a recent textbook on the grammars of English. Again it is an ambiguous sentence:

The man who visited my sister regularly begged her to marry him.

Did the man regularly visit my sister and, perhaps, only once beg her to marry him? Or did he visit her only occasionally but make a repeated nuisance out of his begging that they unite in matrimony? As the author of the text quite correctly points out, you can't tell. But it is also true, as he does not point out, that as you *say* this sentence you will give it one meaning or the other. This time you do it with pauses. Note what happens if you lengthen ever-so-little your pronunciation of "sister" and pause slightly after it, resuming tempo for the rest of the sentence. Or, conversely, don't pause at all after "sister" but instead do it after "regularly." Then you have assigned the sentence the other meaning. In this case, as with the dog biscuits above, we note that the segmental phonemes are identical in each version. We have to conclude, then, that the *pause* we place after "sister," or after "regularly," is phonemic. And it is. It is the kind of phoneme that we call "juncture."

As you can already understand, the following discussion of the suprasegmental phonemes is going to be a challenge to your ability to read imaginatively, as well as to my ability to explain clearly, for we are going to have to try to communicate through cold paper and type something of the warmth, the rhythm, the music of the spoken language. It will help if you will actually read the examples aloud to yourself, listening to how they sound and observing what causes the differences being discussed—as you probably did with the so-called ambiguities above. One thing we will inevitably come to appreciate is that writing, marvelous accomplishment though it is, the base of our civilization and all that, is an impoverished instrument compared to the flexibility, the subtleties and the nuances of speech. Punctuation is a sorry and inadequate substitute for the suprasegmentals.

We need to recognize at the outset that there is less agreement about the suprasegmental phonemes than there is about the segmentals—not that anyone challenges their existence, which is readily demonstrable, but there is disagreement as to just how many such phonemes there are. One widely published analysis says there are four phonemes of stress, four of pitch, and four of juncture, and that is the approach we will consider here, but you should be aware that this is not universally accepted. Perhaps the difficulty is something like that of dialects, only more complex. It may be that in fact we don't all use these intonation patterns (i.e., suprasegmentals) in exactly the same way and that as we listen to another speaker we are constantly engaged in a small act of "translation," converting his patterns into our own —much as we supply the /r/ when we listen to a speaker from one of the so-called "r-less" dialect areas (assuming, that is, we are not ourselves r-less), as in *far* and *beer*. It is true that often when you ask a speaker to pronounce a given sentence, trying to get him to illustrate a particular intonation pattern, he will not say it "right." It's frustrating. We are dealing here with very slight shadings, often difficult to describe. Doubtless the most amazing thing about them is that with all their complexity, their difficulty, their subtlety, we all—as speakers of English—recognize them and react to them and, indeed, produce them, quite oblivious to the virtuosity of the performance we are engaged in. As we become consciously aware of some of its many details we may well be like Molière's character who was surprised and delighted to find he had been speaking prose all his life.

Let's begin with stress. Most simply, it is the degree of volume a speaker gives to part of an utterance. It is relative. That one speaker might have a louder voice than another is irrelevant, as is the fact that at times he will speak louder than at others. We are talking about the little extra oomph he will give to a syllable within an utterance. For a simple example consider this word: /ɪnsɛns/. If you pause to think you will realize that it isn't one word but two, depending upon how you stress it. If you pronounce the first syllable louder than the second—/ɪ́nsɛns/—you have a noun designating a fragrant smoke; if you give the additional volume to the second syllable—/ɪnsɛ́ns/—you have a verb meaning "to make angry." We see that in this minimal pair the segmentals are the same; the difference in meaning is caused by the placement of the stress. Therefore, stress is phonemic by definition.

It is also easy to demonstrate that in English we have four levels of stress. Take this sentence: "He bought a new windshield wiper." If you rattle this off as you might in a routine observation (try it once or twice or several times) you'll come to realize that not all the syllables are equally loud, and if you're saying it in the way most of my students do you'll conclude that the one syllable that sticks out most prominently is the /wɪn/ of "windshield." At the same time, you'll observe that the other syllables, though not as loud as /wɪn/, are not all the same either. Two of them seem louder than their mates: /nu/ and /waip/. Finally, you note that the /šil/ of "windshield," while not as loud as the already-cited syllables, is still louder than the initial /ə/ (= *a*) or the final /ər/ or "wiper." You can—and should—experiment with pronouncing and listening carefully to a number of phrases like this (e.g., "Hand me the book."), and you will probably convince yourself that English does indeed have four different levels of stress.

These four levels have been given names and symbols. In descending order, from loudest to least loud, they are as follows:

´ = primary
ˆ = secondary
` = tertiary, or third-level
˘ = weak

In a phonemic transcription these symbols are written above the syllables to which they apply.

The problem, so far not resolved, lies in demonstrating convincingly that all four stress levels are indeed *phonemic*. Can we find minimal pairs distinguished by secondary stress in one and tertiary in the other, between third-stress in one and weak in another? Not everyone is convinced we can.

Fortunately, we need not settle this problem. But let's look at a few examples of the kinds of things we do and have been doing all our lives with these stresses. (We'll place the stress marks over standard spelling rather than using phonemic transcription, since it will serve as well here and may be easier to read.)

What is the difference between ăn Énglĭsh têachĕr and ăn Ênglĭsh téuchĕr? Of course. The first one teaches English and the second one is from England. We could easily have an Ênglĭsh Énglĭsh têachĕr, also. (If you try marking out the stress symbols on phrases like this you will discover how easy it is to mark the syllables with primary stress, and how difficult to make up one's mind whether some lesser syllables are secondary or third—or third or weak.)

Here are a few minimal pairs:

I saw him bỳ thĕ líbrary. (near the library)
I saw him bûy the library. (he made a purchase)

He's a ĝiant tácklĕ. (a huge lineman)
He's a Gíant tâcklĕ. (plays tackle for the Giants)

They had a rêcórd sále. (biggest one they've had)
They had a récòrd sâle. (a sale of records)

Or even:

They had a rêcórd récòrd sâle. (biggest sale of lp's ever)

I saw a blâck bírd. (any old bird that was black)
I saw a bláckbird. (a particular kind of bird)

A perhaps-amusing example of this kind of thing involves a radio news broadcast I heard several years ago following a tragic accident in Italy where a great dam had burst, killing hundreds of people. I heard the announcer say this: "Here's some more news about that damn disaster in Italy." This was startling and puzzling because one doesn't expect flip talk about such events. It took me a while to realize that the announcer had under-stressed "damn." Like this:

. . . that dâmn dĭsástĕr. (What he said).
. . . that dám dĭsâstĕr. (What he should have said.)

When you stop to think about it, it is perhaps surprising that we don't all make more blunders with these tiny signals, and yet most of us go on manipulating them, and interpreting them, correctly all day long, quite unaware that we are doing anything special. For instance, an adjective modifying a noun bears less stress than the noun, as in *a prêtty girl* and *a gôod driver*. But when a noun modifies another noun, one of two stress patterns may occur: secondary-plus-primary again, as in *côllege básketball, stûdent téacher*, and *bôy wónder*; or primary-plus-third, as in *bár girl, táxi driver*, and *cóllege stùdent*. There is no way to predict which of the two patterns will occur with noun + noun, but you, as a native speaker, will always get them right.

Let's turn now to a consideration of pitch, which is a matter of the voice rising or falling in the scale. Again pitch is relative within the phrase. That your friend might have a higher pitched voice than yours is not relevant. Let's begin with a consideration of what is usually called the "tag question," like this one:

She's a nice girl, isn't she?

On this particular question your voice would probably be falling throughout the part after the comma: is n't she? And you note that it isn't really a question. It's merely an affirmation we add, expecting possibly a confirmation. But suppose that instead of falling your voice is rising:

She's a nice girl, is n't she?

This is quite a different matter. This is a real question. It's asking for a reply where the other is not. Try these pairs, first with falling pitch on the question parts, then with rising. Note the differences:

We're on time, aren't we?
Johnny behaved this morning, didn't he?
They were undefeated, weren't they?

We find the same kind of difference in other types of questions too. Try it on "What did you say?" In this case the rising pitch seems to say something like "Would you give me that again? I didn't quite hear you." Or it might indicate astonishment. But the same words ending with a dropping pitch constitute a different question. This question does not ask for a repetition of what was said, nor does it express strong feeling. It simply asks unemotionally for information.

Pitch is usually indicated in four levels, from the highest—"4"—to the lowest—"1." Let's consider "She's my sister," made as a simple statement of fact. The voice begins at one's normal pitch level that we designate "2" and continues more or less at that level until it comes to the first syllable of "sister," where it rises abruptly. On the weak syllable of "sister" ("-er") it falls sharply to the lowest level in the sentence. This arrangement of pitches is often called the "normal statement pattern" and could be represented with a diagram:

$$\text{2} \qquad \text{3} \qquad \text{1}$$
$$\underline{\text{She's my}}\,|\,\text{si\underline{s}ter.}$$

This pattern is referred to as "the 2-3-1 pattern."

Suppose we make the statement into a question:

$$\text{2} \qquad \text{3} \qquad \text{3}$$
$$\underline{\text{Is she my}}\,|\,\text{sister?}$$

The voice begins on level 2, as in the statement, and continues more or less level until "sis-" where it rises. This time, however, it does not fall off on the second syllable of "sister" but holds even or continues rising somewhat. This pattern is called 2-3-3.

Actually, though we say the voice holds level until "sis-" you will note that it doesn't really. But it doesn't have any *significant*—or phonemic—change until then. We *can* move the significant change, and when we do we alter the meaning, as in:

$$\text{2} \qquad \text{3} \qquad \text{1}$$
$$\underline{\text{She's}}\,|\,\text{my \underline{s}ister}$$

This might indicate "Not his, but mine." And so on if we move the pitch to the other words: we vary the significance of what is being said.

Incidentally, in the question example just above—"Is she my sister?"—we reversed the statement order of the first two words, but we wouldn't have had to. Pitch alone would make it into a question:

$$\text{2} \qquad \text{3} \qquad \text{3}$$
$$\underline{\text{She's my}}\,|\,\text{sister?}$$

But it would be a question with a somewhat different "flavor" from "Is she my sister?" It would convey a note of surprise, perhaps.

Pitch level 4 is employed to give particular or unusual emphasis. An exasperated mother screams at Junior, who is drawing pictures with her lipstick:

$$\text{2} \qquad \text{4} \qquad \text{1}$$
$$\underline{\text{Leave that a\underline{lo}ne!}}$$

òr,

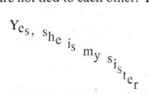

It has probably occurred to you that pitch and stress seem to fall on the same syllable and it is true that they usually go together. But they don't always; they are not tied to each other. You might easily say:

$$Y_{es,}\ _{sh}e\ _{is}\ _{my}\ _{si}_{s}_{t}_{e}_{r}$$

—and you could put the stress anywhere you wished in this sequence of descending pitches.

As was suggested above (with the tag question and with "What did you say?") we do interesting things to our sentences by varying the pitches employed. For instance, we have two principal types of questions, the "yes/no question" and the "information question"—so-called because the first one anticipates "yes" or "no" as an answer, and the second expects some kind of information. Examples of the yes/no are:

> Do you like it here?
> Are you taking chemistry?
> Is that the man you're going to marry?
> Have you lived in Minneapolis very many years?

We observe that these questions normally would have the 2-3-3 pitch pattern, the voice holding level or rising at the end.

The information question on the other hand uses the 2-3-1 pattern just like normal statements:

> How long have you lived here?
> Why did your brother sell his MG?
> What grade did you make in history?
> When did you first learn to like opera?

(These questions are often called "wh- questions" after the words that commonly signal them.)

Note what happens if we change the pitch patterns. If we give a 2-3-3 pattern to "How long have you lived here?" we are indicating that the person has told us and we can't believe our ears. Or perhaps that we didn't hear him and would like a repetition. Similarly, the yes/no 2-3-3 question a student might ask about a teacher—"Is she difficult?"—becomes something quite else with 2-3-1 :

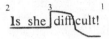

As in "Brother! Is she *ever!*"

It isn't our purpose here to ring all the changes of this sort that we all know—if only subconsciously—but to indicate the kinds of things we achieve in this manner. Once alert to the possibilities, and with an awareness of some of the mechanics involved, it is entertaining to catch them occurring in the speech that constantly envelops us, including especially our own.

The third kind of suprasegmental, the one yet remaining to be discussed, is juncture, and is, as we said, a holding apart, a separating, of adjoining sounds. The usual analysis presents us with four levels of juncture, though it is also common to note the absence of juncture, which is called "close" or "zero" juncture. It isn't quite as empty an exercise as it may seem to note this lack because there are times when the contrast between two utterances is exactly that one has a juncture and the other doesn't. For example, see suggested assignment 1, "juncture," sentences *h* and *i*.

Here we will be satisfied with merely *illustrating* the least of these junctures, the so-called plus juncture. If as a child you played with phrases like "a nice man" as opposed to "an ice man," what you were playing with was plus juncture. The same with "I scream" and "ice cream" in the little jingle that surely we all chanted. In phonemic transcription this juncture is symbolized with $/+/$. Thus the key difference between "It was a great rain" and "It was a grey train" would be $/gret+ren/$ in the former and $/gre+tren/$ in the latter.

The remaining kinds of juncture, in ascending order of degree, are single bar juncture$/|/$, double bar juncture$/\|/$, and double cross juncture $/\#/$.

Single bar juncture was what was involved in the ambiguous sentence we considered earlier: "The man who visited my sister regularly begged her to marry him," but let's look at a different one:

It left the students involved in a state of confusion.

Like the other sentence this one is ambiguous only on paper. What it means depends on "how you read it," or more specifically where you put the single bar juncture. This juncture is characterized by a slight lengthening, slowing, of the last few segmental phonemes just before it, and a quick resumption of tempo once the juncture has been bridged. Our example could be read like this:

It left the students | involved in a state of confusion.

In this case all the students we're talking about have been left confused. But here's another reading:

It left the students involved | in a state of confusion.

With this version not all the students are confused but just the ones who were involved. Apparently there must be other students who are not confused at all. Try reading this sentence in each fashion. Notice how your tempo slows and you l-e-n-g-t-h-e-n out the sounds just before the juncture, and then the juncture once over you steam right along again.

Single bar juncture is not ordinarily reflected in modern punctuation, which tends to be minimal. At times perhaps it should be punctuated. If I had written the sentence about the confused students, and if I had noticed the ambiguity, and if for some reason I didn't want to restate it in a better way, I would conclude that it *had* to have a comma—rulebooks to the contrary—in order to indicate the intended reading. "Clarity above all" should be the writer's motto.

But many students who try to punctuate by ear—maybe they have been told to "put a comma where you hear a pause"—will put unnecessary and sometimes "incorrect" commas where single bar juncture occurs. Because of course they *do* "hear a pause." For example, it is very common in a sentence with a long subject to have single bar juncture between the subject and the predicate—but it is not the fashion in writing to put a comma there and countless students have been criticized for doing it.

> Example: **All** students in the dormitory who have cars | are required to get a parking permit.

The next juncture, called the double bar juncture, is not merely a pause but a particular *kind* of pause, and it's easy to hear once you learn to recognize it. I think you can get yourself to hear it if you count slowly from one to five: one, two, three, four, five. Note that as you say each of these numbers (except five) your voice drops and then rises again. It's like a sag with a hook on the end, which we could represent with diagrams something like this:

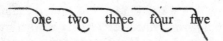

(Please disregard here the other way of counting—with merely a rising pitch.) I suggested that you do this counting slowly only so that you might exaggerate the "dip" and following "hook" of the voice which are characteristic of this juncture. Actually, the same features would be present no matter how fast you counted.

Now, if this juncture was used only in counting it would be of minimal interest, but of course it isn't so confined. We use it all the time. Here is a sample sentence:

El Paso || the westernmost city in Texas || is || perhaps || also the nicest.

The phrase *the westernmost city in Texas* is what we were taught in school to call an appositive and to set off by commas. We can now see that these commas reflect a reality of speech: double-bar juncture. Notice how the same dip and hook occur on "Paso" and on "Texas" as on the numbers in the counting exercise of a moment ago. Notice too how the words following the juncture pick up at about the same pitch level on which the "hook" terminated:

El Paso / the westernmost city of Texas / is . . .

Observe too the effect of the commas—representing double-bar juncture again—surrounding "perhaps." The junctures here would naturally be optional, but including them seems to emphasize the "perhaps." Contrast the effect of saying the same string of words without those two junctures. We quickly see that either would be "correct" but that the effect is different, and if you were writing a sentence like this the criterion would be the effect you wanted.

This same juncture is involved in the distinction between "restrictive" and "nonrestrictive" clauses which troubled so many of us in school. Here is a pair of sentences:

The boys who were fighting in the principal's office | were thrown out of school. (Single bar juncture after long subject.)

The boys, || who were fighting in the principal's office, || were thrown out of school.

The difference is obvious: In the first sentence only the boys who were fighting were expelled and presumably there were some other boys who were not; whereas in the second *all* the boys were fighting and they were *all* thrown out. The junctures in the second sentence, isolating the clause as they do, almost *insist* that it be treated as a little bit of extra information thrown in as lagniappe, something extra on the side.

All this leaves us with just one kind of juncture to examine and it is very simple. It is the double-cross juncture: /#/. It is what you did with your voice on "five" when you counted from one to five a moment ago. Here it is again:

one two three four five six

This time it's on "six," and just as the double bar juncture on the other numbers in the string seems to say to the listener "Don't go away; there's more coming," so the signal on "six" seems to say, "That's all. End of transmission."

Efforts have been made to define the sentence in terms of this double cross juncture, something like: a sentence is a word or group of words ended with double-cross juncture. Thus whether "I went downtown" is a sentence would depend on the intonation pattern:

$$\overset{2}{\underline{I~went~down}}\overset{3}{down}\overset{1}{town}$$

That would be a sentence. But this would not:

$$\overset{2}{\underline{I~went~downtown}}\overset{2}{}$$

because your listener is expecting you to continue, perhaps adding "to buy a shirt." In the same way, with:

$$\overset{2}{\underline{I~went~downtown~to~buy~a~shirt}}\overset{2}{}$$

he will be expecting you to add something else, like "for my brother," and so on until you finally put the double-plus juncture:

$$\overset{2}{\underline{I~went~downtown~to~buy~a~shirt~for~my}}\overset{3}{bro}ther~\overset{1}{}\#$$

Thus the sentence would be nothing like "a complete thought" (whatever that is) nor would it have to have a subject and predicate. It would simply depend on the presence of double-cross juncture. The absence of a double-cross juncture tells the listener that more is to come, and the presence of a double-cross juncture, in conjunction with the syntactic structure, signals the end of a sentence.

We have now considered the suprasegmental phonemes—twelve of them. Our treatment has been brief, but perhaps it has not been superficial *if* we have gained at least an appreciation of how they operate and how wonderfully complex they are—and of how in consort with the segmentals they comprise the sounds of the speech that comes so trippingly on the tongue.

SUGGESTED ASSIGNMENTS

1. The following words, phrases and sentences are illustrative of the points about the suprasegmentals made by Professor Past. Read each item aloud, using as guides the markers of stress, pitch, and juncture.

Stress

  a. èleméntary
  b. èlemêntary êdùcátion
  c. dârk róom
  d. dárkròom
  e. dáncing tèacher
  f. dâncing téacher
  g. He wanted the hêad shíp.
  h. He wanted the héadshìp.
  i. He is hôme síck.
  j. He is hómesìck.
  k. I am an ôutdóor lòver.
  l. I am an ôutdòor lóver.
  m. Nôrth Wéstchester
  n. Nôrthwèst Chéster
  o. a gôod réading còurse
  p. a gòod réading còurse.
  q. I believe thât mân is hónest.
  r. I believe that mán is hónest.
  s. (Regarding a flag waving over a fort)
     That is ôld Òld Glóry.
  t. Gîve mè a drínk.

Pitch

  a. [2]Kate was the[3] wìnner.[1]

  b. [2]She is very[3] hàppy.[1]

  c. [2]She is very[3] happy?[3]

  d. [2]Is she very[3] happy[3]

  e. [2]Let go of my [4]eàr![1]

  f. [2]What did you find in the[3] trunk?[1]

Juncture

  a. The rabbits álso | enjoyed the lettuce. # (as well as we)
  b. The rábbits | also enjoyed the lettuce. # (as well as the carrots)
  c. My younger sister especially | likes to dance. #
  d. My younger sister | especially likes to dance. #

   e. He was beaten | up by the bridge. #

   f. He was beaten up | by the bridge. #

   g. The students who came to the meeting in the gym | had many questions to ask. #

   h. It's all ríght | here in the bóok. #

   i. It's all right here in the bóok. #

   j. Rags ‖ my brown dachshund ‖ likes to curl up in the doghouse. #

   k. I whistled to Rags # who came bounding to meet me. #

   l. At léast ‖ some of the students were rewarded. #

   m. At least some of the students were rewarded. #

   n. You may ‖ if you wish ‖ bring some beer. #

   o. Although the sun was down ‖ it was light enough to play. #

   p. It was light enough to play # although the sun was down. #

2. Read the following sentences aloud so as to bring out more than one meaning.

   a. I have a son, David, who is a doctor.

   b. The soldiers were issued twenty four hour passes.

   c. Do you want tea or coffee?

   d. Roger slipped on his shoe.

   e. His desire to be certain remained steadfast.

   f. Bryan faced a charge of shooting back in 1947.

   g. He's going to Chicago, isn't he?

   h. This one particularly needs attention.

   i. I suspect that you were right there.

   j. The women are out shooting the men.

   k. Do you know how happy people ought to be?

   l. I have instructions to leave.

   m. He found the library books.

   n. The Israeli city fathers appointed an Arab deputy chief engineer in charge of roads.

   o. They work out in the field.

   p. Are my sentences all right?

FURTHER READINGS

Bronstein, Arthur J. *The Pronunciation of American English*. New York: Appleton-Century-Crofts, 1960. On standards of prouunciation, see pp. 3–18; on assimilation, pp. 207–215.

Fries, Charles C. *The Teaching of English*. Ann Arbor, Mich.: George Wahr Publishing Company, 1949. See pages 46–73 for one of the best treatments of standards of pronunciation.

Hall, Robert A., Jr. *Linguistics and Your Language*. New York: Doubleday & Company, Inc. (Anchor Books), 1960. On the sound system, see Chapter 6.

Kenyon, John Samuel. *American Pronunciation*, 10th ed. Ann Arbor, Mich.: George Wahr Publishing Company, 1961. On the sound system, see especially pp. 33–73; on assimilation, pp. 76–80.

————. "Cultural Levels and Functional Varieties of English," *College English,* Vol. 10 (October 1948), pp. 31–36.

Robertson, Stuart, and Frederick G. Cassidy. *The Development of Modern English,* Englewood Cliffs, N.J.: Prentice-Hall, Inc., 1954. On the sound system, see pp. 52–76; on assimilation, pp. 79–80; on spelling and spelling reform, pp. 353–374 (there is a useful bibliography on p. 374); on pronunciation, Chapter 12.

Sapir, Edward. *Language.* New York: Harcourt Brace Jovanovich, Inc., 1921. On the sound system, see Chapter III.

Thomas, Charles Kenneth, *Phonetics of American English,* 2d ed. New York: The Ronald Press Company, 1958. On standards of pronunciation, see pp. 253–260.

8
LINGUISTIC GEOGRAPHY

Some Words Stop at Marietta, Ohio

Gledhill Cameron

Linguistic geography, also called dialect geography, is the systematic study of language differences within a specified area, usually a country or a part of a country. The differences are those of pronunciation, vocabulary, and grammar. To get accurate information, trained linguists hold long interviews with native informants, who have been carefully selected so as to offer a representative sampling of the speech of the area.

When all the information has been collected and edited, it is made public by a series of maps (see pages 218, 222, 223) or by books and articles. As a result, we get a detailed account of both regional and social dialects.[1] One caution must be urged here. As you study the data

From *Collier's*, June 25, 1954. Reprinted by permission of the author. Copyright 1954.

[1] The 416 informants for the *Linguistic Atlas of New England* were classified into these types:

"Type   I: Little formal education, little reading and restricted social contacts.

Type II: Better formal education (usually high school) and/or wider reading and social contacts.

Type III: Superior education (usually college), cultured background, wide reading and/or extensive social contacts.

Type A: Aged, and/or regarded by the field worker as old-fashioned.

Type B: Middle-aged or younger, and/or regarded by the field worker as more modern."

From Hans Kurath, *Handbook of the Linguistic Geography of New England* (Washington, D.C.: American Council of Learned Societies, 1939), p. 44.

With this information we can generalize on the social class using any given pronunciation, word, or grammatical form. In other words, we can decide which forms are standard English and which are nonstandard English, also called "substandard English" and "vulgate." [eds.]

in the readings of this section, you must remember that this information pertains to the SPOKEN language, and may or may not be true of the written language.

The first reading below by Gledhill Cameron, is an entertaining but sound report on the field work of the linguistic geographer.

What language do you speak? Would you call it "plain American"? If so, you may be surprised to learn that despite the vast influence of radio, TV, the movies, magazines, books and national advertising, many of the words and expressions you use every day might not even be understood by people elsewhere in the United States—who also speak "plain American."

If you're a housewife, do you make bacon and eggs in a frying pan—or, as many other American women do, in a *spider, creeper, or drip-drop*? When you clean house, do you *straighten up* or *tidy up*, *rid up* or *redd up* (as women do in some parts of New England, Ohio and Indiana); *make ménage* (as in New Orleans), or *muck out* (as in some Colorado mining communities)?

If Junior sneaks away from school, do your neighbors say he *skips*, *bags* or *lays out of* school, or that he *plays hooky* or *hooks Jack*? When he reports on how he spent his time, does he tell you he climbed trees, or that he *clim, clum, clome, cloom, clam* or *clammed* them? If he ate too many green apples, does he get sick *to, at, in, with* or *about* his stomach?

To chart the differences in vocabulary, grammar and pronunciation from one American community to another, a small band of language experts—professors and graduate students representing a number of universities—has been traveling around the country for the last 20 years, asking people what words they use for all sorts of simple, everyday objects and actions. They have compiled long lists of variants for everything from the words for the clavicles of a chicken (*wishbone, witch bone, pull bone, pully bone, lucky bone, merry-thought*) to our expressions for the woman who's going to have a baby (she might be *in health, in the family way, in preggety, on the road to Boston, fragrant* or *footbroke*—the last a local Southern expression derived from an African word).

Sometimes the linguistic geographers use tape or disc recordings, but most of their minutely detailed data are collected in thousands of bulky notebooks, in a special phonetic script which can reproduce about 400 differences in vowel sounds alone. Using this script, the interviewers write down the casual conversations of men and women all over America exactly as they talk on their own front porches (*stoops, piazzas, galleries*).

The linguistic fieldworker must be part historian and part sociologist; he must also have in him the spirit of the bloodhound and more than a trace of the gossip. He will go wherever he can find an informant willing to give the six to 20 hours it takes to answer his questions, which cover from 500 to 800 items of everyday speech. The language experts have carried their notebooks into saloons, cotton fields, race tracks, mines, hospitals, schools, court-houses, shops and factories. One linguist obtained a fruitful interview while riding around in a patrol car with the chief of police of a small Southern town, then got another by sitting for hours on a sidewalk curb, chatting with his subject.

A second researcher spent one whole day quizzing a hard-working barber; another day talking to a railroad-crossing watchman who kept a nervous lookout for the road detective (visitors, inquiring professors included, were contrary to regulations); another day perched on a tractor interviewing a farmer; and another in a hospital, where the subject was recovering from an unexpected operation which had interrupted their first interview.

The information so exhaustively collected is going into a colossal work titled *Linguistic Atlas of the United States and Canada* (Canada is included to cover colloquial expressions which ignore the international boundary). When the atlas is finished, an estimated 10 years from now, it will contain thousands of maps showing local and regional speech differences and the geographical boundaries, called isoglosses, that limit the areas in which the words and expressions are used. The work is being done under the direction of the University of Michigan's Dr. Hans Kurath—an internationally known linguist who has been a leader of the atlas project since its origin in 1929.

AT WORK ON MANY LINGUISTIC ATLASES

The atlas actually will consist of a series of regional sets, the first of which, *Linguistic Atlas of New England*, already has been published. Its six volumes (price for the set: $185) were brought out by Brown University and the American Council of Learned Societies from 1939 to 1943, at a cost of about $250,000. Additional atlases are in various stages of completion, two at the University of Michigan, and others at the Universities of Minnesota, Colorado, New Mexico and California, the University of Washington at Seattle and Louisiana State University. Preliminary studies have been made for still another at the University of Texas.[2]

Three kinds of maps are used by the researchers to plot variations. First there's the lexical map, which shows the different words Americans use to indicate the same object or action. For example, "something extra" is *lagniappe* in New Orleans, something *to boot* in Kentucky, a *brawtus* in Charleston, South Carolina, a *pillon* in New Mexico—all good American words.

The linguists use a second, phonetic map to show differences in the pronunciation of the same words. The classic example is provided by the

[2] For up-to-date information on the progress of the regional linguistic atlases, see the headnote to "Linguistic Atlas Findings," p. 228 [eds.]

old lady in North Carolina who said about her crop of tomatoes, "Oh, we'll eat what we *kin,* and what we *cain't* we'll *can.*"

The morphological map, the third type, indicates differences in grammar. Widespread education is rapidly wiping out grammatical variations, the linguists have found. One Georgia man summed up the changes that are occurring: "I used to say, 'I drink water' and 'I have drinked,'" he proudly told an atlas fieldworker. "Now I say, 'I drink,' 'I drank,' and 'I have drank.'"

Most of the regional departures from the common language of Americans (technically, we all speak what linguists call American English) involve the homey aspects of life: family relationships, kitchens and cookery, farm work, daily chores, children's play and other activities which are relatively immune from outside influences. Some of these localisms are confined to very small geographic areas, says Dr. Kurath. If you say *hook Jack,* meaning to be absent from school without leave, you are most probably from Cape Cod. If you call cows by hollering *chay!,* you're from Williamsburg County, South Carolina. If you're an old-timer from eastern Long Island, you might call a barnyard or cowpen a *pightle* (it rhymes with "title").

New England, which had many isolated settlements in colonial times, still carries the traces of that isolation in its current colloquialisms. A deep-dish apple pie is *apple Jonathan* in Rhode Island, *apple grunt* around Plymouth and on Cape Cod, in Massachusetts, and *apple slump* in the Narragansett-Bay region. A garbage pail is an *orts pail* in Essex County, Massachusetts, and (as far as the researchers can tell) nowhere else. A spring onion is a *rarepipe* only in certain sections of eastern New England.

According to some people in the great valley of Pennsylvania, a horse doesn't whinny, it *laughs,* and a setting hen may be known in the same region as a *clook.*

Judging from research to date, it's only in Indiana that a child coasting down a hill on a sled or wagon goes *bellity-bump*; and only around New London that he goes *belly-kuhchunk!* In the upper Midwest he may go downhill *boy fashion,* and in Louisiana he'll go *scooting* or *head fo'most.* In other parts of the country he may go *belly flop, gut, bunt, bump, bumpus, button, bust, booster, wop, whack, womp, slide, slam, kuhchug* or *grinder.*

A QUAINT TALE OF COURTSHIP

The rural areas retain some of the most colorful speech localisms. In some sparsely settled parts of Maine, for example, you might still hear of a *gorming* (stupid) man who gets *all of a biver* (excited) about a *ding-clicker* (a pretty young woman) and invites her to a *hog-wrestle* (a dance). But he wouldn't propose until he was sure she wasn't *pizen neat* (too neat) or a *drozzel tail* (slovenly person).

It's also in the more remote sections that linguistic geographers report the greatest resistance to interviews. One of the most successful of the atlas fieldworkers is Dr. Raven Ioor McDavid, Jr., of Western Reserve University, Cleveland,[3] a South Carolinian who has conducted chatty sessions with 470 housewives, farmers, lumbermen, miners, businessmen, politicians, Civil War veterans, literary ladies and stenographers all over the country. Dr. McDavid recalls an occasion in Georgia where he couldn't get *anyone* to talk to him. He finally discovered that the small town he was visiting had recently been described by a metropolitan newspaper as a "typical hick town." The citizens were now so sensitive that almost no one was willing to talk to any stranger, whatever his apparent purpose. (The local grocer eventually consented to see McDavid—after insisting that the interview be conducted in the back of his store, at night.)

In his home state of South Carolina, McDavid—who customarily carries 15 or 16 colored pencils, mechanical pencils and fountain pens in his pocket for marking symbols—was accused of being an FBI agent by a man who shut the door on him.

Dr. Harold B. Allen of the University of Minnesota, who has conducted almost 200 interviews for the Atlas of the Upper Midwest, says he was accused of being a Communist spy once, by a hardware merchant in Bemidji, Minnesota. ("Who else," said the hardwareman reasonably, "would ask all those questions?")

The late Dr. Guy S. Lowman, Jr., who did most of the field interviews for the New England, Middle and South Atlantic regions, once came out of a house in West Virginia to find the air let out of his automobile tires. (He had been mistaken for a revenuer.) Another time he was chased out of a house by the irate son of a genteel Southern lady, who felt that the linguist had put an indelicate question to his mother: "Madam, what do you call the male kind of cow?" (Cityfolk may not realize it, but the word "bull" is never used in mixed company in some parts of the country. Among the more polite substitutes linguistic geographers have recorded are the *masculine*, rhyming with "vine" and heard only on Nantucket Island, Massachusetts, and in West Virginia, the *surley*, in eastern New Mexico and some parts of Texas, and, more generally, the *old man*, the *roarer*, the *mister*, the *master, male critter, toro, gentleman cow, preacher cow, beast, brute, jock, major, top cow, tuppin' ox, ranger* and the *he*.)

But fieldworkers get only too hospitable a welcome in most places. That is one of the joys, as well as one of the burdens, of a linguistic geographer's life. In the good cause of recording our American speech, they have eaten veritable mountains of home-made cakes, pies, cookies, breads and biscuits of varying degrees of specific gravity, as well as countless doughnuts (*crullers, olicooks, fat-cakes, fried cakes, riz doughnuts, fossnocks*).

[3] Now at the University of Chicago. [eds.]

McDavid recalls with satisfaction the day he shared a lunch of mule ears or meat pastys (it rhymes with "nasty") with miners in northern Michigan, and heard a classic argument as to whether the pastys, which provide the miners with a substantial midday meal, keep better carried in the shirt or in the boot.

But a home-cooked meal in Georgia in "lay-by-time," when the cotton is opening up and before it's ready to pick, is best remembered as the occasion for what McDavid, who prides himself on "blending in with the foliage," describes as his greatest tribute.

"The lunch was a mess of something pretty greasy and full of red pepper," he says, "but I fell to. I noticed my informant's elderly sister, who had cooked the meal, watching me with great satisfaction. Then she said: 'I could have gone and kilt a chicken, Mr. McDavid. But I figured *you* didn't want to be treated like no preacher.' "

The fieldworkers admit that it is surprising that people are willing to be interviewed and to talk long, readily and freely. Except in the most general way, they aren't told exactly what the interview is about; if they knew, they might become self-conscious—and it's the unguarded response of natural, everyday conversation that the linguist hopes to capture.

Armed with lists of the kinds of words he wants the subject to use, the researcher conducts the interview in as close an approximation to casual conversation as he can. He must also be keenly alert to pronunciation and grammar. McDavid usually starts out with what he calls shotgun questions: "What do you call this room that we're in?" "What are those utensils on the stove?" "What do you call other rooms in the house?" The fieldworker never asks a subject to repeat, and answers are never directly suggested.

"For example," explains Dr. Allen, "I'll say to the person, 'I suppose you fry your eggs in a . . .' then he'll take it from there and fill in 'skillet' or 'frying pan' or whichever word comes most naturally. Often he'll look surprised that I don't know. Each person requires a different approach. We ask about familiar things—expressions of time, weather, farm crops, and utensils, vehicles, animals, food, the family and its relations, the human body, social life and institutions, religion and so on.

"I usually start out by explaining we're making a study of the changing names for things. That pleases the old folks, who have thought all along that kids nowadays are pretty dumb not to know the difference between a 'hame' and a 'chokestrap' (parts of a harness)."

A community is selected for interviews only after a careful study of its history, population shifts and the influence of foreign groups who may have settled there. McDavid wouldn't be surprised, for example, to hear a native of Hudson, New York, say he *ran afoul of* something, instead of *ran across* or *ran onto*. The seafaring expression comes naturally in Hudson because it was settled by whalers from Nantucket, Massachusetts.

Around Marietta, Ohio, he'd be prepared to hear people use such New

England terms as *pail* instead of *bucket, chipmunk* instead of *g...rel*, and *boss!* instead of *sook* when they call a cow—although t... expressions are the more common elsewhere in Ohio. A new England... mercial company once sent an entire community to Marietta early in... settlement days, so that linguists today call Marietta and its environs a... Yankee "speech island."

The linguistic geographer tries to talk to two distinct types of people in each community studied. The first type is an older person with family roots deep in the community, someone with limited education, and with few outside social contacts which might tend to blur or even erase certain localisms from his speech. The second type is younger, usually middle-aged, with more education and broader social contacts or travel experience. In some communities, a third type of informant—representing the "cultivated" speech of the community—is also interviewed. By sampling the speech of these three groups, the linguist can determine which local expressions are used by everyone in the community, which tend to disappear, and, if so, what replaces them as the community grows more educated or "cultured." An interesting discovery: one town's speech vulgarity may be a perfectly acceptable regionalism in another community, even among the "cultivated" inhabitants.

Linguists believe that recording the living language of America for the first time should lead to a more realistic approach to the teaching of English in schools and colleges. For, they ask, isn't it a waste of time for English teachers to try to stop New Englanders from saying "hadn't ought to" when linguistic studies show that this grammatically "wrong" expression is used by nearly everyone in New England, educated or not? Or to try to remove "ain't" from the speech of Southerners, when it is generally accepted in the colloquial speech of cultivated persons in the South?

Thus far, a major fact established by atlas investigations is that although there's a popular idea of Northern and Southern speech, divided by the Mason and Dixon's line in the Eastern part of the country, there are, in fact, three distinct speech areas in the East. The third is a clear Midland dialect area between North and South, corresponding to the Pennsylvania settlement area of early days. The North-Midland speech boundary runs in a westerly direction from below Sandy Hook in New Jersey through northern Pennsylvania; the line separating Midland from South runs in a southwesterly direction from Dover, Delaware, through Baltimore and along the Blue Ridge in Virginia. And in the Eastern states from Maine to South Carolina, linguistic geographers can plot 18 dialect divisions largely created by the original colonial settlements and the subsequent routes of migration.

This Eastern coastal area, oldest in point of settlement, still retains the nation's greatest diversity of speech from one community to another. But then, as the dialect divisions flow westward on the map—the way our population did—they begin to unravel, and strands of the three begin to overlap.

ly

arietta, Ohio

209

round squir-
e second
com-
its

ı ways with him wherever he goes," **Dr.** Kurath
ain types of English were carried westward and
ıl varieties; new words were coined, old words came
es, and words were borrowed from the Indian lan-
lidwest, and from the Spanish of the Southwest. But
lish vocabulary in this country is nevertheless clearly
er settlements on the Atlantic slope."

ɔday is away from regional words and expressions,
ɔ don't anticipate complete uniformity in the speech of
uᴄ..—where the way we talk, as well as the way we live, is
based on the bᴇ⊔ᴄᴧ ịhat men can be different, and still be equal.

"While some vocabulary and grammatical differences may disappear,"
says Dr. McDavid, "the differences in word pronunciation are likely to
persist. I don't think anyone can impose a single set of patterns on Americans—for speech or for anything else."

Regional
and Social Variations

Albert H. Marckwardt

In this selection Albert H. Marckwardt, Emeritus Professor of English
at Princeton University, discusses the origins of American regional
dialects, explains the making of a linguistic atlas, and presents information on the different regional dialects. Professor Marckwardt was
director of the *Linguistic Atlas of the North-Central States*, which includes the states of Wisconsin, Michigan, Illinois, Kentucky, and Indiana,
and part of Ontario.

The English language is spoken natively in America by no less than
145 million persons over an area of some three million square miles.[1]

From *American English* by Albert H. Marckwardt. Reprinted by permission of
the publisher, Oxford University Press, Inc., copyright © 1958.

[1] The population of our country is now over 200 million. [eds.]

Various parts of the United States differ considerably from each other with respect to climate, topography, plant and animal life, economic conditions, and social structure. Sociologists and historians recognize at least six regional cultures within the continental borders of the country. The assumption that differences in culture and environmental background bring about differences in language will[2] justify the inference that the language is likely not to be uniform throughout the country. The American novelist John Steinbeck in his *Grapes of Wrath* offers convincing evidence of the plausibility of this assumption:

> "I knowed you wasn't Oklahomy folks. You talk queer kinda—That ain't no blame, you understan'."
> "Everybody says words different," said Ivy, "Arkansas folks says 'em different, and Oklahomy folks says 'em different. And we seen a lady from Massachusetts, an' she said 'em differentest of all. Couldn' hardly make out what she was sayin'."

Early travelers to America and native commentators on the language agree on the existence of regional differences at an early period in our national history. Mrs. Anne Royal called attention to various Southernisms in the works which she wrote during the second quarter of the nineteenth century, and as early as 1829, Dr. Robley Dunglison had identified many of the Americanisms, in the glossary he compiled, with particular portions of the country. Charles Dickens recognized regional differences in the English he encountered in his first tour of the United States, and William Howard Russell, reporting on Abraham Lincoln's first state banquet, at which he was a guest, mentions his astonishment at finding "a diversity of accent almost as great as if a number of foreigners had been speaking English."

A number of other observers, however, were sufficiently impressed by the uniformity of the language throughout the country to make this a matter of comment. De Tocqueville, in a rather extended treatment of the language of the young republic, flatly declared, "There is no patois in the New World," and John Pickering, along with Noah Webster easily the most distinguished of our early philologists, also remarked on the great uniformity of dialect through the United States, "in consequence," as he said, "of the frequent removals of people from one part of our country to another."

There is truth in both types of comment. People in various parts of the United States do not all speak alike, but there is greater uniformity here than in England or in the countries of Western Europe, and this makes the collection of a trustworthy body of information upon the regional variations in American English a somewhat difficult and delicate matter.

The gathering of authentic data on the dialects of many of the countries of Western Europe began in the latter decades of the nineteenth century.

2 Text slightly but not materially altered by permission of the author. [eds.]

The *Atlas linguistique de la France* followed closely upon the heels of the *Sprachatlas des deutschen Reichs*, and the activities of the English Dialect Society were initiated about the same time. In 1889 a group of American scholars organized the American Dialect Society, hoping that the activities of this organization might result in a body of material from which either a dialect dictionary or a series of linguistic maps, or both, might be compiled. The society remained relatively small, however, and although some valuable information appeared in its journal *Dialect Notes*, a systematic survey of the regional varieties of American English has not yet resulted from its activities.[3]

The past quarter of a century, however, has seen the development of such a survey. Beginning in 1928, a group of researchers under the direction of Professor Hans Kurath, now of the University of Michigan, undertook the compilation of a *Linguistic Atlas of New England* as the first unit of a projected *Linguistic Atlas of the United States and Canada*. The New England atlas, comprising a collection of some 600 maps, each showing the distribution of a single language feature throughout the area, was published over the period from 1939 to 1943. Since that time, field work for comparable atlases of the Middle Atlantic and of the South Atlantic states has been completed, and the materials are awaiting editing and publication. Field records for atlases of the North Central states and the Upper Middle West are virtually complete, and significant beginnings have been made in the Rocky Mountain and the Pacific Coast areas. Surveys in Louisiana, in Texas, and in Ontario are also under way.[4] It is perhaps not too optimistic to predict that within the next twenty-five years all of the United States and Canada as well will have been covered in at least an initial survey.

For a number of reasons it is not easy to collect a body of valid and reliable information on American dialects. The wide spread of education, the virtual extinction of illiteracy, the extreme mobility of the population—both geographically and from one social class to another—and the tremendous development of a number of media of mass communication have all contributed to the recession of local speech forms. Moreover, the cultural insecurity of a large portion of the American people has caused them to feel apologetic about their language. Consequently, they seldom display the same degree of pride or affection that many an English or a European speaker has for his particular patois. Since all dialect research is essentially a sampling process, this means that the investigator must take particular

---

[3] The official journal of the American Dialect Society is now called the *Publication of the American Dialect Society*. This society is now sponsoring the *Dictionary of American Regional English*, an extensive project under the direction of Professor Frederic G. Cassidy of the University of Wisconsin, Madison, and also *American Speech*, a quarterly of linguistic usage. [eds.]

[4] For the current status of the regional atlases and the progress of field work, see the headnote to "Linguistic Atlas Findings," p. 228. [eds.]

pains to secure representative and comparable samples from the areas which are studied. Happily, the very care which this demands has had the result of developing the methodology of linguistic geography in this country to a very high level.

In general, the material for a linguistic atlas is based upon the natural responses of a number of carefully selected individuals representing certain carefully chosen communities, which in themselves reflect the principal strains of settlement and facets of cultural development in the area as a whole. Since the spread of education generally results in the disappearance of local or regional speech forms, and since the extension of schooling to virtually all of the population has been an achievement of the past seventy-five years, it became necessary for the American investigator to differentiate between the oldest generation, for whom schooling beyond the elementary level is not usual, and a middle-aged group who is likely to have had some experience with secondary schools. In addition, it is highly desirable to include some representatives of the standard or cultivated speech in each region, that their language may serve as a basis of comparison with the folk speech. Accordingly, in the American atlases, from each community represented, the field worker will choose at least two, and sometimes three representatives, in contrast to the usual practice of European researchers, who may safely content themselves with one. Moreover, it is equally necessary to make certain that the persons chosen in any community have not been subject to alien linguistic influences; consequently, only those who have lived there all of their lives, and preferably those who represent families who have long been identified with the area in question, are interviewed, although as one moves westward into the more recently settled areas this is not always possible.

Since complete materials are available only for the eastern seaboard and for the area north of the Ohio River as far west as the Mississippi, tentative conclusions relative to the regional variations in American English can be presented only for the eastern half of the country. The principal dialect areas presented in Kurath's *Word Geography of the Eastern United States* are indicated on the map on page 215.

The three major dialect boundaries, it will be noted, cut the country into lateral strips and are labeled by Professor Kurath *Northern, Midland,* and *Southern* respectively. The line which separates the Northern and Midland areas begins in New Jersey a little below Sandy Hook, proceeds northwest to the east branch of the Susquehanna near Scranton, Pennsylvania, then goes westward through Pennsylvania just below the northern tier of counties. In Ohio the boundary dips below the Western Reserve, then turns northwest again, passing above Fort Wayne, Indiana. When it approaches South Bend it dips slightly to the southwest and cuts through Illinois, reaching the Mississippi at a point slightly above Quincy. The other principal boundary, that separating the Southern and Midland areas, begins at a point somewhat below Dover in Delaware, sweeps through Baltimore in something of an arc, turns sharply southwest north of the Potomac, follows the crest of the Blue Ridge in Virginia, and south of the James River swerves out into the North Carolina Piedmont. As we approach the lower part of South Carolina and Georgia the boundary is as yet unknown.

Even these necessarily incomplete results of the survey carried on under Professor Kurath and his associates have modified considerably our previous conceptions of the regional distribution of American speech forms. This modification is brought about principally by adding one concept and eliminating another. The concept thus eliminated has been variously known as Middle Western, Western, or General American. The older view of American dialects, reduced to its simplest terms, recognized the existence of a New England type of speech, a Southern type, and the remainder was generally blanketed by some such term as General American.

It seems clear now that what is neither New England nor Southern—which includes, of course, something between three-quarters and nine-tenths of the continental United States—is far too diverse and lacking in homogeneity to be considered a single major dialect. We know, for example, that there are a significant number of differences, both in vocabulary and in verb inflections, between the folk speech of most of Pennsylvania and that of New York state, and between Michigan and Wisconsin on the one hand, and most of Indiana and large portions of Illinois and Ohio on the other. As our information for the rest of the country becomes available, there can be little doubt that this conclusion will be strengthened.

The concept which has been added is the recognition of a Midland type of speech as distinct from both North and South. An examination of the evidence which Professor Kurath presents in his *Word Geography* leaves no doubt that the speech of this area, though it is by no means uniform, is sufficiently differentiated from both North and South to justify its classification as a major dialect area. This conclusion is supported not only by Atwood's study of the verb forms in the eastern portion of the country but by the available materials from the North Central States.

The map shown on page 215 includes also a few, but not all, of the sub-dialect areas which merit recognition. In the North the principal area is that which separates coastal New England from western New England, New York State, and the territory to the west. In general, this boundary follows the line of the Green Mountains, the Berkshire Hills, and the Connecticut River. The Metropolitan New York area consists of a broad circle with the city itself at the center; the Hudson Valley area encompasses the original Dutch settlements in New York and northern New Jersey, spreading into northeastern Pennsylvania. The Midland area is divided into northern and southern sub-areas, the line of demarcation being just a little south of the Old National Road in Ohio, Indiana, and Illinois. Within the Southern dialect region, the Virginia Piedmont and the Delmarva peninsula constitute distinct sub-areas.

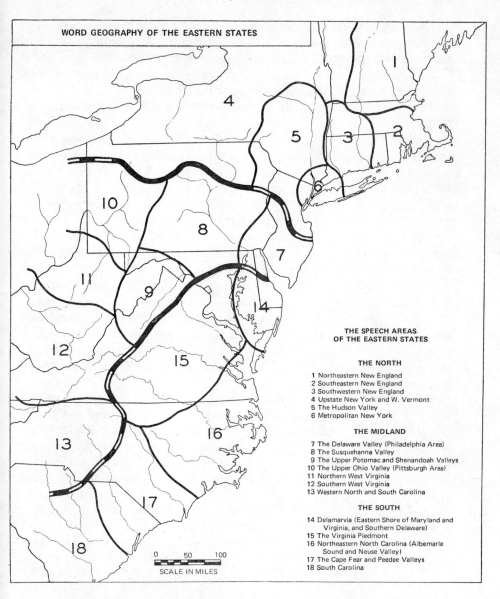

WORD GEOGRAPHY OF THE EASTERN STATES

**THE SPEECH AREAS
OF THE EASTERN STATES**

THE NORTH

1 Northeastern New England
2 Southeastern New England
3 Southwestern New England
4 Upstate New York and W. Vermont
5 The Hudson Valley
6 Metropolitan New York

THE MIDLAND

7 The Delaware Valley (Philadelphia Area)
8 The Susquehanna Valley
9 The Upper Potomac and Shenandoah Valleys
10 The Upper Ohio Valley (Pittsburgh Area)
11 Northern West Virginia
12 Southern West Virginia
13 Western North and South Carolina

THE SOUTH

14 Delamarvia (Eastern Shore of Maryland and
   Virginia, and Southern Delaware)
15 The Virginia Piedmont
16 Northeastern North Carolina (Albemarle
   Sound and Neuse Valley)
17 The Cape Fear and Peedee Valleys
18 South Carolina

0   50   100
SCALE IN MILES

From *A Word Geography of the Eastern United States* by Hans Kurath. Reprinted
by permission of the publisher, The University of Michigan Press, copyright 1949.

Thus far it is the lexical materials gathered in connection with the various atlas projects which have been analyzed most extensively, and as the title of Professor Kurath's work indicates, his plotting of the major dialect areas is based upon vocabulary evidence. For example, characteristic Northern expressions that are current throughout the area include *pail, swill, whiffle-tree* or *whippletree, comforter* or *comfortable* for a thick quilt, *brook, co-boss* or *come-boss* as a cow call, *johnnycake, salt pork*, and *darning needle* for a dragonfly. In the Midland area we find *blinds* for roller shades, *skillet, spouting* or *spouts* for eaves, a *piece* for food taken between meals, *snake feeder* for a dragonfly, *sook* as the call to calves, *armload* for an armful of wood, and one *hulls* beans when he takes off the shells. A quarter *till* the hour is a typical Midland expression, as is the elliptical *to want off*, or *out*, or *in*. The Southern has *lightwood* as the term for kindling, a *turn* of wood for an armful; stringbeans are generally *snap beans*; *hasslet* is the term for the edible inner organs of a pig, *chittlins* for the small intestine; and in this area cows are said to *low* at feeding time.

The sub-dialect areas also have their characteristic forms. In coastal New England, for instance, *pigsty* is the normal term for pigpen, *bonny clapper* for curdled sour milk, *buttonwood* for a sycamore, and *pandowdy* for a cobbler type of dessert. Eastern Virginia has *cuppin* for a cowpen, *corn house* for a crib. *Lumber room* survives as the term for a storeroom. A grasshopper is known as a *hopper grass*, and *batter bread* is used for a soft cornbread containing egg.

As far as the sectors of the American lexicon which reflect regional differences are concerned, the matter is trenchantly summarized in Kurath's *Word Geography*, where the author points out first of all that the vocabularies of the arts and sciences, of industries, commercial enterprises, social and political institutions, and even many of the crafts, are national in scope because the activities they reflect are organized on a national basis. He then goes on to say:

> Enterprises and activities that are regionally restricted have, on the other hand, a considerable body of regional vocabulary which, to be sure, may be known in other parts of the country, even if it is not in active use. The cotton planter of the South, the tobacco grower, the dairy farmer, the wheat grower, the miner, the lumberman, and the rancher of the West have many words and expressions that are strictly regional and sometimes local in their currency.

> Regional and local expressions are most common in the vocabulary of the intimate everyday life of the home and the farm—not only among the simple folk and the middle class but also among the cultured . . . Food, clothing, shelter, health, the day's work, play, mating, social gatherings, the land, the farm buildings, implements, the farm stocks and crops, the weather, the fauna and flora—these are the intimate concern of the common folk in the countryside, and for these things expressions are handed down in the family and the neighborhood

that schooling and reading and a familiarity with regional or national usage do not blot out.

It is not only in the vocabulary that one finds regional differences in American speech. There are pronunciation features as well. Throughout the Northern area, for example, the distinction between [o] and [ɔ] in such word pairs as *hoarse* and *horse, mourning* and *morning* is generally maintained; [s] regularly occurs in *grease* (verb) and *greasy*, and *root* is pronounced by many with the vowel of *wood*.[5] Within the Northern area such sub-dialects as coastal New England and Metropolitan New York also show many characteristic forms; the treatment of the vowel of *bird* is only one of these, and words of the *calf, pass, path, dance* group constitute another.[6] In the Midland area speakers fail to distinguish between *hoarse* and *horse*. Rounding is characteristic of the vowels of *hog, frog, log, wasp* and *wash*, and in the last of these words an *r* often intrudes in the speech of the not too highly educated. The vowels of *due* and *new* will resemble that of *food* rather than *feud*. In the South, *r* is 'lost' except before vowels, as it is in eastern New England and New York City but not in the Northern area generally. Words like *Tuesday, due* and *new* have a y-like glide preceding the vowel, and final [z] in Mrs. is the normal form.[7]

Among the older, relatively uneducated group and even to some extent among the middle-aged informants who have had some secondary schooling there are also regional differences in inflectional forms and syntax. For example, *hadn't ought* for "oughtn't," *see* as a past tense form, *clim* for "climbed" among the oldest sector of the population, *wan't* for "wasn't," *be* in such expressions as *How be you?*, and the choice of the preposition *to* in *sick to his stomach* are all characteristic of the Northern area. *Clum* for "climbed," *seen* for "saw," *all the further* and *I'll wait on you* are to be found in the Midlands, whereas *belongs to be, heern* for "heard," *seed* as the past tense of "to see," *holp for* "helped," *might could* and *mought have* are characteristic of the South.

All of this raises the question as to how the regional forms of American English developed in our three and one-half centuries of linguistic history. The first factor which must be taken into account is settlement history. Where did our earliest settlers come from, and what dialects did they speak? . . . at the time of the earliest settlements, English local and regional dialects were in a stronger position than they are today in that they constituted the natural speech of a greater portion of the English-speaking population and were in customary use farther up the social scale.

[5] See p. 180 for the sounds represented by the phonetic symbols in brackets. [eds.]

[6] The vowel of *bird* is /əi/ in parts of New York City. The vowel of *calf, pass, path*, and *dance* group is /a/ as in *far* in coastal New England. [eds.]

[7] Marckwardt here refers to the pronunciation of *Mrs.* as /mɪz/ or /mɪzɪz/, both commonly heard in the South. [eds.]

Moreover, it is quite unlikely that any single local settlement, even at the outset, ever consisted entirely of speakers of the same dialect. Of ten families of settlers gathered in any one place, two might well have spoken London English, three or four others one of the southern or southeastern county dialects. There would be in addition a couple of families speaking northern English and another two or three employing a western dialect. In the course of their being in constant contact with each other, compromises for the everyday terms in which their dialects differed would normally have developed, and one could reasonably expect to find a southern English term for a water receptacle, a northern word for earthworm, and a western designation for sour milk. Matters of pronunciation would eventually, perhaps after a slightly longer time, be compromised in much the same manner. Moreover, the resultant compromises for various localities would be different. In the first place, no two localities would have had exactly the same proportions of speakers of the various English dialects, and even if they had, the two localities would not have arrived at precisely the same set of compromises. Thus, early in our history we developed, at various points on the Atlantic seaboard, a number of local cultures, each with distinctive social characteristics of its own—including a dialect which was basically a unique blend of British types of speech, supplemented in its vocabulary by borrowings from the Indians and from Dutch and German neighbors.[8]

With the beginning of the nineteenth century, three changes occurred which were to have a profound effect upon the language situation in America. First, the industrial revolution resulted in the growth of a number of industrial centers, uprooting a considerable proportion of the farm population and concentrating it in the cities. The development of the railroad and other mechanical means of travel increased greatly the mobility of the average person. The large-scale migrations westward also resulted in some resettlement and shifting, even among those who did not set out on the long trek. All of this resulted in a general abandonment of narrowly local speech forms in favor of fewer, more or less general, regional types. Some local speech forms have remained even to the present day. These are usually known as relics, particularly when they are distributed in isolated spots over an area rather than in concentration. *Open stone peach*, for example, is a relic for freestone peach, occurring in Maryland. *Smurring up,* "getting foggy," survives as a relic in eastern Maine and more rarely on Cape Cod and Martha's Vineyard.

Even prior to the shifts in population and changes in the culture pattern, certain colonial cities such as Boston, Philadelphia, and Charleston had acquired prestige by developing as centers of trade and foci of immigration. They became socially and culturally outstanding, as well as economically powerful, thus dominating the areas surrounding them. As a

---

[8] See selection by Thomas Pyles on p. 58 [eds.]

consequence, local expressions and pronunciations peculiar to the country-side came to be replaced by new forms of speech emanating from these centers. A fairly recent instance of this is to be found in the New England term *tonic* for soda water, practically co-extensive with the area served by Boston wholesalers. Professor Kurath considers the influence of these centers as second only to the influence of the original settlement in shaping the regional types of speech on the Atlantic seaboard and in determining their geographical boundaries.

Nor was the general process of dialect formation by any means completed with the settlement of the Atlantic seaboard. As the land to the west came to be taken up in successive stages (for example, western New York, Michigan, Wisconsin in the North; southern Ohio, Indiana, and southern Illinois in the Midland area) the same mixtures of speech forms among the settlers were present at first, and the same linguistic compromises had to be worked out. The same processes occurred in the interior South, in Texas, and later on in the Far West. Consequently, the complete linguistic history, particularly with respect to regional forms, of the United States will not be known until all of the facts concerning the present regional distribution of speech forms have been collected, and until these facts have been collated with the settlement history of the various areas and the speech types employed by the settlers at the time they moved in. In its entirety this would necessitate a greater knowledge of the local dialects of seventeenth-century England than we have at present.

Moreover, such environmental factors as topography, climate, and plant and animal life also play their parts in influencing the dialect of an area, just as they did in the general transplanting of the English language to America. The complexity and size of the network of fresh-water streams will affect the distribution and meaning of such terms as *brook, creek, branch*, and *river*. In parts of Ohio and Pennsylvania, for example, the term *creek* is applied to a much larger body of water than in Michigan. It is even more obvious that in those parts of the country where snow is a rarity or does not fall at all, there will be no necessity for a battery of terms to indicate coasting face down on a sled. It is not surprising that those areas of the country where cows can be milked outside, for at least part of the year, will develop a specific term for the place where this is done: witness *milk gap* or *milking gap* current in the Appalachians south of the James River. The wealth of terms for various types of fences throughout the country is again dependent, in part at least, on the material which is available for building them, be it stones, stumps, or wooden rails.

Different types of institutions and practices which developed in various parts of the country also had their effect upon regional vocabulary. Those settlements which did not follow the practice of setting aside a parcel of land for common grazing purposes had little use for such terms as *green* or *common*. The meaning of *town* will vary according to the place and importance of township and county respectively in the organization of local government. The same principle applies equally well to foods of various kinds, which reflect not only materials which are readily available but folk practices as well. The German custom of preparing raised doughnuts as Lenten fare survives in the Pennsylvania term *fossnocks*, shortened from *Fastnachtskuchen.*

Finally, a new invention or development introduced into several parts of the country at the same time will acquire different names in various places. The baby carriage, for example, seems to have been a development of the 1830's and 40's, and this is the term which developed in New England. Within the Philadelphia trade area, however, the article became known as a *baby coach*, whereas *baby buggy* was adopted west of the Alleghenies and *baby cab* in other regions throughout the country. Nor have we necessarily seen an end to this process. Within the last two decades the building of large, double-lane, limited-access automobile highways has been undertaken in various parts of the country, yet the terminology for them differs considerably. In eastern New York, Connecticut, and Rhode Island these are *parkways*, but *turnpikes* in Pennsylvania, New Jersey, New Hampshire, Maine, Massachusetts, Ohio, and Indiana. In New York *thruway* is used, and they are *expressways* in Michigan and *freeways* in California. These would seem to be regionalisms in the making.

SUGGESTED ASSIGNMENTS

1. One can often ascertain the vocabulary items of a dialect by direct questions such as these
   a. What do you call the yellow part of an egg? (*yolk* or *yelk*)
   b. When does *evening* begin? (After midday in the South)
   c. What time does my watch show? (The setting is fifteen minutes before the hour to elicit "a quarter *to, till,* or *of* . . .")

   Write five questions designed to elicit vocabulary items from the following groups. Most of these words are taken from Hans Kurath's *A Word Geography of the Eastern United States.*

   a. *bag, poke, sack*
   b. *sick* (*at, to, till, on*) the stomach
   c. *porch, piazza, stoop*
   d. *creek, brook, run, branch, kill*
   e. *frying pan, spider, skillet*
   f. *you, you-all* (plurals)
   g. *doughnut, raised doughnut, cruller, fried cake, nut cake, fat cake, olicook,*

cookies. (Use an informant east of the Alleghenies for these, and distinguish between the raised and the unraised, sweetened variety.)

h. *pancake, griddle cake, fritter, hot-cake, flannel cake, batter-cake, flapjack*

i. *earthworm, night crawler, fish worm, angle worm, mud worm, angle dog, ground worm, red-worm, rain worm*

j. *pop, soda, tonic, soda pop, soda water*

Choose a speaker from a region other than yours and ask him your questions. Note his responses for class discussion. Although Kurath's material is taken from the eastern seaboard and New England, you can use a speaker from elsewhere because many of these terms have spread.

2. To convey some meanings there is no nationally used word. Instead, there are only various regional words. What, for example, does one call the strip of ground between the sidewalk and the street? Ask as many students as you know from different parts of the country and list the words they use.

3. We have seen that, within the boundaries of our country, there are dialects and subdialects. But we can go further. Any small, closely knit group, such as a family or a group of close friends, is likely to have language peculiarities of its own. It may even be truly said that the speech of every person is unique. This individual speech of a single person we call an *idiolect*. Observe carefully for a week the speech of a person of whom you see a good deal every day. Make a list of the specific ways in which his speech differs from yours—in his pronunciation of words, in his choice of grammatical forms, and in his choice of words and word-combinations. Bring this list to class for discussion.

American Dialects Today

Roger W. Shuy

The two short selections below supplement Professor Marckwardt's preceding account. The first one explains how the dialectologist establishes isoglosses and dialect boundaries. The second shows pronunciation differences between the Northern, Midland, and Southern dialects. Dr. Shuy is Professor of Linguistics at Georgetown University.

From *Discovering American Dialects* by Roger W. Shuy. Reprinted by permission of the author and the National Council of Teachers of English, copyright 1967.

FINDING THE DIALECT AREAS OF AMERICAN ENGLISH

Dialectologists record on maps the pronunciations, words, and grammatical forms which they find in an area. These items are represented by various symbols. Map 1, a map of several Eastern states, illustrates this procedure.[1] The circles indicate the communities investigated. As the legend explains, informants represented by circles say either *corn pone, pone bread,* or *pone.*

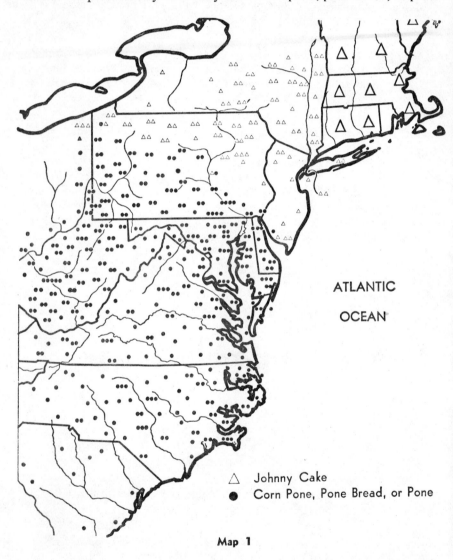

ATLANTIC

OCEAN

△ Johnny Cake
● Corn Pone, Pone Bread, or Pone

Map 1

[1] Adapted from Hans Kurath, *A Word Geography of the Eastern United States* (Ann Arbor: University of Michigan Press, 1949), Figure 116; used by permission of University of Michigan Press.

Informants from the other communities (triangles) say *johnnycake*. Map 2 shows the distribution of the two ways the verb *dive* is used in the past tense in northern Illinois.[2]

Once a number of such maps has been made, the dialectologist looks for similar patterns. Where he finds that one pronunciation or word is used almost entirely in one area, he draws a line which encloses the use of that item. This line, called an isogloss, marks the boundary of the pronunciation, word, or grammatical form. Such isoglosses can be seen in Map 3,[3] where

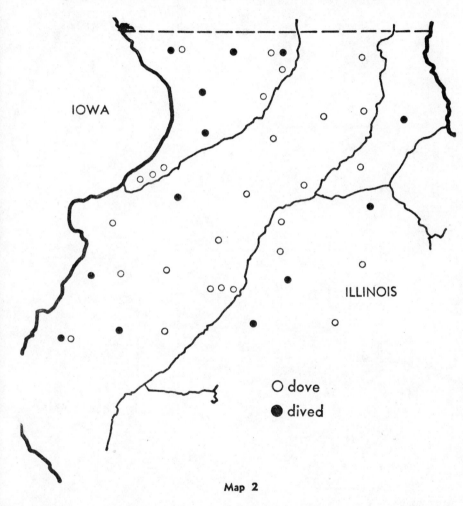

Map 2

[2] Adapted from Roger W. Shuy, "The Northern-Midland Dialect Boundary in Illinois," publication of the American Dialect Society, No. 38, (November 1962), 50; used by permission of the American Dialect Society.

[3] Adapted from Gordon R. Wood, "Dialect Contours in the Southern States," *American Speech* (December 1963), p. 244; used by permission of Columbia University Press, 2960 Broadway, New York, N.Y. 10027.

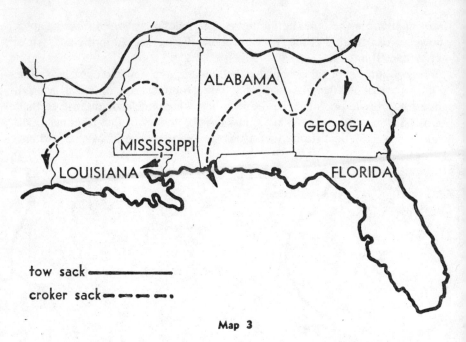

tow sack ————————
croker sack ━━ ━━ ━.

Map 3

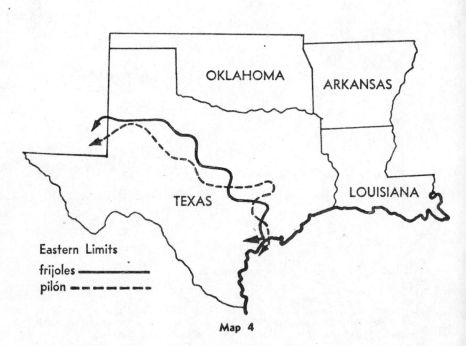

Eastern Limits
frijoles ————————
pilón ━ ━ ━ ━ ━

Map 4

the solid line indicates how far south the term *tow sack* (burlap bag) ex-
tends. The dotted line shows how far north the term *croker sack* (burlap
bag) can be found.[4] The arrows at the end of each line point toward the
areas enclosed by them. Isoglosses marking the distribution of *frijoles*
(pinto beans) and *pilón* (something extra) in Texas are found in Map 4.[5]
Examining these isoglosses, the dialectologist finds patterns of their direction.
He determines whether or not several isoglosses are found in the same place.
One way to do this is to draw several isoglosses on the same map and see
where they coincide. Map 5 shows how this technique was carried out in
northern Illinois. The dark line symbolizes areas where twelve to seventeen

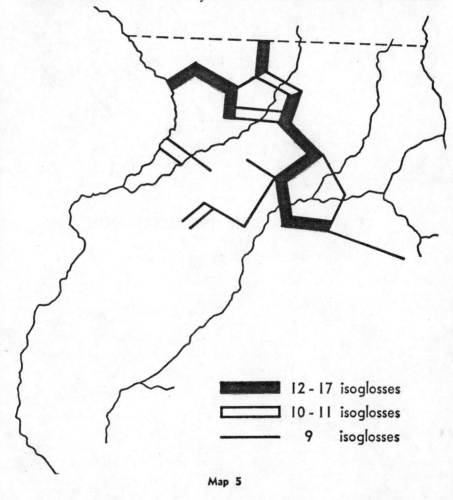

12 - 17 isoglosses

10 - 11 isoglosses

9   isoglosses

Map 5

---

[4] The area between these isoglosses is known as a transition area. [eds.]

[5] Adapted from E. Bagby Atwood, *The Regional Vocabulary of Texas* (Austin:
University of Texas Press, 1962), p. 80; used by permission of University of Texas
Press.

isoglosses pattern identically. The double line describes areas where ten or eleven isoglosses converge. The single line stands for nine isoglosses in the same area.[6]

Using such techniques, then, American dialect geographers have tried to find the major and minor dialect areas of our country. Map 6 shows some of the major boundaries that have been established so far, although a great deal of work remains to be done.

Map 6

DIFFERENCES IN PRONUNCIATION

(See table of sound symbols on page 180. [eds.])

Word	Northern	Midland	Southern
1. cr*ee*k	ɪ and i	ɪ (north (Midland)) i (south Midland)	i
2. p*e*nny	ɛ	ɛ	ɪ—(Southwest)
3. M*a*ry	ɛ e (parts of eastern New England)	ɛ	e
4. m*a*rried	æ (east of Appalachians) ɛ (elsewhere)	ɛ	ɛ
5. c*ow*	ɑʊ	æʊ	æʊ or ɑʊ
6. s*i*ster	ɪ	ɨ (eastern)[7]	ɨ (eastern)
7. f*o*reign	ɔ	ɑ	ɑ
8. *o*range	ɑ (east of Alleghenies) ɔ	ɑ and ɔ	ɑ and ɔ

[6] Such "bundles of isoglosses" establish a "dialect boundary." [eds.]

[7] The symbol /ɨ/ represents the sound many persons make for the vowel of the -*es* plural, as in clas*ses* and church*es*. It is difficult to distinguish this from /ɪ/ and /ə/. [eds.]

9. tomato	o	ə	o or ə
10. coop	u	u (NM), ʊ (SM)	ʊ
11. roof	ʊ	u and/or ʊ	u
12. bulge	ə	ə or ʊ	ə or ʊ
13. farm	ɑ	ɑ or ɔ	ɑ or ɔ
14. wire	ɑɪ	ɑɪ or ɑ	ɑ
15. won't	ə o (urban)	o ɔ	o ɔ
16. fog	ɑ (New England) ɑ and ɔ (Midwest)	ɔ	ɔ
17. hog	ɑ (New England) ɑ and ɔ (Midwest)	ɔ	ɔ
18. on	ɑ	ɔ	ɔ
19. long	ɔ	ɔ	ɑ (eastern Virginia) ɔ (elsewhere)
20. careless	ɨ	ə	ɨ
21. stomach	ə	ɪ	ə

The vowels of these words are pronounced differently in the various parts of our country. The major variants are listed beside the words along with their general distributions.

Consonants sometimes will give clues to the dialect a person speaks. The following generalizations may be helpful:

Word	Northern	Midland	Southern
1. humor	hɪumər	yumər	hɪumər or yumər
2. wash	wɑš or wɔš	wɔrš or wɔɪš	wɔš or wɔɪš or waš
3. with	wɪð and wɪθ (N.Y., Chicago, Detroit = wɪt working class)	wɪθ	wɪθ
4. greasy	grisɪ	grizɪ	grizɪ
5. barn	bɑrn (Eastern North = ban)	bɑrn	bɑrn (East Coast = ban)
6. these	ðiz (N.Y., Chicago, Detroit = diz working class)	ðiz	ðiz
7. which	hwɪč	wɪč	wɪč
8. miss	mɪs	mɪs	mɪz
9. Mrs.	mɪsɨz	mɪsɨz	mɪsɨz or mɪz

SUGGESTED ASSIGNMENT

Here are fifteen groups of words in which dialect differences in pronunciation exist: (a) *barn, dark, far, far away;* (b) *curl, first, bird;* (c) *orange, foreign;* (d) *greasy, Mrs.;* (e) *dog, frog, lot, pot;* (f) *ask, aunt, calf, path;* (g) *ice, mine, time;* (h) *Tuesday, new, tune, duty;* (i) *Mary, merry, marry;* (j) *mourning, morning, horse, hoarse;* (k) *wash, water;* (l) *ought, collar;* (m) *house, out, town, down;* (n) *poor, sure;* (o) *on, from* (in stressed positions, as "Is it *on?*" and "Where are you *from?*") Select five groups and put the words into simple, natural sentences. Then find a student from a part of the country different from yours and ask him to read them. Make a note of the pronunciations that differ from yours and be prepared to contribute these to a class discussion of dialect differences.

Linguistic Atlas Findings

Hans Kurath
E. Bagby Atwood
Harold B. Allen

Work on the regional linguistic atlases for different parts of the United States and southern Canada is in various states of progress. For New England and the Upper Midwest (Minnesota, North and South Dakota, Iowa, and Nebraska) the atlases are now in print. The data have all been collected for the Middle and South Atlantic States, the North Central States, California, Washington, Colorado, and Oklahoma. These collections are a rich mine of primary source material about contemporary English, and researchers are making use of them for books and articles. To date, a small number of books have been published, from four of which the excerpts below have been chosen.

The first three items—*creek, bull, you-all*—are from Hans Kurath's *A Word Geography of the Eastern United States.* This book describes the distribution of vocabulary items and sets forth the dialect and subdialect areas of the Eastern United States. Professor Kurath was the editor of the *Linguistic Atlas of New England* and is now editor of the *Middle English Dictionary* at the University of Michigan.

CREEK[1]

Creek is the most common word for a small fresh-water stream in the Eastern States. It is current everywhere except in the greater part of New England, where *brook* or *river* are the usual terms.

Outside New England, Long Island, and Metropolitan New York *brook* is rare as a common noun, but it appears in the proper names of many streams in the New England settlement area as far west as Erie, Pennsylvania.

The Midland term for a smaller stream is *run*, but in Pennsylvania and the northern half of West Virginia *creek* is now the common noun. However, *run* occurs in the names of many streams in this area. As a common noun, *run* is now characteristic of an area extending from Delaware Bay to the James River (except Lower Delamarvia) and westward to the Shenandoah and the upper reaches of the Potomac in West Virginia. It is also fairly common along the Neuse in North Carolina.

In the South and in the South Midland as far north as the Kanawha Valley *branch* is the usual designation of the tributary of a *creek* or a *river*. *Branch* is also current on Delaware Bay beside *run*.

The Dutch word *kill* for a small watercourse survives only in the names of certain creeks or rivers in the Dutch settlement area, such as the *Batten Kill* in Vermont, the *Catskill Creek* in New York, and the *Schuylkill River* in Pennsylvania.

BULL

The plain term *bull* is current everywhere, and in the North Midland and New York State other expressions are rare. In New England, the South, and the South Midland, however, the plain term is not used by older folk of one sex in the presence of the other. Even many of the younger generation prefer the veiled expressions of the Victorian era.

New England expressions for the bull are: *sire, animal* or *male animal, critter, toro* (New Hampshire and Vermont), *seed ox* (rare), *gentleman cow, gentleman ox* (found also on Chesapeake Bay), and *masculine* (riming with *fine*, on Nantucket).

Southernisms are equally varied: *male* and *male cow* in Virginia, adjoining parts of North Carolina, and on Delamarvia (occasionally also in New England); *beast, stock beast, male beast* in the coastal section of the Carolinas; *stock brute, male brute* in westernmost North Carolina; *steer*

---

[1] The first three items—*creek, bull, you-all*—from Hans Kurath's *A Word Geography of the Eastern United States* are reprinted by permission of the publishers, The University of Michigan Press, copyright 1949.

from southern Maryland to Albermarle Sound; *ox* in the Virginia Tidewater, central West Virginia, and sporadically elsewhere; *gentleman cow* on Chesapeake Bay (also in New England); and *masculine* (riming with *fine*) in southern West Virginia (also on Nantucket). West Virginia further contributes *Durham, jock*, and *major*.

Some of these expressions are now rare or used only jestingly, but in the Southern area such expressions as the *male*, the *beast*, and the *brute* are common, and if one used the plain word *bull* to a lady, one might be in trouble.

YOU-ALL

The form *you* is used as a plural in all parts of the Eastern States. By the side of *you*, the greater part of the Midland and all of the South have the specific, emphatic, or "generous" plural forms *you'ns, you-all*, and *mongst-ye*. All these forms have a possessive case: *you'ns's, you-all's, mongst-ye's*. [See page 231.]

You-all is current throughout the South and the South Midland (in all of West Virginia, except the northwestern section around Wheeling and Parkersburg).

You'ns is the Midland form and occurs in the folk speech of Pennsylvania west of the Susquehanna, in large parts of West Virginia, and in the westernmost parts of Virginia and North Carolina.

The form *mongst-ye* is common in the folk speech of the central part of Delamarvia, and rare instances are found from the mouth of Chesapeake Bay to Albermarle Sound.

The next four items—*dive, lie, he doesn't, ought not*—are from E. Bagby Atwood's *A Survey of Verb Forms in the Eastern United States*.[2] Here Professor Atwood confines his attention to variant verb forms. To get his information, he examined the *Linguistic Atlas* field records of more than 1400 informants, about 400 from New England and about 500 each from the Middle Atlantic states and the South Atlantic states. The late Mr. Atwood was Professor of English at the University of Texas.

DIVE

The preterite is recorded in the context "He (dived) in."
The geographical distribution of the forms is indicated below.
Dived/daivd/ is uncommon throughout N. Eng., N.Y., n. Pa., and e. N.J.; in this whole territory it is used by less than one out of 15 of the in-

[2] Reprinted by permission of the publisher, The University of Michigan Press, copyright © 1953.

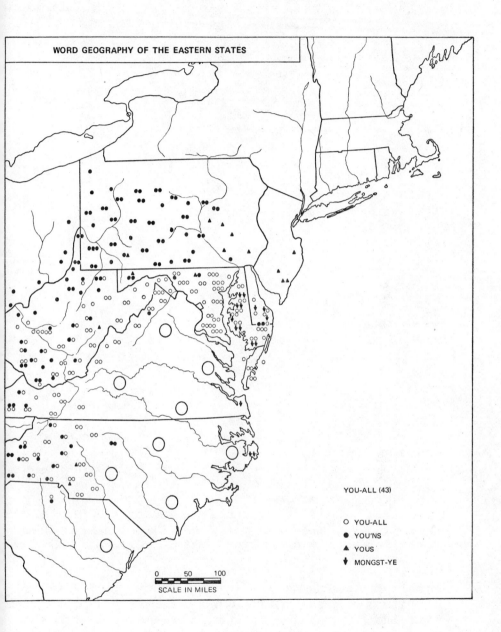

WORD GEOGRAPHY OF THE EASTERN STATES

YOU-ALL (43)

○ YOU-ALL
● YOU'NS
▲ YOUS
↓ MONGST-YE

0   50   100
SCALE IN MILES

From *A Word Geography of the Eastern United States* by Hans Kurath. Reprinted by permission of the publisher, The University of Michigan Press, copyright 1949.

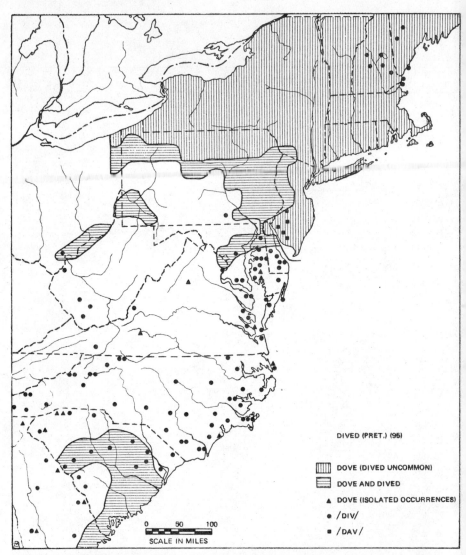

DIVED (PRET.) (95)

⦀	DOVE (DIVED UNCOMMON)
☰	DOVE AND DIVED
▲	DOVE (ISOLATED OCCURRENCES)
●	/DIV/
■	/DAV/

0   50   100
SCALE IN MILES

From *A Survey of Verb Forms in the Eastern United States* by E. Bagby Atwood. Reprinted by permission of the publisher, The University of Michigan Press, copyright 1953.

formants, without distinction as to type (about one eighth of the cultured informants in N. Eng use it). In a belt in n. c. and e. Pa. and along the upper Ohio, *dived* and *dove*/dov/ occur about equally, the former being more common among older informants. Elsewhere in the M. A. S. and the S. A. S.[3] to and including N. C., *dived* heavily predominates on all levels, being limited only by *div* (see above).

[3] The Middle Atlantic States (M.A.S.) include New York, New Jersey, Pennsylvania, eastern Ohio, and West Virginia. The South Atlantic States (S.A.S.) include Delaware, Maryland, Virginia, North Carolina, South Carolina, and approximately the eastern half of Georgia. [eds.]

In the northeastern area indicated on the map *dove* is almost universal. Within the areas of divided usage the more modern informant uses *dove* in more than three fourths of the communities, and at least that proportion of cultured informants choose this form in these areas. There is not the slightest doubt that the area of *dove* is extending itself to the south and west.[4]

South of the Peedee in S. C. *dove* is also fairly common, and it has some currency in coastal Ga. In these areas it is quite frequent in urban and cultured speech somewhat less so in rustic speech.

The form *div*/dɪv/ shows the typical distribution of an archaism, being most common in n.e. N. Eng. and the coastal and mountain areas of the South and the South Midland. About six out of seven of the informants who use it fall in Type I (or Types IA and IIA in N. Eng.), and three N. C. Negro informants use it.[5]

There are five occurrences of *duv*/dʌv/, concentrated in s. N. J. near the mouth of the Delaware.

A few Negro informants use the uninflected *dive*.

LIE

The present infinitive and the preterite are recorded in the contexts "I'm going to (lie) down" and "He (lay) in bed all day."

In general, the present form *lie*/lai/ predominates in all major areas, being used by from three fifths to two thirds of all informants, without any significant geographical distribution. The alternate form *lay* /le/ is slightly more common among Type I informants (about half of whom use it) than among Type II. On the whole, however, *lay* seems characteristic of certain communities, rather than of certain more old-fashioned informants within those communities. Only a scattering of cultured informants give the present form *lay*, and then usually alongside *lie*.

The preterite forms can best be surveyed in terms of their corresponding present forms. The combination *lie : lay* is of very limited occurrence. In n. N. Eng. and in e. N. Eng. (except for a few points in R. I. and e. Conn.) this combination is quite rare outside of cultured speech, and only about half the cultured informants in these areas use it. In s.w. N. Eng. *lie :lay* is universal in cultured usage and occurs among a fair number of noncultured informants as well.

In the entire M. A. S. *lie : lay* is uncommon among noncultured infor-

---

[4] Another characteristic of an advancing form is its appearance in the more populous centers ahead of the main line of advance (in this instance, the Pittsburgh, Baltimore, and Washington areas). Professor Robert Hall has applied the metaphor "parachuting" to this phenomenon.

[5] See footnote, p. 203. [eds.]

mants (being used by less than one twelfth of the group), and is confined to about one third of the cultured group.

In the S. A. S. *lie : lay* is rare in Del., Md., and the Piedmont area of Va., but becomes much more common (and might even be called the dominant popular usage) on the Eastern Shore of Va. and throughout most of N. C. and parts of S. C. A little less than half the cultured informants in the S. A. S. use the *lie : lay* combination.

A much more common practice is the combination of the present *lie* with the *laid*/led/ ("going to lie down" : "laid in bed"). Of those who use the present *lie*, a considerable majority (two thirds in N. Eng. four fifths in the M. A. S.) combine it with the preterite *laid*. Only in N.C. and on the Eastern Shore of Va. is this combination somewhat uncommon. In e. N. Eng. about half the cultured information give *lie : laid;* in the M. A. S. and the S. A. S. something more than half do so.

Some eight informants in N. Eng. and five in other areas use the combination *lie : lied*/laid/. This feature shows no concentration and may represent a groping for a "correct" form rather than habitual usage.

Of those who use the present *lay*, a heavy majority in most areas form the preterite as *laid*. An exception may be found in N. C., where a considerable number use the leveled present and preterite *lay : lay*. This leveling also occurs in a very scattered way in N. Eng. and parts of Pa.

Nearly all Negro informants use the forms *lay : laid;* one (S. C.), however, uses the leveled forms *lie : lie*.

In summary, we may say that as a present form *lie* is predominant in all areas, and that as the preterite of both *lie* and *lay, laid* is very heavily predominant everywhere except in the areas of the S. A. S. mentioned above where *lay* predominates as preterite.

HE DOESN'T

The third person singular of the negative form is recorded in the context "He (doesn't) care."

In contrast to the positive form (*does*), the negative form lacks the inflectional -*s*/z/ among a large majority of informants in all areas.

In N. Eng. *he don't*/dont/ is used by about two fifths of the cultured informants (mostly in the older group) and by more than five sixths of the other types. It is most common in Type IA (nearly nine tenths use it) and decreases in frequency in proportion to the youth and better education of the informants, occurring among only [6]/17 of Type IIIB.

In the M. A. S. *he don't* is all but unanimous in Types I and II, there being but 15 or 20 occurrences of *doesn't* in these groups. Of the cultured informants, nearly three fourths use *he don't* (in a few instances alongside *doesn't*). Cultured informants who use only *doesn't* are mostly to be found in or near New York City or Philadelphia.

In the S.A.S., also, *don't* is universal in Types I and II. About half of the cultured informants use *don't*, occasionally alongside *doesn't*.

OUGHT NOT

The negative form of *ought* is recorded in the context "He (oughtn't) to."

In the southern two thirds of Pa. and nearly everywhere to the southward oughtn't/ɔtənt/ is in universal use in all types. In the South Midland and throughout N. C. phonetic, and probably phonemic, /r/ very generally appears in this form: /ɔrtənt/.

In N. Eng., N. Y., n. Pa., and most of N. J. the usual form is *hadn't ought*. . . . Throughout most of this area nearly all the noncultural informants use this form; however, in s. N. Eng. only about half the informants use it, often alongside *oughtn't* or *ought not*. One third of the cultured informants in N. Eng (nearly all of those who were interviewed in the northeast) use *hadn't ought*. There are only three instances of *didn't ought* in N. Eng.

In a small area of s. Ohio extending northeast from Marietta, and in part of n. e. N. C. *hadn't ought* is also current, though not universal.

The following terms are from Professor Atwood's *The Regional Vocabulary of Texas* and represent Texas usage. They are a selection from the results of 273 field interviews with informants from all parts of Texas. The numbers in parentheses are percentages of possible occurrences.[6]

TEXAS USAGE

YOU (PLURAL).   When addressing more than one person, the usual pronoun forms are *you-all* or *y'all*. Since the former spelling usually implies at least some phonetic reduction, the two may be grouped together, with a frequency of 86 per cent. . . .

The old Midland form *you-uns* (6) is of very infrequent occurrence, and is confined to old and uneducated informants. *You folks* (15) is more common, but shows no geographical concentration, while *you people* occurs only four times. Only a few informants were content with the simple *you* (7) in this situation.

IT WASN'T ME.   The pronoun usually chosen in this phrase is *me* (66). The use of *I* (9) is more characteristic of the educated groups, but constitutes a small minority even here.

[6] From E. Bagby Atwood, *The Regional Vocabulary of Texas*. Reprinted by permission of the University of Texas Press, copyright 1962.

DIVED.   The most usual form past form of *dive* is *dove* (50). This is not an uneducated form; in fact, it is slightly more prevalent among the educated. *Dived* (38) is also in use at all levels. *Div* (6) is only a remnant and is confined to the least-educated informants.

OUGHT NOT.   *Oughtn't* (23) is slightly more prevalent than *hadn't ought* (20), but both of these forms seem to be giving way to *shouldn't* (27).

The information below on *boulevard* is taken from Harold B. Allen's *The Linguistic Atlas of the Upper Midwest*, the two volumes of which appeared respectively in 1973 and 1975. The data in this atlas are based on interviews with 208 informants, many of whom were interviewed by Dr. Allen himself. This information was supplemented by 1064 checklists received by mail. Dr. Allen, before his retirement, was Professor of English at the University of Minnesota and devoted about twenty-five years of his life to this project.[7]

BOULEVARD

No national or standard term exists in the United States for the strip of grass between a sidewalk and the street. The several names elicited by this item, original with the UM Atlas, reveal clear distribution patterns, but no information is available for correlating them with distribution in the eastern part of the nation.

Boulevard, the most frequent term, conspicuously characterizes the Northern speech area of the UM, including the Canadian strip along the border. Indeed, except for single instances of *curb* and *terrace* in Minnesota, the only deviation from the solid monopoly of *boulevard* is the subarea characterized by *berm*.

Unique here in this sense, *berm* is concentrated in Grand Forks, N.D., with decreasing frequency eastward toward Crookston, Mn., and northwestward to Devils Lake and Rolla, N.D. It appeared in a Grand Forks city ordinance as early as 1910. Supplementary verification that the trading zone of Grand Forks is the focal area for *berm*, with a suggestion that even here *boulevard* may be replacing it, appears in a survey made in 1955 of students at Mayville State College, N.D. In a group with homes in northwestern Minnesota and northeastern North Dakota the only students using *berm* outside Grand Forks county were from Traill county, immediately south of Grand Forks, and from Walsh and Pembina counties, immediately north of Grand Forks. But in each of these counties students also use *boulevard*.

The Midland speech territory of the UM is unusually divided into rather clearly defined subareas by the distribution of three principal equivalents of *boulevard*. *Parking*, the most common, dominates with its use in the Midland area of Iowa and South Dakota and in extreme eastern and extreme western Nebraska. Central and west central Nebraska, however, is marked by the use of *curb*, which appears also in northern Iowa. A third term, *terrace*, has scattered instances in northern Iowa and in the southern tier of counties in Nebraska.

Minor variants, all but one of which are in Midland speech territory, are: *grass strip, lawn, tree lawn, park, parking space, parking strip* and *parkway*.

	Mn.	Ia.	N.D.	S.D.	Nb.	Ave.
berm	2%	0%	14%	0	0	—
boulevard	92%	10%	86%	33%	0	50%
curb	2%	5%	0	0	29%	6%
(tree) lawn	2%	8%	0	0	4%	3%
parking	0	60%	5%	48%	46%	28%
terrace	2%	13%	0	0	21%	7%[8]

SUGGESTED ASSIGNMENTS

1. Assume that you are a linguistic field-worker planning an interview with an informant. You want to find out which grammatical forms he uses in sentence situations like those listed below. If you ask him point-blank, he may report the one he thinks to be "correct" instead of what he normally uses. Devise the means whereby you can get him to use the forms in parentheses below, or whatever he naturally uses instead of them, and then go ahead with an interview.

    a. He (*dived   dove*) from the high board.
    b. She (*had drank   had drunk*) all her medicine.
    c. You (*hadn't ought   ought not*) to drive so fast.
    d. Yesterday he (*lay   laid*) in bed all day.
    e. My shirt (*shrank   shrunk*) in the laundry.
    f. It (*don't   doesn't*) matter.
    g. He (*waked up   woke up*) early.
    h. She lives (*on   in*) Broad Street.
    i. This is (*all the further   as far as   all the farther*) I go.
    j. Who (*rang   rung*) the bell?

2. When you have completed the readings, exercises, and class discussions on linguistic geography, write a theme on "Dialect Differences I Have Observed."

---

[8] The information provided by the checklists generally confirms the broad patterns established by the field records. [eds.]

FURTHER READINGS

Allen, Harold B. "Aspects of the Linguistic Geography of the Upper Midwest." *Studies in Languages and Linguistics*, Albert Marckwardt, ed. Ann Arbor: The English Language Institute, University of Michigan, 1964.

————. "The Linguistic Atlases: Our New Resource." *The English Journal* 45: 188–194 (April 1956).

———— and Gary N. Underwood. *Readings in American Dialectology*. New York: Appleton-Century-Crofts, 1971.

American Speech, a Quarterly of Linguistic Usage. This periodical contains many articles on regional speech and linguistic geography, as well as a current bibliography of matters of linguistic interest.

Atwood, E. Bagby. *A Survey of Verb Forms in the Eastern United States*. Ann Arbor: University of Michigan Press, 1953.

————. *The Regional Vocabulary of Texas*. Austin: University of Texas Press, 1962.

Bloomfield, Leonard. *Language*. New York: Holt, Rinehart and Winston, Inc., 1933. See chapter on dialect geography, pp. 321–345.

Francis, W. Nelson. *The English Language: an Introduction*. New York: W. W. Norton, 1965. See pages 223–244, "Regional Variety in English."

Francis W. Nelson. *The Structure of American English*. New York: The Ronald Press Company, 1958. For a short, up-to-date (1958) description of linguistic geography and its accomplishment, see pp. 485–499. Emphasis is on American work.

Hall, Robert A., Jr., *Introductory Linguistics*. Philadelphia: Chilton Company—Book Division, 1964. See pp. 239–252.

————. *Linguistics and Your Language*. New York: Doubleday & Company, Inc., 1960. See pp. 135–166.

Hockett, Charles F. *A Course in Modern Linguistics*. New York: Crowell-Collier and Macmillan, Inc., 1958. See pp. 471–484.

Kurath, Hans. "Area Linguistics and the Teacher of English." *Language Learning*, Special Issue No. 2, March 1961. Also in Harold B. Allen, *Readings in Applied English Linguistics*, 2d ed. New York: Appleton-Century-Crofts, 1964.

————. *A Word Geography of the Eastern United States*. Ann Arbor: University of Michigan Press, 1949.

McDavid, Raven I., Jr. "The Dialects of American English," in W. Nelson Francis, *The Structure of American English*. New York: Ronald Press, 1958.

Publications of the American Dialect Society. This periodical specializes in articles on dialects and linguistic geography.

Reed, Carroll E. *Dialects of American English*. Cleveland: The World Publishing Company, 1967. A simple account, emphasizing Eastern English, with 32 maps.

Shuy, Roger W. *Discovering American Dialects*, Champaign, Ill.: National Council of Teachers of English, 1967. A short, simple, and well-illustrated treatment.

Williamson, Juanita V., and Virginia M. Burke. *A Various Language*. New York: Holt, Rinehart and Winston, 1971. A reader on dialects, including the urban.

9
SOCIOLINGUISTICS: THE STUDY OF SOCIOCULTURAL DIFFERENCES IN LANGUAGE

Black English

Dorothy Z. Seymour

Sociolinguistics is defined by Joshua Fishman of Yeshiva University as "the study of the characteristics of language varieties, the characteristics of their functions, and the characteristics of their speakers as these three constantly interact, change, and change one another within a speech community." [1] Within these limits lies Black English. Linguists are intensively studying the characteristics of Black English today to fill a gap in our knowledge of American English and to furnish useful information to those who teach blacks, especially in the elementary schools. Dorothy Seymour is an editor specializing in linguistics on the staff of an educational publishing company.

In the classroom they made for their desks and opened their books. The name of the story they tried to read was "Come." It went:

Come, Bill, come.
Come with me.
Come and see this.
See what is here.

From *Commonweal*, November 19, 1971. By permission of Commonweal Publishing Company.

[1] *Sociolinguistics*. Rowley, Mass.: Newbury House Publishers, 1971, p. 4.

The first boy poked the second. "Wha' da' wor'?"

"Da' wor' *is*, you dope."

"*Is?* Ain't no wor' is. You jivin' me? Wha' da' wor' mean?"

"Ah dunno. Jus' *is*."

To a speaker of Standard English, this exchange is only vaguely comprehensible. But it's normal speech for thousands of American children. In addition it demonstrates one of our biggest educational problems: children whose speech style is so different from the writing style of their books that they have difficulty learning to read. These children speak Black English, a dialect characteristic of many inner-city Negroes. Their books are, of course, written in Standard English. To complicate matters, the speech they use is also socially stigmatized. Middle-class whites and Negroes alike scorn it as low-class poor people's talk.

Teachers sometimes make the situation worse with their attitudes toward Black English. Typically, they view the children's speech as "bad English" characterized by "lazy pronunciation," "poor grammar," and "short, jagged words." One result of this attitude is poor mental health on the part of the pupils. A child is quick to grasp the feeling that while school speech is "good," his own speech is "bad," and that by extension he himself is somehow inadequate and without value. Some children react to this feeling by withdrawing; they stop talking entirely. Others develop the attitude of "F'get you, honky." In either case, the psychological results are devastating and lead straight to the dropout route.

It is hard for most teachers and middle class Negro parents to accept the idea that Black English is not just "sloppy talk" but a dialect with a form and structure of its own. Even some eminent black educators think of it as "bad English grammar" with "slurred consonants" (Professor Nick Aaron Ford of Morgan State College in Baltimore) and "ghettoese" (Dr. Kenneth B. Clark, the prominent educational psychologist).

Parents of Negro schoolchildren generally agree. Two researchers at Columbia University report that the adults they worked with in Harlem almost unanimously preferred that their children be taught Standard English in school.

But there is another point of view, one held in common by black militants and some white liberals. They urge that middle-class Negroes stop thinking of the inner-city dialect as something to be ashamed of and repudiated. Black author Claude Brown, for example, pushes this point of view.

Some modern linguists take a similar stance. They begin with the premise that no dialect is intrinsically "bad" or "good," and that a nonstandard speech style is not defective speech but different speech. More important, they have been able to show that Black English is far from being a careless way of speaking the Standard; instead, it is a rather rigidly constructed set of speech patterns, with the same sort of specialization in sounds, structure and vocabulary as any other dialect.

Middle-class listeners who hear black inner-city speakers say "dis" and "tin" for "this" and "thin" assume that the black speakers are just being careless. Not at all; these differences are characteristic aspects of the dialect. The original cause of such substitutions is generally the carry-over from one's original language or that of his immigrant parents. The interference from that carry-over probably caused the substitution of /d/ for the voiced *th* sound in *this*, and /t/ for the unvoiced *th* sound in *thin*. (Linguists represent language sounds by putting letters within slashes or brackets.) Most speakers of English don't realize that the two *th* sounds of English are lacking in many other languages and are difficult for most foreigners trying to learn English. Germans who study English, for example, are surprised and confused about these sounds because the only Germans who use them are the ones who lisp. These two sounds are almost nonexistent in the West African languages which most black immigrants brought with them to America.

Similar substitutions used in Black English are /f/, a sound similar to the unvoiced *th*, in medial word-position, as in *birfday* for *birthday*, and in final word-position, as in *roof* for *Ruth*, as well as /v/ for the voiced *th* in medial position, as in *bruvver* for *brother*. These sound substitutions are also typical of Gullah, the language of black speakers in the Carolina Sea Islands.[2] Some of them are also heard in Caribbean Creole. Another characteristic is the lack of /l/ at the end of words. This makes a word like *tool* sound like *too*.

One difference that is startling to middle-class speakers is the fact that Black English words appear to leave off some consonant sounds at the end of words. Like Italian, Japanese and West African words, they are more likely to end in vowel sounds. Standard English *boot* is pronounced *boo* in Black English. *What* is *wha*. *Sure* is *sho*. *Your* is *yo*. This kind of difference can make for confusion in the classroom. Dr. Kenneth Goodman, a psycholinguist, tells of a black child whose white teacher asked him to use *so* in a sentence—not "sew a dress" but "the other *so*." The sentence the child used was "I got a *so* on my leg."

A related feature of Black English is the tendency in many cases not to use sequences of more than just one final consonant sound. For example, *just* is pronounced *jus'*, *past* is *pass*, *mend* sounds like *men* and *hold* sounds like *hole*. *Six* and *box* are pronounced *sick* and *bock*. Why should this be? Perhaps because West African languages, like Japanese, have almost no clusters of consonants in their speech. The Japanese, when importing a foreign word, handle a similar problem by inserting vowel sounds between every consonant, making *baseball* sound like *besuboru*. West Africans probably make a simpler change, merely cutting a series of two consonant sounds down to one. Speakers of Gullah, according to one linguist, have made the same kind of adaptation of Standard English.

[2] For an account of Gullah, see Pyles, p. 62–69. [eds.]

Teachers of black children seldom understand the reason for these differences in final sounds. They are apt to think that careless speech is the cause. Actually, black speakers aren't "leaving off" any sounds; how can you leave off something you never had in the first place?

Differences in vowel sounds are also characteristic of the nonstandard language. Dr. Goodman reports that a black child asked his teacher how to spell rat. "R-a-t," she replied. But the boy responded, "No ma'am, I don't mean rat mouse, I mean rat now." In Black English *right* sounds like *rat*. A likely reason is that in West African languages, there are very few vowel sounds of the type heard in the word *right*. This type is common in English. It is called a glided or dipthongized vowel sound. A glided vowel sound is actually a close combination of two vowels: in the word *right* the two parts of the sound "eye" are really "ah-ee." West African languages have no such long, two-part, changing vowel sounds; their vowels are generally shorter and more stable. This may be why in Black English, *time* sounds like *Tom, oil* like *all*, and *my* like *ma*.

Black English differs from Standard English not only in its sounds but also in its structure. The way the words are put together does not always fit the description in English grammar books. The method of expressing time, or tense, for example, differs in significant ways.

The verb *to be* is an important one in Standard English. It's used as an auxiliary verb to indicate different tenses. But Black English speakers use it quite differently. Sometimes an inner-city Negro says "He coming"; other times he says "He be coming." These two sentences mean different things. To understand why, let's look at the tenses of West African languages; they correspond with those of Black English.

Many West African languages have a tense which is called the habitual. This tense is used to express action that is always occurring, and it is formed with a verb that is translated as *be*. "He be coming" means something like "He's always coming." "He usually comes," or "He's been coming."

In Standard English there is no regular grammatical construction for such a tense. Black English speakers, in order to form the habitual tense in English, use the word *be* as an auxiliary: *He be doing it. My Momma be working. He be running.* The habitual tense is not the same as the present tense, which is constructed in Black English without any form of the verb *to be: He do it. My Momma working. He running.* (This means the action is occurring right now.)

There are other tense differences between Black English and Standard English. For example, the nonstandard speech does not use changes in grammar to indicate the past tense. A white person will ask, "What did your brother say?" and the black person will answer, "He say he coming." "How did you get here?" "I walk." This style of talking about the past is paralleled in the Yoruba, Fante, Hausa, and Ewe languages of West Africa.

Expression of plurality is another difference. The way a black child will talk of "them boy" or "two dog" makes some white listeners think Negroes don't know how to turn a singular word into a plural word. As a matter of fact, it isn't necessary to use an *s* to express plurality. For example, in Chinese it's correct to say "There are three book on the table." This sentence already has two signals of the plural, *three* and *are*; why require a third? This same logic is the basis of plurals in most West African languages, where nouns are often identical in the plural and the singular. For example, in Ibo, one correctly says *those man*, and in both Ewe and Yoruba one says *they house*. American speakers of Gullah retain this style; they say *five dog*.

Gender is another aspect of language structure where differences can be found. Speakers of Standard English are often confused to find that the nonstandard vernacular often uses just one gender of pronoun, the masculine, and refers to women as well as men as *he* or *him*. "He a nice girl" and even "Him a nice girl" are common. This usage probably stems from West African origins, too, as does the use of multiple negatives such as "Nobody don't know it."

Vocabulary is the third aspect of a person's native speech that could affect his learning of a new language. The strikingly different vocabulary often used in Negro Nonstandard English is probably the most obvious aspect of it to a casual white observer. But its vocabulary differences don't obscure its meaning the way different sounds and different structure often do.

Recently there has been much interest in the African origins of words like *goober* (peanut), *cooter* (turtle), and *tote* (carry), as well as others that are less certainly African, such as *to dig* (possibly from *the* Wolof *degan*, "to understand"). Such expressions seem colorful rather than low class to many whites; they become assimilated faster than their black originators do. English professors now use *dig* in their scholarly articles, and current advertising has enthusiastically adopted *rap*.

Is it really possible for old differences in sound, structure and vocabulary to persist from the West African languages of slave days into present-day inner-city Black English? Easily. Nothing else really explains such regularity of language habits, most of which persist among black people in various parts of the Western Hemisphere. For a long time scholars believed that certain speech forms used by Negroes were merely leftovers from archaic English preserved in the ·speech of early English settlers in America and copied by their slaves. But this theory has been greatly weakened, largely as the result of the work of a black linguist, Dr. Lorenzo Dow Turner of the University of Chicago. Dr. Turner studied the speech of Gullah Negroes in the Sea Islands off the Carolina coast and found so many traces of West African languages that he thoroughly discredited the archaic-English theory.

When anyone learns a new language, it's usual to try to speak the new language with the sounds and structure of the old. If a person's first language does not happen to have a particular sound needed in the language he is learning, he will tend to substitute a similar or related sound from his native language and use it to speak the new one. When Frenchman Charles Boyer said "Zees ees my heart," and when Latin American Carmen Miranda sang "Souse American way," they were simply using sounds from their native languages in trying to pronounce sounds of English. West Africans must have done the same thing when they first attempted English words. The tendency to retain the structure of the native language is a strong one, too. That's why a German learning English is likely to put his verb at the end: "May I a glass of beer have?" The vocabulary of one's original language may also furnish some holdovers. Jewish immigrants did not stop using the word *bagel* when they came to America; nor did Germans stop saying *sauerkraut.*

Social and geographical isolation reinforces the tendency to retain old language habits. When one group is considered inferior, the other group avoids it. For many years it was illegal to give any sort of instruction to Negroes, and for slaves to try to speak like their masters would have been unthinkable. Conflict of value systems doubtless retards changes, too. As Frantz Fanon observed in *Black Skin, White Masks*, those who take on white speech habits are suspect in the ghetto, because others believe they are trying to "act white." Dr. Kenneth Johnson, a black linguist, put it this way: "As long as disadvantaged black children live in segregated communities and most of their relationships are confined to those within their own subculture, they will not replace their functional nonstandard dialect with the nonfunctional standard dialect."

Linguists have made it clear that language systems that are different are not necessarily deficient. A judgment of deficiency can be made only in comparison with another language system. Let's turn the tables on Standard English for a moment and look at it from the West African point of view. From this angle, Standard English (1) is lacking in certain language sounds; (2) has a couple of unnecessary language sounds for which others may serve as good substitutes; (3) doubles and drawls some of its vowel sounds in sequences that are unusual and difficult to imitate; (4) lacks a method of forming an important tense; (5) requires an unnecessary number of ways to indicate tense, plurality and gender; and (6) doesn't mark negatives sufficiently for the result to be a good strong negative statement.

Now whose language is deficient?

How would the adoption of this point of view help us? Say we accepted the evidence that Black English is not just a sloppy Standard but an organized language style which probably has developed many of its features on the basis of its West African heritage. What would we gain?

The psychological climate of the classroom might improve if teachers understood why many black students speak as they do. But we still have not reached a solution of the main problem. Does the discovery that Black English has pattern and structure mean that it should not be tampered with? Should children who speak Black English be excused from learning the Standard in school? Should they perhaps be given books in Black English to learn from?

Any such accommodation would surely result in a hardening of the new separatism being urged by some black militants. It would probably be applauded by such people as Roy Innis, Director of C.O.R.E., who is currently recommending dual autonomous education systems for white and black. And it might facilitate learning to read, since some experiments have indicated that materials written in Black English syntax aid problem readers from the inner city.

But determined resistance to the introduction of such printed materials into schools can be expected. To those who view inner-city speech as bad English, the appearance in print of sentences like "My mama, he work" can be as shocking and repellent as a four-letter word. Middle-class Negro parents would probably mobilize against the move. Any strategem that does not take into account such practicalities of the matter is probably doomed to failure. And besides, where would such a permissive policy on language get these children in the larger society, and in the long run? If they want to enter an integrated America they must be able to deal with it on its own terms. Even Professor Toni Cade of Rutgers, who doesn't want "ghetto accents" tampered with, advocates mastery of Standard English because, as she puts it, "If you want to get ahead in this country, you must master the language of the ruling class." This has always been true, wherever there has been a minority group.

The problem then appears to be one of giving these children the ability to speak (and read) Standard English without denigrating the vernacular and those who use it, or even affecting the ability to use it. The only way to do this is to officially espouse bidialectism. The result would be the ability to use either dialect equally well—as Dr. Martin Luther King did—depending on the time, place, and circumstances. Pupils would have to learn enough about Standard English to use it when necessary, and teachers would have to learn about the inner-city dialect to understand and accept it for what it is—not just a "careless" version of Standard English but a different form of English that's appropriate at certain times and places.

Can we accomplish this? If we can't, the result will be the continued alienation of a large section of the population, continued dropout trouble with consequent loss of earning power and economic contribution to the nation, but most of all, loss of faith in America as a place where a minority people can at times continue to use those habits that remind them of their link with each other and with their past.

A History of American Negro Dialects

William A. Stewart

This brief historical sketch combines parts of two articles by William A. Stewart, a leading authority on American Negro dialects. In the original articles Stewart deals with the pedagogical implications of the differences between standard English and nonstandard Negro dialects, and stresses the point that a teacher of reading and of English to young black nonstandard speakers should know the grammatical structures of their language in order to teach effectively. Any student who plans to do educational work in the "inner city" is strongly advised to read both articles.

Of those Africans who fell victim to the Atlantic slave trade and were brought to the New World, many found it necessary to learn some kind of English. With very few exceptions, the form of English which they acquired was a pidginized one, and this kind of English became so well established as the principal medium of communication between Negro slaves in the British colonies that it was passed on as a creole language to succeeding generations of the New World Negroes, for whom it became their native tongue.[1] Some idea of what New World Negro English may have been like

William A. Stewart, "Sociolinguistic Factors in the History of American Negro Dialects" and "Continuity and Change in American Negro Dialects," first published in *The Florida FL Reporter* Vol. 5, No. 2 (Spring 1967) and Vol. 6, No. 1 (Spring 1968). Both are reprinted in Harold B. Allen and Gary N. Underwood, editors, *Readings in American Dialectology* (New York: Appleton-Century-Crofts, 1969), and under the cover title "Toward a History of American Negro Dialects" in Frederick Williams, editor, *Language and Poverty: Perspectives on a Theme* (Chicago, Illinois: Markham Publishing Co., 1969).

[1] In referring to types of languages, linguists use the terms *pidgin* and *creole* in a technical sense which has none of the derogatory or racial connotations of popular uses of these terms. When a linguist says that a variety of language is pidginized, he merely means that it has a markedly simplified grammatical structure compared with the "normal" (that is, unpidginized) source-language. This simplification may be one way in which speakers of different languages can make a new language easier to learn and use—particularly if they have neither the opportunity nor the motivation to learn to speak it the way its primary users do. In addition, some of the unique characteristics of a pidgin language may be due, not to simplification, but to influences on it from the native languages of its users. What is important to realize, however, is that pidginized languages do have grammatical structure and regularity,

in its early stages can be obtained from a well-known example of the speech given by Daniel DeFoe in *The Family Instructor* (London, 1715). It is significant that the Negro, Toby, speaks a pidginized kind of English to his boy master, even though he states that he was born in the New World. A sample of his speech is:

TOBY: Me be born at Barbadoes.
BOY: Who lives there, Toby?
TOBY: There lives white mans, white womans, negree mans, negree womans, just so as live here.
BOY: What and not know God?
TOBY: Yes, the white man say God prayers;—no much know God.
BOY: And what do the black mans do?
TOBY: They much work, much work,—no say God prayers, not at all.
BOY: What work do they do, Toby?
TOBY: Makee the sugar, makee the ginger,—much great work, weary work, all day, all night.

Even though the boy master's English is slightly nonstandard (for example, *black mans*), it is still quite different from the speech of the Negro.

An idea of how widespread a pidginized form of English had become among the Negro population of the New World by the end of the seventeenth century can be gathered from the fact that it had even become the language of the coastal plantations in the Dutch colony of Surinam (that is, Dutch Guiana), in South America. In an early description of that colony, the chapter on the Negro ends with a sample conversation in the local Negro English dialect. The dialogue includes such sentences as *Me bella well* "I am very well"; *You wantee siddown pinkininne?* "Do you want to sit down for a bit?"; and *You wantee go walka longa me?* "Do you want to take a walk with me?" In these sentences, the use of the enclitic vowel in *wantee* recalls the same in DeFoe's example *makee*.[2] Also, the speaker, like Toby, uses *me* as a

---

even though their specific patterns may be different from those of the related un-pidginized source-language of higher prestige. Thus, the fact that the sentence *Dem no get-am* in present-day West African Pidgin English is obviously different from its standard English equivalent "They don't have it" does not necessarily indicate that the Pidgin English speaker "talks without grammar." In producing such a sentence, he is unconsciously obeying the grammatical rules of West African Pidgin English, and these determine that *Dem no get-am* is the "right" construction, as opposed to such ungrammatical or "wrong" combinations as *No dem get-am, No get dem-am, Get-am dem no,* and so forth. If a pidgin finally becomes the native language of a speech community (and thereby becomes by definition a creole language), it may expand in grammatical complexity to the level of "normal" or unpidginized languages. Of course, the resulting creole language may still exhibit structural differences from the original source-language, because the creole has gone through a pidginized stage. . . .

   [2] An enclitic is a lightly stressed word or word-part that is considered as part of the preceding word, like the *-s* in "John's coming" or the *-a* in "I wanna come too." [eds.]

subject pronoun. In the first Surinam sentence, we see an early example of a construction without any equivalent of the standard English verb "to be." Toby also would probably have said *Me weary*, since the *be* in his first sentence was in all likelihood a past-tense marker (as it is in present-day West African Pidgin English)—the sentence therefore meaning "I was born in Barbadoes." In the last Surinam sentence, a reflex of English *along* is used with the meaning of standard English "with." [3] It may or may not be accidental that in the Gullah dialect, spoken by the Negroes along the South Carolina coastal plain, the same phenomenon occurs, for example, *Enty you wantuh walk long me*? "Do you want to take a walk with me?" [4] Some Gullah speakers even still use *me* as a subject pronoun, for example, *Me kyaan brukum* "I can't break it," and enclitic final vowels seem to have survived in such Gullah forms as *yerry, yeddy* "to hear."

Early examples of Negro dialect as spoken in the American colonies show it to be strikingly similar to that given by DeFoe for the West Indies and by Herlein for Surinam. In John Leacock's play *The Fall of British Tyranny* (Philadelphia, 1776), part of the conversation between a certain "kidnapper" and Cudjo, one of a group of Virginia Negroes, goes as follows:

KIDNAPPER: . . . what part did you come from?
CUDJO: Disse brack man, disse one, disse one, disse one, come from Hamton, disse one, disse one, come from Nawfok, me come from Nawfok too.
KIDNAPPER: Very well, what was your master's name?
CUDJO: Me massa name Cunney Tomsee.
KIDNAPPER: Colonel Thompson—eigh?
CUDJO: Eas, massa, Cunney Tomsee.
KIDNAPPER: Well then I'll make you a major—and what's your name?
CUDJO: Me massa cawra me Cudjo.

Again the enclitic vowels (for example, *disse*) and the subject pronoun *me* are prominent features of the Negro dialect. In the sentence *Me massa name Cunney Tomsee* "My master's name is Colonel Thompson," both the verb "to be" and the standard English possessive suffix *-s* are absent. Incidentally, Cudjo's construction is strikingly similar to sentences like *My sister name Mary* which are used by many American Negroes today.

One possible explanation why this kind of pidginized English was so widespread in the New World, with widely separated varieties resembling each other in so many ways, is that it did not originate in the New World as isolated and accidentally similar instances of random pidginization, but rather originated as a lingua franca in the trade centers and slave factories on the West African coast. [5] It is likely that at least some Africans already

---

[3] A reflex is a linguistic form that has come from an earlier form. [eds.]
[4] For further information on Gullah, see pp. 42–69. [eds.]
[5] See, for example, Basil Davidson, *Black Mother; The Years of the African Slave Trade* (Boston: Little, Brown & Company, 1961), particularly p. 218.

knew this pidgin English when they came to the New World, and that the common colonial policy of mixing slaves of various tribal origins forced its rapid adoption as a plantation lingua franca.

In the course of the eighteenth century, some significant changes took place in the New World Negro population, and these had their effect on language behavior. For one thing, the number of Negroes born in the New World came to exceed the number of those brought over from Africa. In the process, pidgin English became the creole mother-tongue of the new generations, and in some areas it has remained so to the present day.[6]

In the British colonies, the creole English of the uneducated Negroes and the English dialects of both the educated and uneducated whites were close enough to each other (at least in vocabulary) to allow the speakers of each to communicate. . . .

Another change which took place in the New World Negro population primarily during the course of the eighteenth century was the social cleavage of the New World–born generations into underprivileged field-hands (a continuation of the older, almost universal lot of the Negro slave) and privileged domestic servant. The difference in privilege usually meant, not freedom instead of bondage, but rather freedom from degrading kinds of labor, access to the "big house" with its comforts and "civilization," and proximity to the prestigious "quality" whites, with the opportunity to imitate their behavior (including their speech) and to wear their clothes. In some cases, privilege included the chance to get an education and, in a very few, access to wealth and freedom. In both the British colonies and the United States, Negroes belonging to the privileged group were soon able to acquire a more standard variety of English than the creole of the field hands, and those who managed to get a decent education became speakers of fully standard and often elegant English. This seems to have become the usual situation by the early 1800's, and remained so through the Civil War. In Caroline Gilman's *Recollections of a Southern Matron* (New York, Harper & Row, 1838), the difference between field-hand creole (in this case, Gullah) and domestic servant dialect is evident in a comparison of the gardener's "He tief one sheep—he run away last week, cause de overseer gwine for flog him" with Dina's " 'Scuse me, missis, I is gitting hard o'hearing, and yes is more politer dan no" (page 254). A more striking contrast between the speech of educated and uneducated Negroes occurs in a novel written in the 1850's by an American Negro who had traveled extensively through the slave states. In Chapter XVII, part of the exchange between Henry, an educated Negro traveler, and an old "aunty" goes as follows:[7]

---

[6] In the West Indies, creole English is usually called patois, while in Surinam it is called Taki-Taki. In the United States, the only fairly "pure" creole English left today is Gullah, spoken along the coast of South Carolina.

[7] Martin R. Delany, "Blake; or the Huts of America," published serially in *The Anglo-African Magazine* (1859). The quotation is from Vol. 1, No. 6 (June 1859), p. 163.

"Who was that old man who ran behind your master's horse?"

"Dat Nathan, my husban'."

"Do they treat him well, aunty?"

"No, chile, wus an' any dog, da beat 'im foh little an nothin'."

"Is uncle Nathan religious?"

"Yes, chile, ole man an I's been sahvin' God dis many day, fo yeh baun! Wen any on 'em in de house get sick, den da sen foh 'uncle Nathan' come pray for dem; 'uncle Nathan' mighty good den!"

After the Civil War, with the abolition of slavery, the breakdown of the plantation system, and the steady increase in education for poor as well as affluent Negroes, the older field-hand creole English began to lose many of its creole characteristics, and take on more and more of the features of the local white dialects and of the written language. Yet, this process has not been just one way. For if it is true that the speech of American Negroes has been strongly influenced by the speech of whites with whom they came into contact, it is probably also true that the speech of many whites has been influenced in some ways by the speech of Negroes.[8]

One of the more important changes which have occurred in American Negro dialects during the past century has been the almost complete de-creolization of both their functional and lexical vocabulary. Although this process actually began long before the Civil War (particularly in areas with a low proportion of Negroes to whites), the breakdown of the plantation system apparently accelerated it considerably, even in the coastal areas of South Carolina and Georgia. In the process, overt creolisms which were so common in early attestations of slave speech, such as *been* for marking past action (with no basic distinction between preterite and perfect); undifferentiated pronouns for subject and object (for example, *me, him*, and *dem* also as subject pronouns and *we* also as an object pronoun), a single subject pronoun form (usually *him* or *he*) for masculine, feminine, and neuter in the third person singular, *-um* (or *-am*) as a general third person (all genders and numbers) object suffix; *no* as a verbal negator, and *for* as an infinitive marker, became quite rare in even the more nonstandard speech of Negroes born after Emancipation.

However, the speed and thoroughness with which the plantation field-hand dialects were thus made more "proper" varied both according to the region and according to the social characteristics of the speakers themselves. Because people learn most of their language forms from others, the change took place more rapidly and completely in areas where speakers (white or Negro) of more-or-less standard varieties of English were present in numbers than it did in areas with a high concentration of field laborers. On the

---

[8] See Raven I. McDavid, Jr., and Virginia Glenn McDavid, "The Relationship of the Speech of American Negroes to the Speech of Whites," *American Speech*, XXVI (1951), pp. 3–17.

other hand, because children generally are more affected by the language usage of other children than by that of grown-ups, and because lower-class child peer groups tend to remain rather isolated from the stylistic innovations of adult discourse, the change took place more slowly and less thoroughly in the speech of young children than it did in that of adolescents and adults.

— The result of this uneven "correction" of the older plantation dialects was that, while they seemed to have died out by the end of the nineteenth century (particularly outside the South Atlantic coastal area and the Mississippi Basin), juvenile versions of them actually continue to survive in many Negro speech communities as "baby talk" or "small-boy talk." That is, the older nonstandard (and sometimes even creole-like) dialect features remained in use principally by younger children in Negro speech-communities—being learned from other young children, to be given up later in life when "small-boy talk" was no longer appropriate to a more mature status. And even though the adult dialects which these child dialects were ontogenetically given up for were also structurally nonstandard and identifiably Negro in most cases, they were still more standard—enough, at least, so that conspicuous retentions of child-dialect forms in the speech of an adult could sometimes result in the accusation that he or she was "talking like a child" or simply "talking bad."

Interestingly enough, the use of an older, more conservative form of Negro dialect as child speech was not always limited to Negroes. In the Old South, many upper-class whites went through a similar linguistic metamorphosis from the nonstandard dialect of their Negro playmates to the relatively standard English of their adult station in life. As John Bennett described the situation for the Charlestonian aristocracy of his day:

> It is true, up to the age of four, approximately, the children of the best families, even in town, are apt to speak an almost unmodified Gullah, caught from brown playmates and country-bred nurses; but at that age the refinement of cultivation begins, and "the flowers o' the forest are a' weed awa!" [9]

It was undoubtedly in this manner that such white southern writers as Joel C. Harris and Ambrose E. Gonzales first acquired their knowledge of the Negro dialects which they immortalized in print.

Over the last two centuries, the proportion of American Negroes who speak a perfectly standard variety of English has risen from a small group of privileged house slaves and free Negroes to persons numbering in the hundreds of thousands, and perhaps even millions. Yet there is still a sizeable number of American Negroes—undoubtedly larger than the number of standard-speaking Negroes—whose speech may be radically nonstandard.

[9] John Bennett, "Gullah: A Negro Patois" *The South Atlantic Quarterly,* **Vol. 7** (Oct. 1908) and Vol. 8 (Jan. 1909), quote from Vol. 7, p. 339. . . .

The nonstandard features in the speech of such persons may be due in part to the influence of the nonstandard dialects of whites with whom they or their ancestors have come in contact, but they also may be due to the survival of creolisms from the older Negro field-hand speech of the plantations.

. . . Although this creole English . . . underwent modification in the direction of the more prestigious British-derived dialects, the merging process was neither instantaneous nor uniform. Indeed, the nonstandard speech of present-day American Negroes still seems to exhibit structural traces of a creole predecessor, and this is probably a reason why it is in some ways more deviant from standard English than is the nonstandard speech of even the most uneducated American whites.

For the teacher, this means that such "Negro" patterns as the "zero copula," [10] the "zero possessive," [11] or "undifferentiated pronouns" [12] . . . should be treated as what they really are—language patterns which have been in existence for generations and which their present users have acquired, from parent and peer, through a perfectly normal kind of language-learning process.

To insure their social mobility in modern American society, these nonstandard speakers must undoubtedly be given a command of standard English. . . . In studying nonstandard Negro dialects and teaching standard English in terms of them, however, both the applied linguist and the language teacher must come to appreciate the fact that even if certain nonstandard Negro dialect patterns do not resemble the dialect usage of American whites, or even those of the speakers of remote British dialects, they may nevertheless be as old as African and European settlement in the New World, and therefore quite widespread and well-established. On various occasions, I have pointed out that many speakers of nonstandard American Negro dialects make a grammatical and semantic distinction by means of *be*, illustrated by such constructions as *he busy* "He is busy (momentarily)" or *he workin'* "he is working (right now)", opposed to *he be busy* "he is (habitually) busy" or *he be workin'* "he is working (steadily)," which the

---

[10] The term "zero copula" refers to the absence of an explicit predicating verb in certain dialect constructions, where standard English has such a verb (usually in the present tense). Compare nonstandard Negro dialect *He old, Dey runnin'*, and *She a teacher* with standard English "He is old," "They are running," and "She is a teacher."

[11] The term "zero possessive" refers to the absence of an explicit suffix in noun-noun constructions, where standard English has such a suffix. Compare nonstandard Negro dialect *My fahver frien'* with standard English "My father's friend."

[12] The term "undifferentiated pronoun" refers to the use of the same pronoun form for both subject and object, and sometimes for possession as well. The pronominal form used may be derived from either the standard English object form, or the subject form. Compare such nonstandard forms as *Him know we, Him know us,* (beside *He know us*) with the standard English "He knows us" to which they are equivalent. Or compare *He fahver* (beside *His fahver*) and *We house* (beside *Our house*) with standard English "His father" and "Our house,"

grammar of standard English is unable to make. Even this distinction g[ ]
back well over a century. One observer in the 1830's noted a request by a
slave for a permanent supply of soap as "(If) Missis only give we, we be so
clean forever," while *be* is absent in a subsequent report of someone's temporary illness with "She jist sick for a little while."

Once educators who are concerned with the language problems of the
disadvantaged come to realize that nonstandard Negro dialects represent
a historical tradition of this type, it is to be hoped that they will become less
embarrassed by evidence that those dialects are very much alike throughout
the country while different in many ways from the nonstandard dialects of
whites, less frustrated by failure to turn nonstandard Negro dialect speakers
into standard English speakers overnight, less impatient with the stubborn
survival of Negro dialect features in the speech of even educated persons,
and less zealous in proclaiming what is "right" and what is "wrong." If this
happens, then applied linguists and educators will be able to communicate
with each other, and both will be able to communicate with the nonstand-
ard-speaking Negro child. The problem will then be well on its way toward
a solution.

SUGGESTED ASSIGNMENTS

1. Standard English (SE) is defined by Otto Jespersen, the eminent Danish grammarian of English, as "the normal speech of the educated class." The American
   linguist C. C. Fries defines it as "the particular type of English which is used in
   the conduct of the important affairs of our people." In other words, we might
   say that Standard English is the prestige dialect of the United States.

   Non-Standard English (NSE), then, is that language that does not fall within
   the boundaries of these definitions. It is the language that is used by those who
   have not been fortunate enough to receive much formal schooling and that
   is not used in the business, professional, and governmental worlds.

   Linguistic studies of the last decade have gradually revealed that in the
   United States there is a black Non-Standard English somewhat different from
   white NSE. This is known in professional writing as NNSE (Negro Non-
   Standard English). In what follows the term Non-Standard English (NSE)
   will be used to include both white and black Non-Standard English.

   Non-Standard English is intrinsically a perfectly good form of expression.
   It can communicate clearly the needs and desires of its users, it can be eloquent
   and persuasive, and it is often vigorous, lively, and colorful. Yet the American
   public through its school system insists that students who speak this social
   dialect called Non-Standard must also learn to use Standard English, the
   dialect of the upper middle class, both white and black; and countless dollars
   are spent yearly to achieve this aim.

This raises thought-provoking questions:

a. Does *everyone* really need to learn to handle SE?

b. What benefits are to be derived, for a speaker of NSE, in learning SE?

c. Should NSE be eradicated and replaced by SE in the schools, or should SE be taught as another dialect to be added to NSE, much as one would add French to English?

d. Is it desirable to be able to switch dialects, choosing SE or NSE as the occasion requires?

e. How can the desire to learn SE be motivated, especially with the black student?

f. For an elementary school teacher this particular question is of tremendous importance at this moment and is being discussed in educational circles: How can the reading of upper middle-class language be taught to black children whose speech deviates radically in pronunciation from the SE norm?

g. It is a fact that millions of NSE speakers are hard-working, intelligent, and useful citizens. How can one avoid the implication that NSE is a badge of inferiority?

h. Could the audio-lingual methods used by foreign language teachers be employed in teaching SE to speakers of NSE?

Your assignment is to find a theme subject suggested by these questions, or similar ones that may occur to you, and write a short paper addressed to a specifically defined class of readers. For example, it might be a paper addressed to a black PTA on why their children are being taught SE. Or it might be addressed to a meeting of young black adults encouraging them to sign up for a night class in the effective use of English.

2. In his Uncle Remus stories, Joel Chandler Harris uses black speech accurately and effectively. Read two of these stories and collect a handful of expressions that are especially colorful or vivid or well stated. For example, Harris uses this comparison: "ez c'am ez a dead pig in de sunshine." How much better could you do in SE?

3. A creolized variety of English known as Gullah, or Geechee, is spoken by American Negroes along the Atlantic coast of South Carolina and Georgia and on the adjacent Sea Islands. Gullah is described on pages 62–69 of this book.) Like all other languages, it is not merely a collection of words but has a systematic grammar. This grammar differs in various respects from Standard English and can be accurately described. This exercise deals with one tiny segment of Gullah grammar.

In Standard English we use forms of the verb *be* in these four patterns:

a. Subject + *be* + adjective
   Ex. He is happy.
       They are abroad.

b. Subject + *be* + noun
   Ex. She was a teacher.

c. Subject + *be* + adverb
   Ex. The box is there.

d. Subject + *be* + past participle.
   Ex. The horses are gone.

Using the Gullah expressions listed below as evidence, describe how Gullah uses *be* in the above four patterns.[13]

a. He very resourceful.
b. We afraid.
c. You gone.
d. You are there.
e. I never see such a thing since I born.
f. I worse.
g. They been there. (*been* = SE *was* or *were*)
h. Earthquake big there.
i. When sun hot. . . .
j. Some dead on the place.
k. Now that is something.
l. When that first storm been here. . . .
m. It is God work. [*God* = *God's*]
n. They say we too old.
o. I satisfied with what him done for me.
p. That man is the meanest man.
q. My husband been my leader.
r. My leader been right there.
s. . . . till he dead.
t. You is a fool.
u. . . . it just as pretty.
v. You be there two hours.

For samples of an urban Non-Standard English dialect, see *Conversations in a Negro American Dialect*, transcribed and edited by Bengt Loman (Washington, D.C.: Center for Applied Linguistics, 1967).

FURTHER READINGS

Burling, Robbins. *Man's Many Voices*. New York: Holt, Rinehart and Winston, 1970. See "Black English," pages 117–134.

Fasold, Ralph W. "Distinctive Linguistic Characteristics of Black English," in James E. Alatis, ed., *Linguistics and Language Study: 20th Roundtable Meeting*. Washington, D.C.: Georgetown University Press, 1970.

Fasold, Ralph, and Walter Wolfram. *Teaching Standard English in the Inner City*. Washington, D.C.: Center for Applied Linguistics, 1970. See "Some Linguistic Features of Negro Dialect," pages 41–86.

Wolfram, Walter, "Black-White Speech Differences Revisited," in Maurice I. Imhoof, ed., *Social and Educational Insights into Teaching Standard English to Speakers of Other Dialects*. Bloomington, Indiana: School of Education, Indiana University, 1971.

[13] These expressions are taken from Lorenzo Dow Turner's *Africanisms in the Gullah Dialect*.

10
USAGE

Differences in Language Practices

Charles Carpenter Fries

Our relationship to knowledge is paradoxical. We have, on the one hand, an insatiable desire for knowledge, a questing spirit that will not be denied. Yet when new knowledge is discovered it is not always welcomed. Indeed, at times it is strongly resisted and comes to be accepted only gradually and reluctantly. One of the hardest things to do is to accept new knowledge that runs counter to what we have been taught. It means giving up old knowledge, relinquishing what we have regarded as established fact. One would think that a "fact," of all things, would remain constant. Yet the history of knowledge is built, in part, on the shattered facts of the past. Astrology and alchemy long ago gave way to astronomy and chemistry. And even today Newtonian physics, long accepted and firmly established, has given way to the more modern theories of Einstein and his successors. So too in language. Until fairly recently, most people accepted unquestioningly principles and rules of usage and grammar laid down by eighteenth-century grammarians. Contemporary linguists, however, have not only challenged but have actually repudiated many of the eighteenth-century views. They assert that just as the "laws" of Newtonian physics can no longer be accepted

From *American English Grammar* by Charles Carpenter Fries. Reprinted by permisison of the author and the National Council of Teachers of English, copyright 1940. Published by Appleton-Century-Crofts.

as an adequate description of the natural universe, so too the "rules" of the eighteenth-century grammarians constitute an outmoded and inaccurate description of our language, both in usage and in grammar.

In the following essay, Professor Fries presents the rationale of the scientific point of view in the study of language, arrives at a sound definition of Standard American English, and discusses the obligation of the schools with respect to differences in language practices. The essay is the introductory chapter of his *American English Grammar*, a revolutionary book in the teaching of English. Before his death in 1968, Professor Fries was Professor of English, Emeritus, at the University of Michigan. The achievement of Professor Fries in helping to bring about a more realistic attitude toward our language, as well as a more accurate description of it, cannot be overestimated. He was the author of numerous articles and books. Especially noteworthy are his *American English Grammar* (1940) and *The Structure of English* (1952).

"English" maintains its place as the most frequently *required subject* of our school and college curriculums because of the unanimous support given it both by the general public and by education authorities. This support rests upon the general belief that the mastery of *good English* is not only the most important asset of the ambitious but also an obligation of every good citizen. There is, however, in many quarters a very hazy idea of the specific elements which make *good English*. A great deal of vigorous controversy ignores all the larger problems of effective communication and centers attention upon the criteria to be applied in judging the acceptability of particular words and language forms. All of this controversy is direct evidence that there do exist many differences in the language practice of English speaking people; for no controversy could arise and no choice be offered unless differing language forms presented themselves in the actual practice of English speech. It is the purpose of this chapter to set forth the general character of these differences and to analyze their significance in relation to the obligations resting upon our schools. The chapter as a whole will therefore present the principles underlying this whole investigation and the point of view which has determined its material and method.

I

Underlying many of the controversies concerning words and language forms is a very common attitude which I shall call here the "conventional point of view." Frequently stated explicitly, sometimes only implied, it appears in most handbooks and manuals of correct English, in grammars and rhetorics, in educational tests and measures, and in many editorials of the press. This conventional point of view assumes not only that there is a correctness in English language as absolute as that in elementary mathematics but also that the measures of this correctness are very definite rules. The following quotations are typical:

A college professor rises to defend 'ain't' and 'it is me' as good English. The reed upon which he leans is majority usage. . . . 'Ain't,' as a legitimate contraction of 'am not,' would not require defense or apology if it were not for widespread misuse. Unfortunately the same cannot be said of 'it is me.' This solecism could not be given the odor of good English by a plurality as great as Warren G. Harding rolled up in 1920. . . . A vast amount of wretched English is heard in this country. The remedy does not lie in the repeal of the rules of grammar; but rather in a stricter and more intelligent enforcement of those rules in our schools. . . . This protest against traditional usage and the rules of grammar is merely another manifestation of the unfortunate trend of the times to lawlessness in every direction. . . . Quite as important as keeping undesirables out of the vocabulary is the maintaining of respect for the rules of grammar, which govern the formation of words into phrases and sentences. . . . Students should be taught that correct speaking is evidence of culture; and that in order to speak correctly they must master the rules that govern the use of the language.[1]

Grammar consists of a series of rules and definitions. . . . Since . . . ninety-five per cent of all children and teachers come from homes or communities where incorrect English is used, nearly everyone has before him the long, hard task of overcoming habits set up early in life before he studied language and grammar in school. . . . Such people are exposed to the ridicule of those who notice the error, and the only way in which they can cure themselves is by eternal vigilance and the study of grammar.[2]

This is a test to see how well you know correct English usage and how well you can select the *rule or principle in accordance with which a usage is correct.* In the left hand column a list of sentences is given. In each sentence there are two forms in parentheses, one correct, and the other incorrect. In the right hand column a list of rules or principles is given, some one of which applies to each sentence. . . .

Sentences	Principles
( ) 1. (Whom) (Who) did you meet?	*a.* The indirect object is in the objective case.
( ) 2. He told John and (I) (me) an interesting story.	*b.* The subject of the verb is in the nominative case.
	c. The object of a verb is in the objective case.

[1] From an editorial in *The Detroit Free Press* (December 9, 1928).
[2] W. W. Charters, *Teaching the Common Branches.* rev. ed. (New York, The Macmillan Co., 1924), pp. 96, 98, 115.

... Read the first sentence in Section I; then mark out the incorrect form. Read the rules Section I, until you find one that applies to this first sentence. Place the letter of this rule in the square preceding the first sentence.[3]

One purpose of this report is to describe and illustrate a method of constructing a grammar curriculum upon the basis of the errors of school children. ... it is apparent that the first step is *to ascertain* the rules which are broken and to determine their relative importance.[4]

The point of view expressed in these quotations, assuming as it does that certain definite rules[5] are the necessary standards by which to measure language correctness, also repudiates *general usage* as a valid guide to acceptability, even the usage of the so-called "educated." The following quotation represents dozens of similar statements:

The truth is, however, that authority of general usage, or even of the usage of great writers, is not absolute in language. There is a misuse of words which can be justified by no authority, however great, and *by no usage however general*.[6]

From this, the "conventional point of view," the problem of the differences in our language practice is a very simple one. Only two kinds of forms or usages exist—correct forms and mistakes. In general, the mistakes are thought to be corrupt forms or illegitimate meanings derived by carelessness from the correct ones. In some cases a grudging acquiescence accepts some forms which are contrary to the rules when these forms are sanctioned by an overwhelming usage, but here the view remains that these forms, although established by usage, are still *incorrect* and must always be incorrect. To this point of view these incorrect forms sanctioned by usage are the "idioms" of the language. In all the matters of differing language practices, therefore, those who hold this point of view regard the obligation of the schools as perfectly clear and comparatively simple—the schools must root out the *mistakes* or *errors* and cultivate the language uses that are *correct according to the rules*.[7]

Opposed to this "conventional point of view" is that held by the out-

---

[3] T. J. Kirby, *Grammar Test,* University of Iowa Standard Tests and Scales.

[4] "Minimal Essentials in Language and Grammar," in *Sixteenth Yearbook* of the National Society for the Study of Education (Bloomington, Ind., Public School Publishing Co., 1917), pp. 86, 87.

[5] For a statement of the development of this point of view see C. C. Fries, *Teaching of the English Language* (New York, Thomas Nelson & Sons, 1927), Chap. I, "The Rules of Grammar as the Measure of Language Errors."

[6] R. G. White, *Words and Their Uses,* rev. ed. (Boston, Houghton Mifflin Company, 1899), p. 14.

[7] "Some better reason than a custom arising from ignorance . . . is needed for changing the English language. It would seem to be still the part of the schools to teach the language *strictly according to rule*, and to place emphasis on such teaching, rather than to encourage questionable liberties of usage." From an editorial in *The Christian Science Monitor*, Boston (February 23, 1923).

standing scholars in English language during the last hundred years. I shall call it here "the scientific point of view." Typical expressions of it abound.

> In considering the use of grammar as a corrective of what are called 'ungrammatical' expressions, it must be borne in mind that the rules of grammar have no value except as statements of facts: whatever is in general use in a language is for that very reason grammatically correct.[8]

> The grammar of a language is not a list of rules imposed upon its speakers by scholastic authorities, but is a scientific record of the actual phenomena of that language, written and spoken. If any community habitually uses certain forms of speech, these forms are part of the grammar of the speech of that community.[9]

> It has been my endeavor in this work to represent English Grammar not as a set of stiff dogmatic precepts, according to which some things are correct and others absolutely wrong, but as something living and developing under continual fluctuations and undulations, something that is founded on the past and prepares the way for the future, something that is not always consistent or perfect, but progressing and perfectible—in one word, human.[10]

> A Grammar book does not attempt to teach people how they ought to speak, but on the contrary, unless it is a very bad or a very old work, it merely states how, as a matter of fact, certain people do speak at the time at which it is written.[11]

In these typical expressions of "the scientific point of view" there is, first of all, a definitely stated opposition to the fundamental principle of the "conventional attitude." All of them insist that it is unsound to take the rules of grammar as the necessary norms of correct English and to set out to make all usage conform to those rules. In these expressions of the scientific view there is, also, a clear affirmation of the fundamental principle of the attitude that usage or practice is the basis of all *correctness* there can be in language.[12] From this, the scientific point of view, the problem presented by the differences in our language is by no means a simple one. Instead of

[8] Henry Sweet, *New English Grammar*. Vol. I (Oxford, Clarendon Press, 1891), p. 5.
[9] Grattan and Gurrey, *Our Living Language* (London, Thomas Nelson & Sons, 1925), p. 25.
[10] Otto Jespersen, *A Modern English Grammar* (Heidelberg, 1909), I. Preface.
[11] H. C. Wyld, *Elementary Lessons in English Grammar* (Oxford, Clarendon Press, 1925). p. 12.
[12] This statement must not be taken to imply that *mere correctness* is to be considered the ultimate ideal of language. The scientific point of view does not in any way conflict with the artistic view of *good English*. See the discussion of "The Scientific and the Artistic Points of View in Language," in C. C. Fries, *The Teaching of the English Language*, pp. 102–121.

having to deal with a mass of diverse forms which can be easily separated into the two groups of *mistakes* and *correct language* according to perfectly definite measures, the language scholar finds himself confronted by a complex range of differing practices which must be sorted into an indefinite number of groups according to a set of somewhat indistinct criteria called "general usage." [13] Those who hold this scientific point of view insist, therefore, that the first step in fulfilling the obligation of the schools in the matter of dealing with the English language is to record, realistically and as completely as possible, the facts of this usage.

This investigation and report assumes as its first principle this scientific point of view with its repudiation of the conventional attitude toward language errors. We shall, therefore, ignore the conventional classification of *mistakes* and *correct forms,* and attempt to outline the types of differences that appear in our American language practices.

II

All of us upon occasion note and use for the purpose of identification the many differences in the speech of those about us. By differences in pitch of voice, for instance, we can usually tell whether the person talking to us over the telephone is a man, or a woman, or a child. . . . In similar fashion we should with little difficulty recognize the speech of a Scot like Harry Lauder as differing from that of a native of Georgia or Alabama. If one could conjure up Shakespeare or Spenser or Milton, he would find their English strange to his ears not only in pronunciation but in vocabulary and in grammar as well.[14] The speech of Chaucer and of Wycliffe would sound even less like English.[15] In other words, even if one ignores such details as separate the speech of every single person from that of any other, there are at least four large types of differences to be noted in our discussion here.

First, there are historical differences. Chaucer used, as we do, *they* as the nominative plural of the pronoun of the third person, but he did not use *their* as the genitive and *them* as the dative-accusative form. Instead, he used the forms *her* or *hir,* for the genitive plural, and *hem* for the dative-accusative or objective forms. In Chaucer's language it was still the practice to distinguish carefully between the singular and plural forms of the past tense of

[13] One should, perhaps, call attention at this point to the fact that the great *Oxford English Dictionary* is the outstanding document in this "scientific view of language." The principle under lying the production of the *Oxford Dictionary,* the very foundation of its method, was the insistence upon use or practice as the sole criterion of the legitimate meaning of words. Compare, for example, the treatment of the word *nice* (especially sense 15) in this dictionary with the usual statements concerning it as given in the conventional handbooks.

[14] This is sixteenth- and seventeenth-century English. [eds.]

[15] This is fourteenth-century English. [eds.]

many verbs. He would say *I rood* (rode) but we *ride (n)*, *he sang* but they *sunge (n)*. In the late sixteenth century it was no longer the practice to distinguish between the singular and plural in the past tense, and Shakspere therefore used *we rode* as well as *I rode*. For him, however, *learn* was often used with the meaning we give to *teach*, and *thou* was frequently used to address those of inferior rank or intimate friends. Thus the language forms of each age have differed in some respect from those of any other time. Constant change is the outstanding characteristic of a live language used by an intellectually active people. The historical changes do not come suddenly, nor do they affect all the users of a language equally. Thus at any time there will be found those who cling to the older methods and those who use the newer fashion. Many of the differences we note in the language of today find their explanation in this process of historical change. These older forms constitute a fairly large proportion of the materials usually called errors by those who maintain the conventional point of view. The so-called double negative, as in "They didn't take no oil with them," is thus a perpetuation of an old practice exceedingly common in the English language for centuries. It was formerly the normal way of stressing a negative. The form *foot*, in such expressions as "He is six foot tall," "The height of the bar is now six foot and two inches," is again the perpetuation of an old practice in the English language which the modern fashion has abandoned. It is an old genitive plural following the numeral. A few other examples out of dozens of such historical differences are *clomb*, usually spelled *clum*, as the past tense of the verb *climb*, instead of *climbed; wrought*[16] as the past tense of the verb *work*, instead of *worked; stang* as the past tense of the verb *sting*, instead of *stung*. Such differences belong not only in this group called "historical differences" but often also to some of the other three groups to be explained below. In fact, the four types of differences are not by any means mutually exclusive classifications but merely loose divisions with convenient labels.

Second, there are regional differences. In the south of England, in early Modern English, the inflectional ending of the verb in the third person singular present indicative was *-eth*, as in "God *loveth* a cheerful giver." [17] In the north of England this inflectional ending was *-es*, as "God *loves* a cheerful giver." Late Modern English has adopted the form that was used only in the northern region. In the language practice of the United States, *gotten* as a past participle form of *get* is fairly general; in England it seldom appears. *You all* as a plural of *you* is especially characteristic of southern United States. In some colleges one takes a course *under* a professor; in others it is *from* one or *with* one; in still others it is *to* one. Some of the dif-

---

[16] One should note that in the case of *wrought* the old form has not the flavor of "vulgar" English as have the other here given but suggests super-refinement.

[17] The Early Modern English period is from 1500 to 1650. The Late Modern English period is from 1650 on. [eds.]

ferences we note in the language practices of those about us find their explanation in the fact that the fashions in one community or section of the country do not necessarily develop in others. Regional or geographical differences show themselves more clearly in matters of vocabulary. That part of an automobile that is called a *hood* in the United States is called a *bonnet* in England. That which they call the *hood* in England we call the *top*. *Lumber*, to most of us in the United States, means *timber*; in England it still means *rubbish*. In some sections of the United States a *paper bag* is usually called a *sack*, in others a *poke*. Such regional differences become especially noticeable when a person from one section of the country moves into another bringing with him the peculiar fashions of the district from which he comes. In the new community these language differences challenge attention and give rise to questions of correctness and preference.

Third, there are literary and colloquial differences. The language practices of conversation differ in many subtle ways from those used in formal writing. Most apparent is the abundance of contractions in the language of conversation. Thoroughly unnatural would sound the speech of those who in conversation did not constantly use *I'm, you'll, isn't, don't, aren't, they'd better, we've*, instead of the fully expanded *I am, you will, is not, do not, are not, they had better, we have*. And in similar fashion the formal writing that habitually employed such contractions would seem equally unnatural because of the impression of very informal familiarity which they would create. Apparent, too, although less obvious are the differences between conversation and formal writing in the matter of sentence completeness. Conversation abounds in groups of words that do not form conventionally complete and logical sentences. Many verbs are omitted; clauses are uttered which are to be attached to the whole context of the conversation rather than to any particular word in a parsable sentence; single words stand for complete ideas. In formal writing the situation demands much more logical completeness of expression, and most of the sentences appear to satisfy the demands of a conventional grammatical analysis. Less apparent but not less real are the differences which arise out of the fact that many perfectly familiar expressions occur practically only in conversational situations and are found very seldom in literary English unless they appear in attempts to report conversation in writing.[18] Occasions seldom arise in anything except conversational situations to use *Who* (or *whom*) *did you call?* or *It is me* (or *I*).

Many assume that the language practices of formal writing are the best or at least that they are of a higher level than those of colloquial or conversational English. When, therefore, they find an expression marked "colloquial" in a dictionary, as is the phrase *"to get on one's nerves"* in Webster's *New International Dictionary*, they frown upon its use. As a matter of fact,

---

[18] Such expressions, used largely in conversational situations, are called colloquialisms. Examples: He came *right away*. That was *real* nice of you. She was *flabbergasted*. Come *quick*. [eds.]

thus to label an expression "colloquial" is simply to say that it occurs in good conversation but not in formal writing.[19] Unless one can assume that formal writing is in itself more desirable than good conversation, the language practices peculiar to conversation cannot be rated in comparison with those of formal writing. Each set of language practices is best in its own special sphere of use; one will necessarily differ from the other.

Fourth, there are social or class differences. Despite the fact that America in its national life has struggled to express its belief in the essential equality of human beings and to free the paths of opportunity from arbitrary and artificial restraints, there still do exist some clear differences between the habits and practices of various social groups. It is, of course, practically impossible to mark the limits of any social class in this country. It is even extremely difficult to describe the special characteristics of any such class because of the comparative ease with which one passes from one social group to another, especially in youth, and the consequent mixture of group habits among those so moving. Our public schools, our churches, our community welfare work, our political life, all furnish rather frequent occasions for social class mixture. All that can be done in respect to such a description is to indicate certain facts which seem generally true for the *core* of any social group, realizing that these same facts may also be true separately of many who have connections with other groups. There are, for example, those who habitually wear formal dress clothes in the evening and those who never wear them. Many of the former frequent the opera and concerts of the best music; many of the latter find their entertainment solely in the movies. The families of the wealthy, especially those whose wealth has continued for several generations, ordinarily mix but little with the families of unskilled laborers; and the families of college professors even in a small city have usually very little social life in common with the families of policemen and firemen.

Just as the general social habits of such separated social groups naturally show marked differences, so their language practices inevitably vary. Pronunciations such as "*ketch*" for *catch* and "*git*" for *get;* and grammatical forms such as "He *seen* his mistakes as soon as he *done* it" or "*You was*" are not the characteristic modes of speech of university professors, or of the

---

[19] The word *colloquial* as applied to English words and structures is frequently misunderstood, even by teachers óf English. Some confuse it with *localism,* and think of the words and constructions marked "colloquial" as peculiarities of speaking which are characteristic of a particular locality. Others feel that some stigma attaches to the label "colloquial" and would strive to avoid as *incorrect* (or as of a *low level*) all words and phrases so marked. The word *colloquial,* however, as used to label words and phrases in a dictionary like Webster's *New International Dictionary* has no such meaning. It is used to mark those words and constructions whose range of use is primarily that of the polite conversation of cultivated people, of their familiar letters and informal speeches, as distinct from those words and constructions which are common also in formal writing. As a matter of fact, even the language of our better magazines and of public addresses has, during the last generation, moved away from the formal toward the informal.

clergymen who preach from the pulpits in our large city churches, or of the judges of the supreme court, or of the presidents of our most important banks, or even of those who habitually patronize the opera. Such language practices, therefore, if used in these particular social groups attract as much attention as a pair of overalls might at an evening gathering where custom demands formal dress clothes. In fact, part of the significance of the social differences in language habits can well be illustrated by a comparison with clothes. Fundamentally the clothes one wears fulfill the elementary practical functions of comfort by keeping one warm and of modesty by avoiding indecent exposure of one's person. These two practical purposes could just as well be accomplished by rather shapeless simple garments produced over a standard pattern for everyone and worn upon all occasions. Such clothes could be made to fulfill their primary functions very efficiently with a minimum of cost. In such a situation, however, aside from the significance of differing degrees of cleanliness, the clothes would show us very little concerning the individuals who wore them. With our present habits of dress the clothes connote or suggest, in a broad general way, certain information concerning the wearers. Among other things they suggest the *circumstances in which we usually see them worn*. A dress suit suggests an evening party (or in some places a hotel waiter); overalls suggest a piece of dirty work or possibly a summer camp. In like manner language forms and constructions not only fulfill a primary function of communicating meaning; they also suggest the circumstances in which those particular forms and constructions are usually employed. If, then, one uses the pronunciations and grammatical forms given earlier in this paragraph, they may serve to communicate his meaning unmistakably, but they will also suggest that he habitually associates with those social groups for whom these language forms are the customary usage and not with those for whom they are not characteristic. We must, therefore, recognize the fact that there are separate social or class groups even in American communities and that these groups differ from one another in many social practices including their language habits.

As indicated earlier the four kinds of differences in language practice here outlined are by no means mutually exclusive. Many historical differences and some sectional differences have become also social differences. For our purpose here the social or class differences are of most concern; other types of differences will be treated only as they bear upon these social or class dialects.

III

In order to grasp the significance of these social differences in language practice for the obligation of the schools one must understand clearly what is meant by "standard" English, and that can perhaps best be accomplished by tracing the course by which a particular kind of English became "standard." As one examines the material written in England during the twelfth and thirteenth centuries—a period from one hundred to two hundred years after the Norman Conquest—he finds a situation in which three things are of especial note:

1. Most of the legal documents, the instruments which controlled the carrying on of the political and the business affairs of the English people, were not written in the English language but in French or Latin. This fact was also true of much of the literature and books of learning familiar to the upper classes.
2. Although some books, especially historical records and religious and moral stories and tracts, were written in English, there was no single type of the English language common to all English writings. The greatest number used what is called the Southern dialect. This particular kind of English had been centered in Winchester, which was the chief city of King Alfred and his successors until the time of the Norman Conquest.
3. There was, therefore, no "standard" English in twelfth and thirteenth century England, for no single type of the English language furnished the medium by which the major affairs of English people were carried on. Instead, English people used for these purposes French, Latin, and at least four distinct varieties of English. The particular kind of English spoken in southern England came nearest to fulfilling the function of a "standard" English because more writings and more significant writings were produced in this type of English than in any other.

In the fourteenth and early fifteenth centuries, however, this situation changed. London had become the political and in some respects the social head of English life in a much more unified England. Many of the major affairs of the realm had to be handled in London. More and more the English language, the English of London, was used in the legal documents of politics and business. Solely because of the fact that more of the important affairs of English life were conducted in this London English rather than in Winchester English, London English became "standard" English. Naturally, then, the growing use of this particular type of English for the important affairs of English life gathered such momentum that even writers to whom other types of English were more natural felt constrained to learn and to use the fashionable London English. Gower, for example, a Kentishman, did not write his native kind of English but practically the same forms, constructions and spellings as Chaucer, a Londoner born. Naturally, too, this London English gained a social prestige because of the fact that its use connoted or suggested relations with the center of affairs in English life, whereas the inability to use London English suggested that one did not have such social contact. "Standard" English, therefore, is, historically, a local dialect, which was used to carry on the major affairs of English life and which gained thereby a social prestige.[20]

Many changes occurred in this dialect of English and these changes especially affected the usage of the younger rather than of the older generations in the centers of fashionable social life. Thus the continued use of the older forms rather than the newer changes always suggested a lack of direct contact with those who were active in the conduct of important matters. In this connotation lay the power of "standard" English to compel the ambitious to conform to its practices.

In America, however, we have had no one recognized center for our political, business, social, and intellectual affairs. More than that, the great distances between various parts of the United States made very difficult frequent actual social contacts in the earlier days. Our coast cities, Boston and New York, maintained direct relations with London long after the earlier settlers had moved west, but the middle western settlements had practically no relations with Boston and New York. This fact can probably explain the differences between our middle-western speech and that of nineteenth century Boston and New York. Because of the fact that New England so long dominated our intellectual life there has been a good deal of feeling in many parts of the United States that the language usages of New England connoted a connection with a higher culture than did the language of the Middle West. Hence the rather widespread attempt to imitate certain New England speech characteristics. On the whole, however, if we ignore the special differences that separate the speech of New England, the South, and the Middle West, we do have in the United States a set of language habits, broadly conceived, in which the major matters of the political, social, economic, educational, religious life of this country are carried on. To these language habits is attached a certain social prestige, for the use of them suggests that one has constant relations with those who are responsible for the important affairs of our communities. It is this set of language habits, derived originally from an older London English, but differentiated from it somewhat by its independent development in this country, which is the "standard" English of the United States. Enough has been said to enforce the point that it is "standard" not because it is any more correct or more beautiful or more capable than other varieties of English; it is "standard" solely because it is the particular type of English which is used in the conduct of the important affairs of our people. It is also the type of English used by the *socially acceptable* of most of our communities and insofar as that is true it has become a social or class dialect in the United States.

[20] "Standard" French, "Standard" Italian, "Standard" Dutch, etc., have similar histories.

IV

With this analysis it is not difficult to understand the nature of the obligation assumed by our schools in respect to the teaching of the English language. Long have we in our national life adhered to the principle that no individual in his attempts to rise to the highest positions should be disqualified by artificial restraints. Our people have been devoted to education because education has furnished the most important tool of social advancement. Our public schools have therefore held to the ideal that every boy and girl should be so equipped that he shall not be handicapped in his struggle for social progress and recognition, and that he may rise to the highest positions. In the matter of the English language it is clear that any one who cannot use the language habits in which the major affairs of the country are conducted, the language habits of the socially acceptable of most of our communities, would have a serious handicap. The schools, therefore, have assumed the burden of training every boy and girl, no matter what his original social background and native speech, to use this "standard" English, this particular social or class dialect. To some pupils it is almost a foreign language; to others it is their accustomed speech. Many believe that the schools have thus assumed an impossible task. Certainly the widespread and almost unanimous condemnation of the results of their efforts convinces us that either the schools have not conceived their task adequately or they have chosen the wrong materials and methods to accomplish it. We shall find, I think, that seldom have school authorities understood the precise nature of the language task they have assumed and very frequently have directed their energies to teaching not "standard" English realistically described, but a "make-believe" correctness which contained some true forms of real "standard" English and many forms that had and have practically no currency outside the classroom.[21]

A few brief statements will serve both to summarize the preceding discussion and to bring into a single view the principles which underlie this investigation and report.

1. All considerations of an *absolute* "correctness" in accord with the conventional rules of grammar or the dicta of handbooks must be set aside, because these rules or these dicta very frequently do not represent the actual practice of "standard" English but describe forms which have little currency outside the English classroom. We assume, therefore, that there can be no "correctness" apart from usage and that the *true* forms

[21] See, for example, H. B. Allen's article "The Standard of Usage in Freshman Textbooks," in *English Journal*, college ed., Vol. 24 (1935), pp. 564–571; and R. C. Pooley, *Teaching English Usage* (New York: Appleton-Century-Crofts, 1946). [The second edition of Pooley's book appeared in 1974, published by the National Council of Teachers of English, 1111 Kenyon Road, Urbana, Illinois 61801. eds.]

of "standard" English are those that are actually used in that particular dialect. Deviations from these usages are "incorrect" only when used in the dialect to which they do not belong. These deviations suggest not only the particular social dialect or set of language habits in which they usually occur, but also the general social and cultural characteristics most often accompanying the use of these forms.

2. It is the assumed obligation of the schools to attempt to develop in each child the knowledge of and the ability to use the "standard" English of the United States—that set of language habits in which the most important affairs of our country are carried on, the dialect of the socially acceptable in most of our communities.

3. The first step in fulfilling that obligation is the making of an accurate and realistic survey and description of the actual language practices in the various social or class dialects. Only after we have such information in hand can we know what social connotations are likely to attach to particular usages.[22]

[22] Much information of this kind is now available. Here are two useful reference books for students:
1. The up-to-date dictionary that you are asked to buy for freshman English. This describes acceptable social usage of verb forms (my shirt *shrunk*), noun plurals (both curriculum*s*), parts of speech (*like* a bonehead should, go *slow*), and pronunciations. In addition, it gives usage labels such as *slang and nonstandard*.
2. Margaret Bryant's *Current American Usage*. This summarizes a great deal of information from research studies in usage. [eds.]

Grammar for Today

Bergen Evans

This article is a reply to an attack on the concept of usage as the determinant of acceptability in language, especially as set forth in Bergen and Cornelia Evans' *A Dictionary of Contemporary American Usage.* In the selection below Bergen Evans defends and illustrates the standard viewpoint held by linguists that usage is the ultimate and only arbiter in linguistic matters.

To teach in our schools the "normal speech of the educated class" (Jespersen), one must find out what it is. This the linguist does. He

From *The Atlantic Monthly* (March 1960). Reprinted by permission of the author.

studies and records the speech of the educated class, as well as that of other speech communities—of criminals, mountain people, the under-privileged, and others. It is this record of educated speech, not a set of arbitrary rules from the past, that brings to light the acceptable usage that is called Standard English. Standard English has wide limits, varying in many ways: according to the speech situation, the region in which it is used, the degree of formality, and age and sex of the user, and the form it takes, either written or spoken. Mr. Evans is Professor of English Emeritus at Northwestern University.

In 1747 Samuel Johnson issued a plan for a new dictionary of the English language. It was supported by the most distinguished printers of the day and was dedicated to the model of all correctness, Philip Dormer Stanhope, Fourth Earl of Chesterfield. Such a book, it was felt, was urgently needed to "fix" the language, to arrest its "corruption" and "decay," a degenerative process which, then as now, was attributed to the influence of "the vulgar" and which, then as now, it was a mark of superiority and elegance to decry. And Mr. Johnson seemed the man to write it. He had an enormous knowl-edge of Latin, deep piety, and dogmatic convictions. He was also honest and intelligent, but the effect of these lesser qualifications was not to show until later.

Oblig'd by hunger and request of friends, Mr. Johnson was willing to assume the role of linguistic dictator. He was prepared to "fix" the pro-nunciation of the language, "preserve the purity" of its idiom, brand "im-pure" words with a "note of infamy," and secure the whole "from being overrun by . . . low terms."

There were, however, a few reservations. Mr. Johnson felt it necessary to warn the oversanguine that "Language is the work of man, a being from whom permanence and stability cannot be derived." English "was not formed from heaven . . . but was produced by necessity and enlarged by accident." It had, indeed, been merely "thrown together by negligence" and was in such a state of confusion that its very syntax could no longer "be taught by general rules, but [only] by special precedents."

In 1755 the *Dictionary* appeared. The noble patron had been given a great deal more immortality than he had bargained for by the vigor of the kick Johnson had applied to his backside as he booted him overboard. And the *Plan* had been replaced by the *Preface*, a sadder but very much wiser document.

Eight years of "sluggishly treading the track of the alphabet" had taught Johnson that the hopes of "fixing" the language and preserving its "purity" were but "the dreams of a poet doomed at last to wake a lexicographer." In "the boundless chaos of living speech," so copious and energetic in its disorder, he had found no guides except "experience and analogy." Irregularities were "inherent in the tongue" and could not be "dismissed or re-formed" but must be permitted "to remain untouched." "Uniformity must be sacrificed to custom[1] . . . in compliance with a numberless majority" and "general agreement." One of the pet projects of the age had been the establishment of an academy to regulate and improve style. "I hope," Johnson wrote in the *Preface*, that if "it should be established . . . the spirit of English liberty will hinder or destroy [it.]"

At the outset of the work he had flattered himself, he confessed, that he would reform abuses and put a stop to alterations. But he had soon discovered that "sounds are too volatile and subtle for legal restraints" and that "to enchain syllables and to lash the wind are equally undertakings of pride unwilling to measure its desires by its strength." For "the causes of change in language are as much superior to human resistance as the revolutions of the sky or the intumescence of the tide."

There had been an even more profound discovery: that grammarians and lexicographers "do not form, but register the language; do not teach men how they should think, but relate how they have hitherto expressed their thoughts." And with this statement Johnson ushered in the rational study of linguistics. He had entered on his task a medieval pedant. He emerged from it a modern scientist.

Of course his discoveries were not strikingly original. Horace had observed that use was the sole arbiter and norm of speech and Montaigne had said that he who would fight custom with grammar was a fool. Doubtless thousands of other people had at one time or another perceived and said the same thing. But Johnson introduced a new principle. Finding that he could not lay down rules, he gave actual examples to show meaning and form. He offered as authority illustrative quotations, and in so doing established that language is what usage makes it and that custom, in the long run, is the ultimate and only court of appeal in linguistic matters.

This principle, axiomatic today in grammar and lexicography, seems to exasperate a great many laymen who, apparently, find two hundred and five years too short a period in which to grasp a basic idea. They insist that there are absolute standards of correctness in speech and that these standards may be set forth in a few simple rules. To a man, they believe, of course, that they speak and write "correctly" and they are loud in their insistence that others imitate them.

It is useless to argue with such people because they are not, really, interested in language at all. They are interested solely in demonstrating their own superiority. Point out to them—as has been done hundreds of times—that forms which they regard as "corrupt," "incorrect," and "vulgar" have been used by Shakespeare, Milton, and the Bible and are used daily by 180 million Americans and accepted by the best linguists and lexicogra-

[1] *Custom* was the eighteenth-century word for *usage*. [eds.]

phers, and they will coolly say, "Well, if they differ from me, they're wrong."

But if usage is not the final determinant of speech, what is? Do the inhabitants of Italy, for example, speak corrupt Latin or good Italian? Is Spanish superior to French? Would the Breton fisherman speak better if he spoke Parisian French? Can one be more fluent in Outer Mongolian than in Inner Mongolian? One has only to ask such questions in relation to languages other than one's own, languages within which our particular snobberies and struggles for prestige have no stake, to see the absurdity of them.

The language that we do speak, if we are to accept the idea of "corruption" and "decay" in language, is a horribly decayed Anglo-Saxon, grotesquely corrupted by Norman French. Furthermore, since Standard English is a development of the London dialect of the fourteenth century, our speech, by true aristocratic standards is woefully middle-class, commercial, and vulgar. And American speech is lower middle-class, reeking of counter and till. Where else on earth, for instance, would one find crime condemned because it didn't *pay!*

In more innocent days a great deal of time was spent in wondering what was the "original" language of mankind, the one spoken in Eden, the language of which all modern tongues were merely degenerate remnants. Hector Boethius tells us that James IV of Scotland was so interested in this problem that he had two children reared with a deaf and dumb nurse on an island in order to see what language they would "naturally" speak. James thought it would be Hebrew, and in time, to his great satisfaction, it was reported that the children were speaking Hebrew!

Despite this experiment, however, few people today regard English as a corruption of Hebrew. But many seem to think it is a corruption of Latin and labor mightily to make it conform to this illusion. It is they and their confused followers who tell us that we can't say "I am mistaken" because translated into Latin this would mean "I am misunderstood," and we can't say "I have enjoyed myself" unless we are egotistical or worse.

It is largely to this group—most of whom couldn't read a line of Latin at sight if their lives depended on it—that we owe our widespread bewilderment concerning, *who* and *whom.* In Latin the accusative or dative form would always be used, regardless of the word's position in the sentence, when the pronoun was the object of a verb or a preposition. But in English, for at least four hundred years, this simply hasn't been so. When the pronoun occurs at the beginning of a question, people who speak natural, fluent literary English use the nominative, regardless. They say "Who did you give it to?" not "Whom did you give it to?" But the semiliterate, intimidated and bewildered, are mouthing such ghastly utterances as a recent headline in a Chicago newspaper: WHOM'S HE KIDDING?

Another group seems to think that in its pure state English was a Laputan tongue, with logic as its guiding principle. Early members of this sect insisted that *unloose* could only mean "to tie up," and present members have compelled the gasoline industry to label its trucks *Flammable* under the disastrous insistence, apparently, that the old *Inflammable* could only mean "not burnable."

It is to them, in league with the Latinists, that we owe the bogy of the double negative. In all Teutonic languages a doubling of the negative merely emphasizes the negation. But we have been told for a century now that two negatives make a positive, though if they do and it's merely a matter of logic, then three negatives should make a negative again. So that if "It doesn't make no difference" is wrong merely because it includes two negatives, then "It doesn't never make no difference" ought to be right again.[2]

Both of these groups, in their theories at least, ignore our idiom. Yet idiom—those expressions which defy all logic but are the very essence of a tongue—plays a large part in English. We go to school and college, but we go to *the* university. We buy two dozen eggs but a couple of dozen. *Good and* can mean *very* ("I am good and mad!") and "a hot cup of coffee" means that the coffee, not the cup, is to be hot. It makes a world of difference to a condemned man whether his reprieve is *upheld* or *held up.*

There are thousands of such expressions in English. They are the irregularities" which Johnson found "inherent in the tongue" and which his wisdom perceived could not and should not be removed. Indeed, it is in the recognition and use of these idioms that skillful use of English lies.

Many words in the form that is now mandatory were originally just mistakes, and many of these mistakes were forced into the language by eager ignoramuses determined to make it conform to some notion of their own. The *s* was put in *island,* for instance, in sheer pedantic ignorance. The second *r* doesn't belong in *trousers,* nor the *g* in *arraign,* nor the *t* in *deviltry,* nor the *n* in *passenger* and *messenger.* Nor, so far as English is concerned, does that first *c* in *arctic* which so many people twist their mouths so strenuously to pronounce.

And grammar is as "corrupted" as spelling or pronunciation. "You are" is as gross a solecism as "me am." It's recent, too; you won't find it in the Authorized Version of the Bible. *Lesser, nearer,* and *more* are grammatically on a par with *gooder. Crowed* is the equivalent of *knowed* or *growed,* and *caught* and *dug* (for *catched* and *digged*) are as "corrupt" as *squoze* for *squeezed* or *snoze* for *sneezed.*

Fortunately for our peace of mind most people are quite content to let English conform to English, and they are supported in their sanity by modern grammarians and linguists.

Scholars agree with Puttenham (1589) that a language is simply speech

---

[2] Evans is objecting to the PRINCIPLE here. The double negative is unacceptable in Standard English, not because two negatives make a positive but because educated persons do not habitually use it. [eds.]

"fashioned to the common understanding and accepted by consent." They believe that the only "rules" that can be stated for a language are codified observations. They hold, that is, that language is the basis of grammar, not the other way round. They do not believe that any language can become "corrupted" by the linguistic habits of those who speak it. They do not believe that anyone who is a native speaker of a standard language will get into any linguistic trouble unless he is misled by snobbishness or timidity or vanity.

He may, of course, if his native language is English, speak a form of English that marks him as coming from a rural or an unread group. But if he doesn't mind being so marked, there's no reason why he should change. Johnson retained a Staffordshire burr in his speech all his life. And surely no one will deny that Robert Burns's rustic dialect was just as good as a form of speech as, and in his mouth infinitely better as a means of expression than, the "correct" English spoken by ten million of his southern contemporaries.

The trouble is that people are no longer willing to be rustic or provincial. They all want to speak like educated people, though they don't want to go to the trouble of becoming truly educated. They want to believe that a special form of socially acceptable and financially valuable speech can be mastered by following a few simple rules. And there is no lack of little books that offer to supply the rules and promise "correctness" if the rules are adhered to. But, of course, these offers are specious because you don't speak like an educated person unless you are an educated person, and the little books, if taken seriously, will not only leave the lack of education showing but will expose the pitiful yearning and the basic vulgarity as well, in such sentences as "Whom are you talking about?"

As a matter of fact, the educated man uses at least three languages. With his family and his close friends, on the ordinary, unimportant occasions of daily life, he speaks, much of the time, a monosyllabic sort of shorthand. On more important occasions and when dealing with strangers in his official or business relations, he has a more formal speech, more complete, less allusive, politely qualified, wisely reserved. In addition he has some acquaintance with the literary speech of his language. He understands this when he reads it, and often enjoys it, but he hesitates to use it. In times of emotional stress hot fragments of it may come out of him like lava, and in times of feigned emotion, as when giving a commencement address, cold, greasy gobbets of it will ooze forth.

The linguist differs from the amateur grammarian in recognizing all of these variations and gradations in the language. And he differs from the snob in doubting that the speech of any one small group among the language's more than 300 million daily users constitutes a model for all the rest to imitate.

The methods of the modern linguist can be illustrated by the question of the grammatical number of *none*. Is it singular or plural? Should one say "None of them is ready" or "None of them are ready"?

The prescriptive grammarians are emphatic that it should be singular. The Latinists point out that *nemo*, the Latin equivalent, is singular. The logicians triumphantly point out that *none* can't be more than one and hence can't be plural.

The linguist knows that he hears "None of them are ready" every day, from people of all social positions, geographical areas, and degrees of education. He also hears "None is." Furthermore, literature informs him that both forms were used in the past. From Malory (1450) to Milton (1650) he finds that *none* was treated as a singular three times for every once that it was treated as a plural. That is, up to three hundred years ago men usually said *None is*. From Milton to 1917, *none* was used as a plural seven times for every four times it was used as a singular. That is, in the past three hundred years men often said *None is*, but they said *None are* almost twice as often. Since 1917, however, there has been a noticeable increase in the use of the plural, so much so that today *None are* is the preferred form.

The descriptive grammarian, therefore, says that while *None is* may still be used, it is becoming increasingly peculiar. This, of course, will not be as useful to one who wants to be cultured in a hurry as a short, emphatic permission or prohibition. But it has the advantage of describing English as it is spoken and written here and now and not as it ought to be spoken in some Cloud-Cuckoo-Land.

The descriptive grammarian believes that a child should be taught English, but he would like to see the child taught the English actually used by his educated contemporaries, not some pedantic, theoretical English designed chiefly to mark the imagined superiority of the designer.

He believes that a child should be taught the parts of speech, for example. But the child should be told the truth—that these are functions of use, not some quality immutably inherent in this or that word. Anyone, for instance, who tells a child—or anyone else—that *like* is used in English only as a preposition has grossly misinformed him and anyone who complains that its use as a conjunction is a corruption introduced by Winston cigarettes ought, in all fairness, to explain how Shakespeare, Keats, and the translators of the Authorized Version of the Bible came to be in the employ of the R. J. Reynolds Tobacco Company.

Whether formal grammar can be taught to advantage before the senior year of high school is doubtful; most studies—and many have been made—indicate that it can't. But when it is taught, it should be the grammar of today's English, not the obsolete grammar of yesterday's prescriptive grammarians. By that grammar, for instance, *please* in the sentence "Please reply" is the verb and *reply* its object. But by modern meaning *reply* is the verb, in the imperative, and *please* is merely a qualifying word meaning "no discourtesy intended," a mollifying or de-imperatival adverb, or whatever you will, but not the verb.

This is a long way from saying "Anything goes," which is the charge that, with all the idiot repetition of a needle stuck in a groove, the uninformed ceaselessly chant against modern grammarians. But to assert that usage is the sole determinant in grammar, pronunciation, and meaning is *not* to say that anything goes. Custom is illogical and unreasonable, but it is also tyrannical. The least deviation from its dictates is usually punished with severity. And because this is so, children should be taught what the current and local customs in English are. They should not be taught that we speak a bastard Latin or a vocalized logic. And they should certainly be disabused of the stultifying illusion that after God had given Moses the Commandments He called him back and pressed on him a copy of Woolley's *Handbook of English Grammar.*[3]

The grammarian does not see it as his function to "raise the standards" set by Franklin, Lincoln, Melville, Mark Twain, and hundreds of millions of other Americans. He is content to record what they said and say.

Insofar as he serves as a teacher, it is his business to point out the limits of the permissible, to indicate the confines within which the writer may exercise his choice, to report that which custom and practice have made acceptable. It is certainly not the business of the grammarian to impose his personal taste as the only norm of good English, to set forth his prejudices as the ideal standard which everyone should copy. That would be fatal. No one person's standards are broad enough for that.

SUGGESTED ASSIGNMENTS

1. Among the usage items in the Evanses' *A Dictionary of Contemporary Usage* that were considered objectionable by its hostile critic were these:

less (fewer) than three
different than (from)
back of (behind)
Who (whom) did you see?
Who (whom) are you looking for?
The data is (are) all in.

See what your desk dictionary has to say about them. All are taken up in *Webster's New Collegiate Dictionary*, 8th edition, (1973).

---

[3] This once popular textbook of freshman composition was filled with prescriptive grammatical rules for "correct English," rules that disregarded usage and spoke with *ipse dixit* authority. [eds.]

2. Many composition textbooks and handbooks contain a section on items of usage, often entitled "Glossary of Usage" or "Glossary of Diction" (sometimes "Faulty Diction"), with comments about the acceptability or nonacceptability of these items as Standard American English and their appropriateness to various language situations. Compare the judgments of any three textbooks about each of the following: *aggravate, different from/different than, due to, enthuse, farther/further, like, who/whom* (interrogative). Then look up each of the items in three dictionaries, compare the dictionary statements with each other and with your original findings, and present your data to the class for discussion.

3. The whole of the English language can be partitioned into various groupings. In the readings of this section, we have seen it divided into two social dialects, standard and nonstandard English. Still another grouping consists of those words that are used in limited areas of discourse, like the special vocabularies of skiers, carpenters, astronauts, skin divers, and so on. Such specialized groups of words are called shoptalk.

   Make a list of shoptalk expressions in a particular area of life with which you are familiar, for example, jazz, trout fishing, hi-fi, boxing, amateur radio work, dog raising, woodworking, painting, stamp collecting, theatre, hot rods. Include only those expressions that you believe are not understood by the general public. Bring them to class, where a discussion of the lists will probably reveal how much of our own language many of us do not know.

4. Running through all varieties of English is a special vein called slang. Slang is a roguish kind of language. At its best it is piquant and picturesque, and holds for us the black-sheep attraction of forbidden pleasures. But when the novelty of a new slang expression wears thin, its sparkle dwindles away and it becomes dull as an old penny. Although slang cannot be defined with precision, most students of language will probably agree that the following statements can be made about it:

   a. It occurs more frequently in speech than in writing.
   b. It is found in both standard and nonstandard English.
   c. It seems to originate from a desire for novelty and freshness of expression.
   d. It tends to change more rapidly than the rest of the language.
   e. It consists largely of these kinds of words:

      (1) Old words with new meanings.
      (2) Newly invented words.
      (3) Standard words used in a figurative sense.
      (4) Words borrowed from shoptalk.
      (5) Clipped words.[4]

   Meet with a friend and see how many slang expressions you can jot down in fifteen minutes. Classify them according to the division under *e*. How would you classify those that you have left over?

---

[4] A clipped word is a word that has been reduced to one of its parts. Examples: *lab, exam, plane, phone, flu, still, co-ed, prom.* [eds.]

FURTHER READINGS

Allen, Harold B., ed. *Readings in Applied English Linguistics,* 2d ed. New York: Appleton-Century-Crofts, 1964. See the section "Linguistics and Usage," pp. 271–341.

Bryant, Margaret M. *Current American Usage.* New York: Funk & Wagnalls, 1962. Summary of research on many problems of usage.

Evans, Bergen, and Cornelia Evans. *A Dictionary of Contemporary American Usage.* New York: Random House, Inc., 1957.

Fries, Charles C. *The Teaching of English.* Ann Arbor, Mich.: George Wahr Publishing Company, 1949. See especially Chapter I, "The Rules of Grammar as the Measure of Language Errors"; Chapter II, "Standards of Acceptable English: Grammar"; Chapter III, "Standards of Acceptable English: Vocabulary."

Hall, Robert A., Jr. *Introductory Linguistics.* Philadelphia: Chilton Books, 1964. On usage, see pp. 444–448.

————. *Linguistics and Your Language.* New York: Doubleday & Company, Inc., 1960. See Chapter I, "Which Should I Say?" and Chapter II, "Right vs. Wrong."

Lamberts, J. J. *A Short Introduction to English Usage.* New York: McGraw-Hill, 1972. Use "Word Index" for specific matters.

Mittins, W. H., Mary Salu, Mary Edminson, and Sheila Coyne. *Attitudes to English Usage.* London: Oxford University Press, 1970. Results of a British survey. Excellent discussion of separate items of usage.

Myers, L. M. *The Roots of Modern English.* Boston: Little, Brown & Company, 1966. On the beginnings of traditional school grammar, see pp. 207–230.

Quirk, Randolph. *The Use of English.* New York: St. Martin's Press, Inc., 1962. On usage see especially pp. 64–68 and 199–215.

Robertson, Stuart, and Frederick G. Cassidy. *The Development of Modern English.* Englewood Cliffs, N.J.: Prentice-Hall, Inc., 1954. See pp. 291–325.

[Remember that a *good, up-to-date* dictionary is useful for some matters of usage, such as part of speech (Come *quick*), principal part of verb (The boat *sunk.*), spelling (*alright*), and area of usage (that is, slang, non-standard, dialect, and so on). eds.]

11
SEMANTICS

Classification

S. I. Hayakawa

Whenever you open your mouth you are likely to make classifications. If you should say, "Today I saw Hubert Humphrey," you would of course be referring to a single, unique individual; this would not be a classification. But think of all the other words you can use to refer to him: *pharmacist, teacher, fisherman, public speaker, Midwesterner, liberal, politician.* In using any of these words to refer to Mr. Humphrey, you are classifying him, that is, you are putting him into a class or group, the members of which possess certain common characteristics. All such nouns are class-words. The class-word we choose to label any specific person or object depends on our purpose. Some such words express and evoke approval; others, disapproval. And the consequences of such classifications can be far-reaching, as you will soon see. Thus it is an important subject that S. I. Hayakawa deals with in this selection from his well-known book. Dr. Hayakawa has been the editor of *ETC.: A Review of General Semantics.*

GIVING THINGS NAMES

The figure below shows eight objects, let us say animals, four large and four small, a different four with round heads and another four with square

From *Language in Thought and Action* by S. I. Hayakawa, copyright, 1939, 1940, by S. I. Hayakawa, copyright, 1940, 1941, by Harcourt Brace Jovanovich, Inc., and George Allen & Unwin, Ltd. Reprinted by permission.

heads, and still another four with curly tails and another four with straight tails. These animals, let us say, are scampering about your village, but since at first they are of no importance to you, you ignore them. You do not even give them a name.

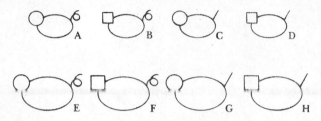

One day, however, you discover that the little ones eat up your grain, while the big ones do not. A differentiation sets itself up, and abstracting the common characteristics of A, B, C, and D, you decide to call these *gogo;* E, F, G, and H you decide to call *gigi.* You chase away the *gogo*, but leave the *gigi* alone. Your neighbor, however, has had a different experience; he finds that those with square heads bite, while those with round heads do not. Abstracting the common characteristics of B, D, F, and H, he calls them *daba*, and A, C, E, and G he calls *dobo*. Still another neighbor discovers, on the other hand, that those with curly tails kill snakes, while those with straight tails do not. He differentiates them, abstracting still another set of common characteristics: A, B, E, and F are *busa*, while C, D, G, and H are *busana*.

Now imagine that the three of you are together when E runs by. You say, "There goes the *gigi*"; your first neighbor says, "There goes the *dobo*"; your other neighbor says, "There goes the *busa*." Here immediately a great controversy arises. What is it really, a *gigi*, a *dobo*, or a *busa*? What is its *right name*? You are quarreling violently when along comes a fourth person from another village who calls it a *muglock*, an edible animal, as opposed to *uglock*, an inedible animal—which doesn't help matters a bit.

Of course the question, "What is it *really*? What is its *right name*?" is a nonsense question. By a nonsense question is meant one that is not capable of being answered. Things can have "right names" only if there is a necessary connection between symbols and things symbolized. . . . That is to say, in the light of your interest in protecting your grain, it may be necessary for you to distinguish the animal E as a *gigi*; your neighbor, who doesn't like to be bitten, finds it practical to distinguish it as a *dobo*; your other neighbor, who likes to see snakes killed, distinguishes it as a *busa*. What we call things and where we draw the line between one class of things and another depend upon the interests we have and the purposes of the classification. For example animals are classified in one way by the meat industry, in a different way by the leather industry, in another different way by the fur industry and in a still different way by the biologist. None of these classifications is any more final than any of the others; each of them is useful for its purpose.

This holds, of course, regarding everything we perceive. A table "is" a table to us, because we can understand its relationship to our conduct and interests; we eat at it, work on it, lay things on it. But to a person living in a culture where no tables are used, it may be a very big stool, a small platform, or a meaningless structure. If our culture and upbringing were different, that is to say, our world would not even look the same to us.

Many of us, for example, cannot distinguish between pickerel, pike, salmon, smelts, perch, crappies, halibut, and mackerel; we say that they are "just fish, and I don't like fish." To a seafood connoisseur, however, these distinctions are real, since they mean the difference to him between one kind of good meal, a very different kind of good meal, or a poor meal. To a zoologist, even finer distinctions become of great importance, since he has other and more general ends in view. When we hear the statement, then, "This fish is a specimen of the pompano, *Trachinotus carolinus*," we accept this as being "true," even if we don't care, not because that is its "right name," but because that is how it is *classified* in the most complete and most general system of classification which people most deeply interested in fish have evolved.

When we name something, then, we are classifying. *The individual object or event we are naming, of course, has no name and belongs to no class until we put it in one.* To illustrate again, suppose that we were to give the *extensional* meaning of the word "Korean." [1] We would have to point to all "Koreans" living at a particular moment and say, "The word 'Korean' denotes at the present moment these persons: $A_1, A_2, A_3 \ldots A_n$." Now, let us say, a child, whom we shall designate as Z, is born among these "Koreans." *The extensional meaning of the word "Korean," determined prior to the existence of Z, does not include Z.* Z is a new individual belonging to no classification, since all classifications were made without taking Z into account. Why, then, is Z also a "Korean"? *Because we say so.* And, saying so—fixing the classification—we have determined to a considerable extent future attitudes toward Z. For example, Z will always have certain rights in Korea; he will always be regarded in other nations as an "alien" and will be subject to laws applicable to "aliens."

In matters of "race" and "nationality," the way in which classifications work is especially apparent. For example, the present writer is by "race" a "Japanese," by "nationality" a "Canadian," but, his friends say, "essentially" an "American," since he thinks, talks, behaves, and dresses much

[1] By the extensional meaning of a word Dr. Hayakawa means "that which it points to . . . in the extensional world," that is, in the world outside your skin. For example, the extensional meaning of "my dog" is the little creature himself that leaps and barks and wags his tail. It is the *thing* referred to in the world you observe. [eds.]

like other Americans. Because he is "Japanese," he is excluded by law from becoming a citizen of the United States; because he is "Canadian," he has certain rights in all parts of the British Commonwealth; because he is "American," he gets along with his friends and teaches in an American institution of higher learning without any noticeable special difficulties. Are these classifications "real"? Of course they are, and *the effect that each of them has upon what he may and may not do constitutes their "reality."*

There was, again, the story some years ago of the immigrant baby whose parents were "Czechs" and eligible to enter the United States by quota. The child, however, because it was born on what happened to be a "British" ship, was a "British subject." The quota for Britishers was full for that year, with the result that the newborn infant was regarded by immigration authorities as "not admissible to the United States." How they straightened out this matter, the writer does not know. The reader can multiply instances of this kind at will. When, to take another example, is a person a "Negro"? By the definition accepted in the United States, any person with even a small amount of "Negro blood"—that is, whose parents or ancestors were classified as "Negroes"—is a "Negro." *It would be exactly as justifiable to say that any person with even a small amount of "white blood" is "white."* Why do they say one rather than the other? Because the former system of classification *suits the convenience of those making the classification.*

There are few complexities about classifications at the level of dogs and cats, knives and forks, cigarettes and candy, but when it comes to classifications at high levels of abstraction,[2] for example, those describing conduct, social institutions, philosophical and moral problems, serious difficulties occur. When one person kills another, is it an act of murder, an act of temporary insanity, an act of homicide, an accident, or an act of heroism? As soon as the process of classification is completed, our attitudes and our conduct are to a considerable degree determined. We hang the murderer, we

---

[2] The level of abstraction refers to the degree of generality of a word. For example, your dog, Duke, might be classified as a *bull terrier,* a *terrier,* a *dog,* an *animal,* a *pet,* or a *creature.* Here each successive term is more general than the preceding one; that is to say, each is on a higher level of abstraction than the one before it. Classifications at high levels of abstraction are extremely general words like *liberty, justice, democracy, officialdom, the American way.* Such words are hard to communicate with because they can mean so many different things. What, for example, does *the American way* mean? To a Russian, fed upon anti-American propaganda, it might mean all the objectionable things he believes Americans do; it would include lynchings, acts of government corruption, illegal price fixing by large corporations, lavish living, gangster activities, oppression of the working man, denial of civil rights to blacks, and many others. But to an American it might mean all of the good things we do: voting at the polls in secret, giving free education to all, allowing private citizens to speak their minds in public, giving voluntarily to charitable organizations, aiding underprivileged nations, and so on. Because the term can include so many thousands of specific acts, it is extremely vague. It is meaningless because it is so meaningful. [eds.]

lock up the insane man, we free the victim of circumstances, we pin a medal on the hero.

THE BLOCKED MIND

Unfortunately, people are not always aware of the way in which they arrive at their classifications. Unaware of the characteristics of the extensional Mr. Miller not covered by classifying him as "a Jew" and attributing to Mr. Miller all the characteristics *suggested* by the affective connotations of the term with which he has been classified, they pass final judgment on Mr. Miller by saying, "Well, a Jew's a Jew.[3] There's no getting around that!"

We need not concern ourselves here with the injustices done to "Jews," "Roman Catholics," "Republicans," "red-heads," "chorus girls," "sailors," "brass-hats," "Southerners," "Yankees," "school teachers," "government regulations," "socialistic proposals," and so on, by such hasty judgments or, as it is better to call them, fixed reactions. "Hasty judgments" suggests that such errors can be avoided by thinking more slowly; this, of course, is not the case, for some people think very slowly with no better results. What we are concerned with is the way in which we block the development of our own minds by such automatic reactions.

To continue with our example of the people who say, "A Jew's a Jew. There's no getting around that!"—they are, as we have seen, confusing the denoted, extensional Jew with the fictitious "Jew" inside their heads. Such persons, the reader will have observed, can usually be made to admit, on being reminded of certain "Jews" whom they admire—perhaps Albert Einstein, perhaps Hank Greenberg, perhaps Jascha Heifetz, perhaps Benny Goodman—that "there are exceptions, of course." They have been compelled by experience, that is to say, to take cognizance of at least a few of the multitude of "Jews" who do not fit their preconceptions. At this point, however, they continue triumphantly, "But exceptions only prove the rule!"[4]—which is another way of saying, "Facts don't count." In extremely serious cases of people who "think" in this way, it can sometimes be observed that the best friends they have may be Isaac Cohens, Isidor Ginsbergs, and Abe Sinaikos; nevertheless, in explaining this, they will say, "I don't think of them as Jews at all. They're just friends." In other words, the fictitious "Jew" inside their heads remains unchanged *in spite of their experience.*

People like this *cannot learn from experience.* They continue to vote "Re-

---

[3] The affective connotations of a word are the feelings that it arouses. [eds.]

[4] This extraordinarily fatuous saying originally meant, "The exception *tests* the rule"—*Exceptio probato regulam.* This older meaning of the word "prove" survives in such an expression as "automobile proving ground."

publican" or "Democratic," no matter what the Republicans or Democrats do. They continue to object to "socialists," no matter what the socialists propose. They continue to regard "mothers," as sacred, no matter which mother. A woman who had been given up both by physicians and psychiatrists as hopelessly insane was being considered by a committee whose task it was to decide whether or not she should be committed to an asylum. One member of the committee doggedly refused to vote for commitment. "Gentlemen," he said in tones of deepest reverence, "you must remember that this woman is, after all, a mother." Similarly such people continue to hate "Protestants," no matter which Protestant. Unaware of characteristics left out in the process of classification, they overlook, when the term "Republican" is applied to both the party of Abraham Lincoln and the party of Warren Harding, the rather important differences between them: "If the Republican party was good enough for Abe Lincoln, it's good enough for me!"

COW₁ IS NOT COW₂

How do we prevent ourselves from getting into such intellectual blind alleys, or finding we are in one, how do we get out again? One way is to remember that practically all statements in ordinary conversation, debate, and public controversy taking the form, "Republicans are Republicans," "Business is business," "Boys will be boys," "Women drivers are women drivers," and so on, are *not true*. Let us put one of these back into a context in life.

"I don't think we should go through with this deal, Bill. Is it altogether fair to the railroad company?"

. "Aw, forget it! *Business is business*, after all." [5]

Such an assertion, although it looks like a "simple statement of fact," is not simple and is not a statement of fact. The first "business" *denotes* transaction under discussion; the second "business" invokes the *connotations* of the word. The sentence is a *directive*, saying, "Let us treat this transaction with complete disregard for considerations other than profit, as the word 'business' suggests." Similarly, when a father tries to excuse the mischief done by his sons, he says, "Boys will be boys";[6] in other words, "Let us regard the actions of my sons with that indulgent amusement customarily extended toward those whom we call 'boys' " though the angry neighbor will say, of course, "Boys, my eye! They're little hoodlums; that's what they

---

[5] In "Business is business" the word *business* shifts its meaning. This expression may be translated "Commercial transactions are matters concerned with profits, not ethics." [eds.]

[6] The word *boy* shifts meaning here, as a translation will show: "Young males of the human species will be mischievous creatures." [eds.]

are!" These too are not informative statements but *directives, directing us to classify the object or event under discussion in given ways, in order that we may feel or act in the ways suggested by the terms of the classification.*

There is a simple technique for preventing such directives from having their harmful effect on our thinking. It is the suggestion made by Korzybski that we add "index numbers" to our terms, thus: Englishman$_1$, Englishman$_2$, . . . ; cow$_1$, cow$_2$, cow$_3$, . . . ; Frenchman$_1$, Frenchman$_2$, Frenchman$_3$, . . . ; communist$_1$, communist$_2$, communist$_3$. . . . The terms of the classification tell us what the individuals in that class have in common; THE INDEX NUMBERS REMIND US OF THE CHARACTERS LEFT OUT. *A rule can then be formulated as a general guide in all our thinking and reading: Cow$_1$ is* NOT *Cow$_2$, Jew$_1$ is* NOT *Jew$_2$; politician$_1$ is* NOT *politician$_2$; and so on. This rule, if remembered, prevents us from confusing levels of abstraction and forces us to consider the facts on those occasions when we might otherwise find ourselves leaping to conclusions which we may later have cause to regret.*

"TRUTH"

Most intellectual problems are, ultimately, problems of classification and nomenclature. Some years ago there was a dispute between the American Medical Association and the Antitrust Division of the Department of Justice as to whether the practice of medicine was a "profession" or "trade." The American Medical Association *wanted* immunity from laws prohibiting "restraint of trade"; therefore, it insisted that medicine *is* a "profession." The Antitrust Division *wanted* to stop certain economic practices connected with medicine, and therefore it insisted that medicine *is* a "trade." Partisans of either side accused the other of perverting the meanings of words and of not being able to understand plain English.

Can farmers operate oil wells and still be "farmers"? In 1947 the attorney general of the state of Kansas sued to dissolve a large agricultural co-operative, Consumers Co-operative Association, charging that the corporation, in owning oil wells, refineries, and pipe-lines, was exceeding the statutory privileges of purchasing co-operatives under the Co-operative Marketing Act, which permits such organizations to "engage in any activity in connection with manufacturing, selling, or supplying to its members machinery, equipment or supplies." The attorney general held that the co-operative, under the Act, could not handle, let alone process and manufacture, general farm supplies, but only those supplies used in the marketing operation. The Kansas Supreme Court decided unanimously in favor of the defendent (CCA). In so deciding, the court held that gasoline and oil *are* "farm supplies," and producing crude oil *is* "part of the business of farming."

"This court," said the decision, "will take judicial notice of the fact that in the present state of the art of farming, gasoline . . . is one of the costliest items in the production of agricultural commodities. . . . Anyway, gasoline and tractors are here, and this court is not going to say that motor fuel is not a supply necessary to carrying on of farm operations. . . . Indeed it is about as well put as can be on Page 18 of the state's Exhibit C where the defendant (CCA) says: *'Producing crude oil, operating pipelines and re-fineries, are also part of the business of farming. It is merely producing synthetic hay for iron horses. It is "off-the-farm farming" which the farmer, in concert with his neighbors, is carrying on.* . . . Production of power farm-ing equipment, then, is logically an extension of the farmers' own farming operations.' " (Italics supplied.)

Is a harmonica player a "musician"? Until 1948, the American Federa-tion of Musicians had ruled that the harmonica was a "toy." Professional harmonica players usually belonged, therefore, to the American Guild of Variety Artists. Even as distinguished a musician as Larry Adler, who has often played the harmonica as a solo instrument with symphony orchestras, was by the union's definition "not a musician." In 1948, however, the AFM, finding that harmonica players were getting popular and competing with members of the union, decided that they were "musicians" after all—a decision that did not sit well with the president of AGVA, who promptly declared jurisdictional war on the AFM.

Is aspirin a "drug" or not? In some states, it is legally classified as a "drug," and therefore can be sold only by licensed pharmacists. If people want to be able to buy aspirin in groceries, lunchrooms, and pool halls (as they can in other states), they must have it reclassified as "not a drug."

Is medicine a "profession" or a "trade"? Is the production of crude oil "a part of farming"? Is a harmonica player a "musician"? Is aspirin a "drug"? The way in which such questions are commonly settled is by ap-peals to dictionaries to discover the "real meanings" of the words involved. It is also common practice to consult past legal decisions and all kinds of learned treatises bearing on the subject. The decision finally rests, however, not upon appeals to past authority, but upon *what people want.* If they want the AMA to be immune from antitrust action, they will go to the Supreme Court if necessary to get medicine "defined" as a "profession." If they want the AMA prosecuted, they will get a decision that it is a "trade." (They got, in this case, a decision from the Court that it did not matter whether the practice of medicine was a "trade" or not; what mattered was that the AMA had, as charged, *restrained* the trade of Group Health Association, Inc., a co-operative to *procure* medical services for its members. The antitrust action was upheld.)

If people want agricultural co-operatives to operate oil wells, they will get the courts to define the activity in such a way as to make it possible. If the public at large doesn't care, the decision whether a harmonica player is or is not a "musician" will be made by the stronger trade union. The question whether aspirin is or is not a "drug" will be decided neither by finding the dictionary definition of "drug" nor by staring long and hard at an aspirin tablet. It will be decided on the basis of where and under what conditions people want to buy their aspirins.

In any case, society as a whole ultimately gets, on all issues of wide public importance, the classifications it wants, even if it has to wait until all the members of the Supreme Court are dead and an entirely new court is appointed. When the desired decision is handed down, people say, "Truth has triumphed." *In short, society regards as "true" those systems of classification that produce the desired results.*

The scientific test of "truth," like the social test, is strictly practical, except for the fact that the "desired results" are more severely limited. The results desired by society may be irrational, superstitious, selfish or humane, but the results desired by scientists are only that our systems of classification produce predictable results. Classifications, as amply indicated already, determine our attitudes and behavior toward the object or event classified. When lightning was classified as "evidence of divine wrath," no courses of action other than prayer were suggested to prevent one's being struck by lightning. As soon, however, as it was classified as "electricity," Benjamin Franklin achieved a measure of control over it by his invention of the lightning rod. Certain physical disorders were formerly classified as "demonic possession," and this suggested that we "drive the demons out" by whatever spells or incantations we could think of. The results were uncertain. But when those disorders were classified as "bacillus infections," courses of action were suggested that led to more predictable results. Science seeks only the *most generally useful* systems of classification; these it regards for the time being, until more useful classifications are invented, as "true."

SUGGESTED ASSIGNMENTS

1. Write a short theme describing a situation you are acquainted with in which a classification makes a real difference. You might consider such classifications as these: resident/nonresident, amateur/professional, junior/senior, drunk/sober, speeding/reckless driving, weed/flower, sane/insane, war/police action, borrowing/stealing.

2. The following letter appeared in a popular syndicated newspaper column:

Dear _____: Please settle an argument. Where I work there is this woman who has silver-gray hair but a young face and a good figure. She must be about 50 but looks younger. She has 12 grandchildren, but she goes swimming with them, rides a bicycle with them, and she belongs to three bowling leagues. She says she never baby-sits with her grandchildren unless there is an emergency. Everyone says I am all wet with my ideas but I think a grandmother should ACT like a grandmother and should be proud of her grand-children and not of her bowling score.

What do you think is the cause of the writer's attitude?

Prejudice:
Linguistic Factors

Gordon W. Allport

The following essay focuses attention on the ways in which classifiers (verbal group-labels) operate in the expression and dissemination of prejudice. Prejudice rests on deep-seated and sometimes unconscious attitudes. An understanding of the extent to which these attitudes are embodied in language that colors our thinking and feelings may make us more sensitive to the inflammatory nature of prejudicial language. It also may enable us to discriminate between informative statements and prejudicial statements. Dr. Allport is Professor of Psychology at Harvard University.

Without words we should scarcely be able to form categories at all. A dog perhaps forms rudimentary generalizations, such as small-boys-are-to-be-avoided—but this concept runs its course on the conditioned reflex level, and does not become the object of thought as such. In order to hold a generalization in mind for reflection and recall, for identification and for action, we need to fix it in words. Without words our world would be, as William James said, an "empirical sand-heap."

NOUNS THAT CUT SLICES

In the empirical world of human beings there are some two and a half billion grains of sand corresponding to our category "the human race." We cannot possibly deal with so many separate entities in our thought, nor can we individualize even among the hundreds whom we encounter in our daily round. We must group them, form clusters. We welcome, therefore, the names that help us to perform the clustering.

The most important property of a noun is that it brings many grains of sand into a single pail, disregarding the fact that the same grains might have fitted just as appropriately into another pail. To state the matter technically, a noun *abstracts* from a concrete reality some one feature and assembles different concrete realities only with respect to this one feature. The very act of classifying forces us to overlook all other features, many of which might offer a sounder basis than the rubric we select. Irving Lee gives the following example:

> I knew a man who had lost the use of both eyes. He was called a "blind man." He could also be called an expert typist, a conscientious worker, a good student, a careful listener, a man who wanted a job. But he couldn't get a job in the department store order room where employees sat and typed orders which came over the telephone. The personnel man was impatient to get the interview over. "But you're a blind man," he kept saying, and one could almost feel his silent assumption that somehow the incapacity in one aspect made the man incapable in every other. So blinded by the label was the interviewer that he could not be persuaded to look beyond it.[1]

Some labels, such as "blind man," are exceedingly salient and powerful. They tend to prevent alternative classification, or even cross-classification. Ethnic labels are often of this type, particularly if they refer to some highly visible feature, e.g., Negro, Oriental. They resemble the labels that point to some outstanding incapacity—*feeble-minded, cripple, blind man*. Let us call such symbols "labels of primary potency." These symbols act like shrieking sirens, deafening us to all finer discriminations that we might otherwise perceive. Even though the blindness of one man and the darkness of pigmentation of another may be defining attributes for some purposes, they are irrelevant and "noisy" for others.

Most people are unaware of this basic law of language—that every label applied to a given person refers properly only to one aspect of his nature. You may correctly say that a certain man is *human, a philanthropist, a Chinese, a physician, an athlete*. A given person may be all of these; but the chances are that *Chinese* stands out in your mind as the symbol of primary potency. Yet neither this nor any other classificatory label can refer to the whole of a man's nature. (Only his proper name can do so.)

Thus each label we use, especially those of primary potency, distracts our attention from concrete reality. The living, breathing, complex individual— the ultimate unit of human nature—is lost to sight. As in the figure following, the label magnifies one attribute out of all proportion to its true significance, and masks other important attributes of the individual.

[1] I. J. Lee, *How Do You Talk about People?*, Freedom Pamphlet (New York, Anti-Defamation League, 1950), p. 15.

Labels of Primary Potency

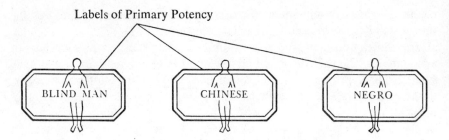

. . . a category, once formed with the aid of a symbol of primary potency, tends to attract more attributes than it should. The category labeled *Chinese* comes to signify not only ethnic membership but also reticence, impassivity, poverty, treachery. To be sure, . . . there may be genuine ethnic-linked traits making for a certain *probability* that the member of an ethnic stock may have this these attributes. But our cognitive process is not cautious. The labeled category, . . . includes indiscriminately the defining attribute, probable attributes, and wholly fanciful, nonexistent attributes.

Even proper names—which ought to invite us to look at the individual person—may act like symbols of primary potency, especially if they arouse ethnic associations. Mr. Greenberg is a person, but since his name is Jewish, it activates in the hearer his entire category of Jews-as-a-whole.

The anthropologist Margaret Mead has suggested that labels of primary potency lose some of their force when they are changed from nouns into adjectives. To speak of a Negro soldier, a Catholic teacher, or a Jewish artist calls attention to the fact that some other group classifications are just as legitimate as the racial or religious. If George Johnson is spoken of not only as a Negro but also as a *soldier*, we have at least two attributes to know him by, and two are more accurate than one. To depict him truly as an individual, of course, we should have to name many more attributes. It is a useful suggestion that we designate ethnic and religious membership where possible with *adjectives* rather than with *nouns*.

EMOTIONALLY TONED LABELS

Many categories have two kinds of labels—one less emotional and one more emotional. Ask yourself how you feel, and what thoughts you have, when you read the words *school teacher*, and then *school marm*. Certainly the second phrase calls up something more strict, more ridiculous, more disagreeable than the former. Here are four innocent letters: m-a-r-m. But they make us shudder a bit, laugh a bit, and scorn a bit. They call up an image of a spare, humorless, irritable old maid. They do not tell us that she is an individual human being with sorrows and troubles of her own. They force her instantly into a rejective category.

In the ethnic sphere even plain labels such as Negro, Italian, Jew,

Catholic, Irish-American, French-Canadian may have emotional tone for a reason that we shall soon explain. But they all have their higher key equivalents; nigger, wop, kike, papist, harp, cannuck. When these labels are employed we can be almost certain that the speaker *intends* not only to characterize the person's membership, but also to disparage and reject him.

Quite apart from the insulting intent that lies behind the use of certain labels, there is also an inherent ("physiognomic") handicap in many terms designating ethnic membership. For example, the proper names characteristic of certain ethnic memberships strike us as absurd. (We compare them, of course, with what is familiar and therefore "right.") Chinese names are short and silly; Polish names intrinsically difficult and outlandish. Unfamiliar dialects strike us as ludicrous. Foreign dress (which, of course, is a visual ethnic symbol) seems unnecessarily queer.

But of all these "physiognomic" handicaps the reference to color, clearly implied in certain symbols, is the greatest. The word Negro comes from the Latin *niger*, meaning black. In point of fact, no Negro has a black complexion, but by comparison with other blonder stocks, he has come to be known as a "black man." Unfortunately *black* in the English language is a word having a preponderance of sinister connotations; the outlook is black, blackball, blackguard, blackhearted, black death, blacklist, blackmail, Black Hand. . . .

There is thus an implied value-judgment in the very concept of *white race* and *black race*. One might also study the numerous unpleasant connotations of *yellow*, and their possible bearing on our conception of the people of the Orient.

Such reasoning should not be carried too far, since there are undoubtedly, in various contexts, pleasant associations with both black and yellow. Black velvet is agreeable, so too are chocolate and coffee. Yellow tulips are well liked; the sun and moon are radiantly yellow. Yet it is true that "color" words are used with chauvinistic overtones more than most people realize. There is certainly condescension indicated in many familiar phrases: dark as a nigger's pocket, darktown strutters, white hope (a term originated when a white contender was sought against the Negro heavyweight champion, Jack Johnson), the white man's burden, the yellow peril, black boy. Scores of everyday phrases are stamped with the flavor of prejudice, whether the user knows it or not.[2]

Members of minority groups are often understandably sensitive to names given them. Not only do they object to deliberately insulting epithets, but sometimes see evil intent where none exists. Often the word Negro is spelled with a small *n*, occasionally as a studied insult, more often from ignorance.

---

[2] I. L. Brown, "Words and White Chauvinism," *Masses and Mainstream* (1950), 3, pp. 3–11. See also *Prejudice Won't Hide! A Guide for Developing a Language of Equality* (San Francisco, California Federation for Civic Unity, 1950).

Connotations are frequently shifting. The term *black* may now be in the process of shifting upward as black people rise in dignity and esteem. [eds.]

(The term is not cognate with white, which is not capitalized, but rather with Caucasian, which is.) Terms like "mulatto" or "octoroon" cause hard feeling because of the condescension with which they have often been used in the past. Sex differentiations are objectionable, since they seem doubly to emphasize ethnic difference; why speak of Jewess and not of Protestantess, or of Negress and not of whitess? Similar overemphasis is implied in terms like Chinaman or Scotchman; why not American man? Grounds for misunderstanding lie in the fact that minority group members are sensitive to such shadings, while majority members may employ them unthinkingly.

THE COMMUNIST LABEL

Until we label an out-group it does not clearly exist in our minds. Take the curiously vague situation that we often meet when a person wishes to locate responsibility on the shoulders of some out-group whose nature he cannot specify. In such a case he usually employs the pronoun "they" without an antecedent. "Why don't they make these sidewalks wider?" "I hear they are going to build a factory in this town and hire a lot of foreigners." "I won't pay this tax bill; they can just whistle for their money." If asked "who"? the speaker is likely to grow confused and embarrassed. The common use of the orphaned pronoun *they* teaches us that people often want and need to designate out-groups (usually for the purpose of venting hostility) even when they have no clear conception of the out-group in question. And so long as the target of wrath remains vague and ill-defined specific prejudice cannot crystallize around it. To have enemies we need labels.

Until relatively recently—strange as it may seem—there was no agreed-upon symbol for *communist*. The word, of course, existed but it had no special emotional connotation, and did not designate a public enemy. Even when, after World War I, there was a growing feeling of economic and social menace in this country, there was no agreement as to the actual source of the menace.

A content analysis of the *Boston Herald* for the year 1920 turned up the following list of labels. Each was used in a context implying some threat. Hysteria had overspread the country, as it did after World War II. Someone must be responsible for the postwar malaise, rising prices, uncertainty. There must be a villain. But in 1920 the villain was impartially designated by reporters and editorial writers with the following symbols:

alien, agitator, anarchist, apostle of bomb and torch, Bolshevik, communist, communist laborite, conspirator, emissary of false promise, extremist, foreigner, hyphenated-American, incendiary, IWW,[3] parlor anarchist, parlor

---

[3] IWW means "International Workers of the World." [eds.]

pink, parlor socialist, plotter, radical, red, revolutionary, Russian agitator, socialist, Soviet, syndicalist, traitor, undesirable.

From this excited array we note that the *need* for an enemy (someone to serve as a focus for discontent and jitters) was considerably more apparent than the precise identity of the enemy. At any rate, there was no clearly agreed-upon label. Perhaps partly for this reason the hysteria abated. Since no clear category of "communism" existed there was no true focus for the hostility.

But following World War II this collection of vaguely interchangeable labels became fewer in number and more commonly agreed upon. The outgroup menace came to be designated almost always as *communist* or *red*. In 1920 the threat, lacking a clear label, was vague; after 1945 both symbol and thing became more definite. Not that people knew precisely what they meant when they said "communist," but with the aid of the term they were at least able to point consistently to *something* that inspired fear. The term developed the power of signifying menace and led to various repressive measures against anyone to whom the label was rightly or wrongly attached.

Logically, the label should apply to specifiable defining attributes, such as members of the Communist Party, or people whose allegiance is with the Russian system, or followers, historically, of Karl Marx. But the label came in for far more extensive use.

What seems to have happened is approximately as follows. Having suffered through a period of war and being acutely aware of devastating revolutions abroad, it is natural that most people should be upset, dreading to lose their possessions, annoyed by high taxes, seeing customary moral and religious values threatened, and dreading worse disasters to come. Seeking an explanation for this unrest, a single identifiable enemy is wanted. It is not enough to designate "Russia" or some other distant land. Nor is it satisfactory to fix blame on "changing social conditions." What is needed is a human agent near at hand: someone in Washington, someone in our schools, in our factories, in our neighborhood. If we *feel* an immediate threat, we reason, there must be a near-lying danger. It is, we conclude, communism, not only in Russia but also in America, at our doorstep, in our government, in our churches, in our colleges, in our neighborhood.

Are we saying that hostility toward communism is prejudice? Not necessarily. There are certainly phases of the dispute wherein realistic social conflict is involved. American values (e.g., respect for the person) and totalitarian values as represented in Soviet practice are intrinsically at odds. A realistic opposition in some form will occur. Prejudice enters only when the defining attributes of "communist" grow imprecise, when anyone who favors any form of social change is called a communist. People who fear social change are the ones most likely to affix the label to any persons or practices that seem to them threatening.

For them the category is undifferentiated. It includes books, movies, preachers, teachers who utter what for them are uncongenial thoughts. If evil befalls—perhaps forest fires or a rocket explosion—it is due to communist saboteurs. The category becomes monopolistic, covering almost anything that is uncongenial. On the floor of the House of Representatives in 1946, Representative Rankin called James Roosevelt a communist. Congressman Outland replied with psychological acumen, "Apparently everyone who disagrees with Mr. Rankin is a communist."

When differentiated thinking is at a low ebb—as it is in times of social crisis—there is a magnification of two-valued logic. Things are perceived as either inside or outside a moral order. What is outside is likely to be called "communist." Correspondingly—and here is where damage is done—whatever is called communist (however erroneously) is immediately cast outside the moral order.

This associative mechanism places enormous power in the hands of a demagogue. For several years Senator [Joseph] McCarthy managed to discredit many citizens who thought differently from himself by the simple device of calling them communists. Few people were able to see through this trick and many reputations were ruined. But the famous senator had no monopoly on the device. . . .

VERBAL REALISM AND SYMBOL PHOBIA

Most individuals rebel at being labeled, especially if the label is uncomplimentary. Very few are willing to be called *fascistic, socialistic* or *anti-Semitic*. Unsavory labels may apply to others; but not to us.

An illustration of the craving that people have to attach favorable symbols to themselves is seen in the community where white people banded together to force out a Negro family that had moved in. They called themselves "Neighborly Endeavor" and chose as their motto the Golden Rule. One of the first acts of this symbol-sanctified band was to sue the man who sold property to Negroes. They then flooded the house which another Negro couple planned to occupy. Such were the acts performed under the banner of the Golden Rule.

When symbols provoke strong emotions they are sometimes regarded no longer as symbols, but as actual things. The expressions "son of a bitch" and "liar" are in our culture frequently regarded as "fighting words." Softer and more subtle expressions of contempt may be accepted. But in these particular cases, the epithet itself must be "taken back." We certainly do not change our opponent's attitude by making him take back a word, but it seems somehow important that the word itself be eradicated.

Such verbal realism may reach extreme lengths.

The City Council of Cambridge, Massachusetts, unanimously passed a resolution (December, 1939) making it illegal "to possess, harbor, sequester, introduce or transport, within the city limits, any book, map, magazine, newspaper, pamphlet, handbill or circular containing the words Lenin or Leningrad.[4]

Such naïveté in confusing language with reality is hard to comprehend unless we recall that word-magic plays an appreciable part in human thinking.

SUGGESTED ASSIGNMENT

The following letter was written to the author of a popular advice column:

Dear _____:
About three weeks ago I met a sailor at a dance. I am 16 and Jim is 19. We liked each other right away and he asked if he could see me again. I asked my mother and she said I couldn't go out with any sailor. I told her I was going to a girl friend's house and I went with him anyway. When I told Jim I lied to go with him he was furious and made me promise I'd never do it again. He asked if he could meet my parents and show them he was respectable. When I asked them if they would please meet Jim they said no. Jane, he's the nicest boy I've ever known, but he refuses to see me without my parents' permission. And they refuse to meet him. What should I do?

Broken Hearted

Answer this letter in such a way that the parents, reading your answer, will learn a lesson about classification and prejudice.

The Environment of Language

Norman Cousins

In the preceding essay, Professor Gordon Allport discussed briefly the connotations of color labels. In this editorial Norman Cousins offers further information on color connotations as they can affect human relations.

From *Saturday Review*, April 8, 1967, p. 36. Copyright 1967, Saturday Review, Inc. Reprinted by permission.

[4] S. I. Hayakawa, *Language in Action* (New York, Harcourt Brace Jovanovich, Inc., 1941), p. 29.

The words men use, Julian Huxley once said, not only express but shape their ideas. Language is an instrument; it is even more an environment. It has as much to do with the philosophical and political conditioning of a society as geography or climate. The role of language in contributing to men's problems and their prospects is the subject of an imaginative and valuable study now getting under way at Pro Deo University in Rome, which is winning recognition in world university circles for putting advanced scholarship to work for the concept of a world community.

One aspect of the Pro Deo study, as might be expected, has to do with the art of conveying precise meaning from one language to another. Stuart Chase, one of America's leading semanticists, has pointed out that when an English speaker at the United Nations uses the expression "I assume," the French interpreter may say "I deduce" and the Russian interpreter may say "I consider." When Pope Paul VI sent a cable to Prime Minister Alexi Kosygin and Party Chairman Leonid Brezhnev on their accession to office, he expressed the hope that the historic aspirations of the Russian people for a fuller life would be advanced under the new leadership. As translated into Russian by the Vatican's own interpreter, the Pope's expression of hope came out in a way that made it appear that the Pope was making known his endorsement of the new regime. The eventual clarification was inevitably awkward for all concerned.

The Pro Deo study, however, will not be confined to problems of precise translation. The major emphasis of the study has to do with something fundamental: the dangerous misconceptions and prejudices that take root in language and that undermine human values. The color of a man's skin, for example, is tied to plus-or-minus words that inevitably condition human attitudes. The words "black" and "white," as defined in Western culture, are heavily loaded. "Black" has all sorts of unfavorable connotations; "white" is almost all favorable. One of the more interesting papers being studied by the Pro Deo scholars is by Ossie Davis, the author and actor. Mr. Davis, a Negro, concluded on the basis of a detailed study of dictionaries and *Roget's Thesaurus* that the English language was his enemy. In *Roget's*, he counted 120 synonyms for "blackness," most of them with unpleasant connotations: blot, blotch, blight, smut, smudge, sully, begrime, soot, becloud, obscure, dingy, murky, threatening, frowning, foreboding, forbidden, sinister, baneful, dismal, evil, wicked, malignant, deadly, secretive, unclean, unwashed, foul, blacklist, black book, black-hearted, etc. Incorporated in the same listing were words such as Negro, nigger, and darky.

In the same *Roget's*, Mr. Davis found 134 synonyms for the word "white," almost all of them with favorable connotations: purity, cleanness, bright, shining, fair, blonde, stainless, chaste, unblemished, unsullied, innocent, honorable, upright, just, straightforward, genuine, trustworthy, honesty, etc. "White" as a racial designation was, of course, included in this tally of desirable terms.

No less individious than black are some of the words associated with the color yellow: coward, conniver, baseness, fear, effeminacy, funk, soft, spirit-less, poltroonery, pusillanimity, timidity, milksop, recreant, sneak, lily-livered, etc. Oriental peoples are included in the listing.

As a matter of factual accuracy, white, black, and yellow as colors are not descriptive of races. The coloration range of so-called white people may run from pale olive to mottled pink. So-called colored people run from light beige to mahogany. Absolute color designations—white, black, red, yellow —are not merely inaccurate; they have become symbolic rather than de-scriptive. It will be argued, of course, that definitions of color and the connotations that go with them are independent of sociological implications. There is no getting around the fact, it will be said, that whiteness means cleanliness and blackness means dirtiness. Are we to doctor the dictionary in order to achieve a social good? What this line of argument misses is that people in Western cultures do not realize the extent to which their racial attitudes have been conditioned since early childhood by the power of words to ennoble or condemn, augment or detract, glorify or demean. Nega-tive language infects the subconscious of most Western people from the time they first learn to speak. Prejudice is not merely imparted or super-imposed. It is metabolized in the bloodstream of society. What is needed is not so much a change in language as an awareness of the power of words to condition attitudes. If we can at least recognize the underpinnings of preju-dice, we may be in a position to deal with the effects.

To be sure, Western languages have no monopoly on words with con-notations that affect judgment. In Chinese, whiteness means cleanliness, but it can also mean bloodlessness, coldness, frigidity, absence of feeling, weakness, insensitivity. Also in Chinese, yellowness is associated with sun-shine, openness, beauty, flowering, etc. Similarly, the word black in many African tongues has connotations of strength, certainty, recognizability, in tegrity, while white is associated with paleness, anemia, unnaturalness, deviousness, untrustworthiness.

The purpose of Pro Deo University in undertaking this study is not just to demonstrate that most cultures tend to be self-serving in their language. The purpose is to give educational substance to the belief that it will take all the adroitness and sensitivity of which the human species is capable if it is to be sustained. Earth-dwellers now have the choice of making their world into a neighborhood or a crematorium. Language is one of the factors in that option. The right words may not automatically produce the right ac-tions but they are an essential part of the process.

SUGGESTED ASSIGNMENTS

1. The following illustration of emotionally toned words is taken, with permis-sion, from the *American Bar Association Journal*, July 1949, p. 559. Underline the favorable words.

The President achieved (notoriety/fame) by (tenaciously/stubbornly), (bitterly/vigorously), (zealously/fanatically) asserting his (bold claims/impudent pretensions) even in legislative councils through his (tools/agents) who (skillfully/cunningly) (insinuated/introduced) themselves into those councils. The Senate being in accord with his (prejudices/principles) (succumbed/yielded) to his (domination/leadership). He was a man of (faith/superstition) and of (obstinacy/strength of purpose) whose policy combined (firmness and courage/bigotry and arrogance) with (cowardice/caution).

He was a (man/creature) of strong (biases/convictions) and belonged in the camp of the (reactionaries/conservatives). His conduct of the Presidency (portended/foreshadowed) a (change/degeneration) of that office into one of (dictatorship/leadership).

2. Think of a campus problem about which you have strong feelings. Then write a letter to the editor of your university paper expressing your point of view with the vigorous use of emotionally toned words. Next, write a second letter conveying the same ideas in objective and impersonal language. What kind of reader do you think each letter would appeal to most?

Contexts

Robert H. Moore

The word *context* means environment, associated surroundings, enveloping situation. One key idea in language study is this: Context determines meaning. Consider, for example, the statement "Indians Scalp Yankees" in the context of an American history book and in that of the sports page, and you get two different meanings. In this essay and the assignments that follow, the idea that context determines meaning is developed and illustrated, and its implication are shown.

An understanding of *why* one person will interpret a word differently from another person is necessary if we are to . . . improve our interpretative abilities. The following quotation from *The Meaning of Meaning* gives us one explanation of why an individual interprets a sign in a certain way:

From *General Semantics in the High School English Program*, pages 77–88, by Robert H. Moore. Reprinted, with alteration, by permission of the publisher, The Ohio State University Press, Columbus, Ohio, copyright 1945.

The effects upon the organism due to any sign, which may be any stimulus from without, or any process taking place within, depend upon the past history of the organism, both generally and in a more precise fashion. In a sense no doubt, the whole past history is relevant; but there will be some among the past events in that history which more directly determine the nature of the present agitation than others.

. . . when a context has affected us in the past the recurrence of merely a part of the context will cause us to react in the way in which we reacted before. A sign is always a stimulus to some part of an original stimulus and sufficient to call up the engram formed by that stimulus.

An engram is the residual trace of an adaption made by the organism to a stimulus.[1]

A sign, according to Ogden and Richards, is not necessarily formed for the purpose of communicating meanings. A symbol, however, is a stimulus provided for the purpose of conveying one person's thoughts or feelings to another person.

When for the first time we see a flash of lightning and hear almost immediately a clap of thunder, we do not perceive a sign! The lightning flash does not lead us to expect a clap of thunder. However, after we have experienced several thunderstorms, a flash of lightning (part of an original stimulus) calls up other details which accompanied flashes of lightning we have seen earlier and leads us to react as we did previously to the entire stimulus. A lightning flash then becomes a sign to us.

The lightning is not, though, a symbol, for it is not formed for the purpose of conveying meanings to anyone. If, however, a small child has heard his parents say, "A thunderstorm is coming," before a storm occurs and "That was the worst thunderstorm we've had all summer," after the storm is over, the word *thunderstorm,* when later spoken by the mother to the child, becomes a symbol to him, since the word is used for the purpose of communicating meaning.

Words, which are verbal symbols, are normally learned by the individual as the child mentioned in the preceding paragraph learned the meaning of *thunderstorm.* That is, they are heard by the individual as part of an actual experience. When heard again they recall to the mind of the hearer the parts of the original experience which accompanied the word.

. . . it is actually through their occurrence together with things, their linkage with them in a "context" that Symbols come to play that important part in our life which has rendered them not only a legitimate object of wonder but the source of all our power over the external world. . . .[2]

---

[1] C. K. Ogden and I. A. Richards, *The Meaning of Meaning,* pp. 52–53.
[2] Ogden and Richards, p. 47.

For communication to take place, there must be a certain amount of experience common to writer and reader. It is in this common or overlapping experience that words get meanings in discourse. The fact that no two persons have any experience precisely identical makes full or perfect communication impossible, and creates the necessity for interpretation. In any discourse, then, the meaning of a word depends upon its total incidence in the past experiences of writer and reader; and upon the situation in which it is being used.[3]

Since the meaning a word has for a person is determined by his past experiences and the present situation, the reader or hearer of any expression can better understand what he hears or reads by taking into consideration the experiential background of the writer or speaker and the conditions under which the words are written or spoken. . . .

A reader or listener must make use of all possible means of determining the meaning intended to be conveyed by the writer or speaker. A clue as to how to go about devising methods for accurately interpreting spoken or written words is given by Bronislaw Malinowski in a supplement to *The Meaning of Meaning*.

A statement, spoken in real life, is never detached from the situation in which it has been uttered. For each verbal statement by a human being has the aim and function of expressing some thought or feeling actual at that moment and in that situation, and necessary for some reason or other to be made known to another person or persons—in order either to serve purposes of common action, or to establish ties of purely social communion, or else to deliver the speaker of violent feelings or passions. Without some imperative stimulus of the moment, there can be no spoken statement. In each case, therefore, utterance and situation are bound up inextricably with each other and the context of situation is indispensable for the understanding of the words. Exactly as in the reality of spoken or written languages, a word without *linguistic context* is a mere figment and stands for nothing by itself, so in the reality of a spoken living tongue, the utterance has no meaning except in the context of situation.[4]

If "utterance and situation are bound up inextricably with each other," it would be hopeless to attempt to understand words without understanding the conditions under which they are spoken and written. The term *context* is often employed to refer both to the conditions surrounding the utterance of a word and to the other words which precede and follow a word in discourse. For purposes of discussion, the different types of context may be classified as physical, psychological, and verbal. The place where words are spoken or written, the time when they are spoken or written, and the activities going on around the speaker or writer make up the physical context.

---

[3] Progressive Education Association, *Language in General Education*, p. 96.
[4] Bronislaw Malinowski, "The Problem of Meaning in Primitive Languages," Supplement I in *The Meaning of Meaning*, p. 307.

The experiential background and the present mood of the speaker or writer constitute the psychological context. The words which are used with any one word or group of words make up the verbal context.

Usually, of course, all the factors discussed in the preceding paragraph are involved whenever a word is spoken. Depending on the particular situation, however, one type of context may give more of a clue to the meaning of an expression than another.

If a passer-by sees a man walk through the gate of a penitentiary and hears him say, "It certainly feels good to be free again," he is able to interpret the word *free* from an understanding of what the man is doing and where he is doing it. In other words, he studies the physical context of the utterance in his effort to interpret it.

If this same passer-by should overhear a man who he knows has been in prison say, "I'm glad to be free again," he would know, regardless of where or under what conditions the words were uttered, that *free* should be understood to mean "out of prison" or "without physical restraint." The psychological context would then provide the clue for correct interpretation of the words.

Next, let us suppose that a person who has recently been released from prison is overheard by a stranger to say, "After three years in prison, I certainly am glad to be free again." The hearer of this remark is able to interpret the word *free* without any previous knowledge of the case and wherever he hears it. A study of the verbal context of the word *free* has guided the hearer to an accurate interpretation of the word. . . .

Although we are sometimes able to tell the meaning of a word when it is used alone, we usually employ words in groups and rely to some extent on the verbal context as an aid to our interpretation of any one word. In our everyday conversation, however, verbal context is incomplete; that is, the hearer must interpret words largely from a study of their physical and psychological contexts.

If, for example, we hear someone shout, "George passed," we can, if we are seated in a stadium on a Saturday afternoon in October or November, and if we are acquainted with the fact that a halfback on one football team is named *George*, determine that the words mean that George, the halfback, threw the ball to one of his team mates. We have been able to interpret through their physical and psychological contexts words which out of their context would be meaningless. The speaker in the situation is, because of our ability to interpret words through their physical and psychological contexts, spared the necessity of saying, "George Miller, the halfback on our team, threw the football to one of his team mates."

If the physical and psychological contexts of the sentence, "George passed," are changed, our interpretation of it will change accordingly. If George's partner in a bridge game says, "George passed," we realize at once that the words are used to convey the information that George, one of the players, declined to bid.

Although the words used in the two different settings are the same, their referents are different. Because, in each instance, we are aware of what is happening and where it is happening, and because we have an understanding of what has preceded the events which are now taking place, we are able to agree with the speaker on the referents of the words.

SUGGESTED ASSIGNMENTS

1. A footnote in the book *Is Anybody Listening?* by William H. Whyte, Jr., and the editors of *Fortune* describes a revealing experience of Stanley Talbott, vice-president of the shoe-manufacturing firm of Joyce, Inc. For two months Mr. Talbott questioned women in Laundromats about the words that provoked in them the most intense reactions. The most "repulsive" word, he discovered, was *habit*. In the light of what you have learned about context, how would you explain this choice? For the other words, with both favorable and unfavorable connotations, see page 35 of Whyte's book.

2. A word receives its connotation as well as its denotation through the past contexts in which one has experienced it, or its referent, or both together. One powerful emotional experience may be enough to load a word with a specific connotation. The child, for example, who is badly frightened by a dog, may ever after carry the psychic scar of this traumatic experience and always feel a fearsome connotation in the word *dog*. Or a series of experiences may build up a connotation. Another child who has had a friendly and playful little dog as a pet may, as a result of repeated pleasant experiences, attach a happy connotation to the same word. Connotations seem to be much more variable than denotations. Select a word which has a strong connotation for you and write an explanation of how it acquired its connotative flavor.

3. Do you know what a *fleep* is? Not yet, but you soon will as you meet the word in a series of contexts that will narrow the meaning step by step and make it specific. The contexts are in this short paragraph:

I have a fleep with me nearly every day. This fleep goes with me everywhere, and I consider it an indispensable part of my life. In appearance it offers an attractive contrast: one part is bright and shiny, the other quietly dull. My fleep outlasts the other parts of my wardrobe, and I can often wear it for several years. Being unobtrusive, it seldom goes out of style. Some people like a stretchy fleep but I prefer the traditional kind. The leather of my fleep is soft and supple so that it gives with every movement of a part of my body. This fleep is very important to my well-being, for without it my trousers would come down. So every morning I buckle it around my waist and step forth to meet the world with a feeling of confidence.

Write a similar paragraph to teach the meaning of *muggle* through a set of contexts. Try to sharpen the meaning with each step, but hold off the precise meaning through as many steps as possible.

4. An advertisement of a French film called "Portrait of Innocence" reported that Bosley Crowther, former movie critic of *The New York Times*, had described it as "sparkling and penetrating." What Crowther had actually written was "While sparkling and penetrating in flashes, it is rather laboriously contrived." To show that quotations out of context can be misleading and even dishonest, find a quotation on a book jacket or in an advertisement and then write a context for it in which its meaning is different from that of the quotation by itself.

5. Often a single context is sufficient to explain an unknown word. Here are some examples:

   a. "At closing they came out stepping from the *fugginess* of tobacco and bright lights into the fresh night air."

   DAPHNE DU MAURIER

   b. ". . . yet when they begin to be well *whittled* with nectar, and cannot think of anything serious . . ."

   ERASMUS

   c. [About a rooster and his hens]
   "And with a *chuk* he them began to call."

   CHAUCER

   Find five words that your classmates probably do not know and put each one in a context so clear that the meaning is immediately apparent.

Ambiguity in College Writing
(To a College Freshman)
Norman C. Stageberg

In college composition textbooks, ambiguity is given scant attention. Yet ambiguity is an ever-present peril to clearness of expression. If you are to read with discernment and write with exactness—and both skills

By permission of the author.

are required for quality college work—you must become acquainted with the wily ways of ambiguity.

Ambiguity should not be confused with vagueness. A vague expression is merely indefinite. A diplomatic statement like "My government will take strong countermeasures . . ." is vague. Often the vague word is one expressing a quality that can exist in varying degrees, like *strong*. An ambiguous expression, on the other hand, has two or more definite meanings. For example, in "The President rejected the Smith Appointment," Smith can be the one who appointed or the one who was appointed.

Throughout your college years you will have much writing to do, from the pencil-gnawing labors of freshman composition to the painstaking preparation of senior reports. In all this writing the paramount literary quality that will be expected of you is clearness; for if your meaning is muddied, other writing virtues are of little use. Your instructors are accustomed to read with a sharp and critical mind. They want precision of statement: they expect you to say exactly what you mean, not approximately what you are muddling over. Thus, clearness should be your topmost writing goal.

Various enemies of clearness can beset you. A long disorderly sentence may misroute your reader as he wanders through a maze of phrases and clauses. A wrong word may baffle him. A careless comma may change your meaning, and a plethora of words may smother your thought. Each of these faults can fog over the lucidity you are striving for.

But the most insidious foe to clearness is ambiguity. Ambiguity means multiple meaning. A word or passage that can be understood in more than one sense is ambiguous. In isolation most words are ambiguous, because individual words have numerous meanings, as a glance in the dictionary will show. But in written discourse words are not isolated. Each is part of a larger whole, and this enveloping whole, this context, normally shuts out the unwanted meanings and permits only the one desired by the writer. For example, the entry *hand* in *Webster's New Collegiate Dictionary* is given eleven principal meanings; yet the meaning of the word is clear in each of the following sentences because of a short stretch of context:

Let's play another *hand*.
The *hand* of the clock pointed to twelve.
Will you give me a *hand* with this tire?
All *hands* on deck!
This wool has a soft *hand*.
I wish to ask for the *hand* of your daughter.

The next sentence, however, is ambiguous:

1. We breathlessly watched the *hand*.

Here the context is not restrictive enough to limit the meaning to a single sense. Thus it becomes evident that the careful control of context can help you to avoid ambiguity.

In college writing there are four types of ambiguity that it will be useful to examine.

The first type is **lexical ambiguity.** This occurs when two or more meanings of a single word are applicable in a given context, as is the case in the following sentence:

2. Buckley's salvos in defense of conservatism were fired first at Yale University.

The reader here does not know whether *at* means "against" or "in the location of." Lexical ambiguity often lurks in common words, as in this sentence:

3. For many purposes they used obsidian or volcanic rock.

Here *or* has two lexical meanings. It can express either an alternative, or an equivalence with the meaning of "that is." Some writers separate the two senses by punctuation, reserving commas for the meaning of equivalence, but this practice is not common enough to be a dependable key to meaning.

The other three types stem from the grammar of English, not from the semantic diversity of individual words, and are known collectively as structural ambiguity. We will take them up one by one.

The second type is **syntactic ambiguity.** This is occasioned by the arrangement of words. It can be illustrated by a story told about Governor Kirk of Florida. When a political opponent once called him

4. a fat ladies' man

the governor wittily retorted, "I like thin ladies too." Here it is the arrangement of /adjective + noun possessive + noun/ that makes the ambiguity possible. When this grammatical sequence occurs, the adjective can modify either the first or the second noun; but if the meaning of the adjective is compatible with that of each noun, the phrase will be ambiguous, unless, as always, the larger context channels the meaning to a single noun.

The third type, **class ambiguity,** occurs when the context allows a word to be interpreted as belonging to two different grammatical classes. A case in point is the tale of the Chinese philosopher who was addressing a class of American students one evening on the subject of Chinese thought. He had just asserted that much wisdom is embedded in old Chinese proverbs when the lights went out. Immediately he said to the class, "Will you please raise your hands?" A few seconds later the lights came on again, whereupon he remarked:

5. You see, many hands make light work.

Silly, of course, but it affords a nice illustration of class ambiguity, in this case an alternation between /adjective + noun/ and /noun + verb/.

The fourth type, **script ambiguity,** is that which occurs in writing (but not in speaking) because written words are not accompanied by the speaking voice. The voice, by variations in stress, pitch, pause, and length, can make countless distinctions in meaning that are not revealed in the written form of the spoken words.

As illustration, it will be instructive to read the opening sentence of a composition written by a sweet freshman girl who was very fond of camping and the out-of-doors:

> **6.** I am an outdoor lover.

In her mind's ear she heard this sentence with high pitch and strong stress on the -*door* syllable, and the sentence expressed her meaning perfectly: I love the out-of-doors. But she failed to realize that the reader of an opening sentence, with no context to guide his interpretation, might put the stress-and-pitch emphasis on the -*love* syllable and get a startlingly different meaning.

To hear for yourself how the voice can make distinctions in meaning, try reading aloud each of these scriptally ambiguous sentences in two ways that will bring out two different senses. The key words are underlined.

> **7.** Our milk has a stable flavor the year around.
> **8.** Sandy enjoys bathing girls.
> **9.** Nixon swears in his new cabinet.
> **10.** The *Tribune* will take pictures of the Salvation Army cooking students.
> **11.** He is going to take over a hundred pigs.
> **12.** I suspect you are right there.
> **13.** People who drink Old Fitzgerald don't know any better.

Script ambiguity is so ubiquitous in English that it would be impossible to list all the grammatical patterns in which it occurs. It will suffice to call your attention to its existence as a threat to clear writing and to present, as sample patterns, two simple grammatical situations in which it is often found.

Situation 1:   Noun + noun head (= modified noun)

> **14.** giant killer

In cases like this the position of the heavier stress determines the meaning. *Giant kíller*, with stress on *killer*, means a killer which is a giant, like a large shark. But *giánt killer*, with stress on *giant*, is a killer of giants. Similarly we use stress to distinguish two meanings in

> **15.** girl watcher
> **16.** 18th century scholar
> **17.** record sale

and many others.

Situation 2:   /Adjective or noun/ + noun head

18. patient counselor

This noun phrase consists of /adjective + noun head/ if we put the stress on *counselor*, and the meaning is "counselor who is patient." But it consists of /noun + noun head/ if the stress is given to *patient*, and the meaning becomes "counselor of patients." The next four examples behave the same way:

19. a French teacher

20. a mercenary chief

21. Boeing says it isn't seeking firm orders yet.

22. old-fashioned glasses

This concludes a quick glance at four general types of ambiguity that you should be aware of—lexical, syntactic, class, and script ambiguities. This classification is not watertight, and you will find that sometimes an actual case will fit into two categories. For instance, the lexical and class ambiguities are merged into a single one in the words of a sign on a seaside shop:

23. Buy your girl a bikini and watch her beam with delight.

Since *her beam* can be either /possessive adjective + noun/, or /object pronoun + verb/, this is a double class ambiguity. But the shift in the grammatical class of *beam* from noun to verb causes a change of meaning from "derrière" to "smile broadly." Thus it is also a lexical ambiguity.

In addition to genuine ambiguities, there is the pseudoambiguity that can mar your writing. Here is an example:

24. Joe Louis and Jack Dempsey moved around the small tables, each adorned with flowers and candles.

In this sentence we really know what the writer means. Nevertheless, the double entendre is momentarily distracting to the reader, and such distractions have no place in precise writing.

Of the four types of ambiguity that we have discussed, the one that is most amenable to specific and detailed explanation is syntactic ambiguity. So let us examine this type a little further. Syntactic ambiguity, you will recall, derives from the arrangement of words. By arrangement of words we mean syntactic structures. The question that arises here is this: Are there certain structures that are especially likely to be ambiguous? The answer is a firm yes. There are a great many structures in English that are potentially ambiguous, and some of these occur with high frequency. They constitute a semantic minefield for the writer. But if you learn the location of the mines, you can proceed with less danger. Therefore we shall now examine a few of the most hazardous structures, those that have blown up many sentences in student writing.

A considerable number of these can be subsumed under the label "Successive Modifiers." SUCCESSIVE MODIFIERS SHOULD ALWAYS BE CONSIDERED AN AUTOMATIC DANGER SIGNAL. And now, here is a series of such structures, grouped into two categories: (A) successive prenominal modifiers; (B) successive postnominal modifiers.

A. SUCCESSIVE PRENOMINAL MODIFIERS

Situation 3:   Adjective + noun + noun head
   25. Oriental art expert
Here the adjective can modify either the first or the second noun. Our Oriental art expert can be an art expert who is Oriental or an expert in Oriental art. And more of the same:
   26. small business man
   27. old car law
   28. gray cat's eye
In the next four situations, the principle is the same as in Situation 3: The first item can modify either the second or the third. We must always remember, of course, that each example has been removed from its context and that a broader enclosing context could obviate the ambiguity.

Situation 4:   Noun + noun + noun head
   29. student poetry discussion
   30. Maine lobster festival

Situation 5:   "More" + adjective + noun head
   31. You get more modern service there.
   32. Use more colorful language.
This case can also be classified as a script ambiguity. If you will listen carefully to your own pronunciation of Example 32, you will perhaps notice that, when *more* modifies *language*, you lengthen it and give it a slightly stronger stress.

Situation 6:   *-ing* particle + noun + noun head
   33. growing boy problem
   34. weeping woman's child

Situation 7:   *-ed.* participle + noun + noun head
   35. painted ladies room
   36. disturbed girls counselor
In each of the foregoing five situations there are two modifiers before the noun head. When three modifiers precede the noun head, the chances for ambiguity are increased; and it is not uncommon to find three readings for this type of pattern, as you will notice in Situations 8, 9, and 10 which follow.

Situation 8:   Noun + noun + noun + noun head
37. summer faculty research appointment
38. English teacher training program

Situation 9:   Adjective + noun + noun + noun head
39. genuine gold coin purse
40. old-fashioned teachers convention hotel

Situation 10:   Adjective + noun + participle + noun head
41. soft wool insulated bag
42. solid steel cutting blade

B. SUCCESSIVE POSTNOMINAL MODIFIERS

In our English system of modification, word-group modifiers follow the noun head. Word-group modifiers include these kinds: prepositional phrase (for example, *of a movie star*), relative clause (for example, *that the public sees*), noun phrase appositive (for example, the corporal, a *thickset man*), and participial phrase (for example, *located near the business district* and *weeping softly*). When two such modifiers of the noun head occur, there is the danger that the second may seem to refer to something other than the noun head. The next five situations, chosen out of many, will serve our purpose here.

Situation 11:   Noun head + prep phrase + relative clause
43. The life of a movie star that the public sees does look glamorous.
In this pattern the writer often intends the relative clause to modify the noun head; but when instead this clause appears to modify the last word of the prepositional phrase, the result is ambiguous.
44. A test over a new subject which is hard and complex requires careful review.

Situation 12:   Noun head + relative clause + prep phrase
45. I was talking about the books that I had read in the library.
This pattern of modifiers is the reverse of the normal order, which is that of Situation 11, and presents great likelihood of ambiguity. In the preceding example, for instance, *in the library* could modify *had read* or *books* or *was talking*, giving three readings to a simple sentence.
46. Carlsen inspected the boat which Bob had bought at the landing.

Situation 13:   Noun head + participial phrase + relative clause

47. There is a bronze statue standing near the fountain which many of the local populace admire.
48. He publishes books filled with color prints which are of excellent quality.

Situation 14: Noun head + relative clause + noun phrase appositive
49. The student who accused his roommate, a thief, dropped out of school.

Situation 15: Noun head + participial phrase + noun phrase appositive
50. The sergeant talking with the corporal, a thickset man, shook his head impatiently.

The thirteen situations above are samples of the hazards of ambiguity in the noun phrase; and if you read alertly you may notice many other ambigual patterns of like nature. Remember that the general warning for all such patterns is: BE WARY OF TWO SUCCESSIVE MODIFIERS.

C. POSTVERBAL SITUATIONS

Turning to the grammatical patterns that follow the verb, we find that the potentially ambiguous situations consist of complements and adverbials. There are at least nine situations involving complements alone, but these are really not common enough to warrant inclusion here. Of all the others, here are three—Situations 16 through 18—that will serve to show what can happen after the verb to perplex your reader.

Situation 16: Verb + noun object + adverb (or prep phrase)
51. Take the big bag upstairs.
52. This portable photocopier reproduces almost anything on white bond-weight paper.

Situation 17: Verb + prep phrase + prep phrase
53. The suspect had stolen away from the house in the darkness.
54. The teacher spoke to the boy with a smile.

Situation 18: Verb + noun object + infinitive phrase
55. The defendant was fined twenty rubles for selling his place in line to buy Czech woolen underwear. (The relevant verb is *selling.*)
We note here that the infinitive, *to buy Czech woolen underwear,* can go with either *place* or *selling.*
56. A California publisher created the CIA program to subsidize student, labor, and cultural groups.
The next four postverbal situations resemble one another in that the concluding adverbial has two verb forms to modify. The adverbial takes

one of four forms: adverb, prepositional phrase, noun phrase, and adverbial clause. Each of these four forms will be illustrated.

Situation 19: Verb + infinitive (+ noun object) + adverbial
  57. I promised to call at ten oclock.
  58. Nixon may act to combat racial discrimination decisively (or *with speed,* or *before Congress opens,* or *next week*).

Situation 20: Verb (+ noun object) + infinitive phrase + adverbial
  59. The Lindbergs watched their grandson cross the platform proudly (or *with pride,* or *when the great hour arrived,* or *that morning*).

Situation 21. Verb (+ noun object) + "and" + verb + adverbial
  60. He repaired the car and returned promptly.
  Here *promptly* might refer to only *returned* or to both *repaired* and *returned.* (Let us digress a moment to point out that there are numerous cases in which a modifier on either side of an *and* is ambiguous in its reference. For instance, in the simple phrase "fellow teachers and administrators," the noun *fellow* might modify only *teachers* or both *teachers* and *administrators.*)
  61. The guide fed the fire and waited until the sun arose.

Situation 22: Verb (+ noun object) + relative clause + adverbial
  62. We might find something that we could do there.
  63. I discovered the purse that was lost in my car.
  64. They found the uranium that they were seeking when the rainy season was over.
  65. The police saw the girl who had been kidnapped last night.
  These twenty grammatical patterns are only a small fraction of the total number of syntactically ambiguous situations, but a study of these few should heighten your sensitivity to other traps of syntax where you might get caught in an equivoque.
  When you have become sensitive to the possibilities of double meanings and have formed the habit of scrutinizing your own writing to locate intrusive and unintended meanings, you have won half the battle against ambiguity. The second half consists of eliminating them. This elimination will usually take place when you are revising and polishing your rough first draft. After you have spotted an offender, you face the question "How can I restate this clearly?" Although each case is a problem in itself, you have at your disposal eight methods of correcting ambiguous expressions. These methods, used singly or in combination, can be of help to you.

  1. SYNONYMY.   As an example let us consider
  66. The doctor made them well.

This sentence can be turned into two clear statements by synonymy: "The doctor made them skillfully" and "The doctor cured them."

2. EXPANSION.   Expanding by the addition of a word or two will sometimes remove an ambiguity.

67. He finished the race last Thursday.

This can be cleaned up with one word: "He finished the race last on Thursday" and "He finished the race on last Thursday."

3. REARRANGEMENT.   Rearrangement means using the same elements in a different order.

68. They are chewing tobacco and garlic.

Rearranging the elements, we can get two readings: "They are chewing garlic and tobacco" and "They are garlic and chewing tobacco."

4. CAPITALIZATION.   Capital letters are sometimes serviceable in making clear a sentence that would be orally ambiguous. Here is one instance: "You should call your Uncle George" and "You should call your uncle George."

5. PUNCTUATION.   Marks of punctuation are frequently the means of correcting or obviating written ambiguities. The next case is a good illustration.

69. The collection of funds has risen to the level of minimum need; thus much is needed to clothe the poor of the parish.

Thus much has two interpretations—"therefore, much. . ." and "this much. . . " A comma gives the first meaning and synonymy the second one.

With the prenominal modifiers a hyphen is very useful. The next case

70. foreign study program

would be clear if written as either "foreign-study program" or "foreign study-program."

6. SPELLING.   The many homonyms in English that can be a source of ambiguity in speech are usually kept clear in writing by spelling, for example, "The governor went hunting bear last week." Rarely will spelling remove a written ambiguity.

7. ALTERATION OF CONTEXT.   Since, in clear writing, it is the context that restricts various meanings of words and structures to a single sense, it is obvious that an ambiguity can sometimes be remedied by making the context sufficiently restrictive. The following example will illustrate:

71. This fall the rich Winchester School District has been plagued with troubles between the teaching staff and the students. The investigator sent by the District School Board, after prolonged inquiry and many interviews, has recommended the hiring of a teacher counselor by the school.

The written words *teacher counselor*, by themselves, can mean "a teacher who counsels" or "one who counsels teachers," and the passage above does not restrict the meaning to either one of these. So let us alter the context: "This fall the rich Winchester School District has been plagued with troubles between the teaching staff and the students. The investigator sent by the District School Board, after prolonged inquiry and many interviews, has reported that the difficulties stem from unstable personalities among the teaching staff itself and has therefore recommended the hiring of a teacher counselor by the school." This new context now makes probable the interpretation of *teacher counselor* as "one who counsels teachers."

8. USE OF GRAMMATICAL SIGNALS.   The English grammatical system provides us with a limited number of forms that can be used as signals in correcting ambiguity. Here are a few illustrations:

a. Gender signals (*his, her, its*)
   72. (ambiguous) The puppy by the girl with the contented look
      (clear) The puppy by the girl with (her/its) contented look
b. Person-thing signals (*who, which*)
   73. (ambiguous) The dog of the neighbor that bothered him
      (clear) The dog of the neighbor (who/which) bothered him
c. Number signals
   74. (ambiguous) One of the freshman girls who seemed downcast
      (clear) One of the freshman girls who (was/were) downcast
d. Coordination signals
   75. (ambiguous) A car which stood behind the garage that was in need of paint
      (clear) A car which stood behind the garage and which was in need of paint

Possibly no combination of these eight methods will seem to work for a particularly obstinate ambiguity you have created. For such cases there is a ninth method: Grit your teeth and rewrite the wretched thing in any way your reader will understand.

It is difficult to write clear prose; yet proficiency in this skill is mandatory for success in most professions that college graduates enter. If you learn to overcome ambiguity in writing, you will have taken one important step toward mastering this valuable skill.

SUGGESTED ASSIGNMENTS

(Note to the instructor: The exercises below are designed to sharpen the students' perception of ambiguity. For the correction of ambiguities, it is perhaps best to work with those occurring in class themes.)

1. In each sentence the word that is lexically ambiguous is italicized. Show the two meanings of each.

    a. *How* will he find his dog when he returns?
    b. Going to the beach is like going to the attic: you are always surprised at what you find in *trunks*.
    c. For just $10 a year you can read *about* 3000 books a year. (advertisement)
    d. We must not disregard romantic visions *of* democracies and autocracies.
    e. He *rented* the house for $110 a month.
    f. I can do this *in* an hour.
    g. She *appealed* to him.
    h. The agents *collect* at the drug store.

2. Point out the class ambiguity in each sentence and indicate its meanings.

    a. Use indelible ink and varnish over it.
    b. You will forget tomorrow.
    c. The enormous gorilla back of Pedro swayed out through the door.
    d. We observed another sail.
    e. The bouncer turned out a drunkard.
    f. We were seated during the intermission.
    g. Fred looked over her bare shoulder.
    h. We decided on the boat.
    i. They stamped upstairs.
    j. They were both happy and excited.

3. These sentences contain prenominal modifier ambiguities, some of which follow patterns not taken up in the preceding essay. Point out the double or multiple meanings of each.

    a. Mabel took a novel course.
    b. Malcolm looked professional in his chef's cap.
    c. Nelson is a champion cow owner.
    d. Would you like a hot evening drink?
    e. Josephine is an Iowa farmer's wife.
    f. Imported gingham shirts were offered for sale.
    g. Where is the dark brown sugar bowl?
    h. Ferrari is the world's largest sports car maker.
    i. Write for free tape recorder and tape catalogue. (This advertisement really appeared.)

4. This is a group of script ambiguities. Read each item aloud in two ways to bring out two meanings.

    a. He was beaten up by the bridge.
    b. Do you have some metal screws?
    c. I consider these errors.
    d. The club will be open to members only from Monday through Friday.
    e. The proposal calls for charging an annual fee of $40 for all faculty parking on campus.
    f. Agatha is a designing teacher.
    g. This country needs a good roads official.
    h. I suspect you were right there.
    i. Smoking chief cause of fire deaths here (headline in the *New York Times*).

5. The varying uses of the present participle (-*ing* form of verb) involve it in several kinds of ambiguity. Point out the -*ing* ambiguities in these sentences.

   a. They are canning peas.
   b. My job was keeping him alive.
   c. The Greek government staged a crackdown on shortchanging employees.
   d. Moving vans, still in their civilian paint, carry guns.
   e. Testing ignorance involves private schools too.
   f. Easy chemistry for nursing students.
   g. His business is changing human behavior.
   h. MacLeish likes entertaining ladies.
   i. Eleanor enjoys growing roses.

6. The following sentences contain ambiguities of specific types not mentioned in your reading. Point out the meanings of each.

   a. She taught the group athletics.
   b. Investigators find makers of aircraft nuts. (headline)
   c. He found the mechanic a helper.
   d. Our spaniel made a good friend.
   e. They are ready to eat.
   f. At dress rehearsals she sang, danced, and tumbled very expertly.
   g. At her bedside were her husband, Captain Horace Brown, a physician, and two nurses.
   h. The seniors were told to stop demonstrating on campus.
   i. Few names are mentioned more often in discussions of students than that of Mikelson.
   j. His job is to post changes in address, telephone numbers, and performance ratings.

7. Read the following "Minutes of a Borough Council Meeting," taken from *The Reader over Your Shoulder* by Robert Graves and Alan Hodge.[1]

Councillor Trafford took exception to the proposed notice at the entrance of South Park: "No dogs must be brought to this Park except on a lead." He pointed out that this order would not prevent an owner from releasing his pets, or pet, from a lead when once safely inside the Park.

THE CHAIRMAN (COLONEL VINE): What alternative wording would you propose, Councillor?
COUNCILLOR TRAFFORD: "Dogs are not allowed in this Park without leads."
COUNCILLOR HOGG: Mr. Chairman, I object. The order should be addressed to the owners, not to the dogs.
COUNCILLOR TRAFFORD: That is a nice point. Very well then: "Owners of dogs are not allowed in this Park unless they keep them on leads."
COUNCILLOR HOGG: Mr. Chairman, I object. Strictly speaking, this would prevent

---

[1] Reprinted with permission of The Macmillan Company from *The Reader over Your Shoulder* by Robert Graves and Alan Hodge. Copyright 1943 by Robert Graves and Alan Hodge. Also by permission of Jonathan Cape Ltd.

me as a dog-owner from leaving my dog in the back-garden at home and walking with Mrs. Hogg across the Park.

COUNCILLOR TRAFFORD: Mr. Chairman, I suggest that our legalistic friend be asked to redraft the notice himself.

COUNCILLOR HOGG: Mr. Chairman, since Councillor Trafford finds it so difficult to improve on my original wording, I accept. "Nobody without his dog on a lead is allowed in this Park."

COUNCILLOR TRAFFORD: Mr. Chairman, I object. Strictly speaking, this notice would prevent me, as a citizen who owns no dog, from walking in the Park without first acquiring one.

COUNCILLOR HOGG (with some warmth): Very simply, then: "Dogs must be led in this Park." [2]

COUNCILLOR TRAFFORD: Mr. Chairman, I object: this reads as if it were a general injunction to the Borough to lead their dogs into the Park.

Councillor Hogg interposed a remark for which he was called to order; upon his withdrawing it, it was directed to be expunged from the Minutes.

THE CHAIRMAN: Councillor Trafford, Councillor Hogg has had three tries; you have had only two—

COUNCILLOR TRAFFORD: "All dogs must be kept on leads in this Park."

THE CHAIRMAN: I see Councillor Hogg rising quite rightly to raise another objection. May I anticipate him with another amendment: "All dogs in this Park must be kept on the lead."

This draft was put to the vote and carried unanimously, with two abstentions.

This assignment is a difficult one. Write a similar dialogue of a Student Senate meeting trying to frame a dormitory rule or a regulation controlling student behavior.

FURTHER READINGS

Black, Max. *Critical Thinking*. Englewood Cliffs, N.J.: Prentice-Hall, Inc., 1955. On ambiguity, see pp. 183–202; on context, see pp. 190–192.

Lee, Irving J. *Language Habits in Human Affairs*. New York: Harper & Row, 1941. An introduction to general semantics.

Ornstein, Jacob, and William W. Gage, *The ABC's of Language and Linguistics*. Philadelphia: Chilton Company—Book Division, 1964. On semantics, see pp. 103–119.

Payne, Stanley L. *The Art of Asking Questions*. Princeton, N.J.: Princeton University Press, 1951. On ambiguity, see pp. 158–176.

Philbrick, F. A. *Understanding English*. New York: Crowell-Collier and Macmillan, Inc., 1944. An engaging and lively introduction to semantics.

Stageberg, Norman C. "Structural Ambiguity: Some Sources." *English Journal*, May 1960.

[2] Cf. the American highway sign "Pass with care."

_____. "Structural Ambiguity for English Teachers." *Teaching the Teacher of English*. Champaign, Ill.: National Council of Teachers of English, 1968.

_____. "Structural Ambiguity in the Noun Phrase." *TESOL Quarterly*, December 1969.

_____. "Structural Ambiguities in English." *Encyclopedia of Education*. New York: Crowell-Collier and Macmillan, Inc. 1970.

Thouless, Robert H. *How to Think Straight*. New York: Simon and Schuster, Inc. 1950. On ambiguity and vagueness, see pp. 132–146.

12
KINESICS: NONVERBAL COMMUNICATION

The Sounds of Silence

Edward T. and
Mildred R. Hall

This essay deals with the communicative aspect of posture, body movements, gestures, facial expressions, and the use of time and space—
all of which, with or without vocal accompaniment, serve to convey
messages. They may be consciously employed or operate below the
threshold of awareness. Edward T. Hall and his wife, Mildred Reed Hall,
present here illustrative cases of nonverbal communication among
English speakers. Mr. Hall is a professor of anthropology at Northwestern University and a specialist in proxemics and intercultural communication. His book, *The Silent Language*, is highly recommended for
further information on this subject.

Bob leaves his apartment at 8:15 A.M. and stops at the corner drugstore
for breakfast. Before he can speak, the counterman says, "The usual?" Bob
nods yes. While he savors his Danish, a fat man pushes onto the adjoining
stool and overflows into his space. Bob scowls and the man pulls himself
in as much as he can. Bob has sent two messages without speaking a syllable.

Henry has an appointment to meet Arthur at 11 o'clock; he arrives at
11:30. Their conversation is friendly, but Arthur retains a lingering hostility.

Originally appeared in *Playboy* Magazine; copyright © 1971 by *Playboy*. Reprinted by permission of the authors and the publisher.

Henry has unconsciously communicated that he doesn't think the appointment is very important or that Arthur is a person who needs to be treated with respect.

George is talking to Charley's wife at a party. Their conversation is entirely trivial, yet Charley glares at them suspiciously. Their physical proximity and the movements of their eyes reveal that they are powerfully attracted to each other.

José Ybarra and Sir Edmund Jones are at the same party and it is important for them to establish a cordial relationship for business reasons. Each is trying to be warm and friendly, yet they will part with mutual distrust and their business transaction will probably fall through. José, in Latin fashion, moved closer and closer to Sir Edmund as they spoke, and this movement was miscommunicated as pushiness to Sir Edmund, who kept backing away from this intimacy, and this was miscommunicated to José as coldness. The silent languages of Latin and English cultures are more difficult to learn than their spoken languages.

In each of these cases, we see the subtle power of nonverbal communication. The only language used throughout most of the history of humanity (in evolutionary terms, vocal communication is relatively recent), it is the first form of communication you learn. You use this preverbal language, consciously and unconsciously, every day to tell other people how you feel about yourself and them. This language includes your posture, gestures, facial expressions, costume, the way you walk, even your treatment of time and space and material things. All people communicate on several different levels at the same time but are usually aware of only the verbal dialog and don't realize that they respond to nonverbal messages. But when a person says one thing and really believes something else, the discrepancy between the two can usually be sensed. Nonverbal-communication systems are much less subject to the conscious deception that often occurs in verbal systems. When we find ourselves thinking, "I don't know what it is about him, but he doesn't seem sincere," it's usually this lack of congruity between a person's words and his behavior that makes us anxious and uncomfortable.

Few of us realize how much we all depend on body movement in our conversation or are aware of the hidden rules that govern listening behavior. But we know instantly whether or not the person we're talking to is "tuned in" and we're very sensitive to any breach in listening etiquette. In white middle-class American culture, when someone wants to show he is listening to someone else, he looks either at the other person's face or, specifically, at his eyes, shifting his gaze from one eye to the other.

If you observe a person conversing, you'll notice that he indicates he's listening by nodding his head. He also makes little "Hmm" noises. If he agrees with what's being said, he may give a vigorous nod. To show pleasure or affirmation, he smiles; if he has some reservations, he looks skeptical by raising an eyebrow or pulling down the corners of his mouth. If a participant wants to terminate the conversation, he may start shifting his body position, stretching his legs, crossing or uncrossing them, bobbing his foot or diverting his gaze from the speaker. The more he fidgets, the more the speaker becomes aware that he has lost his audience. As a last measure, the listener may look at his watch to indicate the imminent end of the conversation.

Talking and listening are so intricately intertwined that a person cannot do one without the other. Even when one is alone and talking to oneself, there is part of the brain that speaks while another part listens. In all conversations, the listener is positively or negatively reinforcing the speaker all the time. He may even guide the conversation without knowing it, by laughing or frowning or dismissing the argument with a wave of his hand.

The language of the eyes—another age-old way of exchanging feelings— is both subtle and complex. Not only do men and women use their eyes differently but there are class, generation, regional, ethnic and national cultural differences. Americans often complain about the way foreigners stare at people or hold a glance too long. Most Americans look away from someone who is using his eyes in an unfamiliar way because it makes them self-conscious. If a man looks at another man's wife in a certain way, he's asking for trouble, as indicated earlier. But he might not be ill mannered or seeking to challenge the husband. He might be a European in this country who hasn't learned our visual mores. Many American women visiting France or Italy are acutely embarrassed because, for the first time in their lives, men really look at them—their eyes, hair, nose, lips, breasts, hips, legs, thighs, knees, ankles, feet, clothes, hairdo, even their walk. These same women, once they have become used to being looked at, often return to the United States and are overcome with the feeling that "No one ever really looks at me anymore."

Analyzing the mass of data on the eyes, it is possible to sort out at least three ways in which the eyes are used to communicate: dominance *vs.* submission, involvement *vs.* detachment and positive *vs.* negative attitude. In addition, there are three levels of consciousness and control, which can be categorized as follows: (1) conscious use of the eyes to communicate, such as the flirting blink and the intimate nosewrinkling squint; (2) the very extensive category of unconscious but learned behavior governing where the eyes are directed and when (this unwritten set of rules dictates how and under what circumstances the sexes, as well as people of all status categories, look at each other); and (3) the response of the eye itself, which is completely outside both awareness and control—changes in the cast (the sparkle) of the eye and the pupillary reflex.

The eye is unlike any other organ of the body, for it is an extension of the brain. The unconscious pupillary reflex and the cast of the eye have been known by people of Middle Eastern origin for years—although most are unaware of their knowledge. Depending on the context, Arabs and others look either directly at the eyes or deeply *into* the eyes of their interlocutor.

We became aware of this in the Middle East several years ago while looking at jewelry. The merchant suddenly started to push a particular bracelet at a customer and said, "You buy this one." What interested us was that the bracelet was not the one that had been consciously selected by the purchaser. But the merchant, watching the pupils of the eyes, knew what the purchaser really wanted to buy. Whether he specifically knew *how* he knew is debatable.

A psychologist at the University of Chicago, Eckhard Hess, was the first to conduct systematic studies of the pupillary reflex. His wife remarked one evening, while watching him reading in bed, that he must be very interested in the text because his pupils were dilated. Following up on this, Hess slipped some pictures of nudes into a stack of photographs that he gave to his male assistant. Not looking at the photographs but watching his assistant's pupils, Hess was able to tell precisely when the assistant came to the nudes. In further experiments, Hess retouched the eyes in a photograph of a woman. In one print, he made the pupils small, in another, large; nothing else was changed. Subjects who were given the photographs found the woman with the dilated pupils much more attractive. Any man who has had the experience of seeing a woman look at him as her pupils widen with reflex speed knows that she's flashing him a message.

The eye-sparkle phenomenon frequently turns up in our interviews of couples in love. It's apparently one of the first reliable clues in the other person that love is genuine. To date, there is no scientific data to explain eye sparkle; no investigation of the pupil, the cornea or even the white sclera of the eye shows how the sparkle originates. Yet we all know it when we see it.

One common situation for most people involves the use of the eyes in the street and in public. Although eye behavior follows a definite set of rules, the rules vary according to the place, the needs and feelings of the people, and their ethnic background. For urban whites, once they're within definite recognition distance (16–32 feet for people with average eyesight), there is mutual avoidance of eye contact—unless they want something specific: a pickup, a handout or information of some kind. In the West and in small towns generally, however, people are much more likely to look at and greet one another, even if they're strangers.

It's permissible to look at people if they're beyond recognition distance; but once inside this sacred zone, you can only steal a glance at strangers. You *must* greet friends, however; to fail to do so is insulting. Yet, to stare too fixedly even at them is considered rude and hostile. Of course, all of these rules are variable.

A great many blacks, for example, greet each other in public even if they don't know each other. To blacks, most eye behavior of whites has the effect of giving the impression that they aren't there, but this is due to white avoidance of eye contact with *anyone* in the street.

Another very basic difference between people of different ethnic backgrounds is their sense of territoriality and how they handle space. This is the silent communication, or miscommunication, that caused friction between Mr. Ybarra and Sir Edmund Jones in our earlier example. We know from research that everyone has around himself an invisible bubble of space that contracts and expands depending on several factors: his emotional state, the activity he's performing at the time and his cultural background. This bubble is a kind of mobile territory that he will defend against intrusion. If he is accustomed to close personal distance between himself and others, his bubble will be smaller than that of someone who's accustomed to greater personal distance. People of North European heritage—English, Scandinavian, Swiss and German—tend to avoid contact. Those whose heritage is Italian, French, Spanish, Russian, Latin American or Middle Eastern like close personal contact.

People are very sensitive to any intrusion into their spatial bubble. If someone stands too close to you, your first instinct is to back up. If that's not possible, you lean away and pull yourself in, tensing your muscles. If the intruder doesn't respond to these body signals, you may then try to protect yourself, using a briefcase, umbrella or raincoat. Women—especially when traveling alone—often plant their pocketbook in such a way that no one can get very close to them. As a last resort, you may move to another spot and position yourself behind a desk or a chair that provides screening. Everyone tries to adjust the space around himself in a way that's comfortable for him; most often, he does this unconsciously.

Emotions also have a direct effect on the size of a person's territory. When you're angry or under stress, your bubble expands and you require more space. New York psychiatrist Augustus Kinzel found a difference in what he calls Body-Buffer Zones between violent and nonviolent prison inmates. Dr. Kinzel conducted experiments in which each prisoner was placed in the center of a small room and then Dr. Kinzel slowly walked toward him. Nonviolent prisoners allowed him to come quite close, while prisoners with a history of violent behavior couldn't tolerate his proximity and reacted with some vehemence.

Apparently, people under stress experience other people as looming larger and closer than they actually are. Studies of schizophrenic patients have indicated that they sometimes have a distorted perception of space, and several psychiatrists have reported patients who experience their body boundaries as filling up an entire room. For these patients, anyone who comes into the room is actually inside their body, and such an intrusion may trigger a violent outburst.

Unfortunately, there is little detailed information about normal people who live in highly congested urban areas. We do know, of course, that the noise, pollution, dirt, crowding and confusion of our cities induce feelings of stress in most of us, and stress leads to a need for greater space. The man who's packed into a subway, jostled in the street, crowded into an elevator and forced to work all day in a bull pen or in a small office without auditory or visual privacy is going to be very stressed at the end of his day. He needs places that provide relief from constant overstimulation of his nervous system. Stress from overcrowding is cumulative and people can tolerate more crowding early in the day than later; note the increased bad temper during the evening rush hour as compared with the morning melee. Certainly one factor in people's desire to commute by car is the need for privacy and relief from crowding (except, often, from other cars); it may be the only time of the day when nobody can intrude.

In crowded public places, we tense our muscles and hold ourselves stiff, and thereby communicate to others our desire not to intrude on their space and, above all, not to touch them. We also avoid eye contact, and the total effect is that of someone who has "tuned out." Walking along the street, our bubble expands slightly as we move in a stream of strangers, taking care not to bump into them. In the office, at meetings, in restaurants, our bubble keeps changing as it adjusts to the activity at hand.

Most white middle-class Americans use four main distances in their business and social relations: intimate, personal, social and public. Each of these distances has a near and a far phase and is accompanied by changes in the volume of the voice. Intimate distance varies from direct physical contact with another person to a distance of six to eighteen inches and is used for our most private activities—caressing another person or making love. At this distance, you are overwhelmed by sensory inputs from the other person—heat from the body, tactile stimulation from the skin, the fragrance of perfume, even the sound of breathing—all of which literally envelop you. Even at the far phase, you're still within easy touching distance. In general, the use of intimate distance in public between adults is frowned on. It's also much too close for strangers, except under conditions of extreme crowding.

In the second zone—personal distance—the close phase is one and a half to two and a half feet; it's at this distance that wives usually stand from their husbands in public. If another woman moves into this zone, the wife will most likely be disturbed. The far phase—two and a half to four feet—is the distance used to "keep someone at arm's length" and is the most common spacing used by people in conversation.

The third zone—social distance—is employed during business transactions or exchanges with a clerk or repairman. People who work together tend to use close social distance—four to seven feet. This is also the distance for conversations at social gatherings. To stand at this distance from someone who is seated has a dominating effect (e.g., teacher to pupil, boss to secretary). The far phase of the third zone—seven to twelve feet—is where people stand when someone says, "Stand back so I can look at you." This distance lends a formal tone to business or social discourse. In an executive office, the desk serves to keep people at this distance.

The fourth zone—public distance—is used by teachers in classrooms or speakers at public gatherings. At its farthest phase—25 feet and beyond—it is used for important public figures. Violations of this distance can lead to serious complications. During his 1970 U.S. visit, the president of France, Georges Pompidou, was harassed by pickets in Chicago, who were permitted to get within touching distance. Since pickets in France are kept behind barricades a block or more away, the president was outraged by this insult to his person, and President Nixon was obliged to communicate his concern as well as offer his personal apologies.

It is interesting to note how American pitchmen and panhandlers exploit the unwritten, unspoken conventions of eye and distance. Both take advantage of the fact that once explicit eye contact is established, it is rude to look away, because to do so means to brusquely dismiss the other person and his needs. Once having caught the eye of his mark, the panhandler then locks on, not letting go until he moves through the public zone, the social zone, the personal zone and, finally, into the intimate sphere, where people are most vulnerable.

Touch also is an important part of the constant stream of communication that takes place between people. A light touch, a firm touch, a blow, a caress are all communications. In an effort to break down barriers among people, there's been a recent upsurge in group-encounter activities, in which strangers are encouraged to touch one another. In special situations such as these, the rules for not touching are broken with group approval and people gradually lose some of their inhibitions.

Although most people don't realize it, space is perceived and distances are set not by vision alone but with all the senses. Auditory space is perceived with the ears, thermal space with the skin, kinesthetic space with the muscles of the body and olfactory space with the nose. And, once again, it's one's culture that determines how his senses are programmed—which sensory information ranks highest and lowest. The important thing to remember is that culture is very persistent. In this country, we've noted the existence of culture patterns that determine distance between people in the third and fourth generations of some families, despite their prolonged contact with people of very different cultural heritages.

Whenever there is great cultural distance between two people, there are bound to be problems arising from differences in behavior and expectations. An example is the American couple who consulted a psychiatrist about their marital problems. The husband was from New England and had been brought up by reserved parents who taught him to control his emotions and to respect the need for privacy. His wife was from an Italian family and had been brought up in close contact with all the members of her large family, who were extremely warm, volatile and demonstrative.

When the husband came home after a hard day at the office, dragging his feet and longing for peace and quiet, his wife would rush to him and smother him. Clasping his hands, rubbing his brow, crooning over his weary head, she never left him alone. But when the wife was upset or anxious about her day, the husband's response was to withdraw completely and leave her alone. No comforting, no affectionate embrace, no attention—just solitude. The woman became convinced her husband didn't love her and, in desperation, she consulted a psychiatrist. Their problem wasn't basically psychological but cultural.

Why has man developed all these different ways of communicating messages without words? One reason is that people don't like to spell out certain kinds of messages. We prefer to find other ways of showing our feelings. This is especially true in relationships as sensitive as courtship. Men don't like to be rejected and most women don't want to turn a man down bluntly. Instead, we work out subtle ways of encouraging or discouraging each other that save face and avoid confrontations.

How a person handles space in dating others is an obvious and very sensitive indicator of how he or she feels about the other person. On a first date, if a woman sits or stands so close to a man that he is acutely conscious of her physical presence—inside the intimate-distance zone—the man usually construes it to mean that she is encouraging him. However, before the man starts moving in on the woman, he should be sure what message she's really sending; otherwise, he risks bruising his ego. What is close to someone of North European background may be neutral or distant to someone of Italian heritage. Also, women sometimes use space as a way of misleading a man and there are few things that put men off more than women who communicate contradictory messages—such as women who cuddle up and then act insulted when a man takes the next step.

How does a woman communicate interest in a man? In addition to such familiar gambits as smiling at him, she may glance shyly at him, blush and then look away. Or she may give him a real come-on look and move in very close when he approaches. She may touch his arm and ask for a light. As she leans forward to light her cigarette, she may brush him lightly, enveloping him in her perfume. She'll probably continue to smile at him and she may use what ethologists call preening gestures—touching the back of her hair, thrusting her breasts forward, tilting her hips as she stands or crossing her legs if she's seated, perhaps even exposing one thigh or putting a hand on her thigh and stroking it. She may also stroke her wrists as she converses or show the palm of her hand as a way of gaining his attention. Her skin may be unusually flushed or quite pale, her eyes brighter, the pupils larger.

If a man sees a woman whom he wants to attract, he tries to present himself by his posture and stance as someone who is self-assured. He moves briskly and confidently. When he catches the eye of the woman, he may hold her glance a little longer than normal. If he gets an encouraging smile, he'll move in close and engage her in small talk. As they converse, his glance shifts over her face and body. He, too, may make preening gestures—straightening his tie, smoothing his hair or shooting his cuffs.

How do people learn body language? The same way they learn spoken language—by observing and imitating people around them as they're growing up. Little girls imitate their mothers or an older female. Little boys imitate their fathers or a respected uncle or a character on television. In this way, they learn the gender signals appropriate for their sex. Regional, class and ethnic patterns of body behavior are also learned in childhood and persist throughout life.

Such patterns of masculine and feminine body behavior vary widely from one culture to another. In America, for example, women stand with their thighs together. Many walk with their pelvis tipped slightly forward and their upper arms close to their body. When they sit, they cross their legs at the knee or, if they are well past middle age, they may cross their ankles. American men hold their arms away from their body, often swinging them as they walk. They stand with their legs apart (an extreme example is the cowboy, with legs apart and thumbs tucked into his belt). When they sit, they put their feet on the floor with legs apart and, in some parts of the country, they cross their legs by putting one ankle on the other knee.

Leg behavior indicates sex, status and personality. It also indicates whether or not one is at ease or is showing respect or disrespect for the other person. Young Latin-American males avoid crossing their legs. In their world of *machismo*, the preferred position for young males when with one another (if there is no older dominant male present to whom they must show respect) is to sit on the base of their spine with their leg muscles relaxed and their feet wide apart. Their respect position is like our military equivalent; spine straight, heels and ankles together—almost identical to that displayed by properly brought up young women in New England in the early part of this century.

American women who sit with their legs spread apart in the presence of males are *not* normally signaling a come-on—they are simply (and often unconsciously) sitting like men. Middle-class women in the presence of other women to whom they are very close may on occasion throw themselves down on a soft chair or sofa and let themselves go. This is a signal that nothing serious will be taken up. Males, on the other hand, lean back and prop their legs up on the nearest object.

The way we walk, similarly, indicates status, respect, mood and ethnic or cultural affiliation. The many variants of the female walk are too well known to go into here, except to say that a man would have to be blind not to be turned on by the way some women walk—a fact that made Mae West rich before scientists ever studied these matters. To white Americans, some French middle-class males walk in a way that is both humorous and suspect. There is a bounce and looseness to the French walk, as though the parts of the body were somehow unrelated. Jacques Tati, the French movie actor, walks this way; so does the great mime, Marcel Marceau.

Blacks and whites in America—with the exception of middle- and upper-middle-class professionals of both groups—move and walk very differently from each other. To the blacks, whites often seem incredibly stiff, almost mechanical in their movements. Black males, on the other hand, have a looseness and coordination that frequently makes whites a little uneasy; it's too different, too integrated, too alive, too male. Norman Mailer has said that squares walk from the shoulders, like bears, but blacks and hippies walk from the hips, like cats.

All over the world, people walk not only in their own characteristic way but have walks that communicate the nature of their involvement with whatever it is they're doing. The purposeful walk of North Europeans is an important component of proper behavior on the job. Any male who has been in the military knows how essential it is to walk properly (which makes for a continuing source of tension between blacks and whites in the Service). The quick shuffle of servants in the Far East in the old days was a show of respect. On the island of Truk, when we last visited, the inhabitants even had a name for the respectful walk that one used when in the presence of a chief or when walking past a chief's house. The term was *sufan,* which meant to be humble and respectful.

The notion that people communicate volumes by their gestures, facial expressions, posture and walk is not new; actors, dancers, writers and psychiatrists have long been aware of it. Only in recent years, however, have scientists begun to make systematic observations of body motions. Ray L. Birdwhistell of the University of Pennsylvania is one of the pioneers in body-motion research and coined the term kinesics to describe this field. He developed an elaborate notation system to record both facial and body movements, using an approach similar to that of the linguist, who studies the basic elements of speech. Birdwhistell and other kinesicists such as Albert Shefien, Adam Kendon and William Condon take movies of people interacting. They run the film over and over again, often at reduced speed for frame-by-frame analysis, so that they can observe even the slightest body movements not perceptible at normal interaction speeds. These movements are then recorded in notebooks for later analysis.

To appreciate the importance of nonverbal-communication systems, consider the unskilled inner-city black looking for a job. His handling of time and space alone is sufficiently different from the white middle-class pattern to create great misunderstandings on both sides. The black is told to appear for a job interview at a certain time. He arrives late. The white interviewer concludes from his tardy arrival that the black is irresponsible and not really interested in the job. What the interviewer doesn't know is that the black time system (often referred to by blacks as C. P. T.—colored people's time) isn't the same as that of whites. In the words of a black student who had been told to make an appointment to see his professor: "Man, you *must* be putting me on. I never had an appointment in my life."

The black job applicant, having arrived late for his interview, may further antagonize the white interviewer by his posture and his eye behavior. Perhaps he slouches and avoids looking at the interviewer; to him, this is playing it cool. To the interviewer, however, he may well look shifty and sound uninterested. The interviewer has failed to notice the actual signs of interest and eagerness in the black's behavior, such as the subtle shift in the quality of the voice—a gentle and tentative excitement—an almost imperceptible change in the cast of the eyes and a relaxing of the jaw muscles.

Moreover, correct reading of black-white behavior is continually complicated by the fact that both groups are comprised of individuals—some of whom try to accommodate and some of whom make it a point of pride *not* to accommodate. At present, this means that many Americans, when thrown into contact with one another, are in the precarious position of not knowing which pattern applies. Once identified and analyzed, nonverbal-communication systems can be taught, like a foreign language. Without this training, we respond to nonverbal communications in terms of our own culture; we read everyone's behavior as if it were our own, and thus we often misunderstand it.

Several years ago in New York City, there was a program for sending children from predominantly black and Puerto Rican low-income neighborhoods to summer school in a white upper-class neighborhood on the East Side. One morning, a group of young black and Puerto Rican boys raced down the street, shouting and screaming and overturning garbage cans on their way to school. A doorman from an apartment building nearby chased them and cornered one of them inside a building. The boy drew a knife and attacked the doorman. This tragedy would not have occurred if the doorman had been familiar with the behavior of boys from low-income neighborhoods, where such antics are routine and socially acceptable and where pursuit would be expected to invite a violent response.

The language of behavior is extremely complex. Most of us are lucky to have under control one subcultural system—the one that reflects our sex, class, generation and geographic region within the United States. Because of its complexity, efforts to isolate bits of nonverbal communication and generalize from them are in vain; you don't become an instant expert on people's behavior by watching them at cocktail parties. Body language isn't something that's independent of the person, something that can be donned and doffed like a suit of clothes.

Our research and that of our colleagues has shown that, far from being a superficial form of communication that can be consciously manipulated, nonverbal-communication systems are interwoven into the fabric of the personality and, as sociologist Erving Goffman has demonstrated, into society itself. They are the warp and woof of daily interactions with others and they influence how one expresses oneself, how one experiences oneself as a man or a woman.

Nonverbal communications signal to members of your own group what kind of person you are, how you feel about others, how you'll fit into and work in a group, whether you're assured or anxious, the degree to which you feel comfortable with the standards of your own culture, as well as deeply significant feelings about the self, including the state of your own psyche. For most of us, it's difficult to accept the reality of another's behavioral system. And, of course, none of us will ever become fully knowledgeable of the importance of every nonverbal signal. But as long as each of us realizes the power of these signals, this society's diversity can be a source of great strength rather than a further—and subtly powerful—source of division.

SUGGESTED ASSIGNMENTS

1. What do these gestures and body movements mean to you and your compatriots?

   a. Shaking hands
   b. A nod of the head (This means "No" in Greece.)
   c. A shrug of the shoulders
   d. A wink of one eye
   e. Lifting the eyebrows
   f. Thrusting out tongue toward a person
   g. A waving of the hand, with arm outstretched and palm down.
   h. Down-pointing thumbs.
   i. An "O" made with thumb and forefinger.
   j. A "V" made with forefinger and second finger
   k. Wrinkling the nose
   l. Clenching the fist and shaking it forward and back.

2. If you are a girl, demonstrate a "come-on" look at a boy. If you are a boy, demonstrate a "let's get acquainted" look at a girl.

3. Special sets of gestures are often used in particular situations, such as

   a. in the army infantry for deploying troops
   b. in a baseball game for conveying information from catcher to pitcher
   c. in a football game as the referee signals the reason for a penalty to the crowd
   d. in a symphony concert as the conductor leads the orchestra
   e. in the flight movement of a plane to signal the tower when its radio is inoperative

   Interview a person who is acquainted with such a special set of gestures and report them to the class.

Communication in Africa

Leonard W. Doob

In African societies, voluntary body movements are an integral part of elaborate social codes and are consciously used to express attitudes and thoughts, as you will observe below in the examples cited. The data in parentheses (name, date, page numbers) refer to Doob's sources, which are listed at the end under "References." Leonard Doob has been Professor of Psychology at Yale University for forty years.

Only a quick glance at African societies is needed to appreciate the tremendous number of relatively voluntary movements that are used to transmit information. The fuller accounts of prevailing customs in this respect provided by some observers may be a function either of their interest in the subject or of a real emphasis within the society on such forms of communicating. Likewise only a brief reference may reflect the investigator's indifference or the society's; unfortunately, . . . negative instances cannot be interpreted unless explicit guidance is provided. Here, for example, is a brief summary of movements that convey information among the Amhara of Ethiopia. Anger is shown by the wide opening of the eyes, by biting the lower lip or a finger, by a knit brow, or by "a furious, intent stare"; melancholy by a wrinkled face; timidity and respect in the young by "turning the eyes to the dust", impatience by rapidly shifting the glance; and greetings or acknowledgment of superordination by rhythmic hand-clapping. In commercial relations, a buyer and seller signify agreement by waving their right hands up and down and then touching each other's palms with the fingers stretched away: Master and servant sit differently: the master pushes his body way back as if to show that a special effort is required to rise; the servant, on the rare occasions when he is permitted to sit in the master's presence, must "sit lightly" (Messing, 1957, pp. 520–521, 574). There is no way of knowing whether the Amhara have a richer or poorer repertoire of such movements than other people.

Unquestionably, no uniform set of meanings is attached to particular body movements, as can be seen when the problem is viewed in cultural perspective. Among the Mbundu of Angola, for example, it might appear that any outside observer ought to be able to comprehend certain gestures. Throwing a mat on the ground and laying the head on one's hands indicates sleep; or fingers are used to signify various numbers. But what is the meaning of the gesture that suggests the stroking of an imaginary bear? Or one in which the head is bent forward with eyes wide open and tongue out? Or one in which the left arm is held up with the fist closed and, while that fist is shaken, the wrist is grasped by the right hand? Clearly an outsider would be foolhardy to guess the meaning of such esoteric signs. He would have to be told that they mean, respectively, an inquiry concerning the health of one's father; a very insulting way of saying "You are a fool"; and extreme anger, so strong that adequate words cannot be found to express one's feelings (Hambly, 1934, pp. 252–253).

The *faux pas* reported by missionaries and other travelers in Africa are indeed evidence that the meanings of movements cannot be transferred from one society to another without running the risk of misunderstanding. Thus the warm gesture of patting a child's head or indicating the height of a plant or animal by a horizontal extension of the hand is considered in some societies to be an evil attempt to cast a spell upon the child, plant, or animal so that growth will cease at the height indicated by the pat or the extension (A. Fraser, 1932, p. 5). Pointing to objects with the index finger in certain areas of Central Africa is a "crude and vulgar" gesture; the polite way to point is by sticking out the lower lip (Nida, 1952b, p. 12). Africans who have frequent contact with Europeans often grow tolerant when outsiders violate their etiquette. The present writer sat with his legs crossed in front of the chief of an Ewe community in Ghana; later he apologized, after learning that the gesture showed disrespect; the chief smiled and indicated that he knew the impoliteness had been unintended.

The messages communicated by voluntary bodily movements are often intimately linked with extremely important values of the society. In particular there is a right and a wrong way to conduct one's body in order to demonstrate respect, but again that way varies and may be displayed in different social contexts:

Ashanti of Ghana—it is insulting to use the left rather than the right hand for gesticulation (Rattray, 1929, p. 164).

Chaga of Tanganyika—children receiving or giving something to an older person are expected to clasp their outstretched right hand with their left one; they must offer seats to old people who enter a hut (Raum, 1940, p. 175).

Ganda of Uganda—inferior people receiving or giving something to a superior person must use both hands; if it is necessary to hold the object in one hand, then the free hand must touch the arm of the hand holding the object (Roscoe, 1911, p. 44).

Luo of Kenya—while speaking, a man and his mother-in-law must turn their backs to each other (Evans-Pritchard, 1950, p. 141).

Mende of Sierra Leone–anyone approaching a chief, including the younger members of his own family, must bend his body, place his hands on his knees, and uncover his head (Little, 1951, p. 192).

Some, perhaps most bodily movements convey information not only to others but also to the communicators themselves. In addition to participating in the vomiting ritual previously mentioned, Zulu warriors about to go into battle also chewed a particular plant which they then spat out in the direction of the enemy.[1] This action they felt would cause the enemy "to make mistakes." No doubt the gesture helped the spitter and his marching contemporaries more than it harmed the enemy. Besides spitting and vomiting, these warriors strengthened themselves in other ways. When summoned to war, they donned a special war dress and would "leap about as if fighting, in order to 'get up steam' " (Krige, 1936, p. 268).

Since the symbolic significance of voluntary movements seems on the whole to be quite arbitrary, it is not surprising to discover that the process of establishing the symbolic link may be extended another step: a gesture can replace words which are themselves symbols, and symbolic words can replace a gesture. The Ashanti in Ghana provide an illustration of the first relation, the Mossi in the Mali and Voltaic Republics, of the second. Among the Ashanti, the way to abuse or slander a paramount chief is to use certain stereotyped phrases ("the child of a fool") or to invoke a special oath ("May your ancestral spirits chew their own heads"); such utterances were once punishable by death. The same abuse or slander may be conveyed by a simple gesture, which consists of "closing the hands, placing the closed fists together, and holding up the thumbs" (Rattray, 1929, p. 310). Among the Mossi, gratitude is expressed by saying "My head is in the dirt." The words represent the custom of demonstrating gratitude by bowing so low that the head is actually pressed into the dirt, "so humbled does one feel because of the graciousness of another" (Nida, 1952a, pp. 134–135).

The third and final form of bodily movement to be considered is a special type of voluntary movement requiring, let praise be uttered, no formal definition: *dancing*.[2]

After surveying some of the literature (most of which seems to be either romantic or arty), the writer feels tentatively that competent observers agree on two points concerning dancing in Africa. First, dancing is important and occurs frequently. Africans allegedly "dance for joy and they dance for grief; they dance for love and they dance for hate; they dance to bring prosperity

---

[1] "In order to bring together 'the hearts' of Zulu warriors being prepared for battle through a series of intricate ceremonies lasting a few days, not more than four warriors at a time had to vomit into specially prepared holes. Here, as it were, was an unusual movement of the body which by its very unusualness may have helped symbolize the seriousness of the situation. Since vomiting is not a voluntary movement but a series of reflexes that must be triggered off by some intervening processes, the warriors drank a mouthful or two of an emetic concocted for them by the war doctors of the king (Krige, 1936, p. 269)," *Communication in Africa*, p. 69. [eds.]

[2] The first was relatively involuntary body movements, with which we are not concerned here because they are not at all comparable with those discussed by the Halls in the preceding selection. [eds.]

and they dance to avert calamity; they dance for religion and they dance to pass the time" (Gorer, 1935, p. 289). Then, secondly, dancing is always linked with other expressive forms: "In the African village singing, clapping, dancing, and drumming are not separate entities, but may be said to constitute one homogeneous art form" (Hailey, 1957, p. 67).

There is, however, less agreement concerning the precise functions performed by dancing, especially with relation to communication. One promising theory suggests that dancing is "an important factor in maintaining the sense of group solidarity" (Krige, 1936, p. 336). This hypothesis need not exclude other functions simultaneously served, such as expressing aggression or communicating—and stimulating—sexual desire. Undoubtedly the fruitful approach is to appraise the medium in each social context. The same writer, for example, indicates that Zulu hunters once danced both before and after the hunt. In advance, they entered "the cattle-kraal of the master of the hunt, where they danced round, boasting of their prowess and stabbing imaginary bucks." Afterwards those who had distinguished themselves received the approval of all as they danced about (ibid., pp. 336, 341–342). Without additional information, without knowing exactly how the dancers themselves felt on the two occasions, it may be reasonable nevertheless to think that before the hunt "solidarity" and morale-building were the important goals, but that later the communication from the audience to the dancers became more significant than the feelings of in-group membership conveyed among themselves. In a different society—the Bemba in Northern Rhodesia—dancing is "for amusement" and also to show respect. The latter feeling may be vividly communicated by the soloist who, while singing and "with vitality and dash," dances in front of the person he would honor (Richards, 1956, p. 59). Like other forms of bodily movement and especially those involving the entire body, dancing must convey to the dancer himself a variety of feelings about himself that he may not ordinarily verbalize.

The people who are permitted to dance on special occasions or in a particular way are usually specified within a society. Men, for example, are likely to have their own dances that are different from those reserved for women. Among the Wolof of Senegal, who have a large number of dance forms, low-caste women may "act in an outrageously flirtatious manner, make risqué remarks, and when dancing perform the indecent actions and postures for which Wolof dancing is notorious." In contrast, high-caste girls generally do not dance in public, and when they do, their dancing is "very restrained" (Gamble, 1957, p. 75). . . .

In passing it must be emphasized that the meaning of nonverbal media can likewise be grasped by tracking down their referents within the society. Consider the following miscellany: a turban of glazed blue cloth; a sword; an alarm clock; two people cowering for half a minute or more; two people stretching out their fingers several times; bowing or kneeling low; the taking off of sandals; one man sitting slightly behind the other; squatting cross-legged; and pulling a sleeve or cloth over one's hands, while offering a gift. As discrete bits of behavior, they become intelligible when it is reported, first, that among the Nupe of Nigeria there is a "social gradation of remarkable thoroughness and indeed conspicuousness' and that the class barriers are communicated and enforced through etiquette and a system of symbols. The turban, the sword, and nowadays the alarm clock are worn or carried to signify high rank. When men of equal rank meet, they cower; if they know each other well, they stretch out their fingers several times. In the presence of superiors, men of lower rank bow or kneel low and remove their sandals; when sitting, they must be behind the others and, if the social distance between the two is great, they must sit cross-legged; when offering a gift, they must conceal their hands under a sleeve or a piece of cloth (Nadel, 1942, pp. 128–129). The content of the communications, indeed the fact that they are communications, thus becomes clear in the Nupe context.

REFERENCES

These are the sources to which Professor Doob refers in parentheses in the above selection.

Evans-Pritchard. "Marriage Customs of the Luo of Kenyo." *Africa*, 1950, *20*, 132–42.

Fraser, Agnes Kenton. *The Teaching of Healthcraft to African Women*. London: Longmans, Green, 1932.

Gamble, David P. *The Wolof of Senegambia*. London: International *African Institute*, 1957.

Gorer, Geoffrey, *African Dances*. New York: Alfred A. Knopf, 1935.

Hailey, Lord. *An African Survey—Revised 1956*. London: Oxford University Press, 1957.

Hambly, Wilfrid I. "The Ovimbundu of Angola." *Field Museum of Natural History, Anthropological Series*, 1934, *21*, 89–362.

Krige, Eileen Jensen. *The Social System of the Zulus*. London: Longmans, Green, 1936.

Little, Kenneth L. *The Mende of Sierra Leone: A West-African People in Transition*. London: Routledge and Kegan Paul, 1951.

Messing, Simon David: *The Highland-Plateau Amhara of Ethiopia*. Ph.D. thesis, University of Pennsylvania, 1957.

Nadel, S. F. *A Black Byzantium: The Kingdom of Nupe in Nigeria*. London: Oxford University Press, 1942.

Nida, Eugene A. *God's Word in Man's Language*. New York: Harper & Row, 1952.

————. *How the Word Is Made Flesh: Communicating the Gospel to Aboriginal Peoples*. Princeton: Princeton Theological Seminary, 1952.

Rattray, Robert S. *Ashanti Law and Culture*. Oxford: Clarendon, 1929.

Raum, O. F. *Chaga Childhood*. London: Oxford, 1940.

Richards, Audrey I. *Chisungu*. London: Faber and Faber, 1956.
Roscoe, John. *The Baganda*. London: Macmillan, 1911.

SUGGESTED ASSIGNMENTS

1. Interview a foreign student to find out what gestures and body movements are conventionalized symbols in his culture. Latin Americans have an especially large repertory. One way to begin such an interview is to begin with meanings, thus: What is your common way of expressing the following meanings without using words?

   a. Let's be friends. I am glad to make your acquaintance.
   b. Let's have a drink.
   c. Let's eat.
   d. What a pretty girl!
   e. I despise you.
   f. I am angry with you.
   g. Hello.
   h. Goodbye.
   i. I am overjoyed to see you after all these years.
   j. Who knows? What's the difference? Who cares?

   He will probably be able to volunteer many more.

2. Watch a TV talkshow that includes both men and women and where there is likely to be a diversity of opinion on a controversial subject. Observe closely the body language of the participants and give an oral report of your findings. Note especially the use of head movements and facial expressions, as well as the use of shoulders, arms, and legs, in relation to tone of voice and statements of agreement and disagreement. Do not forget to observe the body language of listeners as well as speakers. If the panel is large or especially active, it may be expedient to concentrate on a single person throughout the discussion.

FURTHER READINGS

Benedict, Ruth. *The Chrysanthemum and the Sword*. Boston: Houghton, Mifflin, 1946. Mores of the Japanese.
Fast, Julian, *Body Language*. New York: M. Evans and Co., 1970.
Hall, Edward T. *The Hidden Dimension*. New York: Doubleday, 1966. On the use of space by animals and human beings.
_____. *The Silent Language*. New York: Doubleday, 1959. Differences in mores, actions, and concepts between cultures and how one can misinterpret them. Fascinating reading.
Townsend, Elvira. *Latin-American Courtesy*. Santa Ana, Cal.: Summer institute of Linguistics, 1961. Delightful and illuminating.

13
PSYCHOLINGUISTICS

Language and Psychology

John B. Carroll

Psycholinguistics is a new field of study, about twenty years old, that employs the methods and theories of both psychology and linguistics in order to ascertain the intellectual abilities that underlie the acquisition and use of language. The psycholinguist examines and experiments with overt speech behavior. From this activity he attempts to infer those processes and structures in the mind that account for such behavior. John B. Carroll, a professor of educational psychology at Harvard University from 1961 to 1967, is now Senior Research Psychologist for the Educational Testing Service at Princeton University. He is the author of *The Study of Language* and has edited the major writings of Benjamin Lee Whorf.

The language I use in writing is English. A reader who is a native speaker will have little trouble in understanding what I write, nor would he have difficulty in understanding my speech if he were listening to this chapter delivered as a lecture. If the reader has learned English as a foreign language, he might have more difficulty in understanding and might even find himself making quick mental translation into his native tongue. Let us suppose

Chapter 15, "Language and Psychology," by John Carroll, in *Linguistics today,* edited by Archibald A. Hill, © 1969 by Basic Books, Inc., Publishers, New York.

that such a student were listening to me reading this paragraph aloud. Both he and I would be using a language. I have used the language as the medium in which I have encoded my message and if I were reading it aloud, I would be using my vocal apparatus—my lungs, my larynx, and the various parts of my mouth to create a physical sound which could be recorded mechanically on tape or disc, and transmitted by radio. Were he listening to me, the hearer would be engaged in the truly remarkable feat of hearing this physical sound not as a jumble of noises, but as a sequence of speech sound which he recognized as words and sentences in the English language. And he would be engaged in the even more remarkable feat of understanding the concepts and thoughts conveyed in these words, these sentences.

Most of the chapters in this book are concerned only with language, considered as a system of symbols for communicating meanings. The English language is just one of many such systems, and it can be studied in the abstract, by studying the various kinds of units that are involved in a language system—units such as phonemes, words, and sentence structures —with little reference to how the speakers of that language actually use the system in creating and understanding sentences. Study of language systems in the abstract is the province of the science of linguistics. But the study of how people *use* a language system, and how they learn to use it, is the province of psychology, or more specifically, the province of a specialty which has come to be called *psycholinguistics*. For there is a peculiarly intimate relation between linguistics and psychology when we consider language. Developing a theory of language systems in the abstract means developing at the same time a theory of the "competence" of users of the language. That is, a description of a language system states, in effect, what a person must have learned in order to use that language either as a speaker or as a hearer. Since language systems turn out to be remarkably rich and complicated, it follows that a speaker of a language has learned something that is remarkably rich and complicated.

One of the first tasks of the psychology of language is to account for how a child learns this system as his mother tongue. It would appear that one must have a powerful theory of learning to do so; some linguistic theorists have been of the opinion that no currently available theory of learning is sufficiently powerful to do this, but there are eminent psychologists who claim that their theories of learning *can* handle the problem—that, although a language system is complex, the child's learning of that system can be accounted for by appeal to what they consider to be relatively well-established principles of learning, applied in various combinations. The intellectual battle has been joined, but there is no victory in sight for either side. Only in very recent years has the child's learning of language been looked at. Currently the problem is to collect enough data from enough children to enable one to draw some conclusions. For it is not merely a matter of enumerating the words that the child uses or measuring the lengths of his sentences; one must examine in great depth how the various grammatical structures of the child's language change and unfold as they converge toward the grammatical structures of the adult language. At the same time, it is up to the psychologist to re-examine his theories of learning and if necessary to develop new theories. A theory of learning that may be adequate to account for the behavior of a rat in a maze *may* not be adequate to account for a child's learning of, say, grammatical agreement between noun and verb, although some psychologists would argue that there is nothing different in principle between these behaviors. Obviously this is a tremendously complex and theoretical issue; as a psychologist, my sympathies are with those who claim that no totally new learning theory is required to account for the child's learning of language, but rather that our theories of learning only need certain revisions and extensions. But in this I may be totally wrong, and I must admit that there is something unsatisfying about the principles of learning that we have. For example, one of the currently most favored principles of learning, at least among many psychologists, is the principle of reinforcement: briefly, that we tend to learn whatever responses get reinforced or rewarded, that is, whatever responses have satisfying consequences. This principle may indeed explain how learning is *motivated,* but it does not explain how the learning itself takes place or how the individual creates new responses.

Although the learning of complex grammatical rules is difficult to explain, how children learn the meanings of language symbols is not. There is at least a considerable number of language symbols—words like *banana, telephone, drop, yellow, swift*—that correspond to the concepts the child derives from ordinary experience. There is good reason to believe that fairly simple principles of "conditioning" can explain the child's learning of these symbols. Some experimental psychologists have shown how classical Pavlovian conditioning can be used to manipulate the child's use and interpretation of such language symbols. And what is called operant conditioning—as discussed by the American psychologist B. F. Skinner—can be used to teach a child to use a given word to denote a given concept.

Psycholinguistics has also been concerned with the way people learn foreign languages. The debate as to whether the learning of a foreign language by an adult, say, is qualitatively different from a child's acquisition of his native language remains unsolved. Perhaps some of the same learning principles can be invoked in either case, but most of the evidence supports the view that these two forms of learning are different. In learning his native language, a child is at the same time learning new concepts. A person learning a foreign language has already learned these concepts; and he has already learned names for them in his native language. Furthermore, while all normal children learn their native language at about the same pace, people who learn a foreign language after childhood learn at different rates. In fact, some people seem to have considerable difficulty in learning foreign languages, and it is possible to measure various aspects of this aptitude. For example, some people seem to have special difficulties in learning to remember the sounds and words of a foreign language; some people (not always the same ones) have special difficulties in learning the grammatical features. Further, it is possible that people learn foreign languages in different ways. Some learn a foreign language with relatively little reference to their native language system; this seems to happen most frequently when the individual is transferred into the environment of the foreign language and is forced to speak it to communicate. Others learn a foreign language largely as a translation, so to speak, of their native language; this seems to happen frequently when a foreign language is learned from books.

Thus far the learning of linguistic systems—either the native language or a foreign language—has been in question. But the psychology of language is also concerned with how people *use* the language systems they have acquired, that is, with what has been called *performance,* as distinguished from *competence.*

A complete scientific explanation of how people use language is at present far out of reach. Because the use of language is involved in so much of human behavior, the psychology of language ultimately has to explain a large part of human behavior. To progress toward this goal, the psycholinguist, like his colleagues in other fields of science, must often content himself with small steps. Psychology is a field in which there have thus far been very few great discoveries, very few breakthroughs, but over the past fifty years a good deal of progress has been made.

There are different levels on which explanations can be made. The layman who wonders about the workings of the mind probably demands, first of all, an explanation on the neurological level. But there has been little success in explaining language behavior neurologically. To be sure, one can trace back into the brain the nerves that carry auditory messages from the ear, or the nerves that control the various parts of the speech musculature; but next to nothing is known about how language knowledge is stored in the brain or about how the brain works as sentences are formulated. One of the few things that neurologists can agree upon is that in most persons the control center for speech is located in only one hemisphere, usually the left. Postmortem studies of aphasics—persons who have lost the power to speak —show that lesions can occur in various areas of the cortex, and there is some evidence that the location of the lesion is correlated with the type of speech loss. But even this evidence has not helped much in explaining speech behavior.

It is far better to keep to a behavioral level of explanation, relying on careful observation of normal speech behavior and also on carefully designed experiments specifying special conditions and tasks for the language user to reveal some of the relationships between stimulus conditions and speech behavior and—eventually—inferences about the processes that govern these relationships.

In fact, one can derive considerable information from observations of ordinary speech behavior—for example, some idea of what the speaker has learned, and the relative strengths of these learnings. We can count all the words an individual uses in a number of situations and observe which words are used most frequently. Recent studies show that a mathematical theory of word frequency can be developed in such a way as to predict, from the distribution of word frequencies in a fair-sized sample, the size of the vocabulary of the speaker. The resulting sizes of vocabularies are staggering; educated speakers of normal intelligence have vocabularies that extend at least to 100,000 words—though interpretation of such figures depends partly on how the word-unit is defined (for example, are *go, goes, gone,* and *went* different words or variants of the single morpheme *go*?). However words are counted, it is evident that vocabularies are larger than one might expect. Linguistic units constitute what is probably the largest single class of knowledges possessed by the individual. Even words that occur less than once in one million words, like *nepotism, sextant, numismatics, convene,* are immediately recognized and understood by the educated adult. In fact, adult speakers can make fairly accurate judgments of the relative frequency of words, and when these judgments are pooled they show quite a high correspondence to actual word counts. And when adults have to learn to associate arbitrary pairs of words, they are better able to learn pairs consisting of frequently used words than pairs of rare words. Word frequency is a powerful variable, then, in various kinds of speech behavior.

Ordinary observation of speech behavior can also suggest something about the processes of sentence formulation. The normal flow of speech is often interrupted by various kinds of hesitations. In the spoken sentence "The *ah* first thing I want to do is *ah* locate my *ah* suitcase," some of the hesitations may represent periods in which the speaker is actually deciding what he wants to do but they may also represent periods in which he searches for words or grammatical patterns that express his thoughts. Studies of speech hesitation show that they are more likely to occur directly before points of high selectivity—points at which it would be possible to insert any one of a number of words. Hesitations are not likely to occur in the middle of highly automatized sequences, in the middle, for example, of *as a matter of fact.* One theory that arises out of such observations is that the formulation of sentences takes place in two levels or stages: (a) grammatical selection, in which the speaker selects the over-all grammatical frame for the sentence or a part of it (is it to be declarative, or a question?), and (b) word selection, in which particular words are fitted into particular "slots" in the sentence. The theory does not state which of these kinds of selection takes place first; actually they may take place in any order, for in the formulation of a complex sentence there is undoubtedly a succession of various kinds of selections. Although speech must necessarily come out in a temporal order (or, if it is English, "from left to right"), there is evidence to suggest that the speaker formulates large chunks of his sentences all at once. For example, in the question "Who did you come home with?" the last word, *with,* must have been formulated even at the beginning, because it is closely associated with the first word, *who,* as evidenced in another possible form of the question: "With whom did you come home?" One grammatical theory asserts, in fact, that such a question is actually formulated as a derivation of some underlying structure that can be represented as "You come *past tense* home with somebody *question.*" This poses the problem of how a speaker learns to make the complicated series of transformations involved. A simpler explanation is that the learning of the framework of a question like "Who did you come home with?" is quite separate from the learning of the declarative form, "I came home with my sister," say, and that this in turn is quite separate from the learning of the framework of the imperative form," "Come home with my sister."

Ordinary observation also tells something about the kinds of stimulus situations that give rise to various kinds of sentences. In general, declarative sentence structures, for example, are used, when the speaker perceives that he has information to transmit to the hearer; question structures, when he needs some kind of information or action from the hearer.

But ordinary observation has its limitations, for one cannot control conditions as well as one can in a formal experiment. A simple experiment that suggests interesting ideas about how words are stored in memory has been made by Roger Brown at Harvard. This experiment concerned the TOT, or "tip-of-the-tongue," phenomenon: that experience of searching for some word or name that is "on the tip of the tongue" but cannot be recalled. For example, recently I was trying to recall the word *contagious,* but I could only remember *incongrous, contextual,* and *infectious*—all of them similar to the word I sought, in general length (number of syllables), stress pattern, and certain combinations of sounds (*con, -ous*), and one of them, *infectious,* overlapping semantically with the target word (both referred to disease). Brown sought to generate TOT phenomena wholesale. To a group of 56 college students, Brown read definitions of relatively rare words, asking them to write the word referred to if they could recall it. In about 13 per cent of all possible instances, subjects reported a TOT phenomenon—they intuitively felt they knew the word referred to but could not recall it. The subjects were asked to give as much information as they could about each such case; they were asked to report, or guess, the number of syllables, the first letter, words of similar sound, and words of similar meaning. Brown found statistically significant evidence that in the TOT phenomenon the subjects' guesses of the initial letter and the number of syllables of the target word bear a positive relation to the actual characteristics of the target word. In other words, storage of words in memory includes something about their abstract form. It is as if all the words in our memory are stored like cards in a keysort file. The definition causes the subject to select cards that are edge-punched for certain semantic features. For example, what word is referred to by the definition "a navigational instrument used in measuring angular distances, especially the altitude of sun, moon, and stars at sea"? The key semantic features are "navigation," "instrument," and "geometry," and with these you might think of a group of words including *astrolabe, compass, protractor.* Although you can't think of *sextant,* which is the correct word, something you fish up from your memory makes you think of *secant, sextet,* and *sexton.* To continue the analogy to cards in a keysort file: it is as if the card with the word *sextant* in your mental dictionary has that word so faintly written on it that all you can make out is that it has two syllables and the first syllable is something like *sec-* or *sex-.* So you think of words like that, and perhaps you eventually recognize *sextant.*

Of course, most of the time we can instantaneously recall the words we want. The experimental study of the TOT phenomenon slows down the process of word recall so that it can be examined in detail.

Another kind of experiment that has been a favorite of psycholinguists is the free-association experiment, first developed by psychiatrists to study mental inhibitions in psychopathology. The procedure is to announce or expose a word to a subject and ask him to report the first word that comes to mind other than the stimulus word. For example, to the stimulus *light* many persons will respond with *dark*; others will give *lamp, bright, sun, bulb, heavy, day,* and so on. Note that all these words have a *semantic* relation to the stimulus word; only rarely will a subject give a "clang" association based solely on phonetic similarity (*delight, fight*). Of course, if he is asked to give a rhyme, he can usually do so quite easily. Children, even without special instructions, are somewhat more likely than adults to give "clang" associations. Adults usually give words that are the same part of speech as the stimulus word, but children are more likely to give a word that could be used in sequence with the stimulus word in a sentence—to *light,* for example, they tend to respond with *bulb* or *dress.* This difference in the responses of children and adults has been interpreted to mean that as a person grows older, he is more and more likely to organize his memory traces for words into sets of grammatical equivalence classes. James Deese of Johns Hopkins University has analyzed the structure of the associations revealed in the free-association experiment. He shows that these associations are organized in a number of semantic dimensions or categories. He finds that most of the adjectival concepts of our language can be reduced to about forty bipolar concepts—pairs like *Above–Below, Alone–Together, Active–Passive, Alive–Dead.* The free-association technique, therefore, has yielded information on the structure of thought.

In fact, the psychology of language can hardly be studied without at least some reference to the psychology of thinking and concept formation. A large number of words in any language can be regarded as names of concepts. In order to use a word properly, one must have acquired the underlying concepts. Dictionary definitions are frequently attempts to describe the criterial attributes of concepts. The question has often been asked, To what extent does a language direct the course of thought? Evidence from the psychology of the deaf before they have acquired language suggests that they can indeed think without using the *names* of concepts that language offers, but they *must think* with something like concepts. For a person who has learned a language, thinking can certainly be much faster and smoother. Language undoubtedly influences thinking in the way it names and defines concepts. If someone should tell me that there is something called *thrizymia* (which there is not, so far as I know) I would be immediately curious about what it is; the mere existence of a word invites us to inquire into its meaning, or rather, into the nature of the concept that lies behind it. Moreover, we are tempted to conclude that no two words can have exactly the same meaning, even though they may actually refer to the same thing. Jessica Mitford, in *The American Way of Death*, has pointed out that undertakers have tried to veil the meanings of certain words by substituting certain other words with different connotations. For example, in the undertaking world, one does not dig a grave and then fill it; rather, one *opens* and *closes* it. A cemetery is not a cemetery but a *memorial park*. The language psychologist studies the connotations of words as well as the concepts they represent. For example, what is the difference between *nice* and *good?* Both are adjectives expressing favorable evaluation. One psychologist, Charles Osgood of the University of Illinois, has developed a technique, the *semantic differential,* for measuring subtle differences in connotation. *Nice* is found to connote something mildly feminine, *good* is neutral in connotation.[1] Osgood finds three major dimensions inherent in connotative meaning: the "evaluative" dimension—how good or bad the concept is; the "potency" dimension—how big and powerful the concept is; and the "activity" dimension—to what degree the concept suggests active, fast, and perhaps unexpected action. In studies using the semantic-differential technique in different languages, he has found these three dimensions to be universal.

The hypothesis of "linguistic relativity" [2]—the hypothesis that the thinking of the speakers of a given language is affected by the structure of that language—was advanced by the American linguist Benjamin L. Whorf in a famous series of papers published around 1940, just before his death.[3] As a

[1] For more information on the *semantic differential* see Stephen Ullmann, *Semantics: an Introduction to the Science of Meaning*, pages 68–70. [eds.]

[2] The hypothesis of "linguistic relativity," also known as the Whorfian hypothesis, is explained above by Clyde Kluckhohn on pages 38–46. [eds.]

[3] The writings of Whorf are most readily available in John B. Carroll, ed., *Language, Thought, and Reality; Selected Writings of Benjamin Lee Whorf.* Massachusetts Institute of Technology Press, 1956.

former student of Whorf's I led a series of investigations to try to confirm this hypothesis. We explored whether there were any major ways in which the thinking of certain groups of southwestern American Indians when using their own language differed from the thinking of speakers of English. By and large it was extremely difficult to discover any such differences. The differences we did find were trivial and were certainly unrelated to ability to solve problems or to philosophies. In fact, we were impressed again with that marvelous characteristic of language, its power to express any thought and any conception. All languages contain a well-nigh universal set of categories. To be sure, languages differ in the ways they apply and combine these categories, and it is important to observe these differences in making a translation from one language to another. But, if there are differences in the thought processes of speakers of different languages, it is most probable that they are attributable to differences in culture and education and not to differences in language.

SUGGESTED ASSIGNMENT

This is a simple, short, investigative assignment in psycholinguistics, using the "semantic differential." The term *connotation* refers to the suggestiveness that a word has and the associations that it brings to mind. An important part of *connotation* consists of feelings and attitudes. Among many persons and in some textbooks you will find the naïve belief that the connotations of a given word are stable, constant, and universally accepted. This belief is voiced in such sentences as "The word *toad* connotes repulsiveness" and "The word *brother* has connotations of personal warmth and helpfulness."

The semantic differential can be used to ascertain connotations. It is a set of adjectival scales applied to a given word. Here is an example:

friendly								hostile
	1	2	3	4	5	6	7	
thoughtful								thoughtless
unselfish								selfish
warm								cold
helpful								indifferent
good								bad

Pairs of polar adjectives are used in seeking the connotations of a word. Between each pair of adjectives is a scale of seven degrees with the following meanings (using the first pair as examples):

1. extremely friendly
2. quite friendly
3. slightly friendly

4. neither friendly nor hostile; equally friendly and hostile
5. slightly hostile
6. quite hostile
7. extremely hostile

Your assignment is to devise a semantic differential for a word or expression that you suspect has strong or variable connotations for your fellow students and to administer it to a set of subjects. The purpose is to find out one or more of these things: 1. what connotations the word has; 2. how strong these connotations are; 3. what variability of connotations there is among your subjects; 4. what differences in connotation occur between sexes, races, teachers and students, freshmen and seniors, or other groups. Here are a few suggested terms: *beauty contests, coed dormitories, interracial dating, Homecoming, Arab, Jew, Communist, crew cuts, capital punishment, mouse, spot quizzes, election politics, official government pronouncements, chairperson.* In preparing this semantic differential, your main difficulty will be to find a set of polar adjectives that will best elicit the connotations of the term. After the differential has been administered you will face the tough problem of finding a way to interpret the results. In professional practice, elaborate statistical procedures are employed, but for this class assignment, a simple method will be sufficient.

How Children
Acquire Language

Carol L. Smith

Careful and systematic observation of child language had its beginning, in a really meaningful sense, in Jean Piaget's work in the twenties. In the sixties, interest suddenly intensified. Linguists, psychologists, and educators engaged in investigations, experiments, and probings of theory that have resulted in a rapidly growing accumulation of knowledge. This knowledge has practical implications for parents and teachers of children and deepens our speculations on the nature of language and first-language acquisition. Today, the study of children's acquisition of language is an active and promising field of research.

From *Psychology Today: An Introduction*, 2d Edition, pp. 118–125, © 1972 by Communications Research Machines, Inc. Used with permission.

In order to understand the nature of spoken languages and why men are so adept at learning them, it is useful to study the development of speech in children. The factors that affect that development should help reveal the capabilities a child brings to language learning and should help us understand how he applies them in learning the rules of his native language.

EARLY VOCALIZATIONS

Most children do not speak their first recognizable word until about a year old, but before that time they have had a considerable amount of practice at vocalization. At birth, babies can coo and cry. During the next few months the sounds they spontaneously produce increase in frequency and variety. By four or five months they are beginning to babble—to chant various syllabic sounds in a rhythmic fashion. Then slowly they develop the capacity to imitate the sounds made by others and to control the sounds they make. Finally, they learn the names of people or objects—their first words.

Infants' early vocalizations seem remarkably independent of what they hear around them. Their early babbling is a type of motor play and experimentation, and it is not limited to the sounds used in a particular language. Instead, infants seem to make sounds from all languages, including French vowels and German rolled Rs. For the first six months of life, deaf babies cry and babble like hearing children—additional evidence for the spontaneity of early vocalization and its relative independence of hearing.

Hearing the speech of others becomes increasingly important during the second half of the first year. The development of children's ability to imitate others reflects their growing ability to produce sounds voluntarily, although the range of voluntarily produced sounds always lags behind those produced spontaneously. At the end of the first year, the baby not only imitates the sounds of syllables and words but is beginning to mimic the stress and pitch patterns of those who talk with him. Before this time the speech sounds of babies from different communities all sound much the same.

Learning to make syllable sounds and to imitate is good preparation for learning words. By rewarding the baby with enthusiastic bursts of approval when he says something that sounds like a word, parents encourage infants to repeat and practice the sounds that are used in words. Imitation and reinforcement also play a major part in the development of children's vocabulary. But there is a leap to be made before the baby starts using words: he must learn that the sound has meaning, that it is used as a symbol for something else. Generally, his first words refer to the tangible and the visible and are used one at a time, as labels or commands ("Dog!" "Cookie!"). Toward the beginning of the second year, the infant will begin to express himself more precisely by combining two words in an utterance.

At this time he enters a new phase of the language-learning process, during which he learns the complicated rules for combining words into sentences.

RULE LEARNING

Much of the discussion of rule learning that follows is based on the work of R. Brown, from Harvard University, and particularly on a long-term study that Brown and his collaborators, U. Bellugi, C. Fraser, and C. Cazden, did on the speech of three children whom they call Adam, Eve, and Sarah. When the study began, the children were about two years old and were just beginning to combine words in two-word utterances. The researchers visited them in their homes every week or so until Adam and Sarah were five years old (Eve moved away nine months after the study began) and collected many samples of their speech. They studied primarily the children's spontaneous speech rather than their comprehension of what other people said to them, because speech gives a clearer indication of a child's understanding of grammatical forms than do his responses to other people's utterances. The two central questions of the research were: what do children know about the structure of English at different points in their development, and what process do they use to acquire that knowledge?

At age two, a child's speech is not much like an adult's. His utterances are short; his vocabulary is limited to nouns and action verbs; most other parts of speech are missing. Nonessential words are left out, much as they are when someone writes a telegram. People who know the child well can usually understand what his statements mean, and they often respond by expanding his utterances into a well-formed adult sentence. [Below] are some examples of a young child's *telegraphic speech* and his mother's interpretation recorded by Brown and Bellugi.

Child	*Mother*
Baby highchair	Baby is in the highchair.
Eve lunch	Eve is having lunch.
Throw Daddy	Throw it to Daddy.
Pick glove	Pick the glove up.

By age four or five, the child's speech is more adultlike. His utterances have increased in length, and they usually include prepositions, auxiliary verbs, and articles. Furthermore, the child seems to have mastered most of the rules of grammar. Brown and C. Hanlon found Adam—when he was four years and seven months old—saying:

The man's not bad, is he?
I can hold on like a monkey, can't I?
She thought that was a tiger, didn't she?

Questions like these are called *tag questions,* and there is much a child must know to form them correctly. First, he must know that he should use a negative tag such as "can't I?" when he expects a "yes" answer to his question; when he expects a "no" answer, he must use an affirmative tag such as "is he?" In addition, he has to be able to substitute a pronoun for a noun (replacing "man" with "he" in the first example). And he must know how to use auxiliary verbs (such as "did" in the third example.)[1]

How does a child come to master the rules of sentence formation in these few short years? Brown and Bellugi's observations suggest that although the child under age four or five does not follow adult grammatical rules, he seems to be following more primitive rules of his own.

One of the first rules that an English-speaking child may learn concerns word order. For example, a two- or three-year-old might say, "Eat cake" while he is devouring his birthday fare. For an adult, "Eat cake" is a command to another to eat the cake. To be correct, the child should say "I am eating the cake," indicating that he is the actor, that eating is in progress at the present, and that the cake is what is being eaten. . . . The child's sentence does not include all these nuances, and it violates several grammatical rules. But the child has observed one adult rule of word order: he puts "cake" after "eat," indicating that the cake is the object being eaten rather than the agent doing the eating. When a child imitates an adult, he often leaves out words, but he does preserve word order. For example, when Brown and Fraser in 1963 asked children between two and three years old to repeat sentences that were spoken to them, one child typically made these responses . . .

Adult	*Child*
I am drawing a dog.	I draw dog.
I do not want an apple.	I do a apple.
Read the book.	Read book.

---

[1] In reference to verb forms in the tag questions, the child must know the following rules in addition to the yes/no rule above.
    1. If the verb is a single *be* form, this form is repeated in the tag in the negative.
    Example: He *is* your friend, *isn*'t he?
    2. If the verb of the statement is a single affirmative verb form other than *be,* the verb of the tag is *do* in that same form (*does, do, did*) in the negative.
    Example: Mary *likes* peaches, *does*n't she?
    3. If the statement contains a verb phrase, the first auxiliary of the verb phrase is repeated in the tag.
    Examples: That was a hard problem. *was*n't it.
             You *did*n't lose the padlock, *did* you?
    4. Whatever verb form is used in the tag must appear in the first position.
    Examples: That was a hard problem, *was*n't it.
             There is a rabbit under the bush, *is*n't there?
             Jim liked fishing, *did*n't he?
             They aren't going to stay, *are* they?

[eds.]

As the child's speech becomes less and less telegraphic, he begins to use helping verbs (such as "is" and "are"), prepositions, and articles. He also begins to make a type of error called *overregularization*. Overregularization, which is common in the speech of three- and four-year-olds, results from the misapplication of a grammatical rule. For example, the usual rule for forming the past tense of an English verb is to add "ed" to the base. But some verbs, including many common ones, have irregular past tenses: go/went, come/came, drive/drove, fall/fell. The child may learn common words like "fell" and "came" from his parents before he masters the "ed" past-tense rule and produce grammatically correct sentences: "I fell down" and "The cat came home." But once he learns the rule for forming the regular past tense, he is likely to overgeneralize, producing sentences like "He goed to the store" and "I falled down." Similarly, the general rule for forming plurals in English is to add an "s" to a singular noun: "dog" becomes "dogs," and so on. After the child has learned that rule, such words as "foots," "mans," and "mouses" creep into his conversation.

The emergence of any one adult rule is not sudden; one can see it coming for a long while. For example, consider Sarah's acquisition of the "ing" grammatical inflection to form the present progressive, as in "I am eating." At twenty-seven months, Sarah used this form only about half the time that an adult would have used it. Not until sixteen months later did she consistently use it where required. During those months, Sarah did not use the "ing" ending incorrectly so much as skip it sometimes, saying "I eat" where an adult would say "I am eating." A transitional period during which the child sometimes does and sometimes does not use the new form is characteristic of the learning of inflections (including the plural "s," as in "boys," and the past "ed," as in "played," as well as the present progressive "ing").

Some rules are learned somewhat differently, in several steps. When Bellugi studied the development of children's ability to form negative sentences, for example, she found a number of intermediate steps preceding use of the adult rule. A very young child (age two) has a simple rule for forming a negative: he adds the word "no" to a statement: "No want stand." "No gonna fall." "No mom sharpen it." "No write book." "Like it, no." A little later, the child begins to use "not," and he seems to know that he should place "no" or "not" in a special position. He puts it just before the verb: "You not have one." "He not bite you." "I not get it dirty." The last step is to add the necessary auxiliary verb: "You don't have one." "He doesn't bite you." "I don't get it dirty."

As he progresses toward the adult rules, a child does not make all the errors that he conceivably might. Curiously, he seems to learn some rules without making the errors one would expect. The development of the present progressive (I am eating) is a good example. Not all verbs are used in the progressive form. In general, process verbs such as "break" and "play" commonly occur in the progressive—"I am breaking the world track record"; "I am playing by banjo." State verbs such as "know" or "need," however, do not take the progressive. It would sound strange to say "I am knowing how to do this" or "I am needing a hammer." A child just learning to form the progressive might be expected to add the "ing" ending to all verbs randomly, and not to observe the process-state distinction. Yet errors of this type, according to Brown and Bellugi, are rarely made.

The tag question is another form that emerges with remarkably few errors. The rules for the formation of tag questions are complicated, so there are many opportunities for error, but the child rarely makes any. The predecessor of the tag question is, "The lady swallowed the sword, *huh?*" or ". . . , *right?*" Then, quite suddenly "huh?" is replaced by "didn't she?" It is as if the child holds off on trying to use tag questions until he understands all the necessary rules.

Semantics and Grammar

Although there is abundant evidence that children consistently apply rules when they speak, it is a difficult matter to state formally what the rules are. One basic question that needs answering is: are the rules based primarily on semantic or on grammatical relationships?

Sentences can be described in both semantic and grammatical terms. Consider the sentence, "The runner overturned the hurdle." Semantically, a person or *agent* (the runner) initiates an *action* (the overturning), and the *object* (the hurdle) directly receives this action. The meaning of the sentence can be characterized by the semantic relation of agent-action-object. Alternately, the sentence can be described in formal grammatical terms. The *subject* (the runner) dominates the sentence, and there is a predicate composed of a *main verb* (overturned) and a *direct object* (the hurdle). In this sentence, the subject has the semantic role of agent and the main verb that of action. Subjects and verbs, however, will have other semantic roles in different sentences; there is no simple, one-to-one correspondence between grammatical and semantic roles. Consider, for example, the sentence "The hurdle was overturned by the runner."

According to N. Chomsky, the rules that govern speech are based primarily on grammatical relationships rather than on semantic ones. For example, the basic rule of sentence production that says a sentence must have a subject and a predicate is a grammatical rule, not a semantic one. Subject and predicate express a formal relation between parts of a sentence rather than a fixed relation between the meaning of words.

Another rule that governs sentence production is that the verb must agree in number with the subject. Again, this rule is phrased in grammatical terms. There is no easy way to state it in semantic terms. Although the grammatical subject and the semantic agent are often identical, that is not always true. To illustrate, consider the following sentences:

The boy gives presents to the girls.
The girls receive presents from the boy.

In both cases the boy is giving presents to the girls and so is the agent of the action. But only in the first sentence does the verb agree in number with "boy." The verb agrees with the grammatical subject in both sentences; the subject is defined in terms of its relation to the main verb and not in terms of its semantic role.

The rules that govern young children's speech are not necessarily of the same type as those that govern adults' speech. It seems quite possible that the early stages of children's speech rely more heavily on semantic relationships than does adults' speech. Beyond the earliest stages, however, the regularities in children's speech do seem to be based on grammatical rules rather than exclusively on semantic ones.

If that is correct, then we are faced with a problem: how does a two- or three-year-old child begin to learn grammatical rules? Piaget's theory . . . suggests how a child constructs certain semantic concepts during the sensorimotor period, but how he constructs the concepts of subject, predicate, verb, and object at that age is not yet known. Where does his understanding of these relationships come from? It is problems like these that led Chomsky and others to conclude that children are born with a potential ability to understand formal grammatical relations, much as they are born with a potential ability to walk. This innate capacity for the grammatical structure of language, according to Chomsky's theory, helps account for the special linguistic abilities of human beings.

The Order of Acquisition of Rules

So far we have described children's speech as regular and systematic, something that can be characterized as following rules. We have suggested that the rules are grammatical rather than semantic and have even ventured the hypothesis that sensitivity to certain features of language may be innate. Yet even though the child may have this built-in sensitivity, he does not speak like an adult when he begins to talk.

The child seems to learn adult rules in a fairly stable order. There is some variation from child to child, but not a great deal. The children that R. Brown studied mastered the rules of word order first, and then the rules for certain grammatical inflections. There was a definite order of acquisition among the grammatical inflections. For example, the children learned to use the plural "s" (as in "horses") and the irregular past forms of verbs (went, gone) before they began to use the linking verb "to be" ("The cops *are* here") or the third person indicative ("He run*s*"). These two forms, in turn, were acquired before auxiliary verbs ("The cops *are* running in place").

Why do children tend to learn these rules in the same order? There are several possible reasons. First, the frequency with which a form is used in the home might help determine when it is mastered. If a child hears many sentences in which "ing" is attached to verbs, it should be easier for him to figure out when this ending is appropriate. Brown decided to test this hypothesis with the parents of Adam, Eve, and Sarah. In his recent book, *A First Language: The Early Stages,* he reports that the three sets of parents did use different grammatical inflections with different frequencies and that the frequencies were remarkably consistent within each home. However, the forms the parents used most frequently were *not* the ones that the children acquired first. It seems, then, that something other than frequency in parental speech determines the order in which children learn grammatical rules.

Brown found that the *semantic complexity* of a rule is an important determinant of rule learning: the rules that are easiest to understand are mastered first. Semantic complexity refers to the number of meanings that a person must understand in order to use a rule correctly. For example, the rules for the formation of the plural and of the past each requires an understanding of one major meaning. To use the plural correctly, you must understand the concept of number. A given noun is either singular (bed) or not singular (beds). When the noun is not singular, you add an "s." Similarly, to use the past correctly you must understand the idea that something has occurred before right now. Verbs can refer either to some earlier time or not. When they refer to an earlier time, you add "ed" (walked). By contrast, the rule for the formation of a regular third-person verb is semantically more complex. To form it, you must be able to coordinate the meanings of *both* number and earlierness. When the verb is both singular and not earlier, for example, you add an "s" to the main stem of the verb (he walks).

Intuitively, it makes sense that semantic complexity should be an important factor in the order of rule learning. It is hard to imagine how a child could use the past and present tense correctly if he could not differentiate between past and present time. He might perceive that adults sometimes used one form of a verb and sometimes another, but the choice would seem completely arbitrary to him until he could attach distinct meanings to the two forms.

If semantic complexity were the *only* factor affecting the child's discovery of rules, however, forms that have the same meanings would be acquired at the same time. This is not always the case. Sometimes two forms that have the same meanings, such as simple and complex plurals, are acquired at different times. In many of these cases, Brown found, the two forms differ in *grammatical complexity*. Grammatical complexity is a second factor in the order of rule learning. (The table below displays some examples of both semantic and grammatical relations.)

Examples of Semantic and Grammatical Relations

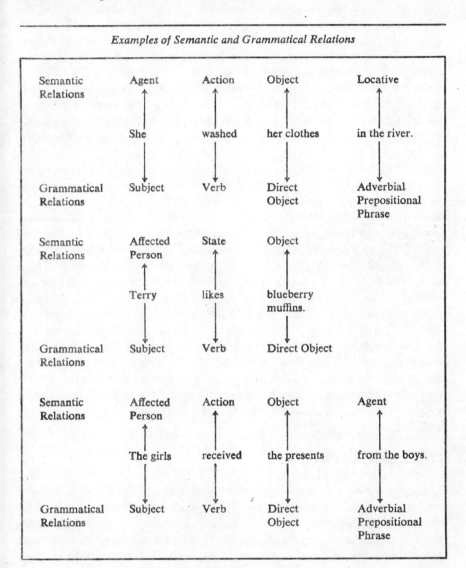

Grammatical complexity refers to the number of steps involved in the derivation of a particular form. For example, compare a simple plural form—a child pointing and saying "apple"—with a more complex plural —"They apples." Although both statements have the same meaning, the second is the more complex grammatically; the child not only pluralized "apples" but also made the pronoun "they" plural, to agree in number with "apples." Cazden analyzed the data from Adam, Eve, and Sarah and found that their performance was better with the simple plurals than with the complex plurals. This finding and others cited by Brown suggest the importance of grammatical complexity in the order of rule learning.

Semantic and grammatical complexity seem to be two important factors in the order of rule learning, but other variables may also be quite important —for example, the *perceptibility* of a given form. Compare the full possessive form, "That is John's hat" with the elliptical possessive, "That is John's." With the elliptical possessive, the "s" can be heard more easily because it is often at the end of a sentence and stressed, whereas the "s" in the full possessive is more likely to be slurred over. Cazden found the performance of Adam, Eve, and Sarah to be much better on the more perceptible form, the elliptical possessive—*even though the elliptical possessive is more grammatically complex than the full possessive.* Apparently, perceptibility may sometimes override grammatical complexity as a determinant of the order of rule learning. However, there are other possible interpretations for the children's performance. The two forms of the possessive differ not only along the dimensions of grammatical complexity and perceptibility but also along that of redundancy of meaning. These multiple differences between any two forms make it difficult to point to any variable as the most important determinant in the order of rule learning.

To summarize, the regularities in a child's speech at different stages suggest that he is learning rules for sentence production. Rule learning is a gradual process: first the child may learn to understand a concept like singular and plural and then, slowly, he begins to notice that plural nouns are marked with an "s." Also, rule learning is not a conscious process. A four-year-old can speak grammatically, but he cannot describe the rules of grammar. Increasing awareness of language rules comes with age.

LATER DEVELOPMENTS

By the age of five most children talk very well. Their sentences are like an adult's in form, although the content of the sentences is restricted. Later developments seem to keep pace with the child's general cognitive advancement. He enlarges his vocabulary as his ability to understand increases and as he is exposed to new things, and he begins to be able to reflect on his own speech.

It takes several years, however, for children to understand fully that words are arbitrary symbols, not intrinsic parts of an object. For example, a group of eight-year-olds was reading a story about how the kangaroo got its name. In the story Captain Cook and his men had landed in Australia and, seeing some strange animals in the distance, asked an Australian what the animals were called. The Australian, not knowing, replied "kangaroo," which in his language meant "I don't know." But Captain Cook and his men went off confident that this strange being was called a kangaroo. The children had a difficult time getting the point of the story because they could not conceive of "kangaroo" as meaning something different from the animal itself. Older children would have easily perceived the two meanings of kangaroo.

F. Kessel reports that between ages five and twelve the child also learns to appreciate the two meanings of an ambiguous sentence. For example: "The duck is ready to eat" could mean either that the duck is the dinner or the diner. Before about twelve years of age, children are unable to pick out the two meanings of the sentence. Around twelve, however, they become able to see the two meanings simultaneously. This and other new abilities with language seem to reflect advances in cognitive development, particularly in the child's capacity to direct his thinking in systematic ways and to deal with hypothetical situations and abstractions.

FURTHER READINGS

Although the bibliography on psycholinguistics is extensive, most of the writing is technical, written by specialists for specialists, and hence is not readily accessible to the lay reader. The five books listed below are useful as starting points in this subject. Each contains a bibliography that will take the questing student further afield.

Brown, Roger. *A First Language: The Early Stages*. Cambridge, Mass.: Harvard University Press, 1973. The author reports the results of important recent studies, including his own, in the acquisition of language. This volume is as clear as a comprehensive and technical book can be.

_____. *Words and Things*. Glencoe, Ill.: Free Press, 1958. This book, designed for the general reader, deals with reference and meaning, phonetic symbolism and metaphor, linguistic determinism, persuasion, and other topics. The presentation is lucid.

Deese, James. *Psycholinguistics*. Boston: Allyn and Bacon, 1970. A short introductory textbook (135 pp.).

Hopper, Robert, and Rita C. Naremore. *Children's Speech: A Practical Introduction to Communication Development*. New York: Harper & Row, 1973. A simple and relatively nontechnical introduction to the study of children's speech.

Slobin, Dan I. *Psycholinguistics*. Glenview, Ill.: Scott Foresman, 1971. A short basic textbook for college students (133 pp.).

14
ETHOLOGY: THE STUDY OF ANIMAL BEHAVIOR

Language and Animal Signals

Claire and
W. M. S. Russell

The question of whether nonhuman animals have language is now under intense investigation. The results of some of these inquiries are presented here by two pioneers in the study of human ethology. Among the many publications of Claire and W. M. S. Russell are *Human Behavior: A New Approach* and *Violence, Monkeys, and Man*. Dr. W. M. S. Russell is a lecturer in Social Biology at the University of Reading, England.

The footnote references to numbered lectures and pages relate to the book in which this article was first printed, *Linguistics at Large*.

. . . If we are seriously to consider whether any animals have languages, we must begin by considering some properties of languages and automatic signal codes. To begin with, human spoken language is generally conveyed by sound; and . . . many animal signals are also calls. But this is not an essential feature of either language or animal signals. There are several different types of true sign or gesture language, evolved for communication between the deaf and the dumb and between monks of religious orders forbidden to talk. These sign or gesture languages are perceived through

From *Linguistics at Large*, edited by Noel Minnis. Copyright by Claire and W. M. S. Russell. Published by Victor Gollancz. Reprinted by permission.

the eyes instead of the ears. Animal signal codes too are often predominantly gestures or postures to be seen by the recipient. In teaching severely handicapped children such as Helen Keller, use has been made of communication by touch, and touch signals are also widely used by animals. Human language is not normally conveyed by smell or taste, though it could conceivably be coded in this way, but elaborate chemical signals are quite common among animals and simpler ones are involved in the human perfume industry. So the use of a particular physical medium or sense is not a crucial feature of language.

Another distinction we can make also cuts across the distinction between true language and automatic signal codes. Both can convey messages about two different kinds of things, which we can sum up as *emotion* and *economics*. We can talk about how we feel about somebody else; we can also talk about natural surroundings, things, techniques and technical aspects of our life in society. In the same way an animal's signals may convey, for instance, a readiness to groom another animal's coat (emotion) or the presence of food or danger (economics). This is an important distinction, but it is no help in deciding what is or is not true language.

The use of symbols or symbolization used to be regarded as unique to human language. This is now known to be nonsense. Symbolization simply means that a set of things or events can be translated into a set of signals, with one signal for each, and that the individual who receives the signals can translate them back into the things symbolized. There is no doubt at all that animals can symbolize in this sense, both as signallers and receivers, as we shall see most clearly in the case of honeybees. A more interesting contrast is that between two kinds of symbols, *representative* and *arbitrary*. A representative symbol has something structurally in common with the thing symbolized.[1] When a herring gull lifts his wrist joints as if about to unfold his wings, and holds his head up straight with beak pointing downwards, this actually *looks like* the beginning of a fighting attack, in which the gull would raise his wings to beat his opponent, and raise his head to peck downwards from above. The raising of the wrist joints and the position of the head are examples of *intention movements*; they symbolize attack, and act as a threat: a gull so threatened will often retreat. On the other hand, an arbitrary symbol bears no particular formal resemblance to the thing it symbolizes. Herring gulls in a conflict between the urges to attack and flee may resolve their problem by doing a third, irrelevant thing derived from some other behavior context—a *displacement activity*, as it is called. They may, for instance, pluck at the grass as if gathering material for a nest. This does not look at all like a real attack, but it also comes to symbolize attack, and acts as a threat which may cause another gull to

---

[1] In other words, a representative symbol resembles in some way the thing it stands for. For example, the highway sign for a sharp right turn shows an arrow which turns at a ninety-degree angle to the right. [eds.]

retreat. Niko Tinbergen has shown that intention movements and displacement activities are the basic units of signal codes in many animal species; animals thus use both representative and arbitrary symbols.

Human language relies heavily on arbitrary symbols. The sound of the word *sun*, for instance, has nothing structurally in common with the sun itself. It is true that we sometimes use representational symbols in language. In spoken language, words that symbolize sounds often resemble the sounds themselves: words such as *thunder* and *hiss* really represent what they symbolize. In American Sign Language, used by the deaf in North America, many signs are arbitrary, but the symbol for *flower* is touching the two nostrils in turn with the tip of the tapered hand, which clearly suggests smelling a flower. Representational effects of a subtler kind are important in poetry, as Pope observed in his *Essay on Criticism.*

> 'Tis not enough no harshness gives offence,
> The sound must seem an Echo to the sense:
> Soft is the strain when Zephyr gently blows,
> And the smooth stream in smoother numbers flows;
> But when loud surges lash the sounding shore,
> The hoarse, rough verse should like the torrent roar.

But, on the whole, the lavish use of arbitrary symbols is a great advantage. Only by arbitrary symbols can we represent such complicated or abstract conceptions as *Institute, Contemporary* or *Arts.* We can see this well in the special case of written language, which advanced from simple picture signs as representational symbols to arbitrary symbols for the sound units of spoken language, and hence for the things which are symbolized in turn by the patterns of sound units making up words.

In the long run, too, arbitrary symbols lend themselves most readily to the formation of many combinations and recombinations. And here we do come to a crucial feature of true language. The signal units of many animals can be put together in many different combinations. Thus the calls and facial expressions of monkeys consist of units which can be combined in many ways. For instance, rhesus monkeys, observed at Whipsnade Zoo by Vernon Reynolds, had a number of different signal units for threat, such as bobbing the head up and down, raising the eyebrows, drooping the eyelids, opening the mouth without showing the teeth, and making a low-pitched noise described as *hough.* A number of different combinations of these units could be observed, according to the intensity of aggression expressed.[2] Even the threat postures of gulls can show a number of different combinations of units signalling various intensities of the urges to attack and flee, as Niko Tinbergen and his colleagues have shown.

[2] V. Reynolds: Dissertation (University of London, 1961).

But these animal signal combinations are both governed and limited by the close relation here between emotion and its expression in vocal and postural and facial symbols. Each signal is tied to a particular emotional state, and signal combinations reflect only combinations of emotions. Some combinations, for instance of units expressing extreme fear with units expressing extreme sexual desire, are simply impossible. Now any symbol units of true language can be uttered in any emotional state. Hence many new combinations become possible, and emotional rules of combination are replaced by logical ones, which we call grammar and syntax. In this way it becomes possible to form at any time totally new combinations of symbols, which the speaker may never have used before, and even combinations which no member of his language-group has ever used before. Human languages vary in their vocabularies or terms of reference, but they all have this potential flexibility. During World War II, when young East Africans were being trained for the Bantu Rifles, a problem arose because there were no words for "red" or "green" in the local language.[3] The problem was easily solved by using the phrases *colour of blood* and *colour of leaves*. By similar means, totally new situations can be described, or totally new possibilities envisaged. This power of producing new combinations is crucial to true language.

R. J. Pumphrey has noted another advantage of detaching symbols from the direct expression of immediate emotion. An alarm call indicating the presence of a lion is given only when the calling animal is feeling the special fear association with seeing or hearing or smelling a lion. The word *lion*, on the other hand, can be used when no lions are about. "Whereas an emotive lion is necessarily in the present, an intelligible lion could be discussed in the future or in the past; and so tradition and forward planning about lions became possible."

True language,[4] therefore, involves the free combination of symbols limited only by logical rules of grammar and syntax, which themselves express *relations between* symbols and hence symbolize *relations between* things and individuals and events. In addition, true language must involve true communication. Compulsive utterance of signals in the absence of other individuals is not true communication. And signalling which produces automatic effects on other individuals is mere interaction. In true communication the signaller transmits information which enables the recipient to behave more freely, to have a greater range of choice and decision; so whereas interaction reduces, communication increases the variability of the recipient's behavior. No doubt the combination of all these qualities is necessary before we can speak of true language, as opposed to an automatic code of signals.

[3] For discussion of language and colour recognition, see R. H. Robins, Lecture 1, p. 31 and Stephen Ullmann, Lecture 4, pp. 83–4. (ed.)
[4] See also Edmund Leach, Lecture 7, pp. 140–1. (ed.)

AN ANIMAL WITHOUT TRUE LANGUAGE

Equipped with these general ideas, we can consider more exactly whether any animals have true languages. To begin with, it is worth glancing at the signal code of an animal which certainly cannot talk, namely the human infant[5]—the word *infant* is simply the Latin root meaning "speechless." Infants have, in fact, a very simple signalling system with at most 8 sound units. These are said to correspond to phonemes, 5 vowels and 3 consonants, but they are certainly not used as elements to be combined in a language. Four kinds of infant cries have been studied in 351 infants in Sweden and Finland, by means of sound spectrographs, which display on a sort of graph called a sonagram the amount of energy produced at different sound frequencies over the time-course of a cry. Birth cries were produced only at birth. Pain cries were produced when the baby was vaccinated. Hunger cries were produced about 4 hours 20 minutes after a feed. Pleasure cries were produced when the infant, after being fed and changed, was lying comfortably in bed or in the mother's or nurse's arms. The sonagrams showed that each kind of cry varied considerably but always differed in definite ways from the other 3 kinds of cry. Each cry was uttered only in its appropriate situation, so there was no question of combining them to produce, say, a sentence like *I was hungry, now I am comfortable*, still less to describe something unusual and new. All this, perhaps, is a bit obvious. But it shows rather clearly what we mean by a simple code as opposed to a true language. Adults have to interpret the signals much as they try to interpret the signals of a cat or a dog.

High-fidelity tape recordings of 6 of each of the 4 kinds of cries were played to 483 adults under 50, including 349 women, and these people were asked to identify the cries as birth, pain, hunger or pleasure cries. They were far from perfectly accurate in their interpretations. Pleasure cries were easiest to recognize, with 85% correct interpretations; then came hunger cries, 68%; pain cries, 63%; and birth cries, which most people hear very rarely, with only 48% correct interpretations. Experience naturally helps in such matters. Children's nurses were better at recognizing pain and hunger cries than mothers who had only had one child each; and, not surprisingly, the top score for recognizing birth cries was obtained by midwives.

If the signals of babies are so relatively difficult to interpret, it will be clear that it takes much work and skill to understand animal signals. The great decoders of animal signal codes, such as Karl von Frisch, Konrad Lorenz and Niko Tinbergen, have had to use as much ingenuity as those of Cretan Linear B or the script of the Mayas. If we are to consider whether any animals have true languages, we shall naturally focus our attention on

[5] See also M. M. Lewis, Lecture 9. (ed.)

the most promising candidates, whose signalling is enormously more elaborate than that of human babies. These animals fall into three groups, which we shall consider in turn, beginning with the extraordinary code of the honeybees. It is simplest to describe this as a language; whether it deserves to be called a true language will appear when we have seen what it does.

THE DANCE OF THE HONEYBEE

In 1788, Pastor Ernst Spitzner reported a surprising fact. When a honeybee finds a good supply of honey, she returns to the hive and there performs a curious circular dance. Spitzner put out some honey, brought 2 bees to it, watched them dance on their return to the hive, and saw that many of their fellow-bees came to the honey-place. He concluded that the returning bees had somehow told their colleagues about the honey. It was a beautiful observation and a true inference, but Spitzner went no further, and it was left to Karl von Frisch, in our own age, to interpret the language of the honeybees. How he made his discoveries can be read in his books. Here we will simply summarize some of what he and Martin Lindauer and their colleagues discovered, beginning with the language of the Carniolan honeybee.[6]

When a honeybee of this race discovers a new source of honey within about 10 m. of the hive, she returns to the hive and regurgitates drops of honey which are eagerly drunk by other bees. Then she begins to dance round in a circle; first she goes one way round, then she reverses and goes the other way round, then another reverse, and so on. This is called the *round dance*. Other bees follow her about, holding their antennae against her abdomen. After dancing, she "refuels" by taking a drop or two of honey back from some other bee, and flies back to the food source, which in natural conditions is a flower or group of flowers. The other bees who followed the dance do not fly after her. They fly out in all directions. But, fairly soon, a lot of them find the new food source. They do so because they have smelt the scent of the flower that clung to the dancer's body, and so look for the right kind of flower. In one experiment, bees informed by a dancer found the right flowers in a section of the Munich Botanical Garden where 700 different plant species were blooming at once. The round dance, therefore, tells the other bees to go out and search the near neighbourhood of the hive; the scent on the dancer's body tells them what flowers to look for.

But honeybees can forage for food at far greater distances than 10 m.[7] They have been known to fly more than 13 km. in search of honey. A

[6] *Apis mellifera carnica.*
[7] "m" means meters, not miles. A meter is about 39 inches. [eds.]

honeybee is only about 13 mm. long, so 13 km. for a bee is the equivalent of about 1000 miles for a human being—not a bad commuting trip. But of course, even at much smaller distances, a round dance would not be much use. If the discoverer of new food told her colleagues to go out and search in all directions for several km., she might just as well save her energy. They would never find the flowers. So when a Carniolan honeybee finds food at a considerable distance from the hive, say between 100 m. and 10 km., she returns to the hive, offers the honey she has found, and then performs a different kind of number, called a *tail-wagging dance*, which is somewhat reminiscent of the Charleston or Black Bottom. She dances along in a straight line for a certain distance, wagging her tail for all she is worth and buzzing away by means of slight vibrations of the muscles that flap her wings in flight. It is as if she was, so to speak, flying on the spot. At the end of this *waggling run*, she stops buzzing and wagging her tail, circles round to one side back to where she started, does another waggling run, circles round to the opposite side, does a third waggling run, circles to the first side, and so on. A number of other bees follow her around, showing special interest in the waggling runs. Bees cannot hear sounds in air, but they can feel the buzzing vibrations through the surface on which the dance is done. Like the round dance, the tail-wagging dance tells the bees who follow it that there is food available, and what flowers to look for, from the smell. But it tells them much more than this. It tells them exactly how far away the flowers are, and in exactly what direction. And so, even at distances of km., the bees who study the dance can fly with precision to the spot indicated and find the honey-bearing flowers.

The distance to the food is conveyed by the tempo of the dance. A quick-step tempo means a relatively nearby food source, a slow foxtrot tempo a more distant one. To be exact, as the distance increases so does the duration of each waggling run. A single waggling run may be inaccurate, but Von Frisch and his colleagues have shown that the bees who follow the dance study several waggling runs and calculate the average duration, which they then translate into distance by a mathematical rule.

The tail-wagging dance is sometimes done on a horizontal surface just outside the hive. When this happens, the dancer indicates the direction of the food by aiming her waggling run in exactly this direction. She can only do this if she can see the sun (or the polarized light of the blue sky, which indicates the position of the sun to bees, though not to us). So actually she is taking up a position in which she sees the sun at the same angle as during her flight to the honey source. The waggling run makes the same angle with the sun as her outward flight did.

But the dance is normally performed in the dark inside the hive, on the *vertical* surface of the comb. Here the angle between the flight path and the sun is translated into the angle between the waggling run and the vertical direction straight upwards. Thus if the flight path was, say, 30° to the right of the sun's position, the waggling run will be 30° to the right of the vertical. This symbolism is remarkable enough, but the dancing bee's achievements go even further. If on the flight there is a sidewind, the bee corrects for the tendency to drift sideways by flying with her body at an oblique angle to the flight path. So the angle at which she sees the sun is not the same as the angle between the sun and flight path. Nevertheless, in the dance, she makes the necessary correction, and tells the other bees the true angle between sun and flight path. More remarkable still, if she has reached her goal (and returned from it) by an L-shaped detour, she uses the angles and lengths of the 2 segments of the flight to calculate the true direction of the goal by straight-line flight, and this is the direction she conveys in her dance, although she has never flown this direct route herself. One critic objected to the idea of a bee calculating, and proposed instead "a kind of 'mixture' of the neuronal learning effects during the segments." As Von Frisch observes, this is "a statement that simply clothes the phenomena in other words."

As for the bees who are following the dance, they are working literally in the dark and can only use touch to find out the angle of the dancer's waggling run with the vertical. They translate this back into a visual angle with the sun, fly off in this direction (allowing for any bending *they* have to do to oppose a sidewind) for the distance signalled by the waggling run tempo, and look for flowers of the scent they smelled on the dancer. Many experiments by Von Frisch and his colleagues show that they duly find the food.

On 14 August 1946, Von Frisch returned from a trip in the mountains to his field base. His daughters told him they had set up a new station with sugar-water for the bees in his experimental hive, but they would not tell him where it was. He must ask the bees! Von Frisch did ask the bees (by observing their dances), and he found the feeding station. On 22 September 1951, while doing some experiments, Von Frisch noticed lively dancing going on in a hive. He decoded the dances, entered the spot indicated on a map, and found it was a place (600 m. away) where a local dealer kept his bees. An assistant went over and found the dealer had just spun down honey from some combs, and then put them out in the sun for his own bees to gather back the remaining traces of honey. The assistant told the dealer Von Frisch's bees were stealing this honey and had told Von Frisch where it was. The dealer told the assistant he had to be joking, and never did believe this story, which, however, is perfectly true.

Even all this does not exhaust the symbolism of the honeybee dances. They can also vary in liveliness and total duration. They are livelier and longer the sweeter the food, the easier it is gathered, the better the weather. When honey is short in the hive, any returning bee will be eagerly badgered for honey drops, and this stimulates her to longer and livelier dances; when there is plenty of honey in the hive, the returning bee will have to search hard for customers, and this makes for shorter and less lively dances. If, of two food sources, one is richer, fewer customers are left for bees returning from the other, so even the relative attractions of different sources are represented. All this makes for flexibility and economy of labour and a readiness to exploit a variety of flowers as each ripens. The dances do not compel a reaction from every bee that the dancer meets; as Von Frisch nicely puts it, there is a most subtle regulation of "supply and demand on the flower market."

So far we have described the language of the Carniolan race of the honeybee. Other races have different dialects. German, North African, Caucasian, Italian and Egyptian honeybees[8] all begin to indicate distance and direction at much shorter distances than the Carniolan race. Italian honeybees, for instance, start indicating these data by a modified tail-wagging dance at about 10 m., as opposed to about 85 m. in the Carniolan bees. All the races indicate distance by dance tempo, but on different scales. Thus Italian honeybees dance slower than Carniolan ones for any distance of the food source. When a colony was made up of Italian and Carniolan bees, misunderstandings arose. When Italian bees danced, Carniolan ones flew too far; when Carniolan bees danced, Italian ones did not fly far enough. Each race was using their own scale to interpret the other's dances. Bees of different species, living in India and Ceylon, the Indian honeybee, dwarf honeybee and giant honeybee,[9] show similar but more extreme differences in tempo scales. The dwarf honeybee dances in the open on top of its comb, which is unprotected from the weather, and thus on a horizontal surface; unlike all the other honeybees, she cannot translate the angle with the sun into the angle with the vertical.

Wonderful as the bee language is in its precise and elaborate symbolism, there are many indications that it is really a matter of automatic signalling and not a true language after all. One experiment will perhaps make this clear. We have mentioned that the Italian bee uses a modified tail-wagging dance at 10 m. At smaller distances, this bee uses round dances in the usual way. On one occasion Von Frisch and his colleagues put a hive of these bees on the concrete foundation of a radio tower, and brought 10 bees a distance of 50 m. straight *up* the inside of the tower to a station with rich sugar water. The 10 bees flew down to the hive and danced "most vigorously" for 4 hours. But the honeybee languages contain no symbols for "up" or "down." All the dancers could do was to perform round dances (indicating that the food source was not far away *horizontally*). Consequently their colleagues all set out and scoured round the neighbourhood of the hive at ground level. Not one of them found her way up to the feeding station high up in the tower right over the hive. In Von Frisch's words, the dancers "sent

---

[8] *A. m. mellifera, intermissa, caucasica, ligustica* and *fasciata*, respectively.
[9] *A. indica, florea, dorsata*.

their hivemates astray—their ability to communicate broke down when faced with the unaccustomed task." Thus the bee language unlike human languages (such as the East African one we mentioned) cannot generate new combinations of symbols to describe a completely unusual event. We are bound to conclude it is not a true language. Studies of other insects suggest origins for both the round and the tail-wagging dances in automatic circling and wagging movements performed by flies and moths, respectively, without any communicative function. The moths even wag their bodies more the further they have just flown. Even the marvellous translation of sun angle into vertical angle can be seen to have developed from a widespread automatic tendency of insects to translate responses to light into responses to gravity in darkness. This arises from the simple fact that an insect can generally move upwards either by going towards the light or, of course, by going against gravity. What the honeybees have evolved from these elements is marvellous indeed, but it is not a true language.[10]

THE VOICE OF THE DOLPHIN

For our next candidates, we can choose animals much more like ourselves —individualistic mammals: the whales, dolphins and porpoises, notably dolphins and above all the best studied and so far the most remarkable species, the Atlantic bottlenose dolphin.[11] Dolphins are, so to speak, the monkeys of the sea: they have evolved many similar aspects of behaviour. Both groups of animals show prolonged and intense parental care for their young, and with this go very long-term relationships between mother and offspring. Amicable relations between 3 generations—grandmother, mother and daughter—have been seen among chimpanzees and in bottlenose dolphins. Male Japanese monkeys and bottlenose dolphins "baby-sit" for the females when these are otherwise occupied; on one occasion, a bottle-

[10] The honeybee signal code introduces us to yet another distinction. The signalling of distance by waggling run duration, and the signalling of angle of flight path with sun by angle of waggling run with vertical, are both examples of *continuous* signalling. Distance and direction vary continuously, and so do the signals for them. In human languages, signalling is normally done by separate or *discrete* signal *units,* such as phonemes, combined in various ways. As we have seen, many animal signal codes are also based on combinations of discrete units, and the whole science of animal behaviour study is based on the description and observation of such units of social behaviour. Signal units may be arbitrary or representational, as we have seen in the case of human words (*sun* and *hiss,* respectively). Continuous signals could in theory be arbitrary—for instance, bees could signal a flight angle of 40° by a dance angle of 10°, an angle of 60° by 11°, 80° by 9°, and so on. But, as Stuart A. Altmann has pointed out, in such a system any slight error in signalling would lead to serious mistakes, so continuous signalling must in practice be representational, as it is in honeybees, with a real formal relationship between signals and events.

[11] *Tursiops truncatus.*

fed baby dolphin, suffering from wind due to a badly composed formula, had his buoyancy relations upset and could not stay upright: he was cured in a rough but effective way by an adult male, who gave him a bang on the belly to empty out the wind. In both groups, mothers become so attached to their babies that they cannot be parted from them even after the baby has died of some illness. A rhesus monkey mother will carry a dead infant around till it is completely decomposed, and the same is observed in dolphin mothers, for instance one observed at sea "supporting the partially decomposed head of a dolphin young with its own head"; it "withdrew support only long enough to surface and breathe, then returned to its burden." Live dolphin infants are normally held at the surface after birth to enable them to take their first breath—for of course dolphins are mammals and need to surface regularly for air.

The prolonged parental care gives young dolphins, like young monkeys, the opportunity for a great deal of play and exploration. They make up a great variety of games. For instance, in captivity in a tank, one young dolphin will put an object over an intake jet and let it go, allowing the current of water to whirl it up towards the surface, where another youngster catches it, and immediately returns it to the jet while the first player goes up to catch it in his turn. Even as adults, dolphins, like monkeys, are highly exploratory animals.

The powerful parental urge is also extended, in both groups, to a care for the welfare and survival of other adults. In the wild, adult monkeys will remove thorns and clean wounds for each other, and a band of monkeys will rush into danger to rescue one of their number who has fallen down a well or been captured by human beings. In the open sea, adult dolphins and also many species of large whales will stand by a wounded comrade; 19th-century whalers knew this well, and would regularly wound a whale without killing it so that they could easily kill his comrades, who would not leave while he was alive; the procedure was risky, because sometimes the comrades managed to release the first victim or even attacked the whaleboats. Dolphins have extended to sick or injured adults the practice of holding the patient's head above water to let him breathe, just as they do with babies. When dynamite is exploded at sea near a school of dolphins, they will all leave the area at once. But on one occasion one dolphin was stunned by the explosion. Two comrades at once came and held the victim's head out of water; when they had to surface to breathe themselves, two others relieved them; the whole school stayed around till the stunned dolphin recovered completely, whereupon all left at once.

In captivity, under crowding stress, monkeys and dolphins can be as cruel as human beings under such pressures. Monkeys will cruelly wound and kill each other, including females and young. Dolphin adult males and females have been observed to bite juveniles and bash them against the tank wall, and one adult male bottlenose dolphin bit and bashed a small female so viciously, drawing much blood, that she had to be separated from him to save her life. But even in captivity, the care for others in distress can also be seen. J. C. Lilly found that sick dolphins often recover without treatment provided they are left with other dolphins, who support them at the surface. He found that dolphins will instantly help sick or stunned *strangers*, even of different species. On one memorable occasion, reported by D. H. Brown, a female Pacific Common Dolphin[12] was giving birth to a stillborn baby, whose fin stuck in the birth canal. Two females of *other* species acted as midwives. One of them[13] pulled out the foetus, and helped the mother to hold the stillborn baby at the surface (in vain, unfortunately). The other female[14] pulled out the afterbirth. On another occasion, Lilly reports that two bottlenose dolphins, male and female, supported a conscious adult female with a back injury at the surface for 48 hours till she recovered. They worked out 10 different methods of keeping her head out of water, the simplest being to hold her tail on the bottom in such a way that she was pushed upright. During this and similar occasions, Lilly has noted prolonged and complicated exchange of calls between the patient and his or her helpers, and it is hard to resist the suggestion that they may be exchanging requests and information in true language, or even discussing what to do.

The dolphin brain resembles the human brain in being very large and having its cerebral cortex (surface layer) very wrinkled, and in certain other respects.[15] But some say the cortex is so wrinkled only for mechanical reasons, because it is very thin, and that in fine structure of layering it is simpler and cruder, and has a lower density of nerve cells, than that of a rabbit. So if we seek for evidence from the dolphin brain about the dolphin's capabilities, we are back where we started. The behaviour observations, however, are so suggestive that in the past two decades people have been seriously studying the calls of the dolphins to find out whether they are a true language.

Dolphins are extremely vocal animals. As Gregory Bateson has put it, "adaptation to life in the ocean has stripped the whales of facial expression." Their heads and bodies are naked, rigid and streamlined, and anyway visibility under water is probably usually not good enough to recognize subtle facial expressions or bodily postures. So nearly all their signalling is by sound. It seems likely from records of their calls that they produce dis-

---

[12] *Delphinus bairdi.*

[13] *Lagenorhynchus* species.

[14] *Pseudorca* species.

[15] Nearly all of the dolphin cerebral cortex, like that of man, is made up of the most recently evolved kind of structures (neocortex); but this may be because the older structures are related to the sense of smell, which is much reduced in these sea animals. It is also said that large areas of the dolphin cortex, as of the human cortex, are not directly concerned with control of muscular activity.

crete vocal signal units in more elaborate sequences or combinations than any other animals, though this leaves open the question whether the rules of combination are emotional or truly logical, with grammar and syntax.

Dolphin calls are of three kinds. They produce sequences of clicks. These are probably used mainly for echolocation ("sound radar") but to some extent for signalling also—among sperm whales, where click sequences are the only calls, they are almost certainly used for signalling. The two other kinds of dolphin calls are pulsed sounds (such as squawks and mews) and whistles, and both these are certainly signals. The pulsed sounds are easily recognized as different-sounding unit calls. The analysis of the whistles can be done by exactly the methods used to analyze certain human languages.

A number of human languages, in North America, East Asia, and Africa south of the Sahara, are said to be *tonal*.[16] That is, much of the meaning of the words is carried by the relative *pitch* at which they are uttered. There are a varying number of pitch levels or *registers*, higher or lower. The voice goes up or down so that syllables are *relatively* higher or lower, and it is the difference or contrast and not the absolute pitch that matters; hence women and boys can talk on average at a higher pitch than men without misunderstandings. Tone may be so important that a language can be almost completely intelligible without hearing vowels and consonants at all. Hence many African tribes construct drums with the same number of registers (pitch levels) as their languages, and can transmit long conversations over long distances by drumming. The distinguishable units of tone languages are often *glides*, in which the voice goes up, down, up and down, down and up, starting and ending at different levels, changing pitch faster or slower, and so on. These units can be represented on paper as *contours*, in which a line goes up and down to represent rising and falling pitch; a contour in the shape of the letter V, for instance, would mean that the voice gets lower and then suddenly rises again in pitch by the same amount; and all other variations can be represented in this sort of way. A similar method was used for writing down music in Georgia in the 8th to 11th centuries A.D.

Some peoples speaking tonal languages have also evolved actual whistling languages which they use in addition. Whistling languages have been studied on Gomera Island in the Canaries, in the village of Aas in the French Pyrenees, and among the Mazatecos, Zapotecos and Tlapanecos of Mexico. Among the Mexican peoples, only the men whistle. It is considered bad form to raise the male voice, so the men began to communicate over the mountain trails by whistling. Women do not normally whistle, but they understand the language and can demonstrate it (with a certain embarrassment). G. M. Cowan heard a young man whistle to a girl for several minutes. It was far more detailed than a wolf whistle, and she understood

---

[16] See also Eugénie Henderson, Lecture 2, pp. 43–4. (ed.)

every word he whistled—finally she answered him back furiously in ordinary words. These whistling languages can also be represented as sets of contours.

John J. Dreher and René-Guy Busnel have tried to study dolphin whistling as if it were a human tonal or whistled language (respectively). The idea is to represent each different whistle unit by a contour, and then try to decipher whole sequences of contours as if one were deciphering sequences of hieroglyphs from some ancient script, or, for that matter, the Georgian medieval musical contour notation, which actually has been deciphered from Georgian musical documents preserved in the monasteries of Mount Athos and Mount Sinai. Such decoding methods depend on analyzing the frequency of different units and how they combine together. In addition, of course, since this is a living language, or at least a living signalling system, the occurrence of each different sound unit and each combination can be related first to what is happening to the signalling dolphin, and second to what other dolphins do in response. Both whistles and pulsed sounds have been studied in this way in Atlantic bottlenose dolphins, and Dreher has also played different whistle units back to dolphins and obtained different complicated responses in the form of actions and long sequences of calls. So far a number of units have been related to simple emotional situations, such as the distress call, a whistle of falling pitch, and the sex yelp of the male. But these are quite on a par with the simple automatic signal codes of many animals. Little progress has yet been made in deciphering long sequences of calls. J. C. Lilly, and later T. G. Lang and H. A. P. Smith, have recorded long exchanges of calls between pairs of dolphins who could not see each other. But many animals will exchange vocal signals, and there is no certain evidence that these are real conversations, though there is some indication that a dolphin can distinguish the naturally changing calls of another dolphin from repeated playback of a standard dolphin call recording.

It was against this background of uncertainty that Jarvis Bastian, in 1966, reported on a highly imaginative experiment. Two Atlantic bottlenose dolphins, a male and a female, were kept in a large tank and trained to work together in pressing paddles to be rewarded by an automat which disgorged fish when the proper paddles were pressed. At a certain stage in the complicated sequence of training procedures, the tank was divided by an opaque partition, with the male on one side and the female on the other. The arrangement was then as follows. Both the male and the female were warned by lamps being switched on that the game was ready to begin. Then another lamp was switched on to give *either* a continuous *or* a flashing light. In the former case, the right-hand paddle must be pressed, in the latter case the left-hand paddle. Now the female could see this signal lamp, but the male *could not see either the lamp or her*. Both dolphins got fish if, and only if, the *male first* pressed the correct paddle on his side of the tank, and *then the female* pressed the correct paddle on her side, there being a pair of paddles for each of them. So the male had to press the correct paddle without seeing the lamp that signalled which paddle to press.[17] On the face of it, he could only do this if *the female told him, by her calls, which paddle to press, when she saw whether the lamp was flashing or steady*. Nevertheless, over many thousands of runs, the male pressed the correct paddle and the dolphins succeeded in earning their reward on more than 90% of the tests. Analysis of the female's calls indicated that she made different pulsed sounds when her lamp was flashing and steady, responding sooner, longer and at faster pulse rate to the steady light; it is quite possible the male, hearing her, could tell the difference between the two kinds of call. The dolphins' success was only prevented if *either* the female was not rewarded with fish (as happened accidentally in two test series through a defect of her automat), *or* her signal light was hidden from her as well as from the male, *or* the barrier between male and female was made sound-proof. It seems certain from this amazing experiment that *in some sense* the female was telling the male whether the light was flashing or steady, so that he could press the correct paddle in response.

Was this true language? The dolphins were surely presented with a most unusual and novel situation and problem, and, unlike the honeybees, they solved it. Were they using a new combination of symbols to deal with this problem in communication? In 1966, the answer was uncertain. But alas! in 1969 Bastian published further findings. It now seemed all too clear that true language was not involved after all. Apparently the female went on giving her different calls in response to flashing and steady light when the barrier was taken down, the male could see the light himself, and the calls were quite superfluous. And she went on doing it after this even after the male had been taken out of the tank before her very eyes and she was "talking" all by herself. This and other detailed evidence made it extremely likely that the female had become conditioned to giving different calls in response to the different light signals, because this *worked* in getting her fish, without realizing that it worked by telling the male what to do; and that the male had become conditioned to pressing different paddles in response to the two different calls of the female, because this also *worked* for him, without realizing why she gave these calls. This is pretty remarkable in itself, and the male did make a very quick transfer from using visual clues (when he could only hear the female's calls); people have said in the past that this easy juggling between the senses was necessary for human language and not present in animals. But, after all, we cannot speak of true language where both signalling and reaction were conditioned and compulsive and not a

---

[17] Very elaborate control experiments ensured that the male could not be guided by noises from the lamps or even by echolocation to find which paddle the female was nearest to, for putting the paddles far apart or side by side made no difference to the results.

true communication between individuals. So the dolphins, so far, like the bees, cannot be said to have a true language. There have been other indications that these enigmatic animals may not be quite so bright as they sometimes appear. One female bottlenose dolphin had a 5-foot leopard shark[18] in a tank with her. She apparently mistook it for a baby dolphin, and held its head repeatedly above water. Dolphins breathe in air, but sharks are fishes and breathe in water, and within a day the wretched shark had suffocated and died. So far this could have been the intelligent use for killing a shark of a technique evolved for saving baby dolphins. But the dolphin really was making a mistake, it seems, for she carried the dead shark about for 8 days as if it were a dead infant, fed little as if in mourning, and would not let divers take the carcass away till it was decomposed. It seems inescapable that this particular dolphin was not very bright, unless she was as short-sighted as Mr. McGoo.[19]

THE MONKEY'S PAW

After honeybees and dolphins, it is natural to turn back to what have always seemed the most hopeful candidates for true animal language, the monkeys and apes (for convenience, we refer to both as *monkeys*). Though, as we have seen, monkeys have much in common with dolphins, they differ from them strikingly in at least one respect. They have agile bodies and mobile faces. Most species have considerable repertoires of calls, and some species living in dense forest rely heavily on these. But many species live partly on the ground and/or in relatively open country, where visibility is good; and these include the species we know most about. Among these monkeys, visual signals, made by gesture, posture and facial expression, are far more important than vocal signals made by calls. Thus in the rhesus monkey[20] colony studied by Vernon Reynolds at Whipsnade Zoo, 73 signal units could be distinguished. Of these 63 were visual signals, and only 10 were calls. In another rhesus community, Stuart A. Altmann recorded a total of 5504 signalling events. Only 5.1% of these social signals involved

---

[18] *Triakis semifasciatum.*

[19] But before dismissing dolphin capabilities altogether, we must make one reservation. As Dreher and Evans have pointed out, not all the work being done on dolphins is being published: much of it is enveloped in military secrecy. Already in 1963, L. Harrison Matthews, then Director of the London Zoo, remarked that "some people are proposing to prostitute their biological work on the Cetacea and involve the animals in human international strife by training them as underwater watch-dogs to guard naval installations from frogmen, or to act as unmanned submarines. Intelligent as the animals may be, they are, unfortunately, not sufficiently intelligent to refuse cooperation and treat their trainers to some of those characteristic underwater noises which, if produced in the air, would be regarded as gestures of contempt."

[20] *Macaca mulatta.*

calls (with or without accompanying gestures), and only 3% consisted of calls alone. Comparable counts have not been made for chimpanzees, among whom the richness and sensitivity of facial expression are considerably greater than among rhesus monkeys.

Unlike the honeybee code, which concerns itself entirely with information about economics—whereabouts of food, weather conditions, state of the hive's food reserves, and so on—monkey signalling is mainly concerned with emotional states and events and interpersonal relationships. Thus 36 vocal units have been distinguished in vervet monkeys[21] by Thomas T. Struhsaker, working in the Amboseli Reserve of Kenya. Only 7 of these refer to events in the natural surroundings (sighting, approach or sudden movement of various kinds of predatory animals); 3 are not really signals (coughing, sneezing, vomiting); the other 26 all refer to different social situations (such as a subordinate monkey appeasing a dominant one nearby, a female protesting she is not in the mood for sex, or several monkeys warning of the approach of a "foreign" group of the same species).

In Struhsaker's study of the vervet monkeys, he found that the calls occurred in at least 21 different situations, and produced at least 22 different responses in the monkeys who heard them. As with the dolphins, studies of the situations evoking different signals and their effects on other individuals have been made in many monkey species, in this case for visual as well as vocal signals. One result of great interest has been the finding that different communities of the *same species* may have different signal codes. This is a special case of the fact that different communities of the same monkey species differ in many aspects of their behaviour, including diet, way of getting food, and even mating taboos. Thus among Japanese monkeys[22] one community scratches up edible roots, another invades rice-fields, others do neither. It appears that young monkeys acquire the customs of their band by imitation and because some of their actions are encouraged, others discouraged, by mothers and leaders. Occasionally a new habit is adopted by a young monkey and accepted by his or her mother, and gradually spreads through the kinship group in the mother's line, and eventually to the whole band (except some of the older monkeys who, like old dogs, will not learn new tricks), being afterwards transmitted to subsequent generations. This has happened, for instance, in a band on Kōshima Island, with the practices of washing sweet potatoes before eating them and separating wheat grains (supplied by human observers) from the sand on which they have fallen by washing out a handful of grain and sand in water. In this way each band has its own *culture*, and this includes its own signal units.[23]

[21] *Cercopithecus aethiops.*
[22] *Macaca fuscata.*
[23] "Symbols are derived out of experience and history–i.e. out of institutions". Colin Cherry, Lecture 13, p. 284. (ed.)

The Kōshima monkeys have acquired a completely new gesture for asking for food. A rhesus monkey community in Regent's Park Zoo used regularly to smack their lips as a friendly gesture and to execute a kind of press-up by bending and stretching their arms as a form of threat; neither gesture was ever seen in the rhesus community at Whipsnade.

Monkey signal codes have been much more studied than those of dolphins, and we know enough about them to be quite sure that they are simply automatic codes of signals which, as we saw earlier, are combined only according to emotional and not according to logical rules. Monkeys certainly have not evolved true languages. But so many combinations are at least possible, and monkey behaviour is so variable and exploratory, that several scientists have tried seriously to teach a *human* language to chimpanzees, the most variable and exploratory of them all. It has long been known that chimpanzees can respond separately to as many as 60 different human words. But then even a seal can do so to 35 words, and an elephant to 20. The real test is whether chimpanzees can be taught to use human words themselves, and to combine them, in appropriate ways. A very intensive attempt to teach a chimpanzee to talk was made some years ago by a married couple, both scientists, K. J. and Cathy Hayes. They adopted a baby chimp called Viki, and brought her up in their house exactly as if she were a human child, but using in addition the most sophisticated methods of teaching available. The result was disappointing. After 6 years of great effort and ingenuity, Viki had learned to utter only 4 sounds resembling English words. From this and other studies, it looked as if chimpanzees cannot be taught a human language.

So matters stood until June 1966, when another scientist couple, R. A. and Beatrice T. Gardner, began work at the University of Nevada with a female chimpanzee between 8 and 14 months old, whom they named Washoe after the county where the University is situated. Benefiting from the Hayes' experience, the Gardners had had an imaginative new idea. We have seen that most monkeys rely more on visual than on vocal signals. Even the actual vocal apparatus of chimpanzees is very different from man's. So instead of trying to teach *spoken* English, the Gardners decided to teach Washoe American Sign Language, as used by the deaf in North America, in which English words or concepts are represented by signs made with the hands; some of these symbols are representational, others are arbitrary, and all can be combined according to principles of English grammar and syntax. The Gardners and their colleagues brought up Washoe in shifts so that she never lacked for affectionate human company. They played all sorts of games with her and seem to have given her a very good time. All the time they were chattering among themselves in Sign Language, for it is known that simply being exposed to adults talking helps human children to learn to talk. They encouraged Washoe to imitate them, prompted her to get a sign right by repeating it themselves or by placing her hands in the right position, introduced plenty of toys and other objects to increase her vocabulary, encouraged her to "babble" with her hands, as a child does with his voice, and rewarded her for correct usage by tickling her, which she greatly enjoyed.

The results of all this were as follows. After 22 months of teaching, Washoe could use 34 words correctly in the appropriate circumstances. (She was only counted as knowing a word if three observers independently saw her use it correctly and without prompting). Whenever Washoe learned a new word, she very soon and quite spontaneously transferred it from a particular object, such as the key of a cupboard, to a whole class of objects, such as all keys. She would spontaneously call the humans' attention to objects by making the correct signs. She used the sign for "dog" when she saw a picture of a dog or even heard a dog bark without seeing it; evidently, like the dolphins, she had the capacity, previously supposed to be unique to man, of transposing patterns from one sense to another.

All this is remarkable, but Washoe did more. Without any prompting and apparently quite spontaneously, as soon as she had about 10 signs in her repertoire, Washoe began to *invent combinations* of signs and use them in a perfectly appropriate way. Among combinations which she invented are:— *open food drink*, for opening the refrigerator; *go sweet*, for being carried to a raspberry bush; *open flower*, to be let through the gate to a flower garden; and *listen eat,* at the sound of an alarm clock signalling meal-time. Just before the Gardners published their first results (in August 1969), Washoe had learned the pronouns *I-me* and *you,* "so that combinations that resemble short sentences have begun to appear." It only remains to add that Washoe's learning was accelerating—she had learned 4 signs in the first 7 months, 9 in the next, and 21 in the last 7 months.

Since Washoe unmistakably combines and recombines signs to describe objects and situations new to her in perfectly appropriate ways, this wonderful experiment seems to have established beyond doubt that a chimpanzee is capable of learning true language. True, at 3 years of age, she only has 34 words; at the equivalent age in terms of development, namely 5 years old, the average human child has a vocabulary of hundreds of words and makes sentences averaging 4.6 words in length. Sheer numerical differences of this kind may be important for the potentialities of human language. But the Gardeners' achievement remains epoch-making. An animal has been taught to use true language, to communicate with human teachers. . . .

Editors' note: Chimpanzees at the University of Oklahoma who have been taught sign language by humans are now using it to communicate among themselves. There is also evidence that they can invent signs of their own. See *Newsweek,* October 1, 1973, p. 69.

SUGGESTED ASSIGNMENTS

1. Most people with pets develop a limited system of communication with their animals that works quite well for simple purposes. They know that their pets understand them because they respond to certain signals of voice, gesture, and other actions. The animals too make signals that their owners understand. Based on your own experience, write a theme in which you describe the communication system you have had with an animal. Would you call this a signalling system or a language? Explain.
2. Interview the trainer in an obedience school for dogs and report orally to the class on the teaching methods and the signals used. A person who has attended a class on obedience training might also be a useful subject for interview.
3. To establish a friendly relation with a strange dog or cat involves attempts at communication. Describe one such encounter you have had, with your successes and failures.

FURTHER READINGS

1. Babies

Irwin, O. C. *Infant Speech: Scientific American Reprint* 417. San Francisco, 1949.

Wasz-Höckert, O. J. Lind, V. Vuorenkoski, T. Partanen, and E. Vallené. *The Infant Cry*. London, 1968, with 45rpm. record.

2. Bees

Von Frisch, K. *The Dance Language and Orientation of Bees*. Translated by L. E. Chadwick. London, 1967.

3. Whales, Dolphins and Porpoises

Andersen, H. T. (Ed.). *The Biology of Marine Mammals*. New York and London, 1969.

Busnel, R. H. G. (Ed.). *Animal Sonar Systems: Biology and Bionics*, Vol. 2. Jouyen-Josas, France, 1966.

Norris, K. S. (Ed.). *Whales, Dolphins and Porpoises*. Berkeley and Los Angeles, 1966.

Tavolga, W. N. (Ed.). *Marine Bio-Acoustics*. Oxford, London and New York, 1964.

4. Monkeys and Apes

Altmann, S. A. (Ed.). *Social Communication among Primates*. Chicago and London, 1965.

Devore, I. (Ed.). *Primate Behavior*. New York and London, 1965.

Gardner, R. A., and B. T. Gardner. "Teaching Sign Language to a Chimpanzee," *Science* 165, pp. 664–72. 15th August, 1969.

Morris, D. *The Naked Ape*. London, 1967.

Moynihan, M. *Some Behavior Patterns of Platyrrhine Monkeys. 1. The Night Monkey* (Aotus trivirgatus). Washington, 1964.

Russell, C., and W. M. S. Russell. *Violence, Monkeys and Man.* London, 1968.

Southwick, C. J. (Ed.). *Primate Social Behaviour.* Princeton and London, 1963.

5. Language and Animal Signals: General

Cornwall, I. V. *The World of Ancient Man.* London, 1964.

Count, E. W. "An Essay of Phasia: on the Phylogenesis of Man's Speech Function," *Homo* 19, pp. 170–227. 1969.

Gerard, R. W., C. Kluckhohn, and A. Rapoport. "Biological and Cultural Evolution: Some Analogies and Explorations," *Behavioral Science I*, pp. 6–34. 1956.

Hastings, H. (Ed.). *Abbé Bougeant: Amusement Philosophique sur le Language des Bêtes.* Geneva and Lille, 1954.

Heinzelin, J. de. "Ishango," *Scientific American Reprint* 613. San Francisco, 1962.

Hockett, C. D. "The Origin of Speech," *Scientific American Reprint* 603. San Francisco, 1960.

Kalmus, H. "Ethnic Differences in Sensory Perception," *Journal of Biosocial Science* Supplement I, pp. 81–90. 1969.

Lenneberg, E. H. *Biological Foundations of Language.* New York and London. 1967.

Métraux, G. S., and F. Crouzet. *The Evolution of Science.* London, 1963.

Oakley, K. "Fire as Palaeolithic Tool and Weapon," *Proceeding of the Prehistoric Society* 21, pp. 36–48. 1955.

Pike, K. L. *Tone Languages.* Ann Arbor, 1948.

Pumphrey, R. J. *The Origin of Language.* Liverpool, 1951.

Russell, C. *Forbidden Fruit.* Stockholm, in press.

Russell, C., and W. M. S. Russell. *Human Behaviour: a New Approach.* London, 1961.

Russell, W. M. S. "Animals, Robots and Man; Signals and Shibboleths," *The Listener* 68, pp. 169–70, 207–8, 213. 2nd and 9th August, 1962.

Russell, W. M. S. *Man, Nature and History.* London, 1967.

Smith, F., and G. A. Miller, (Ed.). *The Genesis of Language.* Cambridge, Mass., and London, 1966.

Thompson, S. *Motif-Index of Fold-Literature,* Vol. 1. Helsinki, 1932.

Tinbergen, N. *The Herring Gull's World.* London, 1953.

Tinbergen, N. *Social Behavior in Animals.* London, 1953.

Woolley, Sir Leonard. *The Beginnings of Civilization.* London, 1963.

EDITORS' ADDITIONAL READINGS

These two readings are short, clear, informative, and entertaining.

Brown, Roger. *Words and Things.* New York: Free Press, 1958. On animal "languages," see pages 155–172.

Lorenz, Konrad Z. *King Solomon's Ring.* New York: Thomas Y. Crowell, 1952. See Chapter 8, "The Language of Animals."

15
STRUCTURAL
AND TRANSFORMATIONAL
GRAMMAR

Revolution
in Grammar

W. Nelson Francis

For two centuries we have been using in English a grammar based on Latin, constructed by British grammarians of the eighteenth century. This grammar is entrenched in our dictionaries and is widely taught in the schools. It is serviceable in certain ways; for example, it gives us a technical vocabulary with which to discuss problems of writing and speaking, and it enables us to analyze English sentences in a rough-and-ready way. But with the advance of linguistic science in recent decades, the structural grammarians find this Latinized grammar too crude an instrument for the thorough linguistic analyses they wish to make. Beginning with new premises, they have been forging new grammars that are highly refined and that enable us to see with greater clarity the marvelously complex structure of our language. W. Nelson Francis discusses these two types of grammars, the Latinized and the scientific, in the important article below. Professor Francis, of Brown University, is the author of *The Structure of American English*, a college textbook that offers an excellent insight into the structural point of view toward grammar.

From *Quarterly Journal of Speech* (October 1954). Reprinted by permission of the Speech Association of America.

I

A long overdue revolution is at present taking place in the study of English grammar—a revolution as sweeping in its consequences as the Darwinian revolution in biology. It is the result of the application to English of methods of descriptive analysis originally developed for use with languages of primitive people. To anyone at all interested in language, it is challenging; to those concerned with the teaching of English (including parents), it presents the necessity of radically revising both the substance and the methods of their teaching.

A curious paradox exists in regard to grammar. On the one hand it is felt to be the dullest and driest of academic subjects, fit only for those in whose veins the red blood of life has long since turned to ink. On the other, it is a subject upon which people who would scorn to be professional grammarians hold very dogmatic opinions, which they will defend with considerable emotion. Much of this prejudice stems from the usual sources of prejudice— ignorance and confusion. Even highly educated people seldom have a clear idea of what grammarians do, and there is an unfortunate confusion about the meaning of the term "grammar" itself.

Hence it would be well to begin with definitions. What do people mean when they use the word "grammar"? Actually the word is used to refer to three different things, and much of the emotional thinking about matters grammatical arises from confusion among these different meanings.

The first thing we mean by "grammar" is "the set of formal patterns in which the words of a language are arranged in order to convey larger meanings." It is not necessary that we be able to discuss these patterns self-consciously in order to be able to use them. In fact, all speakers of a language above the age of five or six know how to use its complex forms of organization with considerable skill; in this sense of the word—call it "Grammar 1" —they are thoroughly familiar with its grammar.

The second meaning of "grammar"—call it "Grammar 2"—is "the branch of linguistic science which is concerned with the description, analysis, and formulization of formal language patterns." Just as gravity was in full operation before Newton's apple fell, so grammar in the first sense was in full operation before anyone formulated the first rule that began the history of grammar as a study.

The third sense in which people use the word "grammar" is "linguistic etiquette." This we may call "Grammar 3." The word in this sense is often coupled with a derogatory adjective: we say that the expression "he ain't here" is "bad grammar." What we mean is that such an expression is bad linguistic manners in certain circles. From the point of view of "Grammar 1" it is faultless; it conforms just as completely to the structural patterns of English as does "he isn't here." The trouble with it is like the trouble with Prince Hal is Shakespeare's play—it is "bad," not in itself, but in the company it keeps.

As has already been suggested, much confusion arises from mixing these meanings. One hears a good deal of criticism of teachers of English couched in such terms as "they don't teach grammar any more." Criticism of this sort is based on the wholly unproved assumption that teaching Grammar 2 will increase the student's proficiency in Grammar 1 or improve his manners in Grammar 3. Actually, the form of Grammar 2 which is usually taught is a very inaccurate and misleading analysis of the facts of Grammar 1; and it therefore is of highly questionable value in improving a person's ability to handle the structural patterns of his language. It is hardly reasonable to expect that teaching a person some inaccurate grammatical analysis will either improve effectiveness of his assertions or teach him what expressions are acceptable to use in a given social context.

These, then are the three meanings of "grammar": Grammar 1, a form of behavior; Grammar 2, a field of study, a science; and Grammar 3, a branch of etiquette.

II

Grammarians have arrived at some basic principles of their science, three of which are fundamental to this discussion. The first is that a language constitutes a set of behavior patterns common to the members of a given community. It is a part of what the anthropologists call the culture of the community. Actually it has complex and intimate relationships with other phases of culture such as myth and ritual. But for purposes of study it may be dealt with as a separate set of phenomena that can be objectively described and analyzed like any other universe of facts. Specifically, its phenomena can be observed, recorded, classified, and compared; and general laws of their behavior can be made by the same inductive process that is used to produce the "laws" of physics, chemistry, and the other sciences.

A second important principle of linguistic science is that each language or dialect has its own unique system of behavior patterns. Parts of this system may show similarities to parts of the systems of other languages, particularly if those languages are genetically related. But different languages solve the problems of expression and communication in different ways, just as the problems of movement through water are solved in different ways by lobsters, fish, seals, and penguins. A couple of corollaries of this principle are important. The first is that there is no such thing as "universal grammar," or at least if there is, it is so general and abstract as to be of little use. The second corollary is that the grammar of each language must be made up on the basis of a study of that particular language—a study that is free from preconceived notions of what a language should contain and how it should operate. The marine biologist does not criticize the octopus for using jet-propulsion to get him through the water instead of the methods of a self-respecting fish. Neither does the linguistic scientist express alarm or distress when he finds a language that seems to get along quite well without any words that correspond to what in English we call verbs.

A third principle on which linguistic science is based is that the analysis and description of a given language must conform to the requirements laid down for any satisfactory scientific theory. These are (1) simplicity, (2) consistency, (3) completeness, and (4) usefulness for predicting the behavior of phenomena not brought under immediate observation when the theory was formed. Linguistic scientists who have recently turned their attention to English have found that, judged by these criteria, the traditional grammar of English is unsatisfactory. It falls down badly on the first two requirements, being unduly complex and glaringly inconsistent within itself. It can be made to work, just as the Ptolemaic earth-centered astronomy can be, but at the cost of great elaboration and complication. The new grammar, like the Copernican sun-centered astronomy, solves the same problems with greater elegance, which is the scientist's word for the simplicity, compactness, and tidiness that characterize a satisfactory theory.

III

A brief look at the history of the traditional grammar of English will make apparent the reasons for its inadequacy. The study of English grammar is actually an outgrowth of the linguistic interest of the Renaissance. It was during the latter Middle Ages and early Renaissance that the various vernacular languages of Europe came into their own. They began to be used for many kinds of writing which had previously always been done in Latin. As the vernaculars, in the hands of great writers like Dante and Chaucer, came of age as members of the linguistic family, a concomitant interest in their grammars arose. The earliest important English grammar was written by Shakespeare's contemporary, Ben Jonson.

It is important to observe that not only Ben Jonson himself but also those who followed him in the study of English grammar were men deeply learned in Latin and sometimes in Greek. For all their interest in English, they were conditioned from earliest school days to conceive of the classical languages as superior to the vernaculars. We still sometimes call the elementary school the "grammar school"; historically the term means the school where Latin grammar was taught. By the time the Renaissance or eighteenth-century scholar took his university degree, he was accustomed to use Latin as the normal means of communication with his fellow scholars. Dr. Samuel Johnson, for instance, who had only three years at the university and did not take a degree, wrote poetry in both Latin and Greek. Hence it was natural for these men to take Latin grammar as the norm and to analyze English in terms of Latin. The grammarians of the seventeenth and eighteenth centuries who formulated the traditional grammar of English looked for the devices and distinctions of Latin grammar in English, and where they did not actually find them they imagined or created them. Of course, since English is a member of the Indo-European family of languages, to which Latin and Greek also belong, it did have many grammatical elements in common with them. But many of these had been obscured or wholly lost as a result of the extensive changes that had taken place in English—changes that the early grammarians inevitably conceived of as degeneration. They felt that it was their function to resist further change, if not to repair the damage already done. So preoccupied were they with the grammar of Latin as the ideal that they overlooked in large part the exceedingly complex and delicate system that English had substituted for the Indo-European grammar it had abandoned. Instead they stretched unhappy English on the Procrustean bed of Latin. It is no wonder that we commonly hear people say, "I didn't really understand grammar until I began to study Latin." This is eloquent testimony to the fact that the grammar "rules" of our present-day textbooks are largely an inheritance from the Latin-based grammar of the eighteenth century.

Meanwhile the extension of linguistic study beyond the Indo-European and Semitic families began to reveal that there are many different ways in which linguistic phenomena are organized—in other words, many different kinds of grammar. The tone-languages of the Orient and of North America, and the complex agglutinative languages of Africa, among others, forced grammarians to abandon the idea of a universal or ideal grammar and to direct their attention more closely to the individual systems employed by the multifarious languages of mankind. With the growth and refinement of the scientific method and its application to the field of anthropology, language came under more rigorous scientific scrutiny. As with anthropology in general, linguistic science at first concerned itself with the primitive. Finally, again following the lead of anthropology, linguistics began to apply its techniques to the old familiar tongues, among them English. Accelerated by the practical need during World War II of teaching languages, including English, to large numbers in a short time, research into the nature of English grammar has moved rapidly in the last fifteen years. The definitive grammar of English is yet to be written, but the results so far achieved are spectacular. It is now as unrealistic to teach "traditional" grammar of English as it is to teach "traditional" (i.e. pre-Darwinian) biology or "traditional" (i.e. four-element) chemistry. Yet nearly all certified teachers of English on all levels are doing so. Here is a cultural lag of major proportions.

IV

Before we can proceed to a sketch of what the new grammar of English looks like, we must take account of a few more of the premises of linguistic science. They must be understood and accepted by anyone who wishes to understand the new grammar.

First, the spoken language is primary, at least for the original study of a language. In many of the primitive languages,[1] of course, where writing is unknown, the spoken language is the *only* form. This is in many ways an advantage to the linguist, because the written language may use conventions that obscure its basic structure. The reason for the primary importance of the spoken language is that language originates as speech, and most of the changes and innovations that occur in the history of a given language begin in the spoken tongue.

Secondly, we must take account of the concept of dialect. I suppose most laymen would define a dialect as "a corrupt form of a language spoken in a given region by people who don't know any better." This introduces moral judgments which are repulsive to the linguistic scholar. Let us approach the definition of a dialect from the more objective end, through the notion of a speech community. A speech community is merely a group of people who are in pretty constant intercommunication. There are various types of speech communities: local ones, like "the people who live in Tidewater Virginia"; class ones, like "the white-collar class"; occupational ones, like "doctors, nurses, and other people who work in hospitals"; social ones, like "club-women." In a sense, each of these has its own dialect. Each family may be said to have its own dialect; in fact, in so far as each of us has his own vocabulary and particular quirks of speech, each individual has his own dialect. Also, of course, in so far as he is a member of many speech communities, each individual is more or less master of many dialects and shifts easily and almost unconsciously from one to another as he shifts from one social environment to another.

In the light of this concept of dialects, a language can be defined as a group of dialects which have enough of their sound-system, vocabulary and grammar (Grammar 1, this is) in common to permit their speakers to be mutually intelligible in the ordinary affairs of life. It usually happens that one of the many dialects that make up a language comes to have more prestige than the others; in modern times it has usually been the dialect of the middle class residents of the capital, like Parisian French and London English, which is so distinguished. This comes to be thought of as the standard dialect; in fact, its speakers become snobbish and succeed in establishing the belief that it is not a dialect at all, but the only proper form of the language. This causes the speakers of other dialects to become self-conscious and ashamed of their speech, or else aggressive and jingoistic about it—either of which is an acknowledgment of their feelings of inferiority. Thus one of the duties of the educational system comes to be that of teaching the standard dialect to all so as to relieve them of feelings of inferiority, and thus relieve society of lin-

---

[1] "Primitive languages" here is really an abbreviated statement for "languages used by peoples of relatively primitive culture"; it is not to be taken as implying anything simple or rudimentary about the languages themselves. Many languages included under the term, such as native languages of Africa and Mexico, exhibit grammatical complexities unknown to more "civilized" languages.

guistic neurotics. This is where Grammar 3, linguistic etiquette, comes into the picture.

A third premise arising from the two just discussed is that the difference between the way educated people talk and the way they write is a dialectal difference. The spread between these two dialects may be very narrow, as in present-day America, or very wide, as in Norway, where people often speak local Norwegian dialects but write in the Dano-Norwegian *Riksmaal*. The extreme is the use by writers of an entirely different language, or at least an ancient and no longer spoken form of the language—like Sanskrit in northern India or Latin in western Europe during the Middle Ages. A corollary of this premise is that anyone setting out to write a grammar must know and make clear whether he is dealing with the spoken or the written dialect. Virtually all current English grammars deal with the written language only; evidence for this is that their rules for the plurals of nouns, for instance, are really spelling rules, which say nothing about pronunciation.

This is not the place to go into any sort of detail about the methods of analysis the linguistic scientist uses. Suffice it to say that he begins by breaking up the flow of speech into minimum sound-units, or phones, which he then groups into families called phonemes, the minimum significant sound-units.[2] Most languages have from twenty to sixty of these. American English has forty-one: nine vowels,[3] twenty-four consonants, four degrees of stress, and four levels of pitch. These phonemes group themselves into minimum meaningful units, called morphemes. These fall into two groups: free morphemes, those that can enter freely into many combinations with other free morphemes to make phrases and sentences; and bound morphemes, which are always found tied in a close and often indissoluble relationship with other bound or free morphemes. An example of a free morpheme is "dog"; an example of a bound morpheme is "un-" or "ex-." The linguist usually avoids talking about "words" because the term is very inexact. Is "instead of," for instance, to be considered one, two, or three words? This is purely a matter of opinion; but it is a matter of fact that it is made up of three morphemes.

In any case, our analysis has now brought the linguist to the point where he has some notion of the word-stock (he would call it the "lexicon") of his language. He must then go into the question of how the morphemes are grouped into meaningful utterances, which is the field of grammar proper. At this point in the analysis of English, as of many other languages, it becomes apparent that there are three bases upon which classification and analysis may

---

[2] For example, /l/ is a phoneme because it is significant, that is, because it can be used to signify differences in meaning. It is the /l/, for instance, that distinguishes *light* from such words as *night, might, sight, tight, right, bite, height*. But there is more than one *l* sound: the last sound in *well* differs from the *l* in *light* in that it is preceded by an *uh* sound. However, the difference between these two *l*'s does not distinguish meaning. Thus these two *l*'s are not two different phonemes but simply two members of the family known as the /l/ phoneme. [eds.]

[3] According to the Trager-Smith system. [eds.]

be built: form, function, and meaning. For illustration let us take the word "boys" in the utterance "the boys are here." From the point of view of form, "boys" is a noun with the plural ending "s" (pronounced like "z"), preceded by the noun-determiner "the," and tied by concord to the verb "are," which it precedes. From the point of view of function, "boys" is the subject of the verb "are" and of the sentence. From the point of view of meaning, "boys" points out or names more than one of the male young of the human species, about whom an assertion is being made.

Of these three bases of classification, the one most amenable to objective description and analysis of a rigorously scientific sort is form. In fact, many conclusions about form can be drawn by a person unable to understand or speak the language. Next comes function. But except as it is revealed by form, function is dependent on knowing the meaning. In a telegraphic sentence like "ship sails today" [4] no one can say whether "ship" is the subject of "sails" or an imperative verb with "sails" as its object until he knows what the sentence means. Most shaky of all bases for grammatical analysis is meaning. Attempts have been made to reduce the phenomena of meaning to objective description, but so far they have not succeeded very well. Meaning is such a subjective quality that it is usually omitted entirely from scientific description. The botanist can describe the forms of plants and the functions of their various parts, but he refuses to concern himself with their meaning. It is left to the poet to find symbolic meaning in roses, violets, and lilies.

At this point it is interesting to note that the traditional grammar of English bases some of its key concepts and definitions on this very subjective and shaky foundation of meaning. A recent English grammar defines a sentence as "a group of words which expresses a complete thought through the use of a verb, called its predicate, and a subject, consisting of a noun or pronoun about which the verb has something to say." [5] But what is a complete thought? Actually we do not identify sentences this way at all. If someone says, "I don't know what to do," dropping his voice at the end, and pauses, the hearer will know that it is quite safe for him to make a comment without running the risk of interrupting an unfinished sentence. But if the speaker says the same words and maintains a level pitch at the end, the polite listener will wait for him to finish his sentence. The words are the same, the meaning is the same; the only difference is a slight one in the pitch of the final syllable—a purely formal distinction, which signals that the first utterance is complete, a sentence, while the second is incomplete. In writing we would translate these signals into punctuation: a period or exclamation point at the end of the first, a comma or dash at the end of the second. It is the form of the utterance, not the completeness of the thought, that tells us whether it is a whole sentence or only part of one.

---

[4] This example is taken from C. C. Fries. *The Structure of English* (New York, 1952), p. 62. This important book will be discussed below.
[5] Ralph B. Allen, *English Grammar* (New York, 1950), p. 187.

Another favorite definition of the traditional grammar, also based on meaning, is that of "noun" as "the name of a person, place, or thing"; or, as the grammar just quoted has it, "the name of anybody or anything, with or without life, and with or without substance or form." [6] Yet we identify nouns, not by asking if they name something, but by their positions in expressions and by the formal marks they carry. In the sentence. "The slithy toves did gyre and gimble in the wabe," any speaker of English knows that "toves" and "wabe" are nouns, though he cannot tell what they name, if indeed they name anything. How does he know? Actually because they have certain formal marks, like their position in relation to "the" as well as the whole arrangement of the sentence. We know from our practical knowledge of English grammar (Grammar 1), which we have had since before we went to school, that if we were to put meaningful words into this sentence, we would have to put nouns in place of "toves" and "wabe," giving something like "The slithy snakes did gyre and gimble in the wood." The pattern of the sentence simply will not allow us to say "The slithy arounds did gyre and gimble in the wooden."

One trouble with the traditional grammar, then, is that it relies heavily on the most subjective element in language, meaning. Another is that it shifts the ground of its classification and produces the elementary logical error of cross-division. A zoologist who divided animals into invertebrates, mammals, and beasts of burden would not get very far before running into trouble. Yet the traditional grammar is guilty of the same error when it defines three parts of speech on the basis of meaning (noun, verb, and interjection), four more on the basis of function (adjective, adverb, pronoun, conjunction), and one partly on function and partly on form (preposition). The result is that in such an expression as "a dog's life" there can be endless futile arguments about whether "dog's" is a noun or an adjective. It is, of course, a noun from the point of view of form and an adjective from the point of view of function, and hence falls into both classes, just as a horse is both a mammal and a beast of burden. No wonder students are bewildered in their attempts to master the traditional grammar. Their natural clearness of mind tells them that it is crazy patchwork violating the elementary principles of logical thought.

V

If the traditional grammar is so bad, what does the new grammar offer in its place?

It offers a description, analysis, and set of definitions and formulas—rules, if you will—based firmly and consistently on the easiest, or at least the most

---

[6] *Ibid.*, p. 1.

objective, aspect of language, form. Experts can quibble over whether "dog's" in "a dog's life" is a noun or an adjective, but anyone can see that it is spelled with " 's" and hear that it ends with a "z" sound; likewise anyone can tell that it comes in the middle between "a" and "life." Furthermore he can tell that something important has happened if the expression is changed to "the dog's alive," "the live dogs," or "the dogs lived," even if he doesn't know what the words mean and has never heard of such functions as modifier, subject, or attributive genitive. He cannot, of course, get very far into his analysis without either a knowledge of the language or access to someone with such knowledge. He will also need a minimum technical vocabulary describing grammatical functions. Just so the anatomist is better off for knowing physiology. But the grammarian, like the anatomist, must beware of allowing his preconceived notions to lead him into the error of interpreting before he describes—an error which often results in his finding only what he is looking for.

When the grammarian looks at English objectively, he finds that it conveys its meanings by two broad devices: the denotations and connotations of words separately considered, which the linguist calls "lexical meaning," and the significance of word-forms, word-groups, and arrangements apart from the lexical meanings of the words, which the linguist calls "structural meaning." The first of these is the domain of the lexicographer and the semanticist, and hence is not our present concern. The second, the structural meaning, is the business of the structural linguist, or grammarian. The importance of this second kind of meaning must be emphasized because it is often overlooked. The man in the street tends to think of the meaning of a sentence as being the aggregate of the dictionary meanings of the words that make it up; hence the widespread fallacy of literal translation—the feeling that if you take a French sentence and a French-English dictionary and write down the English equivalent of each French word you will come out with an intelligible English sentence. How ludicrous the result can be, anyone knows who is familiar with Mark Twain's retranslation from the French of his jumping frog story. One sentence reads, "Eh bien! I no saw not that that frog has nothing of better than each frog." Upon which Mark's comment is, "if that isn't grammar gone to seed, then I count myself no judge." [7]

The second point brought out by a formal analysis of English is that it uses four principal devices of form to signal structural meanings:

1. Word order—the sequence in which words and word-groups are arranged.
2. Function-words—words devoid of lexical meaning which indicate relationships among the meaningful words with which they appear.

---

[7] Mark Twain, "The Jumping Frog; the Original Story in English; the Retranslation Clawed Back from the French, into a Civilized Language Once More, by Patient and Unremunerated Toil," *1601 . . . and Sketches Old and New* (n.p., 1933), p. 50.

3. Inflections—alterations in the forms of words themselves to signal changes in meaning and relationship.
4. Formal contrasts—contrasts in the forms of words signalling greater differences in function and meaning. These could also be considered inflections, but it is more convenient for both the lexicographer and the grammarian to consider them separately.

Usually several of these are present in any utterance, but they can be separately illustrated by means of contrasting expressions involving minimum variation—the kind of controlled experiment used in the scientific laboratory.

To illustrate the structural meaning of word order, let us compare the two sentences "man bites dog" and "dog bites man."—The words are identical in lexical meaning and in form; the only difference is in sequence. It is interesting to note that Latin expresses the difference between these two by changes in the form of the words, without necessarily altering the order: "homo canem mordet" or "hominem canis mordet." Latin grammar is worse than useless in understanding this point of English grammar.

Next, compare the sentences "the dog is the friend of man" and "any dog is a friend of that man." Here the words having lexical meaning are "dog," "is," "friend," and "man," which appear in the same form and the same order in both sentences. The formal differences between them are in the substitution of "any" and "a" for "the," and in the insertion of "that." These little words are function-words; they make quite a difference in the meanings of the two sentences, though it is virtually impossible to say what they mean in isolation.

Third, compare the sentences "the dog loves the man" and "the dogs loved the men." Here the words are the same, in the same order, with the same function-words in the same positions. But the forms of the three words having lexical meanings have been changed: "dog" to "dogs," "loves" to "loved," and "man" to "men." These changes are inflections. English has very few of them as compared with Greek, Latin, Russian, or even German. But it still uses them; about one word in four in an ordinary English sentence is inflected.

Fourth, consider the difference between "the dog's friend arrived" and "the dog's friendly arrival." Here the difference lies in the change of "friend" to "friendly," a formal alteration signaling a change of function from subject to modifier, and the change of "arrived" to "arrival," signaling a change of function from predicate to head-word in a noun-modified group. These changes are of the same formal nature as inflections, but because they produce words of different lexical meaning, classifiable as different parts of speech, it is better to call them formal contrasts than inflections. In other words, it is logically quite defensible to consider "love," "loving," and "loved" as the same word in differing aspects and to consider "friend," "friendly," "friendliness," "friendship," and "befriend" as different words related by formal and semantic similarities. But this is only a matter of convenience of analysis, which permits a more accurate description of English structure. In another language we might find that this kind of distinction is unnecessary but that some other distinction, unnecessary in English, is required. The categories of grammatical description are not sacrosanct; they are as much a part of man's organization of his observations as they are of the nature of things.

If we are considering the spoken variety of English, we must add a fifth device for indicating structural meaning the various musical and rhythmic patterns which the linguist classifies under juncture, stress, and intonation. Consider the following pair of sentences:

> Alfred, the alligator is sick.
> Alfred the alligator is sick.

These are identical in the four respects discussed above—word order, function-words, inflections, and word-form. Yet they have markedly different meanings, as would be revealed by the intonation if they were spoken aloud. These differences in intonation are to a certain extent indicated in the written language by punctuation—that is, in fact, the primary function of punctuation.

VI

The examples so far given were chosen to illustrate in isolation the various kinds of structural devices in English grammar. Much more commonly the structural meaning of a given sentence is indicated by a combination of two or more of these devices: a sort of margin of safety which permits some of the devices to be missed or done away with without obscuring the structural meaning of the sentence, as indeed anyone knows who has ever written a telegram or a newspaper headline. On the other hand, sentences which do not have enough of these formal devices are inevitably ambiguous. Take the example already given, Fries's "ship sails today." This is ambiguous because there is nothing to indicate which of the first two words is performing a noun function and which a verb function. If we mark the noun by putting the noun-determining function-word "the" in front of it, the ambiguity disappears; we have either "the ship sails today" or "ship the sails today." The ambiguity could just as well be resolved by using other devices: consider "ship sailed today," "ship to sail today," "ship sail today," "shipping sails today," "shipment of snails today," and so on. It is simply a question of having enough formal devices in the sentence to indicate its structural meaning clearly.

How powerful the structural meanings of English are is illustrated by so-called "nonsense." In English, nonsense as a literary form often consists of utterances that have a clear structural meaning but use words that either have no lexical meanings, or whose lexical meanings are inconsistent with one another. This will become apparent if we subject a rather famous bit of English nonsense to formal grammatical analysis:

> All mimsy were the borogoves
> And the mome raths outgrabe.

This passage consists of ten words, five of them words that should have lexical meaning but don't, one standard verb, and four function-words. In so far as it is possible to indicate its abstract structure, it would be this:

> All . . . . y were the . . . . s
> And the . . . . . . s . . . . . .

Although this is a relatively simple formal organization, it signals some rather complicated meanings. The first thing we observe is that the first line presents a conflict: word order seems to signal one thing, and inflections and function-words something else. Specifically, "mimsy" is in the position normally occupied by the subject, but we know that it is not the subject and that "borogoves" is. We know this because there is an inflectional tie between the form "were" and the "s" ending of "borogoves," because there is the noun-determiner "the" before it, and because the alternative candidate for subject "mimsy," lacks both of these. It is true that "mimsy" does have the function-word "all" before it, which may indicate a noun; but when it does, the noun is either plural (in which case "mimsy" would most likely end in "s"), or else the noun is what grammarians call a mass-word (like "sugar," "coal," "snow"), in which case the verb would have to be "was," not "were." All these formal considerations are sufficient to counteract the effect of word order and show that the sentence is of the type that may be represented thus:

> All gloomy were the Democrats.

Actually there is one other possibility. If "mimsy" belongs to the small group of nouns which don't use "s" to make the plural, and if "borogoves" has been so implied (but not specifically mentioned) in the context as to justify its appearing with the determiner "the," the sentence would then belong to the following type:

> (In the campaign for funds) all alumni were the canvassers.
> (In the drought last summer) all cattle were the sufferers.

But the odds are so much against this that most of us would be prepared to fight for our belief that "borogoves" are things that can be named, and that at the time referred to they were in a complete state of "mimsyness."

Moving on to the second line, "and the mome raths outgrabe," the first we note is that the "And" signals another parallel assertion to follow. We are thus prepared to recognize from the noun-determiner "the," the plural inflection "s" and the particular positions of "mome" and outgrabe," as well as the continuing influence of the "were" of the preceding line, that we are dealing with a sentence of this pattern:

And the'lone rats agreed.

The influence of the "were" is particularly important here; it guides us in selecting among several interpretations of the sentence. Specifically, it requires us to identify "outgrabe" as a verb in the past tense, and thus a "strong" or "irregular" verb, since it lacks the characteristic past-tense ending "d" or "ed." We do this in spite of the fact that there is another strong candidate for the position of verb: that is, "raths," which bears a regular verb inflection and could be tied with "mome" as its subject in the normal noun-verb relationship. In such a case we should have to recognize "outgrabe" as either an adverb of the kind not marked by the form-contrast "ly," an adjective, or the past participle of a strong verb. The sentence would then belong to one of the following types:

And the moon shines above.
And the man stays aloof.
And the fool seems outdone.

But we reject all of these—probably they don't even occur to us—because they all have verbs in the present tense, whereas the "were" of the first line combines with the "And" at the beginning of the second to set the whole in the past.

We might recognize one further possibility for the structural meaning of this second line, particularly in the verse context, since we are used to certain patterns in verse that do not often appear in speech or prose. The "were" of the first line could be understood as doing double duty, its ghost or echo appearing between "raths" and "outgrabe." Then we would have something like this:

All gloomy were the Democrats
And the home folks outraged.

But again the odds are pretty heavy against this. I for one am so sure that "outgrabe" is the past tense of a strong verb that I can give its present. In my dialect, at least, it is "outgribe."

The reader may not realize it, but in the last four paragraphs I have been discussing grammar from a purely formal point of view. I have not once called a word a noun because it names something (that is, I have not once resorted to meaning), nor have I called any word an adjective because it modifies a noun (that is, resorted to function). Instead I have been working in the opposite direction, from form toward function and meaning. I have used only criteria which are objectively observable, and I have assumed only a working knowledge of certain structural patterns and devices known to all speakers of English over the age of six. I did use some technical terms like "noun," "verb," and "tense," but only to save time; I could have got along without them.

If one clears his mind of the inconsistencies of the traditional grammar (not so easy a process as it might be), he can proceed with a similarly rigorous formal analysis of a sufficient number of representative utterances in English and come out with a descriptive grammar. This is just what Professor Fries did in gathering and studying the material for the analysis he presents in the remarkable book to which I have already referred, *The Structure of English*. What he actually did was to put a tape recorder into action and record about fifty hours of telephone conversation among the good citizens of Ann Arbor, Michigan. When this material was transcribed, it constituted about a quarter of a million words of perfectly natural speech by educated middle-class Americans. The details of his conclusions cannot be presented here, but they are sufficiently different from the usual grammar to be revolutionary. For instance, he recognizes only four parts of speech among the words with lexical meaning, roughly corresponding to what the traditional grammar calls substantives, verbs, adjectives, and adverbs, though to avoid pre-conceived notions from the traditional grammar Fries calls them Class 1, Class 2, Class 3, and Class 4 words. To these he adds a relatively small group of function-words, 154 in his material, which he divides into fifteen groups. These must be memorized by anyone learning the language; they are not subject to the same kind of general rules that govern the four parts of speech. Undoubtedly his conclusions will be developed and modified by himself and by other linguistic scholars, but for the present his book remains the most complete treatment extant of English grammar from the point of view of linguistic science.

VII

Two vital questions are raised by this revolution in grammar. The first is, "What is the value of this new system?" In the minds of many who ask it, the implication of this question is, "We have been getting along all these years with traditional grammar, so it can't be so very bad. Why should we go through the painful process of unlearning and relearning grammar just because linguistic scientists have concocted some new theories?"

The first answer to this question is the bravest and most honest. It is that the superseding of vague and sloppy thinking by clear and precise thinking is an exciting experience in and for itself. To acquire insight into the working of a language, and to recognize the infinitely delicate system of relationship, balance, and interplay that constitutes its grammar, is to become closely acquainted with one of man's most miraculous creations, not unworthy to be set beside the equally beautiful organization of the physical universe. And to find that its most complex effects are produced by the multi-layered organization of relatively simple materials is to bring our thinking about language into accord with modern thought in other fields, which is more and more coming to emphasize the importance of organization—the fact that an organized whole is truly greater than the sum of all its parts.

There are other answers, more practical if less philosophically valid. It is too early to tell, but it seems probable that a realistic, scientific grammar should vastly facilitate the teaching of English, especially as a foreign language. Already results are showing here; it has been found that if intonation contours and other structural patterns are taught quite early, the student has a confidence that allows him to attempt to speak the language much sooner than he otherwise would.

The new grammar can also be of use in improving the native speaker's proficiency in handling the structural devices of his own language. In other words, Grammar 2, if it is accurate and consistent, *can* be of use in improving skill in Grammar 1. An illustration is that famous bugaboo, the dangling participle. Consider a specific instance of it, which once appeared on a college freshman's theme, to the mingled delight and despair of the instructor:

Having eaten our lunch, the steamboat departed.

What is the trouble with this sentence? Clearly there must be something wrong with it, because it makes people laugh, although it was not the intent of the writer to make them laugh. In other words, it produces a completely wrong response, resulting in total breakdown of communication. It is, in fact, "bad grammar" in a much more serious way than are mere dialectal divergences like "he ain't here" or "he never seen none," which produce social reactions but communicate effectively. In the light of the new grammar, the trouble with our dangling participle is that the form, instead of leading to the meaning, is in conflict with it. Into the position which, in this pattern, is reserved for the word naming the eater of the lunch, the writer has inserted the word "steamboat." The resulting tug-of-war between form and meaning is only momentary; meaning quickly wins out, simply because our common sense tells us that steamboats don't eat lunches. But if the pull of the lexical meaning is not given a good deal of help from common sense, the form will conquer the meaning, or the two will remain in ambiguous equilibrium—as, for instance, in "Having eaten our lunch, the passengers boarded the steamboat." Writers will find it easier to avoid such troubles if they know about the forms of English and are taught to use the form to convey the meaning, instead of setting up tensions between form and meaning. This, of course, is what English teachers are already trying to do. The new grammar should be a better weapon in their arsenal than the traditional grammar since it is based on a clear understanding of the realities.

The second and more difficult question is, "How can the change from one grammar to the other be effected?" Here we face obstacles of a formidable nature. When we remember the controversies attending on revolutionary changes in biology and astronomy, we realize what a tenacious hold the race can maintain on anything it has once learned, and the resistance it can offer to new ideas. And remember that neither astronomy nor biology was taught in elementary schools. They were, in fact, rather specialized subjects in advanced education. How then change grammar, which is taught to every-body, from the fifth grade up through college? The vested interest repre-sented by thousands upon thousands of English and Speech teachers who have learned the traditional grammar and taught it for many years is a con-servative force comparable to those which keep us still using the chaotic system of English spelling and the unwieldy measuring system of inches and feet, pounds and ounces, quarts, bushels, and acres. Moreover, this army is constantly receiving new recruits. It is possible in my state to become certified to teach English in high school if one has had eighteen credit hours of college English—let us say two semesters of freshman composition (al-most all of which is taught by people unfamiliar with the new grammar), two semesters of a survey course in English literature, one semester of Shakespeare, and one semester of the contemporary novel. And since hard-pressed school administrators feel that anyone who can speak English can in a pinch teach it, the result is that many people are called upon to teach grammar whose knowledge of the subject is totally inadequate.

There is, in other words, a battle ahead of the new grammar. It will have to fight not only the apathy of the general public but the ignorance and inertia of those who count themselves competent in the field of grammar. The battle is already on, in fact. Those who try to get the concepts of the new grammar introduced into the curriculum are tagged as "liberal" gram-marians—the implication being, I suppose, that one has a free choice be-tween "liberal" and "conservative" grammar, and that the liberals are a bit dangerous, perhaps even a touch subversive. They are accused of under-mining standards, of holding that "any way of saying something is just as good as any other," of not teaching the fundamentals of good English. I trust that the readers of this article will see how unfounded these charges are. But the smear campaign is on. So far as I know, neither religion nor patriotism has yet been brought into it. When they are, Professor Fries will have to say to Socrates, Galileo, Darwin, Freud, and the other members of the honorable fraternity of the misunderstood, "Move over, gentlemen, and make room for me."

Transformational Grammar

William G. Moulton

In the foregoing essay you heard about the revolution against traditional school grammar by the advocates of a new, scientifically oriented grammar called structural grammar. After that essay had been written, a still different kind of grammar came into being as a revolution against structural grammar. This is known as transformational, or generative, grammar. Transformational grammar attempts to explain how children can learn language quickly and effortlessly in a short time and without tutelage, and how all human beings can produce and understand new sentences, sentences they have never heard before. Proponents of transformational grammar take the antibehaviorist position that much of the structure of the language we speak is genetically programmed in us. In other words, we only, of all species, have a special innate capacity and predisposition for learning language. In the essay below, William G. Moulton, Professor of Lingusitics at Princeton University, explains and illustrates how transformational grammar works.

Let us consider an English sentence of the simplest type we can find:

Fire burns.

If we take the forms *fire* and *burns* and put them together in the order *burns fire,* the result is quite meaningless. We have added nothing whatever by arranging the two forms in this way; they mean no more together than they did separately; the whole is no greater than the sum of the parts. But if we put them together in the opposite order, the result is very different: *fire burns.* Here each form retains its separate meaning, and we have also added an element of meaning by the very fact of arranging them in this order. This time the whole *is* greater than the sum of the parts. When two forms are combined in this way, they are said to form a CONSTRUCTION; the added element of meaning is called the CONSTRUCTIONAL MEANING. We can diagram this as follows:

Fire burns.

Here the little circle represents the construction, and the lines running from it lead to the CONSTITUENTS of the construction. The concept "construction" is *the* fundamental one of grammar; grammar itself is the study of constructions.

If we now compare *Fire burns* with such further sentences as *Water boils, Snow melts, Milk spoils,* we see that these latter are also constructions, and that they are constructions of exactly the same type: NOUN plus VERB, arranged in each case in the same order. If we abbreviate SENTENCE as "S," NOUN as "N," and VERB as "V," we can write the following formula for all sentences of this type:

$$S \rightarrow N + V$$

This can be read as: Rewrite SENTENCE as NOUN plus VERB. Such a formula allows us to think of the grammatical code of English as a kind of sentence-generating machine: we feed in a noun and a verb, and out comes a sentence.

Though this sentence-generating device is disarmingly simple, a little thought will show that it is also extraordinarily powerful and productive. It means that, theoretically, we can put any noun in the slot "N" and any verb in the slot "V" and thereby get a sentence. Given 1000 nouns and 1000 verbs, we can thus produce 1000×1000 or a million sentences. The only limitations are semantic ones: at the moment we can make no use of *Fire boils.* . . .

We noted above that the constituents of the construction *Fire burns* are the noun *fire* and the verb *burns.* Let us now consider an expanded version of this sentence: *The fire is burning.* What are the constituents of *this* sentence? . . . In terms of grammatical structure . . . the IMMEDIATE CONSTITUENTS are *the fire* and *is burning.* That is to say, in the sentence *The fire is burning,* the PHRASES *the fire* and *is burning* play the same grammatical roles as do the WORDS *fire* and *burns* in the sentence *Fire burns.* Letting "NP" stand for NOUN PHRASE and "VP" for VERB PHRASE, we can now give a more inclusive formula which will cover both types of sentences:

$$S \rightarrow NP + VP$$

To this there must be added an indication of the two ways in which we can rewrite "NP" and "VP":

$$NP \rightarrow \left\{ \begin{array}{l} \text{noun} \\ \text{article} + \text{noun} \end{array} \right\}$$

$$VP \rightarrow \left\{ \begin{array}{l} \text{verb} \\ \text{auxiliary} + \text{verb} \end{array} \right\}$$

The above formulas are valuable in that they show us how a large number of sentences can be generated. But their value goes far beyond this: they not only permit us to generate sentences; they also provide a structural description of each such sentence, in terms of immediate constituents. If, for example, we use these formulas to generate the sentences *Fire burns* and *The fire is burning,* they give us the following phrase-structure diagrams:

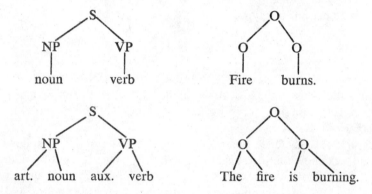

Such diagrams show clearly how each word is related to each other word. Every simple English sentence, we can assume, has the immediate constituents "NP" and "VP." The relationship of "NP" to "S" is that of SUBJECT OF THE SENTENCE; and the relationship of "VP" to "S" is that of PREDICATE OF THE SENTENCE. . . .

The concept IMMEDIATE CONSTITUENT mentioned above is extremely helpful in grammatical analysis, and the term itself needs to be used so often that it is customary to abbreviate it to "IC." We need it, for example, to discuss the relationship between *the* and *fire* in the phrase *the fire.* Here we find that one of the IC's (*fire*) belongs to a class of words ("noun") which can perform the same grammatical function (that of "subject of the sentence") as the phrase as a whole, i.e. one can say both *Fire burns* and *The fire burns.* However, the other IC (*the*) belongs to a class of words ("article") which can *not* perform the same grammatical function ("subject of the sentence") as the phrase as a whole, since there is no such sentence as *The burns.* Of the two IC's in the phrase *the fire,* one is therefore central and the other is subordinate to it. In such cases it is customary to say that the central IC (*fire*) is the HEAD of the construction, and that any subordinate IC (*the*) is an ATTRIBUTE which MODIFIES the head. . . .

Consider now a sentence such as the following:

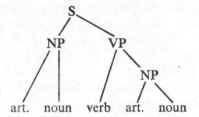

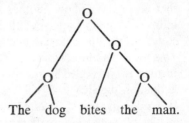

Here we have hit upon an extraordinarily ingenious and economical device. Here we find that a single type of form, an "NP," can appear at two different places and in two different functions. The "NP of S" (*the dog*) is, as before, the SUBJECT OF THE SENTENCE; but the "NP of VP" (*the man*) is the OBJECT OF THE VERB PHRASE. This means that, instead of requiring us to use a different type of form for every different grammatical function, English allows us to use a single type of form in two (and more) grammatical functions: an "NP" can function both as subject of the sentence and as object of the verb phrase. Now, given 1000 nouns and 1000 verbs, we can (theoretically) form 1000 × 1000 × 1000 or a billion different sentences, since any noun can appear in either of two different grammatical slots.

We pay a price for this, however: we must now add something to the grammar which allows us to tell when an "NP" is functioning in which way. As we say earlier, English does this largely by means of word order: *The dog bites the man* vs. *The man bites the dog.* . . . The price which English pays for the freedom of using an NP in two different functions is a sharp restriction on word order. . . .

A further grammatical function of "NP" is illustrated by the following sentence (where "PLACE" stands for "adverbial expression of place," and "prp." is an abbreviation for "preposition"):

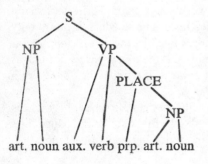

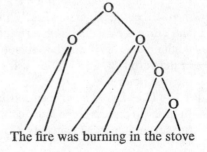

In order to mark this particular use of an NP, English grammar uses not word order but the special type of function word called "preposition." An NP which is in construction with a preposition is said to be the OBJECT OF THE PREPOSITIONAL PHRASE. . . .

If we look back at the sentences given above as illustrations, we will find that all of them show another grammatical feature which lends great flexibility to human language: that of EMBEDDING, of placing slots within slots, etc. In the last sentence given above, for example, the slots "article" (*the*) and "noun" (*stove*) are embedded in the slot "NP" (*the stove*); this in turn is embedded in the slot "place" (*in the stove*); this in turn is embedded in the slot "VP" (*was burning in the stove*); and this, finally is embedded in the slot "S" (*The fire was burning in the stove*).

The phrase-structure diagrams used in the above examples can be thought of as attempts to symbolize visually the abstract underlying patterns that exist somehow in the nervous system of every speaker of English and that he employs whenever he utters a sentence like one of those illustrated. In addition, every speaker has inside himself a stock of words, his LEXICON, from which he draws to fill in these patterns. For example, the abstract diagram

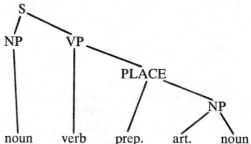

could be filled in with this set of words:

Noun	Verb	Prep.	Art.	Noun
cattle	graze	in	the	pasture

But the speaker's lexicon contains more than mere words; it also contains the grammatical classifications of these words. For example, in his lexicon, the word *cattle* is classified as "Plural." that is, as a noun which is plural only, and *graze* is classified as a verb that requires a subject which is animate but nonhuman. This is why he will automatically put the plural *graze*, not *grazes*, in the verb slot, and why he will not put a word like *books* or *Spaniards* in the first noun slot.

. . . Thus far we have been considering only very simple types of sentences. In order to discuss some more complex types, we first need to introduce three further grammatical concepts. Consider the following pair of sentences:

1. The policeman shot the man.
2. The man was shot by the policeman.

Though we intuitively feel that these are somehow two versions of the "same thing," if we should make structural diagrams of them they would look very different. In (1) the subject is *the policeman*, whereas in (2) the subject is *the man*—even though we still know that the policeman was the one who did the shooting. In (1) the verb has an object *the man*, whereas in (2) it does not—even though we still know that the man was the one who got shot. Even the verbs disagree: *shot* vs. *was shot*. If structural diagrams fail to show the similarity in meaning which we all feel exists between these two sentences, this can only be because something is badly missing in our structural diagrams. And indeed something *is* missing—though it must be shown in quite a different way.

The problem which faces us in this pair of sentences is a very general one; we could find it over and over again in countless other pairs of sentences. It is this: *as we understand* these two sentences, they are almost the same; but *as we say* these two sentences, they are quite different. We can solve this problem by assuming, for any sentence, two levels of grammatical structure: a DEEP STRUCTURE, which represents the way we understand the sentence; and a SURFACE STRUCTURE, which represents the way we say the sentence. Grammatical elements are arranged quite differently in these two kinds of structure. In the deep structure they are arranged in HIERARCHICAL ORDER, corresponding to the structural description of each sentence, in terms of immediate constituents. This type of arrangement corresponds to the way we *understand* the sentence. In the surface structure grammatical elements are arranged in LINEAR ORDER. This type of arrangement corresponds to the way we *say* the sentence, with one element following the other, through the dimension of time (as we speak). In between the deep structure and the surface structure we can assume a set of TRANSFORMATIONAL RULES which convert the hierarchical order of elements in the deep structure into the linear order of elements in the surface structure, and vice versa.

Now we can return to our two sentences. Sentence (1), *The policeman shot the man*, is customarily called "active"; sentence (2), *The man was shot by the policeman*, is customarily called "passive." Because we understand these two sentences as having the same basic meaning, they also have the same basic deep structure—with the same grammatical elements in the same hierarchical arrangement. They differ only in the fact that sentence (2) contains an element "passive" which is lacking in sentence (1). *Without* this element "passive," transformational rules give the linear surface structure that lies behind the spoken sentence (1) *The policeman shot the man*. *With* this element "passive," transformational rules give the very different linear surface structure that lies behind the spoken sentence (2) *The man was shot by the policeman.* In sentence (1), *the policeman* is the subject both in the deep structure and in the surface structure; and *the man* is the object of the verb both in the deep structure and in the surface structure. In sentence (2), the deep structure subject is still *the policeman* (this is the way we understand the sentence), but in the surface structure transformational rules have converted this into the so-called "agent expression" *by the policeman*; and the deep structure object of the verb is still *the man* (this is again the way we understand the sentence), though in the surface structure transformational rules have converted this into the subject.

The transformational principle—deep structure vs. surface structure, connected by transformational rules—plays an essential role in the grammars of all languages. The following paragraphs indicate some of the transformations that we find in simple English sentences.

1. STATEMENT VS. GENERAL QUESTION. *Without* the element "question," transformation rules convert the deep structure *John + live here* into the surface structure *John lives here. With* the element "question," they convert the deep structure *John + live here + Question* into the surface structure *Does John live here*? Note the addition of the meaningless "dummy" auxiliary verb *do.* If the deep structure already contains an auxiliary verb, however, the dummy *do* is not added. Hence the deep structure *John + can live here + Question* gives the surface structure *Can John live here*? Here it is the surface word order alone, without the dummy *do,* which signals the fact that this is a question. The dummy *do* is also not added if the deep structure verb is *be*: deep structure *John + be here + Question,* surface structure *Is John here*? The dummy *do* is optional if the verb of the deep structure is *have.* Deep structure *you + have a pencil + Question* may be transformed in the surface structure either into *Do you have a pencil*? or into *Have you a pencil*? (Where *have* functions as an auxiliary verb, however, *do* is never used: deep structure *you + see John + Perfect + Question* is always transformed into surface structure. *Have you seen John*?, never into *Do you have seen John*?)

2. STATEMENT VS. SPECIFIC QUESTION. In a *general question,* there is no particular grammatical slot that is being questioned; instead, the sentence as a whole is being questioned. In a *specific question,* on the other hand, the notion "question" is directed at some specific grammatical slot; and for this purpose a specific QUESTION WORD is used. Consider the following examples. In a *statement* the grammatical slot *Place* may be filled, for example, by the word *here*: deep structure *John + live here,* surface structure *John lives here.* In a general question the deep structure is the same except for the addition of the element "question": *John + live here + Question,* surface structure *Does John live here*? In a *specific question,* on the other hand, it is precisely the slot "place" that is being ques-

tioned: deep structure *John + live Place-Question*; surface structure *Where does John live?*

English has specific question words for the following grammatical slots:

Nominal:	personal	who/whom
	impersonal	what (e.g. *What is this?*)
	possessive	whose (e.g. *Whose is this?*)
	demonstrative	which (e.g. *Which is this?*)
Adjectival:	demonstrative	which, what (e.g. *which hat, what hat?*)
	possessive	whose (e.g. *whose hat?*)
	descriptive	what kind of
Adverbial:	time	when
	place	where
	manner	how
	cause	why

3. STATEMENT VS. IMPERATIVE. *Without* the element "imperative," transformational rules convert the deep structure *you + will close the door* into the surface structure *You will close the door. With* the element "imperative," they convert the deep structure *you + will close the door + Imperative* into the surface structure *Close the door* (i.e., they delete the elements *you* and *will*). We can surely assume that the deep structure of imperative sentences contains the element *you*, because this is the way we understand them. We can perhaps also assume, as above, that the deep structure of imperative sentences contains the auxiliary verb *will* (or *would*) because precisely this auxiliary shows up in so-called "echo questions": *Close the door, will you?* (or *would you?*)

4. PLAIN VS. EMPHATIC. *Without* the element "emphatic," transformational rules convert the deep structure *John + live here* into the surface structure *John lives here. With* the element "emphatic," they convert the deep structure *John + live here + Emphatic* into the surface structure *John DOES live here.* The presence or absence of the dummy auxiliary verb *do* is governed by the same rules as in (2) above.

5. POSITIVE VS. NEGATIVE. *Without* the element "negative," transformational rules convert the deep structure *John + live here* into the surface structure *John lives here. With* the element "negative," they convert the deep structure *John + live here + Negative* into the surface structure *John does not live here.* The presence or absence of the dummy auxiliary verb *do* is again governed by the same rules as in (2) above.

6. ACTIVE VS. PASSIVE. This is the type of transformation we have already discussed. *Without* the element "passive," transformational rules

convert the deep structure *the policeman + shoot the man* into the surface structure *The policeman shot the man. With* the element passive, they convert the deep structure *the policeman + shoot the man + Passive* into the surface structure. *The man was shot by the policeman.* Note that "passive" can occur only in sentences in which the verb has a direct object. It can *not* occur, for example, in such deep structures as *John + live here,* or in *the journey + last three days.*

7. FULL FORM VS. SUBSTITUTE FORM.   Consider the following example. In answer to the question: "What were John and Mary doing in the jewelry store?," we can reply either: (a) "John was buying Mary a wedding ring," or (b) "*He* was buying *her* a wedding ring." Here *he* and *her* function as SUBSTITUTES for the full words *John* and *Mary*, respectively. Since we *understand* sentence (b) as having the same meaning as sentence (a), we can assume that both have essentially the same deep structure. The only difference is that, in sentence (b), we have chosen to use substitute forms rather than full forms. Once we have done this, transformational rules convert *John* into the surface structure word *he*, and *Mary* into the surface structure word *her*. Substitute words, in contrast to full words, have minimal semantic content. A reasonably full list of English substitute words, arranged according to the types of slots they fill, includes the following:

Nominal:	personal	he, she ⎫ they
	impersonal	it ⎭
	possessive	mine, yours, his, hers, etc.
	demonstrative	this, that (e.g., *This is* . . .)
	modified	one (*this one, the big one*, etc.)
Adjectival:	demonstrative	this, that (e.g., *this man*)
	possessive	my, your, his, her, etc.
	descriptive	such
Adverbial:	time	now, then
	place	here, there
	manner	thus, so
	cause	hence, therefore

Notice how closely these substitute words parallel the question words listed in (2) above. In addition to the above words, English has a word *do* which substitutes for the entire predicate of a sentence. An example is: "*Do you swear to tell the truth, the whole truth, and nothing but the truth, so help you God?*" In the answer "I *do*," the word *do* serves as a substitute for the entire predicate *swear to tell the truth, the whole truth, and nothing but the truth, so help me God.*

8. DELETION BY TRANSFORMATION.   Consider the passive sentence. *The man was shot.* As we understand this sentence, the deep structure has a kind of "dummy subject." That is to say, no information is given as to just who did the shooting; yet we know that *someone* must have done it. We can symbolize this by writing the deep structure as follows: (*someone*) + *shoot the man* + *Passive*, using the parenthesized notation (*someone*) to indicate the dummy subject. Transformational rules now convert this to the surface structure *The man was shot,* with no indication of who did the shooting; that is to say, the dummy subject (*someone*) has been completely deleted from the surface structure. (Note the difference between this sentence and the sentence *The man was shot by someone.* Here the deep structure subject is the indefinite pronoun *someone;* but it is not a "dummy subject," and it is therefore not deleted from the surface structure.)

9. STYLISTIC TRANSFORMATIONS.   We have already pointed out that surface structure word order can serve as a signal of grammatical deep structure. In *The dog bit the man* vs. *The man bit the dog,* it is word order alone which tells us which NP (*the dog, the man*) is functioning as subject of the sentence, and which is functioning as object of the verb. It is also word order which distinguishes the statement *John can live here* from the question *Can John live here?* There are many other cases, however, where word order signals not grammatical meaning but merely shades of stylistic meaning. Example: "*Last Tuesday* I saw Mary in New York" vs. "I saw Mary *last Tuesday* in New York" vs. "I saw Mary in New York *last Tuesday.*" Here transformational rules permit us to place the time expression *last Tuesday* in any one of three different surface positions, with no essential change in meaning.

The grammatical structures that we have been considering thus far allow us to account for many millions, even billions, of English sentences. Yet there is one aspect of grammar that we have not yet considered: the fact that, in English and every other language, it is theoretically possible to say an infinite number of sentences. For example, any sentence we can imagine could always have something further added to it; hence the number of possible sentences is infinite.

How are we to account for this extraordinary property of human language? One type of device which accounts for an infinite number of anything is known, in mathematics, as a RECURSIVE DEVICE. Such a device permits a system to feed upon itself over and over again, theoretically without limit. We can compare this with a mirror, which reflects a man holding a mirror, which reflects a man holding a mirror—and so on and on, without end.

In human language, recursion takes two quite different forms. In CO-ORDINATION, two deep structure sentences are combined so as to produce a single sentence. In SUBORDINATION, one sentence is embedded inside another sentence so as to produce a single sentence. In each case the process is recursive—that is, it can be performed over and over again.

COORDINATION. That is the type: *He smokes cigars + He smokes cigarettes → He smokes cigars and cigarettes.* (We use the symbol "→" to mean "is transformed into.") To understand the power of coordination, we can consider such pairs of sentences as the following (in which we assume the existence of two new detergents, *whiz* and *flash*):

a. *Different subjects:*   *Whiz* washes glasses easily.
                                Flash washes glasses easily.
b. *Different predicates:* Whiz *washes glasses easily.*
                                Whiz *cleans dishes quickly.*
c. *Different verbs:*   Whiz *washes* glasses easily.
                                Whiz *cleans* glasses easily.
d. *Different objects:*   Whiz washes *glasses* easily.
                                Whiz washes *dishes* easily.
e. *Different adverbs:*   Whiz washes glasses *easily.*
                                Whiz washes glasses *quickly.*

If two sentences are in every way identical except that a given slot is filled in the one by X and in the other by Y, they can be combined transformationally by changing this slot to "X *and* Y." Thus we can combine the pairs of sentences (a) through (e) into the following single sentences:

a. *Whiz and Flash* wash glasses easily.
b. Whiz *washes glasses easily and cleans dishes quickly.*
c. Whiz *washes and cleans* glasses easily.
d. Whiz washes *glasses and dishes* easily.
e. Whiz washes glasses *easily and quickly.* . . .

Coordination is a very powerful recursive device, and it can be applied over and over again, leading to such things as *Whiz and Flash wash and clean glasses and dishes easily and quickly.* (Such repeated applications are responsible for the famous phrase *by and with the advice and consent of the Senate.*) . . .

SUBORDINATION. When we transform the structure underlying *He smokes cigars + He smokes cigarettes* into *He smokes cigars and cigarettes,* it is easy to see that two sentences have been combined into one; but we have no way of determining which has been inserted into which. We now need to consider cases in which this question is easily answered—that is, cases in which one sentence is EMBEDDED within the other and is SUBORDI-

NATE to it. Probably the most famous example of embedding in all of English is the following:

This is the cat	1. This is the cat.
that killed the rat	2. The cat killed the rat.
that ate the malt	3. The rat ate the malt.
that lay in the house	4. The malt lay in the house.
that Jack built.	5. Jack built the house.

To the left we give the full sentence, which consists of a series of four successive embeddings; to the right we give the structures which each of the constituent sentences would have if it were used independently. Sentence (5) is first embedded in sentence (4); the resulting sentence is then embedded in sentence (3); the resulting sentence is then embedded in sentence (2); and the resulting sentence is then embedded in sentence (1). At level (1) *This is the cat* is the MATRIX SENTENCE in which all the rest is embedded; at level (2) *the cat killed the rat* is the matrix sentence in which all the rest is embedded; and so on.

In describing subordination we need to consider not only the matrix sentence and the embedded sentence, but also what kind of grammatical slot the embedded sentence fills: a nominal slot, a verbal slot, an adjectival slot, an adverbial slot, etc. In the following examples we shall begin with cases in which the embedded sentence still keeps its "subject + predicate" structure, though it is now marked in some way as a subordinate clause rather than as an independent clause. (We again use the symbol "→" in the meaning "is transformed into.")

Statement, general question, specific question → Nominal clause (i.e. a clause that fills an NP slot). The second sentence is embedded as the subject of the first sentence:

It is true +	→	*It* is true *that he will come.*
He will come	Or:	*That he will come* is true.
It is uncertain +	→	*It* is uncertain *whether he will come.*
Will he come?	Or:	*Whether he will come* is uncertain.
It is uncertain +	→	*It* is uncertain *when he will come.*
When will he come?	Or:	*When he will come* is uncertain. . . .

Statement → Adjectival clause (i.e. a clause that modifies an "NP"— a "relative clause"). The NP of the first sentence is the same as the subject of the embedded sentence:

We saw *the man* +	→	We saw the man
The man spoke		*that/who spoke.*
We saw *the house* +	→	We saw the house
The house burned		*that/which burned.* . . .

Statement → Adverbial clause.

I left *then* + *He came*	→	I left *when he came.*
I left *beforehand* + *He came*	→	I left *before he came.*
I left *afterwards* + *He came*	→	I left *after he came.*
I left *nevertheless* + *He came*	→	I left *although he came.*
I leave *in that case* + *He comes*	→	I leave *if he comes.*
		Etc.

In all of the examples thus far, the embedded sentence still keeps its essential structure. There are other types of embeddings in English in which these shapes are changed. One example: *She sees him* + *He does it* → *She sees him do it.* Here the *he* of the embedded sentence has been collapsed with the *him* of the matrix sentence, and *does* has been transformed to *do.* Another example: *It surprised us* + *He resigned the post* → *His resigning the post surprised us.* Here the embedded sentence has been transformed into an NP which functions as the subject of the embedding sentence. . . .

As a final example of the theory of transformational grammar, consider the following rather complicated sentence: *The man was upset by the boy's being accused of cheating.* As we say this sentence, it consists of a sequence of grammatical elements in simple linear order. As we understand it, however, it consists of a number of grammatical structures in hierarchial order. The theory of transformational grammar attempts to account for these matters by making the following assumptions:

1. The grammatical code provides for two levels of structure:
    a. At the deep level, it produces the structures which underlie the simple sentences (*Something*) *upset the man,* (*Someone*) *accused the boy of* (*something*), *The boy cheated,* and arranges them in the proper hierarchial order.
    b. At the surface level, it produces by transformation the linear structure which underlies the derived sentence *The man was upset by the boy's being accused of cheating.*
2. The semantic code takes the deep structure and from it produces the semantic interpretation which we give to the sentence—that is, the way we understand it.
3. The phonological code takes the surface structure and from it produces the phonological interpretation which we give to the sentence—that is, the way we say it.

If we were to continue with further examples of transformations, we would simply be going more deeply into English grammar, and this is of course not our purpose. . . . All of these transformational rules are part of the "built-in grammatical code" which we carry around inside our heads, and we can call on them at any time to produce or to understand a brand new sentence.

SUGGESTED ASSIGNMENTS

1. Here is an exercise in descriptive grammar on which to try your wings. Collect about twenty sentences containing *some, something, any, anything.* These sentences should be affirmative and negative, and should be in both statement and question form. You can get them from your reading, from spoken discourse, and by asking friends to devise a few for you. Then, using your collected data, write an accurate descriptive statement about how the four words are used that will show a foreigner how to use them as Americans do. Next, test your statement by trying to find exceptions. If you find exceptions, modify the statement to include them. See if your statement will help the Dutch high school students who uttered the following sentences:

   a. I want to ask you any questions about America.
   b. Did you ever hear something about Leonardo da Vinci?
   c. I want to tell you anything about the South Seas.
   d. It is not the use to eat or drink something after that.
   e. I want to tell you anything about dancing.
   f. I do not have some paper today.
   g. Any students think that Greek is easy.
   h. I did not have some money left.

2. As a native speaker of English you have a working knowledge of English grammar; that is, you can construct sentences using the same forms and patterns as other Americans, with the result that you are understood and your language sounds natural. But you are perhaps not conscious of all the complexities of the intricate system that you use so easily. Here is a pertinent exercise. Study the sentences below, all of which were spoken by foreign students. Each group represents one kind of abnormality that makes it non-English. Choose one group and write an explanation of what is wrong in such a way that the speaker will be able to avoid the same kind of mistake in the future. It will not be very helpful merely to show the normal way to express the sentence. You will have to find a principle or general pattern that can be followed.

   a. (1) We have very often clouds.
      (2) I like very much sport.
      (3) You learn quickly English.
      (4) We could take each morning a bath.
      (5) He has been for three weeks minister.
   b. (1) . . . another big house where is a tennis court.
      (2) Before the window is an ivy where lived many birds.
   c. (1) I will be tomorrow there.

(2) We go at nine o'clock to bed.

(3) I went at ten o'clock to the office.

d. (1) What you like with your pancakes?

(2) Why you never come to our class?

(3) To which factory you wrote?

(4) How you like my speech?

3. Here is an exercise that will give you an idea of how a linguistic scientist works with a corpus (collected words, phrases, and sentences) to formulate a grammar. You will find below thirty-eight sentences in Melanesian Pidgin, a language spoken in New Guinea and neighboring islands. These utterances were elicited from speakers of MP by Robert A. Hall, Jr., a linguist at Cornell University. Your assignment is to answer the questions given at intervals, using as your source of information any sentences in the preceding part of the total corpus.

(1) You savvy disfela man?

(2) Long disfela place i-got twofela man i-fight.

(3) Disfela saucepan i-no-good.

(4) Who's 'at i-kaikai-im taro belong me?

(5) Rouse-im alltogether disfela box.

(6) Fireup belong musket i-bigfela.

(7) Alltogether master i-make-im bigfela Christmas.

(1) Do you know this man?

(2) At this place there are two men (who are) fighting.

(3) This utensil is no good.

(4) Who has eaten my taros?

(5) Take away all these boxes.

(6) The explosion of the gun is loud.

(7) All the white men are having a big celebration.

Q. 1. What form do MP nouns have in the plural? (Don't worry about the verbal prefix *i-*. This merely signals that a verb or predicate is about to follow.)

Q. 2. How does MP signal the genitive or possessive, that is, the *of* or *'s* idea?

(8) Police-sergeant i-line-im alla policeboy.

(9) Police-sergeant i-cart-im pass along number-two kee-ap.

(10) Behind i-got place i-got water.

(8) The police sergeant lines up all the native policemen.

(9) The police sergeant carries a letter for the subordinate official.

(10) Then there is a swamp.

Q. 3. How does MP handle the definite article? (i.e., *the*)

Q. 4. How does MP handle the indefinite article? (i.e. *a/an*)

(11) Me no make-im.

(12) All-time all-time em i-fight-im me.

(13) Me no can loose-im you.

(14) Bimeby me go one-time youfela.

(15) Mefela like kitch-im showman.

(11) I couldn't do it.

(12) *He is always hitting me.

(13) I wouldn't desert *you*. (sg.)

(14) I will go with *you*. (pl.)

(15) We want to get a guide.

(16) You-me no got talk.

(16) We (you and I) have nothing to say (in this matter).

(17) Em i-fight-im youfela.

(17) He hits *you*. (pl.)

(18) Em i-fight-im mefela.

(18) He is hitting us.

(19) Em i-got threefela pickaninny finish.

(19) She already has three children.

(20) All i-wind-im deewai.

(20) They blow the flutes.

(21) All-right-im bed.

(21) Make the bed.

(22) Em i-all-right finish.

(22) It is already made.

(23) You go help-im man belong steer.

(23) Go and help the steersman.

(24) Youfela mus' go long bush.

(24) You (pl.) must go to the backwoods.

(25) All i-go finish.

(25) They have gone.

Q. 5. Below are the nominative and objective forms of our English pronominal system. In the blank after each term, place its equivalent in Melanesian Pidgin. If there is no equivalent in the corpus, use a zero.

Q. 6. When you have finished Question 5, study the pattern of the MP pronouns. In the light of this pattern, what forms would you predict that the zero slots might contain? A prediction like this, based on symmetry of pattern, is often made by the linguistic scientist. It is an hypothesis, which the examination of further data may confirm or invalidate.

	Singular			Plural	
Nom.		*Obj.*		*Nom.*	*Obj.*
1. I	_____	me	_____	we _____	us _____
2. you	_____	you	_____	you _____	you _____
3. he	_____	him	_____	them _____	them _____
she	_____	her	_____		
it	_____	it	_____		

Q. 7. What is the distinction between *mefela* and *you-me*, both of which have the same translation in English?

(26) Me razor-im grass belong face.

(26) I am shaving my beard.

(27) Lapun man i-lookout-im pickaninny.

(27) The old man looked after the child.

(28) Bimeby me come.

(28) I will come.

(29) Sun i-burn-im ground.

(29) The sun burns the ground.

(30) I-got dry water.

(30) There is an ebb tide.

(31) Long disfela tin, i-got bull-ma-cow.

(31) In this tin there is beef.

(32) I-got sheepy-sheep?

(32) Is there any mutton?

(33) Me stop here.

(33) I am here.

(34) Me stop policeboy.

(34) I am a native policeman.

(35) Dis-kind man i-no-stop good-fela alltime.	(35) This kind of man is not always good.
(36) Papa i-go finish.	(36) The father is gone.
(37) Man belong long-way place i-kaikai finish.	(37) The foreigners have eaten.
(38) Behind, me cut-im bush.	(38) I shall cut the bush.

Q. 8. Do MP verbs change in form to show past, present, or future time? (For example, English verbs change in form to show past time, as in *beam, beamed,* but do not change in form to show future time, as in *beam, will beam.* Instead, a word must be added to show the future.)

Q. 9. What does the verbal suffix *-im* indicate?

Q. 10. How is the meaning "there is" expressed?

Q. 11. How is the verb *to be* (*am, is, are, was, were*) expressed?

Q. 12. What is the signal for completed action?

Q. 13. How does Melanesian Pidgin show that a happening will occur in the future?

FURTHER READINGS

Aston, Katherine O. "Grammar—the Proteus of the English Curriculum." *Illinois English Bulletin,* November 1967. A 30-page discussion of school, structural, and transformational grammar.

Cattell, N. R. *The New English Grammar.* Cambridge, Mass.: The MIT Press, 1969. A simple, short, and lucid explanation of transformational grammar.

Davies, Hugh Sykes. *Grammar Without Tears.* New York: The John Day Company, Inc., 1953.

Francis, W. Nelson. *The English Language.* New York: W. W. Norton & Company, Inc., 1963, 1965. See pp. 13–68.

Hall, Robert A., Jr. *Linguistics and Your Language.* New York: Doubleday & Company, Inc., 1960. See pp. 97–120.

Laird, Charlton. *The Miracle of Language.* Cleveland: The World Publishing Company, 1953. See pp. 141–210.

Langacker, Ronald W. *Language and Its Structure.* New York: Harcourt Brace Jovanovich, Inc., 1967–1968. On basic concepts of transformational grammar, see pp. 97–140.

Ornstein, Jacob, and William W. Gage. *The ABC's of Languages and Linguistics.* Philadelphia: Chilton Books, 1964. See pp. 80–86.

Postal, Paul, M. "Underlying and Superficial Linguistic Structure." *Harvard Educational Review* 34:246–266. (Special issue, Spring 1964). On transformational grammar.

Sapir, Edward. *Language.* New York: Harcourt Brace Jovanovich, Inc., 1921. See pp. 59–126.

Thomas, Owen. *Transformational Grammar and the Teacher of English.* New York: Holt, Rinehart and Winston, Inc., 1965. A short introduction to transformational grammar.

16
LANGUAGE
AND LITERATURE

Signs and Symbols

Stephen Ullmann

Language binds us together as men; yet, paradoxically, it also divides us. The French speak French, Germans speak German, Italians speak Italian, and the Swiss speak—French, German, Italian, or Rhaeto-Romance. Nor is there any necessary correlation between nationality and language or between race and language. Yet in order to communicate with each other, members of the same speech community must use the same symbols. We say *bread*, the French *pain*, the Germans *Brot*, and the Italians *pane* to refer to the same thing. In each language the symbols are different, but they are equally effective because the symbolic process is the same regardless of the language. Symbols, then, are at the heart of language. Without them we would be unable to communicate with each other. They are instruments of great power.

In our everyday speaking and writing, we are rarely conscious of either the process or the power of the symbols we use. In the language of art, the reverse is true. Symbols are also central in art, and creative artists strive to exploit the power of symbols to the fullest extent—in painting, in sculpture, in the dance, and in literature as well. In the words of the dramatist, the novelist, and the poet, we become more fully aware of the power of symbols. In the essay "Signs and Symbols," Stephen Ullmann, Professor of Romance Philology at the University of Leeds, discusses what a symbol is and how it operates. A short story and a poem, illustrative of symbols in literature, follow the Suggested Assignments.

From *Words and Their Use* by Stephen Ullmann. Reprinted by permission of the publisher, Philosophical Library, Inc., copyright 1951.

The mechanism of language can best be seen at work in a simple speech-situation. Suppose for instance that a child notices an apple and feels an urge to pick it and eat it. To satisfy this desire, the child can do one of two things. If the apple is easily accessible and there are no other obstacles, he can go and get it without any outside help. If he cannot reach it, or if special permission is required, then the collaboration of some second person will have to be enlisted. The child will then articulate a series of sounds arranged into a certain pattern of rhythm and intonation, and forming an utterance such as: "Could you please get me that apple?" The vibrations of air started by the speaker will reach the ear of the hearer who, when the message has been understood, will react. In the simplest case, this reaction will take the form of some practical step, such as the picking of the apple as requested. There may also be more complicated patterns of further linguistic exchanges, with some practical result, positive or negative, at the end.

This situation has been analysed by the late Professor Leonard Bloomfield in "behaviorist" terms, *i.e.* as a chain of stimuli and responses. When the child can pick the apple by himself, there is a simple chain. The sight of the apple acts as an external stimulus and elicits an immediate and practical reaction. When co-operation is required, the external stimulus (S) sets off a linguistic reaction (r): the speaker produces a series of articulate sounds. The soundwaves reach the hearer and act on him as a linguistic stimulus (s). This in its turn gives rise to a practical, external reaction (R) on the hearer's part. Thus: S———r . . . s———R. Between the original stimulus and the final response, a linguistic exchange, an act of speech and interpretation has been fitted in, and as result, the practical step will be taken by someone other than the recipient of the initial stimulus. In other words, a *division of labour* will have been ensured.

On closer inspection, our simple speech-situation will yield further information concerning the linguistic exchange. It shows, for instance, that three factors are involved in any utterance: the speaker, the hearer, and the message. For the speaker, the act of speech is an expression, a means of conveying his thoughts, feelings, or desires. For the hearer, it is a stimulus to take some action or to adopt some kind of attitude. From the point of view of the message itself, it is an act of communication. To use a terse formula advanced by the Austrian psychologist K. Bühler, the act of speech is a *symptom* of the speaker's state of mind, a *symbol* of the message conveyed, and a *signal* to the hearer. . . .

One crucial point, however, remains unexplained in our speech-situation. Why and how did the string of sounds "Could you please get me that apple?" induce the hearer to pick the fruit? To narrow down the problem to its central point, why and how does the string of sounds "apple" denote that particular object and no other, or for that matter any object at all? Clearly there is no natural link between form and meaning in this case. Not only does one fail to see what that link could be, but if a hidden connection did exist, then one would be at a loss to explain the diversity of names for the same object in different languages: *apple, pomme* in French, *manzana* in Spanish, *mar* in Rumanian, *alma* in Hungarian, etc. How did it happen that the word *apple* has, in the minds of all English speakers, become so closely associated with that fruit, that it has established itself as its symbol?

To answer this question it will be necessary to consider signs and symbols on a more general plane, since it is common knowledge that there are many non-linguistic signs and symbols, and that the words of human speech merely take their place in the wider framework of symbolic processes.

If I see heavy clouds in the sky, I interpret this as a *sign* of impending rain. If a dog wants to go out of the room, he signifies his desire by scratching at the door. In the former case, a natural phenomenon has been analysed as an indication of some other phenomenon; in the latter, a sign has been deliberately produced for the benefit of some recipient or recipients. More important, however, is the process of interpretation itself. The famous experiments carried out by the Russian physiologist Pavlov have thrown fresh light on this process. On repeated occasions, Pavlov blew a whistle at a certain pitch when giving food to his dog. Thus, an associative link was established between the sight of the food, its smell, its taste, and the sound regularly accompanying its consumption. All these sense-impressions formed part of one common and recurring experience. Having established this context of sensations, Pavlov one day blew the whistle without producing the food, and found that the dog showed every sign of expectancy, including salivation, which the presence of food would normally evoke. What had happened was that part of an experience had been detached from the rest and, standing by itself, this isolated part was sufficient to call up the remainder of the context. To bring out the most salient feature of signs, Dr. Richards has coined the expressive if somewhat ponderous phrase: "delegated efficacy." An element in a complex experience is singled out to act for the whole, "by proxy," so to speak. We shall then define a sign as *some part of an experience, which is capable of calling up the remainder of that experience.*

A great many signs are used by men in their intercourse with each other. It is convenient to mark off these signs from the rest and to label them *symbols*. Symbols will be defined, for the purposes of our enquiry, as *"those signs which men use to communicate one with another"* (Ogden-Richards). Such symbols can be classified from various viewpoints. They may appeal to different *senses*; sound and sight are of course the most privileged, as their organs are most highly developed, but other sense-impressions may also be brought into play, such as touch in the braille alphabet. There may even arise combinations of diverse sensations, as in an operatic performance where musical effects are accompanied and enhanced by visual devices. From a different point of view, symbols are found to be either *natural* or *conventional*. Natural symbols have some kind of intrinsic link with the thing symbolised.[1] Thus, some gestures are descriptive of the states of mind they reflect. Pictorial or sculptural representations of, say, the goddess of Justice are allegorical, *i.e.*, based on some internal analogy. Again, the cross is a natural symbol of Christendom, not—or at least not primarily—because of any allegorical implications, but through its historical associations, because of the significance of the crucifixion of Christ. On the other hand, the spoken and the written word, the siren as a time-signal or as an air raid warning, the use of black as a sign of mourning, the shaking of the head as a sign of negation, are purely conventional devices; they become unintelligible outside the community where they are established. In China, white and not black is the colour of mourning, and in Turkey, the shaking of the head sig- • nifies assent. Finally, some symbols are *isolated*, whereas others form complex and intricate *systems* such as road signals, naval signals, codes, the deaf-and-dumb alphabet, language, and writing. In recent years, the American philosopher Charles Morris and others have begun to explore the possibility of a comprehensive *theory of signs*, which would examine, classify and correlate all symbolic processes, including human language which is their supreme and most elaborate example.

SUGGESTED ASSIGNMENT

A recent term in our language is *status symbol*, a symbol used to convey prestige upon the possessor, for example, an imported sports car, a Greek-letter fraternity pin, or membership in an exclusive club. Write a theme on one of the following topics:

a. The Use and Abuse of Status Symbols
b. Status Symbols—a Symbol of Inferiority
c. Unusual Status Symbols I have Observed
d. The Ladder of Status Symbols

The following discussion about status symbols in business offices may help you get started: ". . . the American office is a veritable temple of status. Though they may seem almost imperceptible, the symbols are manifested everywhere. Some have a useful purpose—the memo pad 'From the desk of . . .'; the routing slip (should the names on the memorandum be listed by seniority, or alphabetically?); who sits with whom in the company dining room. Others are rooted in propriety: who can call whom by nickname, at what level people may smoke. To what grade of washroom is one entitled? Is the office carpeted or does the occupant rate only linoleum? Some are rooted in functions only marginal: the facsimile signature stamp, for example—evidence that a man's importance is

---

[1] A natural symbol is what the Russells, on page 357, call a representative symbol. It is similar to what it denotes, like a map, or a highway sign with a wiggly line indicating a winding road, or words like *fizzle, roar, hiccup,* and *hiss*. It is also called an "iconic sign" by writers on semiotics, the science of signs. [eds.]

such that he must write to a great number of people, even if he doesn't use the facsimile signature in doing it. All these are favorite topics of office humor, of course, but as this fact itself is witness, the symbols communicate." [2]

[2] William H. Whyte, Jr., and the editors of *Fortune* from *Is Anybody Listening?* (New York: Simon and Schuster, Inc., 1952), pp. 116–117.

The Hoop

Merriam Modell

Much of the interest in "The Hoop" depends upon the use of symbolism. Obviously the hoop itself is symbolic; in order to understand the story, it is necessary to interpret the symbol. The symbolism is clearly evident at the end of the study, but it is not so simple as might appear at first. How do you interpret the last sentence? Where else in the story do you find a hoop or hoop-like situation? This story first appeared in *The New Yorker*, February 14, 1942.

When the little boy came by, Truda was sitting on her usual bench, with only an iron seat partition separating her from the tight row of American nursemaids. Not having much to do, because her Jackie always slept placidly most of the morning, she had watched innumerable older children playing. This little boy, Truda saw immediately, was dressed all wrong, not like an American little boy at all. Voluminous knickers flowed out from his thin calves, and he had high suède shoes on, a stiff shirt with a four-in-hand, and an overcoat styled like a man's. But his hair was the worst. It was cut off in a straight line just below his ears. On his head, tilted to one side, was a large, floppy beret.

"The *Mutter* should not let him so," Truda thought. "Though I know how it is." She shook her head compassionately. "They have not been long in the country and the cloth is yet good, but they should not let him so."

Truda herself took tremendous pains to look exactly like the American nursemaids. Her madam had supplied the white uniforms and paid for the buckskin oxfords, but it was Truda who bought a camel's-hair sports coat.

Also, no matter how sleepy she was at night, she did up her neat black curls in trick devices which she bought in Woolworth's. Correctly dressed, she always wheeled her ten-month-old charge to this bench, hoping stubbornly that the Americans would one day include her in their conversation. "To improve the English," she told herself. But what Truda wanted from them, what Truda wanted from everyone nowadays, was approval. They were so generous with it among themselves.

"You're perfectly right," they kept assuring each other. "That's just what I would have told my madam."

She sighed with pity as she watched the little boy, because he was different.

He was rolling a colored hoop down the cement path, starting it off expertly and keeping it going with a thin wooden wand. He was enjoying himself. And so polite! When his hoop inconvenienced anyone, he bowed and said, "Excuse, please." Truda had known many little boys like that in Hamburg.

Then she saw the gang of American kids come climbing over the crest of a rocky hill near the playground. The first to come was taller than the rest and wore a navy-blue lumberjacket with a camp monogram. He spied the boy with the hoop. "Looka! Detlef!" he shouted and, waving to the others to follow, plunged down over the grass. "Hey, Detlef!" he called. "Hey, c'mon here!"

The German boy, with a timid side glance at the "Keep Off the Grass" sign, lifted his hoop with his wand and stepped over the low railing. "Do you like to roll my hoop, Ritchie?" he asked ingratiatingly.

Ritchie pushed it away. "Only girls roll hoops," he said. "Don't you know it? We're gonna wrestle. You wanna wrestle me, Detlef?"

The German boy shook his head, but Ritchie ignored that, "I already put down all the other kids, so you come next. Here, Martin, hold my watch."

A boy with silver-rimmed glasses stepped forward obediently, stretching out his grimy hand for the watch. The rest formed a loose ring around Ritchie and the German boy, who had not moved.

"Come on," Ritchie said impatiently. He pulled down the zipper on his lumberjacket. "Get your coat off. You can't wrestle with your coat on. I'll give you ten." He lifted the German boy's beret off his head and handed it to the waiting Martin. "Count ten, Martin," he commanded.

Martin started solemnly, "One . . . two . . . three . . ."

The German boy's hand fluttered. "I do not like to wrestle," he said timidly.

"Aw, he doesn't like anything," Ritchie said.

"That's right," agreed a small, fat boy. "Detlef doesen like anything. He doesen like football or swimming or anything. Say"—he winked at the others—"say, Detlef, I'll bet you don't like the United States."

The German boy did not answer.

"See?" the fat one said, throwing up his pudgy hands in an absurdly mature gesture. "I'll bet he doesen like Roosevelt, even. I'll bet he likes Hitler better than Roosevelt."

Detlef shook his head violently. Ritchie stepped closer to him and took hold of his coat sleeve. "O.K., O.K., so you don't like Hitler. But you like Germans, I'll bet!"

The fat boy giggled. "He's gotta like Germans. His mom's a German, his pop's a German. He's gotta like Germans."

Ritchie considered that for a moment. "Excepting them. I mean German Germans. Do you like German Germans?" He thrust out his jaw.

Detlef tugged at his sleeve grimly, as if freeing his coat from Ritchie's grasp was all that mattered.

"C'mon, answer!" Ritchie said.

When Detlef found he was unable to pull himself loose, he burst into tears. "I do!" he screamed. "I do like Germans. There are some Germans good as Americans. There are some Germans better than Americans!"

Ritchie whistled, a thin piercing sound. "That's a lie," he said. "I'm gonna kill you for that lie!"

Truda drew her breath in sharply. "*Komm' hier, Kleiner!*" she called out. "*Setzt Dich hier zu mir.*"

The German boy gazed wildly around. Truda pointed to the empty seat on her left. Gasping, his face convulsed, he broke loose with one tremendous lunge and ran to her. Truda could feel him trembling as he tumbled into the vacant seat. Without thinking, she turned to the American nursemaids. "The poor *Kleiner*," she said, patting the child's shoulder. "The poor *Junge!*"

The girl nearest Truda leaned forward. "Don't let him get away with that," she said. "He deserves all that's coming to him!"

The nursemaid sitting next to her jerked her head toward the American boys, who were standing just beyond the low railing. "They should give him a lesson he won't forget!"

"*Bitte!*" stammered Truda. "*Bitte!*" She looked at their faces, hard and ugly under their white caps.

One of the nursemaids formed a word with her lips. "Ger-man," she said soundlessly to the others.

Truda's heart knocked in her breast. She stared stupidly at the cold faces. Fear was all around her again. She breathed it in as she had breathed it those last years in Hamburg. As she jumped from her seat, she could feel the little German boy's bony hand restraining her. She held her wristwatch in front of her eyes. "Almost twelf," she announced in a loud, false voice. "It iss almost twelf. Time for the *Bub* to haf his lunch. Yes. *Also.*" With a jerk Truda released the brake on the baby's carriage and moved off.

She kept her eyes away from the little German boy, but she knew that the circle of boys, held at bay by her presence, was closing in on him. She pushed at the carriage frantically, shoving it up the hill.

When she did turn to look, she could not see the little German boy at all, only the backs of the others, but she saw the hoop. Someone inside the circle gave it a vicious push and it rolled out into the cement path a way and clattered to the ground. It rocked drunkenly from side to side, and then it was still.

The Span of Life

Robert Frost

The humor and edge of this two-line poem derive from its symbolic nature. Write a paragraph explaining the symbolism.

> The old dog barks backward without getting up.
> I can remember when he was a pup.

Figurative Language

Monroe C. Beardsley

The nature of figurative language, one of the most important and fascinating aspects of language, is often misunderstood. Many people associate figurative language solely with poetry; moreover, they regard it as a kind of poetic decoration, the frosting on the cake merely, sweet and pleasant tasting but not really necessary. Such a view of figurative language is wrong on both counts. Figures of speech, it is true, do play a prominent part in poetry; but they also play an important role in prose, not only in imaginative works such as novels and short stories but also in expository and persuasive works. Indeed, though you may not be highly conscious of it, figures of speech occur frequently in your every-day conversation. And in whatever form figurative language appears—in poetry, prose writing, or ordinary speech—it is an integral and vital part; it is not decorative but functional.

Professor Monroe Beardsley, of Swarthmore College, opens the discussion of figurative language with an examination of the simile and the metaphor.

Take up a book, or article, on education—or start yourself thinking about that subject by asking yourself some questions. What good is it? Should everyone go on to school to the limit of his capacities? Should private and parochial schools be given financial help by the Government? . . . The chances are that you won't read far, or think long, without comparing education, consciously or half-consciously, with something else. Is an education like other things that you believe everyone has a right to? Are the skills and talents of American citizens like natural resources, which ought to be conserved? Is knowledge like tools, or like money, or like a hobby?

This tendency to make comparisons is a fact worth noting about the way we think. Education, for example, is a complicated process, of which we know much less than we should like to know. And when we study a complicated process, we are apt to begin by setting aside some of its complexities. We try to see what light we can throw on it by comparing it with another process we think we understand better. We simplify. If we did not, it is hard to see how we could come to understand anything.

Moreover, such comparisons often fix themselves in the very language we use. Many of the words and phrases that come to mind when we think about education embody comparisons that were made long ago. We speak of education in a number of different ways: (1) eating and drinking: "the omnivorous reader," "undigested facts," "crumbs of information," "ruminating," "swallowing the story whole," "drinking of the Pierian spring"; (2) writing on blank paper or a tablet: "inscribed on the memory," "impressed on the mind," Locke's "*tabula rasa*"; (3) piling up goods in a warehouse or store: "his mind was well stocked," "taking inventory of his knowledge," "loads of learned lumber in his head"; (4) mining: "digging out information," "delving into philosophy"; (5) going on a journey: "adventures of ideas," "traveling in the realms of gold." And there are many others.

These terms are borrowed from simpler activities of human beings and applied to education. At first such a borrowed term may help us to focus upon an important aspect of the process. Thus we may say that one's personality is "molded" by his schooling, because we see that it makes him more of a definite person than he was: it "shapes" his personality, for good or ill. But once we use the term "molded," our thinking will be partly guided by the comparison of teacher with sculptor. And this can easily lead to a serious mistake, if it makes us think that the student is or should be as passive as the clay.

. . . therefore, we must reckon with an important characteristic of language: its power to evoke in our minds the vivid recollection of our sensory experience, the pictures, smells, tastes, sounds, and touch sensations of our waking life. Language does this when it is *concrete*, that is, when it is rich in images.

An *image* is a term that designates characteristics that we can experience by our senses. "Red," "dark cloud," and "pretty girl" are images, because some of the characteristics of these things we can know by direct perception. But "atom," "government," and "civil rights" are not images: these things are conceived, but they are not sensed.

Of course, we can think, and we can understand words, *abstractly*—that is, without imagining concrete things and happenings. And the actual memories that appear to the mind when a word is spoken or heard vary greatly from person to person. When you hear the word "horse," perhaps you imagine a white horse whereas the speaker imagines a brown one; but you won't get into trouble as long as the two horses both satisfy the designation of the term (in having four legs, for example), and as long as you both get the same connotations from the term in its context.[1] The difference in imagination will not hurt your thinking or hinder your communication, if you keep your thinking from being dominated and controlled by these private little pictures. But images can trip the unwary thinker, whether writer or reader, by leading him to wander into interesting but irrelevant thoughts. And so in this chapter we shall look over the principles that will help you manage them, in your ordinary reading and writing.

SIMILE AND METAPHOR

Images become involved in our thinking (for better or for worse) when they enter into what are commonly called "*figures of speech.*" A figure of speech consists in a comparison between two things, which we may label "X" and "Y." Generally one of the things, say X, is the one we are saying something about, and the X-term (or **primary term**) denotes the thing *to*

---

[1] *Designation*, as Beardsley uses the term, means the defining characteristics of a thing. For example, the term *widow* designates the characteristics of being human, being female, having been married, and being one whose husband is dead. *Connotation* means those characteristics that are not strictly a part of the *designation* of a word. [eds.]

which some other thing is compared. In figure of speech we say something about X by comparing Y *to* it; the Y-term (or **secondary term**) denotes the thing which is compared to X.[2] In "love is blind," "love" is the primary term and "blind (person)" is the secondary term. Or when H. G. Wells says that the brain of man is a "food-getting instrument, like the snout of a pig," "brain" is the primary term and "snout of a pig" is the secondary term. When the figurative statement is elliptical, we have to supply part of the terms ourselves.

All figures of speech are comparisons, but not all comparisons are figures of speech. To begin with a simple example, we may say that "James was as angry as a hornet" is figurative, but that "James was angry as John" is *not.* It is not hard to see that there is a difference here, but it is impossible to state the difference exactly without using highly technical language. James and John are evidently much more alike than James and the hornet, for James and John both belong to the same biological species. Thus James and John can *both* be angry, in the same sense of the word. But James and the hornet *cannot* both be angry in the same sense of the word: the hornet doesn't feel the same way, and he doesn't behave the same way. He can't get red in the face or stamp his feet with rage: he can only zoom, buzz, and sting.

Thus there is a distinction between a comparison that is figurative and one that is not figurative, but the distinction is one of degree. Suppose you compare the human heart with a goat's heart, a pump, and a television relay. There is a greater difference between a human heart and a pump than there is between a human heart and a goat's heart. And there is a greater difference between a human heart and a television relay than there is between a human heart and a pump. If the difference is great enough, in a particular case, we say that the comparison is figurative. But "The heart is a pump" is a borderline case: it is figurative in some contexts, but not in others.

It is not possible, or necessary for ordinary purposes, to be very precise about this distinction. The important thing is the degree of difference between the two things compared. When you want to understand a comparison clearly, there are three things to do. First, identify clearly the two terms of the comparison. Second, consider the chief points of likeness and of unlikeness between the two things. And third, examine the context in which the characteristics of the things are stressed. If the two things are *unlike* in some important way that is indicated by the context, then it is reasonable to say that the comparison is figurative.

The teacher of literature, who is skilled in dealing with highly figurative language, must make a number of distinctions. There are, for example, similes, metaphors, analogies, parables, tropes, myths. And besides these there are various technical terms of rhetoric for more special kinds of figure:

---

2 The primary term is also referred to as the *tenor*, the secondary term as the *vehicle* [eds.]

as when we speak of a thing as a person ("personification"), a part as a whole ("synecdoche"), or one thing as another that is associated with it ("metonymy"). These distinctions are useful for analyzing certain kinds of discourse, but ... [here] we are concerned with more general features of discourse. Yet there is one fundamental distinction that any critical reader must make: that is the distinction between a *simile* and a *metaphor*.

A **simile** is an explicit figurative comparison: that is, it is a statement that one thing is like another. Thus it contains a comparative word: "like," "as," "similar," or "same." And we may distinguish further between two kinds of similes: *closed similes* and *open similes*. Compare these two excerpts from a description of international political developments in the summer of 1949:

1. "The international situation was *as tense as* a ball-game tied up in the ninth inning." (*Closed simile.*)
2. "The international situation was *like* a ball-game tied up in the ninth inning." (*Open simile.*)

In both of these figures we have a primary term ("the international situation") and a secondary term ("a ball-game tied up in the ninth inning"). But the first figure not only compares the two things; it specifies the *respect* in which they are compared (the one was "as tense as" the other). Similes that do this we shall call **"closed similes."**

An **open simile** is one that makes no mention of the respect, or respects, in which the two things are to be compared. Thus an open simile, by itself, doesn't give any definite information. It puts us in a frame of mind to note the points of likeness, but it leaves us in suspension. We have to search the context of the simile for an indication of the points of likeness that are relevant to the subject under discussion. *Any* two things are alike in *some* respects: the question is, what are the important, and relevant, respects? Perhaps the writer means that in the international situation the watchers were divided into two hostile groups, or perhaps he means that most people were fearful of the outcome, or perhaps he means that the suspense was likely to continue for some time. The simile, *by itself*, is noncommittal; its specific reference must be supplied by the context.

Thus an open simile is likely to be vague if it is not carefully handled. It might mean a good deal, or it might mean very little. When a poet says that "the evening is spread out against the sky/Like a patient etherized upon a table," we must hold the terms of this comparison in mind until the rest of his poem tells us *how* the two things are alike. The same principle applies to similes when they occur in ordinary discourse.

When the words "like" and "as" are dropped out of a figure, and the primary and secondary terms are jammed together, the figure becomes a *metaphor*. A metaphor does not *state* a comparison, but it *suggests* a comparison. The reporter quoted previously went on to say:

The diplomats made errors, and a few hits, but neither side scored. Everybody muffed the ball, and the peoples of the world breathlessly watched their chosen leaders swinging at wild curves as the international struggle dragged on.

Here is a whole string of metaphors, but take just one: "their chosen leaders swinging at wild curves." Y (a batter vainly trying to hit a badly pitched curve) is compared to X (a national leader dealing with an international crisis). But when we put this situation in the form of a statement, "Their chosen leaders swung at wild curves," we see that the metaphor is elliptical, for part of the comparison is left out. . . .

The simplest sort of metaphor has the form "X is Y": "He is a wolf." The secondary term doesn't have to be a predicate, however. It may be an adjective ("He has a wolfish appetite"), or a verb ("He wolfs his food"). To get the terms of the metaphor straightened out, we can always restate the metaphor in the simple form. We can write: "His appetite is wolfish," "His manner of eating is that of a wolf." This restatement will do violence to the metaphor, and it is not an exact substitute for it; it is merely a device for being clear about the structure of the metaphor. The same device can be applied to those richer metaphors that have added so much to the clarity, and confusion, of recent history: "New Deal," "pump-priming," "maginot-line mentality," "brass hats," "bottlenecks," "fox holes," "underground," "reconversion," "the Iron Curtain," and "Fair Deal."

In figurative language of the richest sort, similes and metaphors are interwoven in a complicated way, and it may take considerable analysis to understand exactly what is being said.

> Life, like a dome of many-coloured glass,
> Stains the white radiance of Eternity,
> Until Death tramples it to fragments.

This remarkable figure has several parts, which can be artificially separated for examination. Ordinary discourse seldom poses such complicated problems. Still, figurative language, even outside poetry, can be quite puzzling. A figure of speech can confuse your thinking, if you are not clear about its primary term and its secondary term, and if you do not recognize what kind of figure it is. . . .

INTERPRETING A METAPHOR

Metaphor is a handy linguistic tool, because it crams so many meanings into a few words. But metaphor is difficult to use skillfully, and, in the hands of a careless or malicious workman, it often gives the reader or listener a good deal of trouble. Metaphor can be a very subtle aid to slanting. And the more meaning that is packed into a metaphor, the harder it is for the critical reader to think *through* it. Therefore, in this section we shall take up the question of finding out just what a metaphor means.

We may begin by noting the common distinction between a "literal" sense and a "metaphorical" sense of a term. The *literal* meaning of "pig" is just its designation: that is, the characteristics of having four legs, having a snout, and so forth. If you say, "The animal in that pen is a pig," this statement *can* be literally true; an animal can have four legs. In this context, the connotations of "pig" are not stressed. But if you say, "That man over there is a pig," it is clear that this sentence *cannot* be literally true. For, if he is a man, he has *not* four legs. So, if this statement is to be true at all, it is not the designation, but only the *connotation*, of "pig" that is being ascribed to the man. In this case "pig" is used *metaphorically*. And this metaphorical statement is (or may be, depending on the context) equal to a number of literal statements: he is greedy, he is gross, he is dirty, he is lazy, he is fat.

We can now give a fairly clear definition of "metaphor." This term covers both statements ("The fire is dying") and noun-phrases ("a dying fire"). Let us consider statements first. We shall say that a statement is "metaphorical" if it has both of the following characteristics: First, it must be *literally* false. That is, the subject cannot possibly have the characteristics designated by the secondary term. Take, for example, the architectural slogan of an earlier decade: "A house is a machine for living." In the ordinary sense of the term, a machine is something that does work; we apply some form of energy (muscular effort, coal, gasoline, falling water) to it, and by the motions of its parts it changes the energy into a different form. This capacity is one of the characteristics designated by the term "machine." But a house is *not* a machine in this sense. Second, a metaphorical sentence *may* be (it does not have to be) true on the level of connotation. That is, the subject *can* have the characteristics connotated by the secondary term. "Machine" connotes the characteristics of being useful, of being designed to fulfill certain specific functions, of not having parts it doesn't need to serve its ends. And (whether or not it ought to be) a house *can* be a machine in this sense.

A noun-phrase may be called a "metaphor" if it can be transformed into a metaphorical statement. In this way we speak of "pork-barrel legislation," "the voice of doom," "a living death" as metaphors.

It is important to keep "literal meaning" (that is, designation) distinct from *etymological* meaning. It is misleading to say, for example, that "budget" (from the French *bougette*) literally means *wallet*. The word "budget" literally means just what the dictionary gives as its *two* standard senses: (*a*) an accumulation, as a "budget of paradoxes" (this meaning seems to be on the way out), and (*b*) a financial statement for the ensuing period. There *is* on record the *obsolete* English sense (*c*) a bag with its contents; that once was one of the designations of "budget," but is not its "literal meaning" today.

This example reminds us of the constantly shifting character of the distinction between the literal and metaphorical senses of words (or between their designations and connotations). When we speak of "dead metaphor" we mean something that *was* a metaphor but is not any longer. "Spinster" is a "dead metaphor." Once it designated *a person who spins* (man or woman). Then, because most such people were unmarried women, it came to connote that characteristic. But when it began to be used very widely in contexts that emphasized this connotation, the connotation came to be so closely linked with the word that *unmarried woman* became the standard meaning, or designation. Today, in the proper context, it can *connote* the characteristic of being one who spins, but it does not now *designate* that characteristic.

When we speak of the "eye of a needle," we do not feel that we are comparing an eye to the aperture of the needle (even though there is more than one respect in which they are similar). This use of "eye" is just one of its designations, the metaphor has "died." But when we read of the "eyes of Night," the context and the personification of Night present a situation in which we *do* feel a comparison of the star to the eye. This is a genuine metaphor. Of course, in between, there will be "half-dead" metaphors, borderline cases, such as, perhaps, "seeing eye-to-eye," in which the comparative element is almost lost and the phrase has practically hardened into an idiom.

It follows that the term "metaphor" is vague; there is no sharp line to divide living metaphors from dead ones. But for a full grasp of any discourse, you must make a good estimate of the amount of life left in its metaphors, especially when you are dealing with material from the social studies or psychology, where the borderline cases are frequent. In these fields, the technical vocabulary is often created by putting a metaphor to death. This is legal, but metaphors sometimes die hard. Hence the vocabulary of Freudian psychiatry has many terms, such as "repression," "censor," "projection," which are not yet fully under control. They are not quite dead enough so that their connotations can be ignored, and they can confuse the writer and reader.

We cannot tell whether a metaphorical statement is true or false until we know its meaning. To *interpret*, or *expand*, a metaphorical statement is to give a list of literal statements which, taken in combination, are equal in meaning to the original statement. In the case of "He is a pig," it may be possible to give a *complete interpretation*, but it would be an almost endless task to list *all* the characteristics wound up together in the meaning of a very rich metaphor. For most purposes this need not trouble us: usually we don't have to know *all* the characteristics connoted—but we do want to know whether a certain *particular* characteristic is connoted or not. Thus we must be able to give at least a *partial interpretation* of the metaphor, to bring out its special bearing upon the point of an argument.

As an example of a partial interpretation, let's consider the sentence

"Russia has drawn an iron curtain across Europe," as it turns up in a discussion of American foreign policy. The first thing to do is to get the *terms* of the metaphor straight. We see that this metaphor is a double one. In the *main* metaphor, drawing an iron curtain is compared to Russian diplomatic and military behavior toward Eastern and Western Europe. But within the secondary term of the main metaphor, the "curtain" is stated to be an "iron" one.

The second step is to consider the connotations of the terms, beginning with the smallest units. You think of the characteristics of curtains (the kind you draw): their tendency to shut out air and light, to billow in a wind, to get dusty. Next you think of the characteristics of iron: its hardness, its brittleness, its uses for war. When you put these two groups of connotations together, they cancel each other out, in part, and in part they coalesce into the image of something that is strong, guarded, hard to penetrate. When you add the characteristics of drawing a curtain (the secrecy and suspense), you have a complicated skein of characteristics that are all wound up together in the meaning of the metaphor. The sentence *says* (whether it is true or false) that Eastern and Western Europe are being prevented from communicating with each other; that this is keeping information from getting into and out of Eastern Europe; that the lack of communication is entirely the fault of the Russians; that the boundary line is manned by armed troops —and there are many other meanings.

Clearly, when you ask whether the metaphorical sentence is *true* or not, you find that it is, in fact, a bundle of different statements, some of which may be true and some false. When metaphors turn up in the course of an argument, it is not safe to take them as they appear and leave it at that. You must interpret them; that is, you must break them down a bit, in order to make explicit exactly what is, and what is not, being stated.

SUGGESTED ASSIGNMENTS

1. Identify the primary and secondary terms in these metaphors and indicate the points of likeness and unlikeness.
   a. High overhead a hawk swung at anchor.
   b. She fished the rejected poem out of the waste basket.
   c. Every man in the room was trying to get her wavelength but couldn't tune her in.
   d. If I should live to be
      The last leaf on the tree
         In the spring. . . .
2. Robert Burns begins a well-known poem with two open similes:
   My love is like a red, red rose
      That's newly sprung in June:

My love is like the melodie
That's sweetly played in tune.

Does *love* refer to his beloved or to the feeling of his heart? Jot down all the points of likeness for each simile and bring them to class for discussion. What do these many points of likeness suggest to you about the role of the reader in interpreting figurative language?

3. Students make considerable use of metaphors drawn from sports: I didn't get to first base with him; I got thrown for a loss in that exam. Choose one sport with which you are familiar and in ten minutes write as many metaphors as you can which are derived from it.

4. Language, it has been said, is a graveyard of dead metaphors. Using an unabridged or an etymological dictionary, look up the etymology of the following and report the live metaphors they once contained: *examine, investigate, depend, fret, grenade, magazine* (= periodical), *seminary, error, scruple, impede, obstruct, stagnate, ardent.*

5. Skillful speakers often employ metaphors that are drawn from the occupations of their listeners. For example, a political speaker might want to say that the promises of the other party sound fair but are not to be trusted. Here is the way he might express this idea metaphorically to different audiences:
   a. (To bankers) The Republicratic promises are nothing but watered stock.
   b. (To airplane pilots) The Republicratic promises are nothing but bent beams that will lead you to a crash on a mountain side.
   c. (To Texas ranchers) The Republicratic promises are nothing but loco weeds. They look edible and nourishing, but if your stock eats them, you will lose your herd.
   d. (To housewives) The Republicratic promises are the good berries on top of the basket.

   Imagine yourself as an educational speaker touring the country. One idea you wish to express forcefully is this: The higher one advances in his education, the more difficult the work becomes. If you were speaking in a mountain area you might use this metaphor: The higher one climbs up the peak of education, the rockier the way becomes. Now, describe three other groups whom you might address and write metaphors fitting the background of each to express your idea.

6. The metaphors that we accept, consciously or unconsciously, can become a strong influence in our thinking and on our actions. If, for instance, a college president or dean or professor accepts the metaphor that a college is a brain *factory*, the implications can be something like these:
   a. Every student, like an object on the assembly line, should receive exactly the same educational treatment: take the same standardized courses taught in the same way. And when a given number of operations have been performed on a student (as shown by his credit hours earned), he is a finished product, identical with the others.
   b. Every instructor, like an assembly-line worker, has one special job to do, and does it the same on every student.
   c. In time of haste, as in war, or of overcrowding, the assembly-line can be

moved faster. Thus we can get more of the same products in less time, for example, doctors in six years instead of eight years.

Assume that the dean of instruction in your college accepts this metaphor: A college is a nursery which grows many kinds of trees, shrubs, flowers, and plants. Write out the implications that this metaphor might have on your educaitonal life.

7. A "mixed metaphor" occurs when two or more metaphors are used together, the secondary terms of which are incongruent. The effect is sometimes ludicrous. Point out the mixed metaphors in the following examples:

   a. If you concentrate all your fire power on one man and he is not the nominee, Crommelin warned, the rug will be pulled out from under your house.

   b. As a politician . . . Bennett was supreme in his ability to walk a straight fence and keep both ears to the ground.

   c. This ulcerous gap that the spiral of inflation breeds. . . .

   d. The novelist must forge in the crucible of his imagination a new vision of the world.

   e. (From a college weekly newspaper) "The idea was hatched about two years ago by Larson, but it didn't actually catch fire until about two months ago when Larson and Nagel, the co-directors, jumped in feet first. Since then things have been really snowballing for the trio." (The *New Yorker*, which reported this mixed metaphor, commented: "No moss growing on those red-hot snowballs!")

8. Below, you will find one of the famous Lucy poems by Wordsworth. Read the poem carefully, noting especially the use of figurative language and the choice of words for emotive effect. Next, study the second version, which includes the stanzas and lines that the poet rejected in the process of composition. Finally, write an analytical theme explaining why you think the poet made these rejections.

SHE DWELT AMONG THE UNTRODDEN WAYS

She dwelt among the untrodden ways
    Beside the springs of Dove,
A Maid whom there were none to praise
    And very few to love:

A violet by a mossy stone   5
    Half hidden from the eye!
Fair as a star, when only one
    Is shining in the sky.

She lived unknown, and few could know
    When Lucy ceased to be;   10
But she is in her grave, and oh,
    The difference to me!

WILLIAM WORDSWORTH
(1770–1850)

SHE DWELT AMONG THE UNTRODDEN WAYS

[First stanza rejected:]
[My hope was one, from cities far,
Nursed on a lonesome heath;
Her lips were red as roses are,
Her hair a woodbine wreath.]

She dwelt among the untrodden ways	*1*
Beside the springs of Dove,	*2*
A Maid whom there were none to praise	*3*
And very few to love:	*4*
A violet by a mossy stone	*5*
Half hidden from the eye!	*6*
—Fair as a star, when only one	*7*
Is shining in the sky.	*8*

[Fourth stanza rejected:]
[And she was graceful as the broom
That flowers by Carron's side;
But slow distemper checked her bloom,
And on the Heath she died.]

She lived unknown, and few could know	*9*
When Lucy ceased to be;	*10*
But she is in her grave, and oh,	*11*
[Long time before her head lay low	9R
Dead to the world was she:	10R
But now she's etc.]	11R
The difference to me!	*12*

9. In E. A. Robinson's "Mr. Flood's Party," the theme is dramatically represented by Mr. Flood and given emotional and intellectual depth by means of
interrelated allusions and images focused on a central symbol. The theme
is the transcience of life; the central symbol is the jug. Read the poem carefully several times. Note especially all the jug and juglike references. Then
write a theme on the symbolic significance of the jug in "Mr. Flood's Party."
In the line "The bird is on the wing, the poet says," the allusion is to the
Rubaiyat of Omar Khayyam; the relevant stanzas are as follows:

Come, fill the Cup, and in the fire of Spring
Your winter-garment of Repentance fling:
   The Bird of Time has but a little way
To flutter—and the Bird is on the Wing.

Whether at Naishapur or Babylon,
Whether the Cup with sweet or bitter run,
   The Wine of Life keeps oozing drop by drop,
The Leaves of Life keep falling one by one.

MR. FLOOD'S PARTY

Old Eben Flood, climbing alone one night
Over the hill between the town below
And the forsaken upland hermitage
That held as much as he should ever know
On earth again of home, paused warily.
The road was his with not a native near;
And Eben, having leisure, said aloud,
For no man else in Tilbury Town to hear:

"Well, Mr. Flood, we have the harvest moon
Again, and we may not have many more;
The bird is on the wing, the poet says,
And you and I have said it here before.
Drink to the bird." He raised up to the light
The jug that he had gone so far to fill,
And answered huskily: "Well, Mr. Flood,
Since you propose it, I believe I will."

Alone, as if enduring to the end
A valiant armor of scarred hopes outworn,
He stood there in the middle of the road
Like Roland's ghost winding a silent horn.
Below him, in the town among the trees,
Where friends of other days had honored him,
A phantom salutation of the dead
Rang thinly till old Eben's eyes were dim.

Then, as a mother lays her sleeping child
Down tenderly, fearing it may awake,
He set the jug down slowly at his feet
With trembling care, knowing that most things break;
And only when assured that on firm earth
It stood, as the uncertain lives of men
Assuredly did not, he paced away,
And with his hand extended paused again;

"Well, Mr. Flood, we have not met like this
In a long time; and many a change has come
To both of us, I fear, since last it was
We had a drop together. Welcome home!"
Convivially returning with himself,
Again he raised the jug up to the light;
And with an acquiescent quaver said:
"Well, Mr. Flood, if you insist, I might.

"Only a very little, Mr. Flood—
For auld lang syne. No more, sir; that will do."
So, for the time, apparently it did,
And Eben evidently thought so too;

For soon amid the silver loneliness
Of night he lifted up his voice and sang,
Secure, with only two moons listening,
Until the whole harmonious landscape rang—

"For auld lang syne." The weary throat gave out;
The last word wavered, and the song was done.
He raised again the jug regretfully
And shook his head, and was again alone.
There was not much that was ahead of him,
And there was nothing in the town below—
Where strangers would have shut the many doors
That many friends had opened long ago.

Interpretational Hypothesis of Matthew Arnold's "To Marguerite"

Seymour Chatman
Morse Peckham

In "To Marguerite," discussed below, the relationships between the tenor (= primary term) and vehicle (= secondary term) inform the whole poem. The functional nature of this relationship is clearly revealed in the analysis following the poem. Morse Peckham is Distinguished Professor of English and Comparative Literature at the University of South Carolina; Seymour Chatman is Associate Professor of Speech at the University of California at Berkeley.

SWITZERLAND
Matthew Arnold (1822–1888)

5: TO MARGUERITE—CONTINUED

Yes! in the sea of life enisled,
With echoing straits between us thrown,

From *Word, Meaning, Poem*, by Seymour Chatman and Morse Peckham, 1961. Reprinted by permission of the authors and Thomas Y. Crowell Company.

Dotting the shoreless watery wild,
We mortal millions live *alone*.
The islands feel the enclasping flow,
And then their endless bounds they know.

But when the moon their hollows lights,
And they are swept by balms of spring,
And in their glens, on starry nights,
The nightingales divinely sing;
And lovely notes, from shore to shore,
Across the sounds and channels pour—

Oh! then a longing like despair
Is to their farthest caverns sent;
For surely once, they feel, we were
Parts of a single continent!
Now round us spreads the watery plain—
Oh might our marges meet again!

Who order'd, that their longing's fire
Should be, as soon as kindled, cool'd?
Who renders vain their deep desire?—
A God, a God their severance ruled!
And bade betwixt their shores to be
The unplumb'd, salt, estranging sea.

Arnold published this poem under various titles: "To Marguerite, in Returning a Volume of the Letters of Ortis" (1852), next as number V in the sequence of poems called "Switzerland" with the title as simply "To Marguerite" (1853), next as number VI in that series and with the same title (1854), then as number VII but with the new title "Isolation" (1857), again as number 7 of "Switzerland" with the title as given above (1869), and finally as number 5 (1888). Since these titles were used at various times for other poems in the same series, this poem is best identified and remembered by its first line.

Of these various titles only that of 1857, "Isolation," is the kind of title that gives some information about the poem itself. "Insula" in Latin and "isola" in Italian, "île" in French, and "isle" or "island" in English all have the same meaning. The land of an island is separated by the surrounding sea from other land. Hence an "isolated" person is separated from other persons. What physically isolates a prisoner from society is concrete: stone walls and bars. What emotionally isolates an individual from society is a sense of separation from others because he does not share with them feelings which emotional communication makes possible. All these uses are metaphorical developments of "to be an island." In the first line the poem states that it is true, emphatically true ("Yes!"), that we are islands in the sea of life. The separating medium, then, is life itself, or the conditions of existence in which we find ourselves. Between us are echoing straits. Two questions arise here. Why "echoing" and why "thrown"? An echo is the return of one's voice to oneself by other than a human agency. The word brings out the failure of communication between the islands, or individuals. Although isolated individuals may attempt to establish emotional communication with others, they "hear only their own voices," i.e. they experience no answering emotional response. "Thrown" implies that some power external to the conditions of life is responsible for the existence of the straits. But that power is not identified. It raises the expectation that it will be. Whether that expectation will be fulfilled or disappointed remains to be seen. The "wild" or wilderness of the water is appropriate because it is consistent that there is no communication, as we have seen, between the islands; and thus the wild is shoreless. But this word raises a question. Do not islands have shores? Yes, but so do continents. The sea of life, then, is different from the actual seas of the earth which are bordered by the shores of continents. In the sea of life, the conditions of existence in which we find ourselves, there are no continents, continuous bodies of lands; there is no such thing as human solidarity. Thus "we mortal millions live alone," each separate on his own little island. The italicization of *alone* is a typographical device to indicate emphasis.

At first glance, lines 5–6 seem to add nothing to what has been said, until we consider "feel" and "know." The metaphor is now extended. Not only are human beings isolated; they are also aware of being isolated. They are clasped or firmly caught in the "flow" or continuously changing medium of isolation. When the individual feels that he is inescapably separated from other human beings by the continuously shifting conditions of experiences, then he is aware, consciously, of his "endless bounds." This last phrase is a paradox, since a "bound" or frontier *is* an "end" or limit. Thus the phrase means "boundless bounds," or "no bounds at all." The phrase is a way of saying, "There are no bounds, no frontiers, to the personality; that is, one personality never genuinely impinges on, confronts, meets, and contacts another personality." The two lines, then, are concerned with the raising of an emotional response to the level of an intellectual conception.

This explains the force of the "But" in the first line of the next stanza (l. 7): "In spite of their knowledge, in spite of their intellectual certainty that this isolation is the condition of life and always will be——." The implication is that a longing for communication and a sense of solidarity and communication with other human beings will appear and will be felt. The rest of this stanza, then, is concerned with the conditions under which such a longing will occur. Having established that the metaphor of "island" equals "individual human personality" and "sea" equals "conditions of existence," the poet now speaks for a time entirely in terms derived from the vehicle. When the moonlight shines into the dark and hidden places of the islands, when the sweet winds of spring blow across them, when the nightingales, the

birds of spring and love, sing on perfect nights, and their notes are heard·
across the straits, the sounds, and the channels, then the islands feel in their
deepest caverns a desire which is like despair, that is, a desire which involves
an awareness that the desire cannot be gratified. With "feel" the language
of the tenor is reintroduced. If the whole preceding passage is expressed in
the language of the tenor, we have something like this: When the individual
finds himself experiencing a great sensuous gratification (the moonlit spring
nights) and a great emotional gratification (the song of the nightingales
from island to island), that is, considering the traditional significance of the
nightingale, when he is in love (the poem, after all, is addressed to a woman)
and finds himself experiencing the feeling of communication, then, the very
depths of his personality (the farthest caverns), he experiences a longing
which he knows cannot be gratified. The "for" in line 15 connects the ensuing statement with the preceding one. It implies, "We are justified in feeling
this longing. Surely, all men at one time were part of a single, continuous
human solidarity ('Single continent'). Although the conditions of life separate us from each other, we have a terrible longing to experience that continuity" (that is, in the language of the vehicle, that the islands' edges or
marges ["bounds," l. 6] meet and the islands join together to form a single
continent).

In the next stanza the voice of the islands has ceased and the poet
speaks. In "order'd" is picked up and developed the implication of "thrown"
in line 2. The conditions of life do not merely exist; they were made that
way. A new metaphor is now introduced. The vehicle is the kindling and
then cooling or extinguishing of a fire. The tenor is the arousing and then
suppression of emotional desire, or longing, among human beings. The longing is suppressed as soon as felt, because it is futile ("vain"); and it is futile
because he has already raised the feeling of isolation to intellectual certainty
(ll. 5–6), and because he has further concluded that longing is hopeless.
Again the question is asked (l. 21): "What force makes it impossible that
the deep desire of the islands for communion be satisfied?" The poet again
shifts into the language of the basic vehicle of the poem. "A God decreed
that islands should be separate and that between their shores should always
exist the unfathomable, salty, and separating sea." In the language of the
tenor: "Some force which we cannot control or understand" (i.e. it is "a
God," not the Christian God or some particular non-Christian God; the
God involved is not identified) "is responsible for the fact that some barrier
always prevents the emotional communication of human beings with one
another and that that barrier is at once incomprehensible ('unplumb'd'),
sterile or destructive of emotional gratification ('salty'), and capable of
making us feel like strangers to one another, people with nothing in common
('estranging')."

The poem, then, is concerned with the emotional isolation of human
beings from each other, with the desire that that isolation should be tran-

scended or destroyed, and with the knowledge that that desire can never be gratified, even in love under the most sensuously and aesthetically perfect conditions.

SUGGESTED ASSIGNMENT

Printed below is Shakespeare's "Sonnet LXXIII." A magnificent example of metaphor in action, it is built on a series of figures (one basic figure in each quatrain) revolving about the same central idea. Study the poem carefully until you think you understand it as fully as you can. Then write a detailed explanation of the basic metaphor in either quatrain two or three, making clear the points of comparison between tenor and vehicle. William Empson's famous discussion of the last line of the first quatrain is an example of how you might proceed: ". . . the comparison holds for many reasons; because ruined monastery choirs are places in which to sing, because they involve sitting in a row, because they are made of wood, are carved into knots and so forth, because they used to be surrounded by a sheltering building crystallised out of the likeness of a forest, and coloured with stained glass and painting like flowers and leaves, because they are now abandoned by all but the grey walls coloured like the skies of winter, because the cold and Narcissistic charm suggested by choir-boys suits well with Shakespeare's feeling for the object of the Sonnets, and for various sociological and historical reasons (the protestant destruction of monasteries; fear of puritanism), which it would be hard now to trace out in their proportions; these reasons, and many more relating the simile to its place in the Sonnet, must all combine to give the line its beauty, and there is a sort of ambiguity in not knowing which of them to hold most clearly in mind. Clearly this is involved in all such richness and heightening of effect, and the machinations of ambiguity are among the very roots of poetry." [1]

SONNET LXXIII

That time of year thou mayst in me behold
When yellow leaves, or none, or few, do hang
Upon those boughs which shake against the cold,
Bare ruin'd choirs, where late the sweet birds sang.
In me thou see'st the twilight of such day   5
As after sunset fadeth in the west,
Which by and by black night doth take away,
Death's second self, that seals up all in rest.
In me thou see'st the glowing of such fire,
That on the ashes of his youth doth lie,   10
As the death-bed whereon it must expire

[1] William Empson, *Seven Types of Ambiguity,* rev. ed. (London, Chatto and Windus, 1949), pp. 2–3.

Consum'd with that which it was nourish'd by.
　This thou perceiv'st, which makes thy love more strong,
　To love that well which thou must leave ere long.

WILLIAM SHAKESPEARE
(1564–1616)

Phonetic Symbolism in Poetry

Norman C. Stageberg
Wallace L. Anderson

Here are two Rumanian words: *mic* (rimes with pick) and *mare* (pronounced with the *a* of *far* and the *e* of *fiancé*). One of these two words means big; the other means small. Judging by the sound alone, try to match the two words with the right meanings. Later, try it on your friends. If most of them say that *mic* means small, which is correct, then you have in the word an example of phonetic symbolism, the congruence of sound and meaning.

The essay below is a discussion of how phonetic symbolism operates in poetry. Two short poems, illustrative of phonetic symbolism, follow the essay.

Phonetic symbolism is a natural correspondence between sound and sense. There are words, writes Otto Jespersen, eminent Danish linguist, "which we feel instinctively to be adequate to express the ideas they stand for, and others the sounds of which are felt to be more or less incongruous with their signification ... everybody must feel that the word *roll* ... is more adequate than the Russian word *katat'*." [1] This is to say, the very sounds of the word *roll* make it more expressive of its sense than the sounds of its

[1] *Language, Its Nature, Development, and Origin* (London, George Allen and Unwin, 1922), p. 398.

Russian synonym *katat'*. Psychological experiments and the study of primitive languages both affirm correspondences of sound and sense.[2] As a simple example of psychological evidence, try the following experiment on your friends. Show the two drawings reproduced below and ask your friends to match these with the meaningless words *taketa* and *naluma*. If most of them agree about which word goes with which drawing, then it appears likely that some correspondence does exist between the sounds and the visual impressions.[3]

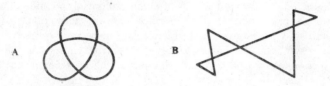

Phonetic symbolism in poetry is of three kinds: (1) speech sounds which imitate actual sounds; (2) speech sounds which have been so arranged as to make them difficult or easy to articulate; (3) speech sounds which in themselves suggest meaning; these are called phonetic intensives.

ONOMATOPOEIA.   The simplest kind of phonetic symbolism consists of speech sounds which imitate actual sounds, such as we hear in the words *sizz* and *roar*. Such imitation is called onomatopoeia. Onomatopoetic words are found in many languages. For example, the meaning of the English onomatopoetic word *murmur* is expressed by *omumu* in Tahitian, by *murmuru* in Tamil, and by *marmara-* in Sanskrit. In Zulu the word *bomboloza* means to rumble in the bowlels.

The human speech organs, however, are incapable of articulating with exactness many of the sounds of nature; hence the speech sounds used to represent natural sounds are often only approximate. For instance the English *whisper*, the French *chucoter*, the German *flüstern*—the English *bow-wow* and the French *gnaf-gnaf*—are all attempts, inexact but suggestive, to represent natural sounds. The reason for the success of such inexactly

[2] See, for example:
Edward Sapir, "A Study in Phonetic Symbolism," *Selected Writings of Edward Sapir* (Berkeley, University of California Press, 1949), 61–72.
Wolfgang Köhler, *Gestalt Psychology* (New York, Liveright Publishing Corp., 1929), p. 242.
[3] Adapted from Wolfgang Köhler, *Gestalt Psychology* (New York, Liveright Publishing Corp., 1929), pp. 242–243. See also G. W. Hartmann, *Gestalt Psychology* (New York, The Ronald Press Company, 1935), pp. 147–148.
Also: "There is no doubt that synaesthetic combinations and associations permeate all languages and that these correspondences have been, quite rightly, exploited and elaborated by the poets." René Welleck and Austin Warren, *Theory of Literature* (New York, Harcourt Brace Jovanovich, Inc., 1949), p. 164.

imitative sounds has been explained by the English philologist Henry Bradley, who has pointed out that the resemblance of an onomatopoetic word to the sound it names.

> . . . consists not so much in similarity of impression on the ear as in similarity of mental suggestion. For instance, it is not at all literally true that a gun, or a heavy body impinging on a door, "says bang." But the sequence of the three sounds of which the word consists is of such a nature that it can easily be uttered with force, so as to suggest the startling effect of a sudden violent noise, while the final consonant admits of being prolonged to express the notion of a continued resonance. In this instance and in many others, the so-called "imitative" word represents an inarticulate noise not so much by way of an echo as symbolically. That is to say, the elements composing the sound of the word combine to produce a mental effect which we recognize as analogous to that produced by the noise.[4]

As examples of onomatopoeia in poetry we may cite Pope's *the torrent roars*; Nashe's bird calls, *cuckoo, jug-jug, pu-we, to-witta woo*; and Poe's description of the susurrus of silk, *the silken sad uncertain rustling*.

An onomatopoetic word may express, not only a sound, but the being which produces the sound, as in the English *peeweet*, in the Australian *twonk*, which means frog, and in the Annamese *cupcup*, which means a tiger, the sounds resembling those made by the tiger when stalking his prey. An onomatopoetic word may also express the sound plus the movement that causes it, as in *tap* and *bubble*, for example, Tennyson's

Bubbled the nightingale and heeded not.[5]

Words sometimes lose their onomatopoetic quality as in the course of time they undergo changes of sound. For example, the Latin *pipio*, a peeping bird, is now English *pigeon*, its original imitative force having been lost through a series of sound changes. But language also takes on new onomatopoetic words as human beings invent new combinations of sound that seem expressive of meaning. If, for instance, we should be told that a car *whooshed* by or that a *yakity-yak* issued from a room in the women's dormitory, we should have no difficulty in understanding these imitative words, even though we had never heard them before.

[4] *The Making of English* (New York, The Macmillan Company, and London, Collier-Macmillan, Ltd., 1904), p. 156.

[5] Of this line from *The Princess*, Tennyson remarked:
"When I was in a friend's garden, I heard a nightingale singing with such a frenzy of passion that it was unconscious of everything else, and not frightened though I came and stood quite close beside it. I saw its eye flashing and felt the air bubble in my ear through the vibration." *The Works of Tennyson*, with notes by the author, ed. by Hallam, Lord Tennyson (New York, The Macmillan Company, 1923 edition), p. 916.

EXERCISE

Point out the onomatopoetic words in the following passages.

1. *(Description of the sounds of serpents)*
    A dismal universal hiss

JOHN MILTON

2. ... the sea, playing on the yellow sand,
    Sends forth a rattling murmur to the land.

CHRISTOPHER MARLOWE

3. *(Description of the sound of ice-laden branches)*
    ... they click upon themselves.

ROBERT FROST

4. The myraid shriek of wheeling ocean-fowl,
    The league-long roller thundering on the reef,
    The moving whisper of huge trees that branched
    And blossomed in the zenith, or the sweep
    Of some precipitous rivulet to the wave.   5

ALFRED, LORD TENNYSON

5. When the hounds of spring are on winter's traces,
        The mother of months in meadow or plain
    Fills the shadows and windy places
        With lisp of leaves and ripple of rain.

ALGERNON C. SWINBURNE

6. I hear lake water lapping with low sounds by the shore.[6]

WILLIAM BUTLER YEATS

7. And the plashing of waterdrops
    In the marble fountain
    Comes down the garden paths.[7]

AMY LOWELL

---

[6] Reprinted with permission of The Macmillan Company from *Collected Poems* by William Butler Yeats. Copyright 1906 by The Macmillan Company. Renewed 1934 by William Butler Yeats.

[7] From Amy Lowell, *Complete Poetical Works* (Boston, Houghton Mifflin Company, 1955).

8.   The moan of doves in immemorial elms
     And murmuring of innumerable bees.[8]

ALFRED, LORD TENNYSON

9.   How often, these hours, have I heard the monotonous
     crool of a dove.[9]

WALTER DE LA MARE

EASE OF ARTICULATION.   The second kind of sound symbolism consists of speech sounds which have been so arranged as to make them difficult or easy to articulate. Clusters of consonant sounds which require difficult or labored muscular effort seem appropriate for the description of difficult or violent movement, or for harsh effects, for example, Pope's

When Ajax strives some rock's vast weight to throw.

On the other hand, words that move easily in utterance, unimpeded by difficulty of articulation, seem fitting for the description of smooth and easy movement, for example, Milton's description of the road from the universe to Hell,

Smooth, easy, inoffensive down to Hell.

Here the effortless transitions between *smooth* and *easy* and *inoffensive* suggest the easiness of the decent.

EXERCISE

1.   Of the two passages below by Milton the first describes the opening of the gates of Hell; the second, the opening of the gates of Heaven. Point out how the sounds help to indicate the manner of the opening of each.

a.   Then in the key-hole turns
           Th' intricate wards, and every bolt and bar
           Of massy iron or solid rock with ease.
           Unfast'ns. On a sudden op'n fly,

----

[8] If the sounds in these lines are reproduced in a line of different meaning, for example,

More ordure never will renew out midden's pure manure,

the suggestiveness of the original is lost. The lesson is clear: onomatopoeia cannot by itself convey meaning; it can only fortify the sound impressions described by meaningful words. This example is taken from Laura Riding and Robert Graves, *A Survey of Modernist Poetry* (Garden City, New York, Doubleday & Company, Inc., 1928), p. 37.

[9] From Walter de la Mare, *The Complete Poems of Walter de la Mare* (London, The Society of Authors, 1969).

With impetuous recoil and jarring sound,
Th' infernal doors, and on their hinges grate
Harsh thunder.

b.   Heaven op'n'd wide
Her ever-during gates, harmonious sound
On golden hinges moving.

2. The two following passages by Milton deal with movement. The first describes Satan's struggle as he makes his difficult way through a turbulent chaos. The second describes a dance of nature. In what parts of these lines do the sounds themselves seem to reinforce the sense?

a. So he with difficulty and labour hard,
Moved on, with difficulty and labour he.

b. The sounds and seas with all their finny drove,
Now to the moon in wavering morrice move,
And on the tawny sands and shelves
Trip the pert fairies and the dapper elves;

3. In the following poem by Thomas Hardy there are many consonant combinations that are hard to say. These consist of the end group in a word plus the beginning consonants of the following word. Read the poem aloud to find out these consonant clusters and see what purpose they serve in the poem as a whole.

IN TENEBRIS, I

Wintertime nights;
By my bereavement-pain
It cannot bring again:
Twice no one dies.

Flower-petals flee;   5
But, since it once hath been,
No more that severing scene
Can harrow me.

Birds faint in dread:
I shall not lose old strength   10
In the lone frost's black length:
Strength long since fled!

Leaves freeze to dun;
But friends cannot turn cold
This season as of old   15
For him with none.

Tempests may scath;
But love cannot make smart
Again this year his heart
Who no heart hath.   20

Black is night's cope;
But death will not appal
One who, past doubtings all,
Waits in unhope.

THOMAS HARDY

PHONETIC INTENSIVES.[10]   The third kind of phonetic symbolism consists of speech sounds which in themselves suggest meaning; these are called phonetic intensives.[11] An example occurs in the word *flare*, whose initial sounds, [fl], carry a suggested meaning of moving light. The origin of the association between phonetic intensives and their meaning is unclear. For instance, we do not know whether the initial [fl] in some words suggests moving light because of some inherent fitness between the sounds [fl] and their meaning, or because the accidents of linguistic history have produced words like *flash, flare, flame, flicker*, whose initial [fl]s and similar meanings have caused [fl] to become associated with moving light. Nevertheless, words containing such phonetic intensives may have a special intensity because the denotation of the word as a whole is strengthened by the suggested meanings of some of the sounds it contains. Let us examine the word *glimmer* as an example. Its [gl] has behind it a meaning of light, borne out by such words as *glow, glare, glint, gleam, glisten*; its [ɪ] suggests smallness, as in *dim, bit, sip, chip, slim*; its [ɚ] indicates repetition, as in *twitter, flicker, flutter, sputter, chatter*. Thus these three sounds in *glimmer* suggest the meaning of a small repeatedly moving light, and in so doing intensify the denotative sense of the word as a whole.

Of the many phonetic intensives found in poetry, we shall discuss only a few here.

Three pairs of sounds are employed with great frequency. The vowels [u], as in *doom*, and [o], as in *woe*, are used to suggest a state of feeling that may be loosely described by terms like *melancholy, unhappiness*, and *mournfulness*; thus words like *gloom, forlorn, moan, sorrow* are in frequent use, and the [u] or [o] sounds may dominate a passage concerned with unhappiness. The vowels [i], as in *peep*, and [ɪ], as in *drip*, suggest smallness, exemplified in *wee, teeny, thin, wink, flicker, trickle*. At the ends of words the sounds [l], spelt *-le*, and [ɚ], spelt *-er*, suggest the frequent repetition of

[10] Known also as "phonesthemes."
[11] For the pronunciation of the symbols in brackets, see Table of Sound Symbols on page 180.

an action. Of these our language has countless examples, such as *clatter, jingle, glitter, sparkle, twinkle, ripple, mutter, shatter, trickle.* In some words, a closing [l] suggests the repetition not of an action but of some visual detail, as in *dapple, stipple, freckle, bramble, bristle.*[12]

Of the consonants used as phonetic intensives we have already mentioned [fl] for moving light and [gl] for light. Among others at the beginnings of words, [b] gives the impression of impact, as in *bang, bump, bounce, bat*; [bl] carries the idea of impetus and use of breath or air, as in *blow, blast, bluster, blizzard*; [gr] suggests roughness and coarseness, as in *grind, grit, gravel, gride, grate*; [skr] indicates a grating impact or sound, as in *scratch, scrape, scrabble, scrannel*; [sp] indicates a point, as in *spire, spark, spot, spout, spike, spade*; [str] has the sense of thinness and narrowness, as in *strait, strip, stream, strap, street.*

Of the consonants at the end of words [p], [t], and [k] give the sense of an abrupt stoppage of movement, whereas [ʃ], spelt *-sh,* indicates an unabrupt stoppage of movement. These contrasting effects become evident when we compare *clap* with *clash, bat* with *bash,* and *smack* with *smash.* In the end position an [n], or [ŋ], spelt *-ng,* after a vowel suggests resonance, as in *clang.*

Knowledge of the meanings of phonetic intensives is sometimes helpful in understanding why particular words in poems seem to be especially appropriate and even inevitable. A double caution, however, is needed. First, we must bear in mind that this kind of phonetic symbolism is operative only when the sense of the word as a whole is related to the sense of the phonetic intensive which it contains. The [fl] in *flea,* for example, and the [ɪ] in *big* have no suggestive power because the potential meanings of these sounds, respectively moving light and smallness, are outside the areas of meaning of the words themselves. Second, we must understand that an automatic stimulus-response relationship does not exist between the phonetic intensives and their imputed meanings. Rather, the meanings are latent, and rise to the surface of consciousness only when the enclosing context—its sense, feeling, and general import—offers conditions favorable to their emergence. Such conditions may be brought about by a poet's delicate and sensitive handling of language, and it is then that these intensives flash into life and help create that vividness and intensity of experience that is sometimes attributed to "word magic." For example, the atmosphere of the next poem, with its slow rhythm and low-keyed imagery, builds up a feeling of sadness. In this context the [o] sounds release their latent suggestiveness to reinforce the total impression.

[12] In a study of over 600 English monosyllables. Professor F. W. Householder found that the vowel [ʌ], as in *mud,* has, in the large majority of cases, a general meaning of "undesirable." "On the Problem of Sound Meaning, an English Phonestheme," *Word,* 2:83–84 (1946). [eds.]

ALL DAY I HEAR

All day I hear the noise of waters
    Making moan,
Sad as the sea-bird is, when going
    Forth alone,
He hears the winds cry to the waters'   5
    Monotone.

The grey winds, the cold winds are blowing
    Where I go.
I hear the noise of many waters
    Far below.   10
All day, all night, I hear them flowing
    To and fro.[13]

JAMES JOYCE

On the contrary, the [o] sounds have no suggestion of melancholy in

More hope arose within his joyous heart
As, note by note, the bugles nearer blew.

because the context is not sympathetic to such a meaning.

The phonetic intensive in a word may be given special emphasis by the repetition of the sound in other words in the passage. A. E. Housman, for example, uses this means of strengthening the effect of *snap*: "And sharp the link of life will *snap*."

SUGGESTED ASSIGNMENTS

In the italicized words of the following quotations point out each phonetic intensive and its suggested meaning.

1. She is a winsome *wee* thing.

ROBERT BURNS

2. Now fades the *glimmering* landscape on the sight.

THOMAS GRAY

3. A late lark *twitters* from the quiet skies.

WILLIAM E. HENLEY

[13] From *Collected Poems* by James Joyce. Copyright 1918 by B. W. Huebsch, Inc., 1946 by Nora Joyce. Reprinted by permission of The Viking Press, Inc., the executors of the James Joyce Estate, and Jonathan Cape, Ltd.

4.   ... crickets *jingle* there.

WILFRED OWEN

5.   *Blow, blow,* thou winter wind.

WILLIAM SHAKESPEARE

6.   The *moan* of multitudes in *woe.*

JOHN MASEFIELD

7.   The birds sit *chittering* in the thorn.

ROBERT BURNS

8.   The naked stars ... *glinting* on the puddles.

SIEGFRIED SASSOON

9.   Down the road someone is practicing scales
     The notes like little fishes vanish with a *wink*
        of tails.[14]

LOUIS MACNEICE

10.   [A FOLK PRAYER]
      From ghoulies and ghosties and long-legged beasties
      And things that go *bump* in the night,
      Good Lord, deliver us.

ANONYMOUS

11.   ... the *flickering* gunnery rumbles.

WILFRED OWEN

12.   [DESCRIPTION OF THE SONG OF A WOODLARK]
      Teevo, cheevo cheevio chee:
      O where, what can that be?
      Weedio-weedio: there again!
      So tiny a *trickle* of song-strain.[15]

GERARD MANLEY HOPKINS

13.   This is the way the world ends
      Not with a *bang* but a *whimper.*[16]

T. S. ELIOT

[14] From Louis Macneice, *Collected Poems,* 1925–1948. New York: Oxford University Press © 1963.
[15] From Gerard Manley Hopkins, *Poems of Gerard Manley Hopkins.* New York: Oxford University Press, copyright 1918.
[16] From T. S. Eliot, *Collected Poems of T. S. Eliot, 1909–1935.* New York: Harcourt Brace Jovanovich, Inc.

14.　I turned about and looked where branches break
　　　The *glittering* reaches of the flooded lake.[17]

WILLIAM BUTLER YEATS

15.　Three jolly gentlemen
　　　　　At break of day
　　　Came *clitter-clatter* down the stairs
　　　　　And galloped away.[18]

WALTER DE LA MARE

16.　The mugger *cracked* his whip and sang.

W. W. GIBSON

17.　The moon, *dwindled* and *thinned* to a fringe of
　　　a fingernail held to the candle.[19]

GERARD MANLEY HOPKINS

18.　When will return the glory of your prime?
　　　*No more—*Oh, never *more*!

PERCY BYSSHE SHELLEY

19.　[DESCRIPTION OF A SALOON BAR]
　　　. . . the *glush* of
　　　squirting taps plus *slush* of foam knocked off.[20]

E. E. CUMMINGS

20.　Water *ruffled* and *speckled* by galloping wind.

F. S. FLINT

21.　What sound was dearest in his native dells?
　　　The mellow *lin-lan-lone* of evening bells.

ALFRED, LORD TENNYSON

22.　A full sea *glazed* with muffled moonlight.

ALFRED, LORD TENNYSON

23.　The street-lamp *sputtered*,
　　　The street-lamp *muttered*.[21]

T. S. ELIOT

[17] Reprinted with permission of The Macmillan Company from *Collected Poems* by William Butler Yeats. Copyright 1933 by The Macmillan Company. Renewed 1961 by Bertha Georgie Yeats.

[18] From Walter de la Mare, *The Complete Poems of Walter de la Mare.* London: Society of Authors, 1969.

[19] From Gerard Manley Hopkins, *Poems of Gerard Manley Hopkins.* New York: Oxford University Press, copyright 1918.

[20] From E. E. Cummings, *Fifty Poems.* New York: Duell, Sloan and Pearce, copyright 1939. Copyright 1940 by E. E. Cummings.

[21] From T. S. Eliot, *Collected Poems of T. S. Eliot, 1909–1935.* New York: Harcourt Brace Jovanovich, Inc.

24. [DESCRIPTION OF THE STRIDENT PIPES OF SHEPHERDS]
And when they list, their lean and flashy songs
Grate on their *scrannel* pipes of wretched straw.

JOHN MILTON

25. [DESCRIPTION OF A SNAKE AT A WATER TROUGH]
He sipped with his *straight* mouth . . .
And *flickered* his two-forked tongue . . .[22]

D. H. LAWRENCE

26. [DESCRIPTION OF A KNIGHT, ENTERING A DARK CAVE]
His *glist'ring* armour made
A little *glooming* light, much like a shade.

EDMUND SPENSER

27. [DESCRIPTION OF THE CHARIOT OF THE SON OF GOD]
And from about him fierce Effusion roll'd
Of smoke and *bickering* fire, and *sparkles* dire.

JOHN MILTON

Bredon Hill

A. E. Housman

The following poem presents a life-death opposition with a corresponding contrast of mood. The change of mood from joy to gloom is accompanied by, and strengthened by, a change in imagery that moves from

a summer scene to a winter one. Sound symbolism also plays a supporting role. At what points and by what specific vowel does sound function symbolically in "Bredon Hill"? The name of the hill, by the way, is pronounced as if it were spelled Breedon.

In summertime on Bredon
      The bells they sound so clear;
Round both the shires they ring them
      In steeples far and near,
      A happy noise to hear.   5

Here of a Sunday morning,
      My love and I would lie,
And see the coloured counties,
      And hear the larks so high
      About us in the sky.   10

The bells would ring to call her
      In valleys miles away:
'Come all to church, good people;
      Good people, come and pray.'
      But here my love would stay.   15

And I would turn and answer
      Among the springing thyme,
'Oh, peal upon our wedding,
      And we will hear the chime,
      And come to church in time.'   20

But when the snows at Christmas
      On Bredon top were strown,
My love rose up so early
      And stole out unbeknown
      And went to church alone.   25

They tolled the one bell only,
      Groom there was none to see,
The mourners followed after,
      And so to church went she,
      And would not wait for me.   30

The bells they sound on Bredon,
      And still the steeples hum.

'Come all to church, good people,'—
   Oh, noisy bells, be dumb;
   I hear you, I will come.   35

The Harbor

Carl Sandburg

The basic structure of "The Harbor" is relatively simple. It consists of
two contrastive images. But though the structure is simple, the poem has
a rich complexity because there are so many points of contrast—in
imagery, movement, feeling, idea, and sound. Read the poem aloud
slowly and carefully. Note the patterns of sound in both vowels and
consonants. Study the use of sound in relation to the imagery and ideas
in the poem. Then write a paper entitled "Sound Symbolism in 'The
Harbor.' "

Passing through huddled and ugly walls
By doorways where women haggard
Looked from their hunger-deep eyes,
Haunted with shadows of hunger-hands,
Out from the huddled and ugly walls,

I came sudden, at the city's edge,
On a blue burst of lake,
Long lake waves breaking under the sun
On a spray-flung curve of shore;
And a fluttering storm of gulls,

Masses of great gray wings
And flying white bellies
Veering and wheeling free in the open.

Poetry and Stylistics

Archibald A. Hill

The idea that form gives meaning is basic not only to descriptive linguistics but also to literary criticism. In the next essay, a renowned linguist uses the formal principle of analogy to interpret three well-known poems, with illuminating results. Professor Hill was the executive secretary of the Linguistic Society of America for many years and is the author of *Introduction to Linguistic Structures*.

I shall discuss here the use that three poems make of a single stylistic device. The device is analogy. There is nothing new in saying that poets make use of analogies; the familiar critical terms metaphor and simile describe two main types of them. What I shall try to show is that development of the analogy is the device by which the poet gives stylistic unity to his poem, and makes it meaningful in ways beyond the meaning of sober, everyday sentences. We shall see that the device is characteristic of poetry, and that it may lead to meanings . . . [that are] in conflict with the linguistic [meaning] . . .

Our first poem is this from Sandburg:

LOST [1]

> Desolate and lone
> All night long on the lake
> Where fog trails and mist creeps,
> The whistle of a boat
> Calls and cries unendingly
> Like some lost child
> In tears and trouble
> Hunting the harbor's breast
> And the harbor's eyes.

From *Essays on the Language of Literature*, edited by Seymour Chatman and Samuel R. Levin (Boston: Houghton Mifflin Company, 1967). Copyright 1967 by Archibald A. Hill. This article was presented as part of the Peters Rushton Seminars in Contemporary Prose and Poetry, the University of Virginia, 21 September, 1956. Reprinted by the kind permission of the author.

The poem obviously offers no very great difficulty in understanding. The whistle of a boat reminds the poet of a lost child crying, and that seems clear enough. The analogy is overt, since the poet tells us flatly "like some lost child." Yet the simple over-all structure is not quite all that is here, since the separate parts of the two halves of the analogy are brought into a more detailed relationship with each other. The whistle is to the boat on the lake, as tears are to the child away from its mother. The phrase "the harbor's breast," compresses a subanalogy. "Breast is to mother, as X is to harbor." Note that we are left to supply the identity of the missing X—one of two places in the poem where we meet such an implicit analogy. The X is not hard to supply: in this case it is the mooring at which the boat comes to rest. The second X, of course, is in the compressed phrase, "harbor's eyes," where eyes are to mother as X is to harbor—evidently harbor's lights.

Sandburg's little poem is obviously a simple one. If it has interest it must somehow be in the analogies around which it is built. We can point to a number of ways in which these analogies are interesting. The first one is of no literary importance, though of interest to us in this particular kind of study. By throwing together items which belong to the two halves of his analogy—*eyes* which belong with the child-mother half, and *harbor* which belongs with the boat-harbor half, Sandburg gives us a phrase which is compressed—"harbor's eyes"—and leaves one term in his proportional analogy as an unsolved X, which the reader must supply. The reader can be relied on to solve it, since the structure of the analogy forces the solution. This sort of unsolved X is one of the principal ways in which an analogy is made to say something which is there stylistically, but linguistically not present at all.

Second, the poem starts with a simple comparison. Probably none of us have failed to respond to the loneliness of a train or boat whistle at night. The ascription of human emotional value to such a sound is a commonplace, and might be considered one of the tritest comparisons a poet could make. It is the points of correspondence, as the single general analogy is worked out in a series of linked subanalogies, that give the poem structure, unity, and some sense of originality. Further, as by now we might expect of a poetic structure, it always suggests correspondences with the metaliterary world of cultural values—we can extrapolate from literary structure to a structure of meanings. For me, at least, the lost boat, compared to a child who has lost the security of its mother's breast, suggests an identification with the society we live in. We, too, are lost, and long to return to a simpler society in the childhood of the world. The Sandburg poem is simple, indeed, but the stylistic structure is certainly more meaningful than would be the linguistic statement—"that boat sounds like a lost child."

From Sandburg, we can turn to a lyric by Emily Dickinson.

The Soul selects her own society,
Then shuts the door;

On her divine majority
Obtrude no more.

Unmoved she notes the chariot's pausing
At her low gate;
Unmoved, an emperor is kneeling
Upon her mat.

I've known her from an ample nation
Choose one;
Then close the valves of her attention
Like stone.

The Sandburg and Dickinson poems are alike in using analogies, and in having easily discoverable surface meanings. The simplest reading of this second poem might be to say that the soul chooses friendships in an arbitrary way. Yet when we leave this first message, we find that Emily Dickinson operates throughout with a series of different but related analogies, all of which leave unsolved X's, and as we shall see, the solution of the X's greatly modifies the surface, linguistic meaning of the several sentences. In the Sandburg poem, we found a single overtly stated general analogy, with sub-analogies, and unsolved X's were found only in the subanalogies.

Let us start with the first two lines. The analogy is complex to state, and would have to be in a form something like this:

The soul selects X^1	as X^2 selects society
The soul shuts X^3	as X^2 shuts a door

In spite of the large number of unsolved X's, it is still not difficult to supply identification:

The soul selects a companion	as a housedweller lets in society
The soul shuts her avenues of emotional communication	as a housedweller shuts the door

The overall comparison is of a soul dwelling in the body, to a human being dwelling in a house.

The next two lines offer another analogy. *Choice* (of society) is to the soul as *majority* is to X. Our question is, then, in what kind of entity can we equate majority with choice? I know of only one such entity, and so only one candidate for the solution of this particular X. It is a parliamentary body. The soul is now various, a world of its own, selfgoverning and democratic. Part of the concept is old—a poet in an older and more aristocratic society said "My mind to me a kingdom is." It seems peculiarly American, however, to compare the soul, even in this indirect fashion, with Congress.

The choice of the soul has been called a divine majority—I think you would agree that the soul is here pictured as a divine body politic, with something of the majesty of government.

Yet note the next verse, simpler in its related analogies. The soul rejects visitors, as X (who has a low gate with a mat) rejects charioteer and emperor. The X is a housedweller again, but the house is surely a cottage. There is again something peculiarly American in identifying an individual soul with the majesty of government, and, in turn, in placing that government in a cottage where it can reject an emperor.

It is in the last verse of the poem that the real surprise lies. The analogy runs something like this.

> The soul selects one individual from a nation
>   (as X^1 selects one X^2 from a host of X^2s)
> The soul closes her attention immutably
>   as X^1 closes its valves like stone

The analogies can not, I think, be solved without remembering the previous ones, which have already established the soul as a living being with an exterior dwelling, having doors that can be closed.

What is this X^1 to which we have several clues—that it selects one item, closes something called valves, and is like a stone afterward? I am quite sure that the analogies force a single answer, and that the answer is therefore a part of the poem, though the answer is nowhere stated in the poem. Only one type of living being has valves which close like hinges—a bivalve mollusc, as probably some of you have already guessed. Further, it is not a clam, but an oyster, since the oyster "selects"—though the term is in quotes—a grain of sand, as the soul selects her "one" from an ample nation.

Notice how the analogies transform the poem. There could scarcely be a more superficially unpromising comparison than to say the soul is like an oyster. Yet the analogies carry us straight to a comparison of the one selected by the soul, of whom she makes a friend, to the grain of sand selected by the oyster, of which it makes a pearl. In this particular poem, I do not see how the final meaning can be reached without solution of the implicit analogies, though of course, we can like the poem without understanding it. Yet I can not believe that the grain of sand and pearl, nowhere mentioned, are not a part, indeed the most important part, of the total design. And as with Sandburg, the analogies carry us far out into cultural correspondences. The recluse Emily Dickinson speaks of love and friendship in terms which imply wounding, then healing and transformation. All of us know these contradictory impulses towards privacy and companionship, of which so much of human relationship consists. Emily Dickinson has given us a model of a conflict in our cultural values, and has presented a solution. Stylistic structure has transcended language, and enabled Emily Dickinson to say to us what can not—or can not easily—be said in sentences of prose.

The last of these poems is different from either of the others, first because it has been so institutionalized that we accept it without thinking about it, or really reading it, merely as a part of our traditions. Second, because it can be read and valued highly, without working out the analogies it contains; it can give, indeed, the impression of being completely understood with none of the analysis we gave to Emily Dickinson. The analogies must therefore, if study of them is to be justified, modify or increase the understanding of the poem enough to make their exposition worth the effort, and must not spoil our appreciation of the poem.

COMPOSED UPON WESTMINSTER BRIDGE, SEPTEMBER 3, 1802

Earth has not anything to show more fair:
Dull would he be of soul who could pass by
A sight so touching in its majesty:
This City now doth, like a garment, wear
The beauty of the morning; silent, bare,
Ships, towers, domes, theatres, and temples lie
Open unto the fields, and to the sky;
All bright and glittering in the smokeless air.
Never did sun more beautifully steep
In his first splendour, valley, rock, or hill;
Ne'er saw I, never felt, a calm so deep!
The river glideth at his own sweet will:
Dear God! The very houses seem asleep;
And all that mighty heart is lying still!

I do not need to comment on the surface meaning of the poem. All of us recognize that Wordsworth saw the city in unwonted beauty, and was moved by it with a religious emotion. All of us can share the emotion. Let us see how study changes this, and whether it enriches it.

We can pass over the first three lines as not relevant to our purpose; they contain no important analogies. The first analogy is in line 4—

"This City now doth, like a garment, wear
The beauty of the morning."

That is, beauty of the morning is to the city as garment is to X. Only human beings—normally at least—wear garments. The city is then like a human being. The garments are next described—"silent, bare, ships, towers, domes, theatres, and temples lie open unto the fields, and to the sky." The garment is not like a suit of clothes, or an overcoat. It is such as to reveal the city and its structures. We can express all this by an analogy which builds on the first one—

The city wears a garment which reveals its structures, as human being of X type wears a garment which reveals its body.

The garment which thus reveals beauty is not the sort of garment we talk about as worn by men or children. It is like the garment of a beautiful woman, and the city is not like a human being merely, but like a woman.

The woman-city, further, lies in calm and beautiful morning sleep. As well as the city and its parts, there is another set of entities in the poem. They are *fields*, *sky*, and *river*. These can easily be grouped as belonging to non-manmade nature, opposed in principle to the man-made city. There is no commoner attitude in our literature than the truism that God made the country, but man made the town—true or not, we all know the attitude. Yet the relation of these representatives of nature is not given here as one of conflict with the city. The woman-city.

"lies open unto the fields, and to the sky."

And below

"The river glideth at his own sweet will."

The analogy can be constructed thus:

Nature is to the city, as X is to woman.

I submit, therefore, that language and situation in this poem force the conclusion that this final missing X is lover—and that nature and city are compared to man and woman in the sleep of lovers.

I am aware enough that these analogies, thus made overt, might be thought of as shocking. Yet they need not be, and should not be. A further statement in the poem throws light on how we are to view the comparison

"The sun . . . in his first splendour . . ."

One way of reading the line would be to take it as a reference merely to the first light of this particular September 3. But throughout the poem there are hints that the scene is touched by a lost beauty—the air is smokeless, for instance, though presumably Wordsworth's negative statement implies that it was not often so. Wordsworth uses *temples* instead of the more prosaic and realistic *churches*, as if he would suggest a past more beautiful than the usual present. For these reasons, I believe that *first splendour* refers rather to the dawn of the world, than to the dawn of September 3. City and nature are as lovers, but lovers with an innocence and beauty lost since Eden.

I do not think I need to carry the central woman-city analogy much further into the metaliterary realm of value and cultural correspondence. It is enough to say man and nature are reconciled, released, and united, as men and women are in love. Wordsworth did not often talk so of the works of man, and I think we can agree that he is a greater poet for the vision of a reconciliation which he grasped that morning on the bridge. The analogies are, I believe, the central structure of the poem—they are the way in which the larger unity of style is made to transcend the limitations of the micro-linguistic.[2] Wordsworth's success could not be achieved, I think, without them. His success, in turn, is a revealing example of the way in which poetry is language, yet more than language, and different from it.

SUGGESTED ASSIGNMENTS

1. Read carefully the following poem, "The Isle of Portland,"[3] by A. E. Housman. The island mentioned contains a lighthouse and a prison.

> The star-filled seas are smooth to-night
> From France to England strown;
> Black towers above the Portland light
> The felon-quarried stone.
>
> On yonder island, not to rise,
> Never to stir forth free,
> Far from his folk a dead lad lies
> That once was friends with me.
>
> Lie you easy, dream you light,
> And sleep you fast for aye;
> And luckier may you find the night
> Than ever you found the day.

In line three the reader may be led off the grammatical path by the words *black towers*. If *towers* is a noun and the subject of the clause, what is the verb? If *towers* is a verb, what is its subject?

Since inversions are common in poetry, a reader must clearly understand the syntax before attempting to interpret a poem.

2. The poem below was written by Thomas Gray. It is a satire upon Cambridge University as a seat of ignorance. The poem was probably written upon Gray's return to Cambridge after an absence of three years.

HYMN TO IGNORANCE

A FRAGMENT

> Hail, horrors, hail! ye ever gloomy bowers,
> Ye gothic fanes, and antiquated towers,

---

[2] By "microlinguistic" Hill means "the world of language as a system and pattern, the world of sentences, clauses, phrases, words, and word elements." [eds.]

[3] From "A Shropshire Lad"—Authorised Edition—from *The Collected Poems of A. E. Housman*. Copyright 1939, 1940, © 1959 by Holt, Rinehart and Winston, Inc. Copyright © 1967, 1968 by Robert E. Symons. Reprinted by permission of Holt, Rinehart and Winston, Inc.

Where rushy Camus'[1] slowly-winding flood
Perpetual draws his humid train of mud:
Glad I revisit thy neglected reign,   5
Oh take me to thy peaceful shade again.

But chiefly thee, whose influence breathed from high
Augments the native darkness of the sky;
Oh, Ignorance! soft salutary power!
Prostrate with filial reverence I adore.   10
Thrice hath Hyperion[2] roll'd his annual race,
Since weeping I forsook thy fond embrace.

Oh say, successful dost thou still oppose
Thy leaden aegis 'gainst our ancient foes?
Still stretch, tenacious of thy right divine,   15
The massy sceptre o'er thy slumb'ring line?
And dews Lethean through the land dispense
To steep in slumbers each benighted sense?

If any spark of wit's delusive ray
Break out, and flash a momentary day,   20
With damp, cold touch forbid it to aspire
And huddle up in fogs the dangerous fire. . . .

As you read this poem, did you keep grammatical relationships clear? Let's see. In line seven, what is the grammatical function of *thee* in the sentence? Remember here that the eighteenth century forms of the personal pronoun in the second person singular were: nominative, *thou;* possessive, *thy;* objective, *thee.* In line seventeen what other verbs is *dispense* parallel with, and what is *dews Lethean* the object of?

[1] The river Cam. [eds.]
[2] A sun god of the Greeks. [eds.]

Name Index

Subject Index